# Children's
# Literature
# Review

# Guide to Gale Literary Criticism Series

**When you need to review criticism of literary works, these are the Gale series to use:**

**If the author's death date is:**

**You should turn to:**

After Dec. 31, 1959
(or author is still living)

### CONTEMPORARY LITERARY CRITICISM

for example: Jorge Luis Borges, Anthony Burgess,
William Faulkner, Mary Gordon,
Ernest Hemingway, Iris Murdoch

1900 through 1959

### TWENTIETH-CENTURY LITERARY CRITICISM

for example: Willa Cather, F. Scott Fitzgerald,
Henry James, Mark Twain, Virginia Woolf

1800 through 1899

### NINETEENTH-CENTURY LITERATURE CRITICISM

for example: Fedor Dostoevski, George Sand,
Gerard Manley Hopkins, Emily Dickinson

1400 through 1799

### LITERATURE CRITICISM FROM 1400 TO 1800
### (excluding Shakespeare)

for example: Anne Bradstreet, Pierre Corneille,
Daniel Defoe, Alexander Pope,
Jonathan Swift, Phillis Wheatley

### SHAKESPEAREAN CRITICISM

Shakespeare's plays and poetry

Antiquity through 1399

### CLASSICAL AND MEDIEVAL LITERATURE CRITICISM

for example: Dante, Plato, Homer, Sophocles, Vergil,
the Beowulf poet

*(Volume 1 forthcoming)*

---

## Gale also publishes related criticism series:

### CHILDREN'S LITERATURE REVIEW

This ongoing series covers authors of all eras.
Presents criticism on authors and author/illustrators
who write for the preschool to junior-high audience.

### CONTEMPORARY ISSUES CRITICISM

This two volume set presents criticism on
contemporary authors writing on current issues.
Topics covered include the social sciences,
philosophy, economics, natural science, law, and
related areas.

ISSN 0362-4145

volume 9

# Children's Literature Review

Excerpts from Reviews,
Criticism, and Commentary
on Books for Children

**Gerard J. Senick**
Editor

**Melissa Reiff Hug**
Associate Editor

Gale Research Company
Book Tower
Detroit, Michigan 48226

## STAFF

Gerard J. Senick, *Editor*

Melissa Reiff Hug, *Associate Editor*

Susan Miller Harig, *Senior Assistant Editor*

Motoko Fujishiro Huthwaite, *Assistant Editor*

Sharon R. Gunton, *Contributing Editor*

Lizbeth A. Purdy, *Production Supervisor*
Denise Michlewicz Broderick, *Production Coordinator*
Eric Berger, *Assistant Production Coordinator*
Robin L. DuBlanc, Kelly King Howes, *Editorial Assistants*

Victoria B. Cariappa, *Research Coordinator*
Jeannine Schiffman Davidson, *Assistant Research Coordinator*
Vincenza G. DiNoto, Daniel Kurt Gilbert, Maureen R. Richards, Filomena Sgambati, Valerie J. Webster, *Research Assistants*

Linda M. Pugliese, *Manuscript Coordinator*
Donna Craft, *Assistant Manuscript Coordinator*
Maureen A. Puhl, Rosetta Irene Simms, *Manuscript Assistants*

Jeanne A. Gough, *Permissions Supervisor*
Janice M. Mach, *Permissions Coordinator, Text*
Patricia A. Seefelt, *Permissions Coordinator, Illustrations*
Susan D. Nobles, *Assistant Permissions Coordinator*
Margaret A. Chamberlain, Sandra C. Davis, Mary M. Matuz, *Senior Permissions Assistants*
Colleen M. Crane, Kathy Grell, Josephine M. Keene, *Permissions Assistants*
H. Diane Cooper, Dorothy J. Fowler, Yolanda Parker, Mabel E. Schoening, *Permissions Clerks*

Arthur Chartow, *Art Director*

Frederick G. Ruffner, *Publisher*
Dedria Bryfonski, *Editorial Director*
Christine Nasso, *Director, Literature Division*
Laurie Lanzen Harris, *Senior Editor, Literary Criticism Series*
Dennis Poupard, *Managing Editor, Literary Criticism Series*

Copyright © 1985 by Gale Research Company

Library of Congress Catalog Card Number 75-34953
ISBN 0-8103-0334-5
ISSN 0362-4145

Computerized photocomposition by
Typographics, Incorporated
Kansas City, Missouri

Printed in the United States

# CONTENTS

Preface   7

Authors to Appear in Future Volumes   11

Appendix   237

Cumulative Index to Authors   249

Cumulative Index to Nationalities   255

Cumulative Index to Titles   257

Aliki (Liacouras Brandenberg)
1929-   . . . . . . . . . . . . . . . . . . . . . 15

John (Mackintosh) Burningham
1936-   . . . . . . . . . . . . . . . . . . . . 33

James Howe   1946-   . . . . . . . . . . . 54

Monica (Ince) Hughes   1925-   . . . . . . 61

James (Jacob Hinrich) Krüss
1926-   . . . . . . . . . . . . . . . . . . . . 80

Hugh (Francis) Lewin   1939-   . . . . 89

David (Thompson Watson) McCord
1897-   . . . . . . . . . . . . . . . . . . . . 93

Gerald (Edward) McDermott
1941-   . . . . . . . . . . . . . . . . . . . . 105

Bruno Munari   1907-   . . . . . . . . . . 121

(Ann) Philippa Pearce (Christie)
1920-   . . . . . . . . . . . . . . . . . . . . 131

Dr. Seuss   1904-   . . . . . . . . . . . . . . 160

Seymour Simon   1931-   . . . . . . . . 198

Mildred D(elois) Taylor   19??-   . . . . 223

Vera B. Williams   1927-   . . . . . . . . 230

# PREFACE

As children's literature has evolved into both a respected branch of creative writing and a successful industry, literary criticism has documented and influenced each stage of its growth. Critics have recorded the literary development of individual authors as well as the trends and controversies that resulted from changes in values and attitudes, especially as they concerned children. While defining a philosophy of children's literature, critics developed a scholarship that balances an appreciation of children and an awareness of their needs with standards for literary quality much like those required by critics of adult literature. *Children's Literature Review* (*CLR*) is designed to provide a permanent, accessible record of this ongoing scholarship. Those responsible for bringing children and books together can now make informed choices when selecting reading materials for the young.

## Scope of the Series

Each biannual volume contains excerpts from published criticism on the literary works of authors and author/illustrators who create books for children from preschool to junior-high age. The author list for each volume is international in scope and represents the variety of genres covered by children's literature—picture books, fiction, folklore, nonfiction, poetry, and drama. The works of approximately fifteen to forty authors of all eras are represented in each volume. Although earlier volumes of *CLR* emphasized critical material published after 1960, recent volumes have expanded their coverage to encompass criticism written before 1960. Since many of the authors included in *CLR* are living and continue to write, it is necessary to update their entries periodically. Thus, future volumes will supplement the entries of selected authors covered in earlier volumes as well as present criticism on the works of authors new to the series.

## Organization of the Book

An author section consists of the following elements: author heading, author portrait, author introduction, excerpts of criticism (each followed by a bibliographical citation), and illustrations, when available.

- The **author heading** consists of the author's full name followed by birth and death dates. The portion of the name outside the parentheses denotes the form under which the author is most frequently published. If the majority of the author's works for children were written under a pseudonym, the pseudonym will be listed in the author heading and the real name given on the first line of the author introduction. Also located at the beginning of the introduction are any other pseudonyms used by the author in writing for children and any name variations, including transliterated forms for authors whose languages use nonroman alphabets. Uncertainty as to a birth or death date is indicated by a question mark.

- An **author portrait** is included when available.

- The **author introduction** contains information designed to introduce an author to *CLR* users by presenting an overview of the author's themes and styles, biographical facts that relate to his or her literary career, a summary of critical response to the author's works, and information about major awards and prizes the author has received. Where applicable, introductions conclude with references to additional entries in biographical and critical reference series published by Gale Research Company. These sources include past volumes of *CLR* as well as *Contemporary Authors, Something about the Author, Yesterday's Authors of Books for Children, Contemporary Literary Criticism, Twentieth-Century Literary Criticism, Nineteenth-Century Literature Criticism, Dictionary of Literary Biography,* and *Authors in the News.*

- **Criticism** is located in three sections: **author's commentary** and **general commentary** (when available) and within individual **title entries,** which are preceded by **title entry headings.** Criticism is arranged chronologically within each section. Titles by authors being profiled are highlighted in boldface type within the text for easier access by readers.

The **author's commentary** presents background material written by the author or by an interviewer. This commentary may cover a specific work or several works. Author's commentary on more than one work appears after the author introduction, while commentary on an individual book follows the title entry heading.

The **general commentary** consists of critical excerpts that consider more than one work by the author being profiled. General commentary is preceded by the critic's name in boldface type or, in the case of unsigned criticism, by the title of the journal.

**Title entry headings** precede the criticism on a title and cite publication information on the work being reviewed. Title headings list the work's title as it appeared in its country of origin; titles in languages using nonroman alphabets are transliterated. If the original title is in a language other than English, the title of the first English-language translation follows in brackets. The work's first publication date is listed in parentheses following the title. Differing U.S. and British titles of works originally published in English follow the publication date within the parentheses.

**Title entries** consist of critical excerpts on the author's individual works, arranged chronologically by publication date. The entries generally contain two to six reviews per title, depending on the stature of the book and the amount of criticism it has generated. The editors select titles that reflect the entire scope of the author's literary contribution, covering each genre and subject. An effort is made to reprint criticism that represents the full range of each title's reception —from the year of its intitial publication to current assessments. Thus, the reader is provided with a record of the author's critical history.

• Selected excerpts are preceded by **explanatory notes,** which provide information on the critic or work of criticism to enhance the reader's understanding of the excerpt.

• **A complete bibliographical citation** designed to facilitate the location of the original book or article follows each piece of criticism. An asterisk (*) at the end of a citation indicates that the essay or book is on more than one author.

• Numerous **illustrations** are featured in *CLR.* For entries on author/illustrators, an effort has been made to include illustrations that reflect the author's style as represented in the criticism. Entries on major authors who do not illustrate their own works may also include photographs and other illustrative material pertinent to the authors' careers.

## Other Features

• A list of **authors to appear in future volumes** follows the preface.

• An **appendix** lists the sources from which material has been reprinted in the volume. It does not, however, list every book or periodical consulted for the volume.

• *CLR* volumes contain **cumulative indexes** to authors, nationalities, and titles.

The **cumulative index to authors** lists authors who have appeared in *CLR* and includes cross-references to *Contemporary Authors, Something about the Author, Yesterday's Authors of Books for Children, Contemporary Literary Criticism, Twentieth-Century Literary Criticism, Nineteenth-Century Literature Criticism, Dictionary of Literary Biography,* and *Authors in the News.*

The **cumulative nationality index** lists authors alphabetically under their respective nationalities. Author names are followed by the volume number(s) in which they appear. Authors who have changed citizenship or whose current citizenship is not reflected in biographical sources appear under both their original nationality and that of their current residence.

The **cumulative title index** lists titles covered in *CLR* followed by the volume and page number where criticism can be found.

## Acknowledgments

No work of this scope can be accomplished without the cooperation of many people. The editors especially wish to thank the copyright holders of the criticism included in this volume, the permissions managers of many book and magazine publishing companies for assisting us in securing reprint rights, and the staffs of the Kresge Library at Wayne State University, the University of Michigan Library, the Detroit Public Library, and the Wayne Oakland Library Federation (WOLF) for making their resources available to us. We are also grateful to Anthony J. Bogucki for his assistance with copyright research.

## Suggestions Are Welcome

In response to various suggestions, several features have been added to *CLR* since the series began:

- Since Volume 3—**Author's commentary,** when available, which presents the viewpoint of the author being profiled.

   —An **appendix** listing the sources of the criticism in each volume.

- Since Volume 4—**Author portraits** as well as **illustrations** from works by author/illustrators, when available.

   —**Title entries** arranged chronologically according to the work's first publication; previous volumes listed titles alphabetically.

- Since Volume 5—A **guest essay,** when available, written specifically for *CLR* by a prominent critic on a subject of his or her choice.

- Since Volume 6—**Explanatory notes** that provide information on the critic or work of criticism to enhance the usefulness of the excerpt.

   —A **cumulative nationality index** for easy access to authors by nationality.

- Since Volume 8—Author entries on retellers of traditional literature as well as those who have been the first to record oral tales and other folklore.

   —More extensive illustrative material, such as holographs of manuscript pages and photographs of people and places pertinent to the authors' careers.

Readers are cordially invited to write the editor with comments and suggestions for further enhancing the usefulness of the *CLR* series.

# AUTHORS TO APPEAR IN FUTURE VOLUMES

Aardema, Verna 1911-
Adams, Adrienne 1906-
Adams, Harriet S(tratemeyer) 1893?-1982
Adams, Richard 1920-
Adler, Irving 1913-
Aesop 620?BC-564?BC
Anderson, C(larence) W(illiam) 1891-1971
Arnosky, Jim 1946-
Asbjörnsen, Peter Christen 1812-1885 and Jórgen Moe 1813?-1882
Asch, Frank 1946-
Asimov, Isaac 1920-
Avery, Gillian 1926-
Avi 1937-
Aymé, Marcel 1902-1967
Bailey, Carolyn Sherwin 1875-1961
Ballantyne, R(obert) M(ichael) 1825-1894
Banner, Angela 1923-
Bannerman, Helen 1863-1946
Barrett, Judi(th) 1941-
Barrie, J(ames) M(atthew) 1860-1937
Baum, L(yman) Frank 1856-1919
Baumann, Hans 1914-1985
BB 1905-
Beatty, Patricia 1922- and John 1922-1975
Behn, Harry 1898-1973
Belloc, Hilaire 1870-1953
Benary-Isbert, Margot 1889-1979
Benchley, Nathaniel 1915-1981
Berenstain, Stan(ley) 1923- and Jan(ice) 1923-
Berger, Melvin 1927-
Berna, Paul 1910-
Beskow, Elsa 1874-1953
Bianco, Margery Williams 1881-1944
Bishop, Claire Huchet
Blades, Ann 1947-
Blake, Quentin 1932-
Blos, Joan W(insor) 1928-
Blyton, Enid 1897-1968
Bodecker, N(iels) M(ogens) 1922-
Bond, Nancy 1945-
Bonham, Frank 1914-
Branley, Franklyn M(ansfield) 1915-
Branscum, Robbie 1937-
Brazil, Angela 1869-1947
Breinburg, Petronella 1927-
Briggs, Raymond 1934-
Bright, Robert 1902-
Brink, Carol Ryrie 1895-1981
Brooke, L(eonard) Leslie 1862-1940
Brown, Marc 1946-
Brown, Marcia 1918-
Brown, Margaret Wise 1910-1952

Buff, Mary 1890-1970 and Conrad 1886-1975
Bulla, Clyde Robert 1914-
Burch, Robert 1925-
Burchard, Peter 1921-
Burgess, Gelett 1866-1951
Burgess, Thornton W(aldo) 1874-1965
Burnett, Frances Hodgson 1849-1924
Burton, Virginia Lee 1909-1968
Butterworth, Oliver 1915-
Caines, Jeannette
Carle, Eric 1929-
Carlson, Natalie Savage 1906-
Carrick, Carol 1935-
Childress, Alice 1920-
Chönz, Selina
Christopher, Matt(hew) 1917-
Ciardi, John 1916-
Clapp, Patricia 1912-
Clark, Ann Nolan 1896-
Clarke, Pauline 1921-
Cleaver, Elizabeth 1939-
Cohen, Barbara 1932-
Colby, C(arroll) B(urleigh) 1904-1977
Colman, Hila
Colum Padraic 1881-1972
Cone, Molly 1918-
Conford, Ellen 1942-
Coolidge, Olivia 1908-
Coolidge, Susan 1835-1905
Cooney, Barbara 1917-
Cormier, Robert (Edmund) 1925-
Courlander, Harold 1908-
Cox, Palmer 1840-1924
Cresswell, Helen 1934-
Crompton, Richmal 1890-1969
Cunningham, Julia 1916-
Curry, Jane L(ouise) 1932-
Dalgliesh, Alice 1893-1979
Daugherty, James 1889-1974
d'Aulaire, Ingri 1904-1980 and Edgar Parin 1898-
de la Mare, Walter 1873-1956
de Regniers, Beatrice Schenk 1914-
Dickinson, Peter 1927-
Dillon, Eilís 1920-
Dodge, Mary Mapes 1831-1905
Domanska, Janina
Duncan, Lois S(teinmetz) 1934-
Duvoisin, Roger 1904-1980
Eager, Edward 1911-1964
Edgeworth, Maria 1767-1849
Edmonds, Walter D(umaux) 1903-
Epstein, Sam(uel) 1909- and Beryl 1910-
Ets, Marie Hall 1893-
Ewing, Juliana Horatia 1841-1885
Farber, Norma 1909-
Farjeon, Eleanor 1881-1965

Field, Eugene 1850-1895
Field, Rachel 1894-1942
Fisher, Dorothy Canfield 1879-1958
Fisher, Leonard Everett 1924-
Flack, Marjorie 1897-1958
Forbes, Esther 1891-1967
Forest, Antonia
Freeman, Don 1908-1978
Fujikawa, Gyo
Fyleman, Rose 1877-1957
Galdone, Paul 1914-
Gardam, Jane 1928-
Garfield, Leon 1921-
Garis, Howard R(oger) 1873-1962
Garner, Alan 1935-
Gates, Doris 1901-
Gerrard, Roy
Giblin, James Cross 1933-
Giff, Patricia Reilly 1935-
Ginsburg, Mirra 1919-
Goble, Paul 1933-
Godden, Rumer 1907-
Goodrich, Samuel G(riswold) 1793-1860
Gorey, Edward 1925-
Goudge, Elizabeth (de Beauchamp) 1900-
Graham, Lorenz B(ell) 1902-
Gramatky, Hardie 1907-1979
Greene, Constance C(larke) 1924-
Grimm, Jacob 1785-1863 and Wilhelm 1786-1859
Gruelle, Johnny 1880-1938
Guillot, René 1900-1969
Hader, Elmer 1889-1973 and Berta 1891?-1976
Hale, Lucretia Peabody 1820-1900
Harnett, Cynthia 1893-1981
Harris, Christie 1907-
Harris, Joel Chandler 1848-1908
Harris, Rosemary (Jeanne) 1923-
Haugaard, Erik Christian 1923-
Haywood, Carolyn 1898-
Heide, Florence Parry 1919-
Hill, Eric
Hoberman, Mary Ann 1930-
Hoff, Syd(ney) 1912-
Hoffman, Heinrich 1809-1894
Holland, Isabelle 1920-
Holling, Holling C(lancy) 1900-1973
Hughes, Langston 1902-1967
Hughes, Shirley 1929-
Hunter, Mollie 1922-
Ipcar, Dahlov 1917-
Iwasaki, Chihiro 1918-
Jackson, Jesse 1908-1983
Jacobs, Joseph 1854-1916
Janosch 1931-
Jeschke, Susan 1942-

Johnson, Crockett 1906-1975
Johnson, James Weldon 1871-1938
Jonas, Ann
Jones, Diana Wynne 1934-
Jordan, June 1936-
Judson, Clara Ingram 1879-1960
Juster, Norton 1929-
Keith, Harold 1903-
Kelly, Eric P(hilbrook) 1884-1960
Kennedy, Richard 1932-
Kent, Jack 1920-
Kerr, Judith 1923-
Kerr, M. E. 1927-
Kettelkamp, Larry 1933-
King, Clive 1924-
Kipling, Rudyard 1865-1936
Kjelgaard, Jim 1910-1959
Kraus, Robert 1925-
Krauss, Ruth 1911-
Krumgold, Joseph 1908-1980
La Farge, Oliver 1901-1963
La Fontaine, Jean de 1621-1695
Lang, Andrew 1844-1912
Langton, Jane 1922-
Lasky, Kathryn 1944-
Latham, Jean Lee 1902-
Lauber, Patricia 1924-
Lavine, Sigmund A(rnold) 1908-
Leaf, Munro 1905-1976
Lenski, Lois 1893-1974
Levy, Elizabeth 1942-
Lewis, Elizabeth Foreman 1892-1958
Lightner, A(lice) M. 1904-
Linklater, Eric 1899-1974
Lofting, Hugh 1866-1947
Lunn, Janet 1928-
MacDonald, George 1824-1905
MacGregor, Ellen 1906-1954
Major, Kevin (Gerald) 1949-
Mann, Peggy
Marshall, James 1942-
Martin, Patricia Miles 1899-
Masefield, John 1878-1967
Mayer, Mercer 1943- and Marianna 1945-
Mayne, William 1928-
Mazer, Norma Fox 1931- and Harry 1925-
McClung, Robert M(arshall) 1916-
McGovern, Ann
McNeer, May 1902- and Lynd Ward 1905-
Meader, Stephen W(arren) 1892-1977
Means, Florence Crannell 1891-1980
Meigs, Cornelia 1884-1973

Merriam, Eve 1916-
Merrill, Jean 1923-
Miles, Betty 1928-
Milne, Lorus 1912- and Margery 1915-
Minarik, Else Holmelund 1920-
Mizumura, Kazue
Molesworth, Mary Louisa 1842-1921
Morey, Walt(er) 1907-
Mukerji, Dhan Gopal 1890-1936
Naylor, Phyllis Reynolds 1933-
Neville, Emily Cheney 1919-
Nic Leodhas, Sorche 1898-1969
Nichols, Ruth 1948-
North, Sterling 1906-1974
Nöstlinger, Christine 1936-
Olney, Ross R(obert) 1929-
Ormondroyd, Edward 1925-
Ottley, Reginald
Oxenbury, Helen 1938-
Parish, Peggy 1927-
Peck, Richard (Wayne) 1934-
Peck, Robert Newton 1928-
Peet, Bill 1915-
Perl, Lila
Perrault, Charles 1628-1703
Petersham, Maud 1890-1971 and Miska 1888-1960
Petry, Ann (Lane) 1908-
Pfeffer, Susan Beth 1948-
Picard, Barbara Leonie 1917-
Politi, Leo 1908-
Prelutsky, Jack
Price, Christine 1928-1980
Provensen, Alice 1918- and Martin 1916-
Pyle, Howard 1853-1911
Reeves, James 1909-1978
Richards, Laura E(lizabeth) 1850-1943
Richler, Mordecai 1931-
Robertson, Keith 1914-
Rockwell, Anne 1934- and Harlow
Rodgers, Mary 1931-
Rollins, Charlemae Hill 1897-1979
Ross, Tony 1938-
Rounds, Glen 1906-
Saint-Exupéry, Antoine de 1900-1944
Sandburg, Carl 1878-1967
Sandoz, Mari 1896-1966
Sawyer, Ruth 1880-1970
Scarry, Huck
Scott, Jack Denton 1915-
Seredy, Kate 1899-1975
Seton, Ernest Thompson 1860-1946
Sharmat, Marjorie Weinman 1928-
Sharp, Margery 1905-

Shotwell, Louisa R(ossiter) 1902-
Sidney, Margaret 1844-1924
Silverstein, Alvin 1933- and Virginia 1937-
Sinclair, Catherine 1880-1864
Skurzynski, Gloria 1930-
Sleator, William 1945-
Slobodkin, Louis 1903-1975
Smith, Doris Buchanan 1934-
Smucker, Barbara (Claassen) 1915-
Snyder, Zilpha Keatley 1927-
Spence, Eleanor 1928-
Sperry, Armstrong W. 1897-1976
Spykman, E(lizabeth) C. 1896-1965
Spyri, Johanna 1827-1901
Steele, William O(wen) 1917-1979
Stevenson, James 1929-
Stevenson, Robert Louis 1850-1894
Stolz, Mary 1920-
Strasser, Todd 1950?-
Stratemeyer, Edward L. 1862-1930
Streatfeild, Noel 1897-
Taylor, Sydney 1904?-1978
Taylor, Theodore 1924-
Ter Haar, Jaap 1922-
Titus, Eve 1922-
Tolkien, J(ohn) R(onald) R(euel) 1892-1973
Treadgold, Mary 1910-
Trease, Geoffrey 1909-
Tresselt, Alvin 1916-
Treviño, Elizabeth Borton de 1904-
Tudor, Tasha 1915-
Turkle, Brinton 1915-
Udry, Janice May 1928-
Unnerstad, Edith 1900-
Uttley, Alison 1884-1976
Ventura, Piero 1937-
Vincent, Gabrielle
Vining, Elizabeth Gray 1902-
Voigt, Cynthia 1942-
Waber, Bernard 1924-
Wahl, Jan 1933-
Walter, Mildred Pitts
Wells, Rosemary 1943-
Wiese, Kurt 1887-1974
Wilkinson, Brenda 1946-
Williams, Barbara 1925-
Yates, Elizabeth 1905-
Yonge, Charlotte M(ary) 1823-1901
Zemach, Harve 1933-1974 and Margot 1931-
Zion, Gene 1913-1975

Readers are cordially invited to suggest additional authors to the editors.

# Children's
# Literature
# Review

# Aliki (Liacouras Brandenberg)

## 1929-

American author/illustrator of picture books and nonfiction, reteller, and illustrator of picture books, fiction, and nonfiction.

Aliki is recognized as a versatile author whose books are both entertaining and informative. Gearing her works to a preschool through middle grade audience, she creates nonfiction on scientific and historical subjects, easy-reading biographies of prominent Americans and Europeans, fiction that is usually amusing and often sensitive, and adaptations of Greek folktales. Her works contain concise language and illustrations which range from jovial cartoons to paintings in the style of illuminated manuscripts. Warmth and enthusiasm permeate Aliki's books; she invests many of them, including her nonfiction titles, with a playful sense of humor.

Aliki began her career by writing biographies of such figures as Johnny Appleseed, George Washington Carver, and William Penn. These works, which center on the lives of personages for whom Aliki has affection, present a generalized approach to their subjects without sacrificing character or atmosphere. Topics that she enjoys or wants to learn about are the basis for Aliki's nonfiction works on dinosaurs, fossils, mammoths, mummies, and food; in these books, she explains complex facts and processes as simply as possible so that young readers can learn effortlessly about the burial rites of ancient Egypt or how a dinosaur skeleton is assembled. Although her fiction is generally lighthearted, Aliki gives several of these works a strong emotional base. *The Two of Them* and *At Mary Bloom's,* for example, treat the closeness between generations, while *We Are Best Friends* centers on the feelings that children experience when their friends move away. Aliki also retells folktales from her ancestral homeland, Greece, in a direct, colloquial style.

Observers note that Aliki's illustrations both complement and amplify her texts. Utilizing such mediums as gouache, pen and ink, and watercolor, she creates a variety of pictures to match the format and mood of her books. A childlike, primitive style characterizes Aliki's early works, which are drawn simply and colored brightly. Later books such as the Greek folktale *Three Gold Pieces* present readers with more dramatic, often opulent illustrations. With *My Visit to the Dinosaurs,* Aliki introduces an illustrative technique that helps distinguish her informational books—the inclusion of running commentaries, often in speech balloon style, that comment on the main text. Frequently presented as conversations between children and other characters, these voice-bubbles provide an entertaining, human reaction to the subject under discussion while supplying clarification and new knowledge. Aliki also uses this technique in several of her fictional works, most notably *June 7!*. Perhaps Aliki's most successful illustrations are those for *A Medieval Feast,* which depicts a fifteenth-century royal banquet. Modeling her watercolor paintings on actual tapestries and illuminated manuscripts, Aliki is acclaimed for capturing the beauty of her sources without losing her artistic individuality.

When she was five years old, one of her teachers predicted that Aliki would become an artist. Upon graduation from the

*Photograph by Alexa Brandenberg. Courtesy of Aliki Brandenberg*

Philadelphia College of Art, she worked in advertising and display, painted murals, taught art and ceramics, and had her own line of greeting cards. Aliki married author Franz Brandenberg in 1957 while traveling in Europe. They settled in Switzerland, where she created her first book, *The Story of William Tell,* after discovering that Tell was Swiss. After returning to America, Aliki began illustrating the works of other authors, including her husband. While she was creating the pictures for a volume of publisher Thomas Y. Crowell's "Let's-Read-and-Find-Out" series of science books for children, she was inspired to create an original book for the series, which now includes much of her nonfiction.

Aliki's books often reflect her own activities and experiences. *Corn Is Maize* and *A Medieval Feast,* for example, are based on her interest in food and cooking. She spent two years researching *A Medieval Feast*—going to museums, taking photographs, and developing a picture file she had started in high school. *The Two of Them,* however, may have the strongest personal connection to Aliki. Highlighting the mutual love of a small girl and her grandfather, the story is based on Aliki's own relationship with her father, to whom the book is dedicated.

Most critics acclaim Aliki for creating books that are exceptional both visually and textually. Praised for her thorough research, simplicity, and attention to detail, Aliki is also appreciated for the appealing humor and engaging qualities of her books. She is considered an author whose unique approaches and fresh presentations provide children with learning experiences that are both enjoyable and profitable.

Aliki won the New York Academy of Sciences Children's Science Book Award in 1977 for *Corn Is Maize*. She has also received several child-selected awards and has had her works put on exhibition.

(See also *Something about the Author*, Vols. 2, 35.)

---

## AUTHOR'S COMMENTARY

[*In the following excerpt, Margaret Carter interviews Aliki, who comments on the sources of her ideas for books.*]

Aliki produces books as different in subject as *Digging Up Dinosaurs* to *We Are Best Friends*, from *Mummies Made in Egypt* to a tale about a crocodile *Use Your Head, Dear*.

And in doing so she is fulfilling a teacher's prophecy to her parents: "Your daughter will be an artist one day". The teacher must have had long sight for Aliki at the time was just five years old. "I had drawn a picture of our family—three girls and a boy and I put in Peter Rabbit's family too, because it struck me that they were three girls and a boy too!" . . .

It is Aliki's meticulous attention to detail allied to an individual way of presenting facts which has led to universal praise from critics and a stream of awards. . . .

"It's best for me to know nothing about a subject when I begin" she says, "that way I have to get it right. Because I am not a scientist I can perhaps approach the subject with fresh eyes."

*Digging Up Dinosaurs* and *Mummies Made in Egypt* are not just mines of detailed easily-presented information: they somehow manage to distil a sense of their period. They become facts set against their background. Yet *Dinosaurs* has another dimension. Underneath the craggy skeletons of Stegosaurus, Iguanodon or Tyrannosaurus Rex are tiny pictures of the humans who have come to look at these million-year old survivors. It is a curious dichotomy of vision which the artist has turned into a comment on her subject matter. It sets a frame on the pictures and puts two worlds into perspective. "Wait for me . . . you know too much . . . Are you scared?" say the little scurrying figures along the bottom of the pages while above them the great relics loom with fossilised indifference.

"I have twenty-minute books and two-year books" Aliki explains. "A book is inside me without my knowing it and then something—an experience or a remark—will trigger it off. *We Are Best Friends*, for instance, was prompted by a remark made to me about how a little boy was missing his friend who had moved away. It made me think how lonely children can be."

The idea of *A Medieval Feast* was first suggested in New York. "We were discussing what my next book should be. My publishers know that I have to love the subject—and they know I love cooking and somehow the idea of a feast came up. But what period? And where? And then someone made a chance remark that medieval feasts must have ruined families when the King came to stay. Suddenly everything fell into place. It must be a medieval feast and it could only be set in Britain."

The research absorbed her for two years. . . . "Everything" she says, "is absolutely authentic." You will find no anach-

ronism among the beautifully detailed and ordered pictures. The book progresses like the feast it portrays—from the preparation, the cleaning, the hunting, the presentation. . . .

Yet perhaps the most moving of Aliki's books has never been published in Britain. *The Two of Them* is a litany of love drawn in memory of her father. In simple lines it recounts the love of a small girl for her grandfather who has died. It tells the things they did together "he made me a bed . . . he made me a ring." But fiction is never really fiction and Aliki still wears the green stone ring her father made for her. "We never questioned his love. He used to get up at three in the morning to buy the best fruit, the best vegetables for our shop. Then when he retired he had time for all kinds of things that had been inside him all those years of work—making a ring, making music."

Without knowing it she is answering my question "Were there other artists in your family?" It is obvious that all the family are artists in the art of living.

*Margaret Carter, "Cover Artist—Aliki," in* Books for Your Children, *Vol. 19, No. 1, Spring, 1984, p. 9.*

---

## GENERAL COMMENTARY

### CHARLOTTE S. HUCK AND DORIS YOUNG KUHN

[Aliki] has written and illustrated some outstanding easy-vocabulary picture biographies for the beginning reader. Her texts are brief and simple, but they avoid the pitfalls of too much repetition and stilted language patterns. The childlike pictures create a feeling of true colonial primitives. In *The Story of Johnny Appleseed*, this author-illustrator has captured the humor and simplicity of the legendary Johnny Appleseed. Delicately illustrated period pictures reflect the warmth and gentleness of the Quakers in *The Story of William Penn*. Their belief in the simple life is shown in the sharp contrast of William's plain dress with the King of England's curls and frills. William Penn practiced what he believed, and his fairness in treating the Indians proved to the world that men can live as brothers if they choose. This quiet picture biography somehow conveys the dignity and greatness of the man. The same dignity and simplicity is communicated in *A Weed Is a Flower, the Life of George Washington Carver*. Again, Aliki has made meaningful for the youngest reader, the inspiring story of the man who was born a Negro slave but lived to become one of America's greatest research scientists. Unfortunately, in *George and the Cherry Tree*, Aliki perpetuates the old Parson Weems myth of the ever-truthful George and his cherry tree. (p. 283)

*Charlotte S. Huck and Doris Young Kuhn, "Biography and Historical Fiction: Well-Known Biographers of Juvenile Literature," in their* Children's Literature in the Elementary School, *second edition, Holt, Rinehart and Winston, Inc., 1968, pp. 283-89.\**

### BERNARD J. LONSDALE AND HELEN K. MACKINTOSH

[Aliki Brandenberg] works in an amazing variety of media—clay, silver, enamel, papier-mâché, mosaic, and collage—using the medium that she feels best fits the mood and style of each story.

Mrs. Brandenberg shows her versatility both in text and illustrations in *Keep Your Mouth Closed, Dear*. . . . Charles is a young crocodile whose parents are dismayed by the problems that result every time he opens his mouth.

With illustrations in pastel colors resembling Greek friezes and simple text, Mrs. Brandenberg has written a picture biography for young children. *Diogenes: The Story of the Greek Philosopher* . . . relates the dramatic events in the life of a great man. Even with the slight text, young listeners and readers catch a glimpse of life in ancient Athens and Corinth, while making the acquaintance of Diogenes. (p. 234)

> *Bernard J. Lonsdale and Helen K. Mackintosh, "Picture-Story Books: Contemporary Author-Illustrators," in their* Children Experience Literature, *Random House, 1973, pp. 232-56.\**

---

## THE STORY OF WILLIAM TELL  (1960)

[Aliki] has made a gay picture-book in the Continental manner out of the story of William Tell and the apple. The colour is excellent and the simple bold pictures sprawl enticingly across the pages. Such a jolly book must not be taken too seriously, but there is a snag. The story is so greatly simplified for small readers that it reads as a direct incitement to political assassination. There was surely more to Tell than one arrow in an apple and another in Gessler.

> *A review of "The Story of William Tell," in* The Junior Bookshelf, *Vol. 25, No. 3, July, 1961, p. 127.*

Another version [of William Tell's story] might well be shrugged off as old hat. Nothing could be further from the truth with this one. Aliki has taken it and dressed it up as fresh as the daisies with some of the most gorgeous illustrations I have seen. The characters jump off the page with the sheer audacious simplicity of their presentation. To anyone who wants something wonderful for children of seven to eight I heartily recommend it.

> *H. Millington, in a review of "The Story of William Tell," in* The School Librarian and School Library Review, *Vol. 10, No. 6, December, 1961, p. 567.*

---

## THE WISH WORKERS  (1962)

A nonsense tale with a moral—but so beautifully presented by this gifted author-artist that one can forgive the obviousness of the text. It is a story about a dissatisfied little bird that used up his three wishes in such absurd ways that he was still unhappy. And then another bird pitied his fate, and used her wish to make him what he was before. Of course they lived happily ever after. Enchanting pictures in bright flat color and pencilled grays—with humor and imagination.

> *A review of "The Wish Workers," in* Virginia Kirkus' Service, *Vol. XXX, No. 13, July 1, 1962, p. 553.*

The theme is old, but the simple text and gaily imaginative illustrations by the author in lovely colors have modern charm. Recommended for any library seeking fresh, original picture books which can be enjoyed by preschool children and beginning readers.

> *Allie Beth Martin, in a review of "The Wish Workers," in* School Library Journal, *an appendix to* Library Journal, *Vol. 9, No. 3, November, 1962, p. 39.*

Imaginative bird drawings are paired with a modern Aesop fable of a songbird that felt the plumage was greener on the other side of the fence. . . . The writing is direct, the moral

clear, but the sense of magic lags once or twice. All in all, worth while, though.

> *Earl W. Foell, "Quiet Please," in* The Christian Science Monitor, *November 15, 1962, p. 2B.\**

The plot may be overworked and the story inconsequential and boring to adults, but the modern drawings of the fantastic bird Wish Workers and the other birds, flowers, and trees of the forest have great fun and vitality, and are in such lovely, clear, porcelain-like colors that the book is very beautiful to look at if not to listen to.

> *Ruth Hill Viguers, in a review of "The Wish Workers," in* The Horn Book Magazine, *Vol. XXXIX, No. 1, February, 1963, p. 50.*

---

## THE STORY OF JOHNNY APPLESEED  (1963)

Johnny Appleseed, a generously lanky figure, strolling alone through warm colored autumn forests, happy with his own thoughts, or surrounded by relaxed, smiling children—is captured in artistically designed illustrations. The use of color is exceptional; autumn sunset shades and cold winter blues and whites are effective. The illustrations complement a lively text in a book which will be a valuable addition to any child's own collection or the public library's children's room.

> *A review of "The Story of Johnny Appleseed," in* Virginia Kirkus' Service, *Vol. XXXI, No. 17, September 1, 1963, p. 859.*

Aliki has a remarkable way of capturing the spirit of a small child's paintings and lighting them up with the genius of the adult painter of true primitives. The result, as here, is quaint, humorous, realistic, and somehow beautiful. Johnny Appleseed, the New Englander who wandered through the Middle West in the early days distributing seeds of apple trees . . . , could not be a better subject for Aliki's gifts. This makes a charming and gay picturebook for the 4-7's. The text is brief, cheerful, and full of action.

> *Millicent J. Taylor, "Peopling the Past," in* The Christian Science Monitor, *November 14, 1963, p. 7B.\**

In telling this tale, Aliki has simplified it to a degree that may be understandable to children, but will not excite them. Her **"Story of Johnny Appleseed"** is pleasant, but its generalizations diminish the real John Chapman, whose life was one of action, saintliness and courage. The pictures are bright and cheerful but like the text, they tend to sweeten rather than reveal.

> *Barbara Wersba, in a review of "The Story of Johnny Appleseed," in* The New York Times Book Review, *January 26, 1964, p. 26.*

A version of the Johnny Appleseed story, simplified, but with enough aspects of both the real events and the tall-tale embroidery to give children an idea of the character. The illustrations are gay and attractive; the text is a bit fragmented in construction, since it does not provide any linkage between anecdotes.

> *Zena Sutherland, in a review of "The Story of Johnny Appleseed," in* Bulletin of the Center for Children's Books, *Vol. XVII, No. 8, April, 1964, p. 121.*

[The] old-timer tale offers wonderful chances for Aliki's brilliantly coloured, sparkling style and for her delicate use of small decorative features, like birds, flowers and apples. The pictures are a joy to look at and they contain enough action (the approach of friendly Indians, the growth of orchards) to keep a small child interested.

> *Margery Fisher, in a review of "The Story of Johnny Appleseed," in her* Growing Point, *Vol. 4, No. 1, May, 1965, p. 524.*

### GEORGE AND THE CHERRY TREE (1964)

In case anyone has survived Washington's birthday without telling the smug I-cannot-tell-a-lie myth of Parson Weems to small children in his immediate vicinity, here is a retelling that avoids the horrid phrase, gives little George a natural little-boy manner and retains the heroism (and it *was* heroism, if true) of admitting a wickedness in the face of dire threats. Our adult timidity was aroused by the dangerously toppling huge tree in one picture—those woodcutters should certainly be scampering to safety to the cry of "timber"—and by the idea of allowing a forceful small boy to have his new axe in his bedroom at night! We enjoyed the little book, nevertheless, both for the pleasant account and the bright, forceful pictures which are unmistakably colonial but amusingly stylized.

> *Margaret Sherwood Libby, "A Gift for the King," in* Book Week—New York Herald Tribune, *February 23, 1964, p. 18.*

Another book by Aliki! That is enough to say. Quaint, brightly colored, peasant-style pictures just close enough to those a child would paint for himself yet skillful, humorous, and decorative. No matter that it keeps alive the fictitious legend. . . ! The tale is told with tongue-in-cheek. The preschool set will pore over this book, and primary graders will proudly read the large print and simple account for themselves.

> *Millicent J. Taylor, in a review of "George and the Cherry Tree," in* The Christian Science Monitor, *May 7, 1964, p. 2B.*

[*George and the Cherry Tree*] infuses new fun, drama and atmosphere into the old clergyman's apocryphal yarn about our first President. The pictures, with their slightly stylized figures, are remarkable for draftsmanship, color-sense, humor and vigor.

> *Ethna Sheehan, in a review of "George and the Cherry Tree," in* America, *Vol. 110, No. 24, June 20, 1964, p. 848.*

### THE STORY OF WILLIAM PENN (1964)

The text is brief and direct. Aliki's accompanying pictures are stylized and (within the boundaries necessary to the dignity of the subject) amusing. William Penn's England, his goals in settling a Quaker colony in the New World and his relations with Indians and early settlers make this book simple, basic non-fiction for the first two grades. The colors used in the illustrations have a water base which manages to capture both the bright Indian approach to dress and the rich soberness of the Quaker shades.

> *A review of "The Story of William Penn," in* Virginia Kirkus' Service, *Vol. XXXII, No. 17, September 1, 1964, p. 892.*

Visually, Aliki's easy-to-read picture book about William Penn is a refreshing introduction to history. Her delicately tinted, decorative illustrations, primitive in style, have the flavor of the period. The text, though, is stiff and bland, giving only the bare facts. . . . That much is left out of this simplified account is to be expected, but what is sorely missing is narrative pace and excitement.

> *Alice Low, in a review of "The Story of William Penn," in* The New York Times Book Review, *November 8, 1964, p. 38.*

Many seem to find Aliki's "primitive art" approach to history most alluring; others are less entranced by what is becoming more and more a definite mannerism: all the people have small legs. Nevertheless, this is one of the best of her biographies for very young children. It does not attempt to compress Penn's whole life into a limited number of pages, but concentrates mainly on his Quaker beliefs and his effort to live in peace and brotherhood with the Indians.

> *Alice Dalgliesh, in a review of "The Story of William Penn," in* Saturday Review, *Vol. XLVIII, No. 13, March 27, 1965, p. 33.*

### A WEED IS A FLOWER: THE LIFE OF GEORGE WASHINGTON CARVER (1965)

The complete self-containment that has often been identified as an aspect of true genius is not the easiest thing to convey in a book for the youngest readers, but Aliki has accomplished it in her text and picture biography of George Washington Carver. There is a storyteller's rhythm apparent in the words that describe him and his life which is evident when the book is read aloud. The illustrations are faithful to his times and his condition. His shoulders are usually bent over some task, humble or scientific, but Dr. Carver ages beautifully in these full color pages, going from small boy to young man (with a fiercely proud mustache) to a Gandhi-esque old age. The line is stylized, the color vivid. Again, it is rare to find a simplified biography true both to its subject and the interests of early childhood.

> *A review of "A Weed Is a Flower," in* Virginia Kirkus' Service, *Vol. XXXIII, No. 19, October 1, 1965, p. 1039.*

Here is a beautifully illustrated, factually correct, direct expository narrative of the life and important work of George Washington Carver written for preschool and beginning-school children. It is a model of the type of writing that should be used in all books about science and scientists for younger children. This story of Carver's life will give inspiration to all youngsters, and particularly those from disadvantaged homes. (p. 173)

> *A review of "A Weed Is a Flower: The Life of George Washington Carver," in* Science Books, *Vol. 1, No. 3, December, 1965, pp. 172-73.*

Gentle reverence and warm sentiment radiate from Aliki's picture-book. . . . As in Aliki's earlier introductions to Johnny Appleseed and William Penn, her new portrait is framed with stunning, stylized illustrations at once sophisticated and child-like. They are a spring garden bloom of color and a graceful expression of Carver's love of plants. Somehow though, the sweet and sunny text, with its few facts and simple generalizations, presents only a modest glimpse of the distinguished

*From* The Story of William Penn, *written and illustrated by Aliki. Prentice-Hall, 1964. © 1964 by Aliki Brandenberg. All rights reserved. Published by permission of Prentice-Hall, Inc., Englewood Cliffs, NJ 07632.*

Negro scientist whose experimental work enabled him to better the lot of the South and his people.

> *Margaret F. O'Connell, in a review of "A Weed Is a Flower: The Life of George Washington Carver," in* The New York Times Book Review, *January 30, 1966, p. 22.*

A read-aloud biography that is written in simple, rather dry, style and has balanced—if skimpy—coverage; the title refers to the statement (imputed to Dr. Carver) that a weed is a flower growing in the wrong place. The text is adequate; the illustrations—all of which are good and some of which are quite lovely in the use of color and mass, and in layout of text and painting—have a curious lack of reality, since many of the Negro faces look Andean or Polynesian and in a few of the pictures Dr. Carver does not look like himself. One pleasant new note: Aliki paints her characters in a realistic range of skin tones.

> *Zena Sutherland, in a review of "A Weed Is a Flower: The Life of George Washington Carver," in* Bulletin of the Center for Children's Books, *Vol. 19, No. 6, February, 1966, p. 93.*

---

## KEEP YOUR MOUTH CLOSED, DEAR (1966)

Anything that comes graphically close to exaggerated pregnancy gets a sniff (with some justification) from most adult

women and a belly laugh from the junior set. . . . However, this book is for very young children and it tries to make the point, in captions and illustrations, that swallowing interesting things is an uncomfortable habit, as many a three year old knows (sometimes secretly). Aliki's little alligator, like Waber's Lyle the Crocodile, has an expressive, mobile face. He's also got a big mouth that everything, including an alarm clock, falls into. . . . Finally, the vacuum hose fell in his mouth and sucked everything out. Shudderingly extreme? For dainty adults it is. But for early childhood, it plays straight to their often shattering sense of the comedy in anatomy.

> *A review of "Keep Your Mouth Closed, Dear," in* Virginia Kirkus' Service, *Vol. XXXIV, No. 18, September 15, 1966, p. 972.*

Aliki's understated prose yields gracefully to the wonderfully witty drawings of the little animal's distress as his mother tries to curb his troubling habit by sealing his snout with, in turn, a zipper, a paper bag, a large sock, and a series of Band-Aids. . . . Aliki adds to the central joy by providing the careful reader-looker with warm details, like the little wooden crocodile that is one of Charles's toys, or the way Charles's tail dips down casually into a water bucket while he is up on a ladder helping his mother wash the windows. An altogether winning creation. (p. 4)

*Richard Kluger, "Crocodile Smiles," in* Book Week—World Journal Tribune, *Fall Children's Issue, October 30, 1966, pp. 4-5, 8.\**

When little readers arrive at the startling twist that ends the family's woes, they'll want to investigate Aliki's story, an absolute romp, all over again—and again. The laugh-out-loud events get extra kicks from the author's illustrations, nifty black-and-white drawings that are backgrounds for the characters, shown in appropriate green. (pp. 108, 110)

*A review of "Keep Your Mouth Closed, Dear," in* Publishers Weekly, *Vol. 217, No. 4, February 1, 1980, pp. 108, 110.*

---

### THREE GOLD PIECES: A GREEK FOLK TALE   (1967)

Aliki's illustrations for this retelling of a Greek folk tale are her best to date. A submissive Greek peasant went to work as a servant to a wealthy Turk who gave him only three gold pieces for his 10 years of labor and took even these away in exchange for three pieces of valuable advice. The narrative is rather weak for reading aloud, but it is simple enough for second graders to manage on their own. The illustrations, most in brilliant full color, are as intricately yet gracefully crowded as Turkish oriental rugs; particularly excellent is the portrayal of the Turk's parlor. The contrasts between the rustic home of the Greeks, and cosmopolitan Constantinople are clearly depicted.

*Elinor Cullen, in a review of "Three Gold Pieces," in* School Library Journal, *an appendix to* Library Journal, *Vol. 13, No. 8, April, 1967, p. 61.*

[The story] exudes an almost Biblical quality with its virtuous hero triumphing over worldly temptations. Though its melancholy tone may not be to everyone's taste, Aliki's rich, Oriental illustrations are moving and, in themselves, worth the asking price.

*Eleanor Dienstag, in a review of "Three Gold Pieces," in* The New York Times Book Review, *April 30, 1967, p. 26.*

The books were for children from 4 or 5 to 8 or 9. The children were 5, 8, and 10. So this report involves the views of a looker, a reader, and a critic.

"I'll show you something," said Looker, as she and her brothers conducted their seminar on the big bed. She gave a magicianly flourish to bending back the covers of *Three Gold Pieces* . . . so all could see that the front and back made a single glowing picture. In an interior of Byzantine splendor it portrayed the black-mustached hero and the white-mustached old man who took his only three gold pieces in exchange for ambiguous but invaluable advice.

"I like the floor and the candles and the everything, except the men," said Looker, revealing a familiar bias. Certainly Aliki has provided marvelous colors and strong staring-eyed black-and-white illustrations for the Greek folk tale she has straightforwardly retold here.

"Nice," said Critic, "but it's like all the other ones, it's just not what I think of for children. . . . They read about space or TV—you know, characters on TV—or old stories like 'Cinderella.'. . . This is sort of a copy of a story told in a different way. . . . It would be good to read to a person just learning about books."

*Roderick Nordell, "Hero with a Black Mustache," in* The Christian Science Monitor, *May 4, 1967, p. B2.\**

Jubilant, dramatic, exotic color distinguishes . . . **Three Gold Pieces**. Certain to become a favorite in any storyteller's repertoire, this version of the Greek tale . . . conveys the spirit of Greece, the opulence of Constantinople, and the innate wisdom of the common peasant. Aliki's faithfulness to pictorial detail—down to the very coils of the nobleman's *nargilch*—merits reward.

*Virginia A. Tashjian, "A Wealth of Tales," in* Book Week—Chicago Sunday Sun-Times, *May 21, 1967, p. 18.\**

Aliki illustrates this in gorgeous and appropriately exotic colours. A shade strong to English tastes, but splendid nevertheless. The almost unrelieved melancholy of the hero is strongly appealing. Even in his final good fortunes only a hint of a smile shows below the huge bush of his moustache. (p. 160)

*A review of "Three Gold Pieces," in* The Junior Bookshelf, *Vol. 32, No. 3, June, 1968, pp. 159-60.*

---

### NEW YEAR'S DAY   (1967)

This description of New Year's Day, hardly a significant holiday in the life of American children, is trivial. After a brief description of historical New-Year observances, holiday traditions from many different countries are noted. The relevance of folk customs in such countries as Belgium, Hungary, and Scotland, is questionable, while the characterization of New Year's Eve in this country is inane.

*Marguerite M. Murray, in a review of "New Year's Day," in* School Library Journal, *an appendix to* Library Journal, *Vol. 14, No. 1, September, 1967, p. 107.*

A book that is simply written and enhanced by lively, amusing illustrations of scenes of celebration, past and present. The text is slight, not because of the author's treatment, but because there is really little to say about the holiday's origin: it is simply an occasion that marks a fresh start in time.

*Zena Sutherland, in a review of "New Year's Day," in* Bulletin of the Center for Children's Books, *Vol. 21, No. 4, December, 1967, p. 53.*

---

### THE EGGS: A GREEK FOLK TALE   (1969)

["The Eggs"] is a cheater cheated story, in which a sailor who owes an innkeeper for food consumed six years ago is charged an inflated price to discharge his debt. A sharp lawyer gets him off and all ends well. The Mediterranean colors are inviting and sunny, but none of the characters is appealing, least of all the wife whose sole contribution is "Heaven forbid that anything should happen to the caique."

*Nora L. Magid, in a review of "The Eggs," in* The New York Times Book Review, *Part II, May 4, 1969, p. 53.*

Good for storytelling or for reading aloud, this tale has an easy, colloquial style of writing and illustrations (some in color, others black and white) that capture both the atmosphere of the setting and the humor of the plot.

Zena Sutherland, in a review of "The Eggs: A Greek Folk Tale," in Saturday Review, Vol. LII, No. 45, November 8, 1969, p. 64.

The style of the retelling is excellent, with no distractions in the way of excess verbiage, direct in approach and natural in dialogue. The illustrations have vigor and humor.

Zena Sutherland, in a review of "The Eggs: A Greek Folk Tale," in Bulletin of the Center for Children's Books, Vol. 23, No. 4, December, 1969, p. 53.

With subtle humor Aliki retells a tale about a rascally innkeeper who over-reaches himself. . . . Carrying the story are beautiful, expressive, often humorous illustrations brilliantly colored on alternate double-page spreads; colors, characters, and backgrounds all reflect the Mediterranean setting.

Laura F. Seacord, in a review of "The Eggs," in School Library Journal, an appendix to Library Journal, Vol. 16, No. 7, March, 1970, p. 127.

## DIOGENES: THE STORY OF THE GREEK PHILOSOPHER (1969)

[Diogenes: The Story of the Greek Philosopher presents] the ancient but timely wisdom of this early flower child who gave up wealth and worldly comforts to go forth, a lantern in his hand, searching for an honest man. . . .

Diogenes is pictured as an ascetic—an impressive, saintly, rather remote hero whose growth in virtue and self-control is charted in a series of (alas! somewhat disconnected) anecdotes. . . . The illustrations are equally dignified. With a serene, classic beauty they resemble portions of a Grecian frieze.

Mary Lynne Bird, in a review of "Diogenes: The Story of the Greek Philosopher," in The New York Times Book Review, August 24, 1969, p. 20.

Pleasantly illustrated, and written in a simple but rather flat style, this is a book designated as a read-aloud book by the publisher. The biography of Diogenes seems not likely to appeal to many young children, although the style and format are appropriate for that audience. For the independent reader who might be interested in the subject the book is superficial.

Zena Sutherland, in a review of "Diogenes: The Story of the Greek Philosopher," in Bulletin of the Center for Children's Books, Vol. 23, No. 6, February, 1970, p. 91.

In Diogenes: The Story of the Greek Philosopher, the illustrator-writer Aliki has adapted the style of classical Greek fresco painting in the telling of a life of that historical culture. The Greeks' "way of seeing the world" as realized in their paintings became our way of encountering a member of that culture, imaginatively, across time. The surfaces of the pictures, which relate scenes of Diogenes' life, have been carefully worked to resemble the plaster of a fresco. We view them as from one remove, as reproductions of frescos, documentation. But in contrast to this distancing effect . . . are the noon-bright, Mediterranean colors of the illustrations of alternating spreads (the rest are in black and white), which beam forth and delight us with an animated richness and immediacy of color that seems entirely a given, a natural resource of Diogenes' world. No wonder, we think to ourselves on seeing these pictures, the philosopher . . . felt the need for almost nothing he did not already have, around him or inside him. It is not so much a

moral as an atmosphere or climate of well-being and reassurance that readers are offered. The accompanying text is spare as Diogenes. (p. 21)

Leonard S. Marcus, "Life Drawings: Some Notes on Children's Picture Book Biographies," in The Lion and the Unicorn, Vol. 4, No. 1, Summer, 1980, pp. 15-31.*

## MY VISIT TO THE DINOSAURS (1969)

What this dinosaur book has that others don't is what might be called human interest—also a sense of humor. My Visit . . . is that of a little boy, his father and littler sister to see the skeletons in the museum (of Natural History, N.Y., but it hardly matters), which occasions some explanation—beginning with the Brontosaurus—of how a skeleton is put together, of how fossils were found and of what paleontologists (explained) learned from them. Then, beginning again with the benign Brontosaurus, we have a descriptive gallery of dinosaurs . . . that get fiercer and fiercer-looking. . . . "I was glad Tyrannosaurus Rex wasn't alive any more. When you go to the museum, you will see what I mean." How can you wait? (pp. 930-31)

A review of "My Visit to the Dinosaurs," in Kirkus Reviews, Vol. XXXVII, No. 17, September 1, 1969, pp. 930-31.

[My Visit to the Dinosaurs provides] generally accurate, occasionally oversimplified information about the prehistoric animals. The accompanying illustrations, some in mustard, blue, and green, depict both museum-goers and animals adequately. Although this makes the point that dinosaur bones are to be found at the Museum, and might therefore be useful as visit-encouraging, supplementary material, Clark's True Book of Dinosaurs (Children's Pr., 1955) and Holsaert's and Garland's Dinosaurs (Holt, 1959) cover a greater variety of the "terrible lizards" and give better explanations of what exactly a fossil is.

Ann D. Schweibish, in a review of "My Visit to the Dinosaurs," in School Library Journal, an appendix to Library Journal, Vol. 16, No. 5, January, 1970, p. 47.

[The] illustrations are good, the human figures in pictures of the exhibit a contrast to the size of the skeletons, and the pictures of individual dinosaurs are detailed enough for identification. The text gives a few facts about each and gives some background information about dinosaur fossils and paleontological research. The author writes as simply as is commensurate with the use of accurate terminology; no writing-down, no padding. Another fine book in a good beginning science series.

Zena Sutherland, in a review of "My Visit to the Dinosaurs," in Bulletin of the Center for Children's Books, Vol. 24, No. 1, September, 1970, p. 2.

## FOSSILS TELL OF LONG AGO (1972)

This may not be the most complete book about fossils, but it's certainly the most enjoyable. . . . In the museum we see not only dinosaur bones but crying babies, shouting children and a worried guard, and in the end the children are given the green light to make their own fossil—"Not a one-million-year-old

From Three Gold Pieces: A Greek Folk Tale, *retold and illustrated by Aliki. Pantheon Books, 1967.*
*First printing © copyright, 1967, by Aliki Brandenberg. All rights reserved. Reprinted by permission of*
*Pantheon Books, a Division of Random House, Inc.*

fossil but a one-minute-old 'fossil' "—by making an imprint of their hands in clay. The kids Aliki draws seem to be having fun, and it's no wonder because the author . . . mixes paleontology and playfulness in a way that shows she's far from an old fossil herself.

A *review of "Fossils Tell of Long Ago," in* Kirkus Reviews, *Vol. XL, No. 10, May 15, 1972, p. 581.*

This factually accurate, clearly written text will be welcomed by primary graders who are usually captivated by fossils and dinosaurs. The large print and special format will encourage beginning readers, and the illustrations are in the same appealing style as other Aliki books in the Let's-Read-and-Find-Out Science Books series. Julian May's *They Turned to Stone* (Holiday, 1965) covers most of the same information at the same level, and the illustrations are more carefully detailed and realistic than Aliki's, which have a note of humor to recommend them yet do give adequate detail to clarify the text.

Mary Neale Rees, *in a review of "Fossils Tell of Long Ago," in* School Library Journal, *an appendix to* Library Journal, *Vol. 19, No. 1, September, 1972, p. 111.*

The altogether excellent presentation puts us in touch with the ongoing quest of science for a better picture of the long yet continuing evolution of our planet and its inhabitants; the il-

lustrations heighten interest and help involve one in the developing text. Here is a compelling, fascinating book.

O. Robert Brown, Jr., *in a review of "Fossils Tell of Long Ago," in* Childhood Education, *Vol. 49, No. 2 (November, 1972), p. 86.*

**Fossils** . . . is a well-executed, useful addition to the series. As some of the concepts like millions of years of time, fossilization, imprints and extinct animals may need explanation, the book would be best used with the aid of an adult. The print, format and illustrations are excellent and serve well to describe a process which might be quite abstract to a young child if he had never seen an actual fossil. With little text and many illustrations, the author has done a good job in surveying fossil development, fossil discovery and the role of fossil study in natural history. The book concludes with possible activities for aspiring young paleontologists which are within their domain and are fruitful, absorbing and instructive.

Sonja M. Wieta, *in a review of "Fossils Tell of Long Ago," in* Appraisal: Children's Science Books, *Vol. 6, No. 3, Fall, 1973, p. 5.*

The book seems to sacrifice not only technical accuracy, but also clarity, for the sake of simplicity. Try as I may to view the book as a ''fun thing'' created to be seen through the eyes of a child, I cannot help but note inconsistencies: ''. . . a fossil is made of stone'' (p. 2), but ''. . . some fossils can be eaten''

(p. 15); technical inaccuracies: "coal is a fern encased in mud" (p. 11); and misleading activity suggestions: "fossils can be found almost anywhere, if you just look for them" (p. 27).

*Ronald J. Kley, in a review of "Fossils Tell of Long Ago," in* Appraisal: Children's Science Books, *Vol. 6, No. 3, Fall, 1973, p. 5.*

---

### JUNE 7! (1972)

Anyone who has attended a family reunion will recognize what's going on at this increasingly crowded and chaotic birthday party. From the time that "my father's parents, who are my mother's parents-in-law, who are my grandparents, whose granddaughter I am, walked in," the feted child gamely explicates the relationships while the black and white pages (with touches of green for the household plants) become more and more crowded with a mix of mod to feebly hobbling in-laws, great-aunts and third cousins. . . . [It] will be a picnic for everyone, from reading aloud grown-ups on down, to follow the unadvertised visual subplots: the silent drama at the bathroom door, the young cousins' romps and rivalries, the adults' continuing one-way conversations. Circle *June 7th!*

*A review of "June 7!" in* Kirkus Reviews, *Vol. XL, No. 17, September 1, 1972, p. 1019.*

Look at this picture book many times, each time following a different relative through the ever-increasing crowd. . . . Children from small families may laugh, wondering if such gatherings can be so; children and parents with large families may laugh, knowing very well that there *are* such reunions.

*Patricia Tonkin, in a review of "June 7!" in* Childhood Education, *Vol. 49, No. 6 (March, 1973), p. 317.*

[Aliki] has a simplicity of line and an eye for detail that children seek out. *June 7!* is a pseudo autobiographical picture book for in it she introduces all the relations who come to celebrate her birthday. . . . Through the use of 'balloon-speak' we learn a little of the conversations that ensue between different members of the family, but there are so many of them that it is easy to become confused about who is related to whom.

Black and white line drawings are brightened with green in this picture book which will bring a smile or two, but which will, I think, add little to Aliki's reputation.

*Edward Hudson, in a review of "June 7!" in* Children's Book Review, *Vol. V, No. 2, Summer, 1975, p. 55.*

---

### THE LONG LOST COELACANTH AND OTHER LIVING FOSSILS (1973)

The long-lost coelacanth now turns up with appalling frequency on juvenile science shelves, but somehow Aliki's tongue-in-cheek animated cartoons tell us more than we've learned in older, more serious treatments—including the proper pronunciation (*see*-la-kanth), the fish's evolutionary relationship to other crossopterygians (paddle-fins) and just what it means to be a living fossil. Another simple demonstration of what *Fossils Tell of Long Ago.* . . .

*A review of "The Long Lost Coelacanth: And Other Living Fossils," in* Kirkus Reviews, *Vol. XLI, No. 8, April 15, 1973, p. 458.*

Aliki's book will attract five- and six-year-olds as well as teenage readers with the tangible presence of a distant animal past. Although errors exist, compounded in millions of years (horse shoe crabs lived not merely 30 million years ago but closer to 200 million years ago), either figure remains more than one might imagine even in dreams.

A more serious flaw, especially where young readers are concerned, is the final double-page spread showing two small, frightened children meeting a full-sized, ferocious, living dinosaur!

*Sally Cartwright, "Books to Make Nature Lovers," in* The Christian Science Monitor, *May 2, 1973, p. B4.\**

Some of the excitement that paleontologists may have experienced when the first coelacanth was discovered has found its way into this book and acts as a springboard from which to provide the primary school child with much general knowledge about fossils. It is to be regretted that the author has taught the reader how to pronounce the difficult word in the title but has not also provided for other difficult names in the text. . . . [There] are numerous pictures to help the young reader to imagine life as it was a long time ago. This most useful first book could be used to introduce the subject of fossil life, and it might indeed stimulate a youngster to find out more about this subject.

*A review of "The Long-Lost Coelacanth and Other Living Fossils," in* Science Books, *Vol. IX, No. 2, September, 1973, p. 169.*

The importance of [the discovery of this ancient fish] is successfully explained, along with a basic description of the animals known as "living fossils." The material on the coelacanth is interesting and accurate, but it emphasizes the animal's history and omits pertinent information about its life today. For instance, the similarity of eating habits and digestive tracts in the coelacanth and shark families is not discussed. Nevertheless, the black-and-white drawings, occasionally highlighted with blue and green, are attractive, and this will be a good addition to simple science materials for most collections.

*Margaret Bush, in a review of "The Long-Lost Coelacanth and Other Living Fossils," in* School Library Journal, *an appendix to* Library Journal, *Vol. 20, No. 2, October, 1973, p. 105.*

---

### GREEN GRASS AND WHITE MILK (1974)

Aliki's lesson for the urban and suburban picture-book set on cows and dairying is simpler than Wright's *Look at a calf . . .* but perhaps less effective for its use of drawings instead of photographs. Still, despite an occasionally coy text there are informative basics here, like the reason a cow chews its cud and the way its four stomachs prepare food for transformation into milk. . . . A brief look at factory milk processing is also included, plus simple instructions for making butter and yogurt.

*A review of "Green Grass and White Milk," in* The Booklist, *Vol. 70, No. 19, June 1, 1974, p. 1101.*

The format is appealing: the easy-to-read, sometimes chatty, text is complemented by pleasantly humorous cartoon drawings. This is far superior to Darby's antiquated *What Is a Cow* (Benefic, 1963) or Whitney's simplistic *Let's Find Out about Milk* (Watts, 1967).

*Sylva Manoogian, in a review of "Green Grass and White Milk," in* School Library Journal, *an appendix to* Library Journal, *Vol. 21, No. 1, September, 1974, p. 72.*

For the city slicker who can only read about farm life rather than experience it, this book is recommended. (But even the youngest farm child knows better than to milk a cow as pictured on page 13. The farmer is in direct line of a swift kick from his cow!) . . . [Aliki's] recipes for butter and yogurt have not been tested by this reviewer, but the instructions seem adequate and safe.

*A review of "Green Grass and White Milk," in* Science Books, *Vol. X, No. 3, December, 1974, p. 262.*

It is hard to determine the age group toward which this book is directed. The early pages suggest kindergarten and first grade but the later pages would not hold the attention of little children. It is doubtful if anyone attracted by the pictures will also be interested in the intricacies of the diagram of the milk processing plant. The diagram of the cow's four stomachs that seem to terminate in a large tube of milk running directly into the udder is not only physiologically inaccurate but the idea is unpleasant. I object also to the gross inaccuracies of the drawings of the cows. The cow in the dark barn has extremely short hind legs, and seems rather to have feet with heels than lower legs with hocks. The calf in the field does not look like a calf and has a docked tail. The short staccato sentences of the printed text seem to be directed toward the young child and may bore the older one who might be interested in the subject matter of later pages. And why raise the question on the last page as to green grass and white milk if it is to be left untouched?

*Esther H. Read, in a review of "Green Grass and White Milk," in* Appraisal: Children's Science Books, *Vol. 8, No. 1, Winter, 1975, p. 5.*

---

### CORN IS MAIZE: THE GIFT OF THE INDIANS (1976)

At a younger level than other introductions and more attractively than most, Aliki describes—in characteristically concise sentences and in pictures leavened with warmth and regard—how corn is planted, fertilized and harvested, how American Indians have cultivated and used it through the centuries (plus how they saved the Pilgrims' lives with it), and how present strains probably evolved from an early wild plant. Aliki depicts the young farmers and feasters, both ancient and modern, as native Americans, and she conveys the central place of corn in the Indians' lives in telling pictures of the gods and festivals it inspired, a few sustaining words about the celebrants' praise and dependence, and no unfortified filler.

*A review of "Corn Is Maize: The Gift of the Indians," in* Kirkus Reviews, *Vol. XLIV, No. 4, February 15, 1976, p. 201.*

An engaging description. . . . A successful blend of social studies, science, and history for seven to ten year olds, the clear text is augmented by accurate diagrams and cheerful black-and-white and four-color wash illustrations.

*Diane Holzheimer, in a review of "Corn Is Maize: The Gift of the Indians," in* School Library Journal, *Vol. 22, No. 8, April, 1976, p. 58.*

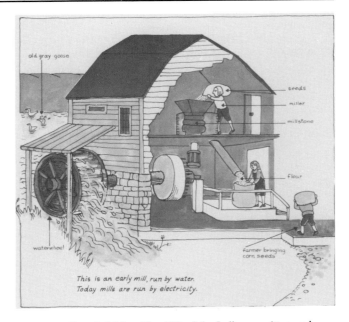

old gray goose

seeds

miller

millstone

flour

waterwheel

farmer bringing corn seeds

*This is an early mill, run by water. Today mills are run by electricity.*

[That this book] demonstrates accuracy is not enough. A hodge-podge of information about the nature, development, history, and use of corn contains too many complex ideas, resulting in confusion rather than clarity. Keeping the facts straight is difficult, as the story skips back and forth in time in a disorderly fashion. Garish green-and-yellow drawings do not help to illustrate the corn silks' turning "from a creamy color to dark red to brown." Worse, the author is guilty of stereotyping blacks and native Americans.

*Ruth M. Stein, in a review of "Corn Is Maize: The Gift of the Indians," in* Language Arts, *Vol. 53, No. 6, September, 1976, p. 696.*

Aliki's new book gives her readers food for contemplation while they munch, and children will come away from this book with some new ideas and new information. . . . Aliki leads her readers through [the] complicated ideas using simple prose and with exciting illustrations. This book should be available to as many readers as possible before next year's crop of corn arrives. (pp. 162-63)

*Helen J. Stern, in a review of "Corn Is Maize: The Gift of the Indians," in* Science Books & Films, *Vol. XII, No. 3, December, 1976, pp. 162-63.*

In 30-odd nicely drawn pages with lots of yellow and green tint and a very brief text the story of maize is told for readers in the early grades. Surprising in the richness of its content, this little book is notably engaging in its warm portrayal of Indian farmers north and south. . . . The well-known artist-author has long had an interest both in corn and in American Indian culture; they have flowed together charmingly in this excellent little book, a model of economic ethnobotany for third-graders.

*Philip Morrison and Phylis Morrison, in a review of "Corn Is Maize: The Gift of the Indians," in* Scientific American, *Vol. 235, No. 6, December, 1976, p. 134.*

Aliki's thorough research, her easy-going narration and delightful illustrations make this one of the best picture books on the Let's-Read-and-Find-Out Science lineup. Period and modern scenes in the artist's quaint style enliven the history of maize.... Aliki concludes with pictures of her own cornhusk doll and wreath, and directions for making them.

*A review of "Corn Is Maize: The Gift of the Indians," in* Publishers Weekly, *Vol. 221, No. 21, May 21, 1982, p. 77.*

---

## AT MARY BLOOM'S (1976)

On the first page of this book, the young narrator announces that her mouse just had babies. She decides to tell her neighbor, Mary Bloom, but realizes that if she rings the doorbell the baby will cry, the dogs will bark, the owl will shiver, the hamsters will hide, and so on, for Mary Bloom's apartment is filled with all kinds of animals. So she telephones, instead, and Mary Bloom says, "Babies! Come show me right away!" All that the narrator had been afraid would happen did when the phone rang, but when she arrives later with the mice all is quiet. Then together she and Mary celebrate the births with a freshly baked cake. The repetition of the text makes this an excellent choice for use with very young children, who will certainly enjoy joining in. The simple line drawings are minimally hued with light shades of pink, green, and brown. Although I generally try to avoid using this description, it is apt in this case—truly delightful!

*Barbara Dill, in a review of "At Mary Bloom's," in* Wilson Library Bulletin, *Vol. 51, No. 2, October, 1976, p. 133.*

Lively drawings add to the humor of an engaging story that has animals as an appealing subject, a repeat pattern that is not abused by being overdone, a warm friendship between a child and an older neighbor, and a pervasive enjoyment of creatures—any kind of creature, especially any kind of new creature.... Great fun.

*Zena Sutherland, in a review of "At Mary Bloom's," in* Bulletin of the Center for Children's Books, *Vol. 30, No. 3, November, 1976, p. 37.*

---

## WILD AND WOOLLY MAMMOTHS (1977)

Here's a Let's Read and Find Out Science book with the unusual touch in text and pictures which have endeared Aliki to young readers. The book is a clear and inviting history of the long-vanished mammoth with details on why it failed to survive as well as a source of information on other creatures of the distant past.

*A review of "Wild and Woolly Mammoths," in* Publishers Weekly, *Vol. 211, No. 11, March 14, 1977, p. 95.*

[*Wild and Woolly Mammoths*] should appeal to many children, attracted by the amusing, cartoonlike wash drawings and brief text.... The book tells about cave paintings, Stone Age man's hunting methods, artifacts made from mammoth bodies, and Thomas Jefferson's interest in fossils. The author states that "not one live wooly mammoth has been seen for 11,000 years."

With such imagination and integration of related subject matter, the book is a model of interesting factual writing for children.

*Sarah Gagné, in a review of "Wild and Woolly Mammoths," in* The Horn Book Magazine, *Vol. LIII, No. 5, October, 1977, p. 557.*

This is a delightful little book.... The cartoon-like illustrations are delightful, and some of the captions lend a pleasant, comical air to the text. Of the better selections are included a map showing the land bridge across the Bering Strait, methods used by early people in hunting the mammoth, human uses of mammoth bones and tusks, and characteristics of mammals. The author mentions that the imperial mammoth lived three million years before the wooly mammoth and discusses the Columbian mammoth, but there is no inclusion of the mastodon. Aliki does state that dinosaurs were long extinct before the mammoths made their appearance, but she does not make clear the link through the mastodons. Since children tend to hear of mammoths and mastodons together, it would appear that a distinction between them would be in order. Another omission is the matter of proboscidean dentition. The fact that modern elephants have four sets of teeth and eventually tend to die of indigestion or starvation was also omitted. However, for a book aimed at a very young audience, *Mammoths* is accurate and interesting.

*Philip Kutner, in a review of "Wild and Woolly Mammoths," in* Science Books & Films, *Vol. XIII, No. 4, March, 1978, p. 221.*

---

## THE MANY LIVES OF BENJAMIN FRANKLIN (1977)

[Benjamin Franklin is projected] in a short, simple chronology and in ink and wash drawings (often several frames to the page) with hand-lettered captions that elaborate on the text. Aliki is sketchiest on Franklin's most significant life, the political one..., and she lacks Jean Fritz's talent for striking just the right, light note. (An early caption reads, "Ben wanted to be a sailor so he could travel"; the accompanying picture has a sweet young Mom explaining "No Ben. Your brother was a sailor and he drowned"—an efficient but odd way to tell it.) Her approach overall is pleasant and unimposing and Franklin is a subject who takes well to the informality—but this is neither first-class Aliki nor notable among the many lives of Benjamin Franklin.

*A review of "The Many Lives of Benjamin Franklin," in* Kirkus Reviews, *Vol. XLV, No. 22, November 15, 1977, p. 1199.*

The multiple accomplishments of Ben Franklin are presented in a conventional, lifeless text and in pen-and-watercolor cartoons with crude hand-lettered balloon dialogue and captions. Unfortunately, the occasional attempts at humor, abandoned after the first few pages, fail to capture Franklin's wit. Aliki's biography is accessible to a young audience because of its simple language and pictures that children can "read" for themselves but it is no more than a faint echo of Ingri and Edgar Parin d'Aulaire's *Benjamin Franklin* (Doubleday, 1950), which presents more information and gives readers a feeling for, as well as knowledge of, the man.

*Stephen D. Roxburgh, in a review of "The Many Lives of Benjamin Franklin," in* School Library Journal, *Vol. 24, No. 5, January, 1978, p. 75.*

Children wanting wider scope than that of Monjo's entertaining *Poor Richard in France* . . . may have their notions of Franklin firmed up here in an equally humorous but more broadly concerned biography. Aliki's captioned cartoons—lightly lined and washed—expand or punctuate her easy text. . . . [Franklin's] inventiveness and multifaceted career as a writer, printer, politician, and diplomat are all touched on to comprise an efficient, lightweight introduction for picturebook readers.

> *Denise M. Wilms, in a review of "The Many Lives of Benjamin Franklin," in* Booklist, *Vol. 74, No. 9, January 1, 1978, p. 744.*

[The] text serves adequately as an introduction, but it is a bit staccato in its treatment, and the pictures (colorful, framed, and—on some pages—crowded) have captions that are difficult to read because of small print. Occasionally the text-illustration combination may be confusing, as when the text states that "Before long they had two children to help them," while one of the facing strips shows three children; only upon reading the small handprinted caption below the middle picture does the reader learn that the second son died at the age of four.

> *Zena Sutherland, in a review of "The Many Lives of Benjamin Franklin," in* Bulletin of the Center for Children's Books, *Vol. 31, No. 7, March, 1978, p. 105.*

---

### THE TWELVE MONTHS: A GREEK FOLKTALE   (1978)

A humble woman who sees good in all the seasons is rewarded, while a greedy woman, expecting the same but only able to find fault, is punished. Aliki is at her best when writing and illustrating folklore—as this beautifully designed book, with its carefully written text and distinctive pen drawings capturing the strong contrasts of the familiar motif, amply demonstrates.

> *Stephen D. Roxburgh, in a review of "The Twelve Months: A Greek Folktale," in* School Library Journal, *Vol. 25, No. 3, November, 1978, p. 39.*

Aliki's pen drawings for the Greek tale show a soft-eyed heroine and unmistakenly nasty neighbor; scenes are simple but strongly evocative—always in tune with the story's emotional ups and downs.

> *Denise M. Wilms, in a review of "The Twelve Months: A Greek Folktale," in* Booklist, *Vol. 75, No. 8, December 15, 1978, p. 681.*

[It] is not the just outcome so much as the way it's arrived at that makes this memorable. It would have been more so, however, had the pictures—black-and-white pen drawings—been colored to reflect the changing moods and succeeding seasons.

> *A review of "The Twelve Months," in* Kirkus Reviews, *Vol. XLVII, No. 1, January 1, 1979, p. 1.*

---

### THE TWO OF THEM   (1979)

Quite different from Aliki's usual, fun-filled books is her new work, a moving but unsentimental story that seems based on her own childhood. Exquisite paintings in inspired colors stress the deep love one reads about, between a grandfather and his granddaughter. . . . Throughout all the girl's young life, the two are inseparable—at work and at play. Then the day comes when . . . her grandfather begins to fail with the days. As their roles are reversed, we see the granddaughter giving the old

*From* The Two of Them, *written and illustrated by Aliki. Greenwillow Books, 1979. Copyright © 1979 by Aliki Brandenberg. All rights reserved. By permission of Greenwillow Books (A Division of William Morrow & Company, Inc.).*

man the same tender care he had given her, until she has to say "good-night forever" to her beloved friend. This is a picture book that parents who read to their children will probably appreciate even more than will the young.

> *A review of "The Two of Them," in* Publishers Weekly, *Vol. 216, No. 11, September 10, 1979, p. 75.*

Just as beautiful a picture of the vital connection between young and old as Farber and Hyman's more complex *How Does It Feel to Be Old?*. . . . [The] child is movingly and comfortingly shown to be the important extension of ongoing life and love. Aliki's accompaniment of warm-toned illustration is dramatically simple but deeply satisfying. (pp. 497-98)

> *Betsy Hearne, in a review of "The Two of Them," in* Booklist, *Vol. 76, No. 6, November 15, 1979, pp. 497-98.*

In an understated, almost symbolic text and in pictures full of gentleness and warmth of feeling, the story is told of the great mutual love of an old man and his granddaughter. . . . The eloquent illustrations in muted full color and the smaller soft-pencil drawings show the life the two shared as well as the tenderness and pure pleasure implicit in their relationship. As effective in its own way as Miska Miles's *Annie and the Old One* (Atlantic-Little), the book transcends the labored introductions to geriatrics which have proliferated in contemporary children's literature and describes with sensitivity and truth the changing seasons of human life.

*Ethel L. Heins, in a review of ''The Two of Them,'' in* The Horn Book Magazine, *Vol. LV, No. 6, December, 1979, p. 651.*

Aliki's predilection for Keene-eyed cuties has its most unmitigated expression here, which only brings out the inherent sugary quality of the whole soft-focus mood piece. Dewy-eyed parents might love it; a red-blooded grandfather is as likely to choke on it.

*A review of ''The Two of Them,'' in* Kirkus Reviews, *Vol. XLVII, No. 24, December 15, 1979, p. 1427.*

Probably not since the Alm Uncle has a grandfather been so devoted and beloved as the one in this story. While the book's sincerity cannot be doubted, one has to wonder whether young listeners will interpret correctly its focus on *The Two of Them.* Didn't the girl have a mother or a father? Didn't he have a wife? Keynote sentences such as the one with which the book opens (''The day she was born,/ her grandfather made her a ring/ of silver and polished stone,/ because he loved her already.'') owe a stylistic debt to Goffstein; and the idea that children grow up to cherish those who have cared for them has been explored recently in Sally Wittman's *A Special Trade* (Harper, 1978). The warm, gentle illustrations use crayon areas and pencil lines for rich and glowing effects.

*Joan W. Blos, in a review of ''The Two of Them,'' in* School Library Journal, *Vol. 26, No. 5, January, 1980, p. 53.*

---

## MUMMIES MADE IN EGYPT (1979)

When an 8-year-old in the Egyptian wing of the Penn Museum announced that he wished he could read the hieroglyphics, I handed him Aliki's **''Mummies Made in Egypt.''** First he identified the Ankh, the Shen, and the Protective Eye of Horus. Then, still consulting the book, he investigated the mummies in their multiple layers of bandages, the coffins and the canopic jars with the innards. His reaction to the news that the brains had been drawn out through the nose by metal hooks was matter-of-fact. (p. 30)

The child plans to acquire the book. And well he might. Particularly for the museum-goer, it is a fine source. It begins with a parade of the Egyptian gods and goddesses of the dead, all in familiar profile; it explains the symbols and the foundations of the belief in the afterlife; and it goes from a description of the early burial practices, which resulted in natural mummification, to the elaborate rituals of the wealthy and the powerful, which were performed by priests and embalmers and required 70 days.

Each step is pictured and described, from the inital rites over the new corpse to the procession and the entombment. The art, adapted from the real article and rendered frieze-style, is stunning, and the text is uncompromisingly informative and clear. (p. 31)

*Nora Magid, in a review of ''Mummies Made in Egypt,'' in* The New York Times Book Review, *November 18, 1979, pp. 30-1.*

Aliki has kept the well-paced, simple but informative text to a minimum and allowed the colorful, richly suggestive illustrations to speak for themselves. The explanation of the steps of the mummification process and of the religious signficance of each part of the burial ritual is uncondescending and nicely accented with clear, well-labeled diagrams and with scenes inspired by tomb paintings. A top choice for any collection on ancient Egypt, and a good source for information for readers of this age group. (pp. 52-3)

*Barbara C. Campbell, in a review of ''Mummies Made in Egypt,'' in* School Library Journal, *Vol. 26, No. 5, January, 1980, pp. 52-3.*

The author's own full-color drawings, many in the style of ancient carvings, are the highlights of this delightful book. Although part social studies, a good portion of the text describes the scientific methods used by the ancient Egyptians to prepare the body for burial so as to last for thousands of years. The text is printed as separate sentences, and the language is, unfortunately, often stilted and technical for the age level for whom the book seems intended. . . . [It] will be useful for the study of Ancient Egypt by primary and elementary grades as a good deal of information is given about the religion and tombs of the dead. The illustrations will be enjoyed by all ages. (pp. 15-16)

*Sallie Hope Erhard, in a review of ''Mummies Made in Egypt,'' in* Appraisal: Children's Science Books, *Vol. 13, No. 2, Spring, 1980, pp. 15-16.*

This delightful book correctly places mummification in its cultural setting. . . . It is written in a simple, direct and easy-to-read style, printed in large type, and lavishly illustrated with paintings by the author. . . . Captions under the illustrations provide information beyond that which is given in the text. This book will give parents and teachers accurate answers to questions children ask about mummification and should be a welcome addition to elementary school libraries.

*Gus W. Van Beek, in a review of ''Mummies Made in Egypt,'' in* Science Books & Films, *Vol. XV, No. 5, May, 1980, p. 281.*

Without being squeamish or gory, this book approaches the process of mummification and succeeds in demystifying it. In clear, direct statements and rich, multicolored illustrations adapted from paintings and sculptures found in ancient Egyptian tombs, Aliki describes this process in detail. Diagrams are used to reduce a complex procedure to its essentials, as we are taken step-by-step through the logic of mummification and are introduced to the meaning behind each ritual. (p. 66)

*Mummies Made in Egypt* highlights Aliki's career as a fine author/illustrator of books which capture the texture of other civilizations, particularly ancient ones. In clear strong language and with beautiful illustrations, she has created a book with wide appeal to children. It may, in fact, be peculiarly comforting: children often wonder about death, and literature for them has only recently begun to explore some of their questions in fiction. Here, this informational book ends on a note of cheerful acceptance: ''At last, the mummy was in its eternal resting place and on the way to its new life.'' (p. 68)

*Roni Natov, in a review of ''Mummies Made in Egypt,'' in* Archaeology, *Vol. 33, No. 5, September/October, 1980, pp. 66, 68.*

I have not come across a clearer exposition of the whys, wherefores and purposes of the Egyptian custom of mummification. (p. 243)

This is a pleasant book to pore over and handle and a clear introduction for budding Egyptologists. (p. 244)

*D. A. Young, in a review of "Mummies Made in Egypt," in* The Junior Bookshelf, *Vol. 44, No. 5, October, 1980, pp. 243-44.*

---

### DIGGING UP DINOSAURS (1981)

Aliki, whose earlier **"My Visit to the Dinosaurs"** was designed to engage the would-be dinosaur buff, now offers a follow-up for the already hooked. Her purpose, in the words of her young narrator, is to explain "where [the dinosaurs] came from and how they got into the museum." (This same winning girl also boasts, "I'm not afraid of dinosaurs anymore. Sometimes I call them 'you bag of bones' under my breath.")

**"Digging Up Dinosaurs"** works on two levels. The main body of the text is straightforward and informative. The time-consuming, often back-breaking and tedious, and sometimes dangerous work of paleontologists, geologists, photographers, draftsmen—Aliki is careful to point out that "there are draftswomen, too"—and other specialists is described, as is the process by which skeletons are transported from the field to the museum, then reconstructed and copied. Aliki has also included a running commentary that poses and answers questions suggested by the story itself. Peopled with very real children who fight and tease and say whatever comes to their minds, this comic-book annotation clips along, zigging and zagging like any kid in a museum who's been told to behave. Moreover, though younger readers may need an adult's help to decipher its tiny hand-written print, this subtext provides additional material for discussion between parent or teacher and child.

Some of the book's humor will undoubtedly escape its readers: How many 8-year-olds will understand why a worker standing by the partially exposed head of a dinosaur mutters, "Alas, poor Brontosaurus"? But Aliki's main text and energetic drawings will appeal to any child who hungers for extra information on those endlessly fascinating "bags of bones."

*Susan Bolotin, in a review of "Digging Up Dinosaurs," in* The New York Times Book Review, *March 8, 1981, p. 30.*

Aliki's noted style of using dialogue in cartoon bubbles to enhance the text falls short in this overview of the history of dinosaurs and how their homes are excavated and displayed. The distraction makes the book more difficult to read. However, the overabundance of information seems to be well researched and accurately presented. An acceptable balance of

From Digging Up Dinosaurs, *written and illustrated by Aliki. Thomas Y. Crowell Co., Inc., 1981. Copyright © 1981 by Aliki Brandenberg. All rights reserved. Reprinted by permission of Harper & Row, Publishers, Inc.*

male and female "experts" are pictured. "There are drafts-women, too." Why not use draftsperson?

*Sharron McElmeel, in a review of "Digging Up Di-nosaurs," in School Library Journal, Vol. 27, No. 10, August, 1981, p. 52.*

This book is both more, and less, than what might be expected of a science text for the young reader.

It is less because it offers relatively little insight into the "how," "when," and "where," or the all-important "why" of lo-cating and recovering fossils. Indeed, one could come away from this book with the impression that paleontologists do their fossil hunting wherever and whenever it might be fun, and with little purpose beyond that of public exhibition and the "gee whiz" level.

On the other hand, and quite apart from the scientific content of the text, there is much that is of value here for its insights into field procedures, professional specialization and teamwork and behind-the-scenes activities of museum exhibit prepara-tion, as well as for its subtle (perhaps too subtle to be perceived by the targeted age group) visual and verbal glimpses of be-haviors and responses to museum exhibits on the part of mu-seum visitors.

It is probably not a book which should be selected for library inclusion on the basis of its scientific content; but it may be of value as a source of thematic extension and embellishment in a collection where a solid basis of scientific information already exists.

*Ronald J. Kley, in a review of "Digging Up Dino-saurs," in Appraisal: Science Books for Young Peo-ple, Vol. 14, No. 3, Fall, 1981, p. 9.*

This is a lovely little book which contains a surprising wealth of information, packaged in a way that should appeal to chil-dren from five to ten years old. Accurate paintings of dinosaur skeletons and impressions of the living creatures are accom-panied by a simple text intelligible to beginning readers. . . . The idea sounds crude, but Aliki has, in fact, managed to combine text, illustration and voice-bubbles in such a way that a young reader is led painlessly through the book, while a slightly older reader is likely to be hooked, his attention caught, wherever he may open the book.

My own five year old liked the illustrations and the dinosaur names, although the main text was just a little over his head; my nine year old, who has a low boredom threshold, zipped through the book and pronounced the length and balance be-tween pictures and words "just right". There are many intro-ductory dinosaur books, but for that age range I know of none better. And Aliki has even taken the trouble to include a short but useful index. Ideal for first—and perhaps middle—school libraries.

*John Gribbin, "Down among the Dinosaurs," in The Times Educational Supplement, No. 3429, January 15, 1982, p. 34.*

This is an unusual and most appealing dinosaur book. On the first page readers join a motley crowd of museum visitors depicted in front of an awesome *Apatosaurus* skeleton. It is just like a Saturday afternoon at the Natural History Museum. A number of the visitors are exclaiming in wonder, a few are misbehaving and, of course, there is one young person who appears to be quite an expert on the exhibit. This engaging

young character (a girl as it happens) then goes on in the following pages to give a fascinating account of the many procedures involved in the excavation, preservation and even-tual reconstruction of dinosaur fossils. The information is well researched and answers many of the perennial questions with conscientious attention to scientific detail. At the same time Aliki brings a delightful levity to this intriguing subject. Her drawings have a refreshing *naïf* quality which together with her cunning use of speech balloons, an interestingly varied layout, and a beautifully simple text combine to make a mas-terpiece of picture-book presentation.

*William Edmonds, in a review of "Digging Up Di-nosaurs," in The School Librarian, Vol. 30, No. 1, March, 1982, p. 39.*

The language is clear and simple. In many illustrations, extra information and human reaction is provided in a pleasant way: dialogue balloons, as in a comic strip. Both the pictures and dialogue are humorous and intriguing. We found only one error of fact: Dinosaurs have not been discovered in Antarctica. A few statements also need to be updated: shellac is no longer used in the field, and has been replaced by more effective hardening chemicals. The restored parts of skeletons are now colored differently from the original bone so that the observer can tell which parts may represent the imagination of the re-storer. The book states that "the dinosaur skeleton looks just as it once did." Actually, it looks just as the paleontologist *theorizes* that it once did.

*Frank C. Whitmore, Jr. and Susan H. Whitmore, in a review of "Digging Up Dinosaurs," in Science Books & Films, Vol. 17, No. 4, March-April, 1982, p. 215.*

---

## WE ARE BEST FRIENDS (1982)

When Robert announces his family's impending move, Peter says, "You can't move away. We are best friends." Robert is realistically both expectant and curious, and, of course, his family goes anyway. The remaining tale of Peter's anger, slow forgiveness and building of new friendship is lifelike and re-assuring. Despite some choppy dialogue in the opening ex-changes, a real sense of a child's growth is created and filled with vivid detail: frog catching, fort building, letters painstak-ingly written. Full-palette watercolor illustrations bring the young boys to cheery life. . . . **Best Friends** will be enjoyed by primary graders alone or in groups, and especially appreciated by those confronted with a move—their own or a friend's.

*Carolyn Noah, in a review of "We Are Best Friends," in School Library Journal, Vol. 28, No. 6, February, 1982, p. 63.*

Bright pictures, busy but not overcrowded, add zest to a direct, ingenuous text. . . . This isn't a new theme or a new treatment; the appeal is in the fact that events are seen from a child's viewpoint and described in a child's forthright way.

*Zena Sutherland, in a review of "We Are Best Friends," in Bulletin of the Center for Children's Books, Vol. 35, No. 10, June, 1982, p. 182.*

Brightly lit pictures in cheerful primary colors portray with just a stroke of the pen the misery of losing a friend who must move away and the tentative beginnings of a new companion-ship. . . . Details of school and home abound in the lively pictures, which variously feature a clutch of interested cats, dogs, or frogs. In a manner which is sympathetic but not sentimental, the happy combination of pictures and text responds comfortingly to the unhappiness of the child who has been left behind.

> *Ethel R. Twichell, in a review of "We Are Best Friends," in* The Horn Book Magazine, *Vol. LVIII, No. 4, August, 1982, p. 388.*

If you are five to seven or eight, don't miss **We Are Best Friends**. . . . Its theme, best friendship, is one of abiding interest, and is treated here with an understanding wit. "You can't move away," says Robert. "We are best friends. What will you do without me?. . . Who will you fight with? Nobody fights like best friends . . . You can't move away. You will miss me far too much." Note the subtlety. What does he *really* mean?. . . The pictures are apt and entertaining; we can see the actual letters for ourselves.

> *Naomi Lewis, "Feather, Fur and Fantasy," in* The Times Educational Supplement, *No. 3492, June 3, 1983, p. 44.\**

The theme is serious, the treatment honest and uncompromising, but, in word and picture, Aliki spills her saving humour over the subject, illuminating it and bringing its relevance home to the reader. A lovely book in conception and in every detail of its realisation.

> *M. Crouch, in a review of "We Are Best Friends," in* The Junior Bookshelf, *Vol. 47, No. 4, August, 1983, p. 157.*

---

### *A MEDIEVAL FEAST* (1983)

[Aliki is a] meticulous researcher. . . . [*A Medieval Feast*] absorbed her for 24 months, 12 hours a day, taking her through 50 to 60 books and contributing to a file thick with photos, sketches and correspondence. The subject is itself a gargantuan effort—planning, preparing for, serving and eating a royal banquet some time around the year 1400. The point of view is that the lord of the manor so honored was certainly hard pressed to provide for the king and the entire royal entourage at the banquet. But, to the surprise of none familiar with Aliki's work, the heart of the book is its illustrations. They are as detailed and delicate, strong and substantial as the best illuminated manuscripts or medieval tapestries, both of which were the basis of the pictures.

Discussing the research, Aliki mentions in particular the Unicorn tapestries at the Cloisters in New York City, the *Book of Hours of the Duke of Berry,* the *Luttrell Psalter,* also the Metropolitan Museum's publication on medieval cookery, *Fabulous Feasts.* . . .

As in her earlier picture book, **Mummies Made in Egypt** . . . , as well as in **Digging Up Dinosaurs, Corn Is Maize** and others in the Let's-Read-and-Find-Out series for Crowell, the pages of **A Medieval Feast** are packed full of facts. These science primers inform, entertain and delight in a way that is particularly Aliki's, using script and different typefaces, with frieze frames and borders. One doesn't have to be a kid to devour each page, intent on not missing a single bit of information it contains. (p. 134)

[The] illustrations in *A Medieval Feast* seem to spring from the copy. Here, in colors that glow like gems, the illustrations attend assiduously to detail, with scenes of the medieval manor, its gardens, preserves and waters, the interiors and the outlying serf quarters bordered with fruits and flowers, wildlife, game and fish, vegetables and herbs, all of the period. Nor is a larger sense of the subject lost in the exactness. In the double-page spread of the kitchen, dogs leap onto tables for bones, a pig

The kitchen was a separate stone structure built on to the main house.

It was connected by a long passageway to the Great Hall, where the feast would take place. There were cupboards along the way to store the prepared food.

*From* A Medieval Feast, *written and illustrated by Aliki. Thomas Y. Crowell Co., Inc., 1983. Copyright © 1983 by Aliki Brandenberg. All rights reserved. Reprinted by permission of Harper & Row, Publishers, Inc.*

is being spitted, a deer's head awaits the knife and pools of blood spread freely—all the heated hustle and business of a kitchen at full tilt comes through. This latest offering overflows with humor too. No expression-alert child will miss the meaning on the faces of the sated feasters as the last and grandest in a long procession of grand courses is carried into the banquet hall. (p. 135)

*Dulcy Brainard, in an interview with Aliki Brandenberg, in* Publishers Weekly, *Vol. 224, No. 4, July 22, 1983, pp. 134-35.*

The preparation, presentation and consumption of the splendid feast offers an occasion to dazzle the king—and us—with dishes that appealed to the eye as much as (or perhaps more than) to the palate. . . . The sapphire blues, plum reds and warm ochres of Aliki's elaborate watercolors recall the enameled pages of illuminated manuscripts and create a pageant of activity as colorful as it is instructive. . . . (It might have been helpful to have included a bibliography of visual and other sources.) Aliki has provided us with a veritable feast of a book.

*Patricia Dooley, in a review of "A Medieval Feast," in* School Library Journal, *Vol. 30, No. 1, September, 1983, p. 114.*

The impressive feast depicted in this tale by Aliki seems more a treat for the reader than it is for the king who eats it. The king is present only from mid-morning until dark of the feast day, but the reader is involved throughout the weeks of preparation. . . .

Not every young reader is going to be interested in the making of a medieval feast. But for the curious, there is more than enough here to inform and satisfy. Although the text is somewhat dry, the pictures are not. Taking their inspiration from old tapestries and illuminated manuscripts, but not bound by them, they are filled with colorful, juicy detail.

*Ellen Rudin, in a review of "A Medieval Feast," in* The New York Times Book Review, *October 16, 1983, p. 37.*

[Aliki] captures the vigorous industry required to prepare for the King and Queen's large entourage. . . .

The factual, well-researched content is both visually and aurally appealing. The illustrations are rich and textured, reminiscent of illuminated manuscripts: plush velvets, rich brocades, coarse homespuns, gold-encrusted linens, rich tapestries, and brilliant jewel-emblazoned mosaics depicting manor scenes and activities.

The visual lushness is well served by a prose style that has a rhythmic cadence and immediacy that engages the reader. "You are there" and involved.

The book is a perfect 'gateway' to many original and creative activities. Based upon the book and other references, children could devise the menu for a many-coursed medieval feast; they could illustrate, in the style of an illuminated manuscript, a "Medieval Dictionary" containing words like cockentrice, trenchers, poaching vessels, and capon.

*Geneva T. Van Horne, in a review of "A Medieval Feast," in* Language Arts, *Vol. 61, No. 2, February, 1984, p. 181.*

[Despite] the attempts to create a sense of an illuminated manuscript, the overgeneralized stylistic mode eventually defeats the purpose of the book. The brevity and general nature of the text and illustrations which serve as the primary source of information are inadequate. Readers examining illustrations closely to see how each activity is done will be frustrated and annoyed by too few supporting details. The lack of clarity permeating this illustrated manuscript will curtail its usefulness in researching life in the Middle Ages.

Curious child readers deserve more than this book is prepared to offer. (p. 182)

*Ronald A. Jobe, in a review of "A Medieval Feast," in* Language Arts, *Vol. 61, No. 2, February, 1984, pp. 181-82.*

[*A Medieval Feast*] has all the visual appeal of an admirable picture-book, but it is also quite a serious contribution to medieval studies and would have a place in at least the upper classes of the primary school. . . . All the details are authentic, and in order to sustain the period mood Aliki has matched her style to that of the illuminated manuscript without, it must be added, losing her own individuality. There is much here to enjoy and to study, especially the marginal decorations which are far more than merely ornamental. (pp. 115-16)

*M. Crouch, in a review of "A Medieval Feast," in* The Junior Bookshelf, *Vol. 48, No. 3, June, 1984, pp. 115-16.*

---

## USE YOUR HEAD, DEAR (1983)

Young Charles, an absent-minded alligator, is "'dear and sweet and means well'" but simply cannot concentrate on the task at hand. Whether at home or at school, he creates chaos—storing the dustpan in the refrigerator, feeding his father's lunch to assorted pets, confusing story time with bedtime and bath time with bedtime. All the usual remedies—tying strings on his fingers, knotting his tail, putting "THINK" signs on his cap—prove ineffective until Father Alligator produces the perfect present for a nonthinker's birthday—an invisible thinking cap which, once acquired, cannot be lost. Both text and illustrations are notable for the care with which they develop the thoroughly childlike story. The words are fresh and funny, precise complements for expressive line drawings highlighted by the authoritative green shapes of the alligator characters and by the quarter-inch borders defining each double-page spread. As winsome as its reptilian protagonist, the book readily demonstrates that the most effective picture book is not necessarily the most elaborate, that there is artistic merit in restraint and enduring appeal in simplicity.

*Mary M. Burns, in a review of "Use Your Head, Dear," in* The Horn Book Magazine, *Vol. LIX, No. 6, December, 1983, p. 697.*

[Charles' forgetfulness is ] in the style of Amelia Bedelia, but without her literal-mindedness. . . . The story is very slight, but the green bordered pictures filled with lively green alligators are endearing while the black-and-white line drawings of home and school provide humorous details. Not as zippy as its predecessor [*Keep Your Mouth Closed, Dear*] but an acceptable story time selection.

*Hara L. Seltzer, in a review of "Use Your Head, Dear," in* School Library Journal, *Vol. 30, No. 4, December, 1983, p. 51.*

The illustrations are breezy and funny, the humor of the situation is of the right kind to appeal to preschool children, and the style is adequate; the plot is a bit silly and has a rather inconclusive ending.

*Zena Sutherland, in a review of "Use Your Head, Dear," in* Bulletin of the Center for Children's Books, *Vol. 37, No. 5, January, 1984, p. 81.*

The hilarious muddle-headed doings of this engaging character will endear him to young listeners and readers, and adults will find added pleasure in the splendid drawings: father reads Proust (upside down) and mother is seen to exclaim 'Give me strength'. A thoroughly enjoyable picture-story book for the young. And parents could do worse than emulate the tolerance and understanding of Charles's mother and father.

*Jill Bennett, in a review of "Use Your Head, Dear," in* The School Librarian, *Vol. 32, No. 1, March, 1984, p. 36.*

[This] is a most attractive picture book. With great skill, the artist/author has matched the humorous quality of the illustrations with a few lines of simple, easily read text on each page. It should certainly appeal to most children between 4 and 7 years of age.

*A. Thatcher, in a review of "Use Your Head, Dear," in* The Junior Bookshelf, *Vol. 48, No. 2, April, 1984, p. 63.*

---

### FEELINGS (1984)

Unmistakably: *I'll Be You and You Be Me* in color—and, alas, flatter, less inspired. But in these pages of pictured dialogues, episodes, and whatever—including just plain pictures and picture-strips—there are multitudinous illustrations of feelings that youngsters will recognize and presumably respond to. . . . Aliki is a conceptualizer and storyteller . . . , [and this] is evident throughout the book. There's a pastoral landscape, looking rather like John Burningham, labeled "feeling quiet"; there's a girl in a room crowded with toys, who pronounces herself "BORED." (Says one little birdie to another: "She sounds lonely to me.") There's a child's version of a *New Yorker* cartoon—a youngster peers from backstage into a huge, dark auditorium: "You're next, Joanna. Don't be nervous." There's a page on which a little boy mimes different feelings (angry, sad, proud) for a little girl to guess—something that Margaret Wise Brown once thought of having Thurber do. There's at least one story, the six-part **"Birthday,"** that rings amusing, explicit changes on feelings (and has as much substance as many a whole book). Perhaps children accustomed to thinking and talking about feelings will take this all as a matter of course—an outcome both desirable and regrettable.

*A review of "Feelings," in* Kirkus Reviews, *Juvenile Issue, Vol. LII, Nos. 18-21, November 1, 1984, p. J-86.*

Small, bright-colored figures act out a wide range of emotions in a series of short dialogues. A comic-strip format emphasizes the linear development of what is so often universally felt by young children. The feelings dealt with are triggered by common experiences, such as spring weather, a birthday party invitation, the death of a pet; or they are depicted as temperamental opposites—selfishness and generosity, loneliness and conviviality, serenity and rambunctiousness. A pair of small birds perched in the corner of most pages provide visual continuity and a running commentary on the action. (pp. 748-49)

*Charlotte W. Draper, in a review of "Feelings," in* The Horn Book Magazine, *Vol. LX, No. 6, November & December, 1984, pp. 748-49.*

Some of the hand-printed words are, in addition to the tiny figures, so small they are hard to see; others are larger and more accessible. This does portray a spectrum of feelings in a way that will make most children able to recognize them as familiar—but it's a patchy format: some of the material is in strip form, some full cartoons, some pages have one large figure and some have one or no words.

*Zena Sutherland, in a review of "Feelings," in* Bulletin of the Center for Children's Books, *Vol. 38, No. 4, December, 1984, p. 59.*

Anger, worry, fear, contentment, excitement, and more are held up for scrutiny in a format that is visually unusual. There are lots of tiny pictures and words that often proceed comic-book style, though larger scenes and an occasional spread sometimes break the rhythm. A lighthearted mood prevails; the fresh, colorful execution lends grace beyond what often passes for bibliotherapy. Adults sharing this with children should find it inspiring for discussion.

*Denise M. Wilms, in a review of "Feelings," in* Booklist, *Vol. 81, No. 7, December 1, 1984, p. 520.*

Unfortunately, the coverage of so many feelings is superficial, and the book fails to promote understanding. The pages are a hodgepodge of small cartoons depicting everyday situations that elicit certain emotions. Some pages have as many as 20 scenes, with dialogue printed in tiny uneven letters. The total effect is confusing and chaotic, especially for young children. There are several unflattering stereotypes. In **"The Birthday: a Story in Six Parts"** an overweight girl is happily consuming her third piece of cake and ice cream while the other children discuss her rudeness, selfishness and embarrassing behavior. Aliki's intent is unclear. In other vignettes, girls are envious and jealous, boys are brave and courageous. Some emotions (grief, boredom, nervousness and love), which are each given one simple, sometimes humorous illustration with a minimum of dialogue, are sensitively handled and a welcome diversion from the confusion of the rest of the book. A better choice is George Ancona's *I Feel—a Picture Book of Emotions* (Dutton, 1977). His revealing, uncomplicated photographs explore a few emotions in greater depth. Aliki's illustrations are childlike and her characters' faces expressive. Children will enjoy the cartoon format, and teachers and counselors may be able to use parts for discussion starters, but this is not a book for young children. (pp. 60-1)

*Diane S. Rogoff, in a review of "Feelings," in* School Library Journal, *Vol. 31, No. 6, February, 1985, pp. 60-1.*

# John (Mackintosh) Burningham

## 1936-

English author/illustrator and illustrator of picture books, fiction, and nonfiction.

The creator of a wide variety of books for children from pre-school through the middle grades, Burningham is often praised as one of the leading artists in contemporary children's literature. He is also recognized for his thorough understanding of his audience and for his accurate appraisal of adults, especially parents, as they interact with children. Conceiving his works in pictures, Burningham uses text mainly to add information to his illustrations.

Burningham's works range from folktales and fantasies to realistic sketches of daily life; several of his books, such as *Would You Rather...*, *The Shopping Basket*, and *Avocado Baby* interweave reality and fantasy. Five of Burningham's first six works—*Borka: The Adventures of a Goose with No Feathers*; *Trubloff: The Mouse Who Wanted to Play the Balalaika*; *Humbert, Mister Firkin and the Lord Mayor of London*; *Cannonball Simp*; and *Harquin: The Fox Who Went Down to the Valley*—are animal fantasies that combine abundant text with bold illustrations. In *Mr Gumpy's Outing*, a story about a patient farmer and his guests, Burningham adds detail, sly humor, and subtle colors to his pictures while reducing his narrative to a basic storyline. His eight "Little Books," a series of picture books for preschoolers, treat subjects familiar to small children in childlike crayon drawings and simple text.

With *Come Away from the Water, Shirley* and *Time to Get Out of the Bath, Shirley*, Burningham satirizes the dichotomy between children and parents by juxtaposing the splendor of Shirley's active imagination and her parents' bland reality. Succeeding books continue to burlesque adults through broad humor and fantasy. With *Granpa*, however, Burningham depicts the relationship between a little girl and her grandfather with sensitivity; observers note that this work is the first contemporary picture book about death for a preschool audience. Burningham has also published fold-out concept books which use jovial humor to explain basic words and number facts, a collection of paintings on the changing seasons, a well-received ABC, and a travelogue describing his eighty-day trip around the world.

The illustrations in Burningham's first six works were immediately hailed for the drama and striking beauty of their colorful backgrounds as well as for the humor of their line drawings. These works utilize such mediums as india ink, gouache, photostats, and cellulose; with *Mr Gumpy's Outing*, Burningham began working in a more restrained, economical style which relies on crayon, watercolor, and colored pencil. Reviewers praise Burningham's integration of text and picture and note that his illustrations successfully convey mood, atmosphere, and the thoughts of his characters. In the "Shirley" series, for example, Burningham draws Shirley's parents in faded colors on the left-hand pages, which depict Shirley's actual environment and her mother's mundane comments. The wordless right-hand pages, however, celebrate the joy of Shirley's fantasy world with bright, splashy paintings.

*Photograph by Christina Gascoigne. Courtesy of John Burningham*

Burningham attended A. S. Neill's Summerhill school, an experimental institution where lessons were not compulsory; he spent much of his time experimenting with color in the school's art room. At seventeen, Burningham declared himself a conscientious objector and spent two years of alternative service in such occupations as forestry and social work. He started attending evening art classes while working on a farm. After winning a scholarship to London's Central School of Art, Burningham designed stage sets, magazine cartoons, Christmas cards, and cereal packets as well as posters for the London Transport and British Transport Commission which were often featured on subways. "I started writing and illustrating children's books," he says, "as a means of getting my work published." He has also created a series of large murals for children's rooms.

Critics applaud Burningham for his originality, inventiveness, humor, illustrative range, and technical proficiency. Although reviewers disagree on the quality of his writing, they consider Burningham an author whose works speak directly to children with respect and relevance.

Burningham was awarded the Kate Greenaway Medal in 1964 for *Borka* and in 1971 for *Mr Gumpy's Outing*, which also received an honorary award from the Biennale of Illustrations Bratislava in 1971 and the *Boston Globe-Horn Book* Award in 1972.

(See also *Something about the Author*, **Vol. 16** and *Contemporary Authors*, **Vols. 73-76.**)

## AUTHOR'S COMMENTARY

Why does anyone write children's books? Is it because they have a story to tell? Or because they need the money? Or is it simply vanity?

I don't know why I write children's books. I don't think I am a writer. I find it difficult to express myself in words. Drawing is hard enough, but there I feel I have more chance. My early attempts at commissioned illustration were not particularly successful. My work, I was told, was unsuitable for the usual commercial outlets. In fact I have done various kinds of commissioned work, but there were still a good many things I was interested in doing for which there seemed to be no ready market. Ideally, of course, one would be able to sit down in an enormous studio and produce whatever work one wanted, then wait for recognition: but unfortunately one has to live. . . . The next best thing is to find work which is satisfying and for which one gets paid.

I enjoy making children's books—and I use the word "making" rather than writing because I think of my books as a series of drawings held together by a thread of text. I enjoy it because it allows me to work with the maximum freedom and to carry out my own ideas. I like using colour, and although colour litho reproduction has many limitations, it gives me a lot of scope. But it is by no means all fun. Just as with making anything, there are moments one really enjoys but most of the time it feels like an endless struggle.

Sometimes people seem to have the idea that drawing for children is a kind of self-indulgence, that it must necessarily be easier than drawing for adults. This is not true. For one thing, you cannot patronise children. They are not, after all, less intelligent than adults: they just have less experience. I think it is very dangerous to set out with the idea in mind "I know what children like." Personally, I have no idea what children like or want, nor do I try to find out. They probably like all kinds of things which I don't. It is just a fortunate coincidence that they seem to get on with what I produce.

Besides, generally speaking, it is not children who buy the books. It is their mothers and fathers and uncles and aunts who buy them, at least to begin with, because *they* like them, and because these are the books they would like their children to like. There are very few excuses for an adult to buy picture books, and I think that secretly they might well enjoy them as much as most fathers enjoy playing with toy trains.

Looking back at the work of the great writers and illustrators of children's books, I do not find that one ever grows out of them. They contain as much for adults as for children because the person who made them was concerned to satisfy himself as well as his readers. This is an attitude which anyone who embarks on creative work must have if he is to achieve anything. Tenniel's illustrations for *Alice*, Ernest Shepard's for *The Wind in the Willows* and Edward Lear's drawings for his own books all have this quality of leaving something to the imagination.

I try not to make my own drawings too formal and finished so that the child who is reading or looking can have the maximum freedom to imagine for himself. The sense of finding something out is as important in pictures as it is in words, and there are some things which can be said better for children in pictures because pictures are more immediate and can convey feelings which would be longwinded and complicated to describe verbally.

As for my own future plans: I intend to go on writing children's books because I like doing them and because there are many more that I want to do. I hope, too, that my books will get better as my drawing improves with experience and new ideas come to mind. I have many other interests and I cannot tell how these will develop as time goes on. Three years ago I did not know I would be writing children's books. I still have a lot to learn and, for the present, I write them for reasons that are partly practical and partly personal. Like most things in life, it is a compromise but I find it a satisfying one, and I can only hope the children find it satisfying too. (pp. 139-41)

> John Burningham, "Drawing for Children," in The Junior Bookshelf, *Vol. 28, No. 3, July, 1964, pp. 139-41.*

## GENERAL COMMENTARY

**FRANK EYRE**

An artist whom many critics link with Wildsmith is John Burningham. . . . His colour is almost equally brilliant, but more controlled, more immediately accessible, and there are many who consider that his books appeal to more children than do Wildsmith's. He has illustrated many books, of many kinds. Like Wildsmith, he has done an *ABC*, but he has also done a number of beautiful books of his own, including *Trubloff, Cannonball Simp, Humbert, Mr. Firkin, and the Lord Mayor of London, Seasons, Harquin* and *Mr Gumpy's Outing* all lit by a controlled delight in colour and a strong sense of fun. . . . It is difficult to think of any twentieth-century artist, with the possible exceptions of Ardizzone and Ernest Shepard, who has given children more pleasure. . . . (p. 50)

> Frank Eyre, "Books with Pictures," in his British Children's Books in the Twentieth Century, *revised edition, 1971. Reprint by E. P. Dutton & Co., Inc., 1973, pp. 38-58.*

**JOHN ROWE TOWNSEND**

John Burningham seems to me to be essentially a comic artist. In *Borka* . . . [and *Trubloff*], the flat, slabby, idiosyncratic pictures show people and animals self-possessed, even smug, however unlikely their situations. The composedly-deadpan manner extends to the (extremely tall) stories of these books, told without a twitch of the lips. Never let it be thought odd that a mouse should play the balalaika or travel a vast distance on skis. . . . [Of Burningham's more recent books, *Mr Gumpy's Outing*] is the most appealing. Mr Gumpy takes two childen and a growing number of domestic animals on a boat trip, and they all do just what they're told not to do (which always seems particularly funny to the very young). Disaster follows, but is quickly surmounted, for it all takes place in a world in which disaster doesn't stand a chance. (p. 325)

> John Rowe Townsend, *"Picture Books in Bloom: Britain," in his* Written for Children: An Outline of English-Language Children's Literature, *revised edition, 1974. Reprint by The Horn Book Incorporated, 1981, pp. 321-30.*

JEAN RUSSELL

New parents and grandparents are often anxious to give books to babies, but after looking at alphabet and simple rhyme books find there is very little choice amongst the brilliantly coloured, complicated picture story book collections. One author who does answer their need is the artist John Burningham for he has the ability to capture in his simple drawings the essence and spirit of his characters—whether animals or people and portray them in a way that little children respond to. The poetic, resigned Mr. Gumpy (in **Mr. Gumpy's Outing**) is like every child's favourite aunt—no matter how badly you behave, how much of a nuisance you are, she will still treat you with the courtesy due to a visiting princess. The exhuberance of Mr. Gumpy's friends who are allowed on the raft on condition that ''you don't squabble'' (to the children), ''don't muck about''— (to the pig), ''don't flap'' (to the chickens) etc, is matched only by his majestic indifference to the catastrophe that inevitably follows when they do all of these things. In the classic way of children's books Mr. Gumpy and his friends finish their outing with a splendid tea at Mr. Gumpy's house. Babies need books about the world immediately around them, but they also need to be gradually introduced to the wonders and magic of a world as yet unimagined—and what better place for that journey to begin than through a book on your father's lap.

To meet the needs of these home based tinies Burningham has created a series of little square books about the most familiar of everyday objects. . . . They are ideal to tuck into a pram for those odd moments when a familiar distracting peacemaker is needed during a walk or visiting trip. (p. 6)

Once familiar with looking at books on his parent's knee the two and three year old is ready to point, shout, laugh and enjoy joining in the story. **The Shopping Basket** . . . is the latest in a long line of marvellously humourous, idiosyncratic tales told by John Burningham. Steven sets off down the street to the stores to get the shopping for his Mother, but on the way home meets various animals—a goat, a bear, a monkey—who each demand something from his shopping basket—bananas, oranges until gradually reducing his load, they precipitate a crisis with Steven's Mother. The book says much about the relationships between Mothers and their sons, counting and most of all imagination.

**Cannonball Simp** is another story which captures emotion in a comforting kind of way. Simp is like every family's mongrel dog . . . fat, small, ugly, greedy, loyal, but full of charm and native wit, which enables Simp to escape from the dog pound, and find a new friend, a new home, and a new role in the circus in **Cannonball Simp**. When you are two and three years old you need an uncomplicated story with a strong emotional pull. **Borka the story of the goose with no feathers** has just that. . . . Borka is laughed at by all the other young geese because she has no feathers. The goose doctor can find nothing wrong with her and so the only thing to do is for her mother to knit her a grey woollen jersey. Even that has its problems as it became wet and soggy when she tried to swim, and when

So Mrs Plumpster got out her knitting needles and set to work. Of course she could not knit real feathers, but she made a kind of grey woollen jersey as much like feathers as she could.

When she had finished, she called Borka and tried it on her. Borka was delighted, and flapped around with joy, because she had always been chilly at night.

*From* Borka: The Adventures of a Goose with No Feathers, *written and illustrated by John Burningham. J. Cape, 1963. © 1963 by John Burningham. All rights reserved. Reprinted by permission of Jonathan Cape Ltd, on behalf of the author.*

the winter came the other geese migrated. Borka is left behind. The glowing soft colours of the almost dead-pan pictures heightens the wit and humour that lurks in odd corners of the story. Of course, Borka solves her problems, and like Andersen's ''Ugly Duckling'' finds true happiness in the end—but still without feathers. (pp. 6-7)

Perhaps the most striking quality of John Burningham's pictures is their very Englishness—Mr. Gumpy is the most pastoral hero of our times; imagine being undefeated by the logistics of packing all those assorted animals and children in your motorcar or punt for a treat. Even Burningham's pictures from *Around the World in 80 Days* are an English interpretation of the wonders of the world as he saw them.

More recently a note of sophisticated humour has crept into John Burningham's books with the dream-like sequence in *Time To Get Out Of The Bath, Shirley*. Left hand page represents Mother with typical comments ''You haven't left the soap in the bath again, have you?'' Right hand page shows Shirley escaping down waste pipe on the back of rubber duck. . . .

And again in *Would you Rather*—''have supper in a castle, Breakfast in a balloon, have Monkey to tickle, a bear to read with, a cat to box with or a goat to dance with—''and so it goes on—fabulous when you're only three. John Burningham really knows children and parents. (p. 7)

*Jean Russell, ''Cover Artist: John Burningham,'' in* Books for Your Children, *Vol. 16, No. 1, Spring, 1981, pp. 6-7.*

## ELAINE MOSS

Where are the children, we may ask ourselves sometimes— and we always mean, where are they physically. Yet most of the time even when we can see them they are somewhere else altogether in their imagination. John Burningham brilliantly conveys this 'double life' in two barrier-breaking picture books [*Come Away from the Water, Shirley* and *Time to Get Out of the Bath, Shirley*]. Yes, Shirley's body is wandering round on the beach being talked at by over-fussy parents. . . . But in her mind (the deeply coloured paintings, always on right-hand pages) she is having an adventure with pirates and hidden treasure. . . . Burningham quietly demands that the reader should look and leap and look again.

*Elaine Moss, ''Picture Books for Young People, 9-13: 'Come Away from the Water, Shirley' and 'Time to Get Out of the Bath, Shirley','' in her* Picture Books for Young People: 9-13, *1981. Reprint by The Thimble Press, 1982, p. 14.*

## SHEILA A. EGOFF

[The] fascination with structural division as well as open-ended narrative is apparent even in the work of a fairly traditional picture-book creator such as John Burningham. In his ''Shirley'' books [*Time to Get Out of the Bath, Shirley* and *Come Away from the Water, Shirley*] he fractures the unity of text and pictures for a quite different purpose. The left-hand pictures and brief text carry the mother's adjurations, while the right-hand wordless pictures show Shirley's imagination at work as she ignores her mother's ''do's'' and ''don'ts,'' lost as she is in a classic pirate fantasy adventure. In a lighthearted but ironic manner Burningham thus expresses simultaneously a too frequent adults' view of children—they have no real sense of the child mind—as opposed to children's own secret desires. The last two wordless pictures are indicative of the long road the picture book has traveled even since Sendak. While his King

Max sails happily home in his little boat to his supper, Burningham's Shirley is shown in her boat as a pirate queen blithely departing from reality. In the final left-hand realistic picture she is a child again, but one being dragged home (as her back shows) by her parents. (p. 253)

There seems to be a high correlation in content and visual image between the still-living books of the past that are beloved by children and those new ones that appeal today. The creators of such works are indubitably contemporary, but they are also storytellers whose artwork and text match, at least to some degree, the suspense and the representational art style of earlier periods. . . .

John Burningham exhibits most of these qualities. He is not concerned with the dark and complex aspects of childhood, bibliotherapy, or social adjustment. But neither is he simplistic. He offers the profound pleasure of comedy, rather than mere humor, and a deep understanding of a child's imagination, particularly in his ''Shirley'' books which show how well he is able to penetrate a child's imagination. In his ''Mr. Gumpy'' books . . . he uses the classic comic genre in miniature form, taking a combined society of children and animals through a free-form chaos to a harmonious resolution. In *Mr. Gumpy's Outing* the children and animals squabble and fight, upsetting the boat; then they happily return home to the symbolic tea table. In *Mr. Gumpy's Motor Car* Burningham makes use of the traditional folktale's artful cumulation, but then comes the slowing down. When the children and animals suddenly decide to push the car, stuck in the mud:

> They pushed and shoved and heaved
> and strained and gasped and slipped
> and slithered and squelched.

Burningham uses a variety of themes and techniques of art, but he always keeps them within a child's comprehension. Many modern picture-book creators begin simply enough but gradually seem determined to push the genre to its utmost limits. Burningham's ''Mr. Gumpy'' books were preceded by his tales of anthropomorphized animals in natural surroundings: [*Borka, the Adventures of a Goose with No Feathers; Trubloff, the Mouse Who Wanted to Play the Balalaika;* and *Harquin, the Fox*]. These are strongly plotted little tales reminiscent of the best animal fantasy picture books of the 1940s and 1950s. His art style for the most part is best described as a combination of the representational and the impressionistic. His *Harquin, the Fox* owes much to Caldecott in its rhythmic sweep of the English countryside, as does its unsophisticated and good-natured humor.

In his ''Little Books,'' Burningham has taken the picture book to its utmost simplicity, but with the ''art that conceals art.'' His children, busy about their homely little affairs, are a cross between Schultz's Charlie Brown and Sendak's Brooklyn children, but they have an appeal all their own. These are for *very* young children and are true to G. K. Chesterton's observation that, ''A child of seven is excited by being told that Tommy opened a door and saw a dragon. But a child of three is excited by being told that Tommy opened a door.'' Burningham does not give a three-year-old a dragon in the books *The Blanket, The Cupboard, The Dog, The Friend*. In them he depicts a little boy playing with pots and pans in his mother's kitchen, or losing his blanket, or quarreling and then making up with a friend. They are so true to life as to take an adult aback with a wry appreciation of the small, but nailed-down details of infant life, while a very young child can recognize its own activities on the pages of a book without adult commentary. Perhaps Burningham's greatest contribution to the picture book in both words and art is to remind us that children can still be charmed by simple things. (pp. 267-68)

> Sheila A. Egoff, "Picture Books," in her Thursday's Child: Trends and Patterns in Contemporary Children's Literature, *American Library Association, 1981, pp. 247-74.**

### VALERIE WILLSHER

The pictures [in Burningham's **"Little Books"**] are rather dependent on the text for interest and are therefore not all that absorbing for the child who is too young to understand or listen to the words. In *The Friend,* for example, of the nine illustrations, three show two boys standing with no other interest in the picture.

> Valerie Willsher, in a review of "Little Books," in Signal, No. 38, May, 1982, p. 107.

### JOSEPH H. SCHWARCZ

Counterpointing [between text and illustration] has been developed to great depth by John Burningham in his *Shirley* books. They are moving stories, because on one level they are simply funny; on another, they exhibit the tragic lack of communication between parents and their children. . . . The text to the left is just a wearisome rustle of words. The wordless story to the right tells a not-too-absorbing adventure. When the two are juxtaposed, they document the hermetic isolation of the child's fantasy world from the adults' reality. Again we are let in on a secret—how little parents seem to know about their children. . . . (pp. 17-18)

[Here] we find the mutual infringement of outer and inner reality, albeit as contrast, the fantasy plot compensating for the frustrations of reality, dynamic independence versus static

overprotectiveness, creating a common message. It teaches us that the human mind and human behavior are more complex than meets the (in this case, mother's) eye. . . . It says something about the polyphonic ability of the human being.

The fact that illustrators can put their symbols and configurations to serious use and still create pictures so naturally humorous or dramatic, or both, on levels enjoyable for children and suitable to their perception and experience, is an important achievement. (p. 175)

> Joseph H. Schwarcz, "Relationships between Text and Illustration" and "The Role of the Illustration in the Child's Aesthetic Experience," in his Ways of the Illustrator: Visual Communication in Children's Literature, *American Library Association, 1982, pp. 9-22, 169-96.**

### BOOKS FOR KEEPS

John Burningham's status as one of the world's most popular and respected author-illustrators for children seems safe as houses—except that his own house . . . looks distinctly unsafe at present: its frontage is obscured by a forest of scaffolding. An apt image of its owner? It's a tempting connection to make since for all his two dozen titles in print, three million copies sold and two Kate Greenaway Medals won, John Burningham still refuses to take his Establishment as a fact. 'I'm one of those ungrateful people who having done something feels that's just history and asks what comes next or whether it can be done again . . . I suppose it's the neurosis of any author or artist that they can't remain inactive for very long because they feel insecure unless they're working.'

His own history includes a dazzling debut (**Borka: The Adventures of a Goose with No Feathers**) . . . as well as an assortment of successes such as the **Mr Gumpy** books, the classic **Come Away from the Water, Shirley** and the unforgettable **Would You**

*From* Mr. Gumpy's Outing, *written and illustrated by John Burningham. Holt, Rinehart and Winston, 1970. Copyright © 1970 by John Burningham. Reprinted by permission of Holt, Rinehart and Winston, Publishers.*

*Rather . . .* , all of them essential occupants of any bookshelf worthy of a child's second glance.

Yet John Burningham himself maintains he doesn't much like the process of book illustration and tries to 'avoid it in any way I can.' Also he feels 'to some degree the prisoner of my own success' and declares 'I'm not really very interested in children's books.' . . .

And even while insisting that 'there's nothing worse than a great sheet of white paper' and that starting on a new project is 'a bit like taking up exercises again—a sort of stumbling about with drawings' he can't seem to resist the activity. The conversation in which he advanced these claims was punctuated by the compulsive scratch-scratch-scratch of crayon on paper. (p. 14)

The appeal of the Burningham style is international in the contrast it presents between a deliberately naïve and childlike draughtsmanship and a supremely sophisticated range of materials: crayons, charcoal and pastels, printers' ink, indian ink, cellulose and gouache. It's a style which emerged as fully-formed almost from the start though he'd claim that 'I'm more controlled now . . . there are fewer happy accidents. One must change. If you're trying to get movement in a child or animal which has been my concern recently with a lot of things I've been doing then there's no point in trying to get that and put in as many colours as one can in the background. It's about isolating what it is one's trying to do at the time. So much depends on the subject matter.' . . .

It's typical of him that he refuses to exploit his own success. *Mr Gumpy's Outing,* for example, a tale of a punting expedition written and drawn with superb deadpan humour, won him his second Kate Greenaway Medal and was followed by the equally popular *Mr Gumpy's Motor Car.* A whole series might have resulted but for his intense dislike of repeating himself. So we're still waiting for the third *Mr Gumpy* book. In the intervening decade or so we've been treated instead to the hilarious mismatch between fantasy and reality of his two *Shirley* books, another series that might-have-been. Only with his short books for beginning readers has he committed himself to a continuing format—*The Baby, The Blanket, The Dog,* etc. Here, too, though, he was swift to vary his approach. Soon words themselves became his subject matter and then numbers. . . . The latter books, *Number Play,* are especially ingenious and were especially challenging to undertake. 'I worked for three months on multiplication before I decided it was impossible.'

His latest book *Granpa* takes a new kind of risk. 'It's sad only because it introduces death. The relationship, which I think is very intriguing, between grandparents and grandchildren reflects the fact that we no longer live in an environment which gives us time with our own children. When he's saying "we used to do this, that and the other" she's switched off but it doesn't matter because they're both muttering away—she's also going on about her own concerns. The book's based partly on observation and partly on my memories of my own grandfather.' Eventually, in a harrowing double-spread which depicts the child facing Granpa's empty chair, the relationship is broken—though the book closes with a wordless affirmation that life can't help perking up. 'I'm quite pleased with it as a book,' he says, 'but I've no idea how it's going to be received and what children are going to make of it. There's a hair's breadth difference between success and failure with this sort of thing.' Given the Burningham track record, the odds must be heavily on the former. (p. 15)

*"Authorgraph No. 29: John Burningham,"* in Books for Keeps, *No. 29, November, 1984, pp. 14-15.*

---

## BORKA: THE ADVENTURES OF A GOOSE WITH NO FEATHERS (1963)

Comedy is still more appropriate to geese, and John Burningham has made the most of it in his tale of *Borka,* who is born without feathers, is scorned for his knitted jacket, escapes to hard work on a ship and finds romance in Kew Gardens. The illustrations are done in bold, thick washes of colour, at times almost like plasticine, and the result is odd and attractive.

*Margery Fisher, in a review of "Borka," in her* Growing Point, *Vol. 2, No. 6, December, 1963, p. 251.*

[Burningham] has a rich sense of humour and an equally rich feeling for colour. *Borka* . . . is exceedingly funny in conception, and has a story which is developed with consistent absurdity. It is also a very beautiful book, for which Mr. Burningham, who knows perfectly well how ridiculous geese look, also knows that they have a grotesque beauty, and that their world is one of exquisite form and colour. The great double-spreads . . . glow with the oranges and purples and greys of autumn. So hilarious and lovely a book is a major contribution to the long and glorious history of the English picture-book.

*A review of "Borka," in* The Junior Bookshelf, *Vol. 27, No. 6, December, 1963, p. 335.*

This is a deceptive picture book, rich in color and texture, but unfortunately, the story is trite and hackneyed—the animal of unconventional appearance rejected by his kind. . . . Too bad this is merely acceptable. . . .

*Allie Beth Martin, in a review of "Borka: The Adventures of a Goose with No Feathers," in* School Library Journal, *an appendix to* Library Journal, *Vol. 10, No. 8, April, 1964, p. 52.*

From end paper to end paper, this is a delightful picture book. . . . There is humor, boldness and verve in the story . . . and in the well-drawn pictures, bright and childlike yet with original and interesting coloring. The text is printed comfortably large for the beginning reader to enjoy. Children of nursery age will giggle at Borka weeping in the reeds, Borka solemnly seated at the captain's table aboard a tug, and Borka smug and happy in Kew Gardens. . . . Slight, but distinctive and funny. (pp. 34-5)

*A review of "Borka," in* Book Week—The Sunday Herald Tribune, *May 10, 1964, pp. 34-5.*

In *Borka: The Adventures of a Goose With No Feathers,* John Burningham uses colours to great advantage. The book makes a great impression because of the effective contrast of the illustrations, which are both in black and white line drawings and in colour. The colours convey well the mood of the story; dark colours are used to express a sense of mystery and strangeness, bright colours gaiety. Like Wildsmith, Burningham uses his pages to full advantage. Sometimes the pictures scurry across the pages, giving the scene more vigour and increasing the sense of adventure. (pp. 18-19)

*P. Osazee Fayose, "Aesthetic Qualities of Nigerian Children's Books," in* Bookbird, *Vol. XV, No. 3 (September 15, 1977), pp. 14-19.**

A classic story. . . . Burningham's lovely pictures make this a book to cherish and to read again and again to all the family. It is just the sort of old family favourite that ought to be in everyone's holiday luggage.

> *A review of "Borka: The Adventures of a Goose with No Feathers," in* Books for Your Children, *Vol. 13, No. 3, Summer, 1978, p. 8.*

---

### TRUBLOFF: THE MOUSE WHO WANTED TO PLAY THE BALALAIKA   (1964)

Here is a real artist, one perhaps who has not yet quite found his form but who possesses unmistakably the true fire. In *Trubloff* he gets a great deal of fun and a measure of beauty out of a charmingly absurd story of a mouse with musical aspirations. Very good stuff, this, and admirably produced.

> *A review of "Trubloff," in* The Junior Bookshelf, *Vol. 28, No. 5, November, 1964, p. 288.*

[This] is one of four picture books that have given me most pleasure this year. The musical son of the Trub family comes out from behind the panelling of the Parlour Bar to learn to play, and ends up leading the family band. Exquisitely comical and beautiful snow and pub scenes, a superb use of mouse physiognomy. For everyone.

> *Margery Fisher, in a review of "Trubloff: The Mouse Who Wanted to Play the Balalaika," in her* Growing Point, *Vol. 3, No. 6, December, 1964, p. 433.*

Trubloff is a magnificently drawn mouse, illustrated in full-color by the same talented English hand that did *Borka*. Trubloff has so much character, visually, that you might find it possible to persuade yourself that the story was worth the illustrative effort. . . . Only the eye is satisfied here, but very well satisfied indeed.

> *A review of "Trubloff: The Mouse Who Wanted to Play the Balalaika," in* Virginia Kirkus' Service, *Vol. XXXIII, No. 16, August 15, 1965, p. 818.*

[Despite] the happy title, Trubloff is a strangely sad-eyed and joyless mouse, and despite the musical theme, I found the story static. . . . Mr. Burningham's somber drawings, composed heavily in umber and muted pinks and oranges, are undeniably evocative; his deep-etched style reminds me of Rouault. *Trubloff* is strong as art, a bit flat as story.

> *Richard Kluger, "The Glottis Got Us," in* Book Week—The Sunday Herald Tribune, *September 12, 1965, p. 28.\**

To begin with, no one listens to [Trubloff], and if that doesn't get the children on his side, the fact that he's in trouble for being late to bed is sure to.

John Burningham's full-color pictures of a characterful little mouse pursuing his vocation regardless of the opposition of man and nature are as fascinating as his story.

> *Patience M. Daltry, "Imagination Needs No Visa," in* The Christian Science Monitor, *November 4, 1965, p. B1.\**

---

### ABC   (1964)

The mannerisms of this interesting artist are easy to pick out in this delectable alphabet. Either he assembles many examples of one thing on a page (mice, dogs, pigs, runners) and ingeniously varies them, or he illustrates one object largely and forcefully (tractor, queen, volcano). Typical are the long-nosed people and the delicacy of incidental decoration, and one or two pictures recall Burningham's splendid railway posters, especially the exotic jungle which is drawn with real intensity. The production is sumptuous, the letters beautifully placed on pages of various colours, and the whole effect is amusing and enlivening.

> *Margery Fisher, in a review of "A.B.C.," in her* Growing Point, *Vol. 4, No. 1, May, 1965, p. 524.*

Yes, this glorious ABC costs $4.95, and it's worth every single penny of it. *If* you believe that the first pictures a child sees are the most important pictures he will ever see, for they will establish his standards for color and for design; and *if* you believe that an antic viewpoint will provide him with better protection from the slings and arrows of outrageous fortune than a bullet-proof vest, this is one of the ABCs you will be *sure* he sees.

> *A review of "ABC," in* Publishers Weekly, *Vol. 191, No. 20, May 15, 1967, p. 41.*

[This] stunning alphabet book follows the usual pattern of page layout but is still original in conception and imaginative in execution. . . . [The] conventional "X/x/xylophone" looks most imposing in white against a rich, dark green. The verso pages are each a different background color; the recto pages are a variable joy, some pages being pure design, others striking and colorful paintings in bold style, still others verging on cartoons.

> *Zena Sutherland, in a review of "ABC," in* Saturday Review, *Vol. L, No. 24, June 17, 1967, p. 35.*

["ABC"] is one of those alphabet books with endless talking possibilities—a sort of juvenile conversation piece. H is for house, and there are one-story, two-story, three-story houses; houses with one chimney, houses with two; houses with lots of windows to count. And the dogs—under D of course, Mr. Burningham doesn't play tricks even with the less easy letters— are standing, sitting, stretching, walking, sleeping; while K is for a solidly regal king, complete with the accouterments of kingship—gold crown, black beard, red and purple robe, down to the buttons on his green pointed slippers. And all this in rich, subtle colors.

> *Patience M. Daltry, "Books for the Look and Touch and Say Years," in* The Christian Science Monitor, *August 31, 1967, p. 5.\**

Mr. Burningham's book has a solid color page with upper and lower case of each letter and just the single word describing the facing page. The solid pages are in almost all colors and shades but in each case they are printed to appear textured. The illustrations of the named objects are, with slight exception, shown without any background. This treatment is similar to Celestino Piatti's *Animal ABC* (regarding backgrounds) but Burningham's pictures don't employ such bold, forceful strokes nor such black outlines. . . . Burningham's [illustrations] are gentler and don't make such active use of brilliant color.

Burningham's choice of subjects is rather common. . . . Though there is no text as such to provide humor and though the subjects

*From* ABC, *written and illustrated by John Burningham. Jonathan Cape, 1964. © 1964 by John Burningham. Reprinted by permission of Jonathan Cape Ltd, on behalf of the author.*

are never intermingled like Piatti's, Burningham's pictures themselves are funny in a very gentle manner. His animal groups . . . depict the creatures in varieties of ridiculous poses. His picture of **"Runners"** shows a collection of old men, balding and puffing in their track uniforms. **"Tractor"** has a driver who could not possibly be more bored. There is considerable variety from the dramatic volcano to the busy jungle, the ridiculous king and queen to the majestic lion. The small children we've shown it to have loved this book.

> *Robert Cohen, in a review of "ABC," in* Young Readers Review, *Vol. IV, No. 2, October, 1967, p. 16.*

A superb book in bright, strong, warm colours, drawn with wit and humour. The book is dedicated to A. S. Neill and follows his teaching that children need to be treated with humour because it involves friendliness and laughter. Burningham likes to give chlidren full value and fills his page up, either with one large object, or with numbers of the same species. His ten mice are large and small, fat and thin, smug and worried. His **'P for Pigs',** all twenty of them are pictured from the front, back and side, they are pink, brown and black, tiny and huge; full of character.

> *Pat Garrett, in a review of "ABC," in* Children's Book Review, *Vol. 1, No. 2, April, 1971, p. iv.*

------

### HUMBERT, MISTER FIRKIN, AND THE LORD MAYOR OF LONDON  (1965)

Mr. Burningham gets better all the time. He knows, none better, the beauty of every-day things. He has, too, a remarkable gift for inventing very funny stories and putting them into brief, unobtrusively perfect words. Here is an enchanting story about the scrap-merchant's horse who saved the day, and the Lord Mayor's Show Day at that. Humbert earns his place at the top table at the Banquet. Nonsense is best straight-faced, and best when based on reality. In **Humbert** we have almost a prescription for success, resulting in a book which inspires the most warm and lasting affection. (pp. 27-8)

> *A review of "Humbert, Mr. Firkin and the Lord Mayor of London," in* The Junior Bookshelf, *Vol. 30, No. 1, February, 1966, pp. 27-8.*

Mr. Firkin the scrap dealer plods round London with his horse and cart and at night sleeps over the stable: his nag Humbert feels inferior as he chats in the brewery yard with the Lord Mayor's coach horses. But one day the Lord Mayor in procession is held up by a broken wheel. With Humbert and his master in the crowd, the rest can be guessed. What can't be guessed is the smoky street scenes, the wide-awake good humour of the Burningham faces (people and horses alike), the acute eye for beauty in bricks and city skies and the eye for comical detail too. Enchanting endpapers put the finishing touch to a delectable book.

> *Margery Fisher, in a review of "Humbert, Mr. Firkin and the Lord Mayor of London," in her* Growing Point, *Vol. 4, No. 9, April, 1966, p. 685.*

[Burningham] is so good he's sometimes too good—too much textured sky, too many scarlet-to-purple buildings looking like London on fire, too big a crowd of obese caricatures—but when he concentrates on Humbert and the Lord Mayor, on Mr. Firkin enjoying his sandwich and his pint, he packs a very funny Punch. The plot, however, is just another poor-horse-makes-good.

> *A review of "Humbert," in* Virginia Kirkus' Service, *Vol. XXXV, No. 10, May 15, 1967, p. 596.*

The striking paintings which feature a lumpish horse, who looks like a relative of a Thurber dog, set against an impressionistic view of the London streets are the main attraction of this minimal but good-natured, easy-to-read story. . . . Humbert's moment of glory seems overstressed in the story and will be short-lived with young children.

> *Elinor Cullen, in a review of "Humbert, Mr. Firkin and the Lord Mayor of London," in* School Library Journal, *an appendix to* Library Journal, *Vol. 14, No. 1, June, 1967 p. 159.*

---

### CANNONBALL SIMP (1966)

Unwanted and unloved, [the ugly pug Simp] is deposited near a rubbish dump inhabited by a troupe of melancholy rats; things go from bad to worse, but eventually she joins another troupe—a circus where, with a sad-faced clown, she stars in the turn of turns. The text is no more than a peg for John Burningham's finely observed, technically brilliant paintings. He is not afraid to follow his heart, to draw what he feels he sees rather than serve up the kind of photographic representation characteristic of so many picture-books today. His use of colour is subtle, his vision of things infectious.

> *Kevin Crossley-Holland, in a review of "Cannonball Simp," in* The Spectator, *Vol. 217, No. 7220, November 11, 1966, p. 627.*

Burningham has not been more aggressive in his drawing than in the pathetic story of Simp. . . . Mr. Burningham is still the best author among artists since Ardizzone, but he should try to draw more consistently well. There are some lovely things here, notably the night scenes in which he habitually excels. Some of the other drawings tempt one, reluctantly, to the thought that success may have come too easily to this young artist. (pp. 367-68)

> *A review of "Cannonball Simp," in* The Junior Bookshelf, *Vol. 30, No. 6, December, 1966, pp. 367-68.*

"**Cannonball Simp**" has made me break the newest resolution of the new season: I wasn't going to look at, let alone review, one picture book and/or one book with pictures until I had read a host of pictureless books. But what can I do when a dog like Cannonball Simp wanders in, a black, Piglet-shaped, disarming schnook of a dog? I've never met John Burningham. I've yet to see a picture of John Burningham, but after looking at his wild and glorious creatures and reading the wild and glorious

stories he writes about them, Jonathan Miller is going to have to move to the back of the pedestal: John Burningham is now my favorite Englishman.

> *A review of "Cannonball Simp," in* Publishers Weekly, *Vol. 192, No. 6, August 7, 1967, p. 54.*

[Burningham] follows in amusing animal portraiture and resplendent scene paintings the unhappy incidents and the circus performances which Simp raises from their former boring level by her virtuoso tricks. The artist's interpretive ability rescues an ordinary story from banality. (p. 741)

> *Virginia Haviland, in a review of "Cannonball Simp," in* The Horn Book Magazine, *Vol. XLIII, No. 6, December, 1967, pp. 740-41.*

There are some truly delightful scenes presented [in *Cannonball Simp*]. When Simp has a successful debut she invites the baby elephant, the lion, and the monkey to join her in a celebration. The youngsters will love it.

Some very sensitive children may have a hard time getting past the very sad beginning but this is a case where perseverance will be amply rewarded.

The pictures are charming. A variety of techniques are employed, and the very bold and colorful pages are especially effective. Mr. Burningham's pictures talk directly to young children—he seems instinctively to grasp what little ones like to look at, and he emphasizes just those things.

This is a success story about a cuddly, ugly, little dog that is really quite endearing.

> *Robert Cohen, in a review of "Cannonball Simp," in* Young Readers Review, *Vol. IV, No. 4, December, 1967, p. 16.*

If the story is not remarkably original, it is a pleasant one, and the illustrations, done in a strong, heavy, bright Expressionist style, are distinguished. Some of them have a mordant humor that may be lost on a four-year-old but will make the person reading out loud to him feel well compensated for his conscientiousness. An especially fine illustration, which appears with the words "The circus managers had a look of boredom on their faces as they watched the clown. 'He'll really have to go,' they said," shows four of the most dissolute men imaginable, dressed in evening clothes and almost comatose with ennui.

> *Janet Malcolm, in a review of "Cannonball Simp," in* The New Yorker, *Vol. XLIII, No. 43, December 16, 1967, p. 159.*

---

### HARQUIN: THE FOX WHO WENT DOWN TO THE VALLEY (1967)

Splendid end-papers decorated with foxes and autumn leaves lead to pages of autumnal richness where freakishly-drawn foxes slink through marsh and thicket or sit comfortably at home by the fireside (kettle on hob, family portrait on wall). Pursued by the hunt, Harquin turns the table on them, and the artist enjoys giving his animals a good deal more intelligence than his pink-coated humans.

> *Margery Fisher, in a review of "Harquin: The Fox Who Went Down to the Valley," in her* Growing Point, *Vol. 6, No. 6, December, 1967, p. 1033.*

*From* Humbert, Mister Firkin, and the Lord Mayor of London, *written and illustrated by John Burningham. J. Cape, 1965. Copyright © 1963 by John Burningham. All rights reserved. Reprinted by permission of Jonathan Cape Ltd, on behalf of the author.*

Despite my increasing awareness of misanthropy in the author, I have to report immediate and increasing success of this modern Reynard with children of three to six. The fox has all the best pictures, some of outstanding scenic beauty and arresting design. The appeal to the imagination is strong. The unspeakable squire is a most acceptable villain.

> *Margaret Meek, in a review of "Harquin: The Fox Who Went Down to the Valley," in* The School Librarian and School Library Review, *Vol. 16, No. 1, March, 1968, p. 124.*

The dashing scenes of a fox hunt across an English valley and marsh that fill the center pages of this picture book feature rich colors, movement, and sophisticated caricatures of the English gentry. These give the book a verve and humor which the text alone fails to supply. The story of a young fox who disobediently played in the valley, but who nevertheless managed to outfox the hunt and bring it to a ridiculous end, is a flatly told, contrived vehicle, but, thanks to those forceful illustrations and the humorous ending, the book as a whole will be enjoyed for its slap-dash fun.

> *Nancy Young Orr, in a review of "Harquin: The Fox Who Went Down to the Valley," in* School Library Journal, *an appendix to* Library Journal, *Vol. 15, No. 3, November, 1968, p. 75.*

["Harquin: The Fox Who Went Down to the Valley" is a] sophisticated picture story that may have something in it for children—a fox hunt from the point of view of the fox. . . . Mr. Burningham's pictures are done in a heavy, strong, painterly style, and some of them are satiric. In his picture of the squire dressed in his country squires' clothes and surrounded by his large, stupid dogs, the artist has wonderfully captured the look of peevish resignation that settles on the faces of people who have nothing to do all day.

> *Janet Malcolm, in a review of "Harquin: The Fox Who Went Down to the Valley," in* The New Yorker, *Vol. XLVI, No. 43, December 14, 1968, p. 217.*

The artist uses colors with rich abandon; starting with two galloping huntsmen on the title page, he has made splendid, humorous pictures—many of them doublespreads—full of droll exaggeration and swift-flowing action.

> *Ethel L. Heins, in a review of "Harquin: The Fox Who Went Down to the Valley," in* The Horn Book Magazine, *Vol. XLV, No. 1, February, 1969, p. 40.*

Examples of clearly expressionistic illustrations are those by Peter Parnall and John Burningham. Parnall's illustrations for *The Way to Start a Day,* the 1979 Caldecott Honor book written by Byrd Baylor, are elegant in their simplicity. . . . In sharp contrast are the vital and action-filled paintings that John Burningham did for the modern fairy tale entitled *Harquin, the Fox Who Went Down to the Valley.* The firm lines and the exuberant splashes of color, even the silhouettes of the mischievous fox dashing among the foliage as it teases and evades the huntsmen, exemplify the emotionalism and the abstract qualities so characteristic of expressionism. (p. 11)

Vital, expressionistic paintings in full color complement perfectly the action and mood of this modern fairy tale. . . . A convincing story emphasizing that in every generation there is someone who rejects the advice of his or her elders even though that advice is based on first-hand experience. Be certain to notice the end sheets for the silhouetted scenes of the fox darting in and out of the foliage which highlight so cleverly the taunting behavior of Harquin (and ultimately one of his sons) eluding the huntsmen. (p. 157)

> *Patricia Jean Cianciolo, "Introduction" and "The Imaginative World: 'Harquin: The Fox Who Went Down to the Valley'," in her* Books for Children, *revised edition, American Library Association, 1981, pp. 1-30, 157.**

---

### SEASONS (1969)

The opportunities for the illustrator of children's books can be delightful; but the very wish to make the most of them, together with the publisher's natural desire for the book to make an immediate impact in the bookshop, sometimes produce results which forget the book's real readers.

I'm not sure that there isn't a hint of this even about a handsome new book by a maestro of the form: John Burningham's *Seasons*. . . . John Burningham arrives at the changing moods of the seasons by a sort of gauche, subtle progress through complex veils and sprays and blots of colour, but the result is essentially faithful and familiar: his rimey and glittering winter is particularly successful. My tiny reservation presented itself first as a wish that there were more people doing things—more, say, of the amiably feckless family you see lounging about the back of their van in the harvest scene. Perhaps it's simply that there is too much of what this artist does so well: that you miss—compared with his other books—the little drama, the narrative which *requires* certain activities, certain moods.

> *Quentin Blake, "Child's Eye View," in* Punch, *Vol. 257, December 17, 1969, p. 1015.**

[*Seasons*] makes its impact first as a whole and then calls for the delighted discovery of small points. For instance, though there is no "story" in the text, which consists of a few phrases ("Spring is birds nesting pigs rooting lambs playing ducks dabbling and flowers") divided among the pictures, there is continuity in that each section begins with a country scene (farmhouse, pond, hills in the background, road); it is always the same scene with details that change with the seasons. The humour in the pictures is like that of Burningham's early Underground posters—animals and people are peculiar but nice and they disport themselves against true landscapes. *Seasons* has in particular some really fine skies—a bonfire-lit sky in autumn, a speckled height above harvest fields, a thunder sky dramatically purple. Each picture has its mood and colour scheme. . . . The joy of looking has seldom been better catered for and, to learn to look, children must have the best material.

> *Margery Fisher, in a review of "Seasons," in her* Growing Point, *Vol. 8, No. 8, March, 1970, p. 1481.*

Success continues to come a little too easily to John Burningham. It is tempting to think that, in *Seasons,* instead of brooding over the beauty and fun of the country year and then

distilling the essence of his experience, he has sat down and knocked off a set of charmingly superficial pictures. How much better, too, if this master—when he chooses—of English prose had welded his pictures with a really evocative text rather than these few words dropped casually into the page. Part of the truth seems to be that Mr. Burningham is not really a book-artist; the four big double-folds set into *Seasons* are some indication tht he does not willingly submit to the tyranny—or the discipline—of the page. Such a pity. There is enough here of shrewd observation, humour and feeling for colour to remind us that, when he submits, he is in the front rank of picture-book makers.

> *A review of "Seasons," in* The Junior Bookshelf, *Vol. 34, No. 2, April, 1970, p. 78.*

So many eye-blinking picture books are in fact picture albums, empty of significant content, that it is good to have artistry unadorned, in the service of mood, moment, and surpassingly vibrant views. What "Spring is . . ." or Summer or Autumn or Winter, is not, however, calendar cut-and-dry: summer, for instance, brings "buzzing insects" (and a hapless fisherman fleeing from them), "heat waves" (a heady, heavy champagne sky above a beach and golden pavilions that could be Brighton), and, turning the page, "thunderstorms" sending picnickers, dog, horses scurrying as the lightning above threatens the still glimmer below. Besides the exotically-edged beach there are "foggy days" and especially "endless rain" in winter to remind us of the book's British origin but more than counterbalancing is the tactility of "frost at night," of "ice and snow."

> *A review of "Seasons," in* Kirkus Reviews, *Vol. XXXVIII, No. 16, August 15, 1970, p. 866.*

The descriptive captions accompanying each drawing are terse; the book is meant to be a visual rather than a verbal delight. And though the volume is very English . . . , the intricacy of detail in the paintings, with their almost physically overwhelming color and mood, will insure an exuberant response to the book.

> *Sheryl B. Andrews, in a review of "Seasons," in* The Horn Book Magazine, *Vol. XLVII, No. 3, June, 1971, p. 277.*

Full-page pictures awash with glowing color provide total immersion in seasonal moods. This is a British book, with concepts like "endless rain" and "foggy days," so children will take a bit of nudging by teachers for an understanding of regional and continental differences in climate. The brief word or two of text on each page is sometimes overpowered by color and thus hard to read; but the book's overall effect is one of great beauty. (pp. 102, 104)

> *Lois Belfield Watt, in a review of "Seasons," in* Childhood Education, *Vol. 48, No. 2 (November, 1971), pp. 102, 104.*

---

### MR GUMPY'S OUTING (1970)

Burningham is one of our best author-illustrators. He knows how to put colour into the briefest of sentences, so that they will please the adult reader as well as the child listener. . . . Burningham's pictures are rather thinly coloured but are full of affectionate observation. A nice book.

> *A review of "Mr. Gumpy's Outing," in* The Junior Bookshelf, *Vol. 34, No. 6, December, 1970, p. 346.*

Mr. Gumpy (not quite grumpy) collects a risky punt load of energetic passengers. Each is separately introduced in a country-fresh, full-page watercolor; each can be rediscovered in smaller sketches of the ever more crowded boat. . . . A blessing of a book. Pored over, read aloud or acted out it should bring joy to the nursery.

*Joan Bodger Mercer, in a review of "Mr. Gumpy's Outing," in* The New York Times Book Review, *November 7, 1971, p. 46.*

The illustrations, skillfully drawn cross-hatched brown ink drawings alternating with full-page impressionistic paintings dominantly in muted greens and browns, are outstanding for their very expressive animals and numerous warm, humorous touches—e.g., an around the table scene features a benign sheep sipping through a straw, etc. And, the simple, cumulative text and easy, natural attitudes of Gumpy and company are sure to please the picture-book audience.

*Pamela D. Pollack, in a review of "Mr. Gumpy's Outing," in* School Library Journal, *an appendix to* Library Journal, *Vol. 18, No. 5, January, 1972, p. 50.*

[A requirement of books for the very young is] a use of words that have precision and yet explore the resources of language, deftly and eloquently setting the scene and moving the action along. Not many writers can do this; not many editors recognize its essentiality for the very young.

And the story itself should proceed in a straight line. Tangents and diversions are not for the one- to three-year-old. He is merely confused by extra information, and loses the thread.

**Mr. Gumpy** serves as the classic example; beautifully paced, each character coming alive through his action and speech, with no need for description.

"May I come please, Mr. Gumpy?" said the pig.
"Very well, but don't muck about . . ."

Of course, he does muck about, as we all know he will, and contributes with the children (who squabble), the chickens (who flap) and the goat (who kicks), to the predictable capsize of the boat. But there is no comment, no moralizing, no need for pardon; all is implicit in the action, the dialogue, and of course, the illustrations. (pp. 13-14)

*Dorothy Butler, "Cushla and Her Books," in* Signal, *No. 22, January, 1977, pp. 3-37.**

'Every good boy deserves father' should be the storytime maxim up and down the social scale, wherever there's a father to be had. So, once *The Old Man of Lochnager* has begun to fall apart at the stitching, I suggest something to grab Dad with its humour. What better than John Burningham's **Mr Gumpy's Outing** . . . : impossible to read aloud without a gentle grin, with all the cumulative qualities of a good joining-in story, and tons to talk about. 'How did the pig muck about? What do you think he did?'

*Bernard Ashley, "Six Books to Give Prince William," in* Books for Your Children, *Vol. 17, No. 3, Autumn-Winter, 1982, p. 28.**

Good artists are not automatically good writers. . . . John Burningham's work is a constant pleasure to the eye, but the stories that accompany his pictures can be thin; the well-known **Mr. Gumpy's Outing,** for example, is not particularly memorable in its choice of words, and its narrative is somewhat predictable. (p. 139)

*Russell Hoban, "Beyond the Last Visible Dog," in* Painted Desert, Green Shade: Essays on Contemporary Writers of Fiction for Children and Young Adults, *edited by David Rees, The Horn Book Inc., 1984, pp. 138-52.**

---

## *AROUND THE WORLD IN EIGHTY DAYS* (1972)

[Safely home from his journey in the steps of Phileas Fogg, Mr. Burningham] has turned his sketches, his photographs and his tapes into a handsome book.

If Mr. Burningham has a fault—and he has—it is that he is rather slapdash. His finished drawings often look like initial sketches. The notebook technique consequently suits him well. He is allowed 96 pages for his eighty days and 24 countries, and so he has room only for very brief impressions, of people, landscape and buildings and of his own weary figure. These are much better than the few finished paintings in which the famous Burningham humour is less evident.

There may be some doubt about the potential audience for this book. Despite the picture book format, it is not for his usual youthful readers who could be baffled by the swift change of scene and the brief wisecracking notes. It is, I suppose, mainly for grown-ups. There is a valuable supplementary use for it in

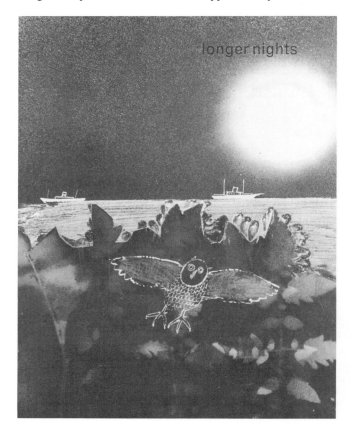

*From* Seasons, *written and illustrated by John Burningham. Cape, 1969. Copyright © 1969 by John Burningham. All rights reserved. Reprinted by permission of Jonathan Cape Ltd, on behalf of the author.*

schools, where it could become a welcome leavening in the lump of geography teaching.

*A review of "Around the World in Eighty Days," in* The Junior Bookshelf, *Vol. 36, No. 3, June, 1972, p. 151.*

The author-illustrator's adventures in 24 countries are described in pithy, droll prose and depicted in paintings of breathtaking beauty and humor. It's a treat to go along on the intrepid tourist's journey. . . .

*A review of "Around the World in Eighty Days," in* Publishers Weekly, *Vol. 216, No. 16, October 15, 1979, p. 67.*

Succinctly captured details and amusing peculiarities of individual countries emerge under Burningham's facile touch. Variations of color and line reflect the ever-changing atmosphere of his travels, while consistency of style unites the entire text. This offers enrichment material for units on other countries, where a knowledgeable adult can interpret and elaborate on the sites visited. Peripatetic travelers of any age will find it an armchair delight.

*A review of "Around the World in Eighty Days," in* Booklist, *Vol. 76, No. 8, December 15, 1979, p. 609.*

[Burningham] recorded his experiences in diary-like jottings and in loose, atmospheric pen-and-pastel drawings that capture the essence of the diverse and colorful stops on his journey. His impressions are perceptive and amusing (the U.S. is depicted as a bespectacled cowboy astride a coke sipping eagle), and some of the subtle humor may be beyond the readers who would be attracted to the picture book format. Older armchair travelers are the best audience for these affable recollections.

*Barbara C. Campbell, in a review of "Around the World in Eighty Days," in* School Library Journal, *Vol. 26, No. 7, March, 1980, p. 128.*

This picture book [is] as witty as it is informative. . . . Essentially a travel book of the tourism period Burningham's *Around the World in Eighty Days* is a record of flashes of insight into people and the places in which they live by a trained observer (with a sense of humour) on the hop.

*Elaine Moss, "Picture Books for Young People, 9-13: 'Around the World in Eighty Days',"* in her Picture Books for Young People: 9-13, *1981. Reprint by The Thimble Press, 1982, p. 44.*

---

## MR GUMPY'S MOTOR CAR (1973)

[Some picture books] make an effort to engage the child's critical sense, his moral judgment or his ability to reason. It's odd to find that most of the better-known names in the field are often content to let these faculties lie dormant: their tales are naive, prettified, inconclusive (and I don't believe that this is simply because they have a younger age-group in mind). In *Mr Gumpy's Motor Car* . . . Burningham has, for instance, given us another Mr Gumpy 'story' not unlike the first. I admire Burningham's long-faced animals and the serene luminosity of his coloured inks and crayons, but not enough *happens*. (p. 780)

*John Fuller, "Irresistible Logic," in* New Statesman, *Vol. 85, No. 2201, May 25, 1973, pp. 779-80.**

*Mr Gumpy's Outing* had an air of inevitability about it—a book not so much put together, painstakingly, over a period of time, as one arriving, complete in all its parts, as soon as it was thought of. Thus, when *Mr Gumpy's Motor Car* was announced, it sounded very much like an act of sheer bravado, a perilous temptation of Providence. What hope was there of finding again the natural ease of that first book?

In the event, Providence has not been as unkind as she could have been, and it says much for *Mr Gumpy's Motor Car* that, while it does not match the standards of its predecessor at least it does not betray them. It follows something of the same pattern as the 'Outing': the car, after three pages, being loaded up with the same assortment of creatures . . . , but instead of the buildup towards the one splendid crisis there is now only the passage of incidents—a rain-storm, the car stuck in the mud and a general cussedness in the matter of pushing it out—and the final swim in Mr Gumpy's river does not offer the full roundness of a conclusion that the tea-party did.

John Burningham has retained a graphic style in the new book very similar to that in the old, with the same hatched colour work and the same use of monochrome sketches to accompany the main pictures. With the red car and at least one very blue sky, the book has a brighter appearance than *Mr Gumpy's Outing*, but brightness—as that volume taught us—is not an absolutely necessary ingredient for the complete success of a picture book.

*Brian W. Alderson, in a review of "Mr Gumpy's Motor Car," in* Children's Book Review, *Vol. 111, No. 4, September, 1973, p. 108.*

"Come for a ride another day," was the closing line in the popular *Mr. Gumpy's Outing*. . . . This is a monotonous recap of that. . . . Once again, [Mr. G., the children, and the farm animals] go for a swim, and again return home, with yet another forecast of more of the same to come in the last line. "Come for a drive another day." The text is easy-to-read and the amusingly cartooned, gently colored illustrations are easy to smile over. Three year olds often prefer this sort of satisfying, familiar, no-surprises reading. But, whichever way adults flip these pages, more is a repetitive bore in Mr. G's case. (pp. 47-8)

*Lillian N. Gerhardt, in a review of "Mr. Gumpy's Motor Car," in* School Library Journal, *Vol. 22, No. 9, May, 1976, pp. 47-8.*

Good man, this Gumpy! He proved it in **"Mr. Gumpy's Outing."** . . .

The strength here is in the rural simplicity and in the colorful illustrations of amiable animals, the countryside in sunshine and under lowering clouds. Those things and the bold type which carries words and phrases for the reader to chew on and roll around on the tongue—"slipped and slithered and squelched." Yes, good man, this Gumpy; Burningham, too.

*George A. Woods, in a review of "Mr. Gumpy's Motor Car," in* The New York Times Book Review, *July 11, 1976, p. 35.*

[A brief text] and enchanting drawings . . . describe the bouncing vehicle and its overload of riders. . . . [The artist] is blessed with a gift for both verbal and visual storytelling; his flow of words describing the muddy crisis matches the charm of his watercolor scenes.

*Virginia Haviland, in a review of "Mr. Gumpy's Motor Car," in* The Horn Book Magazine, *Vol. LII, No. 4, August, 1976, p. 385.*

---

## THE BABY; THE RABBIT; THE SCHOOL; THE SNOW (LITTLE BOOKS) (1974)

More robust and rollicking, here are four glimpses of a child's world, with a first-person narrative in similar mood ("Sometimes I like the baby. Sometimes I don't" seems fair comment on two scenes, one in which the small hero holds baby proudly, the other in which Mother holds Baby and boy holds a dismayed cat.) The crayon pictures are smooth and pointed and convey an entirely convincing view of life that is not at all disturbed by the idiosyncratic treatment of faces and figures.

*Margery Fisher, in a review of "The Baby," "The Rabbit," "The School," and "The Snow," in her* Growing Point, *Vol. 13, No. 6, December, 1974, p. 2535.*

It is a joy to read and handle these four small books, and to see work of this calibre in books for the youngest child who is so often sadly neglected by authors and artists of distinction. This kind of book necessarily imposes certain demands and disciplines which many cannot accept, sensing a curb on their integrity and an invitation to puerility and condescension. Mr. Burningham, however, seems to accept this challenge as one that will exploit equally his usual spontaneous and natural exuberance, and here his gifts are most aptly suited to the small size of the book, the pictures of the familiar and homely, and the minimum of large bold text facing each picture, each of

*From* The Cupboard, *written and illustrated by John Burningham. Cape, 1975, Thomas Y. Crowell Co., Inc., 1976. Copyright © 1975 by John Burningham. All rights reserved. Reprinted by permission of Harper & Row, Publishers, Inc. In Canada by Jonathan Cape Ltd, on behalf of the author.*

which in turn will attract the child and eventually lead him to translate the whole into reading skills. The author-illustrator's earlier larger picture story books about Mr. Gumpy may, with their clear gay characterful drawings and similar attractive large print, have paved the way for this series, and these latest will now form a stepping stone to **"Mr. Gumpy"** and from thence to Mr. Burningham's other work—and to others of repute.

Mr. Burningham has a direct and candid appeal and his rounded illustrations express an honest jocose view of real life and real people. The colours here are just bright enough, the details clear and sufficient, and each picture makes an entity of each page and a statement to match the words opposite.

Charming and delicate, yet jaunty, amusing and robust, they give the youngest child that introduction to fine art which is so vital and necessary in his introduction to books and thence to reading. (pp. 333-34)

*A review of "The Baby," "The Rabbit," "The School," and "The Snow," in* The Junior Bookshelf, *Vol. 38, No. 6, December, 1974, pp. 333-34.*

[Burningham's mini-books are] directed to the same toddler clientele as Gunilla Wolde's Betsy series. . . . In common with Wolde, Burningham's world is peopled with stay-at-home Mommy and kiddies (father power hasn't penetrated the nursery) and nothing happens (*The Snow,* in which the named little boy loses a mitten, is as eventful as they get). The resemblance stops there. English and Swedish imports respectively, the source of the major difference may well be cultural. Burningham, clipped and understated in tone, leaves room to react, while Wolde, with-it and explicit, insists on spelling out everything in imagination-blunting detail. His fluent, effortless texts have the natural sound of a child talking; hers are clearly a well-meaning adult voice. Finally, Burningham's unembroidered pen-and-pastel pictures, no great shakes if held up to his *Mr. Gumpy's Outing* . . . , are drawn with considerably more flair [than Wolde's cartoons].

*Pamela D. Pollack, in a review of "The Baby," "The Rabbit," "The School," and "The Snow," in* School Library Journal, *Vol. 22, No. 4, December, 1975, p. 41.*

Each statement, as bald as the baby itself, is on a page alone, faced by a simple chalky illustration which brings a quiet humour to such straight remarks as "The baby makes a mess with its food". *The Baby* is the best of the four Burningham **"Little Books"** published this year because, being homebound, it has the strongest emotional undertow.

*Elaine Moss, "Picture Books: 'The Baby'," in* Children's Books of the Year: 1974, *edited by Elaine Moss, Hamish Hamilton, 1975, p. 16.*

[In *The School* a] little boy tells us that in school he learns to read, write, and sing. He also says that at school he eats lunch, paints pictures, plays games, and makes friends. Then, after a full day, he returns home.

Colorful, simple crayon illustrations go well with this extremely simple first-person narrative. These same illustrations might be used to encourage discussion. The whole could be used to help prepare a very young child for beginning school.

*Sharon Spredemann Dreyer, in a review of "The School," in her* The Bookfinder, a Guide to Children's Literature about the Needs and Problems of Youth Aged 2-15: Annotations of Books Published

1975 through 1978, Vol. 2, *American Guidance Service, Inc., 1981, No. 105.*

---

### THE BLANKET; THE CUPBOARD; THE DOG; THE FRIEND (LITTLE BOOKS) (1975)

Four more tiny books offering brief, inspired glances at familiar childhood situations. A small boy, whose chubby face belies his obvious force of character, loses and finds his talisman-blanket, turns the cupboard upside-down and is reluctant to tidy it, sometimes enjoys and sometimes can do without his boon companion, enjoys a visit from a friendly dog. The illustrations in fine line and barely-suggested colour are as always alert and in their seemingly casual style reveal the rapidly changing moods of a child in a way that will certainly engage adults and should provoke some recognition of familiarity in children.

> *Margery Fisher, in a review of "The Blanket," "The Cupboard," "The Friend," and "The Dog," in her* Growing Point, *Vol. 14, No. 4, October, 1975, p. 2724.*

Although a good many children have experience of the written form of language when they enter school and gain even more experience from frequent reading-aloud sessions by teachers, there are just as many who lack sufficient knowledge of how print 'sounds' to anticipate sequences. It therefore seems logical that schools should provide a large number of books which capitalise on the experience which all children bring to reading—their familiarity with the spoken form of language. John Burningham's texts are particularly useful for this purpose. Generally he writes in a style which is more akin to speech than writing and the **'Little Books'** series from which [*The Cupboard*] comes is no exception.

> *Cliff Moon, in a review of "The Cupboard," in* The School Librarian, *Vol. 23, No. 4, December, 1975, p. 320.*

As strictly functional as furniture scaled down for the nursery, Burningham's mini-books are made for easy access. The purposely prosaic stories neither demand nor merit much effort. The action sticks close to home. . . . Pen-and-pastel drawings are tastefully done but, like the texts, they're baby food bland.

> *Pamela D. Pollack, in a review of "The Blanket," "The Cupboard," "The Dog," and "The Friend," in* School Library Journal, *Vol. 23, No. 6, February, 1977, p. 54.*

Instead of stretching horizons, the newest four titles in this group focus on familiar things, but ones perhaps not seen in the mirror of a book. Burningham's realizations are completely uncluttered, befitting the smallest listeners' perceptions of their own small world. In this way, he can tell an entire story in about 60 words. . . . Luckily, fewer Briticisms are found than in the last four titles. . . . With charmingly naive crayon illustrations.

> *A review of "The Blanket," "The Cupboard," "The Dog," and "The Friend," in* Booklist, *Vol. 73, No. 12, February 15, 1977, p. 894.*

---

### COME AWAY FROM THE WATER, SHIRLEY (1977)

The secret humour in this book will captivate children because each one will feel he has discovered it for himself. Mother and Father sit stodgily on deckchairs on the beach, delineated in fine line and crayon, addressing admonitory remarks to a child just out of sight ("Don't stroke that dog, Shirley, you don't know where he's been" and so on). On the opposite page, shown in stronger, broader colour, Shirley overpowers the crew of a pirate ship and rows off with their chart to dig up treasure with the dog's help. Part of the fun lies in the precise juxtaposition of parental comment and child's actions, but the whole book is a triumph of expressive technique and an entertaining championing of children's rights. (pp. 3192-93)

> *Margery Fisher, in a review of "Come Away from the Water, Shirley," in her* Growing Point, *Vol. 16, No. 4, October, 1977, pp. 3192-93.*

A child's imagination knows no mundane parental bounds. And John Burningham manages literally to draw and paint . . . the separate togetherness of coexisting worlds. **"Come Away from the Water, Shirley"** is all too brief a masterpiece of humor and affection, with . . . unforgettable illustrations.

> *David Anable, "Shirley Battles Pirates in Deep-Sea Daydreams," in* The Christian Science Monitor, *November 2, 1977, p. B2.\**

[A] rather disappointing John Burningham, . . . cheerfully drawn but dependent on a silent contrast between the verbal narrative . . . [and a visual one]: too sophisticated a device for the rewards it brings, if the lack of interest shown by our usually pro-Burningham children is any guide.

> *Jeremy Treglown, "Shin-Pads," in* New Statesman, *Vol. 94, No. 2433, November 4, 1977, p. 631.\**

John Burningham has produced a two-faced winner. . . . Though its personality is purposely schizoid, the book is as together as Siamese twins. The adequate but bland surface of the parents' scene is drawn in prosaic colored pencil, without depth or background, while Shirley's is shown in colors that glow with the depth of mixed media. Mum and Dad are good solid sorts, sitting there on the grey pebbled shore in practical fold-up chairs, knitting and nodding off behind the papers, as their daughter, on the opposing page, sees sights her parents can't even imagine. The folks have all the lines, the kind children bandage their ears with, . . . while Shirley has all the action, pursuing pirates and finding a treasure trove—in golden silence. (pp. E1-E2)

> *Ann S. Haskell, "Picture Books: The Eyes Have It," in* Book World—The Washington Post, *November 13, 1977, pp. E1-E2.\**

Shirley is one of those innumerable storybook children burdened with perfectly awful parents. . . . While the dull parent/imaginative child theme is hardly new, Burningham's view of it is fresh and fun. Shirley's parents appear . . . virtually immobile in pale pastels; facing them on the opposite page, Shirley goes adventuring in action-packed and richly colored tableaux. Despite **Come Away**'s . . . possible contribution to the generation gap, you can't help but feel good about Shirley. (pp. 42-3)

> *Janet French, in a review of "Come Away from the Water, Shirley," in* School Library Journal, *Vol. 24, No. 4, December, 1977, pp. 42-3.*

This imaginative picturebook . . . is half fantasy and half mundane reality. The juxtaposition will delight young readers unable to comprehend the stuffiness of adults. . . . The whole book is a welcome glorification of the world of the imagination.

*A review of "Come Away from the Water, Shirley,"
in* Book World—The Washington Post, *August 14,
1983, p. 13.*

---

### TIME TO GET OUT OF THE BATH, SHIRLEY   (1978)

**Time to get out of the bath, Shirley** is a clever idea which is concisely and successfully carried out. It is a sequence of fantasies involving adventures in medieval times which pass through young Shirley's mind as her mother carries on a nagging tirade at her while she finishes her bath. Mother's words carry on relentlessly on the left-hand side of the double page spread in rather thin, subdued pictures, while Shirley's own fantasy world opposite is in rich colour. . . . The richness of the fantasy pictures makes an excellent contrast with the dreary reality of the everyday world of dirty towels, soap in the bath, and water on the floor, of her mother's conversation. (pp. 68, 70)

*Lavinia Learmont, "Noah's Ark," in* Books and
Bookmen, *Vol. 23, No. 8, June, 1978, pp. 66, 68,
70.**

The same joke that was so rousing in **Come away from the water, Shirley;** the same zestful humour and ingenuity in placing the mother's routine gestures, words and actions . . . opposite the fancied world entered by way of magic diminution via the plug-hole. . . . A marvellously comical and inventive juxtaposition of everyday taps, toothpaste and domestic admonition with storybook clichés and uninhibited fun.

*Margery Fisher, in a review of "Time to Get Out of
the Bath, Shirley," in her* Growing Point, *Vol. 17,
No. 2, July, 1978, p. 3369.*

Ever since **Mr Gumpy's Outing,** John Burningham has shown how picture books can carry a complete theory of the imagination. . . . This is the artist's non-verbal challenge to everyday phraseology; something very special.

*Margaret Meek, in a review of "Time to Get Out of
the Bath, Shirley," in* The School Librarian, *Vol.
26, No. 3, September, 1978, p. 229.*

Once again, pallid pastel colors are used to characterize the nature of family life while boldly contrasted deep colors and forceful shapes triumphantly express the power of Shirley's personal universe. The end papers are a sly tribute to the ingenuity of English plumbing, the water pipes serving as perches and supports for the inhabitants of a fantasy world. (p. 506)

*Paul Heins, in a review of "Time to Get Out of the
Bath, Shirley," in* The Horn Book Magazine, *Vol.
LV, No. 5, October, 1978, pp. 505-06.*

All the time mother's voice goes droning on, asking questions but, like Pilate, not stopping for the answer. John Burningham keeps his reality and fantasy on opposite pages and never the twain meet. The drawing is as exquisite as the humour.

There are not many words to **Shirley,** but these few are perfect, catching precisely the intonation of speech.

*A review of "Time to Get Out of the Bath, Shirley,"
in* The Junior Bookshelf, *Vol. 42, No. 5, October,
1978, p. 248.*

The delightful illustrations juxtapose the banal, commonplace world of her mother with that of Shirley's outrageously romantic fantasy. The pale pastels of the former contrast with the bright, sunshiny colors of the latter. The humor is very subtle for a picture book. Visual jokes abound: Shirley is a smaller but otherwise almost identical physical replica of her mother; the royal pair appear to be the King and Queen of Clubs; the noble horses would look more at home pulling a milk wagon than as the fiery mounts used in tournaments. The lively endpapers are dominated by a construction of prosaic pipes, surrounded by improbably sized animal and fairy-tale characters who use the plumbing for perches, for holding swings, for growing plants, or for a medieval horse race. The mundane maze of tubing and the fantastic uses to which it is put epitomize the dichotomy of the text.

That's the third and last time I'm asking you whether you want a drink, Shirley

*From* Come Away from the Water, Shirley, *written and illustrated by John Burningham. J. Cape, 1977,
Thomas Y. Crowell Co., Inc., 1977. Copyright © 1977 by John Burningham. All rights reserved. Reprinted
by permission of Harper & Row, Publishers, Inc. In Canada by Jonathan Cape Ltd, on behalf of the author.*

*Barbara H. Baskin and Karen H. Harris, "A Selected Guide to Intellectually Demanding Books: 'Time to Get Out of the Bath, Shirley',*" in their *Books for the Gifted Child, R. R. Bowker Company, 1980, p. 103.*

---

## WOULD YOU RATHER . . . (1978)

Burningham's numerous big, bold, bright watercolor illustrations are the main attraction here. The basic premise seems to be that there are worse things in this world than having to go to bed. For example, "Would you rather be crushed by a snake, swallowed by a fish, eaten by a crocodile or sat on by a rhinoceros?" or "Would you rather be lost in a fog, in a desert, or at sea, in a forest or in a crowd?" or "Perhaps you would rather be asleep in your bed?" Some choice. Admittedly, the "parade of horribles" is presented tongue-in-cheek and there are some pleasant options. . . . But, all in all, this could be anxiety provoking for some kids, especially at bedtime.

*Gemma DeVinney, in a review of "Would You Rather . . . ," in* School Library Journal, *Vol. 25, No. 2, October, 1978, p. 130.*

Favorite childhood pastimes and mind play don't always survive translation to picture-book form, but Burningham's free-floating, storyless imagination-stretcher is consistently felicitous. Warming up with an ingenuously visualized "Would you rather your house was surrounded by water, snow, or jungle," he then entertains, for example: preposterous disaster . . . ; onomotopoetic indigestion ("would you rather be made to eat spider stew, slug dumplings, mashed worms, or drink snail squash"); cost-benefit trade-offs ("would you rather jump in the brambles for 25¢, swallow a dead frog for 50¢, stay all night in a creepy house for a dollar"); and empathetic speculation (the small child who represents "you" throughout is seen living with various animals in their cage, bowl, coop, or whatever). The pictures are wonderfully zesty, childlike, and droll; and Burningham's ending ("or perhaps you would rather just go to sleep in your own bed") makes the whole exercise a choice bedtime book, to inspire any child's musings as (s)he drifts off to sleep.

*A review of "Would You Rather . . . ," in* Kirkus Reviews, *Vol. XLVI, No. 22, November 15, 1978, p. 1241.*

John Burningham takes up the question **Would You Rather . . .** and proceeds to make many good probing jokes. . . . [He] illustrates each predicament in a wide-eyed manner. This seems to me his best book: lucid, unpretentious, funny.

*William Feaver, "That Lear Quality," in* The Observer, *December 10, 1978, p. 38.*

Exhilarating role-playing as a shock-headed lad is offered various unusual alternatives. . . . Dismay (at slug dumplings), glee (riding a bull in a supermarket) and interest (helping a witch make a stew) are illustrated in scenes arranged two or three to a page, each dramatic as well as continuous, each showing comically in lightly applied wash and line the adaptability of an intelligent child.

*Margery Fisher, in a review of "Would You Rather . . . ," in her* Growing Point, *Vol. 17, Nov. 5, January, 1979, p. 3448.*

Burningham, who tells the best stories among modern picture-book makers (Remember **Humbert**?) has rather neglected conventional narrative lately. His experiments are exciting, but one cannot help thinking that something precious is being lost. However, here is another book based on an idea, not a story. Burningham gives us a number of options, some nice, some very nasty, each illustrated in his most hilarious manner. . . . The book is strongly orientated to the child, including the child who normally considers himself too old for picture-books.

*A review of "Would You Rather . . . ," in* The Junior Bookshelf, *Vol. 43, No. 1, February, 1979, p. 15.*

Although I am sure that the four-year-olds to whom this simple-looking book is given get something out of it, there is no doubt in my mind that the best age at which to gorge on its delights is nine or ten. 'Would you rather be made to eat spider stew, slug dumplings, mashed worms or drink snail squash' is an alternative choice that leads straight on to Raymond Briggs's *Fungus the Bogeyman*. . . . And see the boy's face blush in the embarrassingly large pictures that accompany the question, 'Would you rather your dad did a dance in school or your mum had a row in a café?' A tot couldn't care less—but at nine you would sink through the floor!

*Elaine Moss, "Picture Books for Young People 9-13: 'Would You Rather . . . ,'" in her* Picture Books for Young People 9-13, *The Thimble Press, 1981, p. 14.*

---

## THE SHOPPING BASKET (1980)

Steven has gone to the store for his mother, his basket loaded with "six eggs, five bananas, four apples, three oranges for the baby, two doughnuts, and a package of crisps for [his] lunch." Deftly, he handles a bear who threatens to hug the breath out of him if he doesn't give up his eggs: he challenges the bruin to catch an egg and leaves him with it all over his face. Similar schemes prove successful with a banana-hungry monkey, an apple-searching kangaroo, an orange-eating goat, a doughnut-mad pig, and a crisp-loving elephant. We can hardly sympathize with his mom's irritation over how long Steven has taken to do a job so small. Though the resolution is left floating in the air, readers will have poured over details too good to miss. Big, colorful pictures make great fun of the bullying menagerie, while a pyramid layout design of the contents of the basket gives visual clues for each disappearing object. Detail, repetition, and comic vengeance make a story preschoolers will enjoy greatly.

*Judith Goldberger, in a review of "The Shopping Basket," in* Booklist, *Vol. 77, No. 1, September 1, 1980, p. 42.*

This visible subtraction sum, illustrated both in action and in symbol, is executed in strong paint and crayon in the fanciful style that makes the humanising of animals seem as acceptable as it is amusing. A lively domestic joke, robustly expressed in fantastic terms. (pp. 3793-94)

*Margery Fisher, in a review of "The Shopping Basket," in her* Growing Point, *Vol. 19, No. 4, November, 1980, pp. 3793-94.*

Is Burningham sneaking an arithmetic lesson in between lines? Well, not so anyone would notice, with all the fun of seeing Steven, who looks so unprepossessing, facing up to all the commanding animals. Then Burningham gives the joke another turn with a characteristic poke at an obtuse Mom: "How could it have taken so long?" Sly and satisfying.

> *A review of "The Shopping Basket," in* Kirkus Reviews, *Vol. XLVIII, No. 21, November 1, 1980, p. 1389.*

In a simple, brisk text and in droll, brightly colored pictures the author-artist once again shows with tongue-in-cheek solemnity the gap between the imagination of a child and the mundane practicality of an adult. . . . Burningham speaks clearly to the minds of young children; it seems a bit pointless that in the present time of transatlantic copublishing the American editors are fearful of a little ordinary British usage and have translated *shop* into *store*, *packet* into *package*, and *tea* into *lunch*—which isn't even accurate.

> *Ethel L. Heins, in a review of "The Shopping Basket," in* The Horn Book Magazine, *Vol. LVII, No. 1, February, 1981, p. 40.*

**The Shopping Basket** belongs to what one might call the '**Shirley**' branch of Mr. Burningham's work. It deals, that is, with the dreams (and nightmares) that run parallel with the ordinary everyday life of small children. . . . Sound psychology, beautifully exact and humorous drawing, a restrained and rhythmic text, it is all here, adding up to a picture book which falls only a little short of perfection.

> *A review of "The Shopping Basket," in* The Junior Bookshelf, *Vol. 45, No. 1, February, 1981, p. 11.*

[**The Shopping Basket**] is an event-packed shopping expedition which could provide endless talking points for mother and child. . . . It's only a pity that in the end [Steven] gets told off by Mum for being late and an even greater pity that the bananas he has obediently purchased should, in the last illustration, have turned into a bunch of carrots. Publishers ought never to forget that kids have a penetratingly inspectorial eye for such details.

> *Stephen Corrin, in a review of "The Shopping Basket," in* Punch, *Vol. 280, No. 7329, April 29, 1981, p. 680.*

---

*AVOCADO BABY* (1982)

The third Hargraves baby promises to resemble his weedy brother and sister until his appetite is unexpectedly tempted by avocados: then, burglars and bullies are child's play to him. The simple, deadpan text is matched by the bland, unsurprised features of languid parents and by veracious details that clinch the joke, most of all the tidy blue Baby-Gro in which the remarkable infant performs his feats of strength. (pp. 3906-07)

> *Margery Fisher, in a review of "Avocado Baby," in her* Growing Point, *Vol. 21, No. 1, May, 1982, pp. 3906-07.*

A scant 350 words tell matter-of-factly about the Hargraves baby. . . . With mediocre illustrations such a conceit might be as weak as the Hargraves—but Burningham's cartoons, as expertly ingenuous as the words, bring out all the kinetic humor of the situation while maintaining the tone of the text.

> *A review of "Avocado Baby," in* Kirkus Reviews, *Vol. L, No. 13, July 1, 1982, p. 729.*

Is there a better story-teller among artists today than Burningham? He has originality, invention and a rare gift for words. We see him at the top of his form in *Avocado Baby,* a book which will surely be relished equally by the youngest children and the oldest of grandparents. . . . Mr. Burningham gives his story a dreadful authenticity by laying emphasis on the everyday commonplaces of the Hargraves' home. Lovely!

> *A review of "Avocado Baby," in* The Junior Bookshelf, *Vol. 46, No. 4, August, 1982, p. 130.*

The idea is humorous, but the narrative is as limp as a weakly (sic) sit com and trails off formlessly with a baby exploit that is neither climactic nor particularly interesting. The illustrations, which could possibly add the necessary lift, are instead uninventive and even careless. The entire family, for example, appears to wear the same outfits throughout, though the brother's pants waver between blue and red (changing inexplicably in the midst of the final scene). Burningham fans who want the best should stick with *Mr. Gumpy.*

> *Kristi Thomas Beavin, in a review of "Avocado Baby," in* School Library Journal, *Vol. 29, No. 4, December, 1982, p. 47.*

The exploits of this latter-day Popeye are a source of great delight and hilarity to children and provide inspiration for their own tall stories. Look carefully at the endpapers; they may be part of the story too.

> *Jill Bennett, "Picture Books for Learning to Read: 'Avocado Baby'," in* The Signal Review 1: A Selective Guide to Children's Books, *1982, edited by Nancy Chambers, The Thimble Press, 1983, p. 7.*

---

*PIGS PLUS: LEARNING ADDITION; RIDE OFF: LEARNING SUBTRACTION; READ ONE: NUMBERS AS WORDS; FIVE DOWN: NUMBERS AS SIGNS; COUNT UP: LEARNING SETS; JUST CATS: LEARNING GROUPS (NUMBER PLAY)* (1983)

[*Ride off, Count-Up* and *Read One*] introduce the very young to figures and numeracy in the most enlivening way through the antics of children and animals. The folding of these ingenious miniatures is an activity in itself, rearranging and restating the concepts of adding and subtracting, as bears play in the bath, a comically elongated horse entertains a group of boys and girls, elephants don hats, frogs skip. In chalk and line, Burningham's exuberant style proves an admirable medium for children to exercise their wits while enjoying themselves. How to learn without really trying, in fact.

> *Margery Fisher, in a review of "Ride Off," "Count-Up," "Read One," in her* Growing Point, *Vol. 22, No. 2, July, 1983, p. 4108.*

Burningham's whimsical style distinguishes these six preschool mathematics concept books. . . . Addition is the subject of book one, *Pigs Plus*, which shows in each segment how $1 + 1 = 2$ (pigs and their broken-down car), $2 + 1 = 3$ pigs trying to figure out how to get things going again, on up to 5 pigs who finally get under way. The concept of subtraction is displayed in similar fashion in *Ride Off*, book two. This time, however, viewers see 5 children astride a horse until one falls off: $5 - 1 = 4$. The last square introduces zero, as the remaining child loses her seat. Recognizing numbers both in word and symbol is the stuff of *Read One*, book three. . . . In book four, *Five Down: Numbers As Signs,* the pictures portray numbers as physical objects that get broken, so that children might associate

Or would you like to ride a bull
into a supermarket

*From* Would You Rather . . . , *written and illustrated by John Burningham. J. Cape, 1978, Thomas Y. Crowell Co., Inc., 1978. Copyright © 1978 by John Burningham. All rights reserved. Reprinted by permission of Harper & Row, Publishers, Inc. In Canada by Jonathan Cape Ltd, on behalf of the author.*

the symbol with the act of counting the figures in each picture. Three pigs, for example, fumble with a large 3, which tumbles into the water and breaks into three pieces. Book five, *Count Up: Learning Sets,* shows groups of similar things: 1 monkey on a bike, 2 dogs flying a plane, 3 frogs on lilypads, etc., up to 5. Sixth and last is *Just Cats,* which aims to have preschoolers separate the cat protagonists from the various animal groups they meet along the way to picnic. The concepts are basic, but what makes these books shine is the art that carries them through. The light touch with lines, texture, and color that made the author's **"Mr. Gumpy"** books so fresh applies here. There's humor aplenty and carefully planned composition that make these fun for both preschoolers and those sharing the lessons with them. (pp. 355-56)

> *Denise M. Wilms, in a review of "Count Up: Learning Sets," "Five Down: Numbers As Signs," "Just Cats: Learning Groups," "Pigs Plus: Learning Addition," "Read One: Numbers As Words," "Ride Off: Learning Subtraction," in* Booklist, *Vol. 80, No. 4, October 15, 1983, pp. 355-56.*

Each book is in leporello form, with a flap that folds over each section; Burningham uses the device to full advantage, to extend concepts and/or add humor. This is the best kind of toy book: it's ingenious, sturdy, attractive, and useful, with Burningham's pictures maintaining a high standard of visual art.

> *Zena Sutherland, in a review of "Read One," in* Bulletin of the Center for Children's Books, *Vol. 37, No. 4, December, 1983, p. 63.*

The fold-out format is cleverly used, but at £2.50 a book the series is probably aimed at play-schools rather than parents;

the educational ground it covers is really not that great, despite the charm of the drawings. (pp. 24-5)

> *Andrew Clements, "Brightest Is Best," in* New Statesman, *Vol. 106, No. 2750, December 2, 1983, pp. 24-5.**

[In the **"Number Play"** series] an assortment of Mr Burningham's idiosyncratically fat, fubsy and bewildered fauna tumble under and over the flaps upon a concertina fold-out board. Whether or not they will help a pre-school child to master the numerical acrobatics in which the mind can conjure the numbers one to five I don't know, but the drawings, especially the solemn party-goers in *Count Up* and the manic—are they stuffed monkeys or bears?—in *Read One* (the only one of the series with words) are a treat.

> *Victoria Neumark, "Picture Patterns," in* The Times Educational Supplement, *No. 3527, February 3, 1984, p. 31.**

---

*CLUCK BAA; JANGLE TWANG; SKIP TRIP; SLAM BANG; SNIFF SHOUT; WOBBLE POP (FIRST WORDS)* **(1984; U.S. series as** *Noisy Words)*

Burningham's **'First Words'** series is bound to please. Never mind the fact that they ostensibly aim to increase vocabulary. I doubt whether they will, for most of the mono-syllables will already be present in a small child's mind, especially onomatopoeic expressions like slurp, crash or giggle. The glory of these highly skilled crayon-scenes in a child's life is the brilliant way they capture, through facial expression, judiciously exaggerated gesture and precise location, certain familiar situations (gleefully spying on grown-ups, riding in a car, playing on a swing) which are extended into fantasy. Each book (I am commenting on three out of the six published at this time) has a sequential plan. *Sniff shout* explores domestic events mainly of eating and drinking; in *Slam bang* the small boy goes for an exhilarating and alarming ride in a car with a somewhat casual dog as driver; in *Skip trip* a teddy bear is companion in minor accidents and mischief-making. The humour is sly, shrewd and totally disarming; the books seem to me essential to the well-being of alert infants. (pp. 4303-04)

> *Margery Fisher, in a review of "Sniff Shout," "Slam Bang," and "Skip Trip," in her* Growing Point, *Vol. 23, No. 3, September, 1984, pp. 4303-04.*

Remember John Burningham's answer to the reading scheme: *The baby, The blanket, The dog* and the rest? Here is the set for pre-readers, again beating the experts at their own game. For all that I believe that the earliest books should have more than a caption word on each page, I now have to say, it depends on which word. Burningham's inimitable sketches interact with the sounds that children turn into words (cluck baa), the words that accompany actions (skip trip), the words for loud noises (slam bang), not-quite things (*Wobble pop*—which includes: bump, stumble, wipe, squeeze) and musical words (tinkle, strum). It's another example of how imagination takes over from the 'usefulness' of reading and turns it into the game with rules that children learn as play. Three cheers for each one. . . .

> *Margaret Meek, in a review of "First Words: Cluck Baa, Skip Trip, Slam Bang, Sniff Shout, Wobble Pop, Jangle Twang," in* The School Librarian, *Vol. 32, No. 4, December, 1984, p. 345.*

Burningham presents vocabulary concepts in a humorous and subtle manner in his new series. On each page, a hand printed word serves as a caption for a whimsical felt-tip marker drawing of a chubby blond boy and a baby bear acting out the concept. . . . The series name ["**Noisy Words**"] indicates that Burningham is presenting a vocabulary associated with sounds, but so many of the examples are silent activities that this focus is lost. Nevertheless, the pictures are appealing, and the vocabulary concepts can be understood by the intended audience. . . . The **"Noisy Words"** series is an obvious choice for libraries, especially where other Burningham books are popular.

> *Amanda J. Williams, in a review of "Skip Trip," "Sniff Shout," and "Wobble Pop," in* School Library Journal, *Vol. 31, No. 4, December, 1984, p. 68.*

Burningham's illustrations are the big plus in [*Skip Trip, Sniff Shout,* and *Wobble Pop*]. His lines are light and whimsical, and the parade of scenes has an appealing, slightly disheveled look. . . . Besides being useful vocabulary builders, these books may also be used for object identification or simply as a basis for parent-child interaction. A fresh addition to a genre often burdened by inferior art and execution.

> *Denise M. Wilms, in a review of "Skip Trip," "Sniff Shout," and "Wobble Pop," in* Booklist, *Vol. 81, No. 7, December 1, 1984, p. 521.*

John Burningham's *First Words* is a simpler but no less effective series [than Helen Oxenbury's *First Picture Books* series]. A small child is accompanied by toy bear and various animals

in a variety of real and fantasy situations which illustrate a much more interesting range of words than are usually found in 'first concept' books. 'Wobble', 'jangle', 'slump', 'shout'—this last as the cat walks over a precious painting—all sound as good as they look in accurate representations of the meanings of the words. In addition the sequence of pictures builds into a story. (p. 15)

> *Mary Watkins, Lyn Baran, and Lesley Crowthers, "The Proof of the Pudding . . . ," in* Books for Keeps, *No. 30, January, 1985, pp. 15-16.\**

---

### GRANPA (1984)

Only John Burningham could do so much so economically. In 32 pages he depicts a multilayered relationship between an old man and his grandchild, suggests a whole life story for Granpa and shows a small girl reacting to death and bereavement. The whole is simultaneously very restrained and very rich, exceedingly complex and utterly simple. Except for three double spreads which have a special impact because of their difference, Burningham uses the conventions developed in *Mr Gumpy* and the **'Shirley'** books. On the left hand page in two different type faces are words spoken by Granpa and the child; below them in monochrome are line drawings which by showing what the characters are thinking, remembering or imagining provide a commentary on the text and on the full colour right hand page.

John Burningham catches exactly the quality of the relationship, the sense of two separate worlds and a shared one with its own conventions and awarenesses. The feelings of bewilderment and awe that the fact of death arouses in children is caught exactly in a wordless double spread in which a small scrunched up child gazes thoughtfully across the gutter (where the pages are sewn) to the picture on the right hand page of Granpa's empty chair and table. In the next and last page—also without words—we see her running across the landscape pushing baby (brother? sister?) in a pram. Life as always goes on.

I could go on and on about this book. Get it, savour it and share it with individuals or very small groups. It will need tact and sensitivity but I'd dare bet there will be rich rewards.

> *Pat Triggs, in a review of "Granpa," in* Books for Keeps, *No. 29, November, 1984, p. 4.*

In the end [of the book] Granpa fades away. Gently, without mawkishness, the point is made. John Burningham has succeeded in dealing with what, since Victorian times, has been the impossible in picture-book terms: real life death.

> *William Feaver, "Bumps in the Night," in* The Observer, *November 25, 1984, p. 27.\**

While several authors have tried to introduce school-age children to death and the loss of grandparents, I think John Burningham's *Granpa* . . . is the first to take it down to the simplest, picture-book level. It treats the subject gently, poetically—a series of typical Burningham illustrations, spare, immensely evocative, intercut with snatches of dialogue across the generation gap. . . . 'When I was a boy we used to roll our wooden hoops down the street after school'—'*Were you once a baby as well, Granpa?*'. Granpa, though, begins to slow up, becomes chair bound—'Granpa can't come out to play today'—and eventually disappears, leaving the child staring at an empty armchair. Visually it will be marvellously potent for young children, while adults (at whom surely the text is aimed) may find it peculiarly moving.

Andrew Clements, "A Serious Business," in New Statesman, Vol. 108, No. 2803, December 7, 1984, p. 30.*

Like the matchless adventures of Shirley by the sea, **Granpa** is a dialogue in which the speakers only half listen to one another. The child's question 'Do worms go to Heaven' gets a tangential answer suitable for the greenhouse where the old man is potting seedlings—'There would not be room for all the little seeds to grow'. A snatch of rhyme may provoke a rambling addition from the child; double logic obtains when the request 'When we get to the beach can we stay there for ever?' is satisfied with 'Yes, but we must go back for our tea at four o'clock'. The generation gap is neatly summarised in the last two pictures, showing first an empty armchair, then a young woman pushing a pram. The crayon and line pictures are, as always with Burningham, both comic and provocative, sharply expressive of mood and outlook, and the visual annotations in sepia line below the text alternating with full-page colour illustations opposite contribute their own clear narrative element.

Margery Fisher, in a review of "Granpa," in her Growing Point, Vol. 23, No. 5, January, 1985, p. 4375.

[**Granpa** and James Stevenson's *What's Under My Bed?* are two] joyous 'Grandfather' picture-books, from Britain and the States respectively, both revealing under the fun much understanding of the relationship that can exist between the very old and the very young. . . .

John Burningham is master of the happy cross-purposes that can build up in adult/child relationships. In **Granpa** there is, at a superficial glance, no narrative and little relevance in the apparently disconnected scraps of dialogue between child and grandparent. A closer look reveals the fine thread of story linking one opening with the next and the tender, moving association that underlies the funny drawing and the random scraps of text. Burningham has not been more amusing, more wise. I believe however that this is a book about children for adults, and that grown-ups will laugh longest and feel the largest lump in the throat at its beautifully expressed revelations.

M. Crouch, in a review of "Granpa," in The Junior Bookshelf, Vol. 49, No. 1, February, 1985, p. 12.

The jacket drawing of a little girl clinging to her grandfather's shoulders conveys a joyous, adventuresome sharing—but leaves in doubt just what sort of vehicle (a horse-drawn cart, perhaps) they're breezing along in. And the contents—a different shared experience at each opening—are more ambiguous still: deliberately oblique, and inferential. Mostly they pit an adult's matter-of-factness against a child's imaginings. The two are in a greenhouse, where we are supposed to gather from the pictures that Granpa is transplanting seedlings from flats into pots. In Roman type (implicitly, Granpa): "There will not be room for all the little seeds to grow." In italics (implicitly, the little girl): "Do worms go to heaven?" To an adult ear, that may sound a cute non sequitur; most children are apt to take it as simple woolly-headedness. Another scene, one of the simpler to explain, has the pair looking out of the house in a rainstorm: "Noah knew the ark was not far from land when he saw the dove carrying the olive branch," says Granpa; "Could we float away in this house, Granpa?" says the little girl. Then, overleaf, he's saying—with no connection whatever: "That was not a nice thing to say to Granpa." And at the last we have a mini-sequence, totally unforeshadowed, in which Granpa sits in his chair, sick; takes the little girl on his lap; and vanishes, presumed dead (!), as we see her silently gazing at his empty chair. There are ways to make scattered moments, and tenuous feelings, add up—but only in the pictures does the relationship register here.

A review of "Granpa," in Kirkus Reviews, Juvenile Issue, Vol. LIII, Nos. 1-5, March 1, 1985, p. J-3.

# James Howe

## 1946-

American author of fiction, nonfiction, and picture books.

Howe is recognized as a versatile writer whose works show respect for the interests and emotions of his elementary-school audience. The creator of books ranging from comical mysteries to serious nonfiction, he is perhaps best known for his first work, *Bunnicula: A Rabbit-Tale of Mystery,* which he developed into a series with *Howliday Inn* and *The Celery Stalks at Midnight.* These stories present the bumbling attempts of a personable dog and cat team to solve vampire and werewolf mysteries while satirizing the genre with stylish prose, sprightly dialogue, frequent puns, and slapstick comedy. Believing that humor is the greatest gift he can give his readers, Howe invests his fantasies with wit and whimsy. He has also written *The Hospital Book,* an informational work which not only explains medical procedures but also addresses the feelings children experience during a hospital stay, and *A Night without Stars,* a realistic story about friendship in a hospital setting which examines children's fears about surgery.

Interested in writing since childhood, Howe wrote a play at the age of seven and also published a newspaper for the Vampire Legion, an organization he founded when he was nine. A theater major in college, Howe worked as an actor, model, and director as well as a literary agent and social worker. A graduate seminar in playwriting inspired him to become serious about his talent with words. *Bunnicula* was prompted when Howe's wife, Deborah, a writer and actress, suggested that he write a story about a vampire rabbit he had created years earlier. Deborah died of cancer in 1978, shortly after collaborating on *Bunnicula* and *Teddy Bear's Scrapbook.* Now a full-time writer, Howe has also served on the advisory boards of New York's Hospice of St. Vincent's Hospital and other organizations.

Most critics praise Howe's fiction for its strong characterization and sophisticated yet readable style. They note the success of his humor, especially in the *Bunnicula* series, and remark that his use of puns captures the attention of young readers while introducing them to language play. Reviewers consider *The Hospital Book* among the best nonfiction on its subject, and acknowledge Howe as an author whose books fulfill several of children's needs in an often delightful manner.

*Bunnicula* has been the recipient of many child-selected awards. *The Hospital Book* was named a *Boston Globe-Horn Book* Honor Book in nonfiction in 1981 and was nominated for an American Book Award in 1982.

(See also *Something about the Author,* Vol. 29 and *Contemporary Authors,* Vol. 105.)

---

### AUTHOR'S COMMENTARY

[When I wrote *Bunnicula*] with my late wife, Deborah, it was a time of innocence. Writing for our own pleasure, we gave little thought to who might one day read our work. I didn't know much about children's books then, other than those I'd read myself as a child. I certainly knew nothing of contem-

*Photograph by Betsy Imershein*

porary children's book writers; little about children's book publishing.

Children themselves? . . . [We] knew only a handful of children, and rather distantly at that. (p. 156)

As I went on to write other books, however, as my books were reviewed and letters from readers began to arrive, as I spent my days in solitary confinement hunched over a typewriter, as I left that confinement to speak to children and librarians and teachers—as I evolved, in other words, from someone who writes into a *writer*—I began to wonder, "*Who* is my reader?"

In my innocent days, I believed my readers to be innocent, too. But that was before I read David Elkind's *The Hurried Child* (Addison) and Marie Winn's *Children Without Childhood* (Pantheon), before I saw the statistics on teenage pregnancies, on preteen drug and alcohol use, on children committing suicide. It was before I heard the cries that fewer and fewer children were reading, that they were spending their allowances and a good part of their lives on video games and hanging out at the mall waiting in some suspended state for real life to begin—or to end with a nuclear blast.

I asked myself, "Are these junior yuppies decked out in their designer jeans and designer despair really the children out there in the rest of the country? Are these my readers? Is childhood dead?'' Despite the seeming evidence, I wasn't prepared to believe it. Besides, I had evidence of my own. There were the letters I received. The writers *sounded* like children. And there were the grade-school students to whom I spoke. True, they didn't look exactly like the children with whom I grew up. Still—

I was visiting an elementary school in a suburb of Rochester, New York, and the last group of the day was a class of sixth-graders. Sixth-graders, as you may well know, spend an inordinate amount of time being cool. And one thing that is definitely uncool is going to hear a guest author speak.

This particular group had evolved the ''elbow nudge and ceiling stare'' into an art form. One boy caught my eye the moment he came into the room, and I stayed focused on him through my entire talk. He looked like a younger version of Matt Dillon playing an S. E. Hinton character—in *Rumble Fish,* not *Tex.* He hunched his shoulders; he glared through half-open eyelids; he wore a leather jacket. Periodically, he checked out everyone around him to be sure they were checking *him* out. He was a study in ''cool.'' And a challenge. Not once did he give me a sign that I had any right, in his eyes, to exist.

When the session was over, however, young Matt Dillon stayed behind. His hard stare turned shy as he and I were the only ones left in the room. When he was sure we were alone, he brought forth from under his arm a copy of a book I had written. It was **Teddy Bear's Scrapbook** . . . , a book for younger children and, without a doubt, the uncoolest book I had written. ''Do you know what my favorite part of this book is?'' he said to me. ''Tell me,'' I said, ''I'd like to know.'' From somewhere inside the leather jacket and the slicked-back hair, a child came to life. He retold in animated detail one of the silly episodes from the book—and when he was done, he grew quiet again and shy. (pp. 156-57)

I learned from this incident that my reader is not *the hurried child,* but *the hidden child.* (p. 157)

Something I've come across on many school visits is children's fascination with violence and death. When I talk to children about writing, I usually start out by asking for an idea for a story and then develop the story with them. The content of these stories by third- to sixth-graders—regardless of what school or state I'm in—is remarkably similar. Nine times out of ten, within minutes, something violent or sensational will occur.

Recently, while I was in Dayton, Ohio, I asked for an idea for a story, and one of the children said, ''a diseased dog.'' I gritted my teeth and said, ''What disease does the dog have?'' Hands shot up, and from all around me, I heard murmurs of ''cancer'' and ''heart disease.'' I knew I did not want to develop a story along these lines. So I said, ''a *silly* disease.'' The children shifted gears immediately. The disease suggested next was ''chicken pops,'' a condition brought on by drinking too much pop while eating chicken.

That event brought to mind a story told to me by a librarian from Missouri. She was working with a girl on a writing project. The girl started to write a story about a bird, a ''sweet, gentle'' bird. Suddenly, for no apparent reason, the bird became witness to a murder and no longer had anything to do with the story. The librarian pointed out this problem to the child and suggested that she go back to the character of the bird and develop a story from there. When the girl returned with her story completed, the murder was no longer a part of

it. In its place was the tale of a bird forced to make a moral decision about coming to the aid of a cat—its mortal enemy.

Were the children in Dayton under the impression, gathered from television and books they may have read, that for a story to be successful a sensational element, such as a life-threatening illness, had to be a part of it? Was the girl in Missouri ready to abandon her sweet, gentle bird because she was afraid her story wouldn't ''sell''? Did she want to appear more knowing, more sophisticated than she really was? The librarian helped guide the girl back to her truest self, helped her trust her own voice as a writer. In helping her shut out the siren call to be cool and tough and wise, she allowed the hidden child to come out from hiding.

In my responsibilities as a writer for children, I think of myself as both that librarian and that child. Like the librarian, I have the opportunity—and, I believe, the responsibility—to offer children more than a mirror of what is but a window to what might be. I must not simply reflect their jargon, their fads, their current likes and dislikes, but find my way through their maze of disguises to the child, and the person, within. Like the girl, I must recognize my own voice amidst all the voices calling, and when I have heard it and have listened to its story, then I am ready to open my mouth and let the hidden child in me sing out.

In a way, *the hidden child* is a phrase I'm using to describe the inner person. Ultimately, it is the writer's greatest responsibility to write from his or her own inner person, the truest self, to the inner person of the reader. The inner person, the truest self, the child within—these do not change from generation to generation, nor are they affected by fads and whims and marketing trends. Within whatever genre the writer may write, there is a place for truth. That truth allows a popular book to become a book of quality and lasting worth.

When I talk of writing for the hidden child, I don't mean to imply that one should ignore social realities or the impact of television or movies and return to a so-called simpler time. Children are aware of the realities of the world, just as you and I are. But they don't experience them as you or I do. And that is where our responsibilities as adults, and my responsibilities as a writer, come into play.

No, life's less pleasant realities should not be kept out of children's books. But they should be realities that exist within the child's realm, that matter to the child, that are seen through the child's eyes, and over which the child may be able, even vicariously, to exert some influence or control. It is the writer's privilege and responsibility to give children a world they can enter, recognize, at times be frightened of, but which ultimately, they can master and control. We may help them in their struggle to answer questions; we may even raise new questions for them. But we must not leave them feeling stranded in an unfamiliar world where the questions, let alone the answers, are beyond their grasp.

In my books there is an innocence about the children. It is not an innocence of awareness, however, it is not even always an innocence of experience; it is an innocence of biological age. In **What Eric Knew** . . . , a mystery I've recently completed featuring a thirteen-year-old sleuth named Sebastian Barth, part of the plot has to do with drugs, an unfortunate reality in the lives of many children. But the book does not tell the story of a thirteen-year-old with track marks on his arm contemplating suicide. It tells the story of children who do not want drugs to be a part of their lives—and of the older brother of one, a friend of Sebastian's named Ricky, who is trafficking in cocaine.

"'I used to look up to you,'" Ricky says to his brother at one point. "'I used to think you were the greatest thing going. And then . . . you changed. When you didn't get into all those fancy colleges and Dad was getting on your case, you started staying out a lot. Then, last year, I could tell you were messing around with drugs. You just weren't the same. And things weren't the same with us. You weren't my big brother anymore. You were just another bummed-out druggie.'"

The language may be street-wise, but this is a child speaking. He is speaking his anger at a world that messes up older brothers, that pressures them, and him, and the reader to be cool, to go along. He is seeing the world through a child's eyes, and in this case he doesn't like what he sees. In my writing I try to let children know that it's all right not to like what they see. It's all right to resist the pressure to grow up too fast, to give in to peers, to be cool. It's all right to be yourself—and to be true to that self.

Children lack power and control in their lives. Through reading they gain some measure of control. They are able to see something through to a neat resolution; and perhaps through the children in the story, gain a sense of themselves as human beings who are valid and powerful.

As a writer for children, I have many responsibilities—the responsibility to give the reader well-crafted language that is appropriate for the story at hand, to use language that respects the reader's intelligence while stretching his or her appreciation of what language can do, to articulate what the child cannot, to give the child positive values in a world where values have been demeaned, to make demands on the reader's mind and spirit, to entertain, and to make the reader laugh. Humor is the most precious gift I can give to my reader, a reminder that the world is not such a terribly serious place. There is more than video games and drugs and nuclear threats; there is laughter—and there is hope.

In the end, however, my primary responsibility as a writer is to the hidden child in the reader and in myself, and to the belief that—though we are years apart—when I open my mouth to speak, the child will understand. Because in that hidden part of ourselves, we are one. (pp. 158-61)

> *James Howe, "Writing for the Hidden Child," in* The Horn Book Magazine, *Vol. LXI, No. 2, March-April, 1985, pp. 156-61.*

---

### BUNNICULA: A RABBIT-TALE OF MYSTERY (with Deborah Howe, 1979)

The Howes' stylish, exuberant make-believe is the product of unreined imagination and a glinting sense of humor. . . . Harold is a dog who moonlights as an author. His human family, the Monroes, bring home a tiny abandoned rabbit, whereupon Chester, Harold's cat buddy, postulates an alarming theory. Chester claims it's no accident that the rabbit is named Bunnicula after "Dracula," the movie showing in the theater where the Monroes found him. Chester's attempts to act out the vampire story, to warn the family, are hysterically funny but frustrating to the cat. They think Chester needs a psychiatrist. Finally, Chester resorts to starving Bunnicula to death but Harold has a better idea, leading to a gratifying finale.

> *A review of "Bunnicula: A Rabbit-Tale of Mystery," in* Publishers Weekly, *Vol. 215, No. 12, March 19, 1979, p. 94.*

Harold X. (names are changed to protect the innocent) narrates this with all the dignity appropriate to one of his nature and background. . . . Chester's frantic efforts to protect the family through the use of garlic, etc., all backfire into a series of goofy episodes that will offer young readers the entertainment of mystery and spoof. A sure read-aloud. . . .

> *Betsy Hearne, in a review of "Bunnicula: A Rabbit-Tale of Mystery," in* Booklist, *Vol. 75, No. 18, May 15, 1979, p. 1439.*

A talking-dog's story of a vampire rabbit. Uhuh, and this is not one of those madcap affairs that has no natural bounds. . . . Chester's efforts to starve poor Bunnicula—after his other attempts to alert the Monroes fail—give these goings-on some semblance of a plot. But it's a pretty feeble bit of foolishness (except, briefly, for the zucchini bit) which winds up with Bunnicula on a liquid diet that leaves no tell-tale signs. Was he or wasn't he? Your guess is as good as ours.

> *A review of "Bunnicula: A Rabbit-Tale of Mystery," in* Kirkus Reviews, *Vol. XLVII, No. 13, July 1, 1979, p. 741.*

The vampire issue is never clarified, which may disappoint some readers, but the plot is less important in the story than the style: blithe, sophisticated, and distinguished for the wit and humor of the dialogue. If readers like shaggy dog stories at all, they'd have to search hard for a funnier one.

> *Zena Sutherland, in a review of "Bunnicula: A Rabbit-Tale of Mystery," in* Bulletin of the Center for Children's Books, *Vol. 32, No. 11, July-August, 1979, p. 192.*

Fortunately for posterity (8 to 12 division), Chester takes good-natured Harold, the resident dog, into his confidence, and that droopy-eared beast decides to record the strange doings in the Monroe home. Harold, happily, has a fine eye for the comic details of life in a household with pets and children. . . . The intended audience for this mystery-comedy is sure to delight in Chester's vain attempt to finish off the rabbit ravager. And if the tale is somewhat less inspired than the author's original notion of a bunny vampire, few readers are likely to notice or care.

> *Selma G. Lanes, in a review of "Bunnicula: A Rabbit-Tale of Mystery," in* The New York Times Book Review, *September 30, 1979, p. 36.*

A clue to the archness of this book is that the narrator is a dog and his friend the cat is a midnight reader of horror tales. Their owners are Mom and Dad and two kids, who exchange rapid sitcom dialogue so natural you might be sitting en famille in front of your television set. Even the dog's comments might be *your* dog talking. . . . "Bunnicula" is pretty slick bunkula, but quite funny at that.

> *Faith McNulty, in a review of "Bunnicula: A Rabbit-Tale of Mystery," in* The New Yorker, *Vol. LV, No. 42, December 3, 1979, p. 208.*

---

**TEDDY BEAR'S SCRAPBOOK**  (with Deborah Howe, 1980)

With its incomparable humor and the extra ingredient of tenderness, the Howes' second novel is one up on their amazing **"Bunnicula"**.... [The story tells] the exploits of Teddy, who goes through his scrapbook with the little girl who had found him years before in an old trunk and who loves him dearly.

> *A review of "Teddy Bear's Scrapbook," in* Publishers Weekly, *Vol. 217, No. 21, May 30, 1980, p. 85.*

[Teddy Bear's pictures] show him to have been a cowboy, circus performer, news reporter, and Hollywood actor, among other things. Such a checkered career might be inherently appealing, but it's Teddy's inimitable style that makes the stories live. He's a loquacious sort, and not above some charming false modesty in describing his varied successes. Such human dimensions ensure his originality as a charcter; and the wrap-up, in which Teddy and his owner declare their affection for each other, adds a crowning measure of warmth.

> *Denise M. Wilms, in a review of "Teddy Bear's Scrapbook," in* Booklist, *Vol. 76, No. 19, June 1, 1980, p. 1424.*

Whimsey upon whimsey—with lots of inaccessible parody and only one frail thread of emotional continuity.... [In one story, Melinda the movie star] involves Teddy in a rivalry with Lassie that's one of the few down-home jokes here. But better still is the [little girl] narrator's jealousy of each of Teddy's golden-haired admirers—until he assures her [at the book's close] that *her* love for him, in his old and shabby state, is "an even greater love." . . . Trouble is, few youngsters of the indicated age will get that far.

> *A review of "Teddy Bear's Scrapbook," in* Kirkus Reviews, *Vol. XLVIII, No. 14, July 15, 1980, p. 911.*

Just right for the primary grades readers, and the episodic structure of this blithe story makes it just right for reading aloud to younger children.... The light tone, the humor, the yeastiness and wit of the writing style and the adventures themselves . . . have vitality, pace, and some unexpected twists—for example, the abominable snowman proves to be an oversize teddy bear named Clive Neville-Phillips who is a secret contributor to a major literary magazine.

> *Zena Sutherland, in a review of "Teddy Bear's Scrapbook," in* Bulletin of the Center for Children's Books, *Vol. 34, No. 1, September, 1980, p. 13.*

Each captioned snapshot prompts Teddy into a trite and dull story connected with the photo, from **"Teddy on the Range"** (bronco busting in Jackson Hole) to **"Teddy at the Circus"** (rescuing a highwire damsel in distress) to **"Teddy in Hollywood"** (dancing in his big number, "We're in the Honey"). These and other exploits emerge as told to the little girl . . . whose irritating comments and remonstrances punctuate Teddy's alternately boastful and sentimental chatter.... [One] wishes that this particular album had never been dug out of the drawer. Teddy doesn't come across with any endearing panache, and while his language takes on the accents and idioms of his role—"Listen, sweetheart," the tough Chicago reporter begins—no wit informs his words. They become self-conscious and artificial, throwing in gratuitous references that most readers young enough to care about a Teddy Bear story won't appreciate ("this Freud character—he's a big deal in psychology, see—"). Stick with Paddington.

> *Nancy Palmer, in a review of "Teddy Bear's Scrapbook," in* School Library Journal, *Vol. 27, No. 1, September, 1980, p. 60.*

This book should satisfy the need for something just above the Easy Reader level.... The authors did not seem to be able to decide on whether Teddy should be a real teddy bear or an anthropomorphized one, and so I found it hard to suspend disbelief. I also thought the episodes had facile endings. The overall idea of the book, however, and the satisfying finale, might very well give pleasure to those for whom the book is intended.

> *Maureen O'Connor, in a review of "Teddy Bear's Scrapbook," in* Children's Book Review Service, *Vol. 9, No. 2, October, 1980, p. 15.*

---

**THE HOSPITAL BOOK**  (1981)

**The Hospital Book** views hospital procedures from the perspective of a child patient. The photographs [by Mal Warshaw] all show young children, but the vocabulary, sentence construction and descriptions of technical procedures are fairly sophisticated. The text chronicles the major procedures—administrative, diagnostic, surgical and therapeutic—a young patient would be apt to encounter. However, the author is not concerned exclusively with objective descriptions but also addresses children's fears about pain, discomfort and danger and their own reactions to being hospitalized. Some of the hospital staff, Howe writes honestly, are "rushed and tired . . . sometimes they're not such nice people to begin with and sometimes they don't do things the way you would do them yourself." The information-packed book is too much for younger children to handle by themselves. It may be best used to provide basic information to stimulate further conversation between an adult reader and a child listener.... This is the finest book of its kind available.

> *Karen Harris, in a review of "The Hospital Book," in* School Library Journal, *Vol. 27, No. 9, May, 1981, p. 56.*

[The text gives] an excellent introduction to hospital procedures; this is simply enough written to be read, also, to younger children. Howe is candid and comprehensive in his descriptions of procedures, equipment, and personnel and equally candid about pain, differentiating between treatment that is painless (X-ray), uncomfortable but not painful (CAT scan) or painful if brief (drawing blood from a vein). The whole book is permeated by a sense that children are rational people, that telling them exactly what hurts or what's going to happen will evoke their cooperation and tolerance—and when the author addresses the question of stress and reaction, he never implies that children are any more or any less frightened or angry than adults. The text is in second person, and always clear.

> *Zena Sutherland, in a review of "The Hospital Book," in* Bulletin of the Center for Children's Books, *Vol. 34, No. 10, June, 1981, p. 195.*

This is a well-documented photo essay.... Details are presented in a factual but nonthreatening way. The text is reassuring as it shows many aspects of hospital life—treatment room, nurses' station, bedpans, X-ray machines, and operation procedures. People who work there—teachers, lab technicians, dieticians, nurses, and doctors—are also introduced and their jobs are described. An excellent book. Highly recommended.

*Linda Worden, in a review of "The Hospital Book,"
in* Children's Book Review Service, *Vol. 9, No. 11,
June, 1981, p. 94.*

The author does not try to hide the many unpleasantries of the hospital experience. . . . In the chapter, **"How Will I Feel?"**, the author explains that everyone experiences physical and emotional pain in the hospital. He gives the reader many suggestions for dealing with feelings such as anger and fear. Children will appreciate his honesty and attention to detail.

The text is up-to-date, accurate, and quite complete. . . . This is a very well-balanced book. (pp. 22-3)

*Martha T. Kane, in a review of "The Hospital Book,"
in* Appraisal: Science Books for Young People,
*Vol. 14, No. 3, Fall, 1981, pp. 22-3.*

Chapter titles, such as **"What Is Going to Happen to Me?"** **"Who Is That Person?" "What Is That Thing?"** provide clues to content; the inclusion of actual hospital situations in the photographs complements the realistic and pragmatic, but not unsympathetic, approach. The children depicted range in age from preschoolers to young adolescents, thus making the book an excellent choice for a general collection serving readers who have outgrown *Curious George Goes to the Hospital* (Houghton) or *Elizabeth Gets Well* (Crowell). In addition to accuracy of information, the book also provides up-to-date role models: Both men and women are shown as doctors, and fathers share responsibility with mothers for visiting and perhaps helping with patient care. An invaluable resource.

*Mary M. Burns, in a review of "The Hospital Book,"
in* The Horn Book Magazine, *Vol. LVII, No. 5, October, 1981, p. 553.*

This presentation is well done, and it is general enough to apply to all hospital experiences yet specific enough to apply to an individual situation. . . . [This book presents] the anticipated hospital experience in very concrete terms, an approach developmentally necessary for the five- to eleven-year-old-child. The book . . . can be a valuable asset for parents who wish to minimize the potential emotional trauma associated with a child's planned hospital admission. The book can also be utilized by professional staff who teach hospital preparation classes or by staff who need to work with the fears of a child who has been admitted on an unscheduled basis.

*Ruth G. Mullins, in a review of "The Hospital Book,"
in* Science Books & Films, *Vol. 17, No. 3, January-February, 1982, p. 159.*

---

### *HOWLIDAY INN* (1982)

Howe explains that Harold, the dog author of **"Bunnicula,"** has delivered a second manuscript, this sparkling comedy mystery. Harold and Chester, the lofty cat, find themselves in the Chateau Bow-Wow while their family, the Monroes, are on vacation. . . . Nerve-breaking ululations prompt Chester to name the boarding house "Howliday Inn"; he's sure that it harbors werewolves. Harold and Chester are beside themselves when the French poodle Louise disappears; they suspect she's a murder victim like the other cats and dogs who have vanished. . . . The story, with its wonderfully witty dialogue and irresistible characters, is a treat for all ages.

*A review of "Howliday Inn," in* Publishers Weekly,
*Vol. 221, No. 12, March 19, 1982, p. 71.*

The style is chatty, and the animal talk low-key. The plot reads smoothly but could move a bit quicker. The story is strictly for animal enthusiasts who like their pets enough to treat them as humans.

*Jeanette Cohn, in a review of "Howliday Inn," in*
Children's Book Review Service, *Vol. 10, No. 12,
Spring, 1982, p. 117.*

This isn't quite as cohesive or convincing as its predecessor, *Bunnicula* . . . , but the mock-Gothic setup and slapstick animal characters will keep most young readers from realizing that nothing happens for pages at a time. . . . The text is heavy on howling and light on action. However, mystery fans who have enjoyed fare such as the Caulfields' *Incredible Detectives* will relish sorting out Howe's clues, which point to several possible culprits along the way.

*Betsy Hearne, in a review of "Howliday Inn," in*
Booklist, *Vol. 78, No. 18, May 15, 1982, p. 1257.*

*Howliday Inn* is a satire of the whodunit genre. Howe's wry, tongue-in-cheek prose neatly fits cohorts Harold (dog) and Chester (cat) as the two play out their roles as the odd couple of the pet world. . . . Of course, smug Chester coolly solves the "crimes" while befuddled Harold gropes for some understanding, which neither he nor readers gain until it's all neatly and painlessly explained in the end. [Lynn] Munsinger's line drawings . . . effectively [bring] the comedic and appropriately symbolic characters to life. The story may be a bit long for some, but the repartee between the adroit, sophisti-cat and the dog is hilarious. Another hit from the author of *Bunnicula*. . . .

*Jerry Spiegler, in a review of "Howliday Inn," in*
School Library Journal, *Vol. 28, No. 10, August, 1982,
p. 117.*

This is funny, it's occasionally whimsical, and it's written in an appealingly light-hearted style, but it hasn't the cohesion of [*Bunnicula*], and the humor, because it is used almost as filler rather than being incorporated into the forward movement of the story, becomes repetitive.

*Zena Sutherland, in a review of "Howliday Inn," in*
Bulletin of the Center for Children's Books, *Vol. 36,
No. 1, September, 1982, p. 12.*

You'll howl too at the goings on at the kennel and at its denizens not seen in any Disney movie—a jogging bulldog, a jealous pair of French poodles, a mutt, an alley cat, and a pair of dachshunds. . . . Even funnier and more credible than the successful *Bunnicula*. (p. 363)

*Ruth M. Stein, in a review of "Howliday Inn," in*
Language Arts, *Vol. 60, No. 3, March, 1983,
pp. 362-63.*

---

### *A NIGHT WITHOUT STARS* (1983)

From the author of the superior non-fiction *Hospital Book* . . . , a hospital story characterized by the same observant intelligence. The plot is commonplace: Maria goes in for open-heart surgery; is troubled by misinformation supplied by her ignorant friends and by fears brushed off by her loving parents, but finally has the whole procedure explained by a nice new nurse; and, during her stay, becomes friends with [Donald], a sullen, withdrawn boy her age, badly disfigured by a fire, who writes poetry and is called "monster man" by the other children. But

Howe gives these events a fresh, clear life, and he projects all the characters—doctors, nurses, neighbors, friends—with a sharp eye for personal quirks and an amused ear for ethnic speech patterns. . . . [The] story is worth pushing beyond the usual medical-story audience.

> *A review of "A Night without Stars," in Kirkus Reviews, Vol. LI, No. 4, February 15, 1983, p. 184.*

[Howe] brings to the story his knowledge of the workings of a large medical facility and also his understanding of the trauma faced by a hospitalized child. While the book suffers from some superficial characterizations, Maria and Donald stand out as individuals.

> *Kate M. Flanagan, in a review of "A Night without Stars," in* The Horn Book Magazine, *Vol. LIX, No. 2, April, 1983, p. 166.*

Warm, supportive family relationships are portrayed, though the use of footnotes to translate spoken Italian is distracting. Dialogue is stiff and unnatural on occasion, especially between minor characters. But Donald's suffering is real, and his friendship with Maria is touching. The audience shouldn't be limited to children who might be facing surgery.

> *Symme J. Benoff, in a review of "A Night without Stars," in* School Library Journal, *Vol. 29, No. 8, April, 1983, p. 124.*

While [Maria's] story becomes a vehicle for exploring such issues as misinformation from friends, incomprehensible technical information from preoccupied doctors, fear, and the burden of not being able to talk about secret worries, there is also good character development and a strong story line as well. . . . Though the messages are clear and there is some sentimentality in the portrayals, there is also strong characterization and the satisfaction of a happy, credible finish.

> *Denise M. Wilms, in a review of "A Night without Stars," in* Booklist, *Vol. 79, No. 15, April 1, 1983, p. 1035.*

In this serious book, so different from Howe's delicious comedies (**Bunnicula** . . . and **Howliday Inn**), the author weaves incidents of sunny humor and touching portraits of family relationships into an implicit argument for openness in dealing with people needing treatment. The gripping story makes even stronger points than Howe's award winner, **The Hospital Book**.

> *A review of "A Night without Stars," in* Publishers Weekly, *Vol. 223, No. 17, April 29, 1983, p. 51.*

---

## THE CELERY STALKS AT MIDNIGHT (1983)

Howe introduces the third opus by Harold the dog. . . . [The] swift, mad tale . . . begins with the fearful discovery by Chester the Cat: Bunnicula, the vampire rabbit, has slipped from his cage in the Monroe household. Chester dragoons Harold and the puppy Howie—the Monroe boys' new adoptee—into finding the evil bunny before he can do harm. The three wreak havoc in a garbage truck where they upset cans looking for vegetables drained white, and later at a fairgrounds. . . . The laughs growing out of each contretemps scarcely give one time to catch a breath.

> *A review of "The Celery Stalks at Midnight," in* Publishers Weekly, *Vol. 224, No. 11, September 9, 1983, p. 64.*

Chester's again worried that Bunnicula is draining the life and color out of vegetables and is ready to move on to sucking the life-blood out of living creatures, and it's on this premise that all the action takes place. . . . The premise is engagingly silly, and the conversations among the dogs and Chester are amusing, but the idea seems stretched, and, unlike the first book but like the second, the repetitive quality of the episodes weakens the story despite the enjoyable humor of the dialogue. (pp. 30-1)

> *Zena Sutherland, in a review of "The Celery Stalks at Midnight," in* Bulletin of the Center for Children's Books, *Vol. 37, No. 2, October, 1983, pp. 30-1.*

[The rambunctious animal set of **Bunnicula** and **Howliday Inn**] are back with another comic escapade sure to garner an even wider audience. . . . Howe's madcap pace keeps the pages turning, and his tongue-in-cheek humor is child-targeted. (p. 296)

> *Barbara Elleman, in a review of "The Celery Stalks at Midnight," in* Booklist, *Vol. 80, No. 3, October 1, 1983, pp. 295-96.*

[The sequel to **Bunnicula** and **Howliday Inn**] is another startling tongue-in-cheek exposé. Composed in a light-hearted, lively style, the narrative moves briskly from one outrageous pun to another—a technique guaranteed to win the hearts of humorists. . . . Kaleidoscopic action, broad comedy, and appealing format suggest the book as an answer to the need for well-crafted escapist reading. (p. 710)

> *Mary M. Burns, in a review of "The Celery Stalks at Midnight," in* The Horn Book Magazine, *Vol. LIX, No. 6, December, 1983, pp. 709-10.*

The dedication, "To my father, who raised me on corn, ham, and punster cheese," foretells the language plays and slapstick comedy. The fast-paced, very readable plot will appeal to precocious young readers and to intermediate level readers looking for high interest/low reading level stories. Students can find homonyms that create puns and humorous word substitutions in familiar idioms, and try their hand at creating others. The popular vampire theme and suspenseful plot invite dramatization. Writing possibilities include books "by" children's pets. Since Bunnicula never utters a sound, students might write dialogue from this rabbit's point of view. (pp. 539-40)

> *Frances Graham, in a review of "The Celery Stalks at Midnight," in* Language Arts, *Vol. 61, No. 5, September, 1984, pp. 539-40.*

---

## THE DAY THE TEACHER WENT BANANAS (1984)

Versatile Howe's latest invention is a real rib-tickler. . . . [A first-grader] confides gleefully the results of crossed wires that give them a "new teacher," a gorilla, and ship the real teacher to the zoo. The students' lessons in the new math include taking off their shoes and socks and counting on their toes. The drills in writing are even more fun. Although teacher says nothing, just grunts, he is inspiring and very amiable. When the embarrassed principal arrives with the bona fide pedagogue and the gorilla leaves for the zoo, it's a sad parting. But the author figures out a way to end the daffy tale with a neat, happy twist.

> *A review of "The Day the Teacher Went Bananas," in* Publishers Weekly, *Vol. 226, No. 5, August 3, 1984, p. 67.*

**"The Day the Teacher Went Bananas"** will have children howling with delight and asking for it to be read again and again. . . .

Children will ignite with cheers over this "substitute" teacher, and over the book's playful ironies throughout.

> *Darian J. Scott, "Mice and Monkeys, Dogs and Cats," in The Christian Science Monitor, October 5, 1984, p. B9.\**

[This is] a blandly-told nonsense story that should be tremendously appealing to the read-aloud set. Independent readers may secretly enjoy the humor even if they feel lofty about picture books. Unusually, this is a second-person narrative by the members of a primary-grades class. . . . No message, just fun. (pp. 67-8)

> *Zena Sutherland, in a review of "The Day the Teacher Went Bananas," in Bulletin of the Center for Children's Books, Vol. 38, No. 4, December, 1984, pp. 67-8.*

---

### MORGAN'S ZOO (1984)

An animal farce at the level of pleasant/silly, this would read aloud well across a school week—a giggle or a groan of willing disbelief per chapter. Twins Andrew and Allison, middle graders, join forces with gently dotty Morgan, a keeper at the underfunded neighborhood zoo threatened by an order to close and to disperse its tatty collection of "middle-aged mammals" to zoos across the country. . . . [It's] all as impossible and as satisfying as Judy G. and Mickey R. making it from the backyard barn to Broadway.

> *Lillian N. Gerhardt, in a review of "Morgan's Zoo," in School Library Journal, Vol. 31, No. 1, September, 1984, p. 119.*

Howe deftly blends the realism of [the struggles of Morgan, the animals, and the twins to keep the zoo open] with a fine fantasy that has chimps and elephants aiding and abetting the humans every step of the way. Though the ending, which sees the unlikable zoo head involved in a jewel theft, seems forced, children will delight in the story's fun, as well as its messages about ideals and friendship.

> *Ilene Cooper, in a review of "Morgan's Zoo," in Booklist, Vol. 81, No. 6, November 15, 1984, p. 448.*

---

### THE MUPPET GUIDE TO MAGNIFICENT MANNERS: FEATURING JIM HENSON'S MUPPETS (1984)

There is no denying that the Muppets are popular and will attract some readers; the question about this book is, will the cartoon characters that appeal to young children also appeal to readers old enough to be concerned with the proper size of a restaurant tip or when to take a date home from a dance? The advice Howe gives . . . is good, all standard guidance for the uncertain. The fact that it's embedded in often-cutesy anecdotes . . . seems a decided weakness. (p. 88)

> *Zena Sutherland, in a review of "The Muppet Guide to Magnificent Manners," in Bulletin of the Center for Children's Books, Vol. 38, No. 5, January, 1985, pp. 87-8.*

[This] is a happy hodgepodge of etiquette techniques to use in a variety of social situations. Howe tries to cover too wide a territory, and at times his information seems inappropriate for the intended age group. ("The general rule for tipping is to leave 15 percent of the total amount of the bill.") However, many common situations are covered . . . , and children can hardly be intimidated by learning from Gonzo and Fozzie Bear. This is neither as helpful nor as amusing as Marc Brown's *Perfect Pigs: An Introduction to Manners*. . . . Nonetheless, Muppet fans may pick up the book out of curiosity and learn a thing or two in the process.

> *Ilene Cooper, in a review of "The Muppet Guide to Magnificent Manners: Featuring Jim Henson's Muppets," in Booklist, Vol. 81, No. 10, January 15, 1985, p. 719.*

This Muppet guide to etiquette covers all the basics: introductions, conversations, telephone manners, dating, table manners, parties, correspondence and visiting. Writing with clarity and humor, Howe offers four to six pages on each topic. . . . Librarians needing supplementary material on etiquette will find *The Muppet Guide to Magnificent Manners* a useful . . . guide for elementary school children. (pp. 167-68)

> *Kathleen L. Birtciel, in a review of "The Muppet Guide to Magnificent Manners," in School Library Journal, Vol. 31, No. 7, March, 1985, pp. 167-68.*

# Monica (Ince) Hughes

## 1925-

**English-born Canadian author of fiction.**

Hughes is Canada's most renowned writer of science fiction for children and young adults as well as a respected author of realistic and historical fiction. She customarily uses Canada as the setting for her books, often focusing on aboriginal peoples such as the Inuits, Blackfoot Indians, and the Hutterites. Though she places some of her stories in the past and present, Hughes chooses the near future as the usual setting for her works. Centering each of her novels on a major social, moral, or economic issue, she treats such topics as adaptation to alien cultures and climates, erosion of energy and food sources, and the power of computers. Hughes leaves readers with a sense of seriousness regarding these matters, but her works also convey a sense of optimism. Her protagonists are usually adolescents who mature because of personal and societal challenges. By being forced to make moral judgments within conflicting cultures, these characters move from being ordinary and self-centered individuals to responsible but still credible young adults. Hughes hopes that today's youth, like her characters, will analyze their own society and the technological advances of their time to determine what is good and what is harmful.

Hughes brings a knowledge of science and human psychology to her science fiction. Her most ambitious and acclaimed work is the *Isis* trilogy—*The Keeper of the Isis Light, The Guardian of Isis,* and *The Isis Pedlar.* Set on an isolated planet, the series examines the sociological evolution of a colony over three generations and introduces one of Hughes's most enduring characters, Olwen Pendennis. An orphan, Olwen was raised in seclusion by a benevolent robot who altered her body to withstand atmospheric conditions, thus allowing her complete freedom of movement on Isis. Sixteen-year-old Olwen experiences the emotions of love and compassion when an Earth colony moves to her planet. Rejected by her boyfriend, Mark, when he sees her without protective covering, she chooses to remain physically different and live in isolation rather than violate her values by becoming more "human." Hughes examines exploitation in *Ring-Rise, Ring-Set,* which highlights the clash between a technical civilization and a primitive one. Setting her story underground during a future ice age, Hughes relates the injustices that occur when the advanced society imposes its collective will on the Ekoes, a nomadic culture. In addition to this social issue, the author underscores the importance of maintaining an ecological balance.

In her realistic and historical fiction, Hughes continues to probe themes of isolation and identity. Her most impressive work is perhaps *Hunter in the Dark,* which relates how Mike, a teenage boy suffering from leukemia, stalks a deer and in the process comes to terms with his own approaching death. Hughes explores the quest for one's heritage in two contemporary stories, *The Ghost Dance Caper* and *My Name is Paula Popowich!.* An adventure/mystery book, *Ghost Dance* introduces readers to Blackfoot Indian customs as Tom matures spiritually through his acceptance of his half-Indian ancestry. Written for middle-grade readers, *Paula Popowich* describes Paula's search for her unknown father and the discovery of

*Photograph by Russell and Adrienne Hughes. Courtesy of Monica Hughes*

her paternal Ukrainian background. The Canadian gold rush of the late nineteenth century is the background for *Gold-Fever Trail: A Klondike Adventure.* Depicting the dangers encountered by two children who look for their father along the Yukon River, the book provides details on gold prospecting and life in Dawson City. Hughes's first work and her only serious historical novella, *Gold-Fever Trail* was commissioned for use in the grade schools of Alberta.

Born in England but raised in Egypt until the age of six, Hughes was educated in England and Scotland. As a child growing up in London, she was fascinated with history and the beginnings of language. Hughes was especially impressed with the power of words and read adventure and fantasy books extensively. Her father, a mathematician and amateur astronomer, initiated Hughes's interest in astronomy while her mother entertained her with stories of the comet watches of 1910. Hughes lived in Zimbabwe for two years before coming to Canada in 1952; she became a naturalized citizen in 1957. Experience as a laboratory technician for the National Research Council stimulated her to explore the mysteries of space and science more deeply.

Hughes composed an adult novel and the drafts of several others before turning to children's literature. The ideas for her works come from many sources. She keeps extensive files of cuttings from newspapers and magazines and performs meticulous research for each book; events from her own life also initiate plots. Hughes claims that certain incidents make her explore "what would happen if," and she constructs her stories from this point. Her extensive travels and exposure to many cultures also contribute to the variety of Hughes's settings and characters.

Critics generally applaud Hughes for the success of her sociological themes and her psychological characterizations. Reviewers also cite her uncondescending and nondidactic writing style, the plausibility of her plots, and her eye for accurate detail. In view of these achievements, most observers would agree with Gerald Rubio who claims that Hughes is "one of the best Canadian—and perhaps world—authors of juvenile fiction at work today."

Hughes received the Vicky Metcalf Award in 1981, and was given the Canada Council Prize for *The Guardian of Isis* in 1982 and for *Hunter in the Dark* in 1983. *Ring-Rise, Ring-Set* was selected as a Guardian Runner-up in 1983.

(See also *Something about the Author*, Vol. 15 and *Contemporary Authors*, Vols. 77-80.)

---

## AUTHOR'S COMMENTARY

I find writing is a very lonely business, even writing for children, which should be, of course, and is, at the same time very joyful. But when you don't know what you're doing and you confront your inner self sitting all alone at a desk with a pile of blank paper in front of you, then that's the moment you find yourself asking, "Why did I ever begin?" "Why am I doing this?" And quite often, when I get to the difficult part of a book, these same questions come up: "What am I doing?" And, "Why?"

I really don't think I had any choice about becoming a writer. It began with my love affair with books, and *that* began before I can remember. . . .

I think perhaps the most fortunate thing that ever happened to me happened [at the age of 7]. We settled in a London suburb that had what is still, I understand, one of the very best schools for girls in London—the Notting Hill and Ealing High School. (p. 6)

We worked, of course, on our reading and our printing, but besides that we discovered how Early Man lived. We were read aloud to from books on pre-historic man; we took trips to the British Museum to see the Stone Age burials. Besides learning our own writing, we learned to write on clay and wax tablets with a stylus; we learned some cuneiform; we studied hieroglyphs and learned the cartouches of Cleopatra and Ptolemy; we were taught about the Rosetta Stone. And all this . . . in the equivalent of Grade two. (pp. 6-7)

[In Grade three], we went back to the British Museum and we saw the Magna Carta and the Domesday Book. This, of course, is something that can't happen to everyone; I mean, it's just lucky if you go to a terrific school that happens to be situated in London and you can step into the Underground and go to the British Museum.

But it did have a really deep and, until now, unconscious effect on me. I've only just begun to go back and work out why all this has happened: a sense of the magic of words as an essential part of the process of becoming more human, beginning with

Man in his cave, painting the creatures that roamed the Ice Age world and then putting his hand onto the wall next to them. We'll never know, but I think myself that this gesture or "autograph" was designed to gain power over them: "I am here, they are there, and I in my way as Thinking Man have more power than they have who can't draw anything." Then Man would tell stories to explicate his environment, his relationship to other men; tell of the terrors of birth and death and loneliness. And little by little all that storytelling moves forward until we come to the time of writing down one's memories—cuneiform, the hieroglyph, and then finally the simple rounded A, B, C's which are the same forms as we saw in the Domesday Book and the Magna Carta. And they carried this magic of formed letters, words, thoughts forward right into the school and the library of today. There's the whole power of man's self-discovery captured in the written word.

Even now when I'm writing I look at the page and I think, "It's still magic, isn't it?" These scrawls on paper—and you don't have to think about it as your hand actually puts it down—are an incarnation of one's deepest thoughts and emotions solidified into two dimensions right there. I would so much like to see reading and writing brought back into schools with this sense of magic: vibrant, instead of a physiological and psychological exercise which is painful for teachers and students. (pp. 7-8)

I've always known, since that school, that magic lay between the covers of books, and all that was necessary to do to partake of the treasures was to open the covers and plunge in. All the time I was growing up I was reading: *Wind in the Willows, Black Beauty, Coral Island, The Children of the New Forest,* Arthur Ransome, all the books of E. Nesbit. . . . I found in [E. Nesbit's books] the element that is more even to me than adventure, and that is the sense of fantasy, the secret that there is a wellspring of magic just below the surface of everyday life, and that all you have to do is somehow tap it—if you can just find out how. And *she* always does in her books. . . .

[My father] used to talk to me about the stars and point them out to me, and he gave me James Jean's *Mysterious Universe*. I gobbled it up, not understanding half of it, I'm sure, but I could read books, I think, by a sort of process of osmosis. . . . I just drew it all in and, understand it or not understand it, didn't seem to matter; it just became part of my fabric. I didn't worry about things I didn't understand, and so E. Nesbit's world of fantasy and the astronomy of my father were beginning to come together even though I didn't know it at the time. (p. 8)

Then the war came, my father died, and my sister and I were at boarding school. Later on I joined the WRNS [Women's Royal Naval Service], and after the war went to Zimbabwe. And then I came to Canada in 1952.

Canada was really a great shock and it became a catalyst that brought me face to face with myself in a confrontation that led to my first novel—the autobiographical novel, you know, that everybody writes and then hopefully just throws away. (Better out of the way.) I don't mean to be rude when I say that Canada was a shock, but it was totally different in the sense of "place" from anywhere else I had ever been. Europe has a great familiarity about it: you tred on history, you're rubbing elbows with the living and with the memories and ghosts of everybody all piled up through the centuries; it's absolutely crowded with humanity and with tradition. Now Zimbabwe was the opposite of that, really: it was an enigma. It was empty, not crowded the way Europe had been, but it was never lonely. (p. 9)

So I came to Canada and I settled in Ottawa and joined a canoe club. We used to spend weekends on trips up to the Gatineau and the Laurentian lakes. Now, this is where the shock came in. Africa itself is like a Motherland of the human race and I felt totally at home there. But the Laurentian shield seemed to me to deny humanity completely. I used to try to imagine the Indian people who roamed there and canoed on those lakes, and I thought about the Voyageurs and the Coureurs-de-Bois; I knew they were there, but still it seemed to me that the land was rejecting the idea of human feet on its surface. I still have some of that feeling about Canada: it's a marvelous place to fly over, but be wary when you stand on it, be very wary. It has nothing really to do with size; it has to do with the basic myth of the country in some way.

I felt very isolated when I first settled in Ottawa, and a lot of it was due to this feeling that I was not accepted by the land itself. So I wrote out these feelings in an adult novel, which was the first piece of fiction that I ever completed. I'd begun a lot, but I'd never finished anything before.

But then my years became filled with all sorts of other things, and it wasn't until I married and we had moved to Alberta that the need to express my feelings in writing surfaced again seriously. We'd had this long drive with four small children across the apparently unending spaces that lay between Sault St. Marie and Edmonton, and I felt an intensification of that initial contact with the land of Canada that I'd had in the Laurentians. When later on I came to write *Earthdark*, I reached out into those memories and brought out the emotions and fears and all the loneliness that I'd felt in that trip across the Prairies. I used it to describe the feelings of Kepler and Anne as they crossed the Ocean of Storms to the far side of the Moon in their search for Anne's missing father.

I spent the next few years in a creative search just trying to find myself. I had no idea what I was doing. I painted; I embroidered; I wove. And it wasn't until my youngest child went into school that I made the firm decision—a deliberate decision—to start writing again. But I chose juvenile writing purely by chance—except I don't really believe in "chance". I "happened" to go into the library one day and I "happened" to see on a recent acquisition's shelf a book called *Writing for the Juvenile and Teenage Market* by Jane Fitz-Randolph. I just picked it up—I like new books—and I'm always interested in how to do things even if I never do them. So I took it home. You know, I had never thought, in spite of raising four children, in spite of all the reading I had done as a child, I had never thought of writing *for* children. It had never occurred to me as a thing I could do. I think I was caught in the days of "little" books—of "nothings" you know—there were such a lot of them back in the Thirties, Fourties, and Fifties; jolly kids having fun in boarding schools and that sort of thing, and I knew I didn't want to write *that*. I hadn't realized just what an incredible renaissance there had been in children's writing. So I read a great deal. Then I realized how exciting this could be, and that it was worth having a try at it. (pp. 9-10)

The first problem I found was that I didn't know how to make plots "happen". All the books I'd read said, "Write about what you know." But how can you if what you know bears little relationship to where kids are today? What did I know? Life in Egypt in the 1930's with a nanny and going to the country club to see the races? An Edinburgh convent? Boarding

school in Harrogate? Wandering around Britain during the war? Two years in Zimbabwe? Working in Ottawa during the Fifties? I couldn't find anything to relate to young people that I could truthfully talk about. I realized that really I had very few roots and it's hard to write without roots—particularly if you want to write with authority. I just had to go back to those very beginnings of being a human being who had known how to write and how to read, and draw on that authority of just being a human being on earth.

At first I produced a couple of really horrible formula adventures. Then one that was a bit better with an historic background. Suddenly, a year after I'd started, things fell into place—again by "chance". I'd watched a Jacques Cousteau program on television which had to do with setting up an undersea habitat where scientists or engineers could live for two or three days at a time while working at pressures of three or four atmospheres, and so avoid the hazards and the wasted time of continually having to decompress and surface after very, very short work intervals. It was an interesting program, but I found myself saying, "Well, what would it be like if men lived permanently in habitats sixty feet under the surface? If that were their real home for all time?" And then the crucial question popped into my mind: "What would it be like to be a boy growing up in an environment like that?"

When I look back, all this seems incredibly obvious, but, you know, at the time it was like a flash of lightning. I hadn't asked that kind of question before; I had tried to manipulate characters and words to make books "happen". Now I was exploring a territory that in a sense already existed. I had to ask myself the questions and find out the answers to something that in some other world in space and time existed and that I had to bring into a reality on paper here. I began, and I realized that what I wanted to do more than anything was write Science Fiction, simply because the question I had asked *had* to be answered in the future: What would it be like to live under the sea all the time?

From that moment I didn't have trouble with books. It's not to say that writing became easy: it didn't, and it still isn't. I still find . . . that writing is very difficult; it's very aggravating. And in the moment when one dries up and one's mind becomes a desert, it's also rather terrifying; it's a scary way to earn a living when you don't know whether you will have another thought as you sit there staring at the paper. (pp. 11-12)

But then the marvelous moments happen, and they make up for all the rest. Moments when a heroine makes a discovery about herself. (But I didn't know about *that* and I invented her!) When characters say truthful things that *I* didn't put into their mouths. Moments when the hand that's holding the pen connects right through to the mythic levels of one's mind, and the words write themselves. I find myself reading them back and saying, "Yes, that's exactly right, but how did I know that? I didn't know I knew it."

So, where did all the plots come from that had been so hard to find, and that now I was finding so easy? They come from anything, anything in the world around me that stimulates me to ask questions: "What if such and such a thing were to happen?" "What then?" "To whom would this situation happen?" "How would they react?" "How would it change them?"

I've got ideas for books from seeing familiar things in unfamiliar ways, from an emotional reaction, from a domestic crisis, a newspaper cutting, a family incident. The challenge, once one has an idea, is then to turn it into a believable story.

There are several problems—but perhaps "problem" isn't the right word; there are several things one has to be aware of in writing believable stories for children. The first is to get the protagonist into a context where something larger than life, something really emotionally grabbing and important, is going to happen to him or her. And then the second is related to that: how to get the hero and heroine into the position from which they alone can make the decisions or carry out the actions that are really important in the story. In other words, if they are only going to be observers to some scene in which the adults are really doing all the action, it's going to be boring for kids to read. And, with regard to the second point, it's important to avoid—particularly, I think, in Science Fiction—the kind of story that was popular back in the Thirties where the young hero—there were never any girls then; they stayed home and knitted or crocheted—when the hero would jump into a space craft and take off and single-handedly destroy the enemy fleet or whatever it was. And you can't help thinking, "Well, where *is* the army? What are they doing? Where is the Interstellar Police? Come to that, where are this boy's parents and why isn't he at school?" It's all so unrealistic. So it really is important, I think, for believable Science Fiction today to enmesh the hero or the heroine in what is going on—suck them into the action so they are forced to react to it; they are not being puppeted around. I don't want them to be like Nancy Drew who's a female Johnny-on-the-spot all the time; you know, she's always there when the body is discovered.

I'd like to share just a few of the thought processes that went into a couple of plot plans. I won't go into detail but just give you an idea of how very ordinary the substance is that can turn into Science Fiction. The first I'll talk about is **Tomorrow City**. (pp. 12-13)

[While standing at the top of the Alberta Telephone Tower one night], I saw an Edmonton that I'd never seen before: the city stretching out from me as a network of electrical connections, seeming to radiate from the tower where I was standing. And at once there jumped into my mind the idea of the city as a brain; then the tower as the brain-centre with all these electrical connections reaching right out to the horizon as the nerve network. But then I thought, you can't have a book about a brain running a city. What about a computer? The tower as a giant computer designed to make the city a beautiful place for children to grow up in? (Now I've got my linkages started. I have to get more linkages.) Supposing that my heroine is the daughter of the designer. Supposing he has programmed what he knows of her—his daughter, his love for her—he's programmed her and her future needs into the computer to make her the model of the child the city is going to be made beautiful for. Sounds lovely, but of course things have to go wrong. And they have to go wrong naturally, not by the computer just running amuck: they don't do that. Computers make mistakes because the input is faulty. And I have to make the faulty input come from Caroline herself when she tells the computer—not quite knowing what's she saying—"Go ahead and do what you think is best, no matter how silly people may be about the changes."

And, of course, much more has to happen to strengthen that, but basically that was the story of how Caroline became involved in these terrifying events—because she had given the computer the directive to do what it, in its unloving, unfeeling, programmed fashion considered was beautiful for children.

A lot of children ask me when I'm going to write a sequel to **Tomorrow City** because they want to know what happened to Caroline afterwards. And I say there won't be a sequel (I don't think) because Caroline was really a very ordinary girl. Once in her life something tremendously exciting and terrifying happened to her because of her father being the designer of the computer and because of a little slip that she made that caused the computer to go astray. And after that everything followed and she had to face what happened in the story. But that's not going to happen to Caroline again; I think she probably led—quite thankfully—quite a quiet life after that.

**Beyond the Dark River** came about in a totally different way. Again, it was one of these things that happens by "chance" when you're writing: the serendipities that come to writers are just amazing. On this occasion we had a power cut: . . . and we were without electricity and without water (since the water is pumped) for a considerable time. And it was really extremely uncomfortable: cold; you couldn't turn on the tap; you couldn't get a hot meal. It was wretched. I found myself thinking about how much we rely on the trappings of civilization: the things that we originally invented but now are leaning on so heavily that we're in danger of losing our own initiative as human beings. You can turn on a light, you can turn on the tap, you turn up a thermostat, you open a freezer. Could we even survive in a northern climate—I'm thinking of Edmonton—if there was a total disaster that wiped out the whole of civilized structure: electricity, water, heating, comfortable buildings? And I thought, "Probably not. I don't think many of us could survive winter under those circumstances. But who would survive?" And right away I thought of two groups that live close to Edmonton. There's a Hutterite colony south of the city, and the Hutterites, as you may know, are like the old order image: they live very, very simple lives; they came from central Europe and settled in the Northern United States and then in Canada. There are several colonies in Alberta. They live most simply; they live a communal life on a farm; they're extremely self-sufficient and inventive. . . . I was sure they'd survive. Even if there's no gasoline, they'll go back to horse plowing, cultivating; no problem at all.

The second group I felt would survive might be an Indian community, but not the Indians on the Reserve or in the city, I didn't think, because they are too closely linked to all these things that are now destroyed. But in 1968 a band of Ermineskin left the Reserve at Hobbema and went out to start a new life in the foothills, living in the old way, living respectfully with nature, not using all the things we have taken for granted, but learning to live off the land; living in double-walled tepees (which are, I believe, very comfortable in the winter); hunting; fishing; gathering roots: they would survive.

Now the serendipity came when I looked at these two cultures and I realized how absolutely opposite to each other they are. The Hutterite is enclosed; the one source, not only of inspiration but daily living, is the Bible. The Indian looks out to nature; everything around is Holy. And I thought the Indian must be the girl in my story: I saw the Indian way as more the feminine way of looking at things. The Hutterite way of seeing life seemed the more masculine way so I made him the boy. And then all I had to do was to design a story in which in a natural fashion these two disparate people would come together and have an adventure—exploring the old, destroyed city of Edmonton, looking in the University library for an answer to an illness that has attacked the young children in the Hutterite community. And the linkage there is that the Indian girl is the healer for the tribe to whom all the knowledge has been passed down from grandmother to mother and to her.

Then I came to *Keeper of the Isis Light*. The idea for that came from the most simple connection—in a way—and yet the most involved: a newspaper cutting. (I keep them—anything that's interesting, anything that may in some future day a hundred years from now be an idea for a story—or perhaps be a linkage: that's happened, too, with something that I'm already writing and I suddenly find a piece of information I needed that I had cut out ten years ago—it's incredible how one does things like that!) This was a cutting about the young American boy, David, who suffers from a deficient immune system. He spends his entire life—he's eleven years old now—in a room by himself with air that is sterilized; everything that is in the room must be sterilized. He has had no direct communication—skin to skin, lovingly—with a human being from the moment of his birth.

After I had kept this cutting for a long, long time wondering why I was keeping it, I realized that *that* was the connection for me: this extraordinary thing for a human being to be so alone that he had never actually been touched by another human being, except through the equivalent of a space suit. And I wondered, "Would David be lonely? Since he has never known any other life, would he be lonely or would being alone be a perfectly normal way for him to live?" And from that theme I developed *Keeper of the Isis Light*. I felt I had to go right out into space because there's nowhere on Earth left that's lonely enough. Lighthouse stations used to be just about as isolated as you could get with a ship going out only every six months or so; now they get a helicopter every week with newspapers and mail: not nearly isolated enough. So I had to establish a colony on a planet far, far distant . . . from Earth. On it, three people: the mother and father and child who keep the lighthouse, as it would be kept on other planets that are not yet inhabited but someday will be. Then all I had to do was to get rid of the mother and father, and I had the child alone.

But I wanted my character Olwen to be older than a child to face these problems of being alone, being lonely: sixteen years old. If her parents had been killed off when she was in her teens, she would have been so devastated, so reft with loneliness, I don't suppose she'd even have lived. So she had to lose her parents when she was a very small girl. And I thought, "Oh, dear, you know you start this plotting and get so far and then you find yourself with insurmountable difficulties." So there was my insurmountable difficulty: how can I have a child of maybe two years old alone on a planet? If she's going to be brought up by the equivalent of wolves or apes or something, it would turn into a sort of Tarzan book—which might be fun, but it wasn't the book I wanted to write. So I had to compromise: I compromised with "Guardian" (and anyone who has read the book knows who "Guardian" is, and that in a sense it was a fair compromise). He is her protector, her mother and father, her teacher, her close friend.

Having overcome that difficulty, all I had to do to make a plot "happen" was to land a ship from Earth and face this girl who had been happy alone for her entire life with a crowd of eighty strangers from Earth, including twenty teenagers. She has never been exposed to teenagers, doesn't know how to talk to them, how to relate, while they, of course, are a welded group because they had been chosen as a group on Earth. They have come together on this dangerous flight; they have been indoctrinated into a loving family situation so that they are able to cope with this new planet. And now she's the outsider: from being the owner of the planet, she has become the stranger. And from that story developed the whole of the **"Isis"** trilogy, from just a little newspaper cutting. (pp. 13-17)

But no matter where I get the ideas from, from that original thought-outline to the finished manuscript, there is always an intensive search for truth. That's what we writers really do. The truth about my characters: Who are they? How do they think and feel? How are they going to react to the circumstances that I'm going to throw in their way? That's the most important truth: the characters.

The other truth is the background of the story. That is usually not a question of looking inside oneself (which is where I look to find out about my characters) but a question of simple research, reading everything I can about a subject, whether it's about living on the moon or under the sea, or even designing an original planet which is what I had to do with Isis. (And very exciting it was, too, to design a logical planet that kept Newton's laws and wouldn't fall out of the sky or fall into its sun nor have a climate totally at odds with the sun that I placed it in orbit around.)

Research leads one into all sorts of fascinating byways. I found—and I should think that people who write historical fiction for children must find this too—that the hardest part of writing the actual book is knowing what to leave out. You do so much work: I read at least thirty books about the surface of the moon, local conditions, low temperature/low gravity engineering, to find out how the cars would run. What kind of transport system would operate at extremely low temperature, near vacuum conditions? When I sent that particular manuscript of *Earthdark* to the publisher, my editor wrote me back and said, "I was absolutely fascinated with the technology. Now will you please take it out." And it's a hard moment, you know, when you've worked so hard and the material is fascinating. You're dying to share it with the kids. . . . (p. 18)

The point, of course, is—and the same with historical fiction— that if you know a subject totally, then you're not winging it. You can write freely without putting anything much in—but you know it's right, the tiny detail that you do put in—and you know that the background that your hero or heroine comes from is right. You know where they live before they come onto the printed page and *that* gives truthfulness. (p. 19)

*Gold-Fever Trail* was my only serious excursion into history, and I don't think I'll ever dare do it again. I don't really think of myself as a historian, not anymore in any case. . . . But it's a pity in a sense because, you know, there is a tremendous strength in writing history for young people: right away you can overcome this problem of, why is the hero—or, occasionally, the heroine—in these unusual and difficult conditions? . . . The historic context is a marvelous field for people to write in, with great plot possibilities that we can't have writing about today.

But certainly we can read about the past and we can learn from our mistakes in the past and bring a sense of history even when we're writing in the present and also when writing about the future. I think of Science Fiction as history that has, in a sense, not happened yet, where we can learn by our mistakes before we've made them. We can write, for instance, a story about a computer that can take over a city and realize that if we are lazy enough to give up many of our mental powers and our choices to computers to handle, we might find ourselves in a situation in which a computer was running the world. But it's in the future, so we don't have to suffer the consequences. Science Fiction has got that power about it!

And I think Science Fiction is very, very good for young people—particularly today, when they are facing so many difficult choices in life, and we don't even know what kind of choices in their future. Becoming familiar with Science Fiction, I think, helps us reach out fearlessly into that many-branched future and take control, perhaps, of our destiny. It teaches us to ask questions: "What if?" "And then what?" And it teaches us to find answers.

And I think one of the functions of a good writer for children (besides, obviously, being entertaining) is to help them explore the world and the future. And to find acceptable answers to the Big Questions: "What's life about?" "What is it to be human?" As I said before, those are the questions that demand truthful answers, not pat ones. So I think my chief criterion for a story for children—it should be for all fiction in fact, of course, but very especially that written for the young—is that one should write as truthfully as possible, even if it isn't easy or painless. One faces oneself in the darkest inside places of one's memory and one's subconscious, and out of that comes both joy and sorrow. But always—and I think again this is perhaps the second crucial thing for children—always there must come hope.

And then one writes and one scribbles out and then one writes again, and then maybe after half a dozen drafts (as one of my favourite writers, Alan Garner says) maybe—then—a book will emerge. And if it is good enough, it will probably be for children. (pp. 20-1)

> Monica Hughes, "The Writer's Quest," in Canadian Children's Literature: A Journal of Criticism and Review, No. 26, 1982, pp. 6-27.

---

## GENERAL COMMENTARY

**GERALD RUBIO**

Professionals—librarians, teachers, booksellers—familiar with even a few of Monica Hughes' eight published works recognize her as one of the best Canadian—and perhaps world—authors of juvenile fiction at work today. Teenagers—including those who normally have no interest whatsoever in science fiction—respond as favorably, if with less comprehension of the reason: they anticipate each new title with the enthusiasm of *Star Wars* fans about to see *The Empire Strikes Back*. But although Mrs. Hughes' audience is both as devoted and as diverse as George Lucas' and . . . for many of the same reasons, she has yet to attract the critical recognition and wide Canadian readership her work merits. The present . . . [study demonstrates] that the best of her work is as multi-dimensional in theme, scope, narrative content, and literary technique as those works we usually think of as "serious" adult literature. Her work is as superior to what is typical of juvenile fiction as are *Who Has Seen the Wind* and *The Wind in the Willows* (both of which it resembles in many ways). It is not simply "science fiction" any more than *Nineteen Eighty-Four* is: both she and Orwell (and, again, in similar ways) so transcend their nominal common genre that the classification becomes meaningless.

Curiously, few are aware of how essentially Canadian a writer Monica Hughes is. . . . [Not] only are many of her locales and subjects explicitly Canadian, but even the works set in new and distant worlds are permeated by uniquely Canadian themes. Are there, for example, more relevant "Canadian" themes than those central to her novels: the exploitation of natural resources by multi-national conglomerates? or the varieties of alienation experienced by immigrants to "new worlds"? or the importance of adaptation to hostile environments for survival? (p. 20)

Monica Hughes' only Canadian historical novella [*Gold-Fever Trail: A Klondike Adventure*] is, unfortunately, all but unknown outside of Alberta. It is excellent; it should be considered by any teacher in Canada dealing with the Gold-rush period. (The book was originally commissioned as an "assist" for Social Studies programs.)

The simple plot concerns thirteen-year-old Harry and his eleven-year-old sister Sarah, who face separation when their mother dies; their father is prospecting for gold in the Yukon but his whereabouts are unknown. . . . They find their father, of course, after appropriately exciting adventures—including the discovery of some gold for themselves.

The major interest in the novel, however, is the richness of detail used to bring to life the period and the search for gold. The novel is carefully researched, and gives an impressive picture of daily life. (p. 21)

Monica Hughes' first novel [*Crisis on Conshelf Ten*] is epic in scope, structure, and theme. Experimental stations, both on the continental shelves underseas and on the Moon, are imagined as having grown into self-contained societies by 2005, each with its distinctive values and lifestyles. Both Conshelf and Moon societies, however, remain colonies of the United Nations on Earth, and both want independence under U.N. mandate so they can control their own development and stop exploitation of their resources by multi-national conglomerates. (pp. 21-2)

The colonies described in *Crisis on Conshelf* (and in *Earthdark*) are based on fairly straightforward sophistications of presently existing technologies such as SCUBA equipment, underseas exploration vehicles, space modules and shuttles. In addition, all the "facts" about life both underseas and on the Moon—the effects of water pressure and relative gravities on physiology, for example—have been carefully researched and, so far as the science-oriented students I have consulted and I myself can tell, are completely accurate. . . .

The author's problem in *Earthdark* was to flesh out Moon society in such a way that it is consistent with its outlines in *Conshelf* and simultaneously suitable for new themes. In this novel, [the protagonist, Kepler Masterson,] returns to his home on Moon with his father bringing the new U.N. mandate; conglomerate exploitation is, in theory, to cease immediately. Enforcement, however, is impossible until the U.N. mission arrives. The action takes place during the interim. (p. 22)

Kepler rebels in a number of ways, all psychologically realistic and parallel to contemporary adolescent rebellion. (p. 23)

**"The Beckoning Lights"** depicts an encounter with a UFO. (p. 24)

As in the majority of Hughes' works, a central interest is the maturation of the central character. All is told through Julie's point of view, and the way she matures through her response to the encounter is very well handled. (pp. 24-5)

[*Beyond the Dark River*] marks Monica Hughes' break (perhaps temporary, perhaps permanent) with techniques common to her earlier science fiction; the novel is, in many respects, closer to *Ghost Dance Caper* than to *Conshelf*, *Earthdark*, or *Tomorrow City*—works based on extrapolations from existing technology. Like *Ghost Dance*, its materials and themes are strictly Canadian. Does this make it inevitable that the novel will be prized everywhere but in Canada?

The novel is technically science fiction in that it is set in the future; but since our perceptions are alien to the ways in which the protagonists and narrators perceive reality, neither they nor Mrs. Hughes will answer questions about exact dates. For, stylistically, the work is a tour de force in point of view and modes of perception.

Fourteen-year-old Daughter-of-She-Who-Came-After is a member of the Cree tribe; fifteen-year-old Benjamin belongs to a Hutterite Bruderhof.

Both Cree and Hutterite societies are described in sufficient detail to satisfy an adult sociologist; the novel's teenaged protagonists are characters as complex as any modern, intelligent members of such societies. Both alternately accept, then question, the values of their elders; both alternate between taking pride in the positions the societies have assigned them and resenting the obligations and alienations from their peers which these positions impose. (p. 25)

[*The Keeper of the Isis Light*] approaches its subject and themes in a totally different way: it is as different from *Beyond the Dark River* as that is from the earlier "technological" novels.

In many respects it is the best work Monica Hughes has produced; it is, however, so unique that comparisons are not really valid. The time is the very far distant future, and the locale a planet Isis, far across deep space from Earth. . . .

The planet is inhabited by only two "people" as the novel opens: Olwen, a sixteen-year-old girl, and her sole companion, Guardian, a character whom the reader will recognize as a highly sophisticated robot, but whom Olwen assumes to be as human as she. Olwen, because she is idyllically happy and has no memories of any companionship other than Guardian, does not ask questions which will concern the reader until near the end of the novel: How has she come to be on Isis? Where are her parents? Why do colonists from Earth respond to her as they do? All questions, as in a mystery novel, are answered, but the reader should be forewarned that adults are likely to find themselves blubbering through the final scenes like responsive children.

Olwen is unquestionably the most fully realized and complexly drawn character in the Hughes novels, even though ironically placed in so nonrealistic a setting. Although the focus of the novel is on Olwen's character and maturation, there is some adventure (but not nearly so much as in the other novels). Guardian is a variation on the computer in *Tomorrow City*. Contrasting ways of perceiving reality are explored, as in *Dark River*. The problems of maturing youths, coming to terms with their heritages, peers, and environments, are all explored as they have been in all Monica Hughes' novels. (p. 26)

> Gerald Rubio, "Monica Hughes: An Overview," in Canadian Children's Literature: A Journal of Criticism and Review, *No. 17, 1980, pp. 20-6.*

### IRMA McDONOUGH

At Monica Hughes's readings the children deluge her with questions: "Where do you get your ideas? Did you have to do a lot of research about space before you could write *The Keeper of the Isis Light*? What advice would you give to someone who wants to write books?"

She answers: "All writing comes from an author's own experience, not from a book of plots, ready made . . . Yes, I have read many, many books and articles on space, but how my characters act and interact comes from my own knowledge of people . . . Keep your eyes open and keep a journal where you put down things that are important and interesting to you if you want to be a writer."

By their questions and her answers it is obvious that Monica Hughes enjoys a rapport with children. She finds them an exciting, challenging audience. Because she never condescends to children in her books she has a wide readership. She respects children as serious readers and they know it. From her audiences she expects thoughtful questions because she engages children's attention through their intelligence right from the start.

Monica Hughes dislikes the modern adult novel which is "the author's load of despair enlivened with sex and violence." When she decided to become a writer she turned to children's books because she found that they generally lack the despair and sex and violence she disdains. She feels that books influence children more than adults so the children's author has a greater responsibility than the writer of adult books. Hughes knows that children can cope with tragedy in their books, but they should never be divested of hope or dignity by the writer of a story meant for them. . . .

About her own work she is humble. "Sometimes my books grab the celestial fire, but sometimes they are only competent," she says. But all of them have been published as she wrote them, almost entirely unedited. From her first commissioned story, *Gold Fever Trail*, she has moved from a simple historical novella form to the sophisticated science fiction of her latest novel, *The Keeper of the Isis Light*. Each book is a singularly stimulating experience. (p. 11)

Hughes has been rightly recognized as "one of the best Canadian, perhaps world, authors of juvenile fiction at work today" [see excerpt above]. She brings reason and intellect to bear on all of her work. She recognizes three levels of communication in writing fiction: the straight adventure happening to the hero/heroine; the universal that brings the work into commonality with world literature, and the myth level that involves the author's intuitive knowledge about her country's past which is "carried in the genes" from generation to generation. Hughes agrees with Patricia Wrightson, another author who sees the need to recognize the mythology of her own country, in her case the Aboriginal myths of Australia. Myths are part of every person's subconscious. Science fiction writers should be particularly sensitive to interpreting this level in their "mythology of the future."

Monica Hughes writes science fiction not merely to entertain her readers. She says, "Science fiction helps to prepare young readers for the post-agricultural, post-industrial, technological world. The challenge of science fiction is to find new answers to new questions and help children to face the challenge of the future." She sees science fiction as non-threatening reading because it removes the reader from her own world. While pain and loneliness are the same no matter in what galaxy people have to face them, the environments in science fiction are quite different. The human dilemmas they encompass are therefore readily acceptable. The metaphor and analogy the writer uses however must relate to the child reader's frame of reference. (p. 12)

When [Monica Hughes] was young she enjoyed reading Dickens and Stevenson, Blackmore and Nesbit whose works we consider classics. Now Monica Hughes is writing books that will also be considered classics by many new generations of young people. (p. 13)

Irma McDonough, "Profile: Monica Hughes," in In Review: Canadian Books for Children, Vol. 15, No. 1, February, 1981, pp. 11-13.

## NEIL PHILIP

Monica Hughes is not a formula writer. Both her recent novels, **Space Trap** . . . [and **Devil on My Back**] attempt to provide something beyond the momentary thrill. She can be clumsy—**Devil on My Back** is marred by its reliance for its title and the expression of its central theme on a frequently quoted "song" so inexact in its scansion it would be impossible to sing—but in general she writes with fluid confidence. In **Space Trap**, Valerie blunders into a trap while angrily pursuing her resented brother and sister. She is kidnapped across space by aliens who study her as a curiosity. Her feelings of jealousy and spite towards her siblings vie with her deeper attachment in a most interesting way. . . .

**Devil on My Back** is a thoughtful tale about the responsibilities of power and the nature of freedom. Outside the hermetic hierarchy of ArcOne, with its strutting Lords linked in to the computer, and thus all human knowledge, via the infopaks on their necks, its cowed Workers, its mindless Soldiers and its rebellious Slaves, Tomi, son of the overlord, finds a settlement of escaped slaves, who force him to rethink the life he had taken for granted. He returns to ArcOne, only to discover that his father's seeming evil is really cunning diplomacy. The message is simple: if there is hope it lies in the proles.

Neil Philip, "Space Challenge," in The Times Educational Supplement, No. 3545, June 8, 1984, p. 16.*

## SARAH ELLIS

Canada's finest writer of science fiction for children is the English-born Monica Hughes. . . . She has written books in a number of genres, including realistic urban fiction and that Canadian standard, the wilderness survival adventure story. But it is in science fiction that her unique talents are given free rein.

Canadian landscape and history provide interesting models for the science fiction writer. The very factors which have made Canada relatively inhospitable to the writing of epic and mythical fantasy create fertile ground for the writing of science fiction. In the work of Monica Hughes we see how such themes as the disorientation of the newcomer, survival in a hostile and alien landscape, and the challenges of human communication are given narrative strength by being applied to a speculative, futuristic setting. (p. 661)

Like most science fiction the work of Monica Hughes is international in its thrust. She deals with global issues—Earth's overcrowding in the **Isis** books, the coming ice age in **Ring-Rise, Ring-Set** . . . , the possibility of underwater settlement in **Crisis on Conshelf Ten** . . . , mental telepathy in **Beckoning Lights**. . . . But she gives the issues substance in a way that adds a Canadian identity—stories that reveal more about us than much of our realistic fiction does. The story of the settlers on Isis—the story of the newcomer with all its expectation and fear, excitement and loneliness—is very close to the surface in the life of every non-aboriginal Canadian. The landscape of Isis—pockets of habitability in an otherwise large and dangerous land—or the actively hostile natural forces in **Space Trap** . . . all reflect the imagery of much Canadian perception of nature. Monica Hughes's preoccupation with communication—personal, as between Olwen and Mark; interspecies, as between humans and the pink blob-creature "Fifth Daughter"

in **Space Trap**; or across vast distances of space—reflects what has always been a Canadian preoccupation: how to transfer information between distant points. And the documentary element in Hughes's stories, the delight in recording and classifying stars, minerals, plants, and animals is firmly rooted in the tradition of Catherine Parr Traill's early botanical observations, in our realistic animal stories, and in our documentary film tradition.

This documentary flair is also a factor in one of Monica Hughes's great strengths as a science fiction writer—her technical neatness. She always manages to give the essential scientific background economically, without becoming bogged down in hardware. Her obvious delight in invention, in creating a matter-transmitter or a single-organism forest or water-breathing gillmen, is kept firmly in check by a tightly controlled plot.

In terms of readership Hughes is a valuable writer because her books fall into that somewhat sparsely populated territory of science fiction for capable intermediate readers. Her potential appeal to this age group lies in both style and theme. In a genre heavy with the portentous and the solemn, her writing has a lightness and a buoyancy sometimes reminiscent of English fiction of an earlier age. (Her characters are not beyond exclaiming an occasional " 'You're a ruddy little marvel!' ") And the issues she deals with—what it is to be human, the dangers of forgetting your own history, the interaction of immigrant and aboriginal peoples, the role of technology—are posed clearly, in the way that immortality is posed as a clear question in **Tuck Everlasting** (Farrar). Monica Hughes's books can be a fine introduction to the novel of ideas.

And, finally, there is a gentleness to her books that is rare in science fiction. The hairsbreadth escapes, the exotic flora and fauna, the humanoids, the vast intergalactic reaches, the villains and the heroes—all are enclosed in one overriding concern, subtle but ever-present: the value of kindness. This theme seems a rather nonrobust one for science fiction. But Monica Hughes manages to clothe the homey quality in flesh and blood (or in pink blob-tissue or high-technology robot metal) to give it strength and resilience. Hers is a major contribution to the fields of Canadian writing for children and of juvenile science fiction. (pp. 663-64)

Sarah Ellis, "News from the North," in The Horn Book Magazine, Vol. LX, No. 5, September & October, 1984, pp. 661-64.

## KIT PEARSON

Because of one writer—Monica Hughes—Canada shines in the field of science fiction. Perhaps her country's most distinguished writer for children, she is also one of its most prolific, writing realistic fiction as well. Her trilogy, **The Keeper of the Isis Light, The Guardian of Isis,** and **The Isis Pedlar** . . . , although set in the future, is truly Canadian in its theme—immigrants to a new land dealing with the accompanying pressures of prejudice and culture clash. (p. B9)

Kit Pearson, "A Harvest of Children's Books from Canada," in The Christian Science Monitor, October 5, 1984, pp. B8-B9.*

---

## GOLD-FEVER TRAIL: A KLONDIKE ADVENTURE (1974)

A motherless brother and sister, threatened with separation and orphanages, decide to run away and search for their father who, when last heard from, was headed for the Klondike goldfields. Undetected on the crowded ship, they reach Skagway, where they are apprehended by Corporal Jones of the Mounties. Undaunted, they persuade Jones and Sgt. Riley to take them over the Chilcoot Pass to Dawson, where they find lucrative employment, make friends, and are eventually reunited with their father. A fairly standard plot, and one that should appeal to children.

In spite of the fact that Harry and Sarah finds things much too easy, and that the book is too slight to convey the intense excitement of the time and place, it is enjoyable reading. Ms Hughes's prose style is straightforward, lucid and extremely readable, and her characters are believable flesh and blood people, although somewhat too good to be true. Dawson City itself emerges, though not far enough, as a place with a quality all its own. I only wish that the author had spent twice as much time and effort to make the book twice as long and put some meat on the bones of a good, but rather skeletal story. I think that *Gold Fever Trail* shows rich promise and that Monica Hughes should be encouraged. (pp. 49-50)

> *Marion Brown, in a review of "Gold-Fever Trail: A Klondike Adventure," in* In Review: Canadian Books for Children, *Vol. 8, No. 4, Autumn, 1974, pp. 49-50.*

This is a highly cohesive account [of two children searching for their father.] . . . The reader becomes completely engrossed in such situations as the failure to find Mr. Thorpe in Dawson City and in Harry's close call with death from scurvy when he is working on his placer claim out in the goldfields. Another fever—gold fever—nearly overwhelms Harry that winter of 1897 and the reader is not spared from this overpowering ailment. The author skillfully involves the reader from the beginning of the book until he or she completely succumbs. In spite of the fact that the two children mature unnaturally quickly, even acknowledging their experiences, *Gold-Fever Trail* is a book which has high appeal to children and adults alike and can stand on its own as a valuable addition to Klondike literature. (p. 26)

> *Marion Pape, "Yukon Icons," in* The World of Children's Books, *Vol. III, No. 1, Spring, 1978, pp. 25-7.\**

---

### CRISIS ON CONSHELF TEN (1975)

The point of *Crisis on Conshelf Ten* is made early and firmly so that the reader accepts the purpose behind the adventures. A boy born on the Moon comes to Earth for the first time with his father, who has been sent to persuade the government to allow the Moon colony more money and a greater voice in human affairs. Since he finds it hard to adjust to gravity, young Kepler is sent to relations living in an underwater community. Here by accident he discovers the Gillmen, a race evolving in secret who have the same needs as the Moon colony but who are seeking redress through sabotage of essential oil and fishery plants. Kepler's part in the story is as unconvincing as his character is stilted; both are clearly hampered by having to further the political moral of the book, which might have been more spontaneous and attractive if its crisp documentation had been employed in the service of straight adventure. (pp. 2820-21)

> *Margery Fisher, in a review of "Crisis on Conshelf Ten," in her* Growing Point, *Vol. 14, No. 8, March, 1976, pp. 2820-21.*

All the facts of the story are based on theories and possibilities which are at least being discussed today if not in the experi-

mental stages. The plot moves along at a good pace and is not overly interrupted by the explanations and technicalities. However, the characters are not fully developed; they exist primarily to further the exposition of the moral of the story: the immorality of pollution and waste of resources. As well, the ending seems somewhat melodramatic.

It is a fast-moving science fiction read for a summer's day for 10-12 year olds that makes few demands on their intellect.

> *Nancy Ward, in a review of "Crisis on Conshelf Ten," in* In Review: Canadian Books for Children, *Vol. 10, No. 3, Summer, 1976, p. 54.*

[*Crisis on Conshelf Ten* has] several exciting episodes. The dialogue is at times stilted, and the plot peters out in a simplistic ending (the gillmen give in, Hilary is forgiven, and the moon colony wins its vote). However, Hughes' picture of twenty-first century undersea living, where gillmen and people live permanently, is fascinating. Readers intrigued with the futuristic genre may well get caught up in the story.

> *Barbara Elleman, in a review of "Crisis on Conshelf Ten," in* Booklist, *Vol. 73, No. 16, April 15, 1977, p. 1266.*

Kepler manages to convince the revolutionaries . . . to abandon their violent tactics, bringing the action to an unconvincing close. The only redeeming factor is the fascinating background material about what underwater life might be like; however, it only barely makes up for the unbelievable plot and superficial characterizations. Carl Biemiller's *The Hydronauts* (Doubleday, 1970) is a more exciting undersea adventure.

> *Sonia Brotman, in a review of "Crisis on Conshelf Ten," in* School Library Journal, *Vol. 23, No. 9, May, 1977, p. 62.*

---

### EARTHDARK (1977)

*Earthdark* leads the story of a UN Base in Sinus Medic towards the year 2005 but it is not much better than a dozen other current novels about ill-advised excursions on the moon's surface and illicit, diversionary activity in the neighbourhood of Base itself. A new element, though, perhaps, is the sense of conflict between the sociological pull of Earth communities, and the new-world charisma of Moon-conditioned folk. It interferes in the 'romance' between Kepler Masterman and Ann after Kepler's prolonged holiday on Earth. It is about time someone at least hinted at resettlement problems and cultural mutation in an imagined but not impossible dream of colonisation of the spheres.

> *A. R. Williams, in a review of "Earthdark," in* The Junior Bookshelf, *Vol. 41, No. 3, June, 1977, p. 179.*

[In] *Earthdark*, Edmonton author Monica Hughes gives teenage readers science fiction at its best. . . .

The result is pure adventure, complete with spies, thieves and political intrigue, but it's also the sensitive story of two young people who come to know more about each other and themselves.

> *A review of "Earthdark," in* Children's Book News, *Vol. 1, No. 3, December, 1978, p. 2.*

This is an excellent book for young readers who enjoy a realistic science fiction story as opposed to those who demand a time-warping catapult into distant galaxies. The story is dated as happening in 2005 AD when the existence of a manned Moon base does not seem too improbable. The author's description of the Moon and Moon life, and her views of such phenomena as Earth Light and the lunar landscape, as seen through Kepler's eyes, are detailed enough to satisfy the inquisitive reader without being too technical.

As in all good adventure stories there is a last minute twist to the plot which holds the reader's interest to the last page. (pp. 56-7)

*Joan D. Smith, in a review of "Earthdark," in In Review: Canadian Books for Children, Vol. 13, No. 3, June, 1979, pp. 56-7.*

A science-fiction tale dealing with third-world-type complaints of capitalist/imperialist exploitation of colonists and natural resources? Yes, but in this version, the third world country is Moon colony and its exploiter is LEMCON, a huge multi-national mining conglomerate that is milking the moon of its mineral resources but is not interested in developing its potential as a new home for mankind. . . .

For young adults who enjoy spy-story intrigue, this version with its extraterrestrial setting will be appealing. For teachers dealing with questions of developing nations and the responsibility of business towards those from whom they make profits, this book would make interesting supplementary reading for discussion.

*Susan Ratcliffe, in a review of "Earthdark," in CM: Canadian Materials for Schools and Libraries, Vol. VIII, No. 3, Summer, 1980, p. 148.*

---

### THE TOMORROW CITY (1978)

This novel is very strong on theme, adequate in characterisation and predictably weak in setting. Thompsonville is the typical, non-existent town which seems to have no particular place in time or space. Events in the story are rather compressed but it is interesting to trace the gradual—and logical—development of the power of the computer and its predictable lack of feeling. Paradoxically, the computer ends by having a nervous breakdown and blowing a circuit. Recommended; thoughtful reading for the young teenager.

*C.J.C., in a review of "The Tomorrow City," in Book Window, Vol. 6, No. 1, Winter, 1978, p. 28.*

Monica Hughes in **The Tomorrow City** handles the hackneyed idea of a machine taking over men's lives with complete confidence and professional ease. Twelve to 14-year-olds should certainly enjoy this entertaining science fiction and may well be a little fearful that the heroine Caro and her friend David will be killed by the power-crazed computer Cinencom—City Central Computer, called C-Three for short.

The author purposely breaks Law One of the three laws of robotics as stressed by Isaac Asimov, for C-Three does physically injure humans who cross its programmed determination to clean up the city. In fact I was quite startled that Caro is actually blinded by C-Three at the end (despite it being a mistake on C-Three's part) when she and David finally manage to put the menace out of action and thus save the city. This unexpected blindness of the city's young saviour (although a hint is dropped that it may only be temporary) spoilt for me an otherwise most satisfying story.

*Anne Bertoluzzi, "Inter-planetary Adventure," in The Times Educational Supplement, No. 3294, August 18, 1978, p. 17.**

A prediction? A warning? A piece of pure sci-fi? . . .

The process of dehumanisation is chronicled realistically and, even though the activities of C-Three keep the story firmly in the realm of fiction, the plot is engineered convincingly and its sombre undertones are unmistakably sustained.

*G. Bott, in a review of "The Tomorrow City," in The Junior Bookshelf, Vol. 42, No. 5, October, 1978, p. 269.*

The loss of individuality makes a strong theme for Monica Hughes's tale. . . .The end is dramatic but not melodramatic. The deliberate low-keyed, factual style makes belief possible and brings home the point of the story.

*Margery Fisher, in a review of "The Tomorrow City," in her Growing Point, Vol. 17, No. 4, November, 1978, p. 3413.*

Monica Hughes' latest science fiction novel is a convincing picture of the possible effects of computer control. . . .

The plot is very well developed. The pride and anticipation which greets the inauguration of the new computer is not easily laid aside. Its control over the city grows steadily but not overnight. The realization of the true effects of computer control comes slowly. The children's part in the drama is realistically portrayed; their actions and deductions are not beyond the capabilities of their age group. In all, it is a skilfully plotted, gripping look at the possible costs of efficiency. Children of 11-14 years will enjoy the fast-paced story while it raises questions for them about the future. I would recommend it for science fiction collections.

*Nancy Ward, in a review of "The Tomorrow City," in In Review: Canadian Books for Children, Vol. 13, No. 4, August, 1979, p. 30.*

---

### THE GHOST DANCE CAPER (1978)

The Red Indian mystique (or culture, perhaps one might dare to suggest) continues to be a ground of exposition especially where a youngster has a smidgen of Indian blood in his modern veins. Tom besieges his Indian great-grandfather in his quest to "find his Spirit" which leads to a daring museum theft and burglary in reverse in his determination to exploit the mystic "ghost bundle" of Indian lore unobtainable elsewhere. Naturally there is friction between him and purer Americans and a family which disdains all connection with the distant past. The mysteries of Indian beliefs are evocative enough in themselves but the organisation of near grand larceny creates a rivalry in suspense which culminates in a resolution of both factors in the plot. This, with the recent re-printing of *Crazy Weather* [by Charles L. McNichols] encourages the belief that a rich vein of human interest bids fair to providing a rewarding field for revaluation and sympathetic exploitation. (pp. 313-14)

*A. R. Williams, in a review of "The Ghost Dance Caper," in The Junior Bookshelf, Vol. 42, No. 6, December, 1978, pp. 313-14.*

Readers who cannot resist rushing through this exciting and humourous adventure, should read again the minutely detailed crime scenes and note the clever planning and compact construction. The dialogue throughout exactly suits each character. The criminals appear only as shadows yet come alive through ejaculations!

*J. McC., in a review of "The Ghost Dance Caper," in* Book Window, *Vol. 7, No. 1, Winter, 1979, p. 29.*

While the dance description is authentic the major plot line of the narrative . . . is artificial and highly improbable. Monica Hughes is not writing about a half-Indian boy's progress to spiritual maturity amidst traditional or contemporary Blackfoot Indian customs so much as she seems to be condoning juvenile delinquency. Tom never has to answer for the illegalities of his "caper." But he does find his spirit in the form of a bat living in the museum attic, a bat who follows his own path and never gets lost, even in the dark.

Stereotyping clichés like "I just wish I could scalp them" spoken by Tom, and equating success to being a lawyer or a doctor or an Indian chief should be eliminated rather than reinforced as they are in this novel.

For the most part, the language used by Tom and the Indian Chief sounds like British Empire Loyalist from Kingston, Ontario rather than prairie Blackfoot-influenced Canadian English.

Some writers can write well in a literary sense as well as with truth, clarity and passion about an ethnic group not their own, as did Margaret Craven in *I Heard the Owl Call My Name.* Monica Hughes can write well in the literary sense but she fails, as so many people do, to understand the reality of 20th century Indians, and herein lies one of the reasons that stereotyping of Indians still happens, in books, as in everyday life.

*George Kenny, in a review of "The Ghost Dance Caper," in* In Review: Canadian Books for Children, *Vol. 13, No. 2, April, 1979, p. 52.*

---

### BEYOND THE DARK RIVER (1979)

The time is 2026, the setting Canadian, the characters belonging primarily to two races whose traditional isolationalism has helped them to establish a satisfactory life after a nuclear disaster which has left cities ruined and inhabited by starving mutants. Two young people carry the story—Benjamin Gross, who is sent from the Hutterite community which has shaped his personality to find a cure for a mysterious illness among the children, and the so-called 'heathen witch', an Indian girl who has inherited skills of healing and, unusually, an enquiring mind. The author compels belief in her predictive fiction by extrapolating from the known customs and attitudes of North American Indians and the German-American Hutterites, and by interpolating reminders of our own time so that the Canada she imagines seems a plausible development from the present. This is a good story, exciting and well constructed, and its basic premises and challenging predictions are properly related to the thoughts, feelings and traits of her strongly imagined characters.

*Margery Fisher, in a review of "Beyond the Dark River," in her* Growing Point, *Vol. 18, No. 4, November, 1979, p. 3615.*

**Beyond the Dark River,** much the strongest of these three books, [including Paul Biegel's *The Clock Struck Twelve* and Lorna

Baxter's *The White Rose and the Black,* is set] . . . in a vividly realised post-apocalypse Canada. . . .

Although the basic situation is becoming over-familiar, and some of the details of the speed with which knowledge (of, for instance, the importance of salt) has been lost seem unlikely, the book's horrors are skilfully evoked, and the Hutterite settlement convincingly and sympathetically drawn. It is a pity that the Cree society and that of the mutant urban survivors are not presented in similar depth. As it is, the clash of cultures between Benjamin and the Indian girl is the book's central interest and its greatest strength.

If fantasy is not to prove itself a played-out genre, it must once again provide settings as carefully drawn and stories as immediate and exciting as this science fiction.

*Neil Philip, "Apocalyptic Visions," in* The Times Educational Supplement, *No. 3323, February 15, 1980, p. 28.**

In her previous novels Monica Hughes has proved that she can write fast-moving exciting narrative without neglecting to touch on some deep concerns she has about technology's threat to individual freedom in all forms of human thought and expression. In this novel her views are overstated, some plot incidents appear contrived and the developing relationship between the two main characters is not handled successfully. Clearly the author's sympathies lie with the Indians and their natural wisdom so that the helpless plight of the holocaust victims, the religious bigotry of the Hutterite preacher and Brian's rash, ingenuous nature only serve to emphasize the Indians' pastoral nobility. On the other hand this book represents an interesting departure in the author's writing providing young readers with a fresh and imaginative look at problems which already threaten the environment. (pp. 46-7)

*Patrick Verriour, in a review of "Beyond the Dark River," in* In Review: Canadian Books for Children, *Vol. 14, No. 2, April, 1980, pp. 46-7.*

A good book for readers who enjoy being scared stiff! There is something very convincing indeed in this picture of a civilisation in ruins, and the very small crumb of comfort at the end is most acceptable. . . .

This is a well-made, solidly built story, very honest in its presentation and working-out of difficult problems. It is still more a study not only of society but also of individual people being true to their own natures and falling foul of tradition in doing so. The narrow ways of the *Bruderhof* are presented ruthlessly. There is no doubt of young Benjamin's heroism in standing up to the inflexible Preacher. His is a fascinating and convincing study; still better is the picture of the Indian girl who belongs to an even older tradition and one which stands her in better stead in a crisis. When the two are together in the ruined city nightmares become true and Benjamin nearly dies to placate the god of the library! This is the scene which will return to sensitive readers during restless nights. But the horror is held in control by courage and commonsense, and there is much comfort from this. The story ends quietly, with its problems unresolved but with just a little gleam of light at the end of a dark tunnel.

I have missed Miss Hughes' earlier books. On the evidence of this book alone, here is a writer of rare integrity and great narrative powers.

M. Crouch, in a review of "Beyond the Dark River," in The Junior Bookshelf, Vol. 44, No. 3, June, 1980, p. 144.

Characterization is shallow; the story is the thing in this often exciting futuristic fantasy. The part of the book in which the girl tries to help the Hutterites is fairly convincing and plausible, and both Benjamin and the girl engage the reader's emotions. The journey to and from the city, however, is contrived, sensationalistic, and clichéd, and the conclusion, that the sick children are the victims of germs for which the cure is no longer known, is too flat to be satisfying.

*Alethea K. Helbig, in a review of "Beyond the Dark River," in* Children's Book Review Service, *Vol. 9, No. 12, Spring, 1981, p. 107.*

This is the kind of book that leaves you hungry for a sequel. Its two main characters . . . are fully drawn and their makeshift partnership, to retrieve information from a past holocaust abandoned library with which to combat disease is lively and believable. . . .

Off beat enough to be fascinating, the novel possesses a steady honesty in its resolution of conflict and its development of subthemes. Readers should find this a welcome vehicle for evaluating the good and not so good aspects of their own culture. The author's ability to nuance her shift of settings is remarkable; yet the prose is so smooth that it is only when the novel is finished that one recognizes how good it is. It will beg for comparison with LeGuin's *Beginning Place*, although *Beyond the Dark River* is less complex, less mature in mood and tone.

*Judith N. Mitchell, in a review of "Beyond the Dark River," in* Voice of Youth Advocates, *Vol. 4, No. 3, August, 1981, p. 31.*

---

### THE KEEPER OF THE ISIS LIGHT (1980)

*The keeper of the Isis light* is especially for girls of fourteen to sixteen, though not only for them. Sixteen-year-old Olwen has been brought up on the planet Isis in complete solitude except for her guardian, an anthropomorphic robot. Life is idyllic until a party of Earth settlers arrives, when she learns to love and finds she is hated. SF elements abound, are of interest in themselves, and are basic to the plot; but it is Olwen's discovery of her own nature and her own values that is of paramount importance. There is considerable, but unobtrusive, technical skill in the manipulation of the point of view of relation: we see through Olwen's eyes, and share her shock when Mark rejects her. It is difficult to convey the 'feel' of the book. Seeing Olwen's world through her senses and her responses, the reader experiences a refreshing sensation of serene radiance. I can't phrase it adequately. You must read it for yourself.

*Norman Culpan, in a review of "The Keeper of the Isis Light," in* The School Librarian, *Vol. 28, No. 3, September, 1980, p. 293.*

A sixteen year old heroine, a seventeen year old love interest, and a restrictive yet compassionate guardian are attractive ingredients for any novel. In addition, the mystery of why the girl . . . remembers no existence prior to her fifth birthday and of why she must wear a silver jumpsuit with an opaque plastic face-piece when meeting the newly-arrived pioneers increases tension and science fictional involvement. . . .

Francis Molson describes two of Hughes's earlier works in *Anatomy of Wonder* (1981): *Earthdark* is an "above-average adventure story" for young adults with "convincing detail" and *Tomorrow City* is "children's science fiction . . . effectively handled through a convincing plausible scenario and believable characterization." These same qualities reappear in this current work, an above average young adult SF novel of a girl achieving self-awareness. Hughes carefully embeds scientific details. The plot moves quickly from complication to climax. The solution to the mystery does surprise and is plausible.

Unfortunately, *The Keeper of the Isis Light* will not join those SF novels of initiation into man/womanhood by such as Heinlein, McCaffrey, Norton and Panshin which attract readers of all ages. The change in Olwen from innocent happy childhood to compassionate woman lacks conviction.

*Muriel Becker, in a review of "The Keeper of the Isis Light," in* Science Fiction & Fantasy Book Review, *No. 2, March, 1982, p. 21.*

William Faulkner talks about "the old universal truths lacking which any story is ephemeral and doomed—love and honour, and pity and pride, and compassion and sacrifice." And when I thought of these truths the first book that came to mind was a science fiction, an unlikely candidate perhaps, but *The Keeper of the Isis Light* reverberates in the reader's mind long after she reads the last word because these truths enrich Olwen's story. . . . It is only through human relationships that the universal truths become evident, and before the end, love and honour, pity and pride, compassion and sacrifice have changed Olwen. She realizes that loneliness can be terrible but freedom to be herself needs sacrifice and compassion for Mark whom she loves. Oh, it is a most satisfying human story that introduces children to the enormity of unknown space in a credible human context. Hughes has been characterized as the best children's author writing fiction in Canada today. If this is true it is because Hughes realizes that children need to read the truth about the human condition and still retain the dignity and hope that are their right. (pp. 12-13)

*Irma McDonough, "A Creative National Literature for Children," in* In Review: Canadian Books for Children, *Vol. 16, No. 2, April, 1982, pp. 5-13.**

Although much is right in this book—decent social values, believable characters, a logical plot, smooth writing—there is a curious flatness to the story. S.F. buffs won't care, but newcomers to the genre may be put off by the dense print which is unrelieved, as there is not enough dialogue.

*Leslie Bunk Chamberlin, in a review of "The Keeper of the Isis Light," in* School Library Journal, *Vol. 28, No. 8, April, 1982, p. 70.*

The author delivers a double punch when readers realize before Olwen that the arrivals must adapt to the girl, as much as to the land. The plot and the exotic Isis through Olwen's eyes rivet, but the novel falters through anti-climaxes, a weak conclusion, and changes of perspective. A science fiction treatment of prejudice and loneliness. (p. 488)

*Ruth M. Stein, in a review of "The Keeper of the Isis Light," in* Language Arts, *Vol. 59, No. 5, May, 1982, pp. 487-88.*

What is complex and interesting about *The keeper of the Isis light* is that there are three main themes centering on the protagonist, sixteen-year-old Olwen, the most obvious being the issue of colour prejudice. . . . [The Guardian gave Olwen] enlarged lungs, broader nostrils, and a tough, almost reptilian, radiation-resistant skin of a greenish bronze colour, thus granting her the freedom throughout her childhood of a planet where normal humans must take constant precautions except in certain low-lying areas. . . . Once they see her in all her true glory, of course, neither [Mark] nor the other settlers can accept this bipedal green lizard as of their own kind.

The second theme is Olwen's unwavering self acceptance, even in the face of such rejection, and her indignant refusal of possible medical treatment to restore her to normal human form and to dependence on protective clothing and breathing apparatus over much of the planet's surface. But what is perhaps of most lasting interest is her expanding awareness as to the nature and possibilities of human relationships. For many years she has encountered nothing but the placid, even-keel, entirely reasonable responses of her emotionlessly perfect Guardian. Nevertheless, she has been vaguely aware of something missing. The song of the mountain lark, for instance, "was the most beautiful sound on Isis, and yet, in some strange way Olwen could not understand, the beauty seemed to be full of pain. It left her with a strange, aching emptiness . . . , as if she lacked something terribly important, and did not even know what it was." With the settlers' arrival, of course, she begins to realize what has been missing. "Laughter! Guardian never laughed . . . There was a funny feeling inside her, an empty wrenching sort of ache. It was a bit like the way she felt at the song of the upland lark. She suddenly felt she wanted to cry.". . . And soon enough she does cry. But she is glad of even that experience. So much so that, at the end of the book, when it occurs to her that Guardian will long outlive her and be left alone, and he replies that he does not have the capacity to feel emotion or be lonely, she responds in a whisper, "Poor Guardian." (pp. 40-1)

> *James Harrison, "Toward the Last Frontier," in* Canadian Children's Literature: A Journal of Criticism and Review, *No. 33, 1984, pp. 40-5.**

---

## THE GUARDIAN OF ISIS  (1981)

Monica Hughes' space settlement in *The Guardian of Isis* has reverted to "the Primitive Agricultural Stage", and like Townsend's islanders [in *The Islanders*] has rapidly succumbed to a taboo-ridden religion based on deliberately fostered misconceptions of its history. Indeed many of the same themes—including, rather weakly, the feminist one—reappear. But where Townsend's story grows from his characters, Monica Hughes' actors barely begin to be characters at all. They are as spiritless as their barren environment.

> *Neil Philip, "Choppy Seas of Melodrama," in* The Times Educational Supplement, *No. 3389, June 5, 1981, p. 41.**

It is a long time since I was so impressed by a book about the future. Monica Hughes tells a grand story; she is also a serious anthropologist and philosopher and she knows how the human mind works.

We are in the 22nd century. Long ago—but not so long that the events lie beyond memory—a small party of refugees from a shattered Earth made the long trip to Isis and settled in a deep valley, safe from the rarified atmosphere of the mountains and the powerful radiation of Ra. They came with the support of all the technological benefits of civilization, but within two

generations all these have been abandoned. The President rules with virtually autocratic powers, and he deliberately rejects his inheritance. So the people live at a subsistence level in a society dominated by taboos.

This suits most of the community, but Jody, whose ancestors came from the highlands of East Africa, rebels. He seems all set to recreate the lost technology all by himself, but the President, who hates him and his family for historical reasons, has him banished from the valley. Jody takes the high road in search of That Old Woman, the Ugly One, who is death, only to find that the Ugly One is beautiful and that she and her companion, the Guardian of Isis, represent the forces of life. With their help Jody returns to the tribe, saves them from disaster, and quietly reassumes his humble place among them. There are no heroics, but it is clear that here is a future President and one who will overturn the old order.

All this is told with seriousness and dignity, but also with fun, because Jody, although a genius, is also a nice young boy with his instincts unmarred by the restrictive society in which he lives. Monica Hughes brings before us the strange world of Isis in all its beauty, and integrates setting and action and character in exemplary fashion. Her book is an excellent 'read', a tract on society and a relevant commentary on the history of our own times.

> *M. Crouch, in a review of "The Guardian of Isis,"* in The Junior Bookshelf, *Vol. 45, No. 5, October, 1981, p. 212.*

It is helpful to have read *The Keeper of the Isis Light* in order to understand the plot [of *The Guardian of Isis*], but the story in itself is superior science fiction. Jody is an appealing hero, and the character of Guardian, seemingly unemotional but actually kind and loving, is fascinating. (p. 299)

> *Ann A. Flowers, in a review of "The Guardian of Isis," in* The Horn Book Magazine, *Vol. LVIII, No. 3, June, 1982, pp. 298-99.*

[This sequel] answers the question of what happened to the young heroine of the earlier novel. Unfortunately, returning readers will be disappointed. Olwen Pendennis appears only in the latter half and there is no romance. . . .

The lesson presented to the young adolescent reader is clear. Jody's journey [to the Sacred Cave] brought him knowledge, patience and the willingness to do heroic deeds without reward or acknowledgement. What isn't clear are the reasons for the villagers' complicity in their president's paranoia. They acquiesced "For the Good of Isis" in the elimination of education; the subservient, childbearing role of women; and the changing of history. Again, Hughes has not provided enough character motivation for a completely successful adolescent novel.

> *Muriel Rogow Becker, in a review of "The Guardian of Isis," in* Science Fiction & Fantasy Book Review, *No. 6, July-August, 1982, p. 41.*

Hughes has created a compelling character in Jody N'Kumo. He represents the free spirit of human thought unhampered by cultural restrictions which dares to create new patterns. It is a well-written and finely descriptive narrative which contains several ideas worthy of contemplation by young minds.

> *Jody Risacher, in a review of "The Guardian of Isis," in* School Library Journal, *Vol. 29, No. 6, February, 1983, p. 77.*

*HUNTER IN THE DARK* (1982)

This must have been a difficult book to write: it was a difficult book to read—not from the standpoint of style but of story. It is about 16 year old Mike who "has everything".... And then he finds out that he also has leukemia....

Hughes carefully documents the progressive physical stages of the illness, and just as carefully she lets us see the reactions it evokes—his parents' denial of Mike's condition, his girl friend's fright and unfaithfulness, his friend Doug's straight-forward concern....

And through all the physical changes and the medical treatments and the psychological reactions Mike has to find his way to accepting his fate ("Why *me*?"), to make sense of it. Hughes lets Mike take his head to make a solitary hunting trip to bag his first trophy; in fact it is an allegorical journey to come to terms with his life. He does not have a choice of life or death—he must come to death through life.

Hughes has faced a difficult task with integrity. She knows that the outcome of Mike's disease is inevitable; we all know it. And like history it is immutable and just as hard to deal with. There is a sadness attached that allows for no rejoicing in Mike's rage to live. It is a sobering book but an honest one. And young readers deserve honesty.

> *Irma McDonough, in a review of "Hunter in the Dark," in* In Review: Canadian Books for Children, *Vol. 16, No. 2, April, 1982, p. 50.*

*Hunter in the Dark* won two awards prior to publication and it deserves to win more. The novel offers a convincing and particularly Canadian portrait of a young man dealing with cancer and his own coming of age. Hughes manages to treat intelligently these themes of death and maturation while building a narrative of growing interest....

Monica Hughes, previously known for her young-adult science-fiction novels, shows in *Hunter in the Dark* considerable mastery of realistic narrative. Her story line jumps back and forth in time, but always builds towards the hunt when Mike must deal with the reality of death. It is to Hughes' credit, too, that Mike's refusal to kill the deer becomes not only a necessary ending to the book, but a satisfying one.

One might quibble with minor technical flaws in the novel—a few out-of-date references, the wooden and improbable doctor, the painfully long time it takes Mike to discover his blood disease is leukemia—but these are not substantial. *Hunter in the Dark* is generally well written and well edited. The book deserves reading both in school and out as perhaps the most important Canadian young-adult novel of the year.

> *Paul Kropp, in a review of "Hunter in the Dark," in* Quill and Quire, *Vol. 48, No. 4, April, 1982, p. 32.*

[Monica Hughes] writes with a gutsy realism that bodes well for the future of intelligent juvenile fiction in this country.... Hughes spares us none of the humiliation, the emotional fumblings of family and friends, the physical disfigurement, the excruciating pain....

But the life-and-death struggle with leukemia is merely a poignant extra dimension to the novel's central story of survival: a vividly realized solo hunting trip in the Alberta foothills.... Taut and suspenseful, the hunting trip brings us right inside Mike's skin: the thrilling heft of his rifle, the salty taste of fear

as he fights dark November nights and the blackness of his own future. The stalking scenes are especially memorable; Hughes is intimate with the landscape she describes and with the simplicity of life in that place....

The techniques of survival, gun mechanics and hunting lore are all worked effortlessly into the narrative. But most compelling is the recurrent picture of Mike patiently stalking his quarry by imitating the hesitant, browsing pace of a deer. This sustained image of the boy's identification with the very thing he seeks to kill gives force to the moment when he stands, finger on the trigger, a magnificent five-point buck in the cross hairs of his sight. At heart the hunt is Mike's insistent search for himself in the lonely elements of the wilderness, unhampered by hospitals or his cushy urban life. What he finds in the dark out there is his answer to the darkness within. (p. 56)

> *Cathleen Hoskins, "Reading for Sleeping-Bag Adventurers," in* Maclean's Magazine, *Vol. 95, No. 26, June 28, 1982, pp. 56-7.\**

The theme of an adolescent finding maturity with the added complication of a probably-fatal disease could have resulted in a maudlin story, but in the hands of Monica Hughes, this is not allowed to happen. She has produced a touching story. Her detailed description of Mike's odyssey in the Swan Hills bush and his struggles against the elements is faultlessly authentic, as is her characterization. Monica Hughes has produced a number of excellent science fiction books for young adults. This book in a different genre is a prize winner ... and rightly so.

> *Barbara Conquest, in a review of "Hunter in the Dark," in* CM: Canadian Materials for Schools and Libraries, *Vol. X, No. 3, 1982, p. 162.*

Hughes' use of descriptive words is especially good in the first half of the book. Unfortunately, the passage of time through Mike's year of treatment is dispensed with too casually. The strength of the book lies in Mike's clearly drawn motivations. The resolution of the hunting trip logically follows from his thoughts and experiences but the author confuses readers with some ambiguous statements about life and death, marring the climax in retrospect.

> *Karen Perry, in a review of "Hunter in the Dark," in* School Library Journal, *Vol. 29, No. 9, May, 1983, p. 82.*

Hughes captures the rejuvenating stillness of the snow covered wilderness through crisp prose and descriptive words with quiet beauty. Told in the third person this title combines adventure and pathos with philosophical questions. A reader would be in error to dismiss the story as only an adventure tale.... The meaning of violence—human and animal, and the exciting life path of experiential memories that determine life's quality are poetically described in this rite of passage tale with many flashbacks of Mike's pre-hunting trip life and the agonies of leukemia's treatments. Probably best savored slowly by the dedicated reader, this novel is a richly rewarding pleasure.

> *Allan Cuseo, in a review of "Hunter in the Dark," in* Voice of Youth Advocates, *Vol. 6, No. 4, October, 1983, p. 203.*

## RING-RISE, RING-SET (1982)

[Monica Hughes] is one of the most formidable minds among those who today write what may be called, very loosely, science fiction. Her science is sound, but her social conscience and her understanding of the human heart make her fiction outstanding.

She has a completely credible situation in *Ring-Rise Ring-Set*. Not too far in the future a cataclysm has produced a thick band of particles which form a ring around the middle of the earth, keeping the sun away from the polar and temperate zones and launching a new ice age. Technological civilization has survived by going underground, where, in a grimly practical society, the women do the chores and the men search for the means to turn back the ice.

Liza is odd-girl-out. She cannot be reconciled to her role, and she is too impatient to wait to achieve the improved status offered by Master Bix, the enlightened leader of the community. She smuggles herself aboard an expedition into the frozen lands and then, after the breakdown of her crazy plans, finds herself adopted into a tribe of Ekoes, nomads who have come to terms with the cold. Here she finds that she has a part to play in society. But the experiments by which the City expects to defeat the ice threaten the ecology of the wild and so the life of the Ekoes. Liza goes back to plead for her new people. The story ends with a big question-mark still lying over the snow and ice, for the problem is real and the remedy elusive. For Liza, at least, there is immediate, if short-term happiness.

Young people will read this for its drama and heart-ache. They will surely see too the relevance of this situation to their own, in which present benefits threaten long-term disaster. Miss Hughes' novel is a powerful weapon in the conservationists' armoury; it is also a moving and deeply absorbing story of human dilemmas and human strength and weakness.

> *M. Crouch, in a review of "Ring-Rise, Ring-Set,"*
> *in* The Junior Bookshelf, *Vol. 46, No. 4, August,*
> *1982, p. 152.*

Monica Hughes uses description sparingly but it is there when it is needed. *Ring-Rise Ring Set* depends on a forceful contrast between an artificial underground world whose inhabitants obey without question the rules of a circumscribed life, and the real, Canadian Arctic, landscape outside, with its physical dangers and emancipating space. . . . The theme of a clash of cultures, one instinctive and the other intellectual, together with the message of responsibility, one for the other, would have been far less memorable without the pictorial quality of the writing, into which the theme is integrated.

> *Margery Fisher, in a review of "Ring-Rise Ring Set,"*
> *in her* Growing Point, *Vol. 21, No. 3, September,*
> *1982, p. 3954.*

I'm irritated by writers who set up their characters as headstrong and thoughtless then make these qualities land their protagonists in trouble. *Ring-Rise* starts poorly and conventionally in this vein. . . . The novel improves as it progresses though it's short on incident and dodges sex. A few older kids might try it, especially fans of Hughes' better *Isis* novels. . . .

> *Steve Bowles, in a review of "Ring-Rise, Ring-Set,"*
> *in* Books for Keeps, *No. 22, September, 1983, p.*
> *12.*

The story is fairly standard up to [Liza's escape from the city], but it blossoms into a very worthwhile and well-told tale when Liza meets the Ekos (Eskimoes), a tribe she has been taught to fear. Relationships are beautifully drawn from here on, and the dilemma of the two cultures is splendidly presented. The book's particular value lies in the questions it asks. (pp. 48-9)

> *Lance Salway, "A Selection of Novels: 'Ring-Rise*
> *Ring-Set',"* in The Signal Review 1: A Selective
> Guide to Children's Books, 1982, *edited by Nancy*
> *Chambers, The Thimble Press, 1983, pp. 48-9.*

---

## THE ISIS PEDLAR (1982)

### AUTHOR'S COMMENTARY

When I wrote *The Keeper of the Isis Light* to explore aloneness and loneliness, I had no idea what the book would become nor that it would give rise to another question: the relationship of the settlers three generations further on towards Olwen and Guardian. The answer was not a happy one, and I finished *The Guardian of Isis* frustrated that my hero (since he was only twelve) was unable to effect the necessary changes. It wasn't until Mike Flynn sprang into my head that I realized that he was the catalyst for change on Isis.

There are dangers in writing sequels—some of these I had run into in *Guardian*—and the biggest challenge was to plot the story without introducing any new parameters into Isis, which had been a closed society since its beginning. I was enormously relieved to find that I *had* mentioned firestones in *Keeper* and that some of them had been bartered "for books and music-tapes" *before* the arrival of the Earth colony and the non-interference embargo. So Mike could logically possess firestones and, given his personality, would do anything to obtain more.

As I approached the final chapters of *The Isis Pedlar* I was not sure how it would end, and I was happy when the love affair between David and Moira fell into place as part of the necessary healing of Isis, both as a parallel and contradiction to that of Olwen and Mark.

I have been challenged frequently about the "humanness" of Guardian, and all I can say is that he grew quite without my volition, learning, I suppose, through his service to Olwen, the meaning of love. I was surprised, but delighted, when he elected to leave Isis with Mike. I have grown very fond of him and, though I have left Isis for good, I do hope that, somewhere in the Galaxy, I may again meet that odd couple, Michael Flynn and the ex-Guardian of Isis.

> *Monica Hughes, "On the Writing of 'The Isis Ped-*
> *lar',"* in Language Arts, *Vol. 61, No. 1, January,*
> *1984, p. 74.*

---

*The Isis Pedlar* is the conclusion of Monica Hughes' *Isis* trilogy. . . . As told in the earlier books, the settlers who came to the planet Isis have sunk back into primitive superstition. The Guardian, a robot, mourns the death of Olwen, first settler and Keeper of the Light. Before she died, she forbade him to help the settlers, for fear of culture-shock. The Guardian placed the planet in quarantine and sent out a signal to space to prevent travellers landing.

The new book opens with an unscrupulous space trader discovering the quarantine regulation, and deciding to exploit the settlers. Soon his conjuring tricks have them mining for fire-stones, lured by a taste of a drug from another planet. But his daughter Moira, left behind in his space-ship, realises his plan and comes to the rescue. She finds two allies, Guardian, and David N'Kumo, nephew of Jody (hero of the previous book). Eventually the pedlar is unmasked. The furious settlers prepare to stone him to death, and Guardian has to intervene. Jody finds the day has come when, as Guardian predicted, he would take up the leadership of the colony. Guardian leaves Isis as the pedlar's new travelling companion; Moira stays behind to marry David. Superstition gives way to sanity.

Monica Hughes has a particular skill in depicting primitive self-sufficient cultures, whether on our planet or an alien world. The resourceful heroes Jody and David are black, descended from Africans on Earth, and this is necessary for the plot because they can better endure the thin atmosphere of upper Isis. But in *The Isis Pedlar,* her interest in ethnic attributes has created a villain, the pedlar, who is Irish in brogue, in blarney, and in his taste for "the wee tot once in a while". The locutions are unmistakeable. His name is Michael Joseph Flynn, "with his fine clothes and his honeyed words, himself descended from the ancient kings of Ireland", and as he says "I'm nothing but a pedlar with a magic pack on me back and planets galore ahead of me." His spaceship is called *The Luck of the Irish,* it's practically falling to bits, and his daughter has to do the running repairs! The character is well-rounded and humorous, and the author *never* suggests that Flynn is a typical Irishman. But the question at least needs to be asked: given that a con-man was necessary to the plot, how automatic was the decision that he should be Irish?

*Jessica Yates, "Space Invaders," in The Times Educational Supplement, No. 3464, November 19, 1982, p. 34.\**

Monica Hughes's most recent novel, *The Isis Pedlar,* completes and unifies a trilogy which is surely the most impressive achievement in young adult literature to appear in a very long time. Moreover, it is a radical departure from her earlier works: to her usual ingredients of heroic adventure, truth of character, and mythic implications, she here adds broad comedy, romantic love, and even self-parody.

Each of the earlier *Isis* books . . . is a completely self-contained novel of high literary merit. When read together with *The Isis Pedlar* (either in sequence or not), they form a full-scale science-fiction epic concerned with the birth, decay, and subsequent rebirth of a culture during a 90-year period. The same themes, but from different perspectives, are studied in each: isolation (both personal and social) and the particularly Canadian notion of adaptation to a hostile environment. A supernatural god and goddess control the destinies of men. And the society eventually produces an Aeneas-like epic hero who saves it from destruction. . . .

[This] novel's farcical opening scene, its continual shifts from comic sequences to serious ones, its preoccupation with the developing romance between Mike's daughter Moira and David, even the anachronistic title, prevent us from taking the grim side too seriously. *The Isis Pedlar,* in other words, is a daring *tour de force:* it is an aesthetically satisfying conclusion to the *Isis* epic in that it reexamines the major themes of the earlier novels and tends to reconcile them; its style and tone introduce joy and lightness into the trilogy for the first time and thus assure us that Isis's future will be brighter than its past.

*Gerald Rubio, in a review of "The Isis Pedlar," in Quill and Quire, Vol. 49, No. 3, March, 1983, p. 67.*

The book maintains its predecessors' pace and style, but its characters are less appealing; Moira is nagging, Mike is more snake than charmer, and David is but a shadow of Jody. The human outcomes—Guardian volunteers to oversee Mike's interplanetary wanderings and enables Moira to settle happily on Isis with David—seem more convenient than inspired. But the political and sociological themes with their engrossing parallels to Earth retain the same authenticity and wisdom which mark the earlier books. The author uses her created world effectively to explore rather than to evade human nature and its dilemmas.

*Nancy C. Hammond, in a review of "The Isis Pedlar," in The Horn Book Magazine, Vol. LIX, No. 5, October, 1983, p. 583.*

The author has maintained the high quality of storytelling with this completion of the "Isis" trilogy. In the preceding novels, . . . readers were introduced to the concept of how a democracy can go awry when history is allowed to be altered by those in power. *The Isis Pedlar* is more optimistic about the planet's future because a brave new generation arises to regain and reacknowledge the truth. The stereotype of Moira's father as a shiftless, conniving, drunken Irishman is the one negative aspect of this story of adventure, heroism and romance which will please either veteran science fiction readers or those waiting for an introduction to the genre.

*Jody Risacher, in a review of "The Isis Pedlar," in School Library Journal, Vol. 30, No. 2, October, 1983, p. 169.*

*The Isis Pedlar* is great fun. Wittily written, pacey and not taking itself at all seriously, it manages to convey the excitement of a genuine space adventure, while liberally spicing the action with humour. I mean, what can you do after a first line like: "'The Luck of the Irish' burst out of hyperspace like a squeezed grape seed." Abundant fused modules, control panels and computerised hyperdrives to keep junior boffins content through the book's all too short one hundred and twenty pages.

*Bill Boyle, in a review of "The Isis Pedlar," in Books for Keeps, No. 24, January, 1984, p. 10.*

In a satisfying conclusion to her trilogy, the author skillfully constructs a situation remarkably familiar to the reader, yet of a disturbingly incongruous nature. The setting is so crisply and vividly described that the reader feels an immediate empathy for these strange surroundings. A remarkable depth of the character portrayal allows for an insightful glimpse into the society's beliefs, taboos, and superstitions. The splendid richness of the language is illustrated by an astute use of precise vocabulary, diverse syntax, and vibrant dialogue.

The impact of power and authority is explored as Mike promises the leader power. However, the realization of the requisite leadership qualities only emerges in a time of peril. Students will easily relate these concepts to their everyday situation. (pp. 73-4)

*Ronald A. Jobe, in a review of "The Isis Pedlar," in Language Arts, Vol. 61, No. 1, January, 1984, pp. 73-4.*

### THE BECKONING LIGHTS   (1982)

Julia and her twin brother Jack are telepathic, an ability that they try to keep secret from others. But when they accompany their geologist father and two of his students on a field trip into the Rockies and encounter an unidentified flying object, their gift of telepathy becomes critical for the survival of a whole planet. Hughes pays attention to the details of her craft as a science-fiction writer. We find out how the space craft looks, how the aliens support themselves in our atmosphere, how their ship is powered. But she never allows these details to overpower her sense of what makes a good book. The logic of plot and character development is carefully worked out and surely presented. Hughes tells a good story well.

> *Mary Ainslie Smith, in a review of "Beckoning Lights," in* Books in Canada, *Vol. 11, No. 10, December, 1982, p. 11.*

### THE TREASURE OF THE LONG SAULT   (1982)

Monica Hughes wrote both *Beckoning Lights* and *Treasure of the Long Sault* in the early 1970s, well before any of the 10 science-fiction and contemporary novels that established her reputation. . . . *Lights* is as timely, multi-dimensional, and satisfying as the very best of her later work: *Treasure,* by contrast, is an unfortunate resurrection: the most one can say for it is that it shows promise. . . .

[*Treasure of the Long Sault*] is a one-dimensional adventure story which lacks depth of characterization, universality, and the other qualities we have come to expect from Monica Hughes. Worse yet, even though set in the past, it is dated rather than historical. Two young brothers search for Indian treasure along a portion of the St. Lawrence riverbed, temporarily drained during construction of the Seaway. Plotting leads to an admittedly exciting final sequence in which one of the boys is rescued by his father moments before the riverbed is reflooded; instead of maturing (as typical in Hughes), however, the boy is merely punished for his misadventure by having to spend his summer holiday in a cast with a broken ankle. Young readers lacking historical perspective will, I suspect, find references to plans for the future completion of Upper Canada Village confusing; they may also wonder why the more sophisticated metal detectors now so readily available were not used to simplify the search.

> *Gerald Rubio, in a review of "Beckoning Lights" and "Treasure of the Long Sault," in* Quill and Quire, *Vol. 49, No. 2, February, 1983, p. 39.*

### MY NAME IS PAULA POPOWICH!   (1983)

One welcome newcomer, *My Name Is Paula Popowich!,* treats the very typical subject of the search for one's personal history. Paula Herman, nearly 12 years old, has never known any family other than her mother. When one day she discovers that her mother has deceived her about her father's early death and that his name is Paul Popowich, she determines to investigate her own past and to find him. Eventually she learns the truth: her father is indeed dead, but only recently, and she has a loving grandmother who is overjoyed to be united at last with her missing grandchild. Having lived all her life as a German Canadian, Paula finds that she is as well a Ukrainian Canadian, and that she has a proud new second heritage to claim. But first she must reconcile her embittered mother to the change. Paula's family problems and divided loyalties will find an echo

in the lives of many sympathetic young readers with tangles of their own to unravel.

> *Joan McGrath, "Young-Adult Fiction: Tough Subjects for Tough Times," in* Quill and Quire, *Vol. 49, No. 11, November, 1983, p. 22.\**

[*My Name is Paula Popowich!*] has a lot going for it. Hughes is, I think, the foremost Canadian writer for children in the 10-to-14 age group, and she has proven in such previous books as *Hunter in the Dark* that she can be as effective in contemporary settings as in the science-fiction stories with which she is more often associated. Her readers should like Paula, the heroine of this recent book, and be sympathetic to the situation she faces. . . .

Hughes is good at setting up the conflicts that create a good story, but somehow the total effect here is disappointing. There is an unevenness and strange imbalance in the episodes. In a long opening sequence Paula tries to bleach her hair in hopes of becoming blonde like her mother. This does explain something about Paula's self-image and about her relationship with her mother, but the event itself has so little relevance to all that follows that it seems awkward and out of place. The amount of space it gets is disproportionate.

By the end of the story, significant events are dealt with too briefly. For instance, Paula's Ukrainian dancing lessons are very important to her, and she has to win major concessions from her mother to be allowed to take them. And she must be extraordinarily good at them. She moves through several classes to catch up with her age group all in one short paragraph, and then the lessons are barely mentioned again. Quibbles, perhaps, but Hughes has set her own high standards and we can't help but hope she will always live up to them.

> *Mary Ainslie Smith, in a review of "My Name Is Paula Popowich!" in* Books in Canada, *Vol. 13, No. 3, March, 1984, p. 28.*

The latest book from the prolific Monica Hughes is a sensitive story of a young girl's search for her family's past. . . .

*Paula Popowich* has an intriguing and original story and also unobtrusively provides background on Edmonton's Ukrainian community. The book portrays the trials of single parenting and Monica Hughes does not suggest there are simple solutions.

> *A review of "My Name Is Paula Popowich!" in* Children's Book News, *Vol. 6, No. 3, March, 1984, p. 4.*

### SPACE TRAP   (1983)

[*Space Trap*] takes readers into deep space and a faraway future. The story does not possess the mythic resonance of her **"Isis"** trilogy, but should appeal to readers younger than Hughes's usual audience. Valerie, older brother Frank, and infant sister Susan are mysteriously whisked across galaxies, captured by an alien civilization that treats them as specimens to be put in the zoo or the scientific laboratory. The author deftly sorts out the difficulties and keeps us absorbed. Hughes's characters are always recognizable, no matter how remote her settings, but there are occasional traps in this cozy closeness, as when Valerie, reacting to her brother's superior put-downs, says: "This is the thirty-second century, after all. Women have some rights." This kind of transplantation of contemporary attitudes and values to future settings is inappropriate and often jarring.

Peter Carver, *"From the Gripping Yarn to the Gaping Yawn,"* in Quill and Quire, *Vol. 49, No. 11, November, 1983, p. 24.\**

Monica Hughes never allows her plots to get out of hand. Her recent science-fiction novel, *Space Trap* . . . , shows her mastery of writing good stories for young people. The story is an exciting one. . . . This is fantasy that works. The logical plot sequences allow for no confusion, while the sound characterization and quick pace make it highly entertaining. (p. 16)

*Mary Ainslie Smith, "Great Escapes," in* Books in Canada, *Vol. 12, No. 10, December, 1983, pp. 13-14, 16-18.\**

The family involved in this Sci-Fi story are just like the family from which the reader probably comes. Dad goes off on field trips, Mum has computer work to do and the three children argue, quarrel and think they are unjustly put upon. So the reader is at home from the start and will have no difficulty in taking in his stride the customary licence with reality that is the stuff of Sci-Fi. . . .

The people-eating forest is a brilliant idea nicely described. I like Mr. Isnek Ansnek who was able to give instructions to enable one of the children to put him together again from the specimen drawers in which he was kept. He has the usual rational charm of all robots called upon to cope with the stupidities of the human mind and the frailties of the human body.

11-12 year-olds should read this with enthusiasm and perhaps go on to one of the other nine of the author's books.

*D. A. Young, in a review of "Space Trap," in* The Junior Bookshelf, *Vol. 47, No. 6, December, 1983, p. 258.*

Monica Hughes is probably the best of Canadian SF writers for young people, and this book shows her continuing virtues as a writer: a clear story-line with some neat twists in it; an inventive but disciplined mind in creating the details of her other worlds; an economic use of dialogue in developing her characters and their relationships. . . .

The author has fun in making the 'popeyes' find Valerie ugly and in documenting Valerie's fury at being treated as a laboratory animal: as usual, Monica Hughes slips in one or two more serious issues for consideration. It looks as if 'escape from kidnaps' are in vogue. This is one of the better crafted ones for young adolescents.

*Mike Hayhoe, in a review of "Space Trap," in* The School Librarian, *Vol. 31, No. 4, December, 1983, p. 378.*

The world envisaged in *Space Trap* derives from nightmare in a chilling combination of fairy-tale magic and technological dangers. . . .

Freudian symbols and Cold War apprehensions join in a tale of two or three centuries ahead. The implications of ab-evolution and the decline of civilisation are plain enough, but none of the abstract points interfere with a strong story-line backed by ingenious mechanistic and descriptive details.

*Margery Fisher, in a review of "Space Trap," in* her Growing Point, *Vol. 22, No. 5, January, 1984, p. 4194.*

## DEVIL ON MY BACK   (1984)

[*Devil on my Back*] offers a prediction about the future of our world after an 'Age of Confusion' early in the 21st century when an underground centre aptly named Arc One is planned to preserve knowledge and the means of life; seeds are stored and cumulated known facts, skills and ideas are duplicated in access packs which chosen students have attached to their shoulders at the age of initiation into manhood. Like many human plans, this far-sighted one is corrupted in time; in particular, hierarchies grow up and slavery begins. The central character, Tomi, has his pack fitted when he is fourteen and passes the tests by which he is confirmed in a superior status. He has an uneasy feeling that he has succeeded mainly because his father, Lord Bentt, is the final head and arbiter of Arc One, and when the boy is caught in a slave revolt and is helped to escape to the outer world his suspicions are confirmed. Or so he thinks. For in fact the situation in Arc One is far more complex than either he or the escaped slaves who help him have ever imagined and the boy's enlightenment comes together with the reader's discovery that the underground community might indeed save the world. This is a most circumstantial tale, its intricate plot and plausible details firmly grounded in a North American landscape. The father-son relationship, crucial to the story, makes it one of the most moving and thoughtful of Monica Hughes's remarkable sequence of speculative tales.

*Margery Fisher, in a review of "Devil on My Back," in her* Growing Point, *Vol. 23, No. 3, September, 1984, p. 4309.*

Monica Hughes writes carefully and scrupulously. She also raises serious moral issues in her novels, here about the nature of wisdom as opposed to factual knowledge; about the consequences of selfishness and generosity; about the choices which affect the nature and purpose of a community. She handles these with tact, but the result is a fairly slow-moving book, and there are times when her characters slip from their personality and become bearers of moral messages. Lord Tomi's travels in the outside world and his learning about love and loyalty in the free community he encounters are handled in detail. Again, the result is a reflective text which some readers may find slow; and the communalism of the free people is rather idealised, with Healhand, Rowan and Swift seeming to be 'White Indians' in their noble goodness. In sum, I found this a worthy book rather than one likely to enthrall readers of Lord Tomi's age—fourteen. It would be well worth having as a 'sleeper' on the shelves for the more reflective reader to discover and think about, but do not expect extensive borrowing. (p. 260)

*Mike Hayhoe, in a review of "Devil on My Back," in* The School Librarian, *Vol. 32, No. 3, September, 1984, pp. 259-60.*

Coherently conceived and tightly plotted, this disciplined novel is fuelled by the essence of good sci-fi—credibility springing from convincing detail and plausible characters. Moral issues are at the core of the conflicts but they never swamp the pace or pulse of an enjoyable and thoughtful story.

*G. Bott, in a review of "Devil on My Back," in* The Junior Bookshelf, *Vol. 48, No. 5, October, 1984, p. 216.*

[Tomi] finds himself in a secret community of escaped slaves (savages, to him) who live off the land, enjoying their freedom and, to Tomi's embarrassment, openly showing their affection for each other. Few readers will be surprised that Tomi becomes a convert to the simple, healthful way of life; they may, however, be surprised at the twist at the end of the story, both in Tomi's course of action and in its effects. Hughes convincingly creates the society and mores; she develops changes smoothly, and she creates characters that are believable although few are drawn with depth. (p. 149)

*Zena Sutherland, in a review of "Devil on My Back,"* in Bulletin of the Center for Children's Books, *Vol. 38, No. 8, April, 1985, pp. 148-49.*

The combination of a survival story and a futuristic society certainly provides the material for a compelling story if it is executed with a certain skill, and [Hughes] uses these elements to craft a thoroughly readable and enjoyable work of fiction . . . . Although the Lord's decision to return to his community does not seem as motivated by character and situation as it should be, the narrative throughout flows smoothly, and the story builds from scene to scene. The implication of the dénouement—that the young must seek to change their world rather than escape from it—gives the story the kind of philosophical underpinning that characterizes the best of science fiction. (pp. 317-18)

*Anita Silvey, in a review of "Devil on My Back,"* in The Horn Book Magazine, *Vol. LXI, No. 3, May-June, 1985, pp. 317-18.*

Hughes creates a convincing future world in this science fiction adventure. . . . Although the writing is smooth and skillful, Hughes has too little space to develop the themes and issues she raises, let alone to portray convincingly the relationships between characters. As the story progresses, the pace speeds up and even more is left unexamined. Still, Hughes raises some intriguing questions about the uses and the future of technology while providing a flawed but entertaining tale. (pp. 1400-01)

*Carolyn Phelan, in a review of "Devil on My Back,"* in Booklist, *Vol. 81, No. 19, June 1, 1985, pp. 1400-01.*

# James (Jacob Hinrich) Krüss

## 1926-

(Has also written under pseudonym of Markus Polder) German author and author/illustrator of fiction, author of nonfiction, poet, dramatist, scriptwriter, and editor.

One of Germany's most popular children's writers, Krüss is internationally known for creating whimsical stories and poems that promote global peace and encourage appreciation for language. The author of more than seventy books in German, he is also recognized for introducing fantasy to postwar German children's literature. Krüss's works are characterized by their inclusion of sophisticated ideas and strong values, colloquial writing style, and obvious affection for children and childhood. His love of language and respect for literary craftsmanship—an enthusiasm he communicates to his preschool through junior-high audience—is common to all of Krüss's juvenile literature.

Krüss often structures his works by weaving fantasy and poetry into realistic narratives. In *My Great-Grandfather and I,* which recreates a week of Krüss's boyhood, he constructs a story about an eleven-year-old boy who is sent to stay with his great-grandparents. Rudi and Great-grandfather challenge each other to invent fantastic stories and rhymes; Krüss reveals their close family and community life while presenting a collection of diverting tales and poems which introduce young readers to the history of language and the joys of creative writing. *My Great-Grandfather and I* is perhaps Krüss's most highly regarded work. In *Letters to Pauline,* the only book in English translation that Krüss both wrote and illustrated, he employs the epistolary form to portray a fictional correspondence with a little girl in Germany, to whom he sends eight tales which combine nonsense, fantasy, and legend. Fantasies such as *Eagle and Dove,* which describes how the dove escapes with its life by reciting fables to the eagle, and *The Lighthouse on the Lobster Cliffs,* twenty-two stories centering on friendship, also reflect Krüss's fascination with storytelling.

Throughout his career, Krüss has endeavored to articulate the values that he feels help to build peace—respect for the individual, compassion, cooperation, and love of freedom. *My Great-Grandfather, the Heroes and I* and *Coming Home from the War: An Idyll* underscore Krüss's hatred of war. In *My Great-Grandfather, the Heroes and I,* a sequel to *My Great-Grandfather and I,* the great-grandfather expresses Krüss's definition of heroism: true heroism, he says, comes from being faithful to yourself, not to war's false heroics. Perhaps Krüss's most vivid descriptions of his commitment to a united world are the joyful fantasies *The Happy Islands behind the Winds* and *Return to the Happy Islands,* in which he creates a utopian society run democratically by plants and animals.

Krüss was born and raised on Helgoland, a German island in the North Sea, later the setting of *My Great-Grandfather and I* and *My Great-Grandfather, the Heroes and I.* He refers to his brief military experience in *Coming Home from the War,* a memoir that relates his adventures as an eighteen-year-old air force cadet suddenly released in Bohemia at the end of World War II and left to find his way back to Helgoland. Trained as a teacher, Krüss taught briefly in Helgoland. After

serving as the editor of a small newspaper in Hamburg, he moved to Munich in 1950 to teach and write. Short of funds, Krüss took some of the children's poems he had devised for his own pleasure to a radio station and a newspaper and was astonished to have them both broadcast and printed. Following this unexpected debut into children's literature, he composed radio and stage plays for children, both by himself and in collaboration with German author Erich Kästner, to whom Krüss is often compared. Krüss also produced his own children's television program. His poetry, which was printed regularly in newspapers, was later compiled into a collection, *Die kleinen Pferde heissen Fohlen.* Fluent in German, Dutch, English, Serbo-Croatian, Spanish, and his mother tongue, Frisian, Krüss has also published adult works on linguistics.

Critics hail Krüss for his originality and lively facility with language. As a stylist, he is usually considered a distinguished craftsman who writes complex yet accessible works, including tales which are praised for their charm and skillful structure. Most reviewers recognize Krüss as an author who balances the seriousness of his themes with imagination and optimism.

Krüss received the Deutscher Jugendbuchpreis in 1960 for *My Great-Grandfather and I* and in 1964 for *Three by Three.* He won the Hans Christian Andersen Medal in 1968 for his body of work.

(See also *Something about the Author*, **Vol. 8**; *Contemporary Authors New Revision Series*, **Vol. 5**; and *Contemporary Authors*, **Vols. 53-56.**)

## AUTHOR'S COMMENTARY

The great honor, to receive from you the Hans Christian Andersen Award, gives me a happiness that is not less great. And I hope that my happiness is also yours.

That I, who write for the children of different countries and different beliefs and opinions, receive the medal in a country which unifies different nationalities and different beliefs within its borders is as pleasant as it is fitting. It is pleasant because it *is* fitting and fitting, because in the geography of literature this special kind of literature is a sort of Switzerland. In this small territory which is dedicated to peace, where the eye may be open to all things, a hand is never placed upon the sword.

I have the honor also to thank you on behalf of my two co-recipients [José Maria Sanchez-Silva and Jiri Trnka], because with the countries of these two peoples I am personally involved. With the country of José Maria Sanchez-Silva, the Spaniard, in whose farthest province (the Canary Islands) I live, I have a passionate relationship, which is not without complications, but is very deep. With the Czechs and Slovaks I am united by means of the *Golden May*—or *Zlaty Maj*. This is a monthly magazine of criticism of children's literature in which I first proved myself as a writer on this literature.

What unites me with these three countries—with Switzerland, Spain, and Czechoslovakia—are bonds of sympathy, and I believe that in addition to peace, sympathy is necessary to the growth of children's literature.

Sympathy may sound to you a naive word, but I thought about it a great deal. Sympathy stands for flexibility as versus rigidity, a flowing river as against a dam. For me it means standing in front of the cannon to shout: listen, brother, instead of shoot.

Now the writer of books that children read cannot say to a public that is only thinking on the future, "Out with the old men!" for in order to become grown, the children need the help of grownups. So the grown-ups, who bring up children without the use of the stick, metaphorically or otherwise (for example, the writers of so-called children's books), have a duty to explain the beginnings of things—those that are good and those that are bad. But to children, who think in pictures, you cannot explain it theoretically; it has to be done by means of fables, films, legends, stories, and poems.

Jiri Trnka does this with his pictures of genius, as Sanchez-Silva does with his beautiful sad legends. As I myself try to do. And as Sergei Mikhalkov does in his poems, one of which I would like to read.

> Zenya is ten years old today.
> Therefore, to celebrate it,
> They have given him a present
> Of cannons, pistols, guns and tanks,
> Shining, glittering black weapons
> All of them automated.

> "Now," say the grown-ups to each other,
> "He can play at soldiers."
> But while they eat the birthday cake
> And drink the tea to the last drop
> Zenya, lying on the floor,
> Destroys the expensive armory.
> "Alas, what have you done?" they ask.
> "I have done," he says, "what *you* promised to do,
> In conference after conference.
> I have disarmed!"

Let us hope, ladies and gentlemen, that the words of this poet, who is also a member of parliament, will be read by the children of the Soviet Union with very great attention, for children inevitably grow up, and out of the kindergarten rises the new generation. And what this new generation does in the future depends in some sense on those stories that have been told to them in childhood.

If these stories are the right stories, we can perhaps hope that the ancient and noble people of Spain will further live in peace like Switzerland, that my own people will absorb something of the modesty and unpretentiousness of Switzerland, and that for the people of Czechoslovakia the "Golden May" will grow forever. And may there always be for all the people of the world a "Golden May." (pp. 188-89)

> James Krüss, *"The Right Stories,"* in Top of the News, *Vol. 25, No. 2, January, 1969, pp. 188-89.*

## GENERAL COMMENTARY

### BETTINA HÜRLIMANN

*[The following excerpt was originally published in German in 1959.]*

[An] author, who has given a broader foundation to the possibilities of nonsense and unreality, is James Krüss, one of the most prolific of current German authors and one who, by his penchant for the fantastic and his witty conversation-pieces between children, makes considerable demands on his readers. The books of his which have brought a new and original voice to German children's books, cleaving a wide breach in its all too realistic world, are: *Der Leuchtturm auf den Hummer-Klippen* [*The Lighthouse on the Lobster Cliffs*]. . . , *Die glücklichen Inseln hinter dem Winde* [*The Happy Islands behind the Winds*], and *Mein Urgrossvater und ich* [*My Great-Grandfather and I*]. . . . James Krüss is no children's author who, as it were, puts on a special literary hat when he talks to children. He talks his own language, often saying things which they cannot understand at once. He asks questions, he plays with words, and he lets children play with words until they understand what the craft of words actually is. What is more, he gets sea-gulls and clouds to make up poems and in *Mein Urgrossvater und ich* he even gets the old great-grandfather doing it as he teaches his great-grandson to use his native language properly. Towards the end of *Der Leuchtturm* there occurs the beautiful sentence: 'Jetzt brauchen wir nach einer Geschichte nicht mehr zu fragen, ob sie wahr ist, denn jetzt wissen wir, dass schöne Geschichten zugleich wahre Geschichten sind.' ('Now we need no longer ask if a story is true, for now we know that if a story is beautiful it must at the same time be true.') This is a revelation which is new in German children's books.

James Krüss has also set about writing some poems, which were finally collected in a book for young children: *Die kleinen*

*Pferde heissen Pfohlen*. . . . But in spite of the wealth of ideas and images in these poems, Krüss seems to me to be more convincing when he gets the sea-gulls and the clouds to make up his poetry for him.

In his last book, *Timm Thaler* . . . , he reaches back to a theme which is now a classic in imaginative writing—the theme of a child who sells, not in this case his shadow, but his laughter. This profoundly sad and disturbing book reveals a fresh aspect of its author. He has suddenly become very serious and very adult before the eyes of his young readers of yesterday. It is much to be hoped, however, that from time to time he will return to the country of eternal childhood, so welcome has his bold attempt been to bring fantasy into these otherwise all too realistic children's books. (p. 85)

> *Bettina Hürlimann, "Fantasy and Reality," in her* Three Centuries of Children's Books in Europe, *edited and translated by Brian W. Alderson, The World Publishing Company, 1967, pp. 76-92.\**

## MARGERY FISHER

Florentine is the creation of an original writer and one who has no intention of submitting to any rules for what children like or don't like; these two stories [*Florentine* and *Florentine on holiday*], with their fascinating coloured embellishments, are a gorgeous mixture of mischief and nostalgia. Florentine herself is an engaging shrimp of a child whose bright ideas are never in the least appropriate for real life; but somehow, her campaigns to save the city pigeons and to bring light to the life of good-natured Rosa at Tafernwise meet with astonishing success; and in the end the child's negligent parents come to see that she merits better care and attention (not that Florentine will be altered by this, we feel sure). These are richly personal, comic and delightful stories which belong to no particular age.

> *Margery Fisher, in a review of "Florentine" and "Florentine on Holiday," in her* Growing Point, *Vol. 6, No. 1, May, 1967, p. 922.*

## THE JUNIOR BOOKSHELF

[The publication of *Florentine* and *Florentine on Holiday*] is the first English appearance of a celebrated German heroine. James Kruss is a most versatile writer, highly original even if at times he reminds the reader of the creator of *Emil*. Like Kastner, he has a most happy gift for colloquial writing; he talks to the reader man to man.

These two stories of the outrageous Florentine are charming and funny and touched with humanity. Florentine is not splendidly anti-social as, say, Pippi Longstocking. When she takes away the ladder so that Mr. Smeed-Henning descends even more quickly than he intended, we know that it comes from the best of intentions, not from malice.

Physically these two books look like little children's picture-books. In fact they appeal to children a year or so older, and one feels that the format is wrong and so is the episodic treatment. So amusing and complex a heroine deserves space in which to grow; she needs a novel to herself.

> *A review of "Florentine" and "Florentine on Holiday," in* The Junior Bookshelf, *Vol. 31, No. 3, June, 1967, p. 165.*

## ELINOR S. CULLEN

[Krüss's *The Blue Bus; Busy Busy Bettina; Henriette Bimmelbahn; The Jolly Trolley Ride; Ladislaus and Annabella; Rudy Biplane, the Golden Eagle; Seven Frogs Go Traveling;* Wilhelm Reinke's *Ululu, the Midnight Cat;* and Christel Sussman's *Farmer Jensen's Little Horse* and *Michael, the Little Man*] are the first 10 in a series intended to serve as picture books for pre-schoolers and as easy readers on which primary-graders can practice their skills. The bright colors of the full-page . . . illustrations are the books' drawing point. . . . In most cases the texts, all translated from German, seem more complicated than what they have to tell, too difficult and with print too small for first-graders to be able to read comfortably, not interesting enough for older children to want to read.

The best of the group is the series' title offering, *Henriette Bimmelbahn.* This is a pleasant story about a train who, unlike other animated transports of the diligent but plodding Little-Engine-that-Could variety, shuns conformity to jump track and enjoy the freedom she finds. *Rudy Biplane, the Golden Eagle* has less personality than Henriette, although he is a kindred spirit: he decides to keep flying by himself after his pilot retires. *The Blue Bus,* although pictured with a human face, does nothing more out of the way than be trailed by a poodle. *Ladislaus and Annabella* are also animated inanimates, typical of the last-toys-in-the-toy-store-on-Christmas-Eve genre. This cliched story [illustrated by Beatrice Braun-Fock] is also the most poorly illustrated.

Several of the stories feature animals. The most imaginative, *Seven Frogs Go Traveling,* is about a group of frogs who went in search of greener lily pads until they reached what they thought was Egypt but turned out to be their original pond. . . . One of the most complete stories is *Busy Busy Bettina,* in which a girl visiting the zoo inventively soothes the savage bull with sunglasses. As a group, these books provide quantity and variety rather than quality. They are adequate for introductory browsing but offer little promise as stimulus to a sustained interest in reading. (pp. 72-3)

> *Elinor S. Cullen, in a review of "The Blue Bus," & others, in* School Library Journal, *an appendix to* Library Journal, *Vol. 14, No. 9, May, 1968, pp. 72-3.*

---

## DER LEUCHTTURM AUF DEN HUMMER-KLIPPEN [*THE LIGHTHOUSE ON THE LOBSTER CLIFFS*]   (1956)

The lighthouse keeper Johann lives alone and spends most of his time fishing. The seagull Alexandra visits him often and they tell one another stories. Gradually they are joined by Markus Marre, by Aunt Julie, by the Poltergeist Hans and several others. Into the story of storms and daily life are woven other stories of a folk tale or fantastic flavour and the whole makes an entertaining and unusual book, easy to read, yet not unduly juvenile in subject. (pp. 283-84)

> *A review of "Der Leuchtturm auf den Hummerklippen," in* The Junior Bookshelf, *Vol. 24, No. 5, November, 1960, pp. 283-84.*

While lighthouse-keeper Johann and gregarious seagull Alexandra wait, and elderly, bombed-out-of-Helgoland Aunt Julie and South Seas poltergeist Jack-in-the-Net approach in a rowboat, and first Markus Marre, the merman, later an educated Cumulus cloud threaten to swamp it, they exchange stories and story-poems to entertain or detain one another, continuing (with the addition of other storytellers) during a storm on the island and a voyage to Dalmatia. The elaborate *mise en scene* is, however, rendered largely meaningless since the stories are told in a single voice. Moreover, with few exceptions they are didactic fancies of little dimension connected by self-conscious conversations assessing their value. In space and time this falls between Helgoland-based *My Great-Grandfather and I* and *The Happy Islands,* where they eventually fetch up; in inventiveness and charm it doesn't approach either one.

> *A review of "The Lighthouse on the Lobster Cliffs,"* in Kirkus Reviews, *Vol. XXXVII, No. 21, November 1, 1969, p. 1148.*

A collection of 22 uneven stories by the Andersen Award-winning Mr. Krüss. The narratives include such items as a turtle who knits custom-made outfits, the Peepsenburger Mouse Carnival, and a boy who tries to catch a star and succeeds in setting a house on fire. The narrators, an odd assortment of characters such as a poltergeist called Jack-in-the-net, a lighthouse keeper, and a friendly Negro, are involved in a confusing subplot of their own. While many of the stories are cleverly written and smoothly translated, their appeal to American children may be severely limited. The individual tales range from enjoyable to contrived and downright silly, and the cumulative effect is one of self-consciousness. (pp. 121-22)

> *Katherine Heylman, in a review of "The Lighthouse on the Lobster Cliffs,"* in School Library Journal, *an appendix to* Library Journal, *Vol. 16, No. 8, April, 1970, pp. 121-22.*

### DIE GLÜCKLICHEN INSELN HINTER DEM WINDE [*THE HAPPY ISLANDS BEHIND THE WINDS*] (1959)

The Happy Islands were discovered somewhere in the Mediterranean when a smallish freighter accidentally came upon them. These islands are ruled by the plants and animals because men have had such bad experiences ruling other parts of the world. Everybody takes turns ruling because not everybody is good and wise at the same time, and "Happy Day" is the universal greeting.

The Captain and his crew and passengers are given a Cook's Tour of the islands—to Polipopaya, the main island, Mellifera, a blossoming honey island where they learn to have patience with wisdom; Paxos, the Island of Peace where they learn that evil cannot succeed if nobody eats anybody; Jou Jou, the Island of Play; and finally to Torronostro, the island of Towers where they meet the amazing Dr. Cato, a cat who has harnessed the power of sunlight for the benefit of everybody. The Captain says in closing his story: "But even if we will never have such happiness in this world, we can travel with a vision of it. We must know what happiness is before we try to find it."

The bright adventures on the islands, then, come with some strong adult propaganda for peace and wisdom and understanding—highly sophisticated ideas to put before a child, but handled with imagination and intelligence and without preaching. (pp. 14, 16)

> *Elinore Standard, "The Light Fantastic," in* Book Week—World Journal Tribune, *October 30, 1966, pp. 14, 16.\**

This is a well-sustained fantasy, beautifully told with imagination, originality, and an amazing variety of incidents. Highly recommended for reading aloud in families and classrooms.

> *Anne Izard, in a review of "The Happy Islands behind the Winds," in* Library Journal, *Vol. 91, No. 20, November 15, 1966, p. 5750.*

There are flashes of humor in Mr. Krüss's narrative style—the island's interspecies music includes "Divertimento for Mixed Chicken Coop," and there is a Bavarian who slakes his passion for the chase by letting a squirrel chase him. But the book is mostly an explanation of the rotation of duties, of the solar-power economy and of the magical dissipation of hate and the predatory urge.

The idea of giving children a story of a harmonious society began before Swift made his voyage to the Houyhnhnms. It will continue long after the Beatles' Yellow Submarine has gurgled away. But the society needs to be more than charming—which the Happy Islands surely are—to convince children that peace would not be an utter bore.

> *Betsy Wade, in a review of "The Happy Islands behind the Winds," in* The New York Times Book Review, *January 29, 1967, p. 34.*

### MEIN URGROSSVATER UND ICH [*MY GREAT-GRANDFATHER AND I: USEFUL AND AMUSING OCCURRENCES AND INSPIRATIONS FROM THE LOBSTER SHACK ON HELGOLAND TOLD TO THE "LEATHERY LISBETH" AND EMBELLISHED WITH VERSES FROM MY GREAT-GRANDFATHER AND ME, CAREFULLY PUT ON PAPER FOR CHILDREN OF ALL AGES*] (1960)

Great-Grandfather is a retired lobster fisherman in Heligoland who has a penchant for reeling off stories and poems. His 11-year-old great-grandson is sent to stay with him for a week

LETTERS TO PAULINE

*From* Letters to Pauline, *written and illustrated by James Krüss. Translated by Edelgard von Heydekampf Brühl. Atheneum, 1971. English translation copyright © 1971 by Atheneum Publishers. Reprinted with the permission of Atheneum Publishers.*

while the boy's sisters recover from the measles. The two agree to spend the week composing poems and Great-Grandfather suggests that all their poems be about words. The boy fears this will be dull, as may the readers, but the pair manages to come up with some amazingly involved ABC rhymes. In between poems Great-Grandfather tells some delightful tales all of which prove, in one way or another, the importance of words. The book has very little plot, but it does include a very witty and imaginative collection of poems and stories, which will please anyone who enjoys word games. The pen and ink drawings [by Jochen Bartsch] are as lively and good-humored as the text. (pp. 592-93)

> *A review of "My Great-Grandfather and I," in* Virginia Kirkus' Service, *Vol. XXXII, No. 13, July 1, 1964, pp. 592-93.*

The setting on a tiny island is unusual, the customs of a seafaring people add interest, and the characters are priceless. As the grandfather tells stories and he and the boy write their own verses and read them to each other, their comments bring out in the most natural way many of the elements of good style and vocabulary and even how language has evolved through the ages. The whole book is written in a light and humorous vein. Teachers might well use this in classes in language arts. (pp. 120-21)

> *May H. Edmonds, in a review of "My Great-Grandfather and I," in* School Library Journal, *an appendix to* Library Journal, *Vol. 11, No. 1, September, 1964, pp. 120-21.*

[For] seven days the boy and the old man spend blissful hours—interrupted only by the grandmothers' hearty Germanic meals—spinning fantastic tales, making nonsense rhymes, exploring the wonders of language, and indulging in verbal gymnastics. Humor, wisdom, uninhibited family relationships, and above all, joyous fun with words sparkle through the pages of an utterly original, creative book—a book to be read, reread, and shared. (pp. 610-11)

> *Ethel L. Heins, in a review of "My Great-Grandfather and I," in* The Horn Book Magazine, *Vol. XL, No. 6, December, 1964, pp. 610-11.*

"Enchanting" is an expression that occurs in the course of this story, and dangerous though it is to suggest it, there seems scarcely any other single word to express its effect. It does not help much to relate that the work consists of stories told by a great-grandfather to an appreciative small grandson of ten as well as the poems—they are more than mere rhymes—which both compose in competition, mostly on handy pieces of wood. This is the contribution of High-Great-grandfather, who lives above the town, with occasional surprises from High-Grandmother, for all her sniffing at this useless activity in what she terms the "Sodom and Gomorrah" of the old man's workshop. Even Low-grandfather, who lives near the harbour, is discovered to have practised the prevailing vice in verses of propitiation to Low-grandmother. None of this indicates the splendid variety, versatility and originality of the stories which Great-grandfather feels a compulsion to tell at the drop of a hat. And the stories are not all, for they are dominating incidents in the picture of family life and local activity on Heligoland.... The basic situation never seems a mechanical device and no-one may quarrel with the publisher's claim that High-grandfather is "the wise and lively relative that all of us wish we had." It is no surprise to hear that the book was awarded the 1960

Jugendbuchpreis in Germany. One is only surprised that it has not received international recognition.

> *A review of "My Great-Grandfather and I," in* The Junior Bookshelf, *Vol. 28, No. 6, December, 1964, p. 382.*

[Since] the author is re-creating a week of his own boyhood, he brings to life the island people, their customs and their cuisine as a natural, integral part of the story. It is the perfect book to read aloud in family groups for the humor of the conversations begs to be shared. Once adults and children discover together the fun of these rhyming games, they will want to try composing some for themselves.

> *Anne Izard, in a review of "My Great-Grandfather and I," in* The New York Times Book Review, *December 20, 1964, p. 12.*

The story is simplicity itself....

Poems and tales range widely in scene from Rudi's native Heligoland to the China seas and the kingdom of Nowhere. Their moods encompass humour and romance. But this is not a medley of stories strung on a thin narrative thread: its unity derives from Rudi's introduction to the riches of language and the delights of writing. Great-grandfather is a charming mentor on literary matters—how to begin a story, the difficulties of translation, the value of poetry, and many others....

[This book] should appeal to children responsive to words and their magic.

> *Robin Brumby, in a review of "My Great Grandfather and I," in* The School Librarian and School Library Review, *Vol. 13, No. 1, March, 1965, p. 101.*

---

**DIE GLÜCKLICHEN INSELN HINTER DEM WINDE BD. 2 [RETURN TO THE HAPPY ISLANDS] (1960)**

Telling of his remarkable adventures on *The Happy Islands Behind the Winds* . . . , Captain Daworin Madirankowitsch hinted at a return, here accomplished. The trouble is that there are no guidelines for the reader who wasn't along on the first trip, and few ground rules for the fantasy that follows. On each of six successive days, the Captain and passengers visit a different island. . . . It's inventive, it's ingenious, it's sometimes clever (and sometimes coy), but it's mostly disconnected conjuring and it becomes tiresome. Where the first book established the Happy Islands as a sophisticated utopia and had something to say about the essence of happiness, this is largely wish-fulfillment on the confectionery and flying saucer level with occasional sorties into cultural esoterica.

> *A review of "Return to the Happy Islands," in* Kirkus Service, *Vol. XXXV, No. 15, August 1, 1967, p. 878.*

A second voyage to the Happy Islands leads the captain and his crew to fresh discoveries. Musical instruments growing on plants, authors and their characters living together, glaciers of sugar, and a raisin-cake valley are all from the same rich imagination that conceived *Happy Islands Behind the Winds*. This book is in the same mood and format, is equally good for read-aloud, and can stand alone without the first.

> *Anne Izard, in a review of "Return to the Happy Islands," in* School Library Journal, *an appendix to* Library Journal, *Vol. 14, No. 2, October, 1967, p. 175.*

Anyone who accompanied Captain Dado last year when he discovered the **"Happy Islands Behind the Winds"** (or anyone who didn't, for that matter) will want to make this return trip with the entertaining captain. There are firm requisites for enjoying the Happy Islands. You must have a talent for happiness, you must know that happiness is what you have, and that enemies are only undiscovered friends. And you do not hurt nor destroy. These nuggets of wisdom and rightness that glint between the lines do not make this story didactic. It is as fresh and gay and downright funny as flying saucers and sugar bowls, a raisin-cake mountain, towers built by music, and a hundred other wonders can make it. . . . This book belongs on everybody's shelf.

> *Silence Buck Bellows, "A Leprechaun Named O'Toole," in* The Christian Science Monitor, *November 2, 1967, p. B6.\**

---

## TIMM THALER (1962)

Children's writers increasingly insist—no doubt while smiling up their sleeves—that their stories take place on "the most ordinary street," "in a most ordinary house, where a most ordinary family lives" and that this family consists of "a most ordinary father, a most ordinary mother and three most ordinary children . . ." Then begin "the most ordinary miracles," believable even to today's child, who has long had it drummed into him that miracles don't happen. It is the very "ordinariness" of the story that helps him believe in them.

Can we therefore assume that the tale is coming closer to "real life," and if so, how and to what extent? But the main question is, however, whether the miraculous at the core of the tale remains unscathed. And indeed it does. During a ghost game, Astrid Lindgren's Karlsson suddenly loses his ghost costume and, stripped bare and exposed, turns out to be "just the most ordinary Karlsson-on-the-Roof who flies all by himself." . . . [It] turns out that Karlsson is just "an ordinary, fat school boy" who possesses something that "every child could have—a little motor which enables him to fly." So the miracle is exposed, stripped to its mechanical essentials—in what is surely a parody on the explanation of miracles.

And all this kaleidoscopic interplay of facets is surely one of the most integral features of the modern children's tale. This game has a fine literary pedigree—Hans Christian Andersen and Evgeni Shvarts, to name only two, played it. As the fantastic image takes on new facets, becomes more resonant, the game complicates. The man in the checked suit in James Krüss' **Timm Thaler** becomes Baron Lived (Devil, when read from the back; Teufel—Lefuet in the original), the owner of an international concern and later president of the world's largest joint-stock company, the "margarine king." But occasionally we catch glimpses of something grotesque in him, of something supernatural—a parody on the power of the capitalist monopoly. And this omnipotent, diabolical managing director also has many features which are highly reminiscent of the devil in the traditional German "Kasperle" puppet theatre; by the end of the story the likeness is undeniable. Like Koshei the Deathless of the Russian legend, he is vulnerable; the chink in his armour is difficult, but not impossible, to find. His omnipotence is breached by his bewilderment in the face of humankind's unselfish urges—and in this lies his weakness. And so it becomes possible to trick the "poor devil" in spite of all his cunning. Outwitting the devil is surely in complete harmony with the folktale tradition as followed by Pushkin among oth-

ers. We would be hard pressed to list all the guises in which the devil has appeared in literature down through the ages; why should he not become a "margarine king" in the twentieth century, all the more so since Lived's obsession with margarine—an ersatz kind of food at best—is tremendously amusing to the child in its pettiness. The kaleidoscopic intermingling of the various levels of imagery leaves the miracle, when all is said and done, unharmed, "unexposed." This is still a tale, because it still contains a fantastic image, but it has not slipped into the sphere of allegory which always leaves a safety margin between the fantastic image and the abstract concept it shields. It has been claimed that the "triumph of friendship" in the tale of "laughter for sale" practically heralds the death of the tale as we know it. But the allegedly realistic characters of this modern fantastic story (Timm's friends—Johnny the steersman, Mr. Rickert and Kreshimir) are no less conventional and fantastic (in the deliberate "puppet-like" outlines of their appearance and behaviour) than the images of friendship in the Russian folk tale—the mouse who is fed by the young heroine, the apple tree she shakes, etc. And these puppet-like characters, or the forces of good, if you will, are on Timm's side not because they owe him anything, but merely because they want to be . . . (pp. 26-7)

> *Alexandra Issayeva, "The Contemporary Childrens Tale: Images and Intent," translated by Liv Tadge, in* Bookbird, *No. 3 (September 15, 1984), pp. 18-32.\**

---

## DREI MAL DREI: AN EINEM TAG [3 X 3: A PICTURE BOOK FOR ALL CHILDREN WHO CAN COUNT TO THREE] (1963)

It makes a nice change from the "two by two" stories and the repetition of the word three in the verse makes for the quiet amusement of certainty. Altogether, it is a good book to use in settling the smallest children down just before they go to sleep. A clever rhyme that is not overlong and never seems to strain for effect follows the active day of three hunters with three dogs, three cats, three mice, three hens, and three foxes. . . . Well done. Buy three?

> *A review of "Three by Three," in* Virginia Kirkus' *Service, Vol. XXXIII, No. 12, June 15, 1965, p. 571.*

**Three by Three** belongs to a different tradition [than Paul Galdone's *Tom, Tom, the Piper's Son*] and one which is less familiar, for all that its ancestor is our old friend Struwwelpeter. Like other German, as distinct from Swiss and Austrian, books, this is very formal, carefully thought out and admirably drawn, but wanting a little of the sparkle which we look for as an indispensable ingredient of the best picture books for children. **Three by Three** is well worth having in an English edition, but I doubt whether many English children will take it . . . to their hearts.

> *A review of "Three by Three," in* The Junior Bookshelf, *Vol. 29, No. 4, August, 1965, p. 209.*

Hens, foxes, dogs, mice and huntsmen in a symmetrical pattern of pursuit from sun-up to sundown, shown in richly-coloured, heraldically-designed pictures [by Eva Johanna Rubin], governed by a sense of joyous absurdity. The verse that accompanies the pictures is nicely calculated to follow a child's sequence of thought as well as to help counting.

> *Margery Fisher, in a review of "Three by Three," in her* Growing Point, *Vol. 4, No. 6, December, 1965, p. 629.*

A pleasing look-and-listen counting book for the youngest, *3 X 3 Three by Three* by James Krüss, recounts a simple tale in three-line verses. Merriment abounds. . . .

There is ease in the way this book uses language to assist in the development of a single number concept. . . . (p. 75)

> *Constantine Georgiou, "Picture Books and Picture Storybooks," in his* Children and Their Literature, *Prentice-Hall, Inc., 1969, pp. 61-106.\**

For sheer exuberance, it is difficult to imagine anything to excel *Three by Three*. . . . Not strictly a 1-2-3 theme, it develops the concept of three in vivid theatrical pictures that heighten a smart tempo that almost fans the pages. . . . Everyone gets involved in a cumulative chase, but in the end the mice escape the cats, the hens evade the foxes, and the fox hunters go home emptyhanded, leaving the reader happily out of breath. (p. 96)

> *Della Thomas, "Count-Down on the 1-2-3's," in* School Library Journal, *an appendix to* Library Journal, *Vol. 17, No. 7, March, 1971, pp. 95-102.\**

---

## ADLER UND TAUBE [EAGLE AND DOVE] (1963)

As he did in *My Great-Grandfather and I* . . . , the author provides skillfully crafted examples of the short, but completely finished fable. They are told by the dove as a device to keep herself out of the talons of the eagle. Trapped in a tiny crevice in a sheet of rock, the dove discovers she can gain time with her storytelling to dig her way to freedom. In some cases, readers may find themselves as mystified as the eagle about the fables' meaning, but this is good. They bear re-reading and reconsideration. Except for a few clumsy verses, the text . . . is written with style and finesse. A good story is a powerful weapon, just as the dove proves, and this collection is an arsenal.

> *A review of "Eagle and Dove," in* Virginia Kirkus' Service, *Vol. XXXIII, No. 13, July 1, 1965, p. 624.*

James Krüss again—no wonder he is so popular in West Germany. His tale **"Eagle and Dove"** . . . is really a collection of very-well-told short stories. The dove is the storyteller. Trapped in a narrow mountain crevice by an eagle with "a crooked-beaked smile," she plays for time. . . .

In a pleasant change from the usual pattern (baddies all bad, goodies all good), Mr. Krüss allows the eagle to manage a smile that isn't too crooked when the dove eventually escapes.

> *Patience M. Daltry, "Imagination Needs No Visa," in* The Christian Science Monitor, *November 4, 1965, p. B1.\**

---

## PAULINE UND DER PRINZ IM WIND [PAULINE AND THE PRINCE OF THE WIND] (1964)

Each of the nine stories here is introduced by the author speaking in his own voice and then going on to retell a story that Pauline had made up for him. Pauline is a little girl who occasionally arrives at his house and tells a story for the price of a snack. Her imagination is even bigger than her healthy appetite and some of her inventions are charming. Nevertheless, the narrative device is awkward and the author's obvious appreciation of Pauline is indulgent and indulgence carries with it the curse of condescension, however fond it may be. While it is easy to understand an adult appreciating Pauline's precocious gifts, there is the big question of whether youth really speaks to youth and the possibility that her age mates will find that Pauline palls. Some of the stories have short verses in them which may have made more sense in the original German. . . . This isn't up to the author's two outstanding previous books *My Great-Grandfather and I* . . . or *Eagle and Dove*. . . .

> *A review of "Pauline and the Prince of the Wind," in* Virginia Kirkus' Service, *Vol. XXXIV, No. 5, March 1, 1966, p. 242.*

A thoroughly original collection of nine whimsical stories. . . . Similar in concept to the author's *My Great Grandfather and I* in which fanciful poems and stories are interspersed with charming real-life conversation between a child and an adult. Throughout a light, loving atmosphere is created by a charming small child and an adult who recalls and cherishes the magic of childhood. Well worth a wide introduction to children as well as adults. This will be especially enjoyed by a family reading together.

> *Emma Kirby, in a review of "Pauline and the Prince in the Wind," in* School Library Journal, *an appendix to* Library Journal, *Vol. 12, No. 8, April, 1966, p. 95.*

---

## DIE SPRECHMACHINE [THE TALKING MACHINE: AN EXTRAORDINARY STORY] (1965)

Professor Prendergast and his 13-year-old nephew Martin have invented a truly wondrous talking machine capable of making instant translations of animal languages into several human languages as well as of human speech into animal sounds. Their neighbors, pets and people alike, at No. 7 St. Margaret's Road enjoy hearing the thoughts of each other, so the machine is in great demand. When, in the middle of the night, five mice are denied a chance to squeak their minds, one deliberately gnaws through the cat-gut and wooden rods of the machine's coordinator. The Talking Machine, kaput, pours out only gibberish. Or is it only gibberish? Dietrich Lange's brilliant illustrations are humorous and exciting and a perfect complement to a deftly written original text. Good read-aloud material. Will have appeal at many levels of understanding. (pp. 130-31)

> *Jeraline Nerney, in a review of "The Talking Machine," in* School Library Journal, *an appendix to* Library Journal, *Vol. 12, No. 5, January, 1966, pp. 130-31.*

**The Talking Machine** comes from Germany and has some of the technological preoccupations of that country, but the translator [Oliver Coburn] has quite successfully given it an English setting. In fact this is quite literally a story which transcends national barriers. It is about a machine devised by 13 year-old Martin which will translate human speech, regardless of language, into animalese, and *vice versa*. When it is put to the test the machine is only too successful, rendering with ruthless accuracy the opinions which pets hold of their human custodians. In the end the machine breaks down after delivering itself of a spontaneous multi-lingual message. The book may appear at a quick glance to be designed for the very young. It is in fact an excellent sophisticated joke, making considerable demands on those who would enjoy the witty text and complex drawings.

> *A review of "The Talking Machine," in* The Junior Bookshelf, *Vol. 30, No. 1, February, 1966, p. 29.*

*HEIMKEHR AUS DEM KRIEGE [COMING HOME FROM THE WAR: AN IDYLL]* (1965)

The impact of this book that reflects the reactions of an 18-year-old German boy to war, as remembered years later by a sensitive writer, is not as immediate as "A Moment of Silence." Because it *is* remembered, it is more reflective in mood, but its impact is cumulative, thanks to [Krüss's] fine writing. . . . This journey through time and space is a poignant memoir.

> *A review of "Coming Home from the War," in* Publishers Weekly, *Vol. 198, No. 11, September 14, 1970, p. 70.*

The narrator draws from memory impressions of his life in Germany between February and August of 1945. A pause between storms, this was an idyllic time following his release at 19 from the rapidly deteriorating German army and before the restrictions of home and conventional life again took their hold. Foraging without pillaging, unruled but self-regulated, the youth (as seen by the man) becomes freed from the dogma of Hitler, from the idealism of war, from the blind obedience of the soldier. Full of imagery, appealing to a poetic turn of mind, this is of possibly limited appeal, but nonetheless is a worthwhile book to add to general collections.

> *Brooke Anson, in a review of "Coming Home from the War: An Idyll," in* School Library Journal, *an appendix to* Library Journal, *Vol. 17, No. 4, December, 1970, p. 62.*

---

*MEIN URGROSSVATER, DIE HELDEN UND ICH [MY GREAT-GRANDFATHER, THE HEROES AND I: A BRIEF STUDY OF HEROES IN VERSE AND PROSE, MADE UP AND TOLD IN SEVERAL ATTIC ROOMS BY MY GREAT-GRANDFATHER AND MYSELF]* (1967)

A few years later the young boy and the old boy of *My Great-Grandfather and I* . . . are still turning out their brisk, well-turned, disarmingly pointed stories and rhymes in a wonderfully companionable sort of synergistic creativity. Between scribbling in the attic on the backs of wallpaper rolls, they read their efforts aloud to each other and to Uncle Harry, Upper Grandmother and Lower Grandmother. The Young Boy, now fourteen and home from school with a sore foot, and his Great-Grandfather, confined to a wheelchair and nearing the end of his life, fill the rest of the week; this story spans discussing the question around which many of the fables turn: what makes a hero? With tact and understanding the old boy guides the young one to the conclusion that Siegfried was not a hero, that Hercules was and was not a hero, that war is not heroic and that risking one's life is not necessarily heroic. The Great-Grandfather's farewell note to the boy ends "No hero I, yet I think true / To my beliefs: may you be too," and he expresses confidence that whenever he dies his great-grandson will bring him immortality and preserve "my small amount of wisdom" by never again praising false heroes. "I hope this book proves it," ends Kruss, the now grown great-grandson, and we believe that he can rest assured.

> *A review of "My Great-Grandfather, the Heroes and I," in* Kirkus Reviews, *Vol. XVI, No. 22, November 15, 1973, p. 1265.*

Delightfully drawn family relationships add a warm glow to this sequel to the author's recollected rhymes and stories in *My*

*great-grandfather and I*. . . . [Great-grandfather and his fourteen-year-old grandson's] theme is heroes, and great-grandfather teaches the boy to discern different hero types, as well as to distinguish between who is and who is not really a hero. Great-grandfather's slipping health disquiets the boy, but he is comforted by his sage mentor, who reassures him that he is "much tougher than the doctor thinks"—and that he expects to live on in his great-grandson's books. As well he does.

> *A review of "My Great-Grandfather, the Heroes and I: A Brief Study of Heroes in Verse and Prose, Made Up and Told in Several Attic Rooms by My Great-Grandfather and Myself," in* The Booklist, *Vol. 70, No. 10, January 15, 1974, p. 543.*

[The subtitle] sets the mood and tone of the story. . . . Epigrammatic gems are threaded skillfully and appropriately into a unique gathering of stories within a story. Each one is a necessary part of the whole, yet each stands as an entity in itself. The author triumphs because his narrative technique is so intimately a part of the characterization that it never seems artificial or strained. He writes for a special audience of a time and a place remembered from childhood and is a master at depicting the special relationship between the young and the very old. Superb storytelling. . . . (pp. 50-1)

> *Mary M. Burns, in a review of "My Great-Grandfather, the Heroes and I," in* The Horn Book Magazine, *Vol. L, No. 1, February, 1974, pp. 50-1.*

[Great-grandfather] is the voice the author uses to express his philosophy of ethical behavior. The connective tissue of the story establishes the affection between the old man and the boy with warmth and humor, the poems and stories vary in quality, but the stress upon one theme makes the book at times rather heavy going. There are wonderful bits here, but the whole has less cohesion and less narrative flow than most of this distinguished German author's work.

> *Zena Sutherland, in a review of "My Great-Grandfather, the Heroes and I," in* Bulletin of the Center for Children's Books, *Vol. 27, No. 7, March, 1974, p. 112.*

The affection and respect that each "boy" has for the other is well expressed, and the two characters, stories and poems smoothly integrated into the narrative, are lively and humorous with only a subtle suggestion of a moral. Pen-and-ink drawings [by Jochen Bartsch] enhance Krüss' text which is stylistically similar to his *My Great-Grandfather and I* . . . and *The Happy Islands Behind the Winds*. . . .

> *Susan A. Pelavin, in a review of "My Great-Grandfather, the Heroes and I," in* School Library Journal, *Vol. 21, No. 5, January, 1975, p. 47.*

---

*BRIEFE AN PAULINE [LETTERS TO PAULINE]* (1968)

Correspondence between the author, a resident of the Canary Islands, and Pauline, his young friend in Germany, form the basis of James Krüss's newest book. Their letters are fun to read, full of anecdotes and drawings and, most important, stories Mr. Krüss makes up for Pauline, in return for little items she sends him from Germany. The format of the book is pleasing to the eye and the end result is an unusual and entertaining book for younger readers.

*A review of "Letters to Pauline," in* Publishers Weekly, *Vol. 199, No. 7, February 15, 1971, p. 79.*

"Only stories" is Pauline's request of Don Jaime, dismissing the lengthy descriptions and speculations in his first letters from the Canary Islands; later she will ask for silly stories, maybe "one that didn't have a beginning or an ending so there wouldn't be any place for a lesson." The result is that compliant luggage-carrier "Polly Plauz, the Useful Octopus," still carrying on. . . . Don Jaime never quite manages to produce a story "from which one definitely cannot learn anything" . . . and ultimately [Pauline] recognizes that people see and read different things in each; out of their exchange too comes his explanation of why he revises, her understanding of "sailing with the wind," his answer to the teacher who objected to rhymed compositions. Here and there, in his letters or hers, Don Jaime becomes the Famous Author but mostly the correspondence (his letters typed, hers in legible longhand, the stories in print) is crisp and unaffected. And when the stories are good, they are very good—or, as the birzel would say, it's a boo (a modest boon).

*A review of "Letters to Pauline," in* Kirkus Reviews, *Vol. XXXIX, No. 5, March 1, 1971, p. 236.*

The stories Krüss sends [Pauline] have delightful humor (gentle and nonsensical) and wisdom; his letters include descriptions of the Canary Islands while Pauline's display a growing awareness of the people around her. At the end, Krüss sends Pauline a beautiful poem on eternity in answer to a question of hers about whether or not animals can enter heaven. The book's illustrations, black-and-white drawings by the author and Pauline, are suitably amateurish and child-like. This appealing title will give middle-grade readers a view of a warm and mutually respectful adult-child relationship, and many children of Pauline's age will wish they had a friend and pen-pal as charming as James Krüss.

*Jeanette Daane, in a review of "Letters to Pauline," in* School Library Journal, *an appendix to* Library Journal, *Vol. 17, No. 8, April, 1971, p. 107.*

---

### DER TROMMLER UND DIE PUPPE [THE PROUD WOODEN DRUMMER] (1969)

A German fantasy told in stilted narrative rhyme that seems to have become even stiffer in [Jack Prelutsky's] translation. A wooden drummer overhears his next-door neighbor, Widow Mouse, saying that he is a "wooden simpleton, a clown"; grief-stricken, he takes to his bed. When the Widow is told, she becomes apologetic: "'I feel that I'm responsible,' / the Widow Mouse replied. / 'So I shall find some work for him / that he may drum with pride.'" Assigned the job of drumming loud enough to awaken the Widow's incorrigibly late-sleeping children, the drummer succeeds brilliantly, and happily celebrates his triumph and renewed self-esteem with the mouse family and the pretty doll upstairs. The illustrations [by Eva Johanna Rubin], colorful and stylized, reflect the rigidity of the text; the doll and drummer appear appropriately doll-like and wooden. However, the verses and pictures tend to be too mechanical, without flow or continuity from page to page, making it unlikely that young American listeners or independent readers will drum up much enthusiasm for this ossified confection.

*Pat Barnes, in a review of "The Proud Wooden Drummer," in* School Library Journal, *an appendix to* Library Journal, *Vol. 15, No. 9, May, 1969, p. 76.*

The Kruss-Rubin *Three By Three* is a clever construct, the Prelutsky-Rubin treatment of Rudolph Neumann's *Bad Bear* is witty and spirited, but this—despite an immediate outward resemblance—is stiffly and quite garishly illustrated, and the rhymes are frequently forced. Moreover the story—of a downhearted wooden drummer whose pride is restored by the task of awakening Widow Mouse's sleepyhead children—amounts to little more than a tattoo. Even a wooden drummer would demand a more auspicious assignment. (pp. 499-500)

*A review of "The Proud Wooden Drummer," in* Kirkus Reviews, *Vol. XXXVII, No. 9, May 1, 1969, pp. 499-500.*

---

### GROSSVATER LERNER AUF FAHREN [GRANDFATHER LEARNS TO DRIVE] (1971)

The text here is carefully translated from the German: even the left-hand drive of the illustrations is satisfactorily accounted for. The humour is heavy-handed, however, though its literalness may appeal. It depends on the continuing imperception of Grandfather, an elderly Art professor, that his grandson, to whom he insists on recounting every detail of his first drive in a motorcar, already knows everything he can tell him about cars, supplying him each time with the technical terms for his amateur explanations. . . . The salutory moral is somehow drawn that children may know more than their elders in some matters, but by no means in all.

*M. Hobbs, in a review of "Grandfather Learns to Drive," in* The Junior Bookshelf, *Vol. 35, No. 5, October, 1971, p. 298.*

---

### THE TAILOR AND THE GIANT (1972)

Taking two often used characters from folk and fairy tales—a giant and a tailor—the author has created an imaginative original story. Faced with a deadline and the tremendous task of making a coat for the giant, the clever tailor uses psychology to get the job done on time. While most young readers won't fully understand the psychology employed or that the tailor "knew how to enjoy life," they will appreciate the adroit way he enlists the help of the town's young ladies to finish the coat. They can also recognize the human frailty which makes the giant so resent being called ugly that he commissions the "handsomest coat in the countryside" as well as the vanity of the tailor when he shows off for the admiring ladies. At the end, everyone has something of value: the giant his handsome coat, the new seamstresses a skill, and the tailor a thriving business and esteem of the townspeople. The vocabulary and large print will invite readers in second and third grades. . . .

*Mary Katherine Pace, in a review of "The Tailor and the Giant," in* School Library Journal, *an appendix to* Library Journal, *Vol. 19, No. 1, September, 1972, p. 67.*

# Hugh (Francis) Lewin

## 1939-

**South African author of picture books.**

In his *Jafta* series—*Jafta, Jafta—My Mother, Jafta—My Father, Jafta—The Wedding, Jafta—The Journey,* and *Jafta—The Town*—Lewin presents a positive image of childhood in contemporary South Africa. The scope of the series, which focuses on the daily life of Jafta, an exuberant little boy in an unspecified native village, ranges from the warmth and serenity of *Jafta—My Mother* and *Jafta—The Wedding* to the social relevance of *Jafta—The Journey* and *Jafta—The Town*. In the latter books, Lewin depicts Jafta's visits to his father, who works far from home. Originally intending to explain that Jafta's father is imprisoned, Lewin decided not to broach the complex subject of life under apartheid since he was directing his books to children. Lisa Kopper's illustrations, however, occasionally supply details the texts do not address, such as picturing Jafta's father working behind bars. Writing in simple yet lyrical language, Lewin describes Jafta's feelings about himself and his surroundings and laces the stories with regional terms which are defined in the back of each book. A supportive bond within Jafta's family and community underscores the series.

The son of an Anglican parish priest, Lewin initially started to follow the same career. "My father," he wrote in his autobiography *Bandiet: Seven Years in a South African Prison*, "brought me up to believe that all men, rich or poor, should be respected and loved as creatures of God. I have always believed, and still do believe, that all men are equals in the eyes of God." Living as a Caucasian under apartheid, however, incited political and moral conflict in Lewin. While attending Rhodes University, he visited the impoverished black community in Sophiatown. Observing their suffering and hearing them speak about their hatred of the laws imposed on them by the governing whites made Lewin question the dichotomy between the laws and his Christian beliefs. He became an active member of the Liberal Party; frustrated with its ineffectiveness, Lewin joined the National Committee for Liberation (later renamed the African Resistance Movement) in 1962.

The N.C.L. was a secret sabotage group who attempted to shock lawmakers into awareness without causing physical harm, a philosophy which appealed to the nonviolent Lewin. He was involved in three subversive acts during his eighteen months with the organization, and was arrested and imprisoned when South African police conducted mass raids on Leftist sympathizers in 1964. Considered inferior to other inmates because of his status as a political prisoner, Lewin received harsher treatment and fewer privileges but nevertheless earned degrees in English and librarianship through correspondence courses. Upon his release from prison in 1971, he was given the choice to leave South Africa or be placed under twenty-four-hour house arrest. Lewin went to England, where he remained politically active, worked as a journalist, and wrote his first book, *Bandiet*. Wanting to teach his two daughters about childhood in his homeland, Lewin published the first four *Jafta* books in 1981 before moving to Zimbabwe.

*Courtesy of Bell & Hyman Ltd.*

Most critics agree that Jafta's experiences and natural observations successfully introduce children to South Africa while helping them learn about themselves. Some reviewers state that the effectiveness of the series is marred by Lewin's lack of explanation about the hardships of living under apartheid and that he loses the sense of Africa as a multicultural continent by generalizing his characters and settings. Lewin is usually praised, however, for presenting his audience with an affirmative and accessible view of an often unfamiliar culture.

---

## GENERAL COMMENTARY

[The *Jafta* series] raises disturbing questions.

The jacket on the earlier books informs us that the author, born and raised in South Africa but now living in London, was imprisoned for his opposition to apartheid. He wrote these books "out of his desire to introduce his [two daughters] to South Africa and much of the imagery is South African." Readers are thus led to expect far more than these books provide.

A jacket also informs us, "Jafta is not representative of any particular people, but is modeled after a combination of specific individuals. The wedding customs are an amalgam as well." Thus the protagonist and his family are not identified culturally, and therein lies the first problem since it is critical that writers honor the diversity of African societies and those of other people of color by calling them by their group/national names. In this series, both text and illustrations are devoid of any cultural clues. (p. 30)

Most significant, however, is what is—and is not—said about life in South Africa. The author does not so much avoid central questions as get mired and trapped by them. His refusal to deal honestly with central issues does a disservice to the millions of South African children who must live with realities so harsh and pervasive that the only way to avoid talking about them is to avoid talking about South Africa at all. For example, that Jafta's father works in a town far from his family is central to these tales, but readers learn nothing about the context of such realities. Was Jafta's father conscripted to work at a mine? Were he and his family originally sent by the government to a remote "homeland" so that he has to go great distances to find work? Do Jafta and his mother live in one of the "temporary towns" established by women and children who walk as many as 500 miles to live in *relative* proximity to their husbands and fathers? Why, when we see a man that is presumably Jafta's father at work in *Jafta's Father,* is the man shown lifting boxes behind bars? As this same volume closes, Jafta hopes his father will come home. Why doesn't Jafta's mother comfort him and explain things? Not for the Jaftas of South Africa—they know, but for children and adults outside of South Africa who don't know.

Some comments on the specific books in the series follow.

In *Jafta,* the first title in the series, the protagonist is the only human character in the book. . . . When he's shown stamping like a cross elephant or grumbling like a warthog, we are told Jafta doesn't get cross often. Why was it necessary to qualify his anger when there is no such qualification with any other feeling? In addition, many African Americans are likely to consider the sight of Jafta "swing[ing] through the trees like a monkey" offensive since it reinforces an old stereotype.

The poetic text of *Jafta's Mother* conveys Jafta's deep feeling for his mother, the sense of security she provides, her firm discipline and the care she provides. We are told Jafta's mother talks with the children "about today and yesterday, and especially tomorrrow." But what do they talk about? Their history? Their heartache? Their aspirations for liberation? We are not told. Other opportunities to provide information are also ignored; Jafta's mother, for instance, is described as "warm and brown like the earth." That's a nice image but it only describes her racially: the story could be about any number of groups of people.

In *Jafta's Father,* we see father and son doing wonderful things together. Six pages are devoted to their building of a hide-out; why so many pages? I thought perhaps the family would hide there from the South African police, but no. Later, Jafta is sad thinking of his father away in the city working, but as noted above, we learn little about his situation. A friend of Jafta's says his father is not coming back. Does he say this because his own father did not come home? Why does it provoke a fight? Both children must have known about or heard about fathers who didn't come back. Do the children fear Jafta's father will be arrested for not having a pass book? Arrested for being involved in liberation struggles? Drafted for work an even greater distance from home? Dead of disease or killed by police or internalized violence?

*The Wedding* also compares people to animals. Aunts "chatter like a tree full of sakabula birds" (women chatter, men talk). The eldest elder "like an ostrich stretching its neck . . . shouted at the clouds"—an inappropriate and disrespectful treatment of a religious ceremony. Few children's books would handle European or Euro-American weddings or other religious/spiritual ceremonies in such a fashion. And many people of African descent in this country will be offended that an uncle is shown "falling about" as a result of drinking too much beer.

The two most recent books—*The Journey* and *The Town*—share the flaws of the earlier books. *The Town* . . . is perhaps the most distressing because it is clear that the author is writing around issues that he knows exist but has chosen not to deal with.

If books about South Africa cannot reveal some of the realities of life there, perhaps they should not be done at all. (pp. 30-1)

> *Geraldine L. Wilson, in a review of the "Jafta" series, in* Interracial Books for Children Bulletin, *Vol. 15, Nos. 7 & 8, 1984, pp. 30-1.*

---

**JAFTA; JAFTA—MY MOTHER (U.S. edition as *Jafta's Mother*); JAFTA—MY FATHER (U.S. edition as *Jafta's Father*); JAFTA—THE WEDDING (U.S. edition as *Jafta and the Wedding*) (1981)**

These four finely-wrought books [*Jafta, Jafta—My Mother, Jafta—My Father, Jafta—The Wedding*] are the product of a creative partnership [between Lewin and illustrator Lisa Kopper]. They have brought to life Jafta and his family, who live in a South African "homeland". On the surface, Jafta's life is very different from those of British children. He lives in a one-roomed, traditional village house, wears shorts, a bracelet and, at times, a shirt—these are simply the circumstances of his life. There is no trace of the exotic, the "primitive", or the Third-World-unfortunate in the way he is portrayed. He is part of his world: when he describes his feelings in terms of animals, he refers to hyenas, impala, zebra and warthog, as well as rabbits, spiders and snakes. But Jafta's feelings, whether of joy or of rage, are the feelings of all children.

And that is the glory of these books. That which is different is clearly articulated and explained. . . . But there are also the common experiences: Jafta's mother gets angry when he teases his little sister, and she tucks up her children in their blankets at night with a kiss. There are bedtime stories too, told by the village storyteller and listened to by adults and children alike; there is a wedding, with an adorned and beautiful bride, food and drink, music and dancing, all happening out of doors, Jafta's father carries him on his shoulders, builds him a raft and a tree-house—but has to leave his family and go to the city to work in order to support them, so now mother chops the wood.

The language is simple but specific and often poetic. Jafta thinks of his mother as "like the earth—full of goodness, warm and brown and strong".

Knowing South Africa, I welcomed the images of the land so unerringly evoked on every page. . . . [Kopper's illustrations] combine with the text to draw the reader into a world very remote from the British experience. But the 20 seven-year-olds, sitting in an inner London school on a rainy May morning, were entranced. Between them, Hugh Lewin and Lisa Kopper have brought another continent within the grasp of these children's imaginations. This is the kind of depicting image children need of cultures other than their own. These are the kind of children's books of which there can never be enough—comprehensible yet enriching, widening horizons, enchanting and delighting. Sturdy books that will stand up to being perused time and again.

> *Gillian Klein, "Warm, Brown and Strong," in* The Times Educational Supplement, *No. 3389, June 5, 1981, p. 37.*

The two-fold demands of freedom with security, before the adolescent years when the need for freedom usually becomes passionate and paramount, is reflected in domestic stories for the middle years in which adventure moves out from the home and back again or even, in some cases, is drawn simply from a fresh scrutiny of the home itself. This scrutiny is very imaginative in [*Jafta, Jafta—My mother, Jafta—My father, Jafta—The wedding*], in which a small Nigerian boy puts into his own words, almost in the form of lists, what he finds of excitement and satisfaction in his home. Security is implicit in the close contact with his father and mother; the fact that he describes these relationships partly through images and comparisons make his comments very individual, while his joyful acceptance of life is very evident in the 'list' of his own moods and activities, which he sees in parallel with certain animals, confronting a rhinoceros, for example, in a similar pose of bad-temper, impatiently imitating the racing stance of a cheetah, longingly gesturing towards the graceful flight of flamingoes. The family bond is defined more directly in *Jafta—The wedding;* as the small boy comments on his view of his older sister he wonders about his own future. It is impossible to separate text and pictures in these small, absorbing books. The words indicate very simply what children are to recognise in Jafta's circumstances: the pictures confirm these statements in a sensuous, indirect way while they are matching them also in literal terms.

> *Margery Fisher, in a review of "Jafta," "Jafta—My Mother," "Jafta—My Father," and "Jafta—The Wedding," in her* Growing Point, *Vol. 20, No. 2, July, 1981, p. 3909.*

The Other Award, which each year commends four books that help to broaden the range of social values that children meet in their literature, celebrates its seventh birthday this week. . . . Behind the award lies a year of hard work and difficult decisions. . . .

What about the ones that got away? Some of us were sad that the *Jafta* books . . . could not win. These four picture books about a black child living in South Africa had great appeal, freshness and warmth for some panelists.

But we were convinced by others who said that there is no such thing as a generalized "African" way of life, that these books were specifically about the South African homelands and, that being so, fell short of the author's intention to show British children what life under *apartheid* is really like. Seven years ago, the panel might have been delighted to find four well-written nicely illustrated books presenting positive images of black family life. We get choosier as books improve. (p. 20)

> *Mary Hoffman, "A Judge's Story," in* The Times Educational Supplement, *No. 3405, October 2, 1981, pp. 20-1.**

[*Jafta* is a] book with a lot of appeal for young children. There's very little writing on the page, words and illustrations are interlinked, there's some repetition, and an even rhythm that carries the reader forward. It's about Jafta, a delightful brown boy and, although it doesn't tell a story, it does present us with a boy of remarkable insight and knowledge, not only of himself, but of the animals he chooses to be with.

> *Hilary Minns, in a review of "Jafta," in* The School Librarian, *Vol. 29, No. 4, December, 1981, p. 333.*

[Show *Jafta*] to under-fives, and have them, stretching high like a giraffe, or cuddling like a lamb, stamping like an elephant, or scurrying with their fingers like a spider, gleefully reliving the emotion with the movement.

At about five, kids will enjoy the second *Jafta* book, *My Mother.* There's a lot of experience to talk about here—similar or different; and through it all, a *flavour* of Africa, generalised and idealised, but setting the mind free to wander, to leap, and to reflect. (Always dependent, of course, on the adult-with-the-book.)

Fathers are often vague figures, and their love, though longed for, is sometimes in question. In *My Father,* Jafta's father is absent, but very loving and beloved. When Hugh Lewin read these stories in an English school, many children very clearly felt that *My Father* had said something uniquely special to them. I put this story with Felicity Sen's *My Family,* Jeanette Caines' *Daddy,* Beryl Gilroy's *Once Upon a Time,* Shirley Hughes' *Helpers,* and a very few others, as precious picture books about loving dads or other males, white or black.

Originally Jafta's father was in prison (the pictures, unaltered, still vividly suggest the prison bars; and with the new text the visual metaphor remains powerfully apposite) but some people felt adults might find this difficult to explain to a very young child, so he is now separated in a different way—working in the town.

*The Wedding,* about Jafta's sister, though still about Jafta's feelings, has more the tinge of a sociological documentary than the others, and is for slightly older children. Still a lot to talk about, to link the child outside the book with the child inside.

> *Leila Berg, "Nourish the Soil," in* The Times Educational Supplement, *No. 3428, March 12, 1982, p. 38.**

[*Jafta, Jafta and the Wedding, Jafta's Father,* and *Jafta's Mother*] seem more autobiographical than most books for preschoolers. They are told in the first person and I doubt that any young child would describe his mother as being "like the sun rising in the early morning lighting the dark corners." . . . While these books give some insight into South African village life, they are uneven, unattractive, and unsuccessfully stretch Jafta's adventures into too many books.

> *Lelia Davenport Pettyjohn, in a review of "Jafta," "Jafta and the Wedding," "Jafta's Father," and "Jafta's Mother," in* Children's Book Review Service, *Vol. 11, No. 9, April, 1983, p. 87.*

Most American children know little of the life of South Africans; of a child's life in South Africa, practically nothing. These four stories [*Jafta, Jafta and the Wedding, Jafta's Mother,* and *Jafta's Father*] are lighted by the affection of an author born in South Africa remembering his homeland, and are as warm as their gold and brown coloring. Jafta is any little boy, sharing the universal joys and sorrows of childhood, but his are expressed in uniquely African terms. . . . His family is loving and caring; but father must go away to the city for months at a time to earn money, while mother holds the family together until he can return in the spring. Bitterness is unspoken, but it is there. *Jafta and the Wedding* is perhaps the most charming and exciting of the four titles. Big sister Nomsa marries, and the celebration lasts a week. It is a lovely wedding, and a lovely story. Jafta and his family are not representative of any particular people, but are modeled after a combination of specific individuals: the wedding customs too are an amalgam. These titles will be a welcome and much-needed addition to multicultural collections.

> *Joan McGrath, in a review of "Jafta," "Jafta and the Wedding," "Jafta's Mother," and "Jafta's Father," in* School Library Journal, *Vol. 29, No. 9, May, 1983, p. 63.*

This introduction to African wildlife [*Jafta*] suggests possibilities for discussion and movement activities. The text, although limited in its simplistic approach, shows a novel use of simile and metaphor and may indeed be used as a pattern for children to share their own world. (p. 772)

> *Ronald A. Jobe, in a review of "Jafta," in* Language Arts, *Vol. 60, No. 6, September, 1983, pp. 771-72.*

[The *Jafta* Books] exuberantly and lyrically describe the life of a young boy in South Africa. . . . [The] text and pictures capture attention and entrance the reader as they reveal the universal feelings of childhood. The four books, *Jafta, Jafta's Mother, Jafta's Father* and *Jafta and the Wedding,* are based on the life and feelings of children everywhere. At the same time, they introduce young children to the ways and culture of blacks living in South Africa. . . .

*Jafta's Mother* presents a poetic description of mother. And even though this mother lives in South Africa, she displays the concern, love and understanding of mothers the world over.

*Jafta's Father* is a sensitive account of a boy's love for his father. . . .

*Jafta and the Wedding* introduces the traditions of South African festivals. Although the customs and traditions of the wedding in South Africa differ from those in the United States, the universal excitement and warmth and tenderness of being surrounded by family and friends in a time of joy surpasses geographical boundaries.

The poetic language of the books lend them to reading aloud to children. The content will enable a sensitive teacher to help children develop understanding of their own feelings by identifying with a child in another culture. As children and teachers discuss the books, concepts of faraway life can be developed. The reference list of words that are new to children in the United States appears in the back of each book. These words, such as *Mielies* (maize) or *Songololo*, from the Zulu word for centipede, can be used to increase children's knowledge of another culture.

The realistic nature of the books and sensitivity of feelings portrayed is weakened somewhat by attempts to make everything and everyone without flaw. For instance, it's true, all children feel cross, as Jafta does, but after recognizing this fact, he adds, "I don't often get cross." And Jafta's mother, although she does complain and sometimes storms and gets angry, "doesn't often complain, even in the bad times," or "doesn't often storm" as if to avoid any unpleasantness. Nevertheless, this moralizing doesn't destroy the totality of beauty this series of books offers to children and adults.

> *Carol Seefeldt, in a review of the "Jafta" books, in* Curriculum Review, *Vol. 23, No. 1, February, 1984, p. 95.*

---

## JAFTA—THE JOURNEY; JAFTA—THE TOWN   (1983)

[As in the first four *Jafta* stories, *Jafta—the Journey* and *Jafta—the Town* express] basic human emotions in simply worded picture books centered around the day-to-day life of a young boy in rural South Africa. The story lines are moving without forced dramatic embellishments. . . . Both stories are told through the observations and feelings of the child. Children will relate to the simple joys that are expressed in these books, such as riding on a boat for the first time and attending a soccer game with one's father. Likewise, youngsters can easily understand the fear Jafta experiences when he becomes lost in a strange town and the pain of separation he feels when it's time to head home, leaving his father, who must remain in town to earn a living for his family. While the vocabulary is quite simple, Lewin uses regional terminology when it is appropriate, introducing words such as *veld* and *lorries*. A short note in the back of the book explains the meaning of unfamiliar terms.

> *Tom S. Hurlburt, in a review of "Jafta—The Journey" and "Jafta—The Town," in* School Library Journal, *Vol. 31, No. 3, November, 1984, p. 112.*

The stories in these two companion picture books [*Jafta—the Journey* and *Jafta—the Town*] are linked, but each can also stand alone. . . . These books are less successful than their predecessors in articulating Jafta's vibrant personality, and the stories are virtually plotless. The flavor of South African life is conveyed more fully in the illustrations than in the text, which occasionally suffers from stilted phrasing. The books will work best alongside the other *Jafta* stories to convey a tranquil child's-eye view of growing up in a part of the world rarely seen in books for preschoolers.

> *Karen Stang Hanley, in a review of "Jafta—The Journey" and "Jafta—The Town," in* Booklist, *Vol. 81, No. 5, November 1, 1984, p. 370.*

The beauty of the picture books in this series lies in their delightful production—which effectively combines warm sepia illustrations and a simple, expressive text about the way of life in another culture—and in their universal appeal. For although the stories have a specifically African setting, Jafta's emotions are carefully conveyed, showing us a very real picture of a little boy and his family. In *Jafta—The Journey* Jafta and his mother go from their village to visit his father in the town where he works. Jafta's feelings of excitement, frustration and anticipation are vividly captured as slowly they travel by foot, cart and finally bus. In *Jafta—The Town* . . . the little boy is bewildered by all the noise, smells and bustle. This is not such a happy story, as the father lives and works in very poor conditions, and as the visit ends, Jafta wishes 'we could all live together'.

> *"Multicultural Books: The 'Jafta' Books," in* The Signal Review of Children's Books 2: A Selective Guide to Picture Books, Fiction, Plays, Poetry, Information Books Published during 1983, *edited by Nancy Chambers, The Thimble Press, 1984, p. 54.*

# David (Thompson Watson) McCord

## 1897-

American poet.

McCord is often regarded as the foremost contemporary American poet for children. In a series of collections which span four decades, he has created verse to entertain and instruct young readers. McCord's poetry ranges from pure nonsense to emotional yet restrained lyricism. Writing about nature, childhood, and timeless joys like climbing trees, holidays, and make-believe, he enthusiastically invites his audience to explore and appreciate their world. He also introduces children to poetic structure, explaining such forms as the couplet, quatrain, limerick, and haiku by definition and example. Fascinated with the sound and rhythm of words, McCord presents his readers with abundant wordplay and many instances of the possibilities of language. Although his verse is sometimes considered intellectually demanding, he uses a simple, often colloquial style which appeals to children and reveals his craftsmanship and high standards. McCord's poems, especially "Pickety Fence" and "This is My Rock," are often anthologized in collections of poetry for the young.

Although he was born in New York City, McCord grew up on rural Long Island and in New Jersey. Many of his poems are inspired by his boyhood, and his passion for nature permeates his writing. An only child, McCord had recurring bouts of malaria which kept him out of school and free to investigate the outdoors. He learned to identify the rhythms of the earth and to appreciate the beauty of the wilderness as a teenager, when he spent three years in Oregon on his uncle's frontier ranch. McCord began writing verse at fifteen. After receiving his bachelor's degree in physics and mathematics and a master's degree in comparative literature from Harvard, he wrote his first poems for children.

McCord assembled his first collection of poetry for children, *Far and Few,* in 1952. Influenced by Robert Louis Stevenson and Edward Lear, McCord took the title for *Far and Few* from a quotation by Lear. McCord delivered eight lectures on Lear in 1950; Lear's influence on McCord's career is evident in his affection for limericks and nonsense rhymes as well as in the collections of humorous verse he has edited for adults.

McCord has written many books of verse for adults as well as short stories, essays, and a play. He has also been a journalist, and was drama and music critic for the *Boston Evening Transcript* before becoming director of the Harvard Fund Council, a position he held for thirty-eight years. McCord has been Phi Beta Kappa poet at Harvard and other institutions; in 1956, he received the first honorary Doctor of Humane Letters degree ever awarded at Harvard.

Praised as a superior observer of children and nature, McCord is acclaimed as a poet who combines childlike curiosity and wonder with a sophisticated mastery of his medium. The majority of reviewers commend his poetry for its charm and playful humor, literary quality and construction, absence of condescension, and relevance to young readers. A few critics complain that McCord's poems occasionally sacrifice substance for wordplay, but most see him as an author who re-

*Courtesy of David McCord*

spects the intelligence of children and has contributed greatly to their enjoyment of language.

McCord was the first author to receive the National Council of Teachers of English Award for Excellence in Poetry for Children. This award was given in 1977 in recognition of his aggregate body of work.

(See also *Something about the Author,* Vol. 18 and *Contemporary Authors,* Vols. 73-76.)

---

## AUTHOR'S COMMENTARY

When I was twelve, my family headed West to live on my uncle's homestead ranch in the south of Oregon. We lived there three years in all: no light, heat, power; no, not even water, except what we could pump by hand. I milked the cow, raised chickens, did the chores, but had no schooling through the critical years of twelve to fifteen. For one year, once a week, I did take the train to Grants Pass, down the great Rogue River, and was tutored by a fine, wise German lady who spoke four languages and wrote poetry. In the main, though, I was on my own to learn the language of the wild, and learn it on a real frontier; for Jackson County, Oregon, was still a wilderness when I was a boy, and I am very grateful for that rare experience. It taught me more, I think, than anything else about the essential poetry of life. It taught me, in a profusion of wildflowers, in a time of drought, in the terror of a forest fire, to honor the earth itself. (p. 53)

I would like to offer a few of the rules that guide my writing. Although they may not seem to amount to anything, unconsciously they have exercised control whenever I have attempted verse for children. First, just be a child before you grow up and let nothing interfere with the process. Write it all *out* of yourself and *for* yourself as you remember that weasel body with the eagle eyes. Next, never take the phrase "writing verse *for* children" seriously. If you write *for* them you are lost. Ask your brain's computer what you know about a child's mind and what goes on inside it. The answer is zero. What do they think of this new world which you don't even pretend to understand? They do not compare it with the past. It is the only world they know. Don't ever think you are looking at the young; just make sure the young are looking at you. Make your readers believe you are letting them into your own dark life, into your own serene confusion, not you into theirs. Children move forward on a kind of belt line. And when I say they are all the same basically when very young, I am well aware that they change from grade three upward under the flux and impositions and controls of our time—if we have controls. Well, they do move on a sort of belt line, moving steadily through eight grades up through high school, on through college. But the province I am considering is bounded by grades two or three and eight. Now when the young climb on this belt line they are all, or surely 70 to 80 per cent of them, potential poets; but when they leave this belt line—and some of them are thrown off just before they reach the end—I may suppose that only .15 or .25 of them are poets. Something is killed in them. (pp. 53-4)

What does one write about? As I have said, you write out of your own childhood *for yourself*. This is the first principle. Never objectively say there is a little girl, a little boy somewhere. I shall write something that I know will amuse them. I think I saw something that they did or were doing today or something that I overheard—this is what they would like to hear. You will never be a child's poet following that procedure. You will never be a child's poet anyway. Writing verse for children should be strictly a happening in a poet's life. Forget that we live in a baffling world. That isn't the way to approach it. There is a much simpler way. What you have to remember is that Emerson once said, "Every word was once a poem." Don't forget that. Every word except the articles and a few prepositions. Every word *was* once a poem: there is no room for argument. Take *sky, wind, sea, land, valley, mountain, river, cloud, tree, bird*. All these are very simple words. They *must*, each one of them, have been a poem to the man or woman who invented or first said them. One thinks of *sea*, for example: *sea*—with that long *ē* sound of it opening up the way the sea does on the horizon. (p. 56)

Children today are out of touch with the elements. They fly through one, ski and surfboard in another, hot rod over a third. This is one of the great difficulties a poet has to face. The jet has shrunk this world to the size of an orange, and people soar over great tracts of wilderness that they never, in my day, would have dreamed of seeing. But they are not *in* it. They fly into camp equipped with an outboard motor and all the rest of civilization's mess. They don't go in by canoe and portage. I grew up on a noble salmon and steelhead river and I have since fished a great deal in Canada. I once tutored a boy to enter Andover, and we were rewarded by a 120-mile canoe

trip in Canada with one French-Indian guide. Among other things, we caught a baby loon. That in itself was a large experience—the working draft of a poem. Today we would be flown in and flown out. One might as well go camping in a city park. I said to someone a while ago that one of the tragedies of our time is that a boy will have flown to the height of thirty thousand feet before he ever climbs a mountain. All the wonder of going up on his own two feet will come long after he first took wing. Why bother? (p. 57)

The moral is that one ought to make sure that children do know something about the elemental world outside. . . . [The] truth is that children are not in touch with nature. I have talked with too many of them not to know this for a fact. (pp. 57-8)

The other tragedy about ourselves and youth today is that we have lost the art of reading aloud. Children in general (I lack statistics) are not read aloud to unless by teachers and librarians. Especially the librarians. My grandmother read me the Bible through—the King James Version, all the magnificent parts of it—twice before I was twelve. That had a great deal to do with conditioning my instinctive feeling for rhythm and my passionate love of words and the right order of words, and whether adjectives are availing or not—not available, but availing. "Up the airy mountain, / Down the rushy glen," and there you have two adjectives. You are telling children to throw out adjectives, which is sound advice. But suppose you take out *airy* and *rushy*. What is left? "Up the mountain, / Down the glen." But the glory of that fragment is, "Up the *airy* mountain, / Down the *rushy* glen." Children can see that, if a person reads the words slowly aloud. (p. 59)

Finally, there is the matter of humor in verse. The poet writing for children should be sure of his own humor and be at pains to make the reader understand that individual words have humor in them. Light verse to me—if I may stretch a metaphor—is one of the opening doors for children. Take Richard Armour in four lines called "Going to Extremes": "Shake and shake / The catsup bottle, / None will come, / And then a lot'll." Any child can understand that, though it was not written for children. It takes a long while to learn how to be that brief. (p. 60)

And now **"The Walnut Tree."** This poem took me more than fifty years to write, because the event behind it occurred when I was a boy. I was out with my mother, my grandmother, and my uncle in southwestern Pennsylvania, looking at an abandoned farm. While they were off out of sight somewhere, I found this great old walnut tree on the edge of the hill. The tree had a swing with the tallest ropes I ever saw, and the ropes were in pretty good shape. So I took a try, and it swung me right out over the valley. The sight of that valley has haunted me ever since; but of course I was likewise haunted by Stevenson. Oh, how I liked to go up in a swing, yet I did not want to do it his way. I loved Stevenson as a small boy, but this was my swing, not his. So for years I would think about that experience and even trot out pencil and paper in expectation of an idea. But I never wrote a line, good or bad. Then one day, summer before last, I was driving through a dismal part of Lynn, Massachusetts, when a red light stopped me. And right in the red light I saw the poem, took out my pad and pen and wrote the first few lines, went through the green light, pulled up and wrote ten or twelve more, went home and finished it as fast as that. This is what the deep subconscious can do for you. (pp. 65-6)

*David McCord, "Poetry for Children," in* The Library Quarterly, *Vol. 37, No. 1, January, 1967, pp. 53-66.*

GENERAL COMMENTARY

## MYRA COHN LIVINGSTON

It is an uncommon man who can remember, extract, and discern the best of the past, reshape and apply it to the present, and in the process offer others a generous share of his unique celebration of life.

David McCord is such a man: a poet who has not only given to Cambridge, Boston, and academe his myriad talents but during the past twenty-six years has produced a body of work which ranks highest among all poetry written for children in this country. John Ciardi has put it well: "One is too few of him and there is, alas, no second."

There is no second because there is no other American poet who understands, as does David McCord, the high and low points in the English and American tradition of poetry for the young. He is keenly aware of the contributions made by Isaac Watts, William Blake, Edward Lear, Lewis Carroll, Robert Louis Stevenson, Walter de la Mare, Elizabeth Madox Roberts, and others. It is one thing, of course, to be aware of and to comprehend a historical perspective but quite another to translate this into one's own writing. There are many who emulate or imitate the poets of the past. This is not difficult.

What is herculean is to assimilate this past and bring to it the unique voice which characterizes meaningful poetry. David McCord has done this. But he has also cherished, related to, and recalled his own childhood. He has absorbed the sights, sounds, wonders, tastes, and rhythms that have marked his life. The result has been poetry for children, uniquely American, punctuated and crafted with the speech patterns, the rhythms, and the "abiding faith in laughter" of today's children. His understanding of and respect for the sensitivities, interests, emotions, and thoughts of the child coupled with his own abiding curiosity and wonder are what distinguish his work and set him apart from others.

To view David McCord in historical perspective is to recognize that although he has rejected the moral didacticism of Isaac Watts, he is mindful that a child responds to a regular rhythm and rhyme in remembering poetry and that there is verse from which children can learn. He is eager to impart information. It may be facts as mundane as what a chicken eats . . . or the habits of the newt. It may be an amusing approach to the use of correct pronunciation, punctuation, and spelling in such poems as **"You Mustn't Call It Hopsichord"** or **"Spelling Bee."** . . . There may be an occasional warning—not to trust "[s]ly Mr. Halloween" and to be careful in using the word *only*; lessons in how to draw a monkey; and instructions in looking at snowflakes. His poems describe everything from fifty legs of a centipede to hornets' nests, fishing, and how to write verse. What rescues all this from being moralistic, didactic, and encyclopedic is his ability to present his enthusiasms and discoveries with respect for the child's intelligence as well as his glorious wordplay. . . . (pp. 25-6)

Understanding of the child's point of view—the legacy of Stevenson—is of concern to David McCord. In **"No Present Like the Time"** there is not only wordplay but a confrontation with false morality:

"Don't waste your time," they say. Waste time you
    will;
And such as you wish, of course, is yours to squander.
Don't call it wasted when you climb a hill!
Through fields and woods to wander

Is to be young.

This attitude, of course, was also characteristic of William Blake and Lewis Carroll, both of whom believed that time spent in dreaming, play, and laughing is the right of the child. Here David McCord is at one with Blake and Carroll in reacting to the preachments of Watts. The sluggard is not to be viewed with total distaste; one does not have to be continually working like the busy bee who improves "each shining hour." In his poem **"Make Merry"** McCord is very close to Blake's nurse in "Songs of Innocence":

Merry child, make merry!
The sound of laughter dies
So quickly, so contrary
Are the wayward cloudy skies.

Like Blake, McCord recognizes the false nurse in "Songs of Experience," who admonishes the children, "Your spring and your day / Are wasted in play." . . . (pp. 26-7)

McCord's intention in **"Far Away"** and **"The Adventures of Chris"** about the need for play is paramount. . . . There is more to **"The Adventures of Chris,"** however, than a reaction to the moralism of Watts, a kinship with Blake and Carroll, the mystery of de la Mare, or the everyday world of Stevenson and Elizabeth Madox Roberts. It is one of a great number of poems that bear the stamp of David McCord's curiosity and wonder, his belief that apprehension is as important as comprehension, his intuitive understanding of rhythm as a force to carry forth the meaning of the words. Most importantly, it contains a pragmatism and an outlook which are totally American and a vernacular which emphasizes that practicality. It is curiosity that begins this particular poem, the cadence of which is brief and childlike. Other poems—**"Breakfast,"** **"Easter Morning,"** and **"Conversation"**—are but a few which also begin with questions.

**"Take Sky"** names words and sounds but ends on a note that permeates all of McCord's writing—"Man's *first* word: wonder . . . wonder . . ." David McCord is always wondering—about things seen: about the shape of clouds and of islands, about leaves, words, and birds; and about things heard: the sound of trains, clocks, owls, birds, bells, and the elements. In **"August 28"** he combines interest in both shape and sound:

A flock of swallows have gone flying south;
The bluejay carries acorns in his mouth.
I don't know where he carries them or why.
I'm never sure I like the bluejay's cry,
But still I like his blue shape in the sky.

His curiosity and wonder extend to the shape and sound of words. Here he ranges from the intensely cerebral to the most outrageously nonsensical. Echoes of Edward Lear can be felt in **"LMNTL,"** where he writes, "We've hrd a brd, grls gigl''; in **"Pome"**—"a nash a noak anna napple tree"; and in **"Z"**—"When all is zed and done." Simpler to understand by younger children are his **"Scat! Scitten!"** or **"Just Because . . ."** in which

Kittens have paws they don't have pawses,
Lions have maws they don't have mawses.

Word games such as **"Inside Information"** preserve a Carrollinian ring:

Debbie is in DEBt.
You see her? DEB—*B* plus a *t*?

He also enjoys making up odd names—Shadwell Presswood Leeds, Mingram Mo, or Tiggady Rue. Most fascinating of all is **"Dr. Klimwell's Fall,"** for it is Dr. I. Klimwell (*I climb well*—if one is not reading too much into the name) who falls down and must climb up again to view all the wonders of the world. In this very long poem, based on Emerson's quotation "We wake and find ourselves on a stair; there are stairs below us . . . there are stairs above us, many a one, which go upward and out of sight," David McCord sounds a recurring theme of ascension and discovery. This appears in **"Five Chants"** ("Every time I climb a tree") and in **"Up the Pointed Ladder,"** where the climb reveals countless wonders. Noticing everything about him is also felt in **"The Walnut Tree,"** in which the poet recognizes

> That the world begins in the sweep of eye,
> With the wonder of all of it more or less
> In the last hello and the first goodbye.

It is the wonder, too, that sustains apprehension, for McCord well understands that questions cannot always be answered. This is most clearly felt in a poem such as **"Queer."** . . . And certainly in the title poem in his book *Away and Ago*. . . . **"John," "Old Tim Toole," "Where,"** and **"I Have a Book"** may be read on the same level. One can guess that they are autobiographical in nature, as is **"The Walnut Tree," "Dr. Klimwell's Fall,"** and **"Up the Pointed Ladder."** Their quality is haunting. . . . (pp. 27-30)

In his highly symbolic poem [**"Up the Pointed Ladder"**] the reader discovers the boy climbing a ladder, ostensibly for apples. Mindful that he is being watched, that there is danger, he still continues his ascent. Both church spire and pointed ladder emphasize this upward thrust. The view is spellbinding, yet he cannot escape from the watchful eye of tradition, of the mundane world below. Stubbornly he refuses to remain earthbound, dependent on others. No matter how wobbly the ladder, he will hold his place, cherish his view and the literal fruit of his climb. It is the man below who is wild, who may not be "all right," who cannot understand what it is he seeks, and who wishes him to return to the safety of earth. The theme is repeated in another poem, **"Song."** (p. 32)

These two poems, among others, would seem to be David McCord's invitation to the young. One must set goals, climb for the apple, skin the tiger, and somehow make others understand that each individual must aspire to more than the "world below." A boy on a wobbly ladder may become a giant, uncertainty may become certainty—or conversely, certainty may become uncertainty. Refusal to settle for safety or mediocrity, to dream and to climb are the prerogative of youth or of anyone whose sensitivities are attuned to the discoveries of life. There will always be apprehension and more to engage our wonder and curiosity.

But if certain questions cannot be answered, there are others that can be dealt with in straightforward, everyday terms. Here is the pragmatic, practical poet pinpointing a grasshopper's fall (**"The Grasshopper"**), running a stick over the pickety fence (**"Five Chants"**), recognizing that one *should* have said a prayer (**"Waltzing Mice"**), making a list of what Santa Claus forgot last year (**"A Christmas Package"**), asking frankly "Why *Good?* What's Good" about saying good night, or drawing with pad and pencil. The world is a very real place at times, and David McCord never forgets how matter-of-fact children can be. He keeps abreast of the world of TV, laundromats, Little Leaguers, and Rapid Reading. He is alive to the current vernacular of

"man alive," "natch," "the guy's name," "queer stinko stuff," "what's the diff?," "goshawful," and "real fast." An avowed admirer of the poet Elizabeth Madox Roberts for her ability to speak in the language of childhood, David McCord equals and often surpasses her. In **"Wishful"** the house is "flittery with bats." In **"Bridges"** he writes "[t]he big one dizzies me." Nor is any reader likely to forget **"The Star in the Pail,"** in which the reflection "silvered in the water."

In a piece entitled **"Until I Was Ten"** the poet recalls his early years. "I was fascinated," he wrote, "by the sight and sound and shape of everything that moved with rhythm. I was fascinated by everything that had a special motion or made a special noise. For rhythm, not rhyme, is the basis of poetry." It was family members who "made me feel I was not alone in loving the sound of words and the rhythm of words put together in the right order."

Certainly he is a master of rhythm. The lyricism of **"The Walnut Tree"** carries the reader along in backward and forward surges. . . . **"The Star in the Pail"** combines the hush of coming evening, the quiescence of nature with the contrasting rhythmic pattern of a commonplace errand:

> When evening slippered over like the moth's brown
>      wing,
> I went to fetch the water from the cool wellspring.

The carefully crafted rhythms of **"Song"** and **"Suddenly"** attest to an ear alive to the rhythms of nature and of skating in wide sweeps. The choice of trochaic dimeter for the disaster in **"Marty's Party"** must be the envy of any poet.

> Marty's party?
> Jamie came. He
> seemed to Judy
> dreadful rude. He
> joggled Davy,
> spilled his gravy,
> squeezed a melon
> seed at Helen. . . .

The iambic lilt of his story poems as well as the straightforward iambus of his informative verse are, indeed, "the right order." The lugubrious dactyl, in combination with the trochee, is a brilliant choice for a poem about castor oil.

> Ever, ever, not ever so terrible
> Stuff as unbearable castor oil.

There is no precedent for McCord's sure sense and choice of rhythm; he is unequaled.

His use of figurative language is unaffected and wise. He does not burden young readers with overemphasis on poetic devices. Personification occasionally appears. After the fashion of Lear he tells the story of **"Dr. Ping and Mr. Pong."** In **"Whistle"** a Mother Diesel train worries that young Whistle will not blow. Leaves talk through all the seasons in the poem called **"Leaves";** and the sun in **"The Firetender"**

> rises from the dead of night
> And rakes the star-coals up the sky

and later

> watches the reflection spread,
> Then banks the fire and goes to bed. . . .
>
> (pp. 32-4)

Alliteration is often handled with wit. In **"Books Fall Open"** the poet challenges the young reader:

> What *might* you be,
> perhaps *become,*
> because one book
> is somewhere? Some
> wise delver into
> wisdom, wit,
> and wherewithal
> has written it. . . .

Assonance is presented deftly in **"Cocoon,"** when the caterpillar

> sleeps awhile before it flies,
> And flies awhile before it dies. . .

Metaphor and simile are never overpowering. In **"Ants and Sailboats"** the poet matter-of-factly sees sailboats with

> The sails stuck up like tiny thumbs
> And fingernails. . . .

> Or stacked themselves like cards to bunch
> Beyond the islands. . . .
>
> (pp. 35-6)

Onomatopoeia has never been livelier than in **"Five Chants"** (**"The pickety fence"**):

> Give it a lick
> Give it a lick
> Give it a lick
> With a rickety stick

and never more clearly presented to young people than in **"Take Sky,"** where poet invites reader and listener to marvel at the great number of words whose very sound echoes their meaning:

> Three words we fear but form:
> Gale, twister, thunderstorm;
> Others that simply shake
> Are tremble, temblor, quake.
> But granite, stone, and rock:
> Too solid, they, to shock.

"No poet worth his salt," David McCord has written in *Pen, Paper and Poem* . . . , "has ever been able to write the kinds of poems he wanted to write without a basic knowledge of meter, rhythm, rhyme and the established verse forms." A poet may abandon rhyme and forms, "but he will never abandon meter and rhythm." McCord has abandoned neither rhyme nor form. His rhymes, whether in couplet, tercet, quatrain, or other patterns, not only sound a true ring but offer delightful surprises. Enjambment is frequently used in conjunction with closed couplets with grace and wit. . . . (p. 37)

Most amazing is the way in which McCord begins and ends many of his poems, for they seem to spring to mind almost as a part of the stream of consciousness. This he has acknowledged as a legacy from his mother, "who could always find the surprising word to express the surprising idea." **"Three Signs of Spring"** plunges in with "Kite on the end of the twine"; **"Ducks Walking"** opens with "Actually Five"; and in **"Take Sky"** it is as if the reader or the listener were barging in on the poet's thoughts: "Now think of words. Take *sky.*" But the most startling surprises are his endings. In a poem such as **"That's Not,"** in which he explains the difference between

grouse and pheasant, weasel and mink, hare and rabbit—information that could easily turn into a lesson—he writes:

> No rabbit *that.* No, sir! a *hare:*
> long ears, long legs. But not long where
> you're looking. Please learn not to stare. . . .

The endings of **"The Newt," "The Poultry Show," "Dividing," "Alphabet (Eta Z),"** and **"Snake"** are but a few examples of deftly handled material which could easily, in another writer's hand, be ruined by a last line. In **"Pumpkin Seeds"** David McCord talks about carving a pumpkin. In the last two lines of the second stanza he tells us,

> We bring alive a thing that's dead,
> And do it with a sense of love.

It would be impossible for anyone to write *real* poetry for children without this sense of love for bringing things to life.

His poetry for the young is built on a strong foundation of literary tradition. Watts pointed the way towards remembering in rhyme, but the moral overtones and heavy-handedness of his preaching are no fare for today's children. Blake introduced the necessity for joy, dreaming, and play; Carroll the cerebral content of words and games, in addition to joy. Lear and Carroll, the bachelor Victorians, introduced the value of nonsense and wordplay. Stevenson zeroed in on the everyday experience in the life of the child, de la Mare on the mystery. Roberts observed the American scene of childhood with an eye to people and events presented in the language of the child. Such a tradition is felt in many aspects of McCord's work.

What David McCord has added is the invitation to the young people of this country to look about, to be aware, to learn and grow, as he himself has done, with a keen eye and ear for the American landscape, its rhythms, its vernacular, and its subject matter from sky to earth and below. He has never lost the sensitivities of childhood, the love of children, or the knowledge that curiosity and wonder are the lifeblood of the young. His invitation is compelling. It cannot be ignored and is not cast aside because children know that its message is true, that its rhythms and surprises, laughter and wonder are theirs to seize.

In his second book for children, *Take Sky,* David McCord wrote an introductory poem:

> Blesséd Lord, what it is to be young:
> To be of, to be for, be among—
> Be enchanted, enthralled,
> Be the caller, the called,
> The singer, the song, and the sung.

Surely, David McCord is the singer whose songs will be sung as long as there are children to listen. (pp. 37-9)

> *Myra Cohn Livingston, "David McCord: The Singer, the Song, and the Sung," in* The Horn Book Magazine, *Vol. LV, No. 1, February, 1979, pp. 25-39.*

**MARILYN HEERS LARSON**

[McCord's] poetry can be organized into five major categories:

1) Poems about small creatures such as newts, bats, frogs, crickets, ants, etc., or the **"Centipede"** with its rhythm, humor and play on words. . . .

2) Poems written in the first person conveying the thoughts or observations of a child—flying a kite, fishing, eating, drawing, skating, and watching nature. In **"Fred,"** written in one of

McCord's most popular forms, the couplet, one gets a child's-eye look at the home and habits of a flying squirrel. . . .

3) Poems for and about children written from the vantage point of an adult looking back. In **"Make Merry,"** there is a note of urgency (repeated in McCord's comments on the importance of childhood in a person's life: "First be a child before you grow up and let nothing interfere with that process. . . .") . . .

4) Poems for language exploration and word play. In **"Corinna,"** the word "dinner" trips a switch to the down east pronunciation of "Corinner" and from then on the poem becomes hilarious. . . . (p. 23)

5) Poems that demonstrate the writing of verse forms. **"The Cinquain"** is an example of McCord's ingenious way to teach form and structure of verse. It has a content similar to the one McCord uses for the couplet, tercet, villanelle, quatrain, ballade, clerihew, and haiku. The first three cinquains explain the structure and the fourth through eighteenth show the beauty of the form. . . . (pp. 23-4)

The magic and genius of McCord's work lies in his ability to translate the discipline of language and speech into poems about the simple, the detailed, and the complex. The beauty, wonder and humor of life are revealed in his poetry for the young. (p. 24)

> *Marilyn Heers Larson, "David McCord: Poet for the Young," in* Children's Literature Association Quarterly, *Vol 5, No. 2, Summer, 1980, pp. 22-4.*

### ZENA SUTHERLAND, DIANNE L. MONSON, AND MAY HILL ARBUTHNOT

One of the most outstanding and prolific writers of humorous verse for children since the 1950s is David McCord. . . . McCord's poems are not all humorous, but the best of them have a captivating playfulness and ebullience which infectiously communicate an enjoyment of words and word play. (p. 264)

*Take Sky,* McCord's second book of verse for children, is on the whole more completely humorous than *Far and Few.* His **"Write Me a Verse"** should appeal to youngsters wrestling with verse forms. In these poems couplets, quatrains, limericks, and triolets are amusingly defined and illustrated. However, there is also much entertainment in this book for the youngest children. In **"Sing Song," "Three Signs of Spring," "Sally Lun Lundy,"** and many other verses, McCord has a wonderful time playing with the sounds of words. He also makes many clever uses of dialogue. The poems in *Away and Ago* are also light and sunny; in this collection he writes about parties, balloons, baseball, and holidays, and in **"Like You As It"** he plays with words. . . . The poet savors language, but he holds it—like the master craftsman he is—firmly in check. (p. 291)

> *Zena Sutherland, Dianne L. Monson, and May Hill Arbuthnot, "Poetry," in their* Children and Books, *sixth edition, Scott, Foresman and Company, 1981, pp. 255-307.\**

### SHEILA A. EGOFF

David McCord possesses a quieter, less satiric humor than Merriam, and a deeper base of emotion and theme, ranging from bold nonsense to meditative lyricism. But he shares with Merriam the same attentive care for words and the interest in droll language games and stylish illustration of poetic structure. His concern with technical expertise and rhythmic flair is ev-

ident in the antic poem, **"Sometimes"** from *For Me to Say: Rhymes of the Never Was and Always Is* . . . :

> The clouds are full of new blue sky,
> The water's full of sea;
> The apples full of deep-dish pie,
> And I am full of me. . . .

McCord's entire output has been collected in *One at a Time: His Collected Poems for the Young* . . . , a beguiling book of poetry that is predominantly light and playful, but sensitive to childhood's need for wonder, curiosity, and dreaming. (p. 236)

> *Sheila A. Egoff, "Poetry," in her* Thursday's Child: Trends and Patterns in Contemporary Children's Literature, *American Library Association, 1981, pp. 221-46.\**

---

### FAR AND FEW: RHYMES OF THE NEVER WAS AND ALWAYS IS (1952)

An established versifier's first book of poems for children shows thought, humor and sharp tags of image and symbol that aptly hinge its subjects to important phases of daily living. In rhythms always marked but often at sharp variance from poem to poem or stanza to stanza, this poet speaks of the sun, the moon, not being able to stay up at night, a child's private spot in the woods, the reflection of a star in a bucket as it "silvers in the water", a toad—a "private-cellar man"—in its happy hole under the porch. Here are qualities of wit and gentle sentiment agreeable to the whole family.

> *A review of "Far and Few," in* Virginia Kirkus' Bookshop Service, *Vol. XX, No. 15, August 1, 1952, p. 450.*

Mr. McCord is a good poet. He has the requisite wonder, sympathy, tenderness of impression, gayety, fancy and imagination. If sometimes he strives too subtly, for this reader, to implant a between-the-lines suggestion, if sometimes his whimsicality seems very determined, he reports well his notes on life and the world. He has a sensitive ear for the rhythms of nature, and has much satisfaction in transferring these rhythms to verbal forms. He has long practised the art of words, with understanding and discrimination. **"Far and Few"** is his twentieth book. He has learned to make deft, simple, delightful music. . . .

The poet's fascination with sound, his melophilia, recalls the sweet, still resonant rhymes of Laura E. Richards' **"Tirra Lirra."** The reviewer has been very happy, going from **"Far and Few"** to **"Tirra Lirra,"** and then back again to **"Far and Few."**

> *Morris Bishop, in a review of "Far and Few," in* New York Herald Tribune Book Review, *September 7, 1952, p. 6.*

For many years David McCord has been known to readers of poetry as a distinguished craftsman, a man with a keen sense of simple vitality, a vital sense of comedy and an ear for magic. . . . In this new little book, charming in substance as well as format . . . , Mr. McCord gathers together much of his verse written about or for—or as the author puts it—"of" children.

The result will undoubtedly please many children and perhaps more adults, but to this reviewer it is disappointing. There is a certain fierce relevance in the vagaries of children's minds which gives to the idiom in which they declare themselves a quality of surprise which is close to the core of poetry. It never seems contrived, always inevitable. The author of **"Far and Few"** in his attempts to match this aspect of the unsophisticated mind of a child seems often to lose himself in artifice and contrivance.

He does, however, manage in ten or a dozen poems, to present something quite perfect and, when he does, it is apparent that his success comes from falling into the same attitude of spontaneity which governs a child's laughing repetition of sounds by which it is fascinated.

> *Raymond Holden, in a review of "Far and Few: Rhymes of the Never Was and Always Is," in The New York Times Book Review, September 7, 1952, p. 12.*

A completely welcome collection of verse whose strong, individual, fresh rhythms are sure to appeal to the ear, and children will be captivated by the highly contemporary images in certain poems. There is considerable variety of word and technique, ranging from sheerest nonsense to lovely quiet lyric. The author achieves the unusual success of children's poetry that is never cute and never dilutes its meaning; it is clear and fresh and altogether delightful. Recommended for 8-12-year-olds and all who love poetry.

> *Helen M. Brogan, in a review of "Far and Few: Rhymes of the Never Was and Always Is," in Library Journal, Vol. 77, No. 16, September 15, 1952, p. 1521.*

[How] refreshing it was to turn to David McCord's *Far and Few, Rhymes of the Never Was and Always Is*. . . . Here are "loving words" freshly minted and invigorated by their application to what children see and touch, feel and know, instinctively.

Love of poetry is born and bred and nourished by such a book as this and the drawings [by Henry B. Kane], whether of **"The Grasshopper,"** **"The White Ships"** or **"Cocoon,"** are in the mood of rhymes which range from pure nonsense to pure beauty. There is but one thing to say of *Far and Few*, it is indispensable for a children's library. (pp. 310-11)

> *Anne Carroll Moore, in a review of "Far and Few: Rhymes of the Never Was and Always Is," in The Horn Book Magazine, Vol. XXVIII, No. 5, October, 1952, pp. 310-11.*

In his poems for children David McCord likes to introduce new rhythms, new forms of verse. Some, like the poem called **"The Pickety Fence,"** will bring a little child into action as a singing game would. In **"The Grasshopper"** the form of his verse makes a picture that the children will follow with their eyes as well as with their minds. Then there are thoughtful poems, quiet in wording and in feeling like the one called **"This Is My Rock."** . . . It is a heartening thing to have a collection of fresh, new poems for the children as good as these.

> *A review of "Far and Few: Rhymes of the Never Was and Always Is," in The Saturday Review, New York, Vol. XXXV, No. 46, November 15, 1952, p. 68.*

---

## TAKE SKY: MORE RHYMES OF THE NEVER WAS AND ALWAYS IS (1962)

Bananas and cream, ladybugs, kites and castor oil—all find their happy way into these wonderfully crisp lines. We learn never to talk down to glowworms, and not to be surprised at T.V. cowboys who have never seen a cow. The experiences of being measured for height and going to the dentist are as accurately and delightfully presented as the pleasanter ones of making snowmen and going about dressed up on Halloween. Mr. McCord takes simple words—the majority of them monosyllabic—and treats them handsomely, putting them together with expert care into unheard of combinations that will certainly satisfy his young audience. This should be large, because his respect for it and for his medium is profound. He satisfies adventurous longings to be at sea or up in space as deftly as, in **"Write Me A Verse,"** he introduces the couplet, quatrain, limerick and triolet by having his readers join him in the fun of writing them. Nor does he hesitate to have us meet individuals with such perfect names as Mingram Mo and Sally Lun Lundy. (p. 61)

> *William Turner Levy, "Voices that Know How to Say It in Verse," in The New York Times Book Review, Part II, November 11, 1962, pp. 3, 61.**

[David McCord's new book of verse] is written with an elusive and puckish humor that is as hither-and-yon as childhood itself. His initial poem, **"Take Sky,"** sets the mood by collecting word groups that suggest their sound-meanings. The poems that follow play with words as if they were brightly colored balls, sometimes with a flash of deep meaning, but mostly just for fun. In poems like **"Down by the Sea,"** he seems quizzically to anticipate, with a cocked eyebrow, the point of view of the child grown up.

> *Silence Buck Bellows, "I'm Rhyming!" in The Christian Science Monitor, November 15, 1962, p. 3B.**

The poet of the greatly enjoyed *Far and Few* exhibits here his special delight in fun with words and his desire to convey to children the enjoyment of such play and to stimulate them to try various verse forms themselves. The forty-eight poems, beginning with the intriguing "Now think of words. Take *sky* / And ask yourself just why—" include lyrics, delicious nonsense, and the long **"Write Me a Verse,"** containing Professor Swigly Brown's "talk about four kinds of Rime.". . . This diversity of imagination and humor makes a volume that bears dipping into again and again for quiet enjoyment and for reading aloud.

> *Virginia Haviland, in a review of "Take Sky: More Rhymes of the Never Was and Always Is," in The Horn Book Magazine, Vol. XXXIX, No. 1, February, 1963, p. 71.*

Humorous, thought-provoking verse by a literary master (although he does make "produce" rhyme with "noose"!). All 41 will give alert youngsters pleasure in the flexibility of word combinations and will inspire many to creative writing. Adult help may be needed for understanding the verse-lessons part "by Professor Swigly Brown" about couplet, triolet, quatrain, and limerick.

> *Francelia Goddard, in a review of "Take Sky: More Rhymes of the Never Was and Always Is," in School Library Journal, an appendix to Library Journal, Vol. 9, No. 6, February, 1963, p. 53.*

A book of poems, pleasant for independent reading or for reading aloud to younger children. The poetry is rhythmic and imaginative; it has simplicity and humor. A few of the selections are nonsense humor, several of them play happily with words and sounds. One or two serious poems have some lovely lines, as does **"The Leaves"**: "Down flutters every leaf, after twirl and spin, Deleted, spare, and thin In multiple retreat, Feet rustle them. We rake and burn them for the sake of dwelling in their smoke." (pp. 113-14)

> *Zena Sutherland, in a review of "Take Sky: More Rhymes of the Never Was and Always Is," in* Bulletin of the Center for Children's Books, *Vol. XVI, No. 7, March, 1963, pp. 113-14.*

---

### ALL DAY LONG: FIFTY RHYMES OF THE NEVER WAS AND ALWAYS IS   (1966)

This is David McCord's third collection of verses with the subtitle, "Rhymes of the Never Was and Always Is." This is one of those vague, all purpose phrases that allows the poet to include everything he wants. Just so with this collection: the poems are uneven in age level, in quality and in type; there is even a bit of prose. The collection might have benefited from sectioning. But this is quibbling, because there are a number of successful poems. Some of the best are the nonsense poems; Mr. McCord plays perfectly to the young child's ready sense of the ridiculous in such potential favorites as **"Corinna,"** **"Ptarmigan,"** and **"Singular Indeed."** The poet is less successful when he deals with a more sophisticated level of nonsense with an awkward imbalance of seriousness and humor. A few of the poems are not children's poems at all, but reflections from the adult viewpoint, as in **"Walnut Tree."** Then, there are a few totally serious poems that are excellent—**"Elm Seed Blizzard"** is one to check. Yet another type of poem is the short narrative, and here Mr. McCord's rapport with nonsense enters in; these are among his best. Adults using this will have to pick and choose among the types and age levels, but the great plus of this collection is Mr. McCord's facility with a variety of verse forms. Some will come as a challenge to the younger ear, and this in itself is of great value.

> *A review of "All Day Long," in* Virginia Kirkus' Service, *Vol. XXXIV, No. 14, July 15, 1966, p. 685.*

Here is a generous burst of rhymes and rhythms which in varying degrees amuse and surprise. The poet's quixotic fun with oddities in expression and his delight in natural phenomena, too, make this volume, like his *Far and Few* and *Take Sky,* a welcome addition to any library. In short, brisk rhymes or in leisurely speculations, he speaks to many ages, now with "The bumblebee is bumbly, / acting anything but humbly" and the childlike "Hello, skunk cabbage! Where's old skunk? / 'He's rolled up here in the upper bunk'" and with the sophisticated humor of **"Rapid Reading"** and the truly poetic vividness of **"Elm Seed Blizzard."** (pp. 578-79)

> *Virginia Haviland, in a review of "All Day Long: Fifty Rhymes of the Never Was and Always Is," in* The Horn Book Magazine, *Vol. XLII, No. 5, October, 1966, pp. 578-79.*

This collection has much to offer youngsters. Like Ciardi, Merriam, and others of that caliber, Mr. McCord speaks clearly to today's child, with humor, love of life, and love of language. There are no fairies and no cuteness here; robust rhymes only are allowed.

These poems are all simple to read, yet they sing, they dance, they dazzle, and they enchant. They speak of simple things like cloud pictures or a beech tree in serious ways and other simple things like rapid reading and bumblebees in humorous ways. And they speak playfully of language. The author has fun with words and respect for them. . . .

Children should love this collection. It will no doubt be a favorite, as are *Far and Few* and *Take Sky.*

> *Phyllis Cohen, in a review of "All Day Long: Fifty Rhymes of the Never Was and Always Is," in* Young Readers Review, *Vol. III, No. 3, November, 1966, p. 11.*

David McCord likes to call his verses for young people "Rhymes of the Never Was and Always Is." A felicitous phrase, I think. It fitted **"Take Sky,"** and **"Far and Few."** It fits this new collection . . . [**"All Day Long"**]. McCord's playfulness is as skippingly light as ever in tongue-twisters like **"Corinna"** and **"When Monkeys Eat Bananas"** and in a running-punning gag, **"Rapid Reading."** He is at home with both country and urban images, swinging from **"Frog in a Bog"** to **"Laundromat,"** and his language is American at its best: colloquial, comfortable. His eye for nature is observant of details; he conveys enthusiasm without ever sermonizing. (p. 67)

> *Eve Merriam, "The Light and the Slight," in* The New York Times Book Review, *Part II, November 6, 1966, pp. 6, 67.\**

A book of rather light, entertaining poems. . . . The poems are well-suited to reading aloud, although a few that play with words will lose in the translation, such as the poem about ptarmigan, playing on the prefixing of the silent "p" to other words: "ptolerate" or "pterritory." Or, for example, "Supposing though's not tho, but more like thoff, and sough's sow's not a pig that sows, but soff?" The topics are simple but intriguing, the writing has rhythm, humor, and imaginative zest. . . .

> *Zena Sutherland, in a review of "All Day Long: Fifty Rhymes of the Never Was and Always Is," in* Bulletin of the Center for Children's Books, *Vol. 20, No. 5, January, 1967, p. 76.*

A happy collection, mostly in easy rhymed couplets, some representing a light-hearted appraisal of the child's own world, complete with observations on laundromats, bulldozers, and rapid reading ("rabbit reading"), and others to delight the child beginning to notice the oddities of language, e.g., figures of speech, strange spellings, and other word play. A few of the verses are true poetry, especially those about trees. Nature subjects are illustrated with exactitude and lyric sensibility.

> *Margaret Hodges, in a review of "All Day Long: Fifty Rhymes of the Never Was and Always Is," in* School Library Journal, *an appendix to* Library Journal, *Vol. 13, No. 5, January, 1967, p. 68.*

---

### EVERY TIME I CLIMB A TREE   (1967)

Culled from previously published collections, two dozen of Mr. McCord's poems best suited for younger children, many of them nice to read aloud to the very youngest. The writing has both emotional appeal and literary distinction; it comments on the familiar with loving zest and on the unfamiliar with a childlike wonder.

*Zena Sutherland, in a review of "Every Time I Climb a Tree," in* Bulletin of the Center for Children's Books, *Vol. 21, No. 6, February, 1968, p. 97.*

[This is a representative selection from three of David Mc-Cord's other volumes], but not everyone will be taken with it. Mr. McCord is intrigued by words, and while he can sometimes make them assume the flash and color of juggler's balls, too often the glitter conceals a tired subject: "The pickety fence / The pickety fence / Give it a lick it's / The pickety fence / Give it a lick it's / A clickety fence / Give it a lick it's / A lickety fence ..." The book has several dozen poems like this—about a glowworm, and a turtle named Myrtle, and toast spread with jam—but these subjects seem shopworn despite the window dressing. One is only aware of the poet's talent when he abandons wordplay for genuine feeling: "This is my rock, / And here come I / Before the night has swept the sky; / This is my rock, / This is the place / I meet the evening face to face." Perhaps it all comes down to the fact that poetry needs more than words.

*Barbara Wersba, in a review of "Every Time I Climb a Tree," in* The New York Times Book Review, *February 11, 1968, p. 26.*

---

## FOR ME TO SAY: RHYMES OF THE NEVER WAS AND ALWAYS IS (1970)

One of the reasons David McCord is so successful a writer of children's poetry is that he has a relish for fun and games which is like the child's own. Yet he is a sophisticated master of his craft, and the poems in this collection, though light, are polished. Some are on such important matters as breakfast, Santa Claus, or rain, and some merely play with words. One section, **"Write Me Another Verse,"** shows by example and instruction various verse forms. . . . [The] book is great fun to read aloud—in fact, it's hard not to.

*Isaac Asimov, in a review of "For Me to Say: Rhymes of the Never Was and Always Is," in* Saturday Review, *Vol. LIX, No. 4, January 23, 1971, p. 71.*

Innumerable critics—including many who are eminent poets themselves—have mentioned the characteristics of David McCord's work: grace, charm, tenderness, humor, wit, subtlety, ingenuity, joy. And the new collection will be greeted with delight. Here are riddle poems and game poems—poems that celebrate the fun and splendor of words. "Words have more to them than meaning: / Words like *equidistant, gleaning,* / *Paradoxical,* and *glisten.* / All you have to do is *listen.* / That's the way words come to settle / In your mind like molten metal." Included, too, are poems of nature, seasons, birds, bugs, and animals; poems that glorify and vivify everyday experiences and some that contain bits of unobtrusive wisdom. "'No time like the present,' they always used to say, / Meaning—*Get Busy! Do You Hear Me? Don't Delay!* / Much better in reverse (it doesn't have to rhyme): / Simply, simply, *No present like the time.*" One fifth of the book is devoted to an extension of a group of poems included in *Take Sky.* Under the title, **"Write Me a Verse,"** these poems attempted to show the reader how to write the couplet, the limerick, the quatrain, and the triolet by giving specific directions for each in the actual verse form. Now the poet in **"Write Me Another Verse"** shows how to write the ballade, the tercet, the villanelle, the clerihew, the cinquain, and haiku. His "last word" of advice to young writers of verse cannot be stressed too often: "When-

ever you have written a poem of any sort, *always* read it aloud to yourself many times to make sure that your meter (rhythm) is correct, that your rhyme-words are the words you were looking for and *not* words forced upon you because you could not think of anything else."

*Ethel L. Heins, in a review of "For Me to Say: Rhymes of the Never Was and Always Is," in* The Horn Book Magazine, *Vol. XLVII, No. 1, February, 1971, p. 58.*

A collection of gay, occasionally inscrutable poems in which McCord interprets, in his inimitable verbal acrobatic style, a variety of subjects such as how to draw a monkey or play a game of **"Doublets,"** the look and sound of words, arithmetic gazintas, a winter sky, and poor old Mr. Bidery whose garden's awfully spidery.

*A review of "For Me to Say: Rhymes of the Never Was and Always Is," in* The Booklist, *Vol. 67, No. 12, February 15, 1971, p. 494.*

There is not much to say about a new collection of David McCord's poetry except that (1) the poems are, indeed, new; and (2) it is sure to be snapped up, happily, by libraries and their patrons. Most of the verses here are topnotch, from the delightful word-play of **"Mr. Bidery's Spidery Garden"** and **"LMNTL"** to the final series of poems on (and in) various poetic forms: tercet, villanelle, ballade, clerihew, cinquain and haiku. If some selections, like **"Plymouth Rocks, Of Course,"** are comparatively flat, no matter; there are enough gems here to make purchase more than worthwhile.

*Margaret A. Dorsey, in a review of "For Me to Say: Rhymes of the Never Was and Always Is," in* School Library Journal, *an appendix to* Library Journal, *Vol. 17, No. 7, March, 1971, p. 129.*

---

## MR BIDERY'S SPIDERY GARDEN (1972)

Words are obviously "great fun to play with" for David McCord and if it has taken a long time for a volume of his verse to reach Britain, it is all the more welcome now. Like his fellow-American Ogden Nash he enjoys up-ending the normal vocabulary of verse. The title-poem, with its comically invented rhymes, begins mildly enough "Poor old Mr. Bidery. His garden's awfully spidery: Bugs use it as a hidery" and ends abruptly "Pea-picking *is* so poddery!" The crisp, neat patterns of words are often comic but with a twist of thought or a touch of logic behind them and he can make simple lines do a great deal—for example, in *Crows* with its verbal felicities ("I like the great wild clamour of crow hate"), or in the reflective poem *Take sky.* The joking *Write me a verse* offers first lessons in prosody and there is a long, quick-moving tragi-comedy called *Four little ducks.* Sampling, in the long run, doesn't go far enough to suggest the spicy, musical variety of this little book. (pp. 2101-02)

*Margery Fisher, in a review of "Mr. Bidery's Spidery Garden," in her* Growing Point, *Vol. 11, No. 8, March, 1973, pp. 2101-02.*

It is sometimes difficult with verse directed at junior readers to know where inspiration peters out and literary doodling begins. Not that doodling is always unproductive or unrewarding to the reader but it can become tedious as I fear it may do in David McCord's latest offering. On the other hand, the slight intellectual content of most of the pieces allied with the tricksy rhymes and domino-type continuity can exercise a pleasant mesmeric effect. Another possible source of charm lies naturally in the subjects—simple, uncomplicated and near to home: newts, grasshoppers, snails, starfish, mice, owls, Christmas, ducks and more of a similar domestic(?) category. One can like it or loathe it; at least it does not cost half the earth.

> *A. R. Williams, in a review of "Mr. Bidery's Spidery Garden," in* The Junior Bookshelf, *Vol. 37, No. 2, April, 1973, p. 116.*

---

### AWAY AND AGO: RHYMES OF THE NEVER WAS AND ALWAYS IS   (1974)

Boys and girls have a rare treat in store here. This new collection by the eminent poet contains works on a great variety of subjects, including secrets, the Little League, balloons, almost everything including the implications of a word like "only." David McCord has such fun with words, his imagination is so unfettered that he can't fail to appeal even to those who think they don't like poetry.

> *A review of "Away and Ago: Rhymes of the Never Was and Always Is," in* Publishers Weekly, *Vol. 207, No. 5, February 3, 1975, p. 75.*

A new poetry collection marked by McCord's usual wit and originality. For younger children than most of the author's previous verse, many of these rhymes could be read aloud to preschoolers. There are a number of fresh holiday poems and several small gems, e.g., a conversation between a child and toad about school subjects in which the toad comments "my math isn't hard / like how many hops / to the foot round the yard / not counting the stops." Good fun for a wide range of readers.

> *June B. Cater, in a review of "Away and Ago: Rhymes of the Never Was and Always Is," in* School Library Journal, *Vol. 21, No. 9, May, 1975, p. 48.*

**"Away and Ago"** is a collection of fifty-odd accomplished, charming poems, nonsensical or—ah—sensical, about grammar, Easter, balloons, literalness, nursery rhymes, Halloween, girls telling secrets, wizzlebugs, cats—anything, everything. Mr. McCord is a genuine children's poet, original, ingenious, relevant, and rare.

> *Neil Millar, "Of Wizzlebugs and Somber Fire," in* The Christian Science Monitor, *May 7, 1975, p. B5.\**

McCord's playfulness never becomes cute or whimsical; he rejoices in words, he savors them, he teases them—and he is a master craftsman. That's why this, like his earlier collections of poems, is delightful to read aloud or alone. The occasional serious poems are never heavy, and even those speak to a child's concerns, but most of the selections in *Away and Ago* are light in tone whether they are nonsensical or witty. And all of them have a quality of sunny affection, as though the poet were sharing his fun with a friend.

> *Zena Sutherland, in a review of "Away and Ago," in* Bulletin of the Center for Children's Books, *Vol. 28, No. 10, June, 1975, p. 163.*

In a relaxed manner, the author ranges the world of childhood, regarding its inhabitants with realistic affection.... David McCord loves his language and uses it punctiliously; and he

bounces it about like a ball. "Big clocks go *tick,* / Big clocks go *tock.* / The ticking always seems to mock / The tocking." ... Best of all, the author practices his own preachments: "Great poetry—good poetry—is free of jargon. Poets . . . flush the cuckoo adjective out of the nest of nouns and verbs. They seek exactness out of inexactness."

> *Ethel L. Heins, in a review of "Away and Ago: Rhymes of the Never Was and Always Is," in* The Horn Book Magazine, *Vol. LI, No. 3, June, 1975, p. 284.*

---

### THE STAR IN THE PAIL   (1975)

Eminent critics have blessed poet McCord with phrases like "flawless taste, charm, tenderness, grace, lovely humor," etc. And they don't overstate. He has a felicitous collaborator in Marc Simont, the artist who has sparked the pages of this poetry book with pictures of complementary ingenuity. Their joint effort is a winning way to introduce little ones to the world of poetry. **"Hitchhiker"** is the saga of an owl that bums a ride on a witch's broomstick, and a jolly tale it is. For a more brisk exercise, try **"Christmas Eve"**. . . .

> *A review of "The Star in the Pail," in* Publishers Weekly, *Vol. 208, No. 24, December 15, 1975, p. 48.*

From the simplest of objects—a pail, a clock, an animal cracker—and from the commonest of creatures—a starfish, a daddy longlegs, a dog—the poet, as always, extracts wit and imagery, yoking the simplest of words to shapely rhymes and verses. For example, in **"Three Signs of Spring,"** there is a manipulation of repetitive rhyme by which sheer denotation is transformed into connotation: "Kite on the end of the twine, / Fish on the end of a line, / Dog on the end of a whine." Bandying with words, the poet creates humor: "'Would you rather be a starfish / Or an out-beyond-the-bar fish?'" Always ingenious, but never marred by sophistication, the transparent verses have been stripped down to essentials to show and accept things as they are and—at the same time—to show the poet as he is: "Of all the stars in heaven there was one to spare, / And he silvered in the water and I left him there."

> *Paul Heins, in a review of "The Star in the Pail," in* The Horn Book Magazine, *Vol. LII, No. 2, April, 1976, p. 173.*

The subjects are puzzling, the rhymes in many cases are "groaners," and the whole seems like a dry exercise in rhyme and meter: e.g., "Green is go / and red is stop / and yellow is peaches / with cream on top"; "The cow has a cud / the turtle has mud / The rabbit has a hutch / But I haven't much."

> *Barbara Thiele, in a review of "The Star in the Pail," in* School Library Journal, *Vol. 22, No. 8, April, 1976, p. 62.*

The poems are not always McCord's best, but even McCord's second-best is pretty good, and—while the better poems are available in older collections—it's useful to have a book in which there are no poems McCord deems inappropriate for the very young child.

> *Zena Sutherland, in a review of "The Star in the Pail," in* Bulletin of the Center for Children's Books, *Vol. 29, No. 9, May, 1976, p. 148.*

**"The Star in the Pail"** is delicious. David McCord's poems delight the unlost infant in each of us, and Marc Simont's pictures—full-bodied watercolors, lively, humorous, highly accomplished—captivate the eye. Print and paint harmonize like air and sunlight.

The poet has been highly praised by many notable colleagues, including Howard Nemerov, Archibald MacLeish, John Ciardi, and even Ogden Nash; and the praises are deserved. This one is a treasure for adults and children to share.

> *Neil Millar, " 'Bubblegum' and Other Sweet Verse—With Lyric Rhymes to Stall Bedtimes," in* The Christian Science Monitor, *May 12, 1976, p. 25.*

***The Star in the Pail*** contains twenty-six poems selected by McCord from his previously published poems, some originally published as long ago as fifty years. Here are old friends, like **"Our Mr. Toad,"** as well as poems not so well-known, like **"Gone"** and **"The Star in the Pail,"** pieces with sharp and clear images, gentle rhythms, and McCord's genius for seeing and feeling from the child's point of view in an uncomplicated, uncluttered, and ungimmicky way. (p. 199)

> *Alethea K. Helbig, "Trends in Poetry for Children,"*
> *in* Children's Literature: Annual of the Modern Language Association Seminar on Children's Literature and The Children's Literature Association, Vol. 6, *edited by Francelia Butler, Temple University Press, 1977, pp. 195-201.*

---

### ONE AT A TIME: HIS COLLECTED POEMS FOR THE YOUNG (1977)

The collected work of the accomplished, much praised practitioner of children's verse—as it first appeared in ***Far and Few, Away and Ago,*** and other volumes. At 494 pages it's a bit too much light diversion all at once, but teachers and librarians will welcome it for their own convenience.

> *A review of "One at a Time," in* Kirkus Reviews, *Vol. XLV, No. 21, November 1, 1977, p. 1147.*

Even libraries that have the volumes from which many of these poems are collected—***Far and Few, Take Sky, All Day Long, For Me to Say,*** and ***Away and Ago***—will want to invest in this handsome volume for reference, browsing, or classroom use and for the additional poems included. Henry Kane's black-and-white illustrations, varying from naturalistic drawings to cartoon sketches, wear well, as does McCord's longstanding way with words. It's a rich mixture of thought and humor. . . .

> *Betsy Hearne, in a review of "One at a Time: His Collected Poems for the Young," in* Booklist, *Vol. 74, No. 9, January 1, 1978, p. 748.*

Opening David McCord's collected poems, I felt I had stepped into the perfect party: some of the guests are old friends, the rest are people one would like very much to meet. . . .

David McCord is a joyful, exacting teacher who believes that poetry and children should be heard as well as seen. In **"Write Me Another Verse"** he shows by example how to write a ballade, a tercet, a villanelle, a clerihew, a cinquain and a haiku. . . . Playing with the spelling of words, he delights his readers while he instructs them. . . .

Though he loves the games words play, he never loses sight of things words describe: the "beech, / The carefully tailored cut of his grey bark," the rain "driving silver nails / into the shingles overhead," the crickets

> all busy punching tickets
> clicking their little punches.
> The tickets come in bunches,
> good for a brief excursion,
> good for a cricket's version
> of travel (before it snows) to
> the places a cricket goes to.
>
>               **—From "Crickets"**

Sound matches sense in McCord's best poems, and conversation, which he uses often, flows along in meter and rhyme as if these were the natural ornaments of speech. The ghost of Robert Frost, whom McCord praises in his introduction, moves through many of his nature poems and his narratives: "earth's content to hold us with / our dirty shirts and all." Earth's the best place for loving birches, snowy evenings and poetry. . . .

In the list of "Real among the realest books" he appends to **"Books"** I find one serious omission: his own.

> *Nancy Willard, in a review of "One at a Time: His Collected Poems for the Young," in* The New York Times Book Review, *February 26, 1978, p. 27.*

Whether every child will go for the poems of David McCord is questionable, for he sometimes places high demands upon children's powers of analysis, and often upon their vocabularies. Still, many of his poems are irresistible, and the appearance . . . of his collected poems for the young, ***One at a Time,*** gives him a place in American children's poetry comparable to that occupied, on the mainland, by Robert Frost. One never doubts that McCord knows how to fashion a limerick—even to make such a trivial exercise turn into something much more:

> Blessed Lord, what it is to be young:
> To be of, to be for, be among—
>     Be enchanted, enthralled,
>     Be the caller, the called,
> The singer, the song, and the sung.

Not a simple poem to offer a child, that one, but perhaps the child may be tempted by its rollicking form to say it over and over until its meaning begins to dawn on him. (p. 77)

> *X. J. Kennedy and Dorothy M. Kennedy, "Tradition and Revolt: Recent Poetry for Children," in* The Lion and the Unicorn, *Vol. 4, No. 2, Winter, 1980-81, pp. 75-82.*

[***One at a Time*** is an] impressive volume. . . . McCord's wit and thoughtful perception sing in the music of his words. ***One at a Time,*** more than any other single volume, is a key to cultivating poetic taste—to produce children who will read poetry for pleasure. (p. 277)

> *Bernice E. Cullinan with Mary K. Karrer and Arlene M. Pillar, "Poetry and Verse," in their* Literature and the Child, *Harcourt Brace Jovanovich, Inc., 1981, pp. 247-87.*

Perhaps we can do no greater service to you, to the children you teach, nor to the cause of good poetry and good prose than direct you to David McCord's book, ***One At A Time.*** . . . A collection of 450 of his poems for young children, it will capture you, your students, your children and grandchildren as you expose them to the blossoms of this man's careful cultivation. To walk in the poetic garden of this nature lover and joyous human being is an experience all of us—child and adult—should not miss. (p. 39)

> *Allen Raymond, ''David McCord: An Uncommon Man,'' in* Early Years, *Vol. 14, No. 1, August-September, 1983, pp. 37-9.*

---

### SPEAK UP: MORE RHYMES OF THE NEVER WAS AND ALWAYS IS (1980)

What is there to say of David McCord? He is a national resource, and an inexhaustible one. No one has more whatchamacallits and thingamajigs, nor more madly loving rhymes to dance them to. He is not only every literate child's jolly uncle, but a master observer and reporter of nature....

I wish ... that I had space to quote from McCord. I could from many of his past books—lovely rollicking poems about picket fences, the Axolotl, and Chief Wotapotami. But in this book McCord has built his poems like zippers: they are a fine mesh and none of the teeth will come loose without unraveling everything. Read them for yourself if you are willing to have fun. And remember that this inexhaustible man is edging toward 90 by now. He just may have decided to live forever. May it be so. (p. 16)

> *John Ciardi, ''The Essence of Nonsense,'' in* Book World—The Washington Post, *November 9, 1980, pp. 11-16.\**

Of poets who write for the young, the reigning champ in quality and quantity just has to be David McCord.... This new book shows Mr. McCord ... still hoisting his lightweight gloves with verve and pushing them home as usual.

Mr. McCord keeps both up to date and ahead of things. In one poem, a moped stutters as it speeds; in another, jetstream witches' brooms run on bottled stardust....

And as always, Mr. McCord is a wordaholic. Give him a ''persnickety'' or a ''lollapalooza'' and he'll degust the odd word's music and meaning for whole stanzas. If a few of these deliberations call for a pretty patient child, Mr. McCord is also expert in the immediately communicable joys of walking barefoot in ''squeezy black ooze,'' of a roller coaster that makes you feel ''like a ball of twine / ... That's rolling off a roof with no / One there to catch it down below.'' Unlike versifiers who think that, because they're older than children, they're better, David McCord treats every child as his peer. Children will find him factful, fanciful and kind—a voice to listen up to. (p. 50)

> *X. J. Kennedy, ''The Poets Speak,'' in* The New York Times Book Review, *November 9, 1980, pp. 50-1, 62.\**

The 50 poems, about all sorts of things—butterflies, windshield wipers, long words, joggers, worms—are uneven in quality. Some catch McCord's wit, playfulness and disciplined shaping. Others are merely cute or clever; a few are flat and uninspired. Its pleasant, unintimidating format and the humorous sketches

[by Marc Simont] make it attractive, but it is only for larger collections.

> *Marjorie Lewis, in a review of ''Speak Up: More Rhymes of the Never Was and Always Is,'' in* School Library Journal, *Vol. 27, No. 4, December, 1980, p. 60.*

Let me tell what reading the verse of David McCord does to a fellow-versifier. It interferes with the reviewing process. This reviewer, infected with the poems under consideration, came down with symptoms, real or resembling, that necessitated immediate relief. Pen in hand, she filled page after rhyming page—like forcing fluids—in the hope of being restored to normal balance. The outcome remains still in doubt. The patient will probably never be the same. It must be easier to be a nonpoet, simply enjoying the wild, wonderful onbeat balance of McCord's condition without longing to catch it. Once again the poet kicks up his heels ... and cavorts across the pages. Follow him who dare. Let the madness happen, without resistance and interferon. Dance, then, whoever you may be, for he's a trustworthy leader. He knows by heart the planet whereon he circulates, its seasons and sensations, its treasures and trivia: where the bee sucks, how the bittern booms. He takes us to heart as he has taken the world to heart.

> *Norma Farber, in a review of ''Speak Up: More Rhymes of the Never Was and Always Is,'' in* The Horn Book Magazine, *Vol. LVII, No. 1, February, 1981, p. 63.*

With facility and polish, but not much gusto, McCord conducts a staccato conversation on a butterfly sighted in a field; recalls the dubious joys of the roller coaster; looks askance at some conventional representations of animal vocalizations (''lambs *bleat?* ... cows moo? ...''); turns limericks into stiff, enjambment-riddled mouth traps; and bases other rhymes on puns or points of grammar or a list of Persian words. His rhymes might be used as models of light verse technique, but they are all very dry, however accomplished. Word play for little professors.

> *A review of ''Speak Up: More Rhymes of the Never Was and Always Is,'' in* Kirkus Reviews, *Vol. XLIX, No. 3, February 1, 1981, p. 143.*

A steady stream of resounding word-and-phrase play makes these light verses go down easily, though there's not so much to digest as in McCord's more substantial collections. Still, some of the poetry is appetizing—the brief story in **''Worm,''** the quick-sketch landscape in **''Midsummer,''** the plain fun in **''Witch's Broom.''** All are definitely best read aloud for the benefit of McCord's acoustical tricks. For classroom use, there's a broad range of both subject and complexity: **''Joggers''** is a simple, one-page depiction of a fat spaniel laboring beside his athletic family, while the next poem, **''How to Learn to Say a Long Hard Word''** runs five pages with an abstract puzzle quality. Especially for youngsters involved in poetry projects, this could exercise their awareness of form.

> *Betsy Hearne, in a review of ''Speak Up: More Rhymes of the Never Was and Always Is,'' in* Booklist, *Vol. 77, No. 13, March 1, 1981, p. 966.*

# Gerald (Edward) McDermott

## 1941-

**American reteller and author/illustrator of picture books.**

McDermott is well respected for his culturally diverse retellings of archetypal myths and traditional tales. Using mythology as a vehicle to express his interest in magic and transformation, he frequently chooses stories centering on mythic heroes and comic tricksters who undertake quests for self-fulfillment. Regarded as a proficient designer and vibrant colorist, McDermott began his career as a creator of animated folklore films which he later turned into picture books. He enhances his written renditions of tales from Japanese, Pueblo, Greek, Roman, and other sources with illustrations incorporating motifs commonly associated with the civilization featured in the story. In *Anansi the Spider: A Tale from the Ashanti,* for example, he blends the rhythm of this native African language with pictures which utilize the colors and shapes of Ashanti art. McDermott has also composed an original tale with folk elements, *Papagayo, the Mischief Maker,* which conveys the sounds and impressions of a South American jungle while relating how a noisy parrot becomes a hero.

An admirer of painters Henri Matisse and Paul Klee, McDermott creates the majority of his illustrations by using the geometric shapes and limited palette associated with Bauhaus-style design principles. His pictures and collages are angular, abstract, and sophisticated. Most often rendered in intense colors, they usually merge primitive art with contemporary design. Commentators note that McDermott's seemingly simple illustrations mask complex symbols, an observation which critics also extend to his texts. McDermott believes that the picture book illustrator has an obligation to nurture the reader's visual development. A strong proponent of exposing young children to modern art, he finds that children intuitively respond to the abstraction and symbolism in his works.

McDermott began his artistic training at the Detroit Institute of Arts when he was four years old. From ages nine to eleven he enjoyed a career as a radio performer on "Storyland," a show that dramatized folk tales and legends. It was on this program that McDermott learned the rudiments of coordinating sound effects and music with story, a skill he later refined in his films. At Cass Technical High School, a Detroit public school for students gifted in science and the arts, McDermott received formal training in Bauhaus principles. His extracurricular interest in filmmaking led to a part-time job with a television animation studio. After winning a scholarship to New York's Pratt Institute, he took a leave of absence following his junior year to work as a graphic designer for television and to write and produce his first animated film, *The Stonecutter.* Based on a traditional Japanese tale, *The Stonecutter* was created from six thousand drawings inspired by Japanese silk screen prints. McDermott toured Europe, visiting and exchanging ideas with filmmakers in England, France, and Yugoslavia. He returned to Pratt to finish his degree, and began producing and directing a series of acclaimed films on folklore subjects.

Meeting Jungian scholar Joseph Campbell was a milestone in McDermott's career. Campbell served as a consultant on three

© Tana Hoban

of McDermott's films while making the artist aware of the psychological depths of mythology and the possibilities of integrating various cultural symbols into his art. An encounter with editor George Nicholson led McDermott into a new area of artistic expression: he was offered a multivolume contract with Holt, Rinehart and Winston to translate his animated films into picture book format. McDermott lived in the south of France for two years while working on his first book, *Anansi the Spider.* Left without the stimulus and direction provided by music and sound effects, he discovered difficulties in the transition from celluloid to the printed page, and struggled to overcome problems of continuity and emphasis. His success was apparent, however, when *Anansi the Spider* was named a Caldecott Honor Book.

McDermott returned to the United States to work simultaneously on the film and book *Arrow to the Sun: A Pueblo Indian Tale,* a creation story featuring the sun and corn symbols of Pueblo art. In this book, he resolved some of his earlier technical difficulties by utilizing large, wordless spaces and a Rainbow Trail motif to sweep the reader's eye from left to right. *Arrow* won the Caldecott Medal, but the aftermath of the excitement left McDermott artistically barren for a year and a half. His next story, *The Voyage of Osiris: A Myth of Ancient Egypt,* concerns the death and afterlife of the Egyptian god. Since McDermott selects his tales to express his personal change and growth, he has described this work as a reflection of his own death and resurrection as an artist. *Papagayo, the Mischief Maker* came as comic relief after such heavy works as *Voyage* and *Knight of the Lion*, McDermott's longest book and the only one illustrated in black and white. In this adaptation of a twelfth-century Arthurian legend, McDermott deliberately chose to rely on his drawing skill alone rather than his customary use of color and design. With *Sun Flight*, the ancient Greek myth of Daedalus and Icarus, and *Daughter of Earth: A Roman Myth*, which relates the origins of the seasons, McDermott returned to the colorful, modern style of his earlier works.

Most critics applaud McDermott for his straightforward, forceful prose, his artistic proficiency, and the skill with which he converts his films into book form. Some observers express concern that the symbolic, sometimes mature themes of his stories and the stylized, abstract designs of his illustrations may exceed the comprehension of the usual picture book audience. Reviewers nevertheless recognize McDermott as an original interpreter of multicultural myths who stimulates readers of all ages with his powerful art.

In 1973, *Anansi the Spider* was a Caldecott Honor Book and won a Lewis Carroll Shelf Award; *The Magic Tree: A Tale from the Congo* was a *Boston Globe-Horn Book* Honor Book in illustration the same year. *Arrow to the Sun* received the Caldecott Medal in 1975.

(See also *Something about the Author*, Vol. 16; *Contemporary Authors*, Vols. 85-88; and *Authors in the News*, Vol. 2.)

---

### AUTHOR'S COMMENTARY

Imagine an ancient and mysterious figure who sits alone on the desert plain. He wears a dark ceremonial mask, and he is robed in desert hues of ocher, gold, and brown. By his side is a clay pot, decorated with magic symbols, and filled with bits of wood, feather, and stone. From these materials, he will create the feathered shaft that releases a spirit into solar flight.

This is the Arrowmaker, a pivotal figure in the drama of *Arrow to the Sun*. Of all the mythic characters who act out their roles in my books and films, he is the one who especially intrigues and interests me. He is a shaman who possesses the ability to see where others fail to see. He can penetrate the unyielding surface of reality with what has been called the open eye. Wordlessly gazing, the Arrowmaker perceives an essential truth and is inspired to action. He gives his vision tangible form by creating a special arrow that will send the hero on his transcendent journey to the sun. The Arrowmaker has thus acted as a liaison between the everyday world and the realm of dreams. He connects the sphere of the intellect with the sphere of intuition.

Many people believe that the role of the artist is like that of the shaman, and, in fact, this role has grown directly from our archaic need for an interpreter of the image world obscured by common sight. The artist must attempt the shamanic task of penetrating surface reality to perceive a universal truth; that is, he draws out the essence of the idea. In transforming this vision into powerful graphic shape, he hopes to communicate it to others. In the process, he can expand our visual sense and enhance our ability to see with an open eye. The artist, like the Arrowmaker, assists in releasing the imagination.

Imagination. Image-ination. The ability to call up spontaneously the visual forms of our inner life. Children seem to possess the open eye, a direct access to "the unpolluted rivers of perception and imagination." But early in childhood, swiftly, almost inexorably, our natural perceptual responses, instead of being cultivated, are eradicated. Other sensibilities are crushed as well, but visual perception seems particularly susceptible to debasement.... We have all flailed impotently at the most obvious of [the factors which prevent the development of aesthetic consciousness]: an environment cluttered with synthetic junk, the cheapening influence of advertising stereotypes, the banal imagery of television. We continually bemoan their pervasiveness and lament their trivializing influence upon our sensibilities. We have almost ritualized our complaints against these massive realities which are largely beyond our control.

Meanwhile what about the area of visual experience that we as professionals can control—the picture book. Have we brought to our task as broad a knowledge of art as we have of the written word? Do we encourage illustrators and designers to experiment and to push forward beyond conventional solutions? Do we insist that contemporary artists be true to their artistic age? If we have closed ourselves off from the larger field of the fine arts, if we have established a hermetic world, then we limit our ability to distinguish bad art from good art. This is a crucial distinction.... (pp. 349-51)

A picture book of artistic integrity will often be the only place where a child can expand his imagination and direct his gaze toward beauty. In this medium, it is possible to create a dynamic relationship between the visual and the verbal. The techniques of storytelling and the compelling serial imagery together convey the force of exciting ideas. In form and content, the picture book can become an essential element in the child's evolving aesthetic consciousness, and the artist creating a picture book has an opportunity—and a special responsiblity—to nurture the development of his young audience's visual perception.

This certainly sounds like a heavy burden for that cloistered breed, the picture-book artist, separated as he is from the dynamism of modern art. Often shunned by his brethren in other graphic disciplines, he is looked upon as a thumb-sucking regressive, re-creating his nursery fantasies in pastel hues. Can the picture-book artist really be expected to devote himself to raising the art consciousness of a new generation? Perhaps he would if we demanded that he undertake this responsibility. Yet in our sometimes desperate need to be sentimental about childhood, we ask that the picture-book artist produce an art that is easily accessible and realistic in the most trivial sense, reality being the lowest level of cognition.

Often the only expectation of the picture book is that it provide pretty settings for an easy vocabulary or comic-strip clichés that can divert and entertain as they lure the neophyte reader into the realm of words. Once the truly serious task of acquiring reading skills is accomplished, the images cease to be valuable—if indeed they ever were valuable—and they are dispensed with.... The powerful potential of art to communicate what cannot be expressed in words is dismissed and consigned to the nursery along with toys that have been outgrown.

Our language is rich and powerful. We strive to learn it, to master it, to put it at our service as a means of communication and expression. But in our intense effort to verbalize, analyze, and categorize all experience, we tend to overlook the importance of the visual as a means of personal communication and personal expression. This has resulted in a dichotomy between the values we assign to our word-sense and those we assign to our image-sense. We set a goal to acquire a vocabulary, a grammar, and—if we are ultimately to enjoy the riches of our language—a knowledge of literary tradition and contemporary writing. Yet we have no such aspirations for the development of our visual sense. This faculty is held in such low esteem, deemed so expendable, that few of us even have the equivalent of an alphabet. As a result, our natural, spontaneous, child-response to form and color is left untended, to wither away.

What remains is a kind of art-blindness that makes us ill at ease with any but the most banal and representational imagery—that is, those images that can be narrowly defined or put into words. To the extent an image is representational, it narrows interpretation. To the extent an image cancels out interpretation, it sterilizes the imagination. We all know many adults who feel uncomfortable with, if not actually hostile to, images that communicate in an interpretive, stylized, or abstract manner. Yet children, with their open eye, initially feel no such hostility. Indeed, it has been my experience that even the youngest children respond in a direct and receptive manner to the most stylized of images. I believe this quality is manifest in the magic and symbolism of their own paintings.

Our childhood ease with the symbolic can be seen in graphic ways. For example, when I've had the opportunity to share the story of *Arrow to the Sun* with small children, they often react through their art. This Pueblo tale culminates, with the masked celebrants moving rhythmically, in an exultant "Dance of Life." We pretend that the children have also been invited to join in the dance. In order to participate, they are to imagine masks and costumes for themselves—not realistic self-portraits but abstract designs that will serve as symbolic representations. From the hands of eight- and nine-year-olds, gripping fat brushes heavy with paint, come exciting and stylized images. Most of the children make the leap of imagination to this rather abstract concept—to represent themselves in a graphic and symbolic way. They have felt the force of the symbols on the pages of the book and eagerly express themselves in a similar manner. They plunge with delight into a world of color and form and emerge with images of meaning and beauty.

Within a brief time, however, this balance of perception and imagination will be upset. The expression of ideas will become narrowed, and the art will become contrived and awkward. The child's ability to receive the message of symbolic form will rapidly diminish. This will happen because visual expression and communication will be dismissed as invalid. The child's spontaneous image sense will be underestimated and left undeveloped. Eventually, it will be submerged in the deadening tide of inferior visual representation. We cannot hope to reverse this stultifying process until we overcome our denial of the force and value of art and make it an integral part of our lives. (pp. 351-53)

*Gerald McDermott, in the Caldecott Award Acceptance Speech given at the meeting of the American Library Association in San Francisco, California, on July 1, 1975, in* The Horn Book Magazine, *Vol. LI, No. 4, August, 1975, pp. 349-54.*

---

## GENERAL COMMENTARY

### PATRICIA DOOLEY

Despite the many awards won by Gerald McDermott's animated films and picture-books, his work remains controversial for the best of reasons: it is original, thoughtful, and makes few concessions to common children's-book conventions. Both praise and criticism have attended McDermott's attempts to charge the picture-book with "some of the dynamism of modern art," and to keep alive what he believes to be the child's spontaneous response to abstraction. (p. 1)

Except for [*Papagayo the Mischief Maker*] (an original story using folk material) all of the films and books are retellings of myths or traditional tales. It is, indeed, the mythic version of reality, the mythmaker's alternative to "naturalism," that McDermott has sought. He was "drawn to mythology because it offered a starting-point that was filled with mystery and magic and transformation." (p. 2)

Stylized geometric shapes and a restricted palette are part of the vocabulary of an artist formed, as McDermott was, in the Bauhaus manner. The artist also cites Matisse (especially his cut-paper work) and Klee as influences: perhaps it is their ability to combine appealing color with purity of form, to achieve a kind of austere sensuality, that makes them sympathetic figures. McDermott's own colors are vibrant and brilliant, even "fauviste." Unlike much mass-market illustration today, however, his color is not splashed around to compensate for careless design: it is subordinate to, and a functioning part of, the overall graphic and symbolic plan. The use of color as an adjunct to meaning is particularly successful in *Arrow to the Sun*. McDermott's combination of discipline and liberty in color and composition brings him closer to Blair Lent or Leo Lionni, for example, than to Brian Wildsmith. Perhaps he owes something also to the influence of the Douanier Rousseau.

Like the stylized shapes richly colored and organized by the artist, the tales too disguise complexity beneath simplicity. "*Anansi the Spider* is clearly about wholeness"—but so also is it about family relationships, interdependence, and the skills of civilization. *The Stonecutter* is about man's insatiable ambition and thoughtless abuse of power—but so also is it about the relationships balancing the natural world, and the limits of perception. *The Magic Tree, The Voyage of Osiris,* and *The Knight of the Lion* are all about loyalty and betrayal, especially the loyalty between husband and wife.

Mavungu aids the enchanted people of the tree, Papagayo aids the night-creatures when he saves the moon, Anansi's sons restore him to the world, Osiris and the Arrow-Boy are saved and "save" their people, the Knight of the Lion saves his honor and his life. Yet all these tales are in some way about foolishness as well—from the culpable weakness of *The Stonecutter* or *The Magic Tree,* to the innocent imprudence of Anansi (who "falls into trouble") and Papagayo, to the wise folly of the hero, in *Arrow, Osiris,* or *The Knight of the Lion.*

McDermott himself has acknowledged his obsession with "the circular journey of the individual who sets forth on a quest of self-fulfillment" [see excerpt below in the Author's Commentary for *Arrow to the Sun* (1974)]. The theme of self-transformation (successful or failed) appears again in the latest books, where Papagayo is metamorphosed from mischief-maker to benefactor, while *The Knight of the Lion,* like *Arrow,* is about "growth, maturity, continuity, and the miracle of belief in oneself and one's god."

Myth, typically, simplifies to achieve generality, and employs a highly symbolic language to talk about the real world. McDermott's artistic tactics are similar. . . . Rejecting 19th c. "representational" approaches to illustration (Crane, Caldecott, et. al.), and turning away too from the more expressionistic modes of this century, McDermott has deliberately contrived a style at once primitive and contemporary, disciplined by geometry, liberated by color, rigidly conventional in one sense but untrammelled by the demands of naturalism.

The large questions addressed by myth can be particularly well served by an abstract and highly stylized art, such as native folk-art or the Egyptian, Byzantine, and other "hieratic" modes. Reviewers who have criticized McDermott's books for being "cold and uninviting" [see excerpt below by Alice Bach for *The Stonecutter* (1975)] or accused them of "impersonality" and a failure "to humanize the story" forget, perhaps, that it is the nature of myth to be at one remove from the "merely" human. Both myth and hieratic art are concerned not with reflecting the world but with transmuting it in accordance with a conceptual vision. (pp. 3-4)

[It may be] pertinent to ask ... whether the "mystery and magic and transformation" of the artist's vision can be communicated satisfactorily in the 30-odd pages of a picture-book. Once she has seen the animated films, the reader of the books necessarily projects motion into the static figures of the printed pages, and even wills the drawings of *Osiris* into life. Despite painstaking adaptation, the books seem, inevitably, diminished versions of the beautiful, rich, and compelling films. . . .

The two most recent books are ... departures: *Papagayo* because it is an original tale, *The Knight of the Lion* because in it McDermott has striven for a "more emotional approach" to illustration, a spontaneity and a "loosening up." Its black-and-white line is an attempt to capture the "brutal force" of the original 12th c. Celtic Arthurian tale, to suggest its dynamic yet "dark" quality. Thus, an evaluation of McDermott's achievement must perforce await the time when the artist, like his self-transforming heroes, completes his quest "to revivify the dream-world images" of myth and of the artist's imagination. (p. 4)

> *Patricia Dooley, "Gerald McDermott," in* The Children's Literature Association Newsletter, *Vol. III, No. 4, Winter, 1979, pp. 1-5.*

**DAVID E. WHITE**

[Gerald McDermott's] films and most of the books are retellings of myths and traditional tales which are filled with mystery, magic, and transformation. (p. 273)

McDermott sees similarities between his two major types of characters: mythic heroes and tricksters. In discussing the aspects of these characters that interest him, McDermott says,

> All my work is about the process of *becoming*, the transformation to wholeness. Whether I've depicted trickster or hero, they represent two sides of the same coin. The trickster reenacts in a comic way the exploits of the hero. The goal is to integrate these opposite traits. I feel sure it is this aspect of mythology that appeals to me and reflects my own becoming as an artist and a person. I strive to give that idea of transformation a tangible form and share it, communicate it, to others. (pp. 273, 275)

[McDermott acknowledges many] factors, often unconscious ones, as influencing his decision to start a certain project. He feels that, in retrospect, he can trace the choice of all the tales to a very specific emotional state or to a certain period in his life, and that there are very clear links between all the books and the films.

With *The Voyage of Osiris* I'm sure I was attracted to the theme of rebirth and regeneration, a 'return from the dead' so to speak, because I was just emerging from a period of about a year and a half when I hadn't been able to do any art work at all. There had been a tremendous swirl of activity connected with the publication of *Arrow to the Sun,* the subsequent Caldecott Award, and all the traveling and speaking that followed. It was truly exciting, but when all the cheering had died away, I found there came a period where I could not produce a new work. The public exposure connected with winning the Caldecott had been so separate from my life as a creative artist that it took me a long time to get back on the track again. I had become removed from the intimate and private act of sitting alone in a room and creating. As a result, there was a long fallow period. I was very upset that months, then years were passing and I wasn't producing anything new. When I started to work again, I'm sure I chose *Osiris* because I had such empathy with the character as a giver of life, a creator in a certain sense, who is sealed away, bound up, cast away and buried, and then finally re-emerges in a tremendous burst of activity.

Unconscious forces influencing his work were especially strong in his book *The Knight of the Lion.* This ninety-six page picture book version of an Arthurian legend was a radical departure for the artist due to the black-and-white illustrations. McDermott's analysis of his work on this project is especially interesting:

> Over the years, in both films and books, the use of vibrant color had become an important tool for me. I became so adept that I knew which strings to pull to achieve an emotional reaction through color alone. I was concerned that I would begin to design by rote, that it would become a formula, that I would start to repeat myself. By doing *The Knight of the Lion* in black and white, I was challenging myself to conceive the images in a totally different way. I was consciously denying to myself one of my essential tools. There could be no blithe use of a bright color to cover up a lack of conception. Instead, I was forced to draw spontaneously. It was a great release for me. In fact, it has changed my way of working forever.

> Before I saw any of the images for *The Knight of the Lion,* I had instead a tactile sensation. It began when I was trying to conjure up a way of approaching the darkness and mystery of this medieval romance. I was sitting in a chair with my eyes closed, trying to envision the setting, and before I *saw* anything I *felt* in my fingertips the texture of granite. From that physical sensation came the image of rough-hewn granite walls, scarred and discolored with age. I then turned to the drawing board, took a piece of very rough water color paper, and started to almost carve away at it with pen and ink—pushing a black crayon over the surface to get

that same texture that I first felt and then saw. Soon the drawings started to flow. The outpouring of energy for *The Knight of the Lion* astonished me. Until then I had always carefully structured and designed the drawings in my books. I drew them, redrew them, traced them, repositioned them. By the time I finished an illustration it might have gone through six to ten phases of preparation. For *The Knight of the Lion* I would simply sit each day before a blank piece of paper, my hand would start moving, and then I would draw without any preliminary tracing or sketching. I must have done 150 drawings from which I chose 75 to use in the book.

One of the most curious sensations was confronting that blank piece of paper without a preliminary sketch to rely on. I had the same physiological reaction as standing at the edge of a precipice overlooking the sea. It's an attraction-repulsion. You are confronting the void and there's a bit of fear involved. You want to step back from it. At the same time there's a seductive pull that draws you into it. It was that exact sensation, that tightening in the stomach, that I felt every morning when I sat down in front of the drawing board. Sometimes I overcame it in a few minutes or hours. Some days I couldn't overcome it at all. At the moment I did start to draw, however, the sensation vanished and I was free.

For me, *The Knight of the Lion* was like automatic writing. There was a part of me working that came from such a deep and unconscious place that I wasn't at all aware of it. Even now, when I look at some of the drawings, I'm not quite sure who did them.

In a broader sense, I find this process of "taking the leap" occurs each time I begin a new work. Sometimes weeks, even months pass while I stand on the edge, wavering, before plunging in. It's like being a diver and diving deep down inside of yourself.

Because *The Knight of the Lion* and *The Voyage of Osiris* had such serious themes and "delved into realms that were laden with emotion," McDermott then decided to turn to something bright, happy, and original. Years before, while reading trickster tales in preparation for *Anansi,* McDermott had come across the name Papagayo; he never actually found any Papagayo tales suitable for adaption.

I very much wanted to use the character, though, so I jumped off from the idea of a parrot who is a mischief-maker. An additional source was the widespread folk belief in a monster or fantastic creature who devours the moon. I combined these two ideas and decided to write a tale of my own.

It is not unusual for McDermott to find inspiration for his drawings in sources unrelated to the actual story. "Certainly music is an important element. In my films, for example, the music always comes first and the images are generated by the rhythms of the score."

The impetus for the images in *Papagayo* came from a piece of Brazilian jazz the artist was listening to.

It began with a solo percussion instrument, then other instruments joined in and there was a rhythmic building of sound and of melody that developed into a crescendo. I already had the character Papagayo flying around in my head somewhere, but I didn't have a story written. When I was listening to this music I suddenly saw the jungle, the animals of the rain forest coming awake. First one, then several, and then all of them joining in. That awakening became the central event in the story of Papagayo.

Although McDermott has won numerous awards for his works, there are those who criticize the abstractness of his art. He has never felt the criticisms could be supported, although he does admit to "constantly challenging the perceptions of the viewer." McDermott feels the illustrations speak naturally to children because children

don't have the layers and layers of perceptual constrictions that adults have acquired.

If anyone feels that the symbols are obscure, it's because they haven't seen the responses of children to the books, the tremendous involvement and identification they have with the characters. . . . I suppose there will always be a handful of people who refuse to acknowledge that something has happened in the visual arts since the turn of the century. I think that viewpoint acts like a dead hand on innovation. It threatens to rob the child audience of some valuable and exciting visual experiences.

There has been an interesting strain in letters from readers that McDermott has received over the years. The letters, written by parents and teachers of exceptional children, state that McDermott's books have reached these children in ways they are not reached even by materials specifically designed for them. For example, in a suburb of Cleveland, a bus brings exceptional children to the library once a week. "I've been told they make a bee-line for my books." McDermott finds this response intriguing. He tells of a particular experience in Fort Wayne:

The mother of a Down's Syndrome child brought him to meet me and we had a chance to talk before a speech I was about to give. This little boy's favorite book was *Arrow to the Sun*. He had never seen my animated film of the same story, so we sat down together in an empty auditorium and screened it. As the film unreeled, he responded to every twist and turn of the plot. He knew what the drama was and what the forces at work were in this very abstract, almost narrationless film. At the point where the Lord of the Sun appears, the little boy leaned over to me and said in a stage whisper, 'That's the Lord of the Sun, but they're just kidding us. He's really God.' (pp. 275-78)

Clearly, McDermott is in the process of becoming. He is writing original stories, illustrating the writings of others, and exploring different visual expressions of mythological symbolism.

My life and work are inseparably bound up together. If an artist puts himself into his work in the fullest sense—his emotions, his intellect, the symbols from his own psyche—then the work will touch others because it springs directly from the artist's own inner life.

For McDermott, the completion of each book and film has been an "amazement to me, a little miracle. It has been a privilege to do each work, to know it will have an audience, to watch it come to life and fly off on wings of its own." (p. 279)

> *David E. White, "Profile: Gerald McDermott," in* Language Arts, *Vol. 59, No. 3, March, 1982, pp. 273-79.*

---

### *ANANSI THE SPIDER: A TALE FROM THE ASHANTI* (1972)

Those already familiar with McDermott's film version of how Anansi put the moon in the sky (an Ashanti tale) will welcome its adaptation to book form. None of the brilliant color, African design, or language pattern have been lost in the transformation.

For those unfamiliar with the film here at last is a vibrant picture book of one of the famous Anansi stories. Perfect for storytelling this book could well spark enthusiasm for the Anansi stories among a younger audience. Don't let it be lost in the folklore collection.

> *A review of "Anansi the Spider," in* Children's Book Review Service, *Vol. 1, No. 1, September, 1972, p. 2.*

There have been many tales of Anansi, but filmmaker McDermott has created a particularly beautiful book, which children will want to hold, to examine, read and hear repeatedly.... The rhythm of the Ashanti language has been augmented with fas-

*From* Anansi the Spider: A Tale from the Ashanti, *adapted and illustrated by Gerald McDermott. Holt, Rinehart and Winston, 1972. Copyright © 1972 by Landmark Production, Incorporated. All rights reserved. Reprinted by permission of Holt, Rinehart and Winston, Publishers.*

cinating montage illustrations to make a perfect picture book. (p. 86)

> *Judith B. Rosenfeld, in a review of "Anansi the Spider: A Tale from the Ashanti," in* Childhood Education, *Vol. 49, No. 2 (November, 1972), pp. 85-6.*

The story is a pleasant vehicle for a graphic explosion of stylized forms, glossy paper, and colors so bright that the book looks as if it would shine in the dark of an African night. This is a handsome book, but by the end I wished that it were not quite so polished a package. (pp. 86-7)

> *Karla Kuskin, in a review of "Anansi the Spider," in* Saturday Review, *Vol. 1, No. 4, April 14, 1973, pp. 86-7.*

Mr. McDermott's profession means that his chief interest is in devising striking illustrations. These ... seem to be derived from primitive races, and Anansi, the father spider, moves through the pages wearing a witch doctor's mask. The pictures are bold and colourful, but the element of design is so strong that a child may find it difficult to discover what the illustration actually represents, and there is a tendency for the pages to become repetitious. (p. 175)

> *R. Baines, in a review of "Anansi the Spider," in* The Junior Bookshelf, *Vol. 37, No. 3, June, 1973, pp. 174-75.*

Gerald McDermott's **"Prologue"** helps explain the culture which gave rise to the tales of Anansi, and his words reflect the mature theme and symbolism which appear in the story. Like the Ashanti who weave their symbols into their silken fabrics, McDermott weaves their symbols into and throughout his illustrations for the book. His graphic representations of the spider form are evidence of the symbolism contained within the stylized figures.

Within each body of the six sons, an abstract symbol represents the individual's particular skill. Amid geometric landscapes of magenta, turquoise, emerald, and red, the black figures, readily visible, rock across the pages on angular legs.

The white text, highly visible against the brilliant backgrounds, works in and out of the illustrations, adding balance to the compositions on the pages.

Because of the original medium of the tale, the book could well function without a text; accompanied only by the words of an artful storyteller, the illustrations communicate the tale, and though not as artistically cohesive and consistent as ... [*Arrow to the Sun*], the work demonstrates the range of possibilities that this art form offers. (p. 355)

> *Linda Kauffman Peterson, "The Caldecott Medal and Honor Books, 1938-1981: 'Anansi the Spider: A Tale from the Ashanti',' in* Newbery and Caldecott Medal and Honor Books: An Annotated Bibliography *by Linda Kauffman Peterson and Marilyn Leathers Solt, G. K. Hall & Co., 1982, pp. 354-55.*

---

### *THE MAGIC TREE: A TALE FROM THE CONGO* (1973)

Like the similarly spectacular *Anansi the Spider* ..., this is adapted from an animated film and it's difficult not to hear the pulsing jazz music that seems to be visualized on these dynamic, semi-abstract pages, which are distinctly African in patterns and motifs but just as distinctly cinematic in their vibrant color and kinetic energy. McDermott projects in highly stylized figures and succinctly few words the story of a rejected twin who, by pulling off some leaves, accidentally releases several people including a princess from imprisonment in the magic tree. The princess makes him rich and handsome on the condition that he tell no one the source of his good fortune, and they live together happily until, on a visit to his unloving mother, he forgets his vow and tells her his story. In the end it's a purely visual experience, with Mavunga suddenly remembering his promise, rushing back to his home with the princess, and finding only an empty clearing. A dayglo stunner for the jaded eye.

> *A review of "The Magic Tree: A Tale from the Congo,"
> in* Kirkus Reviews, *Vol. XL, No. 20, October 15,
> 1972, p. 1187.*

[This book] is far less compelling to the viewer than its movie counterpart. . . . The simplicity and starkness of the shapes and colors, resembling those found in African art, fit the Congo tale perfectly; and the background of the pictures, softer than those of the author's last book, **Anansi the Spider,** has given the second book far more aesthetic appeal. Although the book stands as a pleasing entity in itself, in comparison with the author's movie—in which movement, color, form, and music are so perfectly blended—the book seems like only the echo of a vibrant voice. (pp. 586-87)

> *Anita Silvey, in a review of "The Magic Tree: A Tale
> from the Congo," in* The Horn Book Magazine, *Vol.
> XLVIII, No. 6, December, 1972, pp. 586-87.*

[This fairy tale from the Congo] is presented with a minimum of text, in highly stylised native-type design on vivid coloured backgrounds. It is very attractive to look at, beautifully suggesting magic and mystery and tangled jungle, but (at any rate on first reading) very difficult to follow. Perhaps this is because it is based on the author's (American) animated film, from which uncaptioned stills are presented as an integral part of the narrative, without explanation, even at climax points like the ending. Once the reader grasps this idea, there is much to enjoy in this novel presentation.

> *M. Hobbs, in a review of "The Magic Tree," in* The
> Junior Bookshelf, *Vol. 38, No. 6, December, 1974,
> p. 338.*

[This folk tale] is remarkable for its illustrations. Intense colours—blues and oranges make a background for the formalised, predominantly black patterns and figures which build up the pictures. The style, like the story, is almost aggressively African; strange, but fascinating.

> *Valerie Alderson, in a review of "The Magic Tree,"
> in* Children's Book Review, *Vol. V, No. 1, Spring,
> 1975, p. 38.*

---

## *ARROW TO THE SUN: A PUEBLO INDIAN TALE* (1974)

### AUTHOR'S COMMENTARY

I've been on a journey past paper mountains, flying men, foolish spiders, talking trees, and the flaming arrows of the solar fire. It has been a journey of discovery through the bizarre and exotic forms of world mythology. The Rainbow Trail has become a path for my work as an artist.

The riches of myth are usually lost to us in adulthood. . . . But myths have a deep appeal and significance for the human mind,

and the task of the artist is to reawaken these images. The purpose of my journey has been to explore and share the evocative qualities of these ancient tales with those still open to the message of myth. (p. 123)

Soon after finishing my first film [**The Stonecutter**], I had the immense good fortune to meet Joseph Campbell. Dr. Campbell has written extensively and eloquently of the relationships between mythology and modern psychology. In his four-volume study, *The Masks of God,* he has traced the evolution of myth and its function in world culture. Campbell has shown that the prime function of mythology is to supply the symbols that carry the human spirit forward, "to waken and give guidance to the energies of life." These ideas, illuminated in Campbell's *The Hero with a Thousand Faces,* became the basis for all my subsequent work. (p. 125)

In each of [my] films, I was concerned with the circular journey of the individual who sets forth on a quest of self-fulfillment. In psychological terms, he must make a break with the past, overcome obstacles to change, and grow. Ideally, the seeker can then return, his full potential realized, and take his place in society with the "wisdom and power to serve others."

This theme finds its fullest expressions in my book and in my film of *Arrow to the Sun*—with a significant difference. In previous works, the circle was broken. Through some weakness or failing, or perhaps sheer foolishness, the protagonist fails in his search, and the ultimate boon is lost. In this Pueblo Indian tale, however, the circle is complete, and the questing hero successfully finishes his journey. It is the symbolism of this beautiful myth that I would like to discuss.

Before I do, however, I want to mention one of my personal artistic trials: the transition from film to printed page. This jarring shift from a medium of time to a medium of space posed some special problems. When George Nicholson, now Editorial Director of Viking Junior Books, put forth the idea of book adaptations of my African folklore films, it seemed an easy task. After all, four thousand discarded animated drawings were stacked up in my studio. Why not simply shuffle through them, choose forty, and send them off to the printer? Because the result would be a souvenir program of the film—a totally unacceptable solution.

We returned to the original film storyboard, and I tried to reconceive the visual material in a series of doublepage spreads. It was an unsettling experience because the control I enjoyed as a film director was lost. There was no longer a captive audience in a darkened room, its gaze fixed upon hypnotic flickering shadows. Gone were the music and sound effects and the ability to guide the viewer through a flow of images with a carefully planned progression. Now the reader was in control. The reader could begin at the end of the book or linger for ten minutes over a page or perhaps merely glance at half a dozen others. As an artist, I was challenged to resolve these problems.

When I began my work on *Arrow to the Sun* . . . , however, I knew from the outset that the book and the film would be conceived concurrently. With the sensitive and patient collaboration of my editor at Viking, Linda Zuckerman, and my art director, Suzanne Haldane, I sought to solve the problems of continuity and design present in the earlier books. The introduction of large areas of quiet space, filled with solid, rich color, improves the pacing. The use of the Rainbow Trail motif, a multicolored band, helps to guide the reader's eye across the page. The elimination of text from many spreads allows the images to speak. These are some of the techniques that eased my passage as an artist. Though story line and character design were shared, the book in form, texture, and color took on a life of its own.

In outline and impact, this ancient, pre-Conquest Pueblo Indian tale is a perfect example of the classic motif of the hero quest. The hero of this myth, which is the creation of a solar-oriented culture, is a young boy who must seek his true father. The object of his search, the Lord of the Sun, embodies the constancy and power of life-sustaining solar fire—a symbol that is central to Pueblo ritual. The sun, in Carl Jung's phrase, is "the classic symbol of the unity and divinity of self."

Corn, the staff of life for the people of the pueblos, is an important companion symbol to the sun. The constant, life-sustaining warmth of the sun nurtures the golden ears of corn. In searching for a graphic motif that would unite these two concepts, I slowly turned an ear of corn in my hands, studying the color, texture, and form. Then I broke the ear in half. At that moment, the symbol hidden beneath the surface was revealed—a moment re-created in my film. The cross section of the ear of corn, with its concentric rings and radiating rays of kernels, forms a perfect image of the sun.

If one looks at the tip of an ear of corn—an important ritual article in Pueblo culture—one sees that four kernels come together to form a quadrilateral sign. I took this flowered cross, with its four kernel rays, and bound it by a solar circle. This became the unifying visual element in my retelling of *Arrow to the Sun.* It first appears as the spark of life, then as the hero's amulet. It identifies him as he proceeds on his journey through a landscape permeated with the golden hues of sun and corn.

The Boy is a child of the divine world and the world of men. He is the offspring of Sky Father and Earth Mother—a lineage he shares with other great heroes of world mythology. (pp. 126-28)

His questing path is the Rainbow Trail—a multihued border motif that appears in the sand paintings, pottery designs, and weaving of the Southwest. It runs through the pages of my book as well; down through the sky to the pueblo, across the earth, blazing up to the sun, framing the drama of the kivas, and bursting forth at the moment of the hero's assimilation to the sun.

The Arrowmaker is encountered on the Rainbow Trail. He is a *shaman*—a man of magical powers. Only he has an open eye and the inner vision required to perceive the Boy's true heritage. He provides the supernatural aid that enables the Boy to continue his journey. The magical arrow that he fashions releases the Boy from his earthbound state, just as one of wisdom opens the closed mind of another. He sends the Boy on the self-revealing way of the father-seeking hero.

Upon passing through the fiery sun door, the Boy confronts the mighty Lord of the Sun. This is hardly the completion of the journey, however, but the beginning of the true challenge. (pp. 128-29)

The Boy must descend into the abyss of the ceremonial chambers—the four kivas—to prove his heritage. He must face these tests and emerge reborn from the dark womb of the kiva. A true hero, he accepts the challenge, "'Father, . . . I will endure these trials.'" Lions, serpents, and bees await the Boy. In the ensuing confrontations, though threatened by these creatures, he is not destroyed. Significantly, neither does he destroy the

animals, for they represent the dark forces of our own unconscious. They are the shadow beings of the dream state, the internal demons that torment us and block our growth. We cannot destroy them, but we can calm them and integrate them with our functions. We can assume their positive qualities and put them at our service.

This interpretation is quite different from the one we might apply to the mythology of the West which is most familiar to us. It represents a kinship and reverence for the natural world that is opposed to Greek and Hebrew tradition. Heracles destroys the titanic snake, the Hydra. He kills the lion, strips it, and wears its skin as a symbol of his dominance. Absolute domination is the message of these myths. But for our Indian hero, the human world and the animal world are reconciled. The Boy assumes the strengths of the lions, even as they become purring kittens at his feet. He overcomes the squirming chaos of the serpents and creates a circle, a symbol of wholeness and unity as is the corn-sustaining sun. (The serpents inhabit the maizefield and devour the corn-destroying rodents.) The bees, which can sting with killing power, instead give the miracle gift of sun-colored honey to the Boy.

The deepest point of the descent into the abyss occurs in the Kiva of Lightning. Here flashes the polar opposite of the constant warmth of the sun. Unpredictable and violent, it shatters the immature form of the Boy. When he emerges from this final crisis, he is reborn and "filled with the power of the sun"—filled with a spiritual awareness born of his trials. If this solar symbolism seems remote, perhaps we should listen to the response of a nine-year-old to *Arrow to the Sun:* "I think that the Lord of the Sun knew all along who the Boy really was, but he made the Boy go through the tests anyway, so that the Boy would know who he was."

The journey on the Rainbow Trail is near its end. The Boy, radiant in his new garments, returns to earth bearing the message of his father. He began as an individual searching for his true identity, isolated from his community. He completes the journey as a self-aware messenger of life-sustaining powers, ready to take his place in the community. . . . Surrounded by the people of his village, joined with the Corn Maiden, watched over by Sky Father and Earth Mother, enclosed within the arc of the Rainbow Trail, the hero steps onto the World Center and joins in the Dance of Life.

The Rainbow Trail of the artist has come full circle. It is not an end, but a continuation, an ever-repeated cycle. The challenge is eternal: to descend again and again into the "image-producing abyss" to discover visual evocations of the compelling myths of mankind. (pp. 129-31)

*Gerald McDermott, "On the Rainbow Trail," in* The Horn Book Magazine, *Vol. LI, No. 2, April, 1975, pp. 123-31.*

---

Gerald McDermott is a sophisticated artist/filmmaker who, instead of listening for the story's own voice, *uses* ethnic material as a vehicle for his spectacular effects. The theme of the Pueblo Indian legend that shapes his *Arrow to the Sun* . . . is familiar to countless diverse cultures and McDermott's clipped text makes it truly anonymous (just as he turns his people into highly stylized dolls—the women might as well be Japanese). Another problem is that McDermott's picture books have their first incarnation as animated films, and though he redoes the drawings for the new format they continue to resemble a series of stills instead of leading viewers from page to page in true picture book fashion. Nor is there any attempt to ease children into the situation or the setting. Nevertheless *Arrow*, based on a boy's journey to his father the sun and the four tests he must undergo to prove himself, does evoke at least the landscape of its origin with its predominantly sun, sand and clay-colored pages and its geometric corn stalks, cliff dwellings and basket designs. Above all *Arrow to the Sun* is so breathtakingly original in its assertive design, strongly male imagery and psychedelic zap that its appeal for audiences well beyond the usual picture-book age justifies its production. But (reluctant as a children's book person must be to admit) it is the flashing, rhythmic, astonishing film that has what it takes to reintroduce folklore as a communal experience for all ages.

Sada Fretz, "Once Upon a Picture," in Book World—
The Washington Post, May 19, 1974, p. 4.*

In keeping with the seemingly endless possibilities for disaster in prize giving, the 1975 Caldecott Medal . . . [was bestowed on *Arrow to the Sun: a Pueblo Indian Tale* ], a work of minor distinction that is entirely alien to the graphic grace and joyful spontaneity of the great English illustrator, Randolph Caldecott (1846-1886), in whose memory the medal was established. (p. 28)

But—irony of ironies—where, more than 100 years ago, Caldecott injected a near miraculous pictorial movement into his wonderfully observed vignettes of rural existence (an animation that fairly promised the advent of motion pictures), McDermott, a thoroughly "now" young man whose artistic career began in film animation, has evolved a picture-book style so static, conventionalized, and bereft of flesh-and-blood content as to suggest what an ultra-sophisticated computer might one day be programmed to produce in the way of children's book illustration.

While Caldecott breathed life into every drawing he ever made, color or black-and-white, McDermott somehow manages to squeeze out any suggestion of it in his work, despite a near-psychedelic palette that makes his artwork virtually jump off the page. And, where Caldecott's pictures flowed effortlessly, one into the next, McDermott's lumber graphically forward with about as much natural grace and motion as those mechanical rabbits that launch dog races.

*Arrow to the Sun*'s story is a freely-adapted Pueblo Indian myth about the creation. "Long ago," the McDermott rendition begins, "the Lord of the Sun sent the spark of life to earth." By the second spread, readers have already been served a veiled immaculate conception, for the spark of life "traveled down the rays of the sun, through the heavens, and it came to the pueblo. There it entered the house of a young maiden." It, in fact, enters the young maiden herself (as an ideogram/illustration of yellow and orange dots parading down a black ribbon from the sun indicates). The spark of life is represented by a cross within a circle decorated by petal-form shapes in each quarter. It looks for all the world like the logo of some flossy Japanese novelty shop.

"In this way," readers next learn, "the Boy came into the world of men." (Who says children's literature has come a long way since the days when the stork delivered babies?) McDermott's representations of mother, son, and assorted Indian characters in the tale are stylized in the extreme. The justification no doubt, is that his flat, expressionless monoliths are meant to remind us of the Kachina dolls common to several pueblo tribes. (Actually, the Boy's mother bears a striking silhouette resemblance to Minnie Mouse.)

Scarcely a whit of bona fide ethnic charm can be found in McDermott's work. His Pueblo Indian art is all contemporary slick, straight from his own sketch pad and cerebellum. A sophisticated colorist, he knows exactly how to make contrast-

The people celebrated his return in the Dance of Life.

*From* Arrow to the Sun: A Pueblo Indian Tale, *adapted and illustrated by Gerald McDermott. The Viking Press, 1974. Copyright © 1974 by Gerald McDermott. Reprinted by permission of Viking Penguin Inc.*

ing colors vibrate, one against the other. But his high-keyed palette and abstracted forms are far too bright and à la mode for the sun-parched earth oranges and browns of the Indian Southwest.

Full of graphic sound and fury, McDermott's flashy spreads signify little. The artwork is, in the end, a facile shorthand, well-suited to a generation brought up on expensively designed symbols that stand for General Motors, Columbia Broadcasting System, First National City Bank, etc. Not so much pictures as simple-minded pictographs, McDermott's illustrations substitute a surface cleverness and primitive visual communication for any lingering content. They are a contemporary graphic equivalent of the old dime novel's classic portrayal of the laconic Indian's response to everything—"Ugh!"

Meanwhile, back at the pueblo, "Boy" is troubled by his lack of a father. With the help of a wise Arrow Maker, he is, in McDermott's theatrical artwork, soon launched toward the sun (shades of American rocketry and space exploration!) and confronts his sire. But, the Lord of the Sun refuses to acknowledge him until he passes through "the four chambers of ceremony"—the Kivas of Lions, Serpents, Bees, and Lightning.

"The Boy was not afraid. 'Father,' he said, 'I will endure these trials.'" This archaic prose, straining to be elevated (or, at the least, elemental) never achieves more than a prissiness bordering on the ludicrous. Seven wordless pages of hoked-up graphic mumbo jumbo follow, during which the mere sight of the hero apparently mesmerizes two fierce lions, causes a pair of vicious snakes to bite their own tails, and impels a swarm of angry bees to instantaneous retreat.

On descending into the Kiva of Lightning, however, Boy himself is "transformed" by white-hot bands of graphic lightning which simultaneously deliver to both him and viewers a quadruple whammy to the eyeballs. When our hero emerges, he is "filled with the power of the sun," a phrase illustrated by a graphic metaphor as clumsy as it is banal: a sort of open envelope spills forth ribbons of McDermott's iridescent colors.

Finally, the Father embraces his now multi-hued offspring and relaunches him earthward to "bring my spirit to the world of men." Readers have had no inkling of what this solar spirit might be—except whimsical, highhanded, and grudging. But never mind that. The Old Testament's Jehovah wouldn't fare much better in a thumbnail character analysis.

That the book's language is brittle and pretentious is surely a secondary consideration in "the most distinguished American picture book." But that the illustrations themselves are barren and zapped up to project indelible images on the child's retina, rather than extend the imagination or mind, seems unfortunate in the winner of a prize bearing Caldecott's name.

What, then, accounts for *Arrow to the Sun*'s success in a year that also saw the publication of Uri Shulevitz's graphic tour de force *Dawn* (Farrar) or William Kurelek's *Lumberjack* (Houghton)? Is there, perhaps, a misdirected social conscience at play? As one librarian recently pointed out in the American Library Association's *Top of the News*, "This is the time of the Indian." Thus, a showy, leaden book about Indians that few Indians would recognize as representing their heritage may have stood a better chance of taking the prize than a genuine work of picture-book art. . . . But, if 1975 was destined to see a book on Indians selected, why not the authentic and movingly beautiful *Songs of the Chippewa* (Farrar) by John Bierhorst, with pictures by Joe Servello? (pp. 28-9)

*Arrow to the Sun* will not make up for 300 years of injustice to the American Indian. Nor can it possibly go down in any serious survey of American juvenile literary history as the best illustrated book of 1974. (p. 29)

*Selma G. Lanes, "A Sign of the Times: The Caldecott Winner for 1975," in* School Library Journal, *Vol. 22, No. 3, November, 1975, pp. 28-9.*

*Arrow to the Sun* is a graphic production of exceptional power and beauty. The geometrical design-motifs are unmistakably derived from Southwest Indian patterns and are highly stylized, but their abstract qualities have been personalized and come across as vital and dramatic. The narrative, based on a Pueblo Indian myth, is terse and straightforward, employing a vocabulary that, for the most part, is within the range of most schoolchildren, though not preschoolers. (p. 196)

This allegory of Pueblo initiation rites seems to be intended as much for adults as for children. I say this because the fine drawings—in themselves a *tour de force*—are highly sophisticated. The author-illustrator has integrated the illustrative and decorative elements of his art-work, eliminating everything circumstantial and concrete; that is, strictly speaking, everything that is inessential. For this reason, *Arrow to the Sun*, at least in its visual aspect, may prove to be less accessible to children than to adults. As far as the story is concerned, the difficulty lies in another direction. The narrative is not communicated within a cultural-historical frame of reference. The result is that even the adult reader is not in a position to grasp the significance of the allegory; still less is he likely to relate the myth to actual initiation rites as performed by Pueblo Indians to this very day. The emotional impact of these rites on Pueblo boys and girls and their function of symbolically incorporating the children into the adult community are not treated. Hence, we have a book which is perhaps too sophisticated pictorially for children, but with a narrative that is too simple and too incomplete for adults. These criticisms aside—they apply to many children's books today—*Arrow to the Sun* is a beautiful book, one that sets a very high standard for graphic productions in its field. (pp. 196-97)

*Leo Schneiderman, "A Miscellany: 'Arrow to the Sun' and Others," in* Children's Literature: Annual of the Modern Language Association Seminar on Children's Literature and The Children's Literature Association, *Vol. 4, edited by Francelia Butler, Temple University Press, 1975, pp. 196-98.\**

I can't agree with Selma G. Lanes's comments about Gerald McDermott's work [see excerpt above]. . . . There's much more to his style than "sophisticated color." I find his pages filled with life, movement, and vitality—those substances which are, in fact, the essence of any mythological tale.

Ms. Lanes completely ignores the literary requirements of mythology. *Arrow to the Sun* is not a 1975 story (except in its universality) and should not be expected to have the same attributes as a book dealing with contemporary situations.

If Ms. Lane prefers other styles of children's illustration, fine. But I'll take the richness of a tale with ethnic, historical, and even religious significance anytime. McDermott has the ability to translate such a story into picture-book form not only with vibrant figures and color but with sensitivity as well.

I'll concur with Ms. Lanes's feeling that the Caldecott Award should go to an artist of equal stature with Randolph Caldecott, and I think in 1975 it did.

*Patrice Harper, "She Likes It," in School Library Journal, Vol. 22, No. 5, January, 1976, p. 2.*

Ah . . . Selma G. Lanes! Do you feel better now that all that vociferous invective and those flatulent eructations are out of your system? I hope so, because both Gerald McDermott and the Caldecott award will not be much ruffled by it.

It is too bad that you do not like bright colors, new (contemporary) art ideas and techniques, and abstract or symbolic approaches in picture books. But then, that is your loss. Personally, I appreciate a well-done change from the usual artistic fare of bland wishy-washy washes, pastel representationalistic epicenes, and the much over-copied squatty distortions of a Sendak. McDermott's art is bold, angular, powerful, sharp, distinctive: I like it.

As far as "McDermott's flashy spreads signify(ing) little," I must strongly disagree. The deep meanings of myth can be passed on in many ways—not only by word but by lonely searching, by brave deed, by facing up to the unknown, by spiritual example, and by the very medium itself (one's work, one's art, one's life). *Arrow to the Sun* has all of these: the medium, color, for example, beyond that of the prominent oranges and browns, illustrates spirit. The white-hot "whammy" is the effulgence of color/spirit seen then in its separate rainbow hues and later in the son and the pueblo dwellers. This solar spirit is their spirit of hope and detailing the search for it much more would subtract from its stark power and universality.

If you, Ms. Lanes, must drag in the mechanical aspects of sex, General Motors, ethnic slurs and other such irrelevant circumvention into an exceptionally well-illustrated, economically stated tale of the creation of the spiritual life of a people, then I must wonder at your bold obfuscation of good book judgment. The book *did* extend *your* imagination—quite vividly, I would say.

*Craighton Hippenhammer, in a review of "Arrow to the Sun," in School Library Journal, Vol. 22, No. 6, February, 1976, p. 2.*

Who is Selma G. Lanes and why is she saying those terrible things about Gerald McDermott? . . . That "*Arrow to the Sun* . . . will not make up for 300 years of injustice to the American Indians" is an absurd finale to a "discussion" that presumes to speak of the book's artistic merits. Nothing . . . will erase 300 years of injustice and to imply Mr. McDermott attempted such a task shows Ms. Lanes is willing to load her critical cannon with any grapeshot available.

Caldecott, Ms. Lanes notes, delivered "visual and imaginative feast(s)" while McDermott renders "static" "conventionalized" "flat" and "expressionless monoliths." This has certainly *not* been the conclusion of the hundreds of students in Tucson who have pleasurably read *Arrow to the Sun* (and enjoyed the film). Many of them have become excited enough by the "conventionalized" pictures to create their own impressions of the story. Far from being dulled by what Ms. Lanes sees as echos of "expensive symbols" children I know have had their imaginations kindled by the vibrant colors and mythological themes of Gerald McDermott's works.

Also, I could not help but sense Lanes' hostility towards the male-oriented character of the story, with a fast backhand to motherhood (or "Minnie Mouse" according to Ms. Lanes' perception). How chic of her to simultaneously slip in Disney and put down conception—immaculate or otherwise.

Gerald McDermott *is* a "now" young man and this *is* the "time of the Indian," but why use these generalities to sharpen a critical hatchet? If Ms. Lanes' personal taste in art is light years distant from anything non-representational and tends towards the schmaltzy—that's her business; but why try so hard to convert others? Surely, the panoramic sweep of picture book artists encompasses enough latitude for a Caldecott *and* a McDermott.

*Burgess Needle, "Shooting Back," in School Library Journal, Vol. 22, No. 7, March, 1976, p. 50.*

*Arrow to the Sun* is brilliant in idea and presentation. This evocation of Red Indian art and legend won a Caldecott Medal, and no wonder, for it is truly an eye-knocker. I wonder what children make of it, even those conditioned to the American Indian image and idiom. English children may be defeated by the strangeness, unless they have learnt . . . to appreciate the potential of geometrical forms. A book for children? Maybe. For adults? beyond question. The design, and the use of words, are equally masterly. Both evoke a remote and strange culture, but both carry a universal message.

*M. Crouch, in a review of "Arrow to the Sun," in The Junior Bookshelf, Vol. 41, No. 5, October, 1977, p. 272.*

[Gerald McDermott] catches the eye of many readers with the graphics of his Medal Book, *Arrow to the Sun*. . . .

The text of this tale remains simple and direct, with few superfluous words; the illustrations are direct as well; bold, vibrant hues of golds, yellows, oranges, browns, magenta, green, and turquoise contrast against the starkness of black backgrounds. McDermott deftly leads the reader's eye from text to illustration, from illustration to text, with strong geometrics and diagonals, intensifying and emphasizing the points he feels important. Although the designs of the pages sometimes become very elaborate within themselves, they manage to retain the simplicity of the Pueblo motifs.

McDermott brings a new look to children's books with *Arrow to the Sun* and creates an original method of handling the retelling of a folk tale. By retaining the simplicity of the language as well as the purity of Indian geometrics and color, he combines them in a unique style to create a powerful vision of Pueblo custom and legend. The book is truly an impressive work and beautiful to hold and experience, and many times it can, and does, function without text. It seems nearly impossible to create a text which is as powerful as the illustrations in this book, so McDermott complements it by a culmination of color, word, and spirit in the ancient Pueblo ceremony—the Dance of Life.

*Linda Kauffman Peterson, "The Caldecott Medal and Honor Books, 1938-1981: 'Arrow to the Sun'," in Newbery and Caldecott Medal and Honor Books: An Annotated Bibliography by Linda Kauffman Peterson and Marilyn Leathers Solt, G. K. Hall & Co., 1982, p. 358.*

---

*THE STONECUTTER: A JAPANESE FOLK TALE* (1975)

A stonecutter's insatiable quest for power is a theme well suited to McDermott's aggressive, highly stylized designs, and the Japanese origin of this version of the "Fisherman and his Wife" idea is acknowledged in the traditional printmaking motifs and architectural forms that are incorporated in his brilliantly colored semi-abstract displays. The pomp of a princely procession, which stirs the envy of a previously contented stonecutter, provides just the occasion for splurge and spectacle that sets off this artist, and later when the stonecutter has himself successively transformed into the sun, a cloud, and a mountain—each form chosen because it is somehow stronger than the last—the elemental forces assert themselves in a series of strong, increasingly ominous scenes that are characterized by a sort of static violence. Another striking performance.

> *A review of "The Stonecutter: A Japanese Folk Tale,"* in Kirkus Reviews, *Vol. XLIII, No. 6, March 15, 1975, p. 300.*

Another triumph for Gerald McDermott. . . . Children will find the forceful print-like illustrations irresistible, particularly because of their brilliant colors and lively spatial arrangement. While McDermott's prose lacks the powerful rhythm of his illustrations, the total effect is both satisfying and successful.

> *Dora Jean Young, in a review of "The Stonecutter: A Japanese Folk Tale,"* in School Library Journal, *Vol. 21, No. 8, April, 1975, p. 46.*

["The Stonecutter"] is an adequate adaptation of a Japanese folk tale. . . . McDermott proves himself once again an accomplished designer. Although the pages shimmer with slick kaleidoscopic patterns, the result is cold and uninviting—instead of pulling us into the book, he hands us a collection of harsh collages.

> *Alice Bach, in a review of "The Stonecutter,"* in The New York Times Book Review, *May 4, 1975, p. 42.*

["The Stonecutter" is] bound to generate the same kind of excitement [as "Arrow to the Sun"].

Opulent, vigorous collages illustrate this cautionary tale of a Japanese stonecutter whose ambition gets the better of him. Artist McDermott uses a treasury of colors to heighten the story's drama: serene sapphire blues and emerald greens melt into velvet reds and amethyst.

However, his highly abstract illustrations are not for everyone—especially younger children, who probably won't be able to identify a character who looks more like a figure in the Japanese alphabet.

But for those who can appreciate the degree of abstraction, **"The Stonecutter"** provides an exhilarating challenge, a trip through a gallery of imaginative art.

> *Jennifer Smith, "A Dragon Who Wanted to Be Noticed,"* in The Christian Science Monitor, *May 7, 1975, p. B4.*\*

---

### THE VOYAGE OF OSIRIS: A MYTH OF ANCIENT EGYPT (1977)

McDermott has bitten off and decorated more of a chunk of ancient Egyptian mythology than primary grade students can digest from a 32-page picture book. In rapid succession, the Pharaoh Osiris, Isis (his sister/wife), the animal-headed Set, ibis-headed Thoth, jackal-headed Anubis, hawk-headed Horus, and Sun-God Ra are introduced by name only—no notes or afterword clarify their roles in the complex structure of Egyptian mythology. The murder of Osiris by Set, the rescue of his corpse by Isis, the destruction of his corpse by Set, the retrieval of his remains, the intervention of Ra—none of this is related

to the flooding and growing season along the Nile, from which the myth arose. This aspect of the Osiris story and the persistent reincarnation themes of Egyptian mythology are tucked away on the jacket copy. In a note about the book on the verso of the title page, the illustrator's technique is identified as opaque watercolor reproduced in five colors. The illustrations are big (mostly full-page) impressions of perspectiveless Egyptian tomb paintings in glowing color. But, they are no more informative about ancient Egyptian art than is the text about ancient Egyptian beliefs.

> *Lillian N. Gerhardt, in a review of "The Voyage of Osiris: A Myth of Ancient Egypt,"* in School Library Journal, *Vol. 24, No. 4, December, 1977, p. 45.*

The Egyptian myth unfolds in sonorous, present-tense prose, but aggressive color is what takes hold and dominates the pages. McDermott is again angular and abstract, tending here toward larger shapes and arrhythmic composition. Striking blues, reds, bright greens, and yellows vie on the page, sometimes to the detriment of pertinent detail, which becomes submerged in the barrage. Compared to earlier works, this is cerebral and visually shrill but of interest as a personalized interpretation of an uncommon story.

> *Denise M. Wilms, in a review of "The Voyage of Osiris: A Myth of Ancient Egypt,"* in Booklist, *Vol. 74, No. 10, January 15, 1978, p. 813.*

Gerald McDermott's **The Voyage of Osiris: A Myth of Ancient Egypt** continues a tradition of fine picture books he began with **Anansi** and continued with . . . **Arrow to the Sun.** A student of the anthropological significance of the ancient myths, McDermott attempts to convey the deeper meanings through both his language and graphic design. Thus his stories appear to be simple and can be enjoyed by younger readers. However, implicit within these simple surfaces are profound themes; thus the works can be enjoyed by all ages. . . . [**The Voyage of Osiris**] is another version of the story of the Sacrificial God, the hero whose sufferings are endured for the betterment of his people and it is a theme to which readers of all ages can respond. The illustrations are characterized by McDermott's fascination with stylized design as a means of conveying message and by his ability to use vivid colors in developing theme and character. Here the major contrasts are between blues and greens on the one hand and reds and oranges on the other. Osiris is associated with the former and his evil brother, Set, with the latter. Thematically life, fertility, and goodness are contrasted with death, aridity, and evil. Not as successful as **Arrow to the Sun, The Voyage of Osiris** is nonetheless a very good book. (pp. 30-1)

> *Jon C. Stott, in a review of "The Voyage of Osiris: A Myth of Ancient Egypt,"* in The World of Children's Books, *Vol. III, No. 2, Fall, 1978, pp. 30-1.*

"Osiris, the Green One, Osiris, Beloved Pharaoh, Osiris, Molder of Civilization . . . Isis, his wife and sister, Isis, giver of wheat and barley, Isis, the Throne."

In this manner, McDermott introduces the two major players and the central myth of Ancient Egyptian civilization. The confrontation of good and evil and the story of betrayal, loyalty, and eternal renewal are simply but powerfully recounted here. (p. 184)

The illustrations incorporate conventions and symbols derived from authentic sources, thus the ubiquitousness of distorted postures and proportions in humans and gods and symbols such as the lotus, papyrus, ankh, and eye of Horus. The brilliant, electric colors are used for background as well as for characters; the unusual images often flow from one body form into another.

This classical myth has heretofore been unavailable to so young an audience. McDermott has minimized its sensual and violent components, preserving those aspects that reveal the values and central preoccupation of the culture. The vocabulary is difficult, including such words as *feted, coveted, coffer,* and *lamentations.* Sentence structure is highly stylized and changes voices, requiring adaptations to comprehend the material. The use of such metaphors as "the Throne" to refer to the heroine also makes demands of the reader; these linguistic forms are rarely used in picture books. The youngster's powers of observation are tested not only on a linguistic but a visual level as the figure of Osiris is concealed or fragmented and dispersed. Similarly, the viewer is confronted with such unconventional presentations as a single image being simultaneously the beard of Osiris and part of the Nile on which floats a boat transporting the dead to the afterlife. This superior interpretation of an ancient story is not only a unique reading and aesthetic experience, but it also clearly demonstrates the unity between the literature of a culture and its social and philosophical values. (p. 185)

> *Barbara H. Baskin and Karen H. Harris, "A Selected Guide to Intellectually Demanding Books: 'The Voyage of Osiris: A Myth of Ancient Egypt'," in their* Books for the Gifted Child, *R. R. Bowker Company, 1980, pp. 184-85.*

---

## THE KNIGHT OF THE LION (1978)

Gerald McDermott has never been much interested in story-telling for its own sake; . . . in his picture books, from "**Anansi the Spider**" to the most recent, "**The Voyage of Osiris,**" he has been gravitating toward the "big" myths of archetypal significance and mystic power. Here, to accompany his version of the Arthurian tale of Yvain, . . . Mr. McDermott has created a series of brooding, weighty black and white illustrations in which the young knight and his companion lion, all Boccioni curves, travel through phantasmagorical landscapes. . . . As told in Yvain's anguished, first-person, present-tense voice, these adventures seem more Oedipal than chivalric. No doubt that's intended, but though the pictures are enjoyably theatrical, the text is stiff and self-conscious. In a field in which many illustrators are content to keep repeating a successful formula, Mr. McDermott is to be commended for trying out new styles and approaches; like all his work, this is an attention-getter. But letting Yvain tell his own story raises awkward questions about his motives for killing a stranger and marrying a lady whom he promptly deserts. This is one example of a tale that would have been more satisfying if told in a lower-key, as if it had happened a long time ago and in a distant country.

> *Joyce Milton, in a review of "The Knight of the Lion," in* The New York Times Book Review, *April 8, 1979, p. 33.*

[The illustrations in **The Knight of the Lion**] are quite unlike McDermott's previous book illustrations: the pictures have the same boldness and some of the stylized quality, but they are rough and stark and often crowded with massing of detail. The story of Yvain . . . is told in present tense, a rather awkward device. The story itself has all of the qualities that have made chivalric tales endure: daring, danger, magic, love, and dedication. It is weakened by the surfeit of florid writing: "Where once leaves flourished, now sings a plumed chorus: a melodious foliage," and by some abrupt developments in the story line, as when the Lady of the Fountain speaks to Yvain for the first time, enraged, "*You* are my husband's slayer! Do you presume to take his place?" and Yvain, who is seeing her for the first time, responds with "I love you, beautiful and gracious lady . . ." An attendant says, when the Lady leaves, "I think she likes you not a little." Turn the page, and suddenly "Amid song of bells, merry shouts and laughter, I am wed to Laudine, the Lady of the Fountain."

> *Zena Sutherland, in a review of "The Knight of the Lion," in* Bulletin of the Center for Children's Books, *Vol. 32, No. 10, June, 1979, p. 179.*

The first-person perspective lends a degree of immediacy that will be needed to carry readers through the long, somewhat inaccessible conventions of chivalry and their levels of meaning. This is not a picture book but an illustrated story. Accompanying drawings are starkly modern—black and white and heavily textured, and minus the degree of angularity that characterized the artist's earlier works. Uniformly dark and dramatic, they emphasize the story's somber, introspective feel, but are unevenly effective: some scenes appear overinked; a few suffer from a too-jumbled composition. As always, though, the spirit is rarified and uncompromising, the substance meaty food for thought and discussion.

> *Denise M. Wilms, in a review of "The Knight of the Lion," in* Booklist, *Vol. 75, No. 22, July 15, 1979, p. 1628.*

Told in the manner of Arthurian epics, the story features rich imagery, clues in verse, faithful attendants, and a lion-mate. Etched black/white textured illustrations are as powerful as any done by McDermott in color. The writing matches the art in drama, and is worthy of standing on its own—something that could not be said of his previous works. A provocative book for the upper grades. The **"Author's Note"** gives the background of the tale and the aesthetics of the book. A well-designed volume. (pp. 323-24)

> *Ruth M. Stein, in a review of "The Knight of the Lion," in* Language Arts, *Vol. 57, No. 3, March, 1980, pp. 323-24.*

### SUN FLIGHT (1980)

Gerald McDermott is [a] prolific and highly regarded writer-illustrator. He has excelled at versions of myths and folktales from a wide range of sources: Africa in **"Anasi, the Spider,"** Japan in **"The Stonecutter,"** Mexico in **"Arrow to the Sun."** Now in **"Sunflight"** . . . he turns to the story of Daedalus and Icarus and their escape from King Minos's labyrinth. The tale is so powerful and so familiar that one comes to Mr. McDermott's version with high hopes, but unfortunately it's not a success. In the past he has adapted the visual style of the culture whose story he is retelling: The Aztec forms of **"Arrow to the Sun"** and the African forms of **"Anansi"** are among the most memorable images in children's books in recent years. But in **"Sunflight"** he has not drawn on Greek or Cretan imagery: instead, he gives us a kind of animated cartoon heroism out of the 1940's—powerfully executed, vigorously colored, but out of touch with the myth itself. This kind of imagery looks fine in motion on a screen, but there's just not enough detail and original observation to work well in print. I'll take the Provensens' versions of the Greek myths any day.

> *John Russell, in a review of "Sunflight," in* The New York Times Book Review, *April 27, 1980, p. 58.*

In this version of the Daedalus and Icarus story, McDermott returns to the lush sun and earth colors of *Arrow to the Sun,*

but adds a good share of sparkling Aegean blue and a dramatic black background for his blue and violet labyrinth. As usual, he is best at semi-abstract backgrounds—the gorgeous skyline of a seacoast town; the Greek-inspired blocks that constitute the labyrinth—and totally unsuccessful at investing his figures with either power or pathos. His depiction of the scorched Icarus falling, head first and wings aflame, is apt; but it is set, characteristically, in the center of an inflated sequence of five essentially wordless double-page displays which tend to undermine that one effective image. As usual too, McDermott's writing suffers from a touch of grandiloquence and an absence of warmth, and as usual the visual spectacle tends to overwhelm the story. Overall, both the telling and the pictures have a distancing effect.

> *A review of "Sun Flight," in* Kirkus Reviews, *Vol. XLVIII, No. 12, June 15, 1980, p. 776.*

The flight and Icarus' death are masterfully executed and, except for a closing paragraph, wordless. Elsewhere there are problems. The story itself has not been successfully isolated from the connecting myths which provide the motivation for its characters: therefore, Minos' wrath toward the architect and his son seems whimsical and the legendary Minotaur deteriorates into some theatrical "ancient ghosts and monsters." McDermott places the labyrinth underground and seals the door, leaving us wondering how so many birds happen in. The abstract use of a Greek motif (a square bending inside itself in snail-like fashion) to represent the maze is ingenious in conception but unappealing in its execution. The vibrant colors of the illustrations throb with life, the figures threatening to burst the boundaries of the page; but only the last few capture both the mood of the tale and the land that generated it. (p. 149)

> *C. Nordhielm Wooldridge, in a review of "Sun Flight," in* School Library Journal, *Vol. 27, No. 2, October, 1980, pp. 148-49.*

## PAPAGAYO, THE MISCHIEF MAKER (1980)

McDermott's original story assumes folktale proportions as it presents the roguish rain-forest parrot Papagayo, whose perpetual noisiness disturbs the day-sleeping night creatures. He becomes a hero, however, when his suggestion of making a great noise works to frighten off an "ancient monster dog" that is eating the night creatures' beloved moon piece by piece. Art for the story is striking; deep tropical colors seem intensified by glossy page surfaces, and they nearly vibrate against the intermittent deep-blue backdrop of a night sky. Figures are stylized, taking shape out of a collagelike blend of individually colored pieces. Geometric and curved shapes merge into a well-balanced whole that's a fitting frame for the story.

> *Denise M. Wilms, in a review of "Papagayo, the Mischief Maker," in* Booklist, *Vol. 76, No. 20, June 15, 1980, p. 1533.*

Using the same strong colors and clear shapes that won him the Caldecott Medal for *Arrow to the Sun,* McDermott journeys to the tropics with Papagayo the parrot. His jungle characters look like collages made from snips of construction paper—bright blues, greens and oranges. Papagayo himself sports no fewer than 10 colors. He and McDermott's monkey, armadillo, butterflies, sloth, frog, possum, bat and—his most wonderful creation—the ghost of an ancient monster dog eating the moon out of the sky, might make a child think he or she could have pasted them up at school. But there is magic in making all these colors and angles work together to such striking effect, and to making characters of his animal figures, which, even when they are mute, are expressive and humorous. When you *have* fed your eyes, go back and read the well-turned prose of this simple tale.

> *Robert Wilson, in a review of "Papagayo the Mischief Maker," in* Book World—The Washington Post, *July 13, 1980, p. 9.*

Brilliant popsicle colors make for appetizing pages, and flat "cutouts" of jungle flora and fauna riot against bright empty backgrounds. The dog-monster is both fearsome and comical: shaggy, toothy, and moon-eyed. Papagayo's exuberance is conveyed by his gaudy but gorgeous body, a vivid patterning of hot pink, orange, wine, turquoise and lime. The visual style is in part an adaptation of native South American geometric art. Similarly the narrative, although original, is based on common folk-motifs (especially myths about the eclipse). But eclipses are rare events: one wonders whether the night-creatures will really have to work themselves into noisy fits every time the moon wanes. Contrary to the jacket-copy, there's not much of a "lesson" here—in fact, as with true folk-tales, one had better not examine the rights and wrongs too closely—but there is plenty of lively entertainment.

> *Patricia Dooley, in a review of "Papagayo, the Mischief Maker," in* School Library Journal, *Vol. 27, No. 1, September, 1980, p. 61.*

---

## DAUGHTER OF EARTH: A ROMAN MYTH (1984)

Once again, as he did in *Anansi the Spider* . . . and *Arrow to the Sun* . . . , McDermott has adapted his artwork perfectly to the origins of the story he is telling. Instead of the bold African batik-like illustrations in *Anansi* or the geometric Pueblo design in *Arrow,* McDermott has used opaque gouache on a prepared surface to mimic the effect of ancient frescos. The story is Ovid's version of how Proserpina is carried off to the Underworld by Pluto—a classical mythological explanation for the origin of the seasons. The writing is straightforward, but it is the illustrations that distinguish this telling. They sweep across borderless pages, giving the illusion of a detail of a larger work not shown. His use of color is dramatic and full, with darker tones and shadows giving sculptural dimension to everything from architectural forms to the folds of gowns. His use of light, like color, is bold and dramatic, thereby underscoring the dif-

*From* Daughter of Earth: A Roman Myth, *retold and illustrated by Gerald McDermott. Delacorte Press, 1984. Copyright © 1984 by Gerald McDermott. All rights reserved. Used by permission of Delacorte Press.*

ferences between the two worlds in which the story takes place. The myth is readily found in anthologies although never before told so handsomely in a single publication. An excellent choice for intermediate students studying Greek and Roman mythology as well as a read aloud for older primary students as an example of a pourquoi story.

> *Patricia Homer, in a review of "Daughter of Earth: A Roman Myth," in* School Library Journal, *Vol. 30, No. 7, March, 1984, p. 162.*

McDermott has been continually drawn in his career to mythic themes, and he is now one of the few contemporary author/ illustrators who can harness their inherent power without trivializing it. He succeeds here, as he does in some of his other works, partly because of his bold, abstract graphic style, partly by the forceful prose he finds to recount these ancient stories. Yet his very success in recreating these mythic essences leads to problems in calling a work like *Daughter of Earth* a picture book for younger children. For McDermott summons up the unsettling, psychosexual dynamics of this particular myth. Proserpina is really a child; Pluto is a driven adult who takes advantage of her. The visual collision of these two facts, as McDermott paints this primal scene, is explosive and unnerving. Clearly, myths are not meant to be taken literally, but rather as metaphor, as archetypal symbol, as a way of describing cosmic events in human terms. I'm afraid, though, that this book, which is true to the spirit of myth, may nevertheless have to struggle for its survival with that spirit of moral outrage that affects our contemporary awareness. (pp. 13-14)

> *John Cech, "Pretty Picture Books, All in a Row," in* Book World—The Washington Post, *May 13, 1984, pp. 13-14.\**

[*Daughter of Earth* is] pictorially inspired by the art of Roman murals, such as those excavated at Pompeii. The retelling is staid and ineloquent, rarely equal to the story's inherent drama, but McDermott's robustly colored spreads explode with energy. The fiery, blood-red hues depicting Pluto's underground kingdom are in vivid contrast to radiant views of sunny earth, and the scene of Ceres laying waste to the landscape after learning of her daughter's abduction is both grim and powerful. Oddly, the exaggerated angularity of Ceres' and Proserpina's faces give them an unpleasantly cartoonish aspect: heavy-lidded, square-faced Pluto, however, is more realistically portrayed. Scholars will appreciate the studied plenitude of historical, literary, and artistic detail, but youngsters will be impressed mainly by the size and showiness of the book's illustrations, making this an effective choice for sharing with large read-aloud groups.

> *Karen Stang Hanley, in a review of "Daughter of Earth: A Roman Myth," in* Booklist, *Vol. 80, No. 20, June 15, 1984, p. 1485.*

# Bruno Munari

## 1907-

Italian author/illustrator and author of picture books.

Munari is internationally known for producing intriguing three-dimensional picture books which reflect his interest in design and form. Recognized as an innovator in the graphic arts, he employs such devices as cutouts, lift-up flaps, and diminishing page sizes to introduce young readers to the possibilities of book construction. By picturing surprises beneath each flap and hole, Munari creates anticipation while helping to further the plots of his stories.

Munari's best-known publications are his books for pre-schoolers, which he began during World War II when he could find no good books for his small son. Munari's first six works—*Animals for Sale; Tic, Tac, and Toc; Who's There? Open the Door!; The Birthday Present; The Elephant's Wish;* and *Georgie Has Lost His Cap*—originally appeared in Italy in 1945 as *I Libri Munari.* Starting in 1957, the English-language translations were published as individual books in an oversize format. Long after *I Libri Munari* was out of print in Italy, the six American editions were reissued in 1970 and again in 1980, evidence of their enduring popularity in the United States.

In 1960, Munari designed an alphabet book specifically for American children. Featuring unusual combinations of familiar objects in large double-page spreads, *ABC* is similar in style to *Bruno Munari's Zoo.* These were the first of Munari's works not to include three-dimensional effects. With *The Circus in the Mist,* which describes a journey through a foggy city to the bright, gay Grand Circus and then home through a dusky park, Munari fashioned a new kind of book for the picture book audience. He uses translucent gray pages to suggest the illusion of mist, black silhouettes that change their images when reversed, and wildly colorful pages to represent the circus scenes. *From Afar It Is an Island,* an introduction to stone collecting, and *A Flower with Love,* an interpretation of Japanese flower arrangement, also demonstrate Munari's fascination with design. A playful sense of humor, both in text and illustration, characterizes many of his works.

Munari's unconventional children's books reveal his varied background as painter, sculptor, graphic artist, photographer, filmmaker, and creator of toys, games, and mobiles. Although he attended the Technical Institute of Naples, Munari has had no formal art training. He started his career in the 1920s as a painter with the Futurists, a group of Italian artists, musicians, and writers who attempted to capture the energy and movement of mechanical processes in their works. In the 1930s, he began making wire mobiles and kinetic sculptures. As a founding member of the *movimento per l'arte concreta,* Munari experimented with polarized light and invented a new technique for producing variations in color. He held a one-man show in Tokyo in 1965 which included his books and research films as well as objects of design and light-polarization. In 1970, Munari was invited to teach basic design and advanced explorations in visual communication at Harvard University; an experimental teaching technique he initiated there became the basis for *Design and Visual Communication,* which has been used as a textbook in art schools. Munari has

*Courtesy of Bruno Munari*

also published such books for designers as *The Discovery of the Circle* and what he terms "libri illeggibili" (wordless books).

Perhaps the most notable achievement of Munari's multifaceted career has been his pioneering efforts in the field of machine art, for which he has served as chief spokesperson. Believing that there is an objective standard of artistic form which all people can comprehend, Munari maintains that industrial design has a special purpose—to educate the ordinary person in an appreciation of good design. He insists that an artist has a duty to know and understand machines, and to create machine-made products that are aesthetically pleasing. In tribute to his diverse contributions, Picasso called him "the new Leonardo."

The majority of English-speaking critics praise Munari's first six books, noting the ingenuity of their inventions, the simple effectiveness of their themes, the originality of their design, and their appeal to children. *ABC* and *Bruno Munari's Zoo* initiated commentary on Munari's technical prowess, and critics now commend his works for their beauty as well as for their successful balance of color, texture, and shape. Frequently deemed an artistic genius, Munari is credited with introducing a new approach to the creation of picture books.

(See also *Something about the Author,* Vol. 15 and *Contemporary Authors,* Vols. 73-76.)

## GENERAL COMMENTARY

### MARIA CIMINO

[*Maria Cimino has translated several of Munari's books into English. Formerly head of the Central Children's Room at the New York Public Library, she has worked in libraries in Florence and Venice and is the author of* The Disobedient Eels and Other Italian Tales.]

Among the most original, imaginative, and beautiful picture books ever made are those of Bruno Munari. Painter, sculptor, photographer, designer of books, toys, and mobiles—he calls them "useless machines"—this Italian artist has a many-sided genius that turns everything he touches into a work of art which, though unmarred by eccentricity, always bears the mark of a distinctive personality. He is a plastic poet who expresses his ideas with a flowing lyrical line, a sensitive eye for color, and an unerring feeling for space.

Munari is very much an artist of his time. His work has its points of contact with that of Mondrian, with the Bauhaus, with Dadaism. He is interested in functional design, in the practical application of modern art, in the experiments of modern architecture. But what he has drawn from these sources has in no way confined the exuberance of his creativity. He moves from one thing to another, a free spirit, bound by no school of art, always in quest of the new.

What is most surprising is the impression of unity one gets from activities so widely dispersed and works so varied in character. There is never any doubt that every one of them, however important or trivial, is the product of the same forceful and sensitive mind. The same balance of gifts is everywhere present in his work: a rich and orderly imagination, spontaneous wit, a constructive capacity that delights in coping with the most difficult problems, a delicate feeling for the harmonies of form, color, and space, and the tact that knows when to leave a work before it begins to be labored or overemphatic. The qualities that are apparent at their simplest and purest in what he calls his *Libri illegibili* (unreadable books) are just as fully present in his picture books for children. The rhythms of form and color and space flow from cover to cover, joining into a complete and harmonious plastic unity. There is the same precise realization of his formal purposes, the same high level of integration, although in the picture books for children he has had to deal with other problems—entertaining a child and arranging the reciprocal relations of text and illustration. (p. 585)

When an artist of Munari's stature applies his ample powers of invention, technical virtuosity, and skill in composition to the picture book, we expect the result to be formally impressive on all counts. We are much more impressed, however, because it is less to be expected, when we find that these powers have been put at the service of a vision which is of the child's world. The tone of the books is pervaded by Munari's insight into the innocent wisdom and guileless humor that are so much a part of childhood. The movement of his simple texts has the easy naturalness of an effortless improvisation, and the pictures, for all their precision of design, share that apparently spontaneous rhythm. Munari is clearly at home in that world and not merely a well-intentioned visitor. (p. 586)

[Most] of his picture books have been designed in a special fashion which Munari has made his very own. Superimposed on the pages there are flaps which, when lifted, change the design and at the same time continue the action of the story. *Mai contenti* [*What I'd Like to Be*; U.S. edition as *The Ele-*phant's Wish*], for example, is a moral tale. Bold full page compositions are divided into large solid areas of bright flat color. Each page shows an animal and asks "Che cosa sogna?" (What does he dream?). By opening the flaps set near each animal's eye we discover his dream. We find that the elephant, tired of being such a heavy animal, dreams of being a bird; the bird has his reason for wishing to be a fish; the fish would like to be a lizard; the lizard a bull; the bull in turn an elephant. And the end carries us back to the beginning with the intimation that the elephant also dreams. The rhythmic effect of the flow of the text and pictorial design uninterrupted from start to finish, produces a sense of variety in unity, which is in fact the basic concept of the book. The little jolts of surprise are so easy and natural in their wit and imagination that the book is not exhausted at one reading. One can go through it again and again and still find pleasure in the sequence. . . .

[Every one of the] books in this series is made of the same elements and every one is different. Whether you follow Gigi looking for his cap in *Gigi cerca il suo berretto* [*Georgie Has Lost His Cap*; U.S. edition as *Jimmy Has Lost His Cap: Where Can It Be?*] or the truckman having trouble bringing home his son's birthday gift in *L'uomo del camion* [*Lorry Driver*; U.S. edition as *The Birthday Present*], you are charmed by a simple effective central idea, brilliantly presented in balanced text and illustration. The pictures flow into each other page after page, their rhythm accentuated by the ingenious interposition of the flaps, and yet each, taken by itself, is a complete composition. The stories combine poetry with realism in an engaging way which is close in spirit to Italian folklore. Two of them, *Il venditore di animali* [*Animals for Sale*] and *Toc toc* [*Who's There? Open the Door!*], are notable for their vividness in the use of color and for the elegant combination of their system of flaps into a simple whole. Another, *Storie di tre uccellini* [*Tic, Tac, and Toc*], is worthy of special comment because of its poignancy.

*Storie di tre uccellini* begins simply: "Would you like to know how the three birds Ciò, Cià and Cì ended up in cages? I'll let each one tell his story." Each bird tells his story in a separate flap. Ciò has the largest flap and the longest story. Cià's are smaller. Both stories, however, end in the same way with their being caged as pets by the same little boy. Cì's flap is very small and his story quite brief. All he says is: "I have no story. I was born in a cage." (p. 587)

[*Nella notte buia (In the Dark of the Night)*] is perhaps the most original, most poetic and impressive book for children he has ever done. Munari says it stems directly from his experiments in designing his *Libri illegibili*, books without text, which consist solely of the play of form and color from page to page with the continuity aided by perforations of irregular shape which reveal a small segment of the succeeding page.

*Nella notte buia* is printed on several different papers varying in their color and texture. Brief in its text and profuse in illustration it covers an imaginative scope that one would have thought impossible to enclose within the pages of a picture book. The first page, printed blue on black, shows a city at night. In the next a cat tries to catch a firefly. The light goes farther and farther away as pages are turned. One follows it through the next day. There is adventure in the city, in the fields, and in a cave through which runs a subterranean stream. At the end it is night again. The text says:

| è notte | it is night |
| forse le lucciole | perhaps the fireflies |

| hanno già acceso | have already lighted |
|---|---|
| i loro lumicini | their little lights |

One turns the page and comes to a black page again with many little perforations through which the small yellow lights are shining. There is a feeling of having lived through a rich experience in this simple poetic book.

Bruno Munari's greatness lies, I think, in his view of the world, which is personal and poetic. His extraordinary originality and his rightness as a creator of children's books rest in turn on the fact that for all his technical proficiency and plastic skills he has been able to retain the fresh eye of childhood and an untrammelled imagination. It is not their formal beauty alone, it is above all their vitality and spontaneity, that make his picture books unforgettable. (p. 588)

> *Maria Cimino, "The Picture Books of Bruno Munari," in* Bulletin of the New York Public Library, *Vol. 60, Nos. 11 & 12, November & December, 1956, pp. 585-88.*

**ELLEN LEWIS BUELL**

When three picture books by the Italian artist Bruno Munari ("**Who's There? Open the Door!**", "**Animals for Sale**" and "**Tic, Tac and Toc**") first appeared in an American edition two years ago they caused something of a sensation among grown-ups and a great deal of pleasure among the children.

Now three more of his books ["**The Elephant's Wish**," "**The Birthday Present**," and "**Jimmy Has Lost His Cap—Where Can It Be?**"] are available. . . . As in the others, Signor Munari ingeniously tells his brief tales by a series of flaps superimposed on his pictures with more pictures (and surprises) concealed beneath those flaps. The illustrations themselves are simple, beautifully composed and richly colored.

Although none of the new titles quite rivals "**Animals for Sale**" for sheer attractiveness or "**Who's There? Open the Door!**" for pictorial suspense, they still have more wit and originality than most picture books. . . . Perhaps the book which children will like best is "**Jimmy Has Lost His Cap**" in which a boy searches through the house, finding unexpected things behind the chair, in the refrigerator and, finally, finds the cap on his own head. And that, as every young child knows is very, very funny.

> *Ellen Lewis Buell, "Three from Italy," in* The New York Times Book Review, *August 30, 1959, p. 28.*

**BETTINA HÜRLIMANN**

[*The following excerpt was originally published in German in 1959.*]

[One] or two big Italian volumes dating from 1945 . . . were the delight of children soon after the war. . . . [Originating from

The elephant is bored with being a big heavy animal. He wishes he could be something else. What do you think he would like to be?

He wishes he could be a little bird who flies and sings.

*From* The Elephant's Wish, *written and illustrated by Bruno Munari. The World Publishing Company, 1959. Copyright © 1945, 1959 by Bruno Munari. Reprinted by permission of Philomel Books.*

Bruno Munari,] they were what we might call high-class novelty books. Perhaps the best of them was *L'uomo del camion* . . . , a book about a lorry driver with a present for his bambino. But he has an accident after going only a few miles along the road for home and this leads him to various changes in his mode of transport. As the vehicles change so this leads in the book to various alterations of page size. Making use of a car, a bicycle, a scooter, roller-skates, and Shanks's pony, finally shrunken and barefooted on a tiny page he reaches his son. This is followed on the next page by the opening of the present to show in full size again an abundance of good things. Fancy tricks, you may say, but they are full of playful ideas which were genuinely sympathetic to the needs of the deprived children of the Second World War. (p. 232)

> *Bettina Hürlimann, "Picture Books in the Twentieth Century," in her* Three Centuries of Children's Books in Europe, *edited and translated by Brian W. Alderson, Oxford University Press, Oxford, 1967, pp. 201-45.\**

## PUBLISHERS WEEKLY

The happiest news for today and for a gaggle of tomorrows is that Bruno Munari's fantastic picture books are back in time for Christmas giving. And back in time to delight the visiting lap-sitters and the grandmothers whose laps they will sit upon. All six titles ("**Who's There? Open the Door!**," "**Tic, Tac, and Toc**," "**The Elephant's Wish**," "**Animals for Sale**," "**The Birthday Present**," "**Jimmy Has Lost his Cap. Where Can It Be?**") are beautiful and visually cleancut. All six are irresistible in line and color. Bound into the heavy white board covers are books of different sizes and shapes and colors, to surprise and delight. Your reviewer has been known to grouse at the current high prices of children's books. . . . But considered as an investment in perpetual pleasure and delight as well as in beauty, [these six] are cheap at any price.

> *A review of "Bruno Munari Books," in* Publishers Weekly, *Vol. 198, No. 23, December 7, 1970, p. 50.*

## SELMA G. LANES

[The appeal of a small child's book] may be almost wholly visual. There are Bruno Munari's large-format picture books which speak directly to the imagination through their graphic invention and wit. Consisting of six to eight heavy board pages, each of Munari's books provides surprising new vistas of visual possibility to children. There is *The Birthday Present*, which is like opening present after surprising present any time you feel like it, not only on your birthday. There is *The Elephant's Wish*, in which the viewer can peep into the minds of several beasts and birds and be privy to their innermost thoughts. There are also *Tic, Tac, and Toc*, a delightful trio of terse bird biographies within one large book, and *Jimmy Has Lost His Cap*, which is like playing a suspenseful game of solo hide-and-go-seek. The world itself seems more magical on closing one of his mind-expanding inventions. (pp. 185-86)

> *Selma G. Lanes, "Once Upon the Timeless: The Enduring Power of a Child's First Books," in her* Down the Rabbit Hole: Adventures and Misadventures in the Realm of Children's Literature, *Atheneum Publishers, 1972, pp. 179-203.\**

## PATRICIA CIANCIOLO

Tempera was used for all of the illustrations that appear in the children's books that Bruno Munari created. Worthy of note are the picture books entitled ***Bruno Munari's ABC, Bruno***

***Munari's Zoo, Who's There? Open the Door!***, and ***The Birthday Present***. His illustrations are very simple and are sharply drawn. Munari uses brilliant hues. Each book evidences a charming sense of humor that is certain to provoke smiles from the young reader. Each picture book reflects Munari's originality and skill as a book designer and his unique style as a tempera artist. (pp. 70-1)

> *Patricia Cianciolo, "The Artist's Media and Techniques," in her* Illustrations in Children's Books, *second edition, Wm. C. Brown Company Publishers, 1976, pp. 58-93.\**

---

## IL VENDITORE DI ANIMALI [ANIMALS FOR SALE]; STORIE DI TRE UCCELLINI [TIC, TAC, AND TOC]; TOC, TOC, CHI È? APRI LA PORTA [WHO'S THERE? OPEN THE DOOR!]   (1945)

A treat is in store for those who appreciate original and truly childlike picture books. . . . Maria Cimino has translated charmingly the extremely brief text, wisely making the tiny changes necessary to have references meaningful to the American child, yet keeping the conversational simplicity of the original. . . .

All [Bruno Munari's] animals are big, boldly drawn and silhouetted in strong color against the white pages. They are beautiful and decorative. The varied sizes and shapes of the colored pages within form changing and interesting patterns as one looks at them. There is real suspense at the nursery level, but such is Mr. Munari's cleverness that he keeps us all at that level, and he always offers a little surprise at the end.

> *"Beautiful, Varied, Original," in* New York Herald Tribune Book Review, *November 17, 1957, p. 3.\**

The first books of the Italian artistic genius, Bruno Munari, to be published in America . . . are easily the most impressively original works of the year, particularly in design and imagination. Each contains sequences of elaborately positioned flaps and foldovers through which the stories progress. . . . And all are done in large, beautifully-hued illustrations.

> *George A. Woods, in a review of "Animals for Sale," "Tic, Tac, and Toc" and "Who's There? Open the Door!" in* The New York Times Book Review, *November 17, 1957, p. 58.*

There is in our house a young bibliophile, aged two and three-quarters, who has been of assistance to us in forming an opinion of some [children's books that seem to make admirable Christmas presents]. When she first saw the three by Bruno Munari, . . . **"who's there? open the door!,"** and **"tic, tac, and toc,"** and **"animals for sale"** (ages one to four)—her reaction was conservative. They have doors that open one within another, holes you can peek through, and pages of diminishing size, and they are quite wonderful. "Those are Valentine books!" she said. "*I* like *children's* books!" Once having heard them, she demanded them over and over. (p. 232)

> *Emily Maxwell, "Christmas for First and Second Readers," in* The New Yorker, *Vol. XXXIII, No. 39, November 23, 1957, pp. 232, 234, 236-39.\**

[These] books have an immediate appeal for children. To that I can testify for I have used them in the Italian editions. Small boys and girls are surprised and pleased by the unusual arrangement of pages. . . . If this kind of thing were poorly and cheaply done, it could be, of course, merely a gadget, but with

Mr. Munari's originality of design and his illustrations in clear colors each book is a work of art. The children love them all, with *Animals for Sale* perhaps a little the favorite.

> *Jennie D. Lindquist, in a review of "Animals for Sale," "Tic, Tac and Toc," and "Who's There? Open the Door!" in* The Horn Book Magazine, *Vol. XXXIII, No. 6, December, 1957, p. 481.*

[These] are animal picture books ingeniously created by an Italian artist. . . . The stories are told in brief imaginative text, brilliantly colored pictures, and clever inserts, peek-throughs, and other devices dearly loved by children. Although luxury items unsuited for circulation the books will give much pleasure when used by the storyteller or for exhibits.

> *A review of "Animals for Sale," in* The Booklist and Subscription Books Bulletin, *Vol. 54, No. 3, January 1, 1958, p. 258.*

---

*L'UOMO DEL CAMION [LORRY DRIVER]* (U.S. edition as *The Birthday Present*); *MAI CONTENTI [WHAT I'D LIKE TO BE]* (U.S. edition as *The Elephant's Wish*); *GIGI CERCA IL SUO BERRETTO [GEORGIE HAS LOST HIS CAP]* (U.S. edition as *Jimmy Has Lost His Cap: Where Can It Be?*) **(1945)**

Libraries which have used with success Munari's earlier picture books . . . will welcome the three new titles. As before the Italian artist tells the stories in clear, brightly colored pictures and a minimum of text, playfully and cleverly utilizing such devices as lift-up flaps to build up a sense of anticipation and surprise.

> *A review of "The Birthday Present," in* The Booklist and Subscription Books Bulletin, *Vol. 56, No. 3, October 1, 1959, p. 89.*

For the reader who can't read and has only just begun to recognize pictures, Bruno Munari has designed a special kind of book to keep small hands and eyes happily busy. There is no automatic page-turning job here. For out of bold bright pictures, smaller pages open out like doors to carry on the story with surprises in smaller pictures. Open a tempting flap and Jimmy's refrigerator is opened too. Turn a pasted-in page on an elephant and see what he wishes to be. This should be a nursery conversation-piece as well as an introduction to books.

> *Pamela Marsh, "Widening Horizons," in* The Christian Science Monitor, *October 1, 1959, p. 9.*

Bruno Munari's made-in-Italy picture books are unlike any others, and trying to describe them in mere words is rather like the old party stunt of describing an egg beater without using your hands. Sturdy, brightly printed pages of different sizes are so assembled that a young reader, in turning them, feels he's looking inside closets, behind chairs, into suitcases, and even into minds. These are not toys but real books, each developing a theme and presenting it in excellent art work with great good humor. . . .

Children love these books, over and over and over.

> *Jean Baron, "Bright Words, Bright Pictures," in* Chicago Sunday Tribune Magazine of Books, *November 1, 1959, p. 12.*

Treasures again for the nursery age! Three more original and striking books by the gifted Italian artist Bruno Munari with the pure clear colors, the bold forms, beautiful and decorative,

and the very genuine understanding of what holds delight for very young children that marked the three that appeared in American editions two years ago, "**Animals for Sale,**" "**Tic, Tac, Toc,**" and "**Who's There? Open the Door!**" This time the artist has rendered his very own slight text into English.

> *"Beguiling Monsters in Gay Picture Books," in* New York Herald Tribune Book Review, *November 1, 1959, p. 3.\**

[The theme of "**The Elephant's Wish**"] is the universal discontent. The elephant is bored with being a big, heavy animal. Lift the flap on his big gray head and see what he'd like to be (a bird). But the bird is bored with flying about and singing. If you lift up the flap on his head, you see he'd like to be a fish. The great pink fish wants to be a green lizard, the lizard a cow, the cow an elephant, and you already know what the elephant wishes he were. This is the first of the Munari books that I ever saw—a friend brought a French edition from Paris, and it was called "**Jamais Content**"—and I still think it is the most engaging. . . .

["**Jimmy Has Lost His Cap**"] is a Surrealistic picture book that begins on the outside cover. Jimmy has lost his cap. Where can it be? . . . Our own three-year-old treats this book as if it were a toy or a game, which is perhaps what the author-illustrator intended it to be. . . .

"**The Birthday Present**" is for a slightly older child who has learned to count from one to ten and is surprised and pleased to learn that it is also possible to count from ten to one. (p. 219)

> *Emily Maxwell, "'A' Is for Andersen, 'B' Is for Belloc, 'C' Is for Christmas, 'D' Is for Darwin, 'E' Is for Elephant, 'F' Is for Frost," in* The New Yorker, *Vol. XXXV, No. 40, November 21, 1959, pp. 219-240.\**

There are few things which are more fun to show to children of five and under than Bruno Munari's picture books which are childlike in their appeal and very original in presentation. In addition, they are distinguished in drawing and design with large clean spaces and clear colors. . . . Parents who discovered [Mr. Munari's first books published in English translation] will welcome three more in which there are books within books and hampers, cupboards and doors to open.

> *Ruth Hill Viguers, in a review of "The Birthday Present," "The Elephant's Wish," and "Jimmy Has Lost His Cap," in* The Horn Book Magazine, *Vol. XXXV, No. 6, December, 1959, p. 473.*

---

*BRUNO MUNARI'S ABC* **(1960)**

Created especially for American children, Bruno Munari's alphabet book is, in one way, less spectacular than that Italian artist's picture-story books which have fascinated youngsters here since they began appearing in American editions. There are none of those ingenious tricks with flaps and fold-overs as in "**Animals for Sale**" and the other stories, but this is, just the same, a handsome volume which shows what a sensitive artist can do with familiar things in a realistic vein. The clear, bright objects, set in effective design against large areas of white, are easy to recognize, and neither too literal nor static. And Signor Munari brings to his selection his own special humor—for instance, the fly which appears on the F pages, whirls in and out and ends up on the Z pages with a zzz.

*From* Bruno Munari's ABC, *written and illustrated by Bruno Munari. The World Publishing Company, 1960. Copyright © 1963 by Bruno Munari. All rights reserved. Reprinted by permission of Philomel Books.*

Ellen Lewis Buell, *"To See and Know," in* The New York Times Book Review, *August 28, 1960, p. 24.*

It is not difficult to imagine an attractive A B C book. Good design with plenty of space, interesting objects skillfully drawn in lovely true colors, and there we have a book to give with pleasure to the very little children just becoming aware of names that go with objects and letters that go with names. However, Mr. Munari's genius does not let him stop with those essentials. He has made an A B C book that is so truly a work of art that one can look at it again and again and never tire, and it has exuberance and wit as well. Because young children are ready to accept anything we give them, nothing can be too good for them. Beauty now can make them receptive to beauty always. Here is beauty and imagination and *fun.* No child should miss it.

*Ruth Hill Viguers, in a review of "ABC," in* The Horn Book Magazine, *Vol. XXXVI, No. 5, October, 1960, p. 399.*

With clean lines and brilliant full-color work, Bruno Munari's **"ABC"** is at once unconventional, yet childlike, modern, yet timeless. A bold and refreshing kind of ABC book, its great simplicity almost conceals its art.... Highly recommended.

Ethel L. Heins, *in a review of "ABC," in* Junior Libraries, *an appendix to* Library Journal, *Vol. 85, No. 2, October 15, 1960, p. 166.*

The presence of verbals [in ABC Books] begins to point to plot, for plot is always the result of action. ***Bruno Munari's ABC*** clearly follows a word-picture format using several words with prepositional phrases for each letter. But the content nurtures seeds of story in its use of a meandering character that provides a thread of continuity. There is no particular surprise in "an Ant on an Apple," but tempo begins to pick up when Munari presents us with "a Crow on a Cup, a Candle, and a Cat in a Cage." On the page for "F" we find "a Fly, a Flower, a Feather, a Fish, and more Flies." The "G" page begins with "still another fly!" before presenting "Glasses in Green Grass and a Gift for you." On the "H" page the fly has lit immediately under "a Hammer over a Hat." He is warned, "look out, fly!" However, when the reader is served "lots of Ice Cream," the insect becomes *persona non grata* with "shoo, fly!" Seemingly, the fly goes about his business. But when on the "V" page he emerges from inside "a Vertical Violet Violin," we learn the true reason for his absence: he has been "a fly on a Voyage." He flits around "a Yellow Yacht" and flies off to star in the finale as "a fly going Zzzz...."

Munari's ABC stirs the yen for story.... (p. 174)

*Mary Agnes Taylor, "From Apple to Abstraction in Alphabet Books," in* Children's literature in education, *Vol. 9, No. 4 (Winter), 1978, pp. 173-81.\**

Munari's alphabet book has been a thing of beauty and on its way to fulfill its destiny as a joy forever since 1960. The superb paintings in full color are the essence of joy and so are the artist's rhythmic definitions, spiced with seemingly impromptu humorous bits that small children relish. They will love, for example, meeting an intrusive fly unexpectedly zooming on objects illustrating letters he has nothing to do with.

*A review of "Bruno Munari's ABC," in* Publishers Weekly, *Vol. 221, No. 23, June 4, 1982, p. 68.*

---

### BRUNO MUNARI'S ZOO (1963)

The animals and birds illustrated are superbly well drawn on pages that are alive with color. However, many of the captions are inane and in some cases inaccurate to silly. For example a picture of a beautiful fox is accompanied by the phrase "The fox hides when he sees the furrier"; or an eyestopping peacock at full fan is given the words, "The peacock stalks proudly because he is the peacock". These are words undermining, rather than underlining, pictures.

*A review of "Bruno Munari's Zoo," in* Virginia Kirkus' Service, *Vol. XXXI, No. 15, August 1, 1963, p. 711.*

Again this Italian artist has made a very beautiful picture book, distinguished in design, brilliant in colors, and enlivened with wit and originality. Opening the book one enters the zoo and sees a notice with such appropriate suggestions as, "The lion will be offended if you pull his tail. It is forbidden to sit on the tortoises or to play with the bears. Applaud the seals." The statements that accompany the animals are far from ordinary: "The parrot was born on a day with rainbow"; "For the hippopotamus the swimming pool is always too small." A pleasure for all ages and a delight for little children.

*Ruth Hill Viguers, in a review of "Bruno Munari's Zoo," in* The Horn Book Magazine, *Vol. XXXIX, No. 5, October, 1963, p. 495.*

Like all of Munari's books, this one can stand up under enthusiastic, repeated scrutiny. Deceptively simple, it begins on the page preceding the title page, and, once inside the zoo, you won't need peanuts and crackerjack. Provocative and

The birds are infinite.

*From* Bruno Munari's Zoo, *written and illustrated by Bruno Munari. The World Publishing Company, 1963. Copyright © 1963 by Bruno Munari. All rights reserved. Reprinted by permission of Philomel Books.*

sometimes funny captions enhance the effectiveness of the bold drawings in vibrant colors. . . . The only thing librarians should find to disagree about in this gay book is which picture they like the best.

> *Patricia H. Allen, in a review of "Bruno Munari's Zoo," in* School Library Journal, *an appendix to* Library Journal, *Vol. 10, No. 3, November, 1963, p. 56.*

Some of the text in this beautiful book of zoo animals—printed in eight colors in Italy—is semipoetic: "The parrot was born on a day with rainbow"; some of it is semihumorous: "A zebra is an animal in striped pajamas"; some plainly and clearly informative: "A tiger is a big cat with stripes." Almost any child, even a very young one, will enjoy it as a picture book; many adults will, too. But it is a book for looking rather than listening because of the small amount of text.

> *A review of "Bruno Munari's Zoo," in* Saturday Review, *Vol. XLVI, No. 45, November 9, 1963, p. 58.*

Original, simple, beautiful as are all Bruno Munari's picture books, this is perhaps as satisfactory a child's first book as one could hope to find. There are many big, handsomely designed animals on stark white pages—among them a magnificent kangaroo as well as a black porcupine and pink flamingos like the delightful ones in **"Animals for Sale,"** a book we have cherished and use as a touchstone in our search for freshness, humor and the bright, bold and clear forms children love.

The only words in the book are the directional signs at the entrance to the zoo, the names of the animals and their outstanding qualities. . . . The words are as unusual, witty and endearing as the pictures.

> *Margaret Sherwood Libby, in a review of "Bruno Munari's Zoo," in* Book Week—The Sunday Herald Tribune, *Fall Children's Issue, November 10, 1963, p. 4.*

An oversize book with a small amount of text and with illustrations of stunning beauty of color and of design. The author does not attempt to include all animals usually found in a zoo, but uses each double-page spread for one creature and one comment, some of these being quips, some matter-of-fact remarks. While most of the text is simple: "The squirrel spends the summer storing nuts for winter," or "A leopard is a big cat with spots," some may need interpretation. "The peacock stalks proudly because he is the peacock," or "The fox hides when he sees the furrier." It is probable that the brief and unhackneyed sentences will be more easily remembered by the small child who later looks at the book by himself than would a more conventional remark.

> *"Bruno Munari's Zoo," in* Good Books for Children: A Selection of Outstanding Children's Books Published 1950-65, *third edition, edited by Mary K. Eakin, The University of Chicago Press, 1966, p. 241.*

---

### NELLA NEBBIA DI MILANO [THE CIRCUS IN THE MIST] (1968)

It's been a long time between Munaris—too long. But he's come back with a magnificent creation that calls for fireworks, stars and wheels, and wild flares bursting in air. In the first half of this book, Bruno Munari shows you, in his unique way, a city in the fog; in the second half, a circus. Cities and circuses will have a new nimbus for you from now on, courtesy of Bruno Munari.

> *A review of "The Circus in the Mist," in* Publishers Weekly, *Vol. 196, No. 21, November 24, 1969, p. 42.*

Bruno Munari is not only an illustrator but an innovator—a master at introducing us to the delights of abstraction by playing with color and form, and he does it superbly in this experiment in bookcraft.

The story is simple—a trip through the foggy city when "birds make only short flights" and even "cats travel at man's pace." This in black on translucent gray paper evoking a synesthesia of silence till we come to the Grand Circus complete with clowns and the high trapeze where colors are hot and pages laced with cutouts. Here fancy roves unrestricted as horns blare and jugglers, literally, lose their heads. And then it's time to "go home across the misty park." Trees and traffic signs are again murky and unreal.

But is that all? The limits are those of your imagination: a trip up Broadway at night . . . and then it's on uptown and back into the dark.

Here is the conscious use of skill, taste and creative imagination. The effect is exquisite perfection in the graphic arts.

> *Ingeborg Boudreau, in a review of "The Circus in the Mist," in* The New York Times Book Review, *December 14, 1969, p. 34.*

Ingeniously using semitranslucent pages, pages of different colors, peepholes, and design to good effect a well-known Italian artist and designer has created a unique and diverting picture book with surprises on every page. There is no real story line but interest is captured and sustained by changing mood and pace. . . . While the book may seem too experimental and gimmicky to many adults, children will undoubtedly find it great fun. (pp. 984-85)

> *A review of "The Circus in the Mist," in* The Booklist, *Vol. 66, No. 15, April 1, 1970, pp. 984-85.*

Every now and again adults ponder the gimmicky things that happen to children's books, shaking their heads over pop-ups and other playthings that masquerade as books. But whatever category Bruno Munari's **"The Circus in the Mist"** . . . belongs to, there is no denying its fascination.

Mr. Munari uses odd shaped unexpected cut-outs so that the same drawing plays a role on several pages. Transparent paper shows the world in a mysterious winter mist and provides abrupt changes of texture to tantalize children's fingers.

In Mr. Munari's brilliant illustrations and in his text there are both jokes—almost slapstick humor—and moments of visual delight.

> *"Why Can a Fly Climb the Wall?" in* The Christian Science Monitor, *April 4, 1970, p. B23.\**

Through grey-white translucent paper are the dim shapes of city scenes, showing through the pages and effectively evoking a sense of a quiet, fog-bound day. The pages then erupt into color: clowns, animals, musicians, bright lights, and all the paraphernalia of a circus; added to this are the inventive use of cut-out pages that distinguish Munari's work, circles that give different effects on each page. Out again, and into the dim mist of the park. The contrast is tremendously effective and the whole book a visual delight; the text is not as strong, some of it firmly descriptive ("... in the mist birds make only short flight.", "... lifting weights is very hard work ...") some of it irrelevant ("... toy boat in a dish and a pocketsize fish ...", "... the train leaves on the dot so suddenly that it scares a little bird ...") but there is a playful quality of humor, often in both text and illustrations, that makes this seem acceptable.

> *Zena Sutherland, in a review of "The Circus in the Mist," in* Bulletin of the Center for Children's Books, *Vol. 23, No. 10, June, 1970, p. 164.*

This visual toy in book form is completely emancipated from any obligation to illustrate a text or tell a story.... The text throughout is a generally uninspired verbal illustration of the highly original pictures; it is falsely poetic and visually annoying when seen in reverse on the transparent pages. Though the format might create a durability problem for libraries, the book is sure to be a hit. Small children will be intrigued by the gimmicks: cut-outs, variety of paper, etc., while older children (if they are properly introduced to the book) will appreciate the visual jokes, clever details and complicated structure.

> *Sada Fretz, "The Circus in the Mist," in* School Library Journal, *an appendix to* Library Journal, *Vol. 17, No. 1, September, 1970, p. 152.*

---

### DA LONTANO ERA UN'ISOLA [FROM AFAR IT IS AN ISLAND] (1971; British edition as Search for a Stone)

The title refers to a jagged "stone," photographed for the endpapers so as to resemble an island many orders of magnitude larger than its actual size, and the rest of the book consists of fancifully captioned photographs of stones with which Munari plays various other games. Munari's commentary might be described as semi-precious ("a family of three stones, all in black suits, bulging out of white belts" describes one photo). What fun there is here is in the pictures—of smooth and spongy and streaked stones, of stones cleverly marked with felt pen drawings (a man rides a bicycle along a stone's white band, a monkey transforms another stone's crisscrossing stripes into jungle vines) that might well inspire emulation, and finally of a real island photographed to look like another small stone. It will be hard to classify or age the book but readers may be just a stone's throw away.

> *A review of "From Afar It Is an Island," in* Kirkus Reviews, *Vol. XL, No. 12, June 15, 1972, p. 670.*

At first sight this book may appear dull, but the ideas within its pages soon bring it to life. It is an imaginative book from Italy ... on the unusual hobby of collecting stones. The author suggests ways of looking at them, not from a geological angle but for imaginative pleasure. For instance he uses the natural markings on a stone as a background for painted figures, or he chooses stones for their unusual shape or surface. Few children could fail to look at stones with new interest after seeing this book.

A book to be shared with parents or teachers or given to a child as a stimulus to his imagination. (pp. 385-86)

From The Circus in the Mist, *written and illustrated by Bruno Munari. The World Publishing Company, 1969. Copyright © 1968 by Bruno Munari. All rights reserved. Reprinted by permission of Philomel Books.*

> *E. Colwell, in a review of "Search for a Stone," in* The Junior Bookshelf, *Vol. 36, No. 6, December, 1972, pp. 385-86.*

Through photographs of rocks arranged in interesting patterns against textured backdrops or with superimposed drawings, Munari introduces young children to the visual and tactile qualities of rocks and stones. Only incidentally factual, the author explores many types of stones (without mentioning their names) in what is essentially a poetic, romantic mood piece. In some instances, he is playful (e.g., Munari draws black images on a white, striated stone), and young children will find this appealing. Older readers may use it as an introduction to geology or art.

> *Marcia Posner, in a review of "From Afar It Is an Island," in* School Library Journal, *an appendix to* Library Journal, *Vol. 20, No. 1, September, 1973, p. 116.*

This small book of remarkable photographs, with a couple of lines of text to a page, is an artist's book, but Bruno Munari's eye sees the real world. Here it is stones he sees: rounded pebbles, glossy or matte, smooth or rough, yellow or sparkling.... A tour de force of imagination, sensitivity and taste, this is a way into clear-sighted view of the world, an artist's pleasure and a beginner's natural history, a slight but real fusion of the outlooks of art and of science.

> *Philip Morrison and Phylis Morrison, in a review of "From Afar It Is an Island," in* Scientific American, *Vol. 229, No. 6, December, 1973, p. 133.*

---

*A FLOWER WITH LOVE*   (1974)

"A flower with love" is Bruno Munari's interpretation of the Japanese art of *ikebana,* his inspiration for the twelve spare compositions of leaves, flowers, moss, etc., displayed here in full-color photographs and described in small paragraphs that give readers suggestions for making gift arrangements of their own. Oddly for Munari, this seems at first to be just a tasteful flower-arranging book—and a second look confirms the impression.

> *A review of "A Flower with Love," in* Kirkus Reviews, *Vol. XLII, No. 20, October 15, 1974, p. 1108.*

A useful addition to craft collections, this explains ikebana, a Japanese art form using natural objects to create decorative arrangements. Using objects found in the garden, backyard, and home, children learn to create beauty from simple things. The color photographs are clear and attractive, and the text is easy to follow.

> *Alice Calabrese, in a review of "A Flower with Love,"* in School Library Journal, *an appendix to* Library Journal, *Vol. 21, No. 4, December, 1974, p. 43.*

Handsome color photographs show a dozen examples of ikebana, the Japanese art of flower arrangement. Munari wisely chooses not to stress the technical aspects of balance and design but to show arrangements that exemplify the restraint of ikebana compositions. Wisely, too, he suggests that the reader not copy them exactly but use them for ideas that embody the concepts of simple arrangements that use "found" containers (bottles, ashtrays, baking dishes, etc.) of weeds, single flowers, branches, vegetables, and so on. No expensive vases or massive bouquets. Each full page photograph is faced by a paragraph of text, occasionally adding a line drawing. The book itself is handsome, and it conveys effectively both the idea of choosing a flower lovingly and of expressing love by a gift of inexpensive beauty. (pp. 135-36)

> *Zena Sutherland, in a review of "A Flower with Love,"* in Bulletin of the Center for Children's Books, *Vol. 28, No. 8, April, 1975, pp. 135-36.*

# (Ann) Philippa Pearce (Christie)

## 1920-

English author of fiction, short stories, picture books, and nonfiction, reteller, scriptwriter, critic, editor, and translator.

Pearce is one of the most highly respected writers of books for children. Although not prolific, she is considered among the foremost of the British writers who emerged at the end of the 1950s, such as William Mayne, L. M. Boston, and Rosemary Sutcliff. Often addressing the events that influence growth and maturity, Pearce's books probe the realities of childhood on many different levels. She employs elements of fantasy and the supernatural to complement the realism of her stories, and often demonstrates how heightened experience or a strong need can cause a supernatural event. Other themes concern the past and its influence on the present and future, social differences caused by class structures, and the loneliness and isolation that can exist within the family unit. Adults play important roles in Pearce's works, rather than being absent or ineffectual as in some other books for young readers. She uses the Cambridgeshire countryside of her childhood as the setting for most of her books, and her precise descriptions and vivid sense of place and atmosphere are often noted.

It is unanimously agreed that Pearce's greatest achievement is *Tom's Midnight Garden*, in which a lonely summer spent with his aunt and uncle leads Tom to discover a magical garden and Hatty, a girl from the past. Essentially, this is the story of a desire for companionship so strong that it breaks through the barriers of time; Pearce firmly links fantasy with reality to suggest the effectiveness of imagination in overcoming limitations. She was praised for the originality of her theory of time and the consistency and logic of her approach. Some critics have called this work the most perfect book ever written for children.

*A Dog So Small* and *The Way to Sattin Shore* are Pearce's other major novels. *A Dog So Small* deals with fantasy in a different manner from *Tom's Midnight Garden*. Triggered by his intense longing for a pet and the loneliness he feels as an excluded child, Ben learns through harsh experience to distinguish possibility from impossibility. The unfolding of his thoughts and emotions is characteristic of Pearce's style, and is represented in several of her other titles, including *The Way to Sattin Shore*. A mystery story in which Kate discovers that her mother and grandmother have been deceiving her about her father's death, *Sattin Shore* is considered one of Pearce's best works for the success of her perception into human relationships and her ability to make characters and places come alive.

Pearce's collections of short stories are often felt to be as successful as her novels. *What the Neighbours Did and Other Stories* concentrates on everyday actions and events while conveying their deeper essence; *The Shadow-Cage and Other Tales of the Supernatural*, a series of ghost stories in the classic tradition, exhibits Pearce's own distinctive approach. In her sole original fairy tale, *The Squirrel Wife*, Pearce emphasizes human emotions and values, thus giving an uncommon immediacy to the genre. *The Battle of Bubble and Squeak*, a book for younger readers which details the upheaval caused when Sid brings home a pair of gerbils, is praised for its insight into

the dynamics of family life. As a collaborator, Pearce provided a novelistic structure for Brian Fairfax-Lucy's autobiographical reminiscence of his Edwardian youth, *The Children of the House;* the work is praised for its unusual viewpoint and for the beauty of its sad though unsentimental ending.

The daughter of a miller, Pearce grew up in the King's Mill House on the River Cam. She swam in the river and fished with her siblings from their canoe, but Pearce was often ill and sometimes lonely. After receiving degrees in English and history from Cambridge, she became a scriptwriter and producer for the Schools Broadcasting Department of the BBC and later worked as a children's editor for two publishing firms. Pearce's vivid recollections of her childhood are the basis for her first book, *Minnow on the Say*, which was written out of her longing for home during a long recuperation from tuberculosis. Her second book, *Tom's Midnight Garden*, was prompted when the Mill House was sold. Focusing on the garden and other parts of the house, Pearce also utilizes some of her father's boyhood experiences in this work. She moved to Suffolk after her marriage and employs this setting in several of her short stories and *The Way to Sattin Shore*, which refers to the estuary where she lived with her husband.

With the exception of *The Way to Sattin Shore*, several of Pearce's later works are considered minor by critics, some of whom have stated that she has yet to regain success on the scale of *Tom's Midnight Garden*. She is also criticized for inconsistent plot construction. It is generally agreed, however, that Pearce's combination of reality and fantasy is unique, and that her writing style and portrayal of human nature have been exceptional throughout her career. Young people attracted to her works have found believable characters and situations with which to identify while discovering a writer of imagination, depth, and quality.

Pearce's awards reflect her stature. She won the Carnegie Medal in 1959 for *Tom's Midnight Garden* and received Carnegie Commendations for *Minnow on the Say* in 1956, *The Shadow-Cage and Other Tales of the Supernatural* in 1978, and *The Battle of Bubble and Squeak* in 1979. Books selected for the International Board on Books for Young People (IBBY) Honour List are *Minnow on the Say* in 1956, *Tom's Midnight Garden* in 1960, and *What the Neighbours Did and Other Stories* in 1974. Works designated as Lewis Carroll Shelf Award winners are *The Minnow Leads to Treasure* in 1959 and *Tom's Midnight Garden* in 1963.

(See also *Contemporary Literary Criticism*, Vol. 21; *Something about the Author*, Vol. 1; *Contemporary Authors New Revision Series*, Vol. 4; and *Contemporary Authors*, Vols. 5-8. rev. ed.)

---

## AUTHOR'S COMMENTARY

*[In the following excerpt from* Books for Keeps, *Pearce is interviewed on her childhood, her career, and her books.]*

Philippa Pearce's cottage stands opposite the Mill House where she spent her childhood. She recalls living there, the youngest of four children, as a very happy time.

'Oh it was lovely, it really was. Although there wasn't much cash we had lots of space. My father ran the mill and because he was the miller he had a narrow strip running up the river for about an eighth of a mile. We had a canoe, we swam, . . . my father fished . . . and in the mill was a wonderful workshop for carpentry and sack-mending and that sort of thing. . . . We used to nip into the mill by a secret way we knew—we were never supposed to do this—and we used to play among the sacks and hide. It was a lovely time.'

Yet surrounded by family there was a sense of being separate, something, perhaps, which makes Philippa Pearce such an acute observer of people, places and feelings. 'I was a bit isolated. My sister was eight years older and the boys did everything together.' She was also ill for a long period. 'I didn't go to school until I was eight or nine. When I did go it was very leisurely. We didn't have afternoon school until I was about thirteen or fourteen. I used to come home at lunchtime and potter around up the river. I don't think it did me any harm.' . . .

[After the war, she] joined the Schools Broadcasting Department and stayed happily for thirteen years as script writer and producer. 'We did adaptations of books. I had to study techniques and structure and what you could do with a book. I began to think it wouldn't be impossible to try to do the same thing myself.' But she was kept fairly busy and it wasn't until 1953 when she got TB and had a long spell in hospital that she began. 'The hospital was in Cambridge; it was a hot summer and I was awfully fed up. I thought of my home and how lovely it would be to be there and to go in the canoe. I began to imagine exactly what it was like. I found I could recreate

it in detail and even feel the texture of the twine that ties the canoe to the landing stage that my brother once made. And then I began to think of a story of two boys in a canoe. I wrote it with the absolute innocence of never having done it before. I just went straight ahead; it was lovely.' . . .

'I went round saying [*Minnow on the Say*] was the only book I was ever going to write; it seemed far safer to say that.' Three years later came *Tom's Midnight Garden*. Like the first book it is rooted in intense personal feelings. 'My father had to retire and they sold the Mill House. Suddenly my childhood was chopped off from me. As they were in the process of selling it I began thinking of writing stories based on the house and the garden and this feeling of things slipping away. It's a terrible feeling. I'm glad I have forgotten what it felt like.' She had the theme, she needed a plot. 'Looking back now at *Minnow on the Say* I think the treasure hunt idea is corny. At the time I wasn't sophisticated enough to see how weak it was, but I did know it was a convention I was borrowing and I was very conscious that the plot was far too involved. I decided this new book would be just about children playing in the garden, nothing more than that. But of course it would have been shapeless. My elder brother and his friends were reading J W Dunne's *Experiment in Time*. I never really understood it properly but it was a sort of theoretical base for the book.'

It fed the real impulse of the book, 'the feeling of time passing, people becoming old. Even though I wasn't old I could see that if you were old you hadn't been old forever.'

The house and garden remain, largely unchanged and uncannily familiar to anyone who knows the book. Philippa Pearce is on good terms with the present owners and their children. Walking round the garden she recreates her childhood and the book. She points out the door in the wall which out-of-time Tom squeezes through like an inexperienced ghost. . . . 'My father did actually walk along the top of this wall as a boy, and he also skated to Ely. All that in the book was based on what he told us. I imagine Hatty as being born about when my father was born, in 1876.'

Two novels published, one a Carnegie winner. Was she beginning to think of herself as a children's writer? 'Well, at that point it was still something I did in my spare time. I wasn't sure whether I would go on writing or not.' (p. 14)

Scenery, places, are important in Philippa Pearce's stories. 'That often comes to me before anything else.' When she married Martin Christie they went to live in Suffolk and she found a new landscape, one which has appeared in the short stories and now most dominantly in her latest book *The Way to Sattin Shore*.

'"Sattin" Shore is a real place; it's a small estuary in Suffolk where we used to live. You approach it along a long road; it was always deserted because you weren't allowed to take a car along. The idea for the story has been lying around in my mind for 15 or 20 years. I wanted to do something with this feeling of going to meet somebody, going to meet somebody for a very important encounter, almost of going to meet your destiny, what you should be or what you were. I wanted that at the heart of it. I still come across boss shots at the beginning of that story dating years back. Kestrel wanted me to call it just *Sattin Shore*; but I wanted it to be *The Way to Sattin Shore* because it was the way into the past, as though the past were a place.'

In the book Kate, the central character, makes several journeys to Sattin Shore to unravel the mystery that surrounds her father whom she believes is dead. There she meets her granny who belongs to the place, and the place which was so important, and in the end she meets her father. It is a moment of great intensity.

'He had been swimming naked, as the place was very deserted: and so Kate saw her father as Eve saw Adam newly created in the Garden of Eden.'

'What I meant, if I "meant" anything was that she needed him so much she almost created him. I wanted him to be absolutely stark naked. At that moment he's the perfect man, the perfect father, the Michelangelo Adam. In some ways he was a weak man. But for Kate he was perfect.'

This encounter becomes even more poignant when Philippa Pearce reveals that her husband died when their daughter was only a few weeks old. But she insists firmly that the book has nothing to do with her daughter. 'It is something *I* have imagined.' (pp. 14-15)

[Philippa Pearce was a part-time children's editor at Andre] Deutsch for five years. 'I loved doing it, and I think I was really helpful to people. . . . Once you get a good writer you don't want to interfere with them.'

About being edited herself she is less happy. 'I don't much like constructive criticism', she smiles, 'so when I finally send it, it is as near perfect as I can make it. Of course there is constructive criticism you have to pay attention to but I dread it, it's drudgery. I think I'm just not good at plots. This latest one caused me lots of problems. I think it was because I was out of practice. I'd translated *Wings of Courage* but nothing very serious and sustained and completely my own for a long time. It took ages.'

Short stories are a different matter. 'I love doing short stories. I don't find them as difficult. I can get a complete idea for a short story whereas when I have written a long book I've never had a complete idea for the whole thing. I have a theme in my mind and one or two strong scenes and then I begin fumbling my way forward,' Like most writers she knows the despair of getting stuck, of not being able to make it work. 'You *can* go on writing, anyone can write a bad book, a book that doesn't take off, where the writing is dead.

'I usually give up and go away and let it work in my mind. There is just one story, **"At the River Gates,"** when I got the whole story in my head between being asleep and being fully awake one morning. It was marvellous. I had never done anything like that before. I'm sure it was lying in wait for me really. It's a lovely feeling.'

Philippa Pearce's short stories demonstrate how well she understands children, their relationships with adults, the strength of their emotions. This quality is also present in *The Battle of Bubble and Squeak*. . . . It was written after Philippa Pearce and her daughter had moved to the village to make it easier to keep the animals Sally loved. Among the cats, dogs, goat, horse, etc. that joined the household were two gerbils.

'It was a terrible time. I don't really take to gerbils but Sally had the chance of getting them and she was radiant at the opportunity; she was about nine. So we had them. Almost all the incidents in the book happened to us: they gnawed holes in the curtains, the cat caught one and we took it to the vet and the vet told us what to do and we saved his life. I invented the rest, but everything about the gerbils was absolutely true.'

'What I wanted to do with that book was make the opening pages deliberately gripping for say a junior child and yet be simple enough for perhaps a younger child, or a junior child who wasn't a very good reader.'

This clear sense of the reader comes very much from Philippa Pearce's years with Schools Broadcasting. 'I very often find myself referring back to that period of my life to get it right. And I have learned an awful lot from teachers and from children, of course. I like talking to children. I prefer talking to children than adults. Adults are so polite you never know when they are bored or not. Children always yawn if they are bored.'

There is a lot of the teacher and a fair bit of the actor in Philippa Pearce. 'I enjoy telling stories; it is lovely holding an audience. I don't usually use my own because although they read aloud alright (I hope), they don't *tell* well. **"The Shadow Cage"** I originally told in a school and another one, **"The Great Sharp Scissors"** will be in my new collection for 5-7's.'

She's working on that now. It's something she started while working on the BBC series Listening and Reading, and she's enjoying writing for a different age. 'I think it keeps you flexible, like gymnastics.' And after that? 'I don't know. I am sure I will want to try, if life lasts out, another long book; but I haven't got one in mind yet. At least I don't think I have. You never know what is lying around in your mind.' (p. 15)

*"Authorgraph No. 23: Philippa Pearce,"* in Books for Keeps, *No. 23, November, 1983, pp. 14-15.*

---

## GENERAL COMMENTARY

### MARGERY FISHER

Personal experience, transmuted by imagination and fine writing—these are found . . . in Philippa Pearce's *Tom's Midnight Garden*. In this story, time loses its limits for two people. First, for Tom, a schoolboy sent to stay with a rather unenterprising aunt and uncle while his brother has measles. (p. 122)

One night the clock strikes thirteen. Tom goes down to investigate, opens the back-door and finds himself not in the concrete yard with dustbins and clothes-lines but in an apparently limitless garden. In this garden it would seem that Tom is a ghost; or so he appears to Hatty, the small girl he meets there and who accepts him as a playmate in her Victorian world. He believes that he can share everything that happens to Hatty before he has to return to the present. This is not to be. Although time stands still in Tom's world while he is in the past, it does not stand still for Hatty. She is growing up even as Tom plays with her, and the magic, the wonder of the garden, the transcending of time must come to an end with the ending of her childhood. This familiar ending to time fantasies is beautifully handled, with great sympathy for the boy who suddenly sees his companion as a young woman. And there is a bold twist to the ending which sends the whole book back on itself, sends the reader rethinking the whole. For Tom, on the very day he is due to go home, meets the owner of the house, old Mrs Bartholomew, who lives in seclusion upstairs. He climbs to her flat, opens the door—and finds that she is Hatty. So, did he go back in the past, or did she create the past with her dreams as she lay in bed, an old woman?

The subtlety of this circumstance is something children may pay more attention to if they reread the book in their late teens.

As a child's story it is magnificent. It is at once philosophical, swift, and gay. The conversations of Hatty and Tom are natural, the incidents probable and presented with beautiful clarity. The style is impeccable—loose-jointed and flexible, colloquial when the occasion demands, at other times rhythmical and poetic. The fantasy will be real to children because it is real to the author. . . . (pp. 122-23)

[*Tom's Midnight Garden*] is a book about people and their feelings. It is also, very much, a book about Time. The author is preoccupied with Time and its problems. Is it circular? Is it continuous? If Hatty carves Tom's private mark on a tree (which in present Time stands in the middle of a new housing estate), will the mark be visible to Tom in the present? And, if so, was it made *now* or *then*? Tom, always conscious of being in two worlds, never finds the answer to this, but he does make one firm attempt to conquer the limits of Time. He visits the garden on one occasion in winter, and finds Hatty skating. As he has no skates, he makes a plan; he begs her to wrap up her skates and hide them in her secret hiding-place (which, in the present, is in Tom's bedroom). Tom then returns to the present, finds the skates, takes them back into the past, and is soon skating blissfully on the Fens, the skates mysteriously duplicated. This bold stroke succeeds by its simplicity. The author, wisely, attempts no explanation. (p. 124)

[In *Minnow on the Say*], one of the best children's books of recent years, young David, whose father is a bus driver, realizes his home life is different from Adam's. He sees the difference in practical terms. Adam lives in a large old house on the river, not in a council house, he has his meals at different times, and he does not always have enough to eat. It is for David's mother to work out how she can offer Miss Codling a cake without hurting her pride, for Mrs Moss realizes the intangible differences which David and Adam can happily ignore. This exquisite story has innumerable threads in its rich canvas—the pervasive presence of the river, every ripple exactly described; the treasure hunt, with its intricate and unexpected ending; the sure handling of a child's joy in living. . . . But one of the most interesting threads is the sensible, subtle treatment of class difference; the contrasting, by implication, of the Moss household, with its safe, small prosperity, and the old house where Miss Codling fights to preserve her standards. (pp. 287-88)

*Margery Fisher, "Travellers in Time" and "Little Birds in Their Nests Agree," in her* Intent Upon Reading: A Critical Appraisal of Modern Fiction for Children, *Hodder & Stoughton Children's Books (formerly Brockhampton Press), 1961, pp. 116-31, 270-96.**

## BRIAN JACKSON

[*A Dog So Small*] is an uncommonly fine book, and completes for Philippa Pearce a remarkable trio of children's stories. In the first, *Tom's Midnight Garden,* a small boy comes to realize that an old woman was once a tough young girl, and, in some lost moment of time, a possible playmate: the strange adventures recreate the continuity of human life, and dissolve the static adult-or-children divisions that a child mistakes for reality. In the second, *Minnow on the Say,* a rather slight plot draws together an enchanting series of episodes—boys growing up together on the banks of a Cambridgeshire river.

All three books concern themselves with growing up, with the real world of childhood. Every child has to live with the double-edged pleasures of fantasy, and learn the art of confining his desires within the realm of the possible. But the vast majority of books published for children today no more recognize this than they recognize the other nine-tenths of childhood. The thing through which they string their narcotic plots is not childhood at all, but a prim and wretched parody of it.

All three books lie on the edge of genuine distinction: almost minor classics for children. They are so good that it disappoints that they are not better. Coming to the end you feel that Miss Pearce either wants her bottom kicking for failing to face the final tasks, or should more kindly be locked away in luxury to write and rewrite until our age has its *Bevis* or its *Treasure Island:* for the ground-plans are here.

*Brian Jackson, "Dog in the Hand," in* New Statesman, *Vol. LXIII, No. 1627, May 18, 1962, p. 726.**

## MARCUS CROUCH

[Philippa Pearce is] a highly intelligent young writer. She is the master of a fine sensitive style. She has imagination and a gift for recapturing the emotions and sensations of childhood. *Minnow on the Say* was a little burdened by its plot, but in atmosphere and in freshness it was the most promising first novel of a children's writer for many years. *Tom's Midnight Garden* fully redeemed this promise. This was a fully mature work, with an original theme developed in a masterly fashion, most understanding treatment of adult and child characters, present and past (for this was a kind of ghost-story), and a hauntingly beautiful evocation of atmosphere. Philippa Pearce's admirers had to wait four years for her next book. So precise, deeply pondering a muse was not to be hurried. (p. 122)

*Marcus Crouch, "Widening Horizons," in his* Treasure Seekers and Borrowers: Children's Books in Britain 1900-1960, *The Library Association, 1962, pp. 112-38.**

## JOHN ROWE TOWNSEND

[*Tom's Midnight Garden*] has not a flaw that I can find, not a trace of untidiness; it is as near to being perfect in its construction and its writing as any book I know. I think only a woman could have written it; girls should like it, and adults, and thoughtful boys, but not the lovers of rough tough stuff. (p. 127)

The book has a profound, mysterious sense of time; it has the beauty of a theorem but it is not abstract; it is sensuously as well as intellectually satisfying. The garden is so real that you have the scent of it in your nostrils. . . .

I have no reservations to make about it. If I were asked to name a single masterpiece of English children's literature since the last war—and one masterpiece in twenty years is a fair ration—it would be this outstandingly beautiful and absorbing book. (p. 128)

Philippa Pearce has written three books while Mayne was writing twenty, and all three are undeniable artistic successes. *Minnow on the Say* . . . has curious parallels with Mayne's work. Here too is an intricately-plotted treasure-hunt, with detective-story elements and with an ingenious relationship between past and present. . . . There is a fine shaping imagination at work throughout.

*A Dog So Small* explores the depths of a child's longing. Ben, the middle child of five, is promised a dog by his grandfather, but the promise cannot be properly kept, and all he gets is a picture of a dog worked in wool. In his disappointment Ben imagines a dog of his own, which he can only see with closed eyes; and while crossing the street, lost to the world, he is run over and goes to hospital. . . .

This is a book which quite young children can enjoy; . . . but there is a subtlety which makes it re-readable at all ages, and it is well worthy of its author's talent. (p. 140)

> John Rowe Townsend, "The New Fantasy" and "Novels for Boys and Girls," in his Written for Children: An Outline of English Children's Literature, 1965. Reprint by Lothrop, Lee & Shepard Co. Inc., 1967, pp. 122-28, 138-44.*

## RUTH HILL VIGUERS

[In Philippa Pearce's *Tom's Midnight Garden*] the idea that time has no barriers was embodied in nearly perfect literary form. No loose ends, no inconsistencies mar the book. Miss Pearce can explain with few words but great conviction such supernatural events as Tom's passing through a closed door or the actual process of a room's transformation from its unfamiliar past appearance to its familiar present. Tom's acceptance of the fact that he can enjoy a garden that had existed long before his birth and friendship with a girl who had played in the garden more than half a century before is wholly believable. The book is a model of what can be done with an intricate theme by a writer endowed with literary style, understanding of children, and a clear insight into her own vision. (p. 477)

The characters are very perceptively drawn [in *The Minnow Leads to Treasure*, published in England as *Minnow on the Say*], but, most important of all, the book has the power to transport the reader into another setting. Unforgettable are the pleasure of sharing an interesting pursuit with a congenial companion, the charm of boating on a beautiful English stream, and the peace and relaxation of summer holidays. (p. 580)

> Ruth Hill Viguers, "Golden Years and Time of Tumult: 1920-1967," in A Critical History of Children's Literature by Cornelia Meigs, Anne Thaxter Eaton, Elizabeth Nesbitt, and Ruth Hill Viguers, edited by Cornelia Meigs, revised edition, Macmillan Publishing Company, 1969, pp. 393-668.*

## ELEANOR CAMERON

In *Minnow* one finds the same devouring awareness of the natural world, the same complexity and maturity of thought . . . , the same artistry of phrasing, and the same unwillingness to compromise in any of these areas because [Philippa Pearce] is writing for children that we find in Lucy Boston's and William Mayne's work. Therefore in her time fantasy one is not in the least surprised to discover, woven into the firmly plotted movement of the story, certain philosophic overtones in her handling of Time as it relates to Tom's gradual understanding of what he has been experiencing in the garden. In this work, too, as in Lucy Boston's, is found what I can only describe as an atmosphere of poetic dimension, tenderness without sentimentality, though expressed quite differently: not so much in paragraphs one can read aloud as examples as in the effect of the book as a whole, in Tom's relationship to the child Hatty and in his almost visceral love for and need of the garden. Here . . . is passionate attachment to place and person. . . . (pp. 118-19)

In a book such as this, . . . one sees the fertile and perceiving mind of the writer joyously at work, unafraid of convolutions (so unexpectedly playing Hatty's time against Tom's Relative Time), ready to explore to the end every possibility opened up by each new pattern of circumstance. Such writers never cease searching for all that any particular pattern will yield. Yet, whatever fresh and original perceptions are arrived at, the results as far as story is concerned will be clear and firm and

satisfying to both the analytical and the aesthetically sensitive adult, as well as to the less consciously critical child. The reader, whoever he may be, will sense a fine proportion, a plausible economy of effect. (pp. 121-22)

> Eleanor Cameron, "The Green and Burning Tree: A Study of Time Fantasy," in her The Green and Burning Tree: On the Writing and Enjoyment of Children's Books, Little, Brown and Company, 1969, pp. 71-136.*

## BRIAN JACKSON

[Philippa Pearce's] achievement, wonderful enough in itself, is representative of how (without forsaking the adult note) a truly gifted writer can now write directly for the child, and for the ordinary child, in a way seldom achieved before. . . .

[*Minnow on the Say* has] plain lucid prose, wholly accessible to a child between 8 and 12. . . . The tale has the hypnotic craftsmanship of a first class detective story. And as the story winds its fascinating course, the book engages the reader even more deeply in the lovely recreation of a boy's life in a small East Anglian village. In doing so, it brings back many childhoods—how tall the walls are, how beckoning the holes in fences, how the fingers reach to caress the dents and bulges in old stonework or to savour the speed and weight and coolness of dripping water or running streams. It spills over with a child's geography, places that only a child would know—like the fallen tree bridge over the river, from where they observe the punters below; or views that a child might specially sense, like the roof-well on Adam's house. . . . (p. 196)

It is, if you like, a very conservative book. Children are expected to be polite to adults, to make things—scraping and varnishing their canoe—not to destroy. There are all the tiny ceremonies of inviting friends to tea, or calling on strangers. Pocket money is earned and carefully counted, and very neatly you pick up the nuances of children and adults observing the codes. . . .

Of course, the boys—being boys—are sometimes rude and destructive, thoughtlessly or at moments of stress. There is the moment when Adam, obsessed by the treasure, suspects treasure under the lovely pinky-yellow rose bush that stands by itself in the garden. . . . (p. 197)

Without being in the slightest moralistic, the book has the rare capacity to create goodness, to make the decencies of life ring true.

Her effects come through her art; her negatives—'a deep, raw hole, empty now of any rose-tree roots'—imply her positives.

And yet there is more; already at least a pre-echo of the Philippa Pearce music, that note of controlled poignancy that is to make *Tom's Midnight Garden* a classic of its literature. You hear something of it with Squeak's tipsy bicycle ride past the bewildered David.

> A voice somewhere down the drive began singing in queer, thin tones that might have come from another world. David felt almost frightened, until he saw that the singer was Squeak Wilson going home, the capacious basket of his tricycle piled high, as usual. He paid no attention to David even when he drew level with him. Now, David could hear the words of his little song:
>
> 'Heigh-ho!'

Heigh-ho!

Heigh-ho! Sweet summer!'

All the sweet summers that David had ever known came drifting into his mind, and last came this one—best of them all, that he had shared with Adam. He heard the swish of the 'Minnow' as they paddled her along the Say; he saw again the moonlight silvering the water-meadows by Jonathan Codling's bridge; he smelt—yes, he really smelt—the delicious scents that follow in their order the summer through—only these were mixed together all at once—hawthorn and cowslips in the meadows; in the garden, apple-mint and clary, honeysuckle and roses. A wave of summer sweetness moved over David as Squeak passed, singing.

I could not imagine J. M. Barrie or Kenneth Grahame or A. A. Milne striking that note, without indulging its plangency. But here the flit of the mind backwards is given to the child—the open adult note is controlled—and the prose implies the cyclic promise of summer, not unstoppable regret for years gone by. (pp. 198-99)

[In *Tom's Midnight Garden,* we note] how clearly the characteristic music sounds now: the precision of place, the child geography, the deep-sunk sense of dream all marvellously fused together. . . . (p. 199)

Again the tale has the same breathless, detective pull. . . .

Who, once having read them, can forget the chapters when boy and young woman skate up the river to Ely?

For it is in these final sections that the art transcends itself. Through scenes of haunting and sometimes painful beauty, Tom perceives that the old woman in the upstairs flat was once a child like Hatty, and that age and life will make Hatty an old woman like her: 'he began to notice, again and again, a gesture, a tone of voice, a way of laughing that reminded him of the little girl in the garden.' It is, if you like, one of the ordinary insights of life; but one, perhaps, we most easily slur over. . . . Philippa Pearce makes you find it, feel it—and for her child audience it is maybe the first uncovering. . . . (p. 200)

[*A Dog So Small* again] has the clean narrative pull, the delicious quiet humour, an essential inwardness as it unfolds his world through a boy's eyes. . . . The chapters where boy and puppies play in the pig sty are marvellously done. . . . (pp. 200-01)

And so too is the closing sequence as dusk falls on Hampstead Heath. It is a very fine book, and yet—coming where it does in her work—it is something of a pendant, a detour. So much is there, but not the music. The theme of obsession (which of course informed the treasure hunt in *Minnow on the Say*) now dominates and fills the gap. There is something of the psychological study about it, and—ever so slightly—the eye slips off the child audience. Characteristically, [Philippa Pearce] no longer relies wholly on her art to do its own work, but—again, ever so slightly—tops up the insights with glimpses of *sententiae:* 'He saw that if you didn't have the possible things, you had nothing.' 'Granny shaded her eyes, looking after them. "People get their heart's desire," she said, "and then they have to begin to learn how to live with it"'.

It seemed at that stage that either *Tom's Midnight Garden* had exhausted the more elusive and precious vein, or that having

hit such brilliant moments the writer was reluctant to make the even more demanding commitment to her talents that was perhaps required.

In the event, she felt her way out of the situation with cautious instinct. . . . [*The Children of the House*] was originally drafted by Brian Fairfax-Lucy, as a tale for adults. Philippa Pearce worked on the existing draft and, as the introductory note says: 'made it one that can be enjoyed and understood by children'. She did a good deal more than that. She made it a classic. The setting could be that of one of the Victorian or Edwardian writers. Four children grow up in a grand country house. (p. 201)

It is a grand loveless childhood, with the four children twined together in mutual and sustaining affection. The servants bring them up, and our images of fathering and mothering come when Elsie the maid or Walter the butler, for a moment, tend the children. The formal parents are defined by their absence . . . .

What takes it out of the standard Victorian mould (as it does E. Nesbit) is a refusal to identify with the assumptions and aspirations of the upper class home—the sense of the house through the servants' eyes, of the eldest daughter denied a useful education, of the old men combing the bins, or the ironic stonebreaker on the roadside. . . . (p. 202)

Compared to her previous books—and perhaps because of the curious joint authorship—it takes some chapters before the vision becomes as freed from its setting as this. And it nowhere has the potent narrative thread.

But it has the music. The beautiful, piercing sense of childhood swept along—and overswept—in the stream of time. The art is superb. The ordinary incidents of childhood—boiling a moorhen's egg, a forbidden hair-clipping, finding a half-crown—lap quietly in the reader's mind: months and years imperceptibly vanish at each chapter's end.

So apt and unforced is the second half, that you may not realise how it is all building up inside you until the marvellous final section, the *adieu*. There is something almost Tchekov-like in those last dozen pages. For one splendid stretch she again meets and tops the great Victorians in their own arbour.

I do not think any age previous to ours could have so brought out Philippa Pearce's talent. Her clean, plain prose opens up her books to any child who reads at all easily. I fear that isn't at all true of many revered classics of the past. Her work brims with life, and with life decent, positive, ongoing. Again one wonders if a critical look at some of our Edwardian inheritance might find that this was precisely what some of them lacked. She writes—mostly—to and for the child: not through the child to other adults. (p. 203)

        Brian Jackson, "Philippa Pearce in the Golden Age of Children's Literature," in The Use of English, Vol. 21, No. 3, Spring, 1970, pp. 195-203, 207.

**DAVID REES**

*Minnow on the Say* employs a familiar formula for a children's book—the successful search for a long-buried treasure, with its usual attendant props, the false clues, villain racing to beat the children in their quest, etc. If the book were no more than this it would scarcely be worth writing about but it is however an unusual book in many respects; and it is worth noting that none of the subsequent novels employs such a well-tried device. The main characters—Adam, David and Miss Codling—are drawn with a convincing detail that immediately places the book on a higher level than its plot suggests. Adam has many of the characteristics of the heroes of *Tom's Midnight Garden* and *A Dog so Small,* particularly their passionate obsession to achieve their hearts' desires. Adam is irrational, often bad-tempered, often depressed; he swings mercurially from one extreme emotion to another.... He is much the most interesting character in the book, and altogether a surprising person to find in a quiet and leisurely English children's novel.

David, in contrast, is practical and down-to-earth, much the sort of son we would expect of Bob Moss, who drives the country buses and grows prize roses. Yet Bob Moss was once known as Bad Bobby Moss, Terror of both the Barleys; and David too, experiences the longing, the unfulfilled desire that torments all Philippa Pearce's heroes. (pp. 40-1)

[Mr Smith] is one of the book's failures. He is observed at such a distance and so unsympathetically as to be scarcely credible. The author is not really interested; Mr Smith is no more than a necessary piece of the plot—the one scene in his house, curtains drawn and weak disembodied voice, is unnecessarily melodramatic, and his relationship with his daughter, Elizabeth, is like that of Mr Rochester and his wife in *Jane Eyre,* and no more convincing. Elizabeth never succeeds in being credible either; and the recognition scene between her and Adam is particularly weak. Melodrama in fact is the book's main weakness; particularly in the last part of the book, one larger-than-life scene succeeds another. There is the death of old Mr Codling (another improbable character), the last-minute race to catch the bus, David's confrontation with Mr Smith at the bus station, David's resolve (out of character) to sink the canoe, and Elizabeth showering David with orchids from a passing train. The last part of the book deteriorates in quality; the pace slackens, too many interviews take place behind closed doors and have to be reported, the denouement is slow and an anti-climax. But it must be said that all the succeeding books are totally free of these particular faults.

The book seems to go wrong at the point where the Smiths enter the story, and perhaps the deterioration is because the author clearly dislikes Mr Smith.... Philippa Pearce's least successful creations seem to be people she dislikes—Mrs Melbourne, Sir Robert Hatton—though these are not as unconvincing as Mr Smith.

Squeak Wilson's fear of everyone, particularly of Adam, is however a very amusing piece of caricature: in fact the behaviour of everybody in the book is seen at one time or another with an amused or ironic eye. (pp. 41-2)

For all its faults, *Minnow on the Say* is an impressive first novel. It could never be mistaken for a book by anybody else, despite its well-worn storyline, for the virtues that delight us in the succeeding books are already there. Ultimately it is not the treasure-hunt, or the Smiths that we remember so much as Miss Codling's anxieties and dignity, the unusualness of Adam, the quiet pastoral background of the Barleys, the boys' and the author's sensuous delight in the river—absent from hardly any page of the book—the warmth and naturalness of David's home and family.

The voice we associate with the later books is already there—the rendering of the sensuous physical world, linking it so often with a past that is only just under the surface, in sentences in which the rhythms and cadences express exactly the right pleasure or sadness that the words mean.

*Tom's Midnight Garden* is the novel more than any other on which Philippa Pearce's reputation rests. It is not without its faults, however, and striking though the imaginative conception of the story is, I am not sure that the two subsequent novels are not better done. The opening chapters seem laboriously written, the characters a little wooden, and measles is certainly not a good enough reason for packing Tom off to his Aunt Gwen's. However when Tom enters the garden, all is well; the writing loses its uncertainty, and seems to change into a triumphantly major key; it is as if the author, having eventually got her central character into the situation she is most interested in, is relieved at being able, at least, to say what she wants to say.... (pp. 42-3)

Like Adam Codling, Tom Long is obsessed by one fixed idea. This is to explain to himself the mystery of the garden, and ultimately to stay in it for ever. Other children in the book, Tom's brother Peter and Hatty Melbourne, are as single-minded and passionately concerned with their own longings as Tom is: Peter with joining Tom in the garden (some of the most moving writing in the book expresses Peter's frustration at being left out of things), and Hatty with finding her own satisfactory modus vivendi in the unsympathetic Melbourne family. Hatty grows up into a spirited and independent woman and as she grows up her longings and frustrations seem to fall away.... [Her] happiness as an adult seems to reinforce a feeling that pervades the whole book, that children of Tom's age experience joy and disappointment with an intensity that adults hardly ever realize: it is the force with which this intensity is expressed that is one of the book's main strengths....

Most moving of all perhaps, in its intensity, is Tom's final attempt to get back into the garden he has lost for ever.... (p. 43)

As well as this intensity, the characters share other characteristics, impulsiveness, unreasonableness, even rudeness; adults as well as children....

In contrast with this feverishness of emotion in almost all the characters the landscape has a cool, unchanging certainty about it; this was the function of landscape, particularly the river, in *Minnow on the Say* and Tom's garden, though its seasons may alter, or lightning on one occasion strike down a tree, is always there, inviting, full of promise....

The 'magic' of the garden is that it is a Garden of Eden, a symbol of Tom's and Hatty's innocence; they have to leave it as they grow up—Tom's appearances become rarer as Hatty grows older; he grows so thin that she can see through him. It is no coincidence that when Tom finds himself excluded finally it is Hatty's wedding day. Hatty is in love with Barty, so she has no more need of her imaginary friend; Tom is banished simply because she doesn't think of him any more. The relationship between Tom and Hatty is like an innocent love affair in this Garden of Eden; and other parallels with the Book of Genesis can be seen—Adam and his descendants were gardeners according to tradition; Adam's sons were Cain and Abel; our gardener is called Abel. Our Abel, however, is in his simplicity and religious devotion, inside Eden with Tom and Hatty, not outside like the Abel of Genesis. However, just as Eden was destroyed so is this garden; sold off by James for building land. (p. 44)

Many people reading the book for the first time, who have not noticed that Mrs Bartholomew and Hatty are one and the same person, speak of the almost unbearable tension as the book proceeds into what is a seemingly inescapable tragedy, and their sense of relief when this is averted, and their delight that the ending is so credible. The fact that the ending is not just a happy coda stuck on so that the reader won't be upset, is because Hatty *is* Mrs Bartholomew, and always was, since before the beginning of the book. In other words, the author knows precisely what she is about. The clues are all there for us, early on. The first appearance of Mrs Bartholomew is when she comes downstairs to wind up the clock, a sort of Father Time figure. A page is spent on showing this seemingly irrelevant character carrying out a seemingly insignificant action, but as the clock is the great link between time past and time present, and Mrs Bartholomew is shown as its keeper or guardian now (just as the angel on the dial is its keeper in time past), it seems clear that the purpose of the scene is to suggest that she has a much more significant connection with the past than Tom, at the moment, realizes. And at the end of the chapter, when Tom enters the garden for the first time, the game is virtually given away by a further apparently irrelevant comment. Mrs Bartholomew 'was lying tranquilly in bed; her false teeth, in a glass of water by the bedside, grinned unpleasantly in the moonlight, but her indrawn mouth was curved in a smile of easy sweet-dreaming sleep. She was dreaming of the scenes of her childhood.' And if the penny still hasn't dropped, we should be wondering not long after why one of the Melbournes' friends is called Barty.

Another reason why the ending seems so effective is because the author herself seems to be growing up as a writer in the process of writing this book. There is a great difference in the quality of the last chapters compared with the first; not only is there simply more certainty and maturity in the way the language of the sentences is put together with their increasing poetry, subtlety of rhythm and cadence, but the insights and sympathies deepen all the time; we feel that the author has a more profound knowledge of Tom and Hatty at the end than she had at the beginning. The same is true of Tom's relationship with the Kitsons, it is developing all the time in sympathy, and in humour. Nevertheless it must be said that the problems of that relationship remain unsolved; Alan and Gwen are no nearer understanding Tom than they were at the beginning, and the debt of gratitude Tom should owe them is scarcely commented on. The speculation about the nature of time grows more thoughtful as the book continues; Tom's ideas on the subject become more complex and adult, and his imaginative leaps seem to hold more truth than Uncle Alan's scientific explanations.

Probably the most impressive writing in the book is the chapter called **'Skating',** not only for its superb evocation of the frost-bound Fenland countryside, but its description of the interior of Ely Cathedral and the tomb of the man who 'exchanged time for eternity'. There is a vivid pictorial rendering of what the eye really sees: 'They skated on, and the thin, brilliant sun was beginning to set, and Hatty's black shadow flitted along at their right hand, across the dazzle of the ice.' Or what the ear really hears—'the ice hissed with their passage.' The certainty with which these things are done shows a great advance on *Minnow on the Say* and if that book can be said to be an unusually interesting first novel, *Tom's Midnight Garden* is nearly a masterpiece.

I can think of only one blemish in her next book, *A Dog so Small,* and that is the somewhat irrelevant story of what happened to the picture after Ben lost it, which seems to show the old unfortunate taste for melodrama. But in Ben Blewitt we have the most interesting of Philippa Pearce's heroes. Though she tells us more than once that Ben is a perfectly ordinary boy, we can scarcely believe her; Ben is surely the oddest person she has ever written about. No other character in her novels departs so far from reality into his private obsession as Ben does; Tom Long's fantasy world was confined to night time but Ben's operates during the day as well as in his dreams, and this leads to real disaster. . . . Ben's problems with his family do not come solely from the fact that he is the odd one out in age; he is also the only one with any real sensitivity or imagination. . . . Ben has an additional problem that none of the heroes of the other novels has to face; there is no possible outlet for his frustrations, no person sufficiently unpleasant for him to dislike, or blame. *A Dog so Small* has no villain. The Blewitt family are remarkable for their niceness, so Ben's troubles turn in on himself. . . . This withdrawal from reality the author suggests is sad and reprehensible. . . . The answer is that the Blewitt parents should have given Ben a dog in the first place; had they known what damage the absence of a dog was causing him they would almost certainly have done so. But they never know, and this points to another sadness in this book—that even in the nicest of families real communication between its members can be impossible.

The construction of *A Dog so Small* is interesting; its opening pages and its conclusion contain the most memorable moments. Like *Tom's Midnight Garden* it opens with the hero's world crashing about his ears; Ben's discovery that he has not been given a dog for his birthday would be so easy to sentimentalize, but in fact the author is quite merciless, showing no let-up in the portrayal of Ben's disappointment, every humorous and uncomprehending remark from his family making the situation worse and worse. Ben is not allowed any escape from the moral dilemma; it would be so easy if he could just quietly hate his grandparents but Grandpa Fitch has written 'TRULY SORY ABOUT DOG' and for Ben there is no way out of that. So Ben's feelings as elsewhere, turn inwards. The last chapter, too, could so easily be a sentimental happy ending. Instead we have something that is psychologically far more truthful; as Granny Fitch says, 'People get their heart's desire, and then they have to begin to learn how to live with it'; Ben makes the miserable discovery that a real dog, given to him at last, is no adequate substitute for the chihuahua of his imagination. It would be a cruelly tragic ending if Ben were to leave Brown on the Heath in the growing dusk; right up to the last page it looks as if he will. But he does not, fortunately. By this I don't mean I necessarily want the book to end happily . . . but the reasons and feelings Ben has for keeping the dog are consistent with the development of his character in the last third of the book. Since the accident he has begun to grow up, to accept, however slowly, the fact that he has to live in the real world— 'He saw that if you didn't have the possible things, then you had nothing.' This book, more than the others, charts the changes and growth of its hero's personality. . . . (pp. 46-9)

The use of caricature is widespread; a number of people and events are seen almost entirely in terms of amused, wry exaggeration. Our first views of Mrs Fitch—coming backwards downstairs—and Mr Fitch tied up in his own dog's lead—are Dickensian and this impression is reinforced when we think of the Blewitt family in comparison with the Cratchits, particularly in the scene of the Christmas preparations. . . . It is caricature of the best sort in that our belief in the reality of these people is never in doubt; the author has as much sympathy for them as amusement. . . .

A boy longing for a dog: it is a common theme in children's fiction: the unusualness of *A Dog so Small* lies in its ability to suggest the sheer pleasure humans can derive from the animal world, and the intensity some people feel for animals, when there is an emotional gap left by the deficiencies of other human beings. The dogs in this novel never cease to be dogs. Philippa Pearce never falls into the obvious cliche of endowing them with human or superhuman feelings. (p. 49)

[Though *The Children of the House* is the] saddest of all the books, there is nevertheless an emphasis on the companionship and pleasures of friendship between the brothers and sisters. . . . [Margaret] we are told 'wished above all for the companionship of the other three'—the very thing that ultimately is denied her; she only wishes to exist as a member of a group, an adjunct of the other three, and this over-riding desire fills her with a singular horror when Hugh and Laura quarrel, and gives the writing a poignancy and total sense of loss when she is separated from them, a feeling not only of loneliness, but of existence being without any further meaning. . . .

Tom is a very different boy from his namesake in *Tom's Midnight Garden*. He is adventurous, a natural leader, even reckless; he never thinks of the consequences of his actions, and often lands the other children and the servants, inadvertently, in trouble. He is particularly thoughtless in the episode involving Margaret's descent in the well, and quite insensitive to her fright. He is, surprisingly, a coward. . . . (p. 50)

A minor theme of the book is Tom's cowardice and his successful attempt to overcome it; his standing up to his parents and daring to point out their faults, not in the heat of the moment, but with calculated forethought, is his first step on the road to his posthumous VC.

Hugh is more in the tradition of Philippa Pearce's previous heroes—Adam, Tom Long, Ben. He has the same passion (an example is his furious disgust with Tom, when Tom wonders whether the stone breaker deserves to be given a shilling) and shrinks from situations of possible violence that his brother Tom might relish. . . .

This sharp distinction of character is necessary in a book in which four people are sharing the same activities. It is worth noting that *The Children of the House* is the only novel of Philippa Pearce's in which girls play a central role, in which we look at the world through the eyes of the girls as well as the boys. There is, of course, Hatty in *Tom's Midnight Garden,* but we rarely observe Tom from her point of view; it is usually the other way round. Less successful creations in *The Children of the House* are the parents, Sir Robert and Lady Hatton, particularly Sir Robert. While it is true that the author is trying to emphasize in this novel that life fifty or sixty years ago is not the pleasant magic world lost beyond recall of *Tom's Midnight Garden,* that one aspect of life that was less satisfactory was the relationship between parents and children, Sir Robert Hatton does not come off as a credible Victorian-Edwardian father, conscious of status, chilling and distant to his children; he seems inhumane, improbable, devoid of any parental feelings at all. . . . (p. 51)

No matter what part of the authorship of the novel belongs to Philippa Pearce, it is as if *The Children of the House* was a deliberate corrective to a view of the past suggested in *Tom's Midnight Garden*. (p. 52)

*The Children of the House* differs from the other three novels in that there is almost no narrative. The plot consists of a series of incidents—punting, the walk to Honeford, the attempt to see Victor—which are connected only by their being shared

by the same four characters; there is no story as *Minnow on the Say* has a story. . . . But we never feel that the book is aimlessly episodic; the style of the writing is its great unifier. In no other novel of Philippa Pearce is this more evident or more successful. It reads like one long prose-poem from its melancholic opening sentence 'No children live at Stanford Hall now' to its last dying echo, the name 'Elsie—Elsie—Elsie' reverberating through the empty rooms. (p. 53)

> David Rees, "The Novels of Philippa Pearce," in Children's literature in education, *No. 4 (March), 1971, pp. 40-53.*

**FRANK EYRE**

[*Tom's Midnight Garden* is the] perfect fantasy of our time. . . . This deeply moving, beautifully written and completely convincing time-fantasy is one of the most perfectly conceived and executed children's books of the past twenty years. (p. 128)

The author makes beautifully subtle and complex use of [the] time-shift. . . .

Such a story in other hands could be mawkish and unconvincing, just another time fantasy. In Philippa Pearce's it becomes almost unbearably moving. A wonderful book, one which children *can* read and enjoy, and many do. . . . (p. 130)

Although it is typical of the author's highly individual outlook that the social problem [in *Minnow on the Say*] should be turned upside down and it is the bus driver's family that leads the happy, secure and well-fed life, while the upper class family is in difficulties, this is not a 'social consciousness' novel. It is a straightforward adventure story, with a long-sustained search for buried treasure by the river; a moderately nasty villain, an old mill, lovable (and unlovable) country characters, and even a happy ending. But the author's style and manner transmute these ordinary ingredients into pure gold and this is a fine book which, although not a fantasy, is unmistakably by the author who was shortly to produce *Tom's Midnight Garden*. To have been runner-up for the Carnegie Medal with one's first book and win it with one's second must be a rare feat, but Philippa Pearce achieved it, and deserved to. (p. 131)

[*The Children of the House*] is, as might be expected, well done, but it is a surprising thing for so original and creative a writer to have done. It will be interesting to see what she does next. Whatever it is, it will be original, imaginative, and written with truth and sincerity, for she creates a real world that is far removed from the imaginary worlds in which so many children's books are set. (p. 132)

> Frank Eyre, "Fiction for Children," in his British Children's Books in the Twentieth Century, *revised edition, 1971. Reprint by E. P. Dutton, Inc., 1973, pp. 76-156.**

**JOHN ROWE TOWNSEND**

In 1965 I said, in *Written for Children*, that if I were asked to name a single masterpiece of English children's literature since the Second World War it would be *Tom's Midnight Garden* [see excerpt above]. . . . Today I would still use it of only one book published since the last war, and the book would still be *Tom's Midnight Garden*. (p. 163)

*Minnow on the Say* was Miss Pearce's first book, and a very attractive one. . . . [The] title has an odd kind of aptness, for the action of the story is quick and light in relation to the slow depth of the setting. On the surface it is a neat treasure-hunt, with ingenious verse clues made still more ingenious by a transposition half way through which requires the same words to be differently interpreted. It is intellectually teasing and pleasing, and pretty much on the level of a good detective novel. The main characters are adequate but not specially interesting, apart perhaps from Adam, a boy in whom one senses already the man he is going to be. But surrounding and underlying it the rural community is strong and solid, and the river Say gives the book its distinctive feeling: suggesting, as a river will in the work of an artist who is fully conscious of it both as thing and as symbol, the changing course of life, the flow of time. (p. 164)

[*A Dog So Small*] is a homely story, with nothing rarefied or 'literary' about it. You might even say it is a bit ordinary; a child's longing for a pet is commonplace, but to explore the depths of this longing is not so common. . . . As elsewhere, Philippa Pearce is perceptive about the relationships of young and old. Grandpa and Granny Fitch are the most rounded and satisfactory characters in the book. . . . The doggy parts of the book are excellent, too. When Grandpa Fitch's bitch Tilly is with her litter in the pigsty you can practically *smell* the puppies and feel them squirming under your hands.

Collaborations are difficult to assess as part of the work of one writer. A successful collaboration is a compound rather than a mixture and the contribution made by each partner can hardly be separated. *The Children of the House* is not exactly a novel: it is an account of Edwardian childhood which hovers on the borders of memory and imagination. The finished book bears the unmistakable stamp of Philippa Pearce; the material must be Sir Brian's, but the tale and telling are now one. (pp. 164-65)

[It is a book that] the reader will not soon forget. (p. 166)

[*Mrs. Cockle's Cat*] has exactly the right picture-book mixture of real-life accuracy and wild invention.

And so to *Tom's Midnight Garden,* which is still Philippa Pearce's best book and still, to my mind, the best book that has ever won the Carnegie Medal. It could not, I think, be deduced from the rest of her work, for all its distinction, that she would write anything quite so good as this. The sense of place and atmosphere, the mastery over words, can be found in *Minnow on the Say* and elsewhere; but the full power of imagination, the perfect shaping, the ear for that particular strain of the still sad music of humanity which is also the music of time, belong only to *Tom's Midnight Garden.*

Tom himself is hardly 'a character': he is any child, any person. He could be you. (pp. 166-67)

If I understand it correctly, the book is concerned with the four-dimensional wholeness of life. In the child the old person is implicit; in the old person the child remains. . . . Books are sometimes said, in a phrase of stereotyped approval, to have an extra dimension. Of *Tom's Midnight Garden* this is no cliché. (p. 167)

There have been many, many time fantasies. Few have had so precise a formal structure, but that would not in itself make *Tom's Midnight Garden* so excellent a novel. There is a profundity of thought and feeling here that goes far deeper than the exposition of a mathematical theory. Successive phases of life, especially the transition from childhood to maturity, are shown symbolically. (p. 167)

If both Then and Now are to be real, we must believe in Then. And we do; for Then is every bit as real as the dustbin-crowded back area and surrounding sea of suburbia that beset the house Now. In Tom's successive visits to the garden—at first ex-

ploring it by himself, then encountering people, and later venturing beyond its bounds—the story quietly takes possession of the past. But in terms of our own perception even the past appears to move. As a symbol of childhood a garden is not static, for in the beauty of any garden is an evanescent sensuousness; today is not as yesterday and tomorrow will not be as today; the season moves on.

A novel for children should, in my view, 'work' at surface level; and *Tom's Midnight Garden* does. The page cries out to be turned; the reader wants to know what happens next; the ending satisfactorily rounds off the story. But there are also echoes and resonances, beauties and mysteries that I believe every reader will be conscious of but none will fully grasp. And at each return to the book the search for what remains elusive can be renewed. *Tom's Midnight Garden* is not a book to be grown out of. I have read it several times and still find it continually rewarding. It is not cosy or jolly; there is nothing to laugh out loud over; but there is joy in it: the joy that is just this side of sadness. (p. 168)

> John Rowe Townsend, "Philippa Pearce," in his A Sense of Story: Essays on Contemporary Writers for Children, *J. B. Lippincott Company, 1971, pp. 163-71.*

## MARCUS CROUCH

[The materials of *The Children of the House*] have the untidiness of real life. . . . The nature of the partnership [between Brian Fairfax Lucy and Philippa Pearce] has not been precisely revealed. In a prefatory note the writer says that Miss Pearce took a story intended for adults and tilted it in the direction of children, and there are some touches—the masterly conclusion and the exploration of the character of the youngest girl, Margaret—which seem to show her fingerprints. (pp. 174-75)

*The Children of the House* is a strong and authentic social document. So recent that Margaret could well be alive today, it shows a way of life infinitely remote. . . . There is no hero in the book, unless it is the house, and that is more like the villain. The author never describes it. . . . The children of the house never use the front door, which is reserved to Sir Robert and his lady and their guests. But it is this incubus which rules the lives of everyone from Papa to the smallest kitchen-maid. (p. 176)

[*Tom's Midnight Garden*] is one of those rare, miraculously individual books which belong to no category and demand absolute acceptance from the reader. (p. 198)

The concluding passages have a perfection unmatched in children's literature.

Part of the wonder of *Tom's Midnight Garden* lies in purely literary qualities. Philippa Pearce is a master of style. Unlike William Mayne, a greater virtuoso performer who is often carried away by the enchantment of his own skill, she is always in control. She uses words as if she had just discovered them. . . . No one, not even E. Nesbit in the 'Arden' books, has managed better the transition from present to past. . . .

[*Minnow on the Say*] is an enchanting story . . . , as fresh and fragile as a spring day. It is structurally disastrous. In three years Miss Pearce learnt all about her craft. The construction of *Tom's Midnight Garden*, its firm development, the subtle variation from episode to episode, is beyond criticism. (p. 199)

[*A Dog So Small*] is a difficult book, its subtle interior action and its deep understanding not fully tuned to the reader's wavelength. (p. 200)

Marcus Crouch, "School—Home—Family" and "Work," *in his* The Nesbit Tradition: The Children's Novel in England 1945-1970, *Ernest Benn Limited, 1972, pp. 161-84, 196-229.**

## PELORUS

There is one children's writer to whom I look for another novel-length story more than I do to any other: Philippa Pearce. Her gifts are unrivalled, the precise qualities of her writing rare and so purely harmonized that they can give excruciating pleasure. It is difficult to avoid over-using superlatives so clearly does her work outdistance anyone else's.

*Tom's Midnight Garden* is the book most people pick out as the peak of her small output to date. And no doubt they are right. . . . [But] it's *A Dog So Small* I find myself reading and re-reading, and wanting to introduce to children, who themselves have made it more popular over the whole range of reading ability and interests than any other critically well-thought-of . . . novel that I can name.

What gives me so much pleasure is that extraordinary combination of Miss Pearce's much-admired style and the diamond-sharp brilliance and clarity of her plots and characters. The touchstone scene, to my mind, is the second chapter of *A Dog So Small,* as subtle and rich and exact as a piece of Bach chamber music. The characters, their responses to the situation, the situation itself, the interplay of emotion described with devastating understatement that hides passions running deep and strong: simple-seeming complexity. I can think only of Jane Austen with whom to draw a comparison among writers outside the specifically children's field.

Well, we haven't got a new full-length story, but we have had, this season, something to go on with—tantalizingly. . . . [In *What the Neighbours Did and other Stories*], there are five new [tales] which reveal that the gifts are still there and in the same strength. . . .

Liking *A Dog So Small* as much as I do, and finding that children like it too, I was surprised at a comment made by Marcus Crouch in his survey, *The Nesbit Tradition: The Children's Novel 1945-1970* [see excerpt above]. . . . "It is a difficult book," he says, "its subtle interior action and its deep understanding not fully tuned to the reader's wavelength." I hope Mr. Crouch meant to speak only for himself, for this reader had no trouble finding the channel on which Miss Pearce was transmitting. (p. 52)

Pelorus, "Notebook," in Signal, *No. 10, January, 1973, pp. 52-4.**

## ISABELLE JAN

Philippa Pearce's books are more direct and consequently more accessible to children [than Lucy Boston's works], though . . . *Tom's Midnight Garden* is perhaps a little too complacent, not withstanding its real charm. . . . [*A Dog So Small*] is a particularly successful attempt at depicting a child's imaginary relationship with an invisible being. Here the reality of the make-believe dog becomes more and more convincing—though the dog remains invisible throughout. And the end, when the spell is broken and everyday life obtrudes, is not contrived and leaves the reader entirely satisfied—a rare achievement in this sort of book, where the difficulty consists in the readjustment to reality, in the manner of presenting the re-entry into existence. (pp. 69-70)

Isabelle Jan, "Through the Looking Glass," *in her* On Children's Literature, *edited by Catherine Storr, Allen Lane, 1973, pp. 56-78.**

## DAVID REES

In England Philippa Pearce is regarded by almost everyone who has any connection at all with the world of children's books as the outstanding author of our time and in America, where she is also widely read and highly respected, she is considered a writer of the greatest importance. *Tom's Midnight Garden*, her masterpiece, is the yardstick with which we tend to measure everything else, and we usually find that everything else does not quite reach it in quality, even if we are forced to admit that in places it does fall short of perfection. It seems to me that on the whole Philippa Pearce deserves her reputation, but we are probably wrong to think of *Tom's Midnight Garden* as simply the best children's novel of the twentieth century. The issue is more complicated than that. It is the best of a certain kind of children's book: the sensitive fantasy set in a timeless English landscape; the gentle, brooding rural story in which British writers excel. But to compare it with a realistic novel that has a harsh urban background—Robert Westall's *The Machine Gunners,* for example—is not altogether possible. Different criteria are involved.

One of the most remarkable things about Philippa Pearce is the smallness of her output: only four novels in nearly a quarter of a century of writing. There have, it is true, been several volumes of short stories, and in 1978, *The Battle of Bubble and Squeak,* a book that is in length about half-way between a short story and a novel. It is a great disappointment that she hasn't written more, but whatever the reasons for this may be, it is a fact that her admirers have to accept. Maybe she has said all she has to say, and has wisely decided not to write just for the sake of pleasing other people. Some of the short stories are superb; "The Tree in the Meadow," for instance, is an object lesson in how to master the genre. But it is the novels on which her reputation rests. . . . (pp. 36-7)

[Philippa Pearce] writes only when she needs to write; her work is an expression of her own feelings and values. One senses behind the text of the books a woman who has suffered a great deal, one whose own childhood was probably unhappy and frustrated. The impression, of course, may be wrong, but one can't help feeling that her peculiar strength and appeal comes from an ability to realize in words—to the point of perfection at times—the sensibility and experience of a very complex and compassionate person. She is one of the great creative artists. (p. 54)

David Rees, "Achieving One's Heart's Desires: Philippa Pearce," *in his* The Marble in the Water: Essays on Contemporary Writers of Fiction for Children and Young Adults, *The Horn Book, Inc., 1980, pp. 36-55.*

## MARGARET MEEK

The openness of young readers to the experience of reading means that authors can create alternative worlds and alternative time. The author writes a story—the oldest, most universal form of told time—and makes narrative time new for new readers. The author's concern is with inventing narrative time *and* with the challenge of making plain for the young 'the backward and dark abysm of time' as an idea. In a book for children, time is a scheme of shifters that the reader takes on in interaction with the text and thus with the author. The most obvious way for an author to exploit this interaction is to count on childhood as the privileged time for dreams, daydreams, fantasies and imaginative play because these are all, in one sense, out of time. And here lies the next challenge: to make time seem *now,* while being never, yet moving *through* time to the end of the story. . . .

Narrative time is its own kind, and reading time, time-within-ness, turns, as Ricoeur suggests, 'a plot into a thought'. This is what happens in the kind of children's books that publishing cataloguers call 'fantasy'. The time scheme of everyday life is abandoned for another. (p. 160)

From Philippa Pearce's *Tom's Midnight Garden* and *The Way to Sattin Shore* it is possible to study the temporal aspects of narrative discourse in books for the young in such a way as to demonstrate the phenomenology of time that children find in story texts created specifically for them. What follows is only a sketch designed to indicate in summary form something of the reading experience that comes from the reader's interaction with writing of this kind. . . .

*Tom's Midnight Garden* is still considered to be a paragon of stories for the young. There are many testimonies to its excellence as an example of the writer's craft. The narration has none of the quirky rhythms that made Garner's early work difficult for inexperienced readers. Part of the fluency of Philippa Pearce's prose is its pacing, the result of a versatile use of pauses and the short sentence. The reader reads at a rate clearly marked by the writer, like the tempo of a score. Its most remarkable effect is the way in which the writer's concern with time becomes the reader's. (p. 161)

Although they are undoubtedly carried along by the narrative and may give scant attention to the surface of the text, readers have to deal with shifters on every page. At the outset, the brothers' anticipated time is spoilt, cancelled: 'They *would have built* a tree house.' '"A child *of your age* needs ten hours' sleep"' begins as a threat. Yet in the few moments of clock-recorded time, Tom spends days in the garden which he knew '*was waiting* for him' although it didn't exist. Tom needs skates for a dream exploit. He actually finds Hatty's in the cupboard where she had left them in her time, so, in garden time, there are 'two skaters on one pair of skates'. At this point in the narrative the reader accepts the possibility without question.

Now, it would be foolish to see in *Tom's Midnight Garden* more than some of the elements of *Remembrance of Things Past,* but they are there. . . . Readers of *Tom's Midnight Garden* come to have an extensive and varied reading experience of time, as order and duration, if not as frequency and repetition. That they also discover how Tom experiences Proust's certainty, 'my dreams were my address', is in itself an anticipation of later literary experiences. My simple point is that literary competences are built up in readers by the discourse diversities of writers. And for all that they are clearly present in Blyton and Dahl, Philippa Pearce offers a wider and more varied play of the text, not least in the matter of shifters.

And yet, the narrative time in *Tom's Midnight Garden* is clearly a device, a way of doing it. Twenty-five years later, years of patient, skilled and meticulous crafting of shorter stories for younger children with whom she has always kept faith and of whose actualities she has always been sensitively aware, Philippa Pearce has written *The Way to Sattin Shore.*

In it there is only linear narrative; no dream time as such weaves a pattern of shifters. This narrative builds the same kind of preoccupation with time as is clear in *Tom's Midnight Garden*

into a story that looks as if it were a succession of events in six months in the life of a child about ten. But it isn't nearly so simple as the surface structure suggests. Here we cannot separate the story from the narration in order to discuss the author's preoccupation with narrative time. Instead, we look at the author's presentation of the complexities of human time to readers who have learned what it is to remember, whose language development can cope with the past and future in the present. They are encountering a storyteller who will teach them how the text is to be read, because it isn't quite like anything they have read before, and who will make their reading into an exploration of narrative discourse about time.

Kate Tranter, the heroine, is the age of most middle-childhood readers of Blyton and Dahl. She is the youngest of three women living in the same house, the other two being her mother and grandmother. She has two brothers. Her father, she thinks, died on the day she was born. (pp. 163-64)

[Before] they have read a page and a half, readers are plunged into a complicated time-scheme of generations and events as they stand with Kate about to cross the hall. They move from events narrated in the order in which they occur to events repeated over time, yet for the reader the events are *now.* On this day, time changes in the Tranter household and a chapter later Kate needs to know, as part of her own puzzle about being in time, what really happened to her father. Her mother and her mother's mother possess part of the story as memory although each *tells* it differently when the time comes to do so. Kate cannot learn about the past until her mother, her grandmother, her father and older brother fit together for her the time just before she was born. Then she can face the future. (pp. 164-65)

Then there is the slow building up of the stories till the past is revealed, some of it to Kate alone. Sometimes time is precise and insistent: 'For three days and nights she thought almost all the time of her father.' Then time has to slow down: '"We must wait for the right time to tell about our dad. The right time, remember, and it's not yet"'.' Or time to make restitution, for only forgiveness can change the past. . . .

Kate, who hates waiting, has to wait to learn what will make the future possible. When it comes, it comes as an intolerable burden, as real as real memory. (p. 165)

*The Way to Sattin Shore* seems to me to present within the conventions of the realistic novel the 'spots of time' which Wordsworth saw as characteristic of childhood and the splendid play of shifters that gives a young reader a grasp of narrative time as a series of mirror-images. As a book it is less dramatic but no less powerful than *Tom's Midnight Garden.* Indeed, its very low key is the more resonant. The plot is a thought; Kate thinking about what it is to understand what happens, what happened and what will happen. Only once does the author step out to talk about time. Kate's father is back.

> Within the Tranter family, the return made a difference—Kate perceived its hugeness like the uprearing of a mountain peak through clearing mist. Years yet to come would show the extent of the difference made to them all, to Fred Tranter included.

By this time Kate has discovered that she has another grandmother alive, and thus another past, another set of memories. Her mother's mother doesn't change the past because she can't forgive her son-in-law, so she stays where she is.

The narrative discourse is very close to the reader. There are some memorable moments: Kate's mother rubbing flour and Kate's Granny watching, at the very time when Kate has to ask her mother about her father and finds she can't. The chance passes. The within-time-ness of the reading is absolutely governed by the way the sentences stop and start, by the counterpointing of narrative time that is as subtle as a fugue. In the end, the story emerges as a perfectly simple read for ten-year-olds and the plot is thought time. (p. 166)

> *Margaret Meek, "Speaking of Shifters," in* Signal, *No. 45, September, 1984, pp. 152-67.**

---

***MINNOW ON THE SAY*** **(1955; U.S. edition as** *The Minnow Leads to Treasure***)**

[Some of the other books to be published by the Oxford Press in 1955] may equal this, the first book by an unusually accomplished beginner, but few can be more satisfying. The story is captivating from the beginning, when young David finds the canoe, Minnow, bobbing against the landing-stage on the river Say. Adam, her owner, becomes his fast friend and the boys embark on a well-plotted search for the treasure hidden by Adam's Elizabethan ancestor. There is a neat balance of hopes and disappointments, and the reader's concern for Adam and his aunt causes him to share their feelings for the shabby old house whose future is threatened with their own, and heightens the suspense. At the same time the aunt's outburst when Adam uproots a prize rose in his mania is a welcome reminder that some things matter more than treasures, and the same sense of proportion is maintained elsewhere. The boys are a well matched, likable pair, and their conversation rings true, while the adults, who might easily have been only "character" parts, *have* character instead. Many children will recognise something of their own fathers in David's—silent, just, but so regretful over David's loss of his wheelbarrow that its recovery is a triumph second only to the grand climax in which the treasure is revealed. And what a relief to meet a bus-driver who is a person instead of a conscientious exponent of lower-middle class virtues! The other characters are just as clearly seen, the humour is quiet but constant, and there is that ingredient of consciousness of the past working in the present—the past of individuals, families, and the town—which always adds a special dimension. The interest of clue-detection during a first reading is replaced in later readings by an appreciation of the clues themselves and by increased pleasure in the people encountered on the search. The final scenes are all that could be desired, the treasure found, all the principal characters gathered together to drink the Flower Wine which provided the last clue, and David and Adam looking forward to the next summer with Minnow on the Say. (pp. 234-35)

> *A review of "Minnow on the Say," in* The Junior Bookshelf, *Vol. 19, No. 4, October, 1955, pp. 234-35.*

Only rarely can a new story for children be praised as standing high above the level of the average, however good that average may be. Of such a quality is *Minnow on the Say.* . . .

The outstanding brilliance of the book lies not in [the] quest theme, but in its penetrating insight into character and the author's ability to convey so much detail with maintained interest in the everyday adventures of two boys with a boat. She has a deep understanding of and sympathy with boys, drawing them with absolute realism and so true to character in their actions and conversations that both David and Adam come

alive. Her backcloth, too, a painting of life in a small village on the river Say and the people who live there, is admirably created and portrayed with the same brilliant clearness.

> *Betty Brazier, in a review of "Minnow on the Say," in* The School Librarian and School Library Review, *Vol. 7, No. 6, December, 1955, p. 439.*

[This story is] one to be put on the shelf with the very best for the intermediate age. We can think of no other which has such an unusual combination of plot, characterization and vivid sense of place. There is a cleverly detailed challenging puzzle. The alert reader is in constant suspense and eager to unravel the clues with the boys. The study of the two heroes, their families and minor characters is perceptive, and dominating the whole book is the wonderful feeling for the river, with all its twists and turns.

> *Margaret Sherwood Libby, in a review of "The Minnow Leads to Treasure," in* New York Herald Tribune Book Review, *March 9, 1958, p. 13.*

Although the plot gets a bit tangled, especially at the last, this flaw is compensated for admirably by several virtues. The boys are completely credible in their behavior, conversation and relationships with others. Most of the minor characters are depicted with humor and insight. The mood of long summer days, the lure of the river, the absorption in the hunt are maintained throughout. The author writes with understanding of the private world of boys, and with deftness maintains the suspense in a good adventure tale.

> *Zena Sutherland, in a review of "The Minnow Leads to Treasure," in* Bulletin of the Children's Book Center, *Vol. XI, No. 9, May, 1958, p. 99.*

For all its search and puzzle, this is no one-dimensional mystery yarn. Here are real people. Loyal David shares something of the desperation which lashes Adam into this last-ditch campaign. There is a villain, but his villainy stems from obtuseness rather than cold-blooded wickedness. And the other grown-ups are all rounded characters, each of whom has an essential function in the dénouement. There are drama and old, remembered heartache in the story, but it is as if it had happened "all on a golden afternoon, full leisurely. . . ." Aided by Edward Ardizzone's dreamy illustrations one sees and almost smells the garden and fields and shares the joys of exploration and discovery.

> *Ethna Sheean, "Search on the River Say," in* The New York Times Book Review, *May 4, 1958, p. 32.*

[*Minnow on the Say* is a] modest classic. . . . Pearce does not rely for effect on heightened emotion, irony, or social observation in this book, but stirs the reader's emotions by understatement, by the smallest of actions, and by the very briefest exchanges of dialogue. Yet the story is filled with perceptions of nature, of family life, and of a leisurely childhood. The two boys do not change but simply add to their perceptions of adult life through their experience. . . . Although another *Minnow on the Say* may never again be written, it is to be hoped that Pearce's sanguine look at childhood and her lucid style do not disappear in the seeming drive of modern writers to push the children's novel ever further into the adult milieu. (pp. 60-1)

> *Sheila A. Egoff, "Realistic Fiction," in her* Thursday's Child: Trends and Patterns in Contemporary Children's Literature, *American Library Association, 1981, pp. 31-65.**

*TOM'S MIDNIGHT GARDEN*   (1958)

AUTHOR'S COMMENTARY

We lived in the mill-house at Great Shelford, on the upper reaches of the River Cam. My father was the miller, and he had been born in the mill-house, for his father—our grandfather—had been the miller there too. The mill-house was large, oblong, plain, grave; it had been built probably in the early nineteenth century. It had a very large garden with old yew trees growing round the lawn; they had archways and alcoves cut into them. There was a big box-bush with a gaping mouth in it: here—so my father said—my grandmother used to stack pots of geraniums in bloom, in the Victorian style.

All this, and much more, I put into *Tom's Midnight Garden*. Nearly all the descriptive detail is real, and exact. (pp. 98-9)

Now, of course, another family lives in the mill-house, and the garden has changed. The garden had already changed since our grandparents' day; it changed in ours—in our last years there the tall fir tree that dominated one corner of the lawn fell. Time changes everything and everybody. . . .

One of the things most difficult to believe—with your imagination as well as with your reason—is the change that Time makes in people. Children themselves often laugh aloud at the idea that they will ever grow old; that old people have ever been children. I tried to explore and resolve this non-understanding in the story of Tom Long and Hatty Melbourne. At the end of the book Tom hugs old Mrs Bartholomew because he realizes she is the little girl he loved to be with.

The garden was the playground—the common ground—of Tom and Hatty as children. The garden provided a powerful image of childhood. The walled garden—the old *hortus conclusus*—represents the sheltered security of early childhood. But Tom climbs the high garden wall and describes to Hatty the extensive and tempting view beyond; and later Hatty leaves the garden to go down to Ely by river. Rivers are emblems of life, moving on, changing, carrying people with them. The Cam carried Hatty on its frozen surface to the turning point of Ely's tower. . . . Hatty went to Ely with Tom, but came back without him. At least, she no longer saw him as a companion—literally: she had outgrown a little boy as a playmate. She saw Tom properly again when she was an old woman, reliving her past. Then, in that moment of full recognition, she received Tom's embrace as the child she once was. The old woman included the child. We all include that. (p. 99)

> *A. Philippa Pearce, " 'Tom's Midnight Garden' ," in* Chosen for Children: An Account of the Books Which Have Been Awarded the Library Association Carnegie Medal, 1936-75, *edited by Marcus Crouch and Alec Ellis, third edition, The Library Association, 1977, pp. 96-9.*

*Pearce stands in the garden of the Mill House, which is featured in the background.* Tom's Midnight Garden *was prompted by her fond memories of this setting. Permission from* Books for Keeps.

*Minnow on the Say* was one of the most remarkable of all first novels. It was so excellent in all respects that wise readers were content to accept it and to ask for nothing more. The second novels of brilliant beginners are so often disappointing. Miss Pearce's successor to *Minnow* has now appeared after three years, and her most enthusiastic admirer need have no fear. Here is no second and inferior *Minnow,* but a book entirely different in every respect except excellence.

*Tom's Midnight Garden*—a poor title for so fine a story—is about a boy spending a reluctant holiday in quarantine with well-intended but unsympathetic relatives. They live in a flat in an old house "oblong, grave, plain," hemmed in among characterless modern houses. At the back of the house is "a narrow paved space" smelling "of sun on stone and metal and the creosote of the fencing." But at night, when old Mrs. Bartholomew's grandfather clock strikes thirteen . . . The story is too good to anticipate further. Sufficient to say that this is an original treatment of a "time" theme, with a brilliant surprise ending—at least it took one reader completely by surprise.

Miss Pearce's magic comes from several sources, from her deep understanding of her characters young and old, from a sense of time, most of all from a mastery of words. Her prose is a miracle of simplicity. Using no tricks, she evokes the atmosphere of the lost garden so vividly that the reader shares Tom's experiences in it and sees with him its ghostly inhabitants. This is a very clever book, but its greatest cleverness is that only on reflection does the reader realise how brilliant the writing is, how sound the observation, with what minute care every detail of the story is fitted into the mosaic. Most children will see none of this, but will surrender readily to its charm and interest and come under the influence of its beauty and wisdom. Don't let us say: "Better (or less good) than *Minnow.*" Merely: "Thank you, Miss Pearce, for a book of rare quality!" (pp. 333-34)

> *A review of "Tom's Midnight Garden," in* The Junior Bookshelf, *Vol. 22, No. 6, December, 1958, pp. 333-34.*

This is a rare book—rare in its theme, the quality of its writing and the success it achieves. The subject matter—the incursions of a boy at midnight into the past to join in play with a little girl who in the present is an old woman living and dreaming of her childhood in the same house, seems altogether unlikely to appeal to older boys and girls. But the writing has the power to capture the imagination so that the young reader becomes caught up in the spell and finds in these magical hours the same urgency that Tom found. Indeed, as Hatty grows into womanhood and her future husband draws her away from childish games, we feel with Tom the poignancy that comes with loss and are solaced when at last he makes friends with the Hatty of old age. Even so, the book would not have come home, had not the children been perfectly conceived and their visions of childhood perfectly realized. . . . [This is a] distinguished addition to children's books. (pp. 399-400)

> *Phyllis Hostler, in a review of "Tom's Midnight Garden," in* The School Librarian and School Library Review, *Vol. 9, No. 5, July, 1959, pp. 399-400.*

There is the most explicit attempt in *Tom's Midnight Garden* to understand the nature of time, one's attitude to it, its relation to one's own existence. Many aspects come over powerfully: the child growing up and changing; the destruction of the garden and its transformation into a housing estate; and a mean little yard mirroring a whole changed pattern of society. But I think that Philippa Pearce's resistance to the new polluted environment loses its impact because it becomes identified with the feelings towards the loss of childhood, which is an inevitable process, whereas the pollution of the environment *need* not be. A place changes, becomes unrecognizable, yet is the same place. . . . (p. 79)

[We] have in this book the sense of Tom's own holiday and the larger sense of Hatty's whole life, and even the background—the objects—changing and being destroyed. The sense of loss, as shown by the central image of the tree falling, is stronger than the sense of creation and growth. This is what the novel emphasizes. Yet these are essential truths about time, in which we are bound to have our achievement and our termination. And it is the truth of *Tom's Midnight Garden* that conflicts with the magical aspect—why the thirteenth hour? Is it not enough to accept that Tom and Hatty are dreaming the same dreams? Is not a dream a valid experience? Given this, one can understand the way that Tom's brother Peter enters one of the dreams—but the way in which Abel sees Tom is not so reconcilable. When the whole movement of the book is to contradict the idea of Time No Longer—for time is continual change—how can this living in the past be anywhere but in dream and memory, which is the only place, as Mrs Bartholomew says, where things stand still? There are other difficulties of course; the skates which were left in the house for Tom years before his birth—so did Hatty meet him in her actual past? There are two movements of time in the book. One is inexorable and uncompromising, but one is fluid.

The beauty and poignancy of course remain. It is a celebration of childhood—but with the apprehension that children suffer keenly. The fact that the weather is always fine—except in the beauty of the frost—shows, as Tom recognizes, the way in which Mrs Bartholomew's mind selects its own images of childhood, ones that suggest her regret. Everything, it seems, should be teaching Tom what he himself will lose and what he will feel. (p. 80)

Tom and Mrs Bartholomew know what they have shared together, and the closeness between the boy and the old woman is finely and delicately described. But *Tom's Midnight Garden* is in many ways hardly a children's book at all; it is a cry from an adult awareness. (p. 81)

> *Lesley Aers, "The Treatment of Time in Four Children's Books," in* Children's literature in education, *No. 2 (July), 1970, pp. 69-81.*

[The] story of the Fall is the key story of contemporary children's literature. *Tom's Midnight Garden* is widely considered the key contemporary children's book . . . and it is to the story of Eden and the Fall that it responds; Tom dreams that 'He went downstairs to go into the garden; but he found that the angel had come down from the clock-face and—grown to giant size—barred the way with a flaming sword.' This essay is an attempt, through an examination of its symbolic base, to understand the potency of Philippa Pearce's story; a story which she herself has defined in terms of 'glimpses of paradise'.

The angel which bars the dreaming Tom's way, presaging his betrayed, incoherent thrashing among the dustbins in chapter 25, is both the cherubim from Genesis 3:24 and the angel of Revelation 10; the connection which Philippa Pearce has made between the two figures is the spark which fires the book. The two angels fuse, like Tom and Hatty 'two skaters on one pair of skates'. The angel of Revelation's promise 'that there should be time no longer' short-circuits history; it is a promise of redemption, of return to the garden. And because there is that promise of return, Philippa Pearce, like Clare, dispenses with temptation and sin; exclusion from her garden springs from the inevitable movement of time. Knowledge of the world crowds out knowledge of the garden. But time comes full circle, and Mrs Bartholomew in old age is as much part of the garden's magic, as innocent of the world, as Tom in childhood.

History is a succession of events; the past a circle of images. In *Tom's Midnight Garden* Hatty's history is Tom's past, Tom's history Hatty's past. They dream each other; or, rather, Hatty dreams Tom, and Tom's brother Peter dreams Hatty for him. That dreams disrupt sequential time is not a new insight, but in a century in which dreams, *pace* Freud, have assumed a new importance, in which they are seen not as disordered imaginings or intermittent portents but as the frames of a deeper truth, dreams have become a precise tool with which to explore temporal as well as psychological dimensions. J. W. Dunne's seminal *An Experiment with Time* provided the philosophical framework, Genesis the symbolic one; the two are linked, perhaps, by a lurking awareness of the ways in which the aboriginal concept of 'the dreamtime' touches our own sense of the loss and recoverability of a perfection outside the linear time.

The intimation that time is not just history (one thing after another) but also the past (which is the present in disguise), and that in dreams the laws of causality and succession can be breached, quivers in *Tom's Midnight Garden* with a luminous intensity. It can be felt in the nervous tick of the grandfather clock, a tick which 'sounded to him like a human heart, alive and beating.' (pp. 21-2)

In much of Helen Cresswell's work the two kinds of time are represented by sea and land, and the characters haunt the shore between the two, between the time that is measured in minutes and the time that is measured in waves; in Natalie Babbitt's *Tuck Everlasting* and in *The Lord of the Rings* mortals and immortals suffer because they are finally answerable to those different measures; both Alan Garner's *Elidor* and William Mayne's *Earthfasts* suggest that for a mortal wholly to embrace the latter is to embrace death; the point of many children's fantasies is that to acknowledge only minutes and never waves is to live an impoverished life.

Nowhere but in *Tom's Midnight Garden*, though, do we find the interdependence of the two times, line and loop, so subtly portrayed. At the point of intersection, at the moment of equilibrium, there is a gate for Tom into the garden. Neither is dispensable: 'Tom felt a tightness round his ribs, as though he were being squeezed apart there. He wanted two different sets of things so badly: he wanted his mother and father and Peter and home—he really did want them, badly; and on the other hand, he wanted the garden.'

*Tom's Midnight Garden* is a work of the most delicate craftsmanship, in which what is said and the means of saying are one and the same.... What I want to suggest is how much the book's distinctive tone, a sort of joyful gravity, depends on the central image of the garden, and its connotations of loss, and promise beyond loss.

Innocence (in a Blakeian sense), childhood, unworldliness, first love: these are the elements of which the special, secret garden is compounded. First love because Tom and Hatty's friendship is a love affair; a love affair which is pre-sexual, unstated, impossible of consummation. The book's intense sadness stems from the reader's awareness, unshared by Tom till the climactic moment on the tower of Ely cathedral, that Tom and Hatty are subject to different kinds of time: as Hatty ages, Tom's visits become less and less frequent, and his appearance more shadowy. The book's moment of epiphany, saved for the very last line, is an affirmation that time the loop can transcend time the line: 'Of course Mrs Bartholomew's such a shrunken little old woman, she's hardly bigger than Tom, anyway: but, you know, he put his arms right round her and he hugged her good-bye as if she were a little girl.' It adds poignancy that . . . Tom himself stands on the wall of the enclosed garden and describes to Hatty the enticements of the outside world; and that the river he sees, on which Hatty skates to womanhood, is inevitably a symbol of linear time.

The garden where Tom and Hatty meet is very much a physical place, described by Philippa Pearce with the same care as it is tended by the significantly named Abel, but it is also a spiritual one; it is this spiritual dimension which Tom, whose footsteps leave no trace, inhabits. Only the guileless—Tom, Hatty, Abel, the animals—can make the connection between the two gardens, the earthly and the ghostly. And even then they must make a choice between the garden and the world. When Tom first meets Hatty the 'half-eaten apple' in her hand foretells her departure. For Tom 'the garden was the thing. That was real' and for the young Hatty the same is true. When she falls from the bough her cold aunt observes that 'She doesn't want to grow up: she wants only her garden'; and that possessive 'her' recognizes the garden as a presence inside Hatty's head as well as outside her house. But when the grown-up Hatty wants to skate to Ely, Tom must 'leave the garden for the time being, and go with her'; and 'leave' has the force of 'forsake'. That phrase 'for the time being' also sets up

reverberations: the book is full of such interesting uses of common or even clichéd phrases about time.

The figure of Abel mediates between the two dimensions in Hatty's garden, allows them to intersect. Without him, they would diverge, as they have in Tom's parents' garden. The book's first chapter is called '**Exile**', and its subject is Tom's bitter sense of loss at his exclusion from that garden, and its apple tree. Even the narrow strip of the Longs' town garden is assimilated to the type of the eternal garden: '. . . there was a vegetable plot and a grass plot and one flower-bed and a rough patch by the back fence. In this last the apple-tree grew: it was large, but bore very little fruit.' What is thrilling in the writing here is Philippa Pearce's dual perception of the garden: as the adult narrator she sees it as a bare, uncherished place, but through Tom's eyes, through the eyes of childhood, it is a place of infinite possibility. What is described is dull, but the tone of the description, that breathless accumulation of 'ands', is exhilarated, loving. When she comes to describe the midnight garden itself the two perceptions blend in a hush of ecstasy.

This description of the Longs' garden shows, too, that *Tom's Midnight Garden* is not a book about nostalgia, not a regretful glance back at a Victorian Golden Age; despite the pollution of the river and the destruction of Hatty's garden, the Edenic garden hovers behind the material world like an indrawn breath.

The reader of *Tom's Midnight Garden* need not be aware of Tom's garden as the Garden of Eden, nor be concerned to work out the metaphysics of time on any more profound level than Tom himself; the book's great virtue is its simplicity, its directness, its entirely specific, believable and enthralling narrative line. But its artistic success lies in the way abstract thought has been caught in concrete images; the way the eternal garden has been fused with the temporal one. It is essentially a drama of emotion, not incident; of image, not argument. It is a book about time, innocence, experience, redemption. Yet it is triumphantly what it sets out to be: a book for children. The treatment of these themes makes it so: for the mystery at the heart of the text is that the relationship between Hatty and Tom is the same as that between author and reader. Philippa Pearce is an adult giving narrative shape, for a child, to her sense of what is lost in the transition from childhood to adulthood, and the grace which enables us to make good that loss. She dreams her reader, to confront her own childhood. And so the book itself becomes an emblem of its story, and a proof of its transcendent theme, that 'He shall deliver the island of the innocent' (Job 22:30). (pp. 22-5)

> Neil Philip, " 'Tom's Midnight Garden' and the Vision of Eden," in *Signal*, No. 37, January, 1982, pp. 21-5.

[*The following lecture was delivered in March, 1982.*]

As many have noted, fantasy is not free of the obligation to be credible.... [Most fantasies set in the here and now] use some rational explanations to achieve credibility as does, for example, Lewis Carroll's *Alice's Adventures in Wonderland*, Mary Norton's *The Borrowers*, and E. B. White's *Charlotte's Web*. One of the few that does not is Philippa Pearce's *Tom's Midnight Garden*. Relying instead on narrative technique, Pearce gradually inspires belief without sacrificing any of the imaginative power of the mystery she unfolds. She never explains Tom's ability to step back into Hatty's world, some seventy years before the novel's present time and sixty or so before

Tom's birth. Using the tools of a master storyteller—an appropriate narrator, psychological characterization, a carefully structured plot, and evocative style—especially the latter—Pearce eases us into exploration of territory still mysterious to the human mind.

Much of *Tom's Midnight Garden*'s credibility arises from Pearce's limiting us to Tom's point of view. Tom Long is an imaginative, lonely, unhappy boy when the novel opens.... His emotional state functions to persuade the reader to believe in the beginning of Tom's midnight adventures in the garden behind the house where the Kitsons live.

Furthermore, Pearce opens the novel in the recognizably ordinary world of England in the mid-twentieth century, in Tom's home and in the Kitsons' flat. Only the grandfather clock in the hall of Mrs. Bartholomew's house, now including the Kitsons' flat, attracts Tom's attention as unusual. (pp. 142-43)

Pearce doesn't introduce fantasy until Chapter III when Tom gets out of bed at midnight, goes downstairs, opens the door at the back of the house in order to see the clock, and discovers [the garden].... The garden, Tom believes, is real. Furious that his aunt and uncle have lied to him, he plans to play in it the following day. If unusual, then, Tom's experience still seems credible.

In Chapter IV, Pearce deepens the fantasy as Tom discovers that there is no garden behind the house, only an old yew tree in a garden strip belonging to the house beyond. That night he plans to climb the fence and examine the tree for clues, but instead he again enters the mysterious garden. In Chapter V, he explores the garden alone, seeing only the gardener as he begins his day's work. Chapter VI summarizes many of Tom's midnight visits and introduces the strangeness of his existence there. He discovers his apparent invisibility to others and his physical inability to affect anything in the garden. Also, he learns that no matter how long he seems to stay in the garden, on his return the clock in the Kitsons' kitchen reads only a few minutes past midnight.

Tom is bothered by what he doesn't understand, but not so bothered that he needs explanations—at least not at first. The reader, too, sharing Tom's delight in the garden, tends to delay questioning the strangeness of Tom's experiences.... By careful selection, accumulation, and startling juxtaposition of details (from different times of the day, parts of a season, seasons of the year), Pearce creates the illusion of timelessness, profusion, and perfection. (pp. 143-44)

With his sense and mind full of the pleasures of the garden, Tom does not seek an explanation of its strangeness until Chapter VII. Here he writes to Peter, "I don't *mind* any of it, except perhaps being invisible to everybody." ... He does, however, question his Uncle Alan about the possibility of going through a closed door, about invisibility, and about time. His uncle dismisses his questions as arising from a dream or a child's fantasy, thus supporting the reader yet disbelieving. By this time, though, descriptions of the garden have created the desire to believe, and readers are, in any case, unlikely to side with Uncle Alan. Insensitive, intellectual, and overly rational, he is an unattractive character. Instead of rational explanations, readers, like Tom, are more likely to immerse themselves in further exploration of the garden's mysteries.

Thus, Pearce disarms doubting readers before plunging deeply into fantasy. (p. 144)

In every possible way, Pearce [shows] the reader that Tom cannot stay in the garden forever—that life does not stand still. Tom, however, hangs on to the hope that he and Hatty can forever remain children in the garden until after he meets Mrs. Bartholomew.... He learns that "never before this summer had she dreamed of the garden so often, and never before this summer had she been able to remember so vividly what it *felt* like to be the little Hatty—longing for someone to play with and somewhere to play." ... Tom recognizes her feelings as his, and the reader has one more piece of evidence which savors of explanation of the mystery. (p. 145)

[The] mystery of *Tom's Midnight Garden* remains unexplained—as much of the novel's appeal. Dreams, psychic bonds between people, an intense emotional need, a magic clock, a thirteenth hour—all are or may be partial explanations of the timelessness of Tom's experience, but we do not care about the logical explanations of these mysteries. The novel maintains our desire to believe and to understand until it ends, and it is completely satisfying because it so deeply involves us in Tom's and Hatty's relationship in the garden. Like *The Secret Garden*, *Tom's Midnight Garden* portrays two children who heal themselves. Delighting in the garden and in one another, they protect each other from isolation and unhappiness, and they learn to love. Indeed, the novel celebrates fantasy for its power to nourish the self. The profuse, timeless, perfect garden is a marvelous symbol of the imagination. Both Hatty and Tom survive deprivation by means of the garden and their relationship. To be sure, Tom seems to err in substituting fantasy for reality long after his need for companionship and play is passed, but then Tom is still a child, outraged by and unreconciled to imperfection and the passage of time. Eventually, he learns to accept change, and, more importantly, he learns that what has been loved is never lost—that it remains inside of him—in dreams and memory. Sharing Tom's point of view, we experience his complex needs and his growth, as Pearce gradually eases us into and then out of the fantasy, leaving us with evocative images of a beautiful garden. Rather than explain to the head, in other words, Pearce uses narrative technique to persuade the heart. Poetry, not science, inspires belief in *Tom's Midnight Garden*. Artistry and not reason is the source of its credibility. (p. 146)

Virginia L. Wolf, "Belief in 'Tom's Midnight Garden'," in Proceedings of the Ninth Annual Conference of the Children's Literature Association: The Child and the Story, an Exploration of Narrative Forms, edited by Priscilla A. Ord, The Children's Literature Association, 1983, pp. 142-46.

Two old women in contemporary children's literature, Mrs. Basil E. Frankweiler in E. L. Konigsburg's *From the Mixed-up Files of Mrs. Basil E. Frankweiler* and Mrs. Harriet Bartholomew in A. Philippa Pearce's *Tom's Midnight Garden*, are noteworthy extensions of the fictional convention of the elderly storyteller used by a number of nineteenth-century writers for children. These characters are story *makers*, who present games of historical detection for the children in their novels. Further, these novels raise interesting questions about time and the possibility for human beings—both young and old—to conquer its inexorable passage. (p. 6)

[*From the Mixed-up Files of Mrs. Basil E. Frankweiler* and *Tom's Midnight Garden* share] a sensitive and sympathetic depiction of the aged. The characters are neither freaks to be feared, nor declining, passive models who accept their disenfranchisement. Mrs. Frankweiler and Mrs. Bartholomew are ordinary enough women who nonetheless possess the power to shape young characters' experiences. Their power comes, not from magical endowment, but from their masterful imaginations. They actually dream up much of the stories of which they are a part. In this respect, they best the old storytellers that precede them in the heritage of children's literature, for they *create* the possibility for the children within the works to perform their own narratives.

In both works, the young characters initially display the diffidence regarding old age that has been transmitted from adults to children in our culture. . . . [In] both novels arresting eyes indicate mysterious depths of personality and experience in these women, territory that children, both characters and readers, come to explore throughout the novels. What is more, the children also discover that the young and the very old are alike in their need to share experience and to have secrets, and in their creative ability to satisfy these needs. (p. 7)

As Mrs. Frankweiler was the mastermind behind the Kincaids' puzzle, Mrs. Bartholomew literally dreams the fantastic adventure that relieves the loneliness Tom feels upon being sent to his aunt and uncle's flat. Pearce provides clues that Mrs. Bartholomew is connected with the Victorian fantasy Tom lives every time the grandfather clock strikes thirteen. Readers are told at the outset, for example, "the lights on the first-floor landing and in the hall were turned out, for the tenants were all in bed and asleep, and Mrs. Bartholomew was asleep and dreaming". . . . Later, readers learn that "Tom's call, sharp like a bird's warning, reached up even to the topmost flat and woke Mrs. Bartholomew from a dream of her wedding one midsummer day some sixty-odd years before". . . . Nonetheless, Tom is not perceived by readers with the same dramatic irony that results in *Mixed-up Files* from knowing Mrs. Frankweiler better than the Kincaids do. For readers, as well as Tom, the denouement of the narrative is the discovery that they already know—and know very well—this old, seemingly unapproachable landlady. They and Tom have been reliving her dreams of her own past. Mrs. Bartholomew is thus perceived by Tom and readers as both the child she once was and, at the conclusion, as the old woman she is in the present of the novel: "You were Hatty—you *are* Hatty! You're really *Hatty!*"

The friendship of Hatty/Mrs. Bartholomew and Tom contrasts with the adversary relationship between Tom and the generation just ahead of him. Like Claudia [in *Mixed-up Files*], Tom is a contemporary counterpart of the "misprized child" in so many fairy tales. Both feel they are unappreciated by their immediate families. . . . Aunt Gwen and Uncle Alan are more fully characterized than the parents in either novel. Still, they are Adults, not individuals, to Tom's way of thinking. While Tom admits in a letter to his brother Peter that his aunt is a very good cook, she remains a shadowy figure in his life, albeit one who does her best to please the boy. Uncle Alan is more clearly perceived by Tom and by readers; he is an obfuscated adult, one whose over-attention to rational explanation precludes fantastic, imaginative experience. He becomes exasperated with Tom's questions about time, since it has never occurred to him to question chronology, to consider the possibility of simultaneous pasts and presents.

In short, Uncle Alan is an example of the longstanding tendency in children's literature to present grownups as butts of satire. . . . (p. 8)

In contrast to Uncle Alan, Young Hatty, who becomes old Mrs. Bartholomew, understands rather than patronizes Tom.

She actually feels his isolation. At the conclusion of the narrative she tells him that before his arrival this summer "never . . . had she been able to remember so vividly what it had *felt* like to be the little Hatty—to be longing for someone to play with and for somewhere to play". . . . She can also empathize with Tom because of her loneliness in old age; in fact, it is what precipitates her retreat through dreaming into the past. Young and old are alike in this novel, too, in their ability to overcome their loneliness and boredom. As with Claudia and Mrs. Frankweiler, Tom's and Mrs. Bartholomew's ingenuity allows them to overthrow the "generation gap" and enjoy each other's company—in *Midnight Garden* the two characters literally share experience. And their solidarity cannot be undone. At the end of the novel, Aunt Gwen describes to her husband Tom's goodbye to Hatty. . . . Readers are left looking forward to another meeting.

The coupling of the old and the young in these two works might be regarded as less than a compliment to either group. Rather than conveying respect toward the old, these works might be said to backfire in their depiction of a society of the powerless, of those with enough time on their hands to live in fantasy worlds, in *Tom's Midnight Garden*, or to play idle games of detection, in *Mixed-up Files*. These works might be charged with the further relegating of the old to the secondary, virtually useless role modern society and earlier children's literature have traditionally assigned them. But I argue otherwise, and base my claim on the attitude taken in the novels toward imagination and toward how time should be spent.

As we have seen, Konigsburg's and especially Pearce's depiction of middle-aged adults does not make that group a club to be belonged to: they are quotidian, unimaginative sorts who, to repeat Mrs. Frankweiler's words, cannot take "time out" to consider anything beyond their immediate circumstances. The young and the old, on the other hand, do take time out to entertain their fantasies and, by so doing, enrich their presents. There is nothing wrong, according to the thinking in the novels, indeed there is something right, with Mrs. Bartholomew's living in the past. . . . Through her power of memory she transcends time—that is, she proves the inscription on her grandfather clock, "Time No Longer." Thus she, like Mrs. Frankweiler, has by her own imaginative ability filled a gap in her present.

The children in the novels also learn, through their communion with old people, that time can be conquered. And this recognition opens up the possibility that the young can find links to the past; they can gain a sense of history. By recognizing the youthful perspectives that underlie Mrs. Frankweiler's and Mrs. Bartholomew's present appearances, children both within and outside the narrative become aware of personal history. People have pasts that continue with them into the present, for example, these two women's husbands, who have both died.

But both these novels provide children with a sense of public history—that is, with the salutary perception of their own historical context. . . . [In] *Midnight Garden*, Tom's fantastic adventure is a trip back in time to Victorian England. Tom, like Claudia Kincaid, is consumed by self-pity because he has been farmed out to his aunt and uncle. Then he involves himself in historical detective work. As he gets to know young Hatty, he becomes increasingly curious about when and how his friend lived. After researching the details of the garden world in various encyclopedias, he concludes, slightly off the mark, that young Hatty is an Early Victorian. This involvement in Hatty's personal past continuing to the more general discovery of public history leads him to overcome his preoccupation with self.

The consideration of time in these novels is not unique among recent literature for children. Many contemporary works combine attention to the old with the subject of human mutability. They typically suggest acceptance of the inexorable passing of time and its implications for humankind: dying is what naturally follows living. What is new is Konigsburg's and Pearce's shared decision not to depict the passive acceptance of the *memento mori* theme. They recognize the transience of life but emphasize their old characters' active overcoming, through imaginative scheming or recollecting, of the effects of time—separation from spouses, lack of contact with children, resulting loneliness. And this triumph turns out to provide an opportunity for young protagonists to use their creative abilities in order to solve historical puzzles and, thereby, their personal problems. In this respect both *From the Mixed-up Files of Mrs. Basil E. Frankweiler* and *Tom's Midnight Garden* are very much a part of the long tradition of children's literature that extols the imagination of young and old alike. (pp. 8, 31)

> *Carol Billman, "Young and Old Alike: The Place of Old Women in Two Recent Novels for Children," in* Children's Literature Association Quarterly, *Vol. 8, No. 1, Spring 1983, pp. 6-8, 31.**

---

## *MRS. COCKLE'S CAT* (1961)

Here is that rarest of books nowadays, a genuine English picture-book, as English as Rowlandson or fish-and-chips.

Philippa Pearce's text is a little long for a picture-book. There are many words to the page, but the words (need one say?) are exquisitely right, with a fine prose rhythm and an inevitable precision of phrase. Her story is original, too, and firmly based in reality, for all that Mrs. Cockle, one windy day, is swept up into the sky on the end of a string of balloons. . . .

[Illustrator Antony Maitland] has matched precisely the warmth and kindliness of Miss Pearce's delightful story. *Mrs. Cockle's Cat* is thoroughly contemporary and original, but it also belongs clearly to the English picture-book tradition.

> *A review of "Mrs. Cockle's Cat," in* The Junior Bookshelf, *Vol. 25, No. 5, November, 1961, p. 269.*

Younger children are seldom treated to writing as superior as Miss Pearce's. Her story of an elderly balloon seller . . . [looking] for her runaway cat, is wonderfully inventive. . . . First and second graders should enjoy the book as well as the pre-schoolers to whom its picture-book format seems to be directed.

> *A review of "Mrs. Cockle's Cat," in* Publishers Weekly, *Vol. 181, No. 12, March 19, 1962, p. 63.*

The author has a pleasantly restrained style, perhaps too sedate for the introduction of the fanciful element after the first pages that give a realistic picture of Mrs. Cockle; the ending is a bit flat.

> *Zena Sutherland, in a review of "Mrs. Cockle's Cat," in* Bulletin of the Center for Children's Books, *Vol. XV, No. 8, April, 1962, p. 130.*

---

## *A DOG SO SMALL* (1962)

### AUTHOR'S COMMENTARY

A book that is worth writing—that the writer really cares about—is only partly *made*. One may be able to make all the parts hold neatly and strongly together, as a carpenter does a good job on a box; but, before that, from the very beginning—perhaps before there is any conscious intention of writing a story—the story must *grow*. An idea grows in the mind, as a tree grows from a seed; it develops with the slowness of natural growth.

The idea of a story springs from experience—from what had been seen and heard and done and felt and thought, going back for weeks, months, perhaps years—perhaps even to birth, or earlier. To say exactly where an idea sprang from may be very difficult; it's much easier to mark its growth—its gaining in strength and in size, and its branchings out. That's what I shall do for one particular story: mine. My concern will be mostly with growth and the encouragement of growth—the cultivation, as a gardener would say; but there will also be something about making, as a carpenter makes. Growth and making can go on together, as long as the second is never allowed to interfere with the first.

Ideas for stories aren't always easily identifiable. One needs to be on the watch, to recognize them; in the beginning, they may not look like stories at all. My idea didn't look like a story; it looked like a person—a boy who longed to have a dog. It began with the longing itself, and at first that was all I knew of the boy. I never did know—and never bothered to wonder—what exactly he looked like: what colour his hair was, or his eyes, whether he was tall or short for his age, or even exactly what his age was. I didn't care about the boy's appearance because I started knowing him from the inside—what he wanted, his thoughts, his feelings; so there was no need to look at him from the outside, as you do with a stranger passing in the street. I knew that at the very centre of that boy—at the heart of him—was his longing for a dog. That was my idea for the story, and from that the boy grew, and the story grew round him, because what he wanted and what he was caused the story.

The idea grew in my mind. The boy's longing was intense—so intense that at last it created what it could not have: the boy imagined a dog for himself. He became absorbed in a waking dream of a dog more wonderful than any flesh-and-blood dog could ever be. The dream couldn't last for ever, so later the boy was alone again, without even an imaginary dog, but with the old longing. Yet that wasn't the end of the story, I was sure, although I didn't yet know what the end would be.

Now, as soon as the boy existed in my mind as a presence, as somebody there, I began trying out different scenes and scenery behind him. Some fitted, some didn't. This was like carpenter's work—fitting the right pieces together, so that they would hold. I tried the boy out, for instance, in various kinds of family and house and district. Only this suited him: a large family living in a pokey house in a back street of London. In the family, the boy had two younger brothers, who did everything together, and two elder sisters, who did everything together; and so my boy, in the middle, was always on his own, and lonely. That was why he longed for a dog, as a companion. But he couldn't have one, because the house was too small, and without any garden, and there was too much traffic in his part of London. Note that in the finished story it seems as if the boy began to long for a dog *because* he belonged to that family, and as if he couldn't have a dog *because* he lived in that house and that district. But, in fact, in my imagining of the story, the exact opposite happened: that family, house, and district were the result of the boy's hopeless longing. They were the only ones that really fitted it.

I tried out different scenes for the boy, some of them only glimpses, others complete scenes, as in a film. One of the scenes that came to me earliest of all was set on Hampstead Heath, late one summer evening. I know the Heath well, and that's when I like it best. Perhaps that was why I put my boy there then. For, when everyone else had gone home, he was still wandering on the Heath; he was the only thing you could see moving in the failing light. There was absolute stillness, too, until he called to somebody or something. I liked the dramatic way his voice cracked the silence. Then there was an answering sound from over the Heath—a dog barking, and out of the dusky distance a dog rushed towards him—a living dog for him alone. The boy and his dog met, overjoyed, and then they went over the Heath together, their shapes melting into the dusk again. And that, I realized, was the end of my story.

So, long before I had the beginning of the story, I had the end—and that was an encouragement, almost a promise. From the first, the end was there as a landmark, a destination to be aimed at.

All the same, this end that I had found asked more questions than it answered. It answered one big question: Did the boy ever get the real dog he longed for? Yes. But it asked others: Where did this dog come from? How did the Heath come into the story? How could the boy have a dog now, and not earlier? Difficult questions, that gave trouble later. Already I looked ahead towards them with anxiety: they appeared as big gaps in the story; and as well as these gaps, there was no beginning. A story without a beginning doesn't look much of a story.

This is just the time when a writer can feel stuck. He may want to give up altogether in despair; or he may feel he'd be justified in *making* the story work out—in forcing it, as one might force a lock. But I believe that forcing can be just as fatal to a story—to the life of a story—as giving up. The life of my story was in the boy, in his longing. Everything had either to grow naturally from that, or be made to fit it, as the family, house and district had been made to fit. The boy himself must never be forced to do anything. If I'd begun doing that, the boy would have become a dummy boy, to be moved about in a dead story.

For me, the important thing at this stage was to wait—to think about the story only when I wanted to; and even then not to think hard, not to reason, but to let the mind rove freely, almost lazily. In any bit of time when one hasn't positively to be thinking of something else, the mind can be wandering about in a half-grown story, exploring its possibilities.

Gradually falling asleep or waking up, dozing—these are often useful times. Sleepiness and sleep free the mind to try out possibilities that might otherwise seem too bizarre; but one of them may fit, or lead to another that fits. You can half-dream the answers to questions.

I've said that you can't force the story along, or you'll almost certainly kill it, or kill that particular part of it. But you can feed its growth. There'll be things that you suddenly remember from long ago, or things you've always known, or things you notice freshly—incidents and details from personal experience. All these you can try out in a story, hoping to nourish its

growth. So the alert, observant part of your mind, the part that notices what goes on round you, can be useful in the story, as well as the part that is meditative, half-dreaming.

Noticing and remembering what had been noticed—these eventually helped me to find the missing beginning of my story. Up to then I had only the end—on Hampstead Heath—and rather a misty middle, which was the boy imagining a dog for himself. I had nothing earlier than that middle, and so I had to work backwards from that. Three things I had seen or heard took me backwards to a beginning.

First of all, up from my memory came something I had noticed in the Greenwich Naval Museum several years before. A section of the Museum was devoted to Nelson, and—as well as all the relics of sea-battles—there was a pretty bronze brooch or medallion of a dog. The label said that this had belonged to Nelson's daughter, when she was no more than an infant. Her father had promised to give her whatever she chose as a present, and she had asked for a dog. But he thought—or perhaps he was persuaded—that a dog was too rough a pet for so young a child. So, to keep his promise, and yet not to keep it, he gave her the representation of a dog in bronze. As I read the explanatory label in the Museum, I thought how bitterly disappointed—perhaps furiously angry—the little girl must have been. Now, years later, with my story growing in my mind, I thought of this again. I wondered what had happened next, for the little girl. Did she go on longing for a dog, as my boy did? And if so . . .

The story of the brooch seemed to fit with the story of the boy and his longing. But the fit couldn't be exact—for one thing, a brooch couldn't be a present for a boy.

Then came the second thing—or rather, it had been there all the time: a little, old-fashioned picture of a dog, embroidered in wool, hanging on the wall in my own home. I had seen it every day for years, but now suddenly I saw it inside the story. The picture might do instead of a brooch.

Lastly, while all this was drifting around in my mind, I happened to have a conversation with a friend, about seeing with your eyes shut. You can often remember the look of a thing more exactly if you close your eyes. And if you have been staring at something very intently, and then shut your eyes, you seem to see with peculiar vividness. And so on . . .

As that conversation continued, I seemed to hear a click in my mind, like the sound of a key turning in a lock, opening something. At last I saw the way through, that my story could go, naturally, without any forcing.

Now I could find a way back from the middle of the story, which I knew, to the missing beginning. In the middle of the story, the boy was imagining a dog. Suppose he saw this imaginary dog only when he had his eyes shut . . . Yes; and suppose this vision came in the first place from staring at a picture of a dog—a picture perhaps like the woolwork picture. He owned the picture—but wait a minute: he didn't want to own a picture of a dog; he wanted to own a real dog. Yes, but that could be the whole point—as it had been with Nelson's little daughter. The boy wanted a real dog, and he was given the representation of a dog instead. That would be a bitter disappointment, if he'd actually been promised a dog as a present—say, on his birthday.

I was there. I had travelled backwards from the middle of the story to what could be rather a good beginning: the boy's birthday, and his expecting a dog.

Finding myself there, at the beginning of the story, I wanted to start writing at once. I knew there were gaps in the story ahead, particularly towards the end. There was some mistiness elsewhere, as well; but both the gaps and the mistiness were a good way ahead. So I didn't let them deter me. I don't believe in putting off writing if one really wants to, even if everything isn't fully planned. After all, one can pause for days, if necessary, between stretches of writing—between chapters, probably—and think ahead again. And if things do go wrong, one can go back afterwards and put them right. That may be a nuisance, but it's less dangerous than putting off writing when one feels ready. The danger then would be that one might forget what was at the tip of one's pen—that one might lose the excitement that often leads to the best writing.

So I started on the first chapter. The story fell into chapters as I went along, and it was only occasionally that I was in doubt where exactly to make a chapter end. In the finished story there were nearly twenty chapters, but long before I could foresee that, I had begun to see that the story was going into a natural pattern of three big sections. These were made by the three different dogs the boy had, one after the other: first, the woolwork picture of a dog; second, the imaginary dog; third, the living dog that came over Hampstead Heath.

The end of the first section—the woolwork dog—actually overlapped a little with the beginning of the next section—the imaginary dog that the boy saw with his eyes shut. This overlap came in the middle of a chapter. I wrote that chapter with particular excitement, because I felt myself at a turning point of the story. After that, the story would be really growing, as a young tree grows, according to its nature—the nature which I had given it. A phrase of dialogue at that turning point also gave me the title for the story when it was finished: *A Dog so Small.* (pp. 140-45)

*Philippa Pearce, "Writing a Book: 'A Dog So Small',"
in* The Thorny Paradise: Writers on Writing for Children, *edited by Edward Blishen, Kestrel Books, 1975, pp. 140-45.*

---

A child's imagination, its intensity, its dangers, and the difficult transition from a dream-world to the light of day—this serious theme is illustrated in a story designed with elegant simplicity. Ben Blewitt, whose father works on the Underground, enjoys the ups and downs of life in a large family; but his energies are set on a dog, and in their London back street this is impossible. Instead, his country grandparents give him the wool picture of a chihuahua sent by their sailor son, and this dog becomes his companion, prancingly real when his eyes are shut. Following this visionary dog, Ben is hurt by a car. The vision has gone, and when his dream is at last fulfilled, he does not at first realise it.

I believe this is Miss Pearce's best book so far. Technically, it is masterly. Every detail of Ben's early morning walk, in the opening chapters, (the pigeon outside the window who knows this is not the crumbgiver, the cat dangerously crossing a Westminster street, the river which recurs in dreams later, the swirl in Ben's mind of scenes from books) every detail points towards the centre of the story, the dangerous flowering of the boy's imagination.

The book has that deeper, oracular meaning we find in the best stories for children. It is also a first-class narrative. . . . Each of the characters has an effect upon the action, and each has

his own way of acting and speaking. Even the park-keeper and the librarian, glimpsed only for a moment, have real personality, and the Fitch grandparents and the Blewitts live on when the book is finished. It is on the precise, concrete details of the story that the theme is supported. Ben's habit of walking with his eyes shut stems logically from a chance remark to Grandpa on Castleford Station, from a fog, from the lack of privacy in Ben's home. Beyond this, everything he does and says makes us realise *why* he develops this habit, this *ordinary* imaginative boy (incidentally, a type familiar enough in real life but too subltle to be often attempted in fiction).

To say that this is a book written on many levels, a book for adults as well as for older childern, is to go only part of the way of conveying the sheer artistry and the warmth of human feeling in it. Young or old, its readers are likely to say, as they shut it, 'Yes, this is what it is like to live with a dream.'

*Margery Fisher, in a review of "A Dog So Small,"
in her* Growing Point, *Vol. 1, No. 1, May, 1962, p. 1.*

---

No book has been more eagerly awaited than the first full-length novel of Philippa Pearce since *Tom's Midnight Garden,* because the only thing one could be sure of was that it would be excellent and unusual. *A Dog So Small* is all that, and more. . . .

Miss Pearce, in addition to her command of words, characterisation and setting, is a master in the invention of complex, unexpected and convincing plots.

It is fair to point out that this is not an easy book. The publisher suggests an age-range of 8-12 which seems grotesquely out. Much of the action goes on in Ben's head, which is difficult enough for many children; and the relationships between Ben and his mother and Ben and his grandfather, which are fundamental to the story, depend for their understanding on hairline subtleties. *A Dog So Small* in fact is likely to be a "minority" book but one which, with its wisdom and sympathy, its profound understanding of human behaviour, its fresh and lively portrayal of town and country society, is likely to be for a few children a rung in the ladder by which they mount to adult life.

*A review of "A Dog So Small," in* The Junior Bookshelf, *Vol. 26, No. 3, July, 1962, p. 139.*

---

This English import may have difficulty finding an American audience. The idea of Ben's longing for a dog of his own is natural enough, and the reader is pleased that he eventually gets one. However, the concept of his fascination for a dog he can see only with his eyes closed is overdeveloped and lengthened almost to the point of becoming a psychopathic problem. Furthermore, Ben's momentary rejection of a large dog because of its size is not quite believable in view of his previous experience with a large dog and his overpowering longing for a real dog. The story is too long, too slow-moving, and too involved with psychological ramifications, but it offers a beautiful reading experience for the special reader.

*Dorothy Winch, in a review of "A Dog So Small,"
in* School Library Journal, *an appendix to* Library Journal, *Vol. 9, No. 9, May, 1963, p. 107.*

---

Beautifully and sensitively written. . . . The other children in the family remain shadowy figures throughout the book; but Ben's parents, and especially his grandparents, emerge as memorable characters, full of concern and unexpected wisdom.

There should be no lack of interest in this extraordinary story of a boy and a dog; it is a moving book and, in many ways, a notable one.

> *Ethel L. Heins, in a review of "A Dog So Small,"*
> *in* The Horn Book Magazine, *Vol. XXXIX, No. 3,*
> *June, 1963, p. 284.*

Because of the spare, selective simplicity of the prose, the weight of metaphor and emotion in the book is carried easily in the character of Ben. First, his position as the middle child of five is shown to be important; the practical outlook of his parents, the giggling chatter of his older sisters and the jostling and cheek of his younger brothers are reason enough for Ben's isolation and his quiet, dogged manner. Then his mood is indicated in phrases that describe, briefly but significantly, an exact gesture, attitude or movement. On Ben's birthday, while the family exclaim and speculate over the Fitches' present, he sits still and silent and his hands 'half-hidden by the wrapping-paper that his mother has picked up from the floor, clenched into angry fists'. His stance in the guard's van on the way back to London—'he sat at a distance, on a crate of chickens, his face turned away from the dog'—is more telling than a direct statement of his feelings would have been. Rich in metaphor and feeling, *A Dog So Small* presents a character created in depth, endowed with individuality, whose problem may be translated into the experience of each and every reader.

> *Margery Fisher, "Who's Who in Children's Books:*
> *Ben Blewitt," in her* Who's Who in Children's Books:
> A Treasury of the Familiar Characters of Childhood,
> *Holt, Rinehart and Winston, 1975, p. 39.*

From time to time the cry is heard, *'Why all this social problem stuff?'* but the best children's books not only have something to say, but rivetting stories to tell. Social awareness can be an added dimension, not a substitute for craft. And the same can be said for a masterly recall of childhood and an understanding of the growing process. All of which are overwhelmingly apparent in . . . [*A Dog So Small*. It] gets right inside the head of an imaginative boy who can't have what he wants . . . and does so in a quiet and brilliant style that made me throw my pen down one night in sheer envy. Twenty years old and enduring, it's a classic of the realistic fantasy which grips every child's mind at times. (p. 30)

> *Bernard Ashley, "Six Books to Give Prince Wil-*
> *liam," in* Books for Your Children, *Vol. 17, No. 3,*
> *Autumn-Winter, 1982, pp. 28-30.\**

---

### THE CHILDREN OF THE HOUSE (with Brian Fairfax-Lucy, 1968)

The Hattons of Stanford Hall belong to the privileged classes but life for the children is one of scant food and strict discipline. . . . It was the servants who gave the children security and affection and the countryside that gave them space and encouragement for adventure. . . . [The] Hattons led a strangely tribal life, ceremonial, ingenious and tolerably happy.

This life is pieced together in one episode after another. A lucid prose style in which every word counts makes these episodes unsensationally vivid. . . .

Lucky the child who acquires a sense of period from reading such books as this, books which do not set out to teach but, by the wealth and choice of detail and by the behaviour of their characters, do pass on the flavour of a particular world. The chronicle of the Hattons begins at the time of the Boer War and ends with the 1914-18 one; a postscript allows a backward glance at the old house now deserted. Brian Fairfax-Lucy writes of a world he knows from inside, Philippa Pearce with intuition about just such periods and estates.

The three interlocking yet separate groups at Stanford are kept precisely clear. We perceive the children's innocently sharp view of servants and parents; the servants are seen on both sides of the baize door; the worried contrivances and remote affection of the parents are demonstrated as they talk to each other, to the servants, to the children. We see how the four children, while accepting rules and influences, remain triumphantly themselves.

This has been a most successful collaboration. There is no visible join or jarring of mood in the book. Humour and grace decorate a confident picture of inheritance and environment.

> *Margery Fisher, in a review of "The Children of the*
> *House," in her* Growing Point, *Vol. 7, No. 1, May,*
> *1968, p. 1121.*

"**The Children of the House**" is an elegant piece of writing, sad but at times wryly humorous. . . . Philippa Pearce has given this chronicle, which is a tragedy in muted tones, shape, form and meaning. Her sense of period is exact, enhanced by an extraordinary flair for dialogue; her love of fun is much in evidence in this re-writing of Brian Fairfax-Lucy's bitter-sweet story.

> *E. D. Moss, in a review of "The Children of the*
> *House," in* Children's Book News, *Vol. 3, No. 4,*
> *July-August, 1968, p. 205.*

This is a most interesting and unusual experiment in authorship. It is collaboration of a sort but not joint authorship in the normally accepted sense. The foreword informs us that Brian Fairfax-Lucy wrote a story for adults and that what we now have is a re-writing of this story by Philippa Pearce for juniors—a case of ghost-writing in which it is not a matter of "as told to" but "from a story by". From Miss Pearce's pen we expect a book to be readable and she has not failed us. She has succeeded in a most interesting way in her presentation of the events in Mr. Fairfax-Lucy's story. . . .

The drawback to the story is the lack of a sense of the passage of time. It is difficult to get a feeling of the ages of the children from one chapter to another, and too abruptly they pass from childhood to a kind of semi-adulthood—at one moment a boyish escapade and the next a commissioned officer. Apart from this, it has a great deal to commend it.

> *A review of "The Children of the House," in* The
> Junior Bookshelf, *Vol. 32, No. 4, August, 1968, p.*
> *237.*

A book designed to leave its readers downcast. . . . Though the theme and tone are more appropriate to an adult short story . . . , this slim, well-written novel may have a certain melancholy charm for pre-teen readers. Presenting an emphatically gloomy statement about a side of aristocratic life seldom well and truly exposed elsewhere in juvenile books, this can also be read as a social document—an interesting, if weird, experience for young readers. (pp. 84-5)

> *Jean C. Thomson, in a review of "The Children of*
> *the House," in* School Library Journal, *an appendix*
> *to* Library Journal, *Vol. 15, No. 3, November, 1968,*
> *pp. 84-5.*

Every so often, one finds a book that speaks for its generation—and **"The Children of the House"** is such a book. . . .

These are the memories of Brian Fairfax-Lucy's childhood—and, as told by Philippa Pearce, they are eloquent. The simplicity, truth, and lack of emphasis in this story are virtually Chekhovian, and it is a stouthearted reader who will not weep.

> *Barbara Wersba, in a review of "The Children of the House," in* The New York Times Book Review, *Part II, November 3, 1968, p. 38.*

Creating a lively, vivid, and humorous book . . . , Mrs. Pearce has succeeded supremely well in bringing to life an actual pre-World War I childhood on an impoverished English estate. Young readers who may not care for a period piece will find this one full of delightful activity: children plotting against strictures, inevitable accidents resulting from adventurous spirits, and triumphs in dealing with austere parents. . . . To the adult reader the book naturally says more—about the way of life and the subtleties and ironies of relationships; but it is a most valid children's story, too, skillfully emphasizing a child's point of view and highlighting many incidents full of fun and surprise. (pp. 689-90)

> *Virginia Haviland, in a review of "The Children of the House," in* The Horn Book Magazine, *Vol. XLIV, No. 6, December, 1968, pp. 689-90.*

## THE ELM STREET LOT (1969)

[Elm Street in North London], to the outward eye a row of terrace houses like any other, is a territory to the children who live there, their cohesion proved by the fact that at school they are known to their peers from other streets as "the Elm Street lot". The six stories that chronicle their adventures were written for the television programme *Jackanory* ten years ago . . . ; the hardback edition seems to me long overdue but at least the passage of time has showed the dateless character of Philippa Pearce's writing. . . .

Elm Street's individuality is supported by the device of "populousness", the method by which an author, defining only a handful of characters, creates the illusion of a far larger cast. . . .

The illusion of populousness is simply and elegantly sustained. . . . (p. 3538)

The quiet humour that illuminates all Philippa Pearce's books rises naturally out of situations in these tales. A bath too big to go through the door, a lost kite, a broken window, a leaking roof, a hamster escaped, a cat run over—each circumstance engages the attention of the neighbourhood in varying ways, and while the energetic improvisations of nine-year-olds sets the tone, there are plenty of hints of more mature confrontations and relationships going on. The simplicity of the book is a matter of selection, not of omission. The style is concrete and precisely phrased; the stories run easily like reminiscences to be listened to but they are complex enough in content for the slow scrutiny of private reading. . . . The artistry of the Elm Street stories, different in scale but not in kind from that of Philippa Pearce's longer books, confirms me in my conviction that there is nobody to equal her in her chosen sphere. (p. 3539)

> *Margery Fisher, in a review of "The Elm Street Lot," in her* Growing Point, *Vol. 18, No. 2, July, 1979, pp. 3538-39.*

As in all Philippa Pearce's stories, the children are real and individual. Elm Street is *their* street and they are curious about all that happens in it for it is a tightly knit community. Naturally the street has its eccentrics like Miss Munson, the timid spinster, and its universally unpopular characters such as Mr. Crackenthorpe. Whatever the happening, the children are there to help or hinder. Here are lively stories told with wit and understanding.

> *E. Colwell, in a review of "The Elm Street Lot," in* The Junior Bookshelf, *Vol. 43, No. 4, August, 1979, p. 209.*

**The Elm Street Lot** is a collection of lively tales about the adventures of a motley crowd of urban kids—a well-used formula, but it still works in the right hands. Philippa Pearce has the golden gift of simple story-telling. I thank her for the hamster called Elaine, and the thing found on the roof ". . . a rusty metal object which Kitty Bates said was a cheese grater".

> *Gerald Haigh, "Tenpence for the Dead Lion," in* The Times Educational Supplement, *No. 3311, November 23, 1979, p. 33.\**

## THE SQUIRREL WIFE (1971)

In this grave and beautiful piece of writing in traditional story-teller's style, magic rises naturally from the impulses of generous or unkind temperaments, with love and loyalty given full value in the working out of the fortunes of two brothers. Philippa Pearce shows no trace of uneasiness in following the patterns, in rhythm and vocabulary, of the fairy-tale tradition which she is not imitating so much as continuing with complete confidence. Like Hans Andersen, she has put human emotion and human values in the forefront of a tale that has its own strong magic.

> *Margery Fisher, in a review of "The Squirrel Wife," in her* Growing Point, *Vol. 10, No. 6, December, 1971, p. 1852.*

What a daring book—balanced so precariously on the edge of mannerism: Miss Pearce's story an attempt at an 'original folk-tale' and Mr. [Derek] Collard's designs eclectic to a degree that should make failure inevitable. Both author and artist teeter, but they never quite topple down.

The tale concerns a Younger Brother who wins from the Green People—faery folk of the forest—a squirrel wife, and it tells how the two of them came to find happiness through sacrifice. It is neither so drastic in its portrayal of the bad, nor so matter-of-fact in its treatment of the strange as true folk tales are, but, on the other hand, it is a modest story, finely controlled in its narrative shape. Similarly its telling does not quite have the ring of a natural folk tale, but, read aloud, it escapes all the worst excesses of so many insensitive imitations.

> *Brian W. Alderson, in a review of "The Squirrel Wife," in* Children's Book Review, *Vol. II, No. 1, February, 1972, p. 11.*

This story keeps faith with age-old fairy-tale traditions, yet is wonderfully fresh, springing surprises all along the way. Not least among its many pleasures are details so precisely stated, they become revelations: Pigs *rootle* on the forest, yes, they do; and the things squirrels build in trees are *dreys*, that's the word!

*Doris Orgel, in a review of "The Squirrel Wife," in* The New York Times Book Review, *March 12, 1972, p. 8.*

Philippa Pearce's near-perfect fairy tale, new yet thoroughly traditional, unfolds like a story recalled from folk memory—as though generations of smoothing tongues had brought it to a final artless form. . . .

While Jack's squirrel-wife shares the secrets of the forest with her simple husband or ingeniously contrives to save him from his brother's treachery, the story never flags. But toward the end, after she is released at last from her enchantment to become a mortal wife, one is somehow reminded of Greta Garbo's heartfelt cry on viewing the ending of Cocteau's film *Beauty and the Beast:* "Give me back my beast!"

*Estelle Miller, in a review of "The Squirrel Wife," in* Book World—Chicago Tribune, *May 7, 1972, p. 4.*

The short tale is constructed of fairy-tale components: a protagonist, Jack, an overworked young swineherd; a species of fairymen—the green people; and the motif of kindness rewarded by magic. Paralleling the seal-wife or fox-wife of folklore is Jack's brown-haired, brown-eyed squirrel-wife. . . . Jack's older brother, jealous of Jack's well-being, caused him to be jailed and lose his squirrel-wife. But a perfectly wrought solution sweetens the tale. . . . Relayed with the directness of a long-known tale, but with more shadings and tenderness, the narrative is as totally pleasing as any long-lived story. The creation of the little wife is charming. . . . A combination of the arts has produced an exceptional book.

*Virginia Haviland, in a review of "The Squirrel Wife," in* The Horn Book Magazine, *Vol. XLVII, No. 3, June, 1972, p. 265.*

---

### BEAUTY AND THE BEAST  (1972)

In a calm, beautifully modulated prose [Philippa Pearce] tells the story in a way to emphasise its intensely human character without losing any of the elusive magical details. Very much a book for connoisseurs but also for reading aloud to a discriminating audience.

*Margery Fisher, in a review of "Beauty and the Beast," in her* Growing Point, *Vol. 11, No. 3, September, 1972, p. 2000.*

Many writers have dealt with this very old tale; but none is more effective than this newest version, with its musical language and its fresh witness to the power of love and faith. . . . A note on roots, sources and interpretations will satisfy the scholarly. (pp. 374-75)

*Lois Belfield Watt, in a review of "Beauty and the Beast," in* Childhood Education, *Vol. 49, No. 7 (April, 1973), pp. 374-75.*

All the enchantment of this fairy tale with its theme of love and compassion appears in a truly lovely picture book. Abridgements in the retelling tighten the essential story, and added inventions are in perfect harmony. . . . In an effective addendum, the author has traced the lineage of the ancient tale and has explained her own modifications—a section that is as interesting as it is informative.

*Beryl Robinson, in a review of "Beauty and the Beast," in* The Horn Book Magazine, *Vol. XLIX, No. 2, April, 1973, p. 137.*

---

### WHAT THE NEIGHBOURS DID AND OTHER STORIES  (1972)

What is simple prose? Most of us would associate it with stories that made obvious points, with little demand on the reader. And colloquial? For folk lore, perhaps, or gang stories. What about this?:

> Then the affair of the yellow dog made the Macys really hate Dirty Dick. It seems that old Mr. Macy secretly got himself a dog. He never had any money of his own, because his wife made him hand it over, every week; so Dad reckoned that he must have begged the dog off someone who'd otherwise have had it destroyed.

Easy, certainly: simple, no. The words give an impression initially of gossip; a boy is chatting about what happened once in his village. He brings place and event to life as much by the manner of his speech as by the details he lets fall (some of which he notices but only partly understands) about independent Dick, who has a tramp's casualness about life, and the couple next door. Relationships with neighbours, private values and social conventions—big themes for a short story, perhaps, but they are all here, implied in the words of a boy whose final comment makes you realise that the whole episode has been cunningly selected to be *his* version, any other points of view being secondary. . . . To use Edward Blishen's invaluable phrase, these stories have "a child's eye at the centre" but they do not reflect an exclusively child-centred world.

It is the world of the Barleys, Great and Little, the Cambridgeshire world of Ben Blewitt's grandparents, the scene of the river adventure of *Minnow* and of Hatty Bartholomew's childhood. . . . In a sense [*Still Jim and Silent Jim*] celebrates—as they all do—that pace and closeness in village life of which one aspect is that crabbed age and youth can and do live together.

Let nobody suppose, though, that these are not stories for children to read. They describe with memory and with verbal skill the doings of childhood—fishing in the stream, exploring water-meadows. . . , learning to dive in the local pond, picking blackberries, always with a special place in the life of family and village. The impeccable art in the stories, the prose that never obtrudes but is always active, pointed, lucid—these are for adults to enjoy consciously and for the young to absorb without having to indulge in any comprehension exercise. Such books form taste, through delight. (pp. 2051-52)

*Margery Fisher, in a review of "What the Neighbours Did and Other Stories," in her* Growing Point, *Vol. 11, No. 6, December, 1972, pp. 2051-52.*

Possibly, the sterility of primer and first-reader stories plus the simple-mindedness of what passes for short stories in magazines for children and young people contribute to turning readers here off the form before they're fairly started. The eight stories in this collection . . . are subtle without being vague and center on single actions with continuing implications. The stories range from light-hearted to thought-provoking—but all have the saving grace of humor. Short stories of any strength written especially for children and offered in a book by one author, rather than in a multi-authored anthology, are a rarity, and these are very good indeed; the short form and the distant setting are worth promoting past the initial indifference of your better-than-average readers.

> *Lillian N. Gerhardt, in a review of "What the Neighbours Did and Other Stories," in* School Library Journal, *an appendix to* Library Journal, *Vol. 20, No. 2, October, 1973, p. 119.*

[Pearce] writes with a hushed expectancy that does not necessarily end in solemnity, but—on many occasions—spills over into humor or into plain realism. . . . [All the short stories] capture the environmental experiences and the domestic adventures of children living in a present-day English village. . . . As in the stories of Sara Orne Jewett, the effect of the narratives depends upon the author's powers of observation and sympathy; and the exquisite simplicity of her style is never precious. (pp. 592-93)

> *Paul Heins, in a review of "What the Neighbors Did and Other Stories," in* The Horn Book Magazine, *Vol. XLIX, No. 6, December, 1973, pp. 592-93.*

[This is] a delightful collection. The writing is direct and simple, the plot lines clean, the characters drawn lightly but with a firm hand; what make the book enchanting are the fluidity of the author's style and the warmth and realism of her conception.

> *Zena Sutherland, in a review of "What the Neighbors Did and Other Stories," in* Bulletin of the Center for Children's Books, *Vol. 27, No. 5, January, 1974, p. 83.*

"**In the Middle of the Night,**" the best story here in Philippa Pearce's collection, is very funny. It's about children illicitly cooking potato cakes and is as finely structured as music; at the last note, sighing pleasurably, you wish for nothing more: a distinct achievement. On the other hand, some of these stories are often oddly unsatisfactory. The tone varies, of course. Two are first person, some slangy, others formal or detached or both. But all have Miss Pearce's strong sense of place, her wit and slyness of observation (adding, incidentally, to her special gallery of obstinate old men). Some may not be children's stories at all. The title one, for instance, shows a small, awful, adult wasteland. The best are too good to be confined to children anyway.

A few, inevitably, work less well—"**Lucky Boy**" perhaps or "**The Great Blackberry Pick**"—though the human observations are as good as ever. I find in some respects, the most interesting story "**Fresh,**" the most introspective, reminding me of the strangeness and intensity of the best of Philippa Pearce's earlier work.

I know from experience the uselessness of asking why a writer isn't working differently. You can only write as you feel able to. Yet it's sad that a writer of this quality appears to have turned so resolutely from certain facets of her talent; and not just her talent for fantasy; her realism was often as powerful. Then I think of the end of her "**The Squirrel Wife**"—significant not so much for the hero's acceptance of the loss of his wife's forest powers, as for his lack of apparent regret. Maybe so. I regret it all the same. But I also know Philippa Pearce must go her own way. And since this collection would be beyond the powers of most of us, it seems churlish not to welcome and enjoy them as they are.

> *Penelope Farmer, in a review of "What the Neighbors Did and Other Stories," in* The New York Times Book Review, *January 20, 1974, p. 8.*

---

### THE SHADOW-CAGE AND OTHER TALES OF THE SUPERNATURAL (1977)

Just as M. R. James lures his readers, word by word and paragraph by paragraph, till they feel the un-ordinariness of the curtains, the sheets on the bed, the dusty old book, so Philippa Pearce leads us—cunningly, with a disarmingly conversational reporting of people's talk and actions—to a state of acceptance. The biscuit barrel, dug out of the guest-room's rich confusion as their grandmother makes it ready for Daisy and Jim, does not simply remind the old woman of the worst moment in her childhood, when her stepmother's hate was most brutally shown—it re-creates the moment, independently, becoming malign by association. (p. 3113)

In many of the stories the supernatural element is skilfully projected from the recognisably ordinary behaviour of ordinary people, part of the fabric of themselves.

This novelistic element makes Philippa Pearce's stories subtly different from those of M. R. James, while inviting comparison for certain qualities of elegance and concentration in the writing. There are other tales in her book whose supernatural apparitions are extra-human in every sense. In the title-story, for example, the whistlers, heard but never seen, lead further back into the past than the agent of their summoning, a dirty glass bottle found by a schoolgirl, containing crusted blood from the experiments of a reputed witch. The green-eyed, lank-haired child who appears in a classroom after the excitement of a fallen tree, in *Guess*, has an inconceivable ancestry. The shiver, the shock of surprise, always come slowly, after an everyday setting has been firmly established—a village school, a mill on the river, a bungalow "in the middle of nowhere in particular". Such clichés of "ghost stories" as attics or isolated, shrub-shrouded mansions, come up as good as new with Philippa Pearce's polishing.

People, their sad or wicked memories, their present alarms and astonishments, are the activators of the stories, but places supply their inspiration and their poetic force. Perhaps the most tightly wrought of all, *The Running-Companion*, shows this fusion of person and place at its most remarkable. A man takes his last training run on the Common in Hampstead with hatred in his heart: step by step his doom follows him. The tale begins coolly and with a certain detachment. (pp. 3113-14)

The plain, measured, disarmingly simple voice of the storyteller quickens and deepens towards the foreseen yet shocking climax. Philippa Pearce works her illusions with the greatest skill, now stating, now surmising, now dropping the lightest of hints, always mindful of the fact that the supernatural belongs to the natural. (p. 3114)

> *Margery Fisher, in a review of "The Shadow Cage and Other Tales of the Supernatural," in her* Growing Point, *Vol. 16, No. 1, May, 1977, pp. 3113-14.*

A new book by Philippa Pearce is always an event and can be expected to be interestingly different from its predecessors. These short stories are not 'ghost' stories in the usual sense of the word, but something much more spine-chilling and evocative of atmosphere. The author has used ordinary things and places as a springboard for her imagination . . . and created with them a feeling of the supernatural and a sense of foreboding that makes the reader almost afraid to turn the page. Each story is unexpected in its ending. . . . The reader is never insulted and deflated by explanations which reduce the happening to the commonplace. Here too is the perceptive observation of character and the felicitous and effective use of words, which the reader has come to expect and appreciate from this author.

> E. Colwell, in a review of "The Shadow-Cage and Other Tales of the Supernatural," in The Junior Bookshelf, Vol. 41, No. 3, June, 1977, p. 182.

Does one have to say that Philippa Pearce is a real writer? Yes, of course, because so many books for children are written by quite other sorts of people. This is not a collection of ghost stories intended to appeal to children of a certain age who, as is well known, like spooky stories. It isn't a way of keeping children quiet for an hour, or a way of persuading them to exercise new-found skills in reading. It isn't designed to make them more understanding, more sensitive or more aware of the world around them. It is not, in short, an educational device. It is literature.

Most children must know the feeling that some places and things are frightening for no obvious reason. Philippa Pearce knows about them: the dark place at the back of the cupboard, the space behind the window of the empty house, the inexplicable nastiness of the old biscuit barrel. She expresses this sense of mystery and menace without in any way explaining it away.

> Dorothy Nimmo, in a review of "The Shadow Cage and Other Tales of the Supernatural," in The School Librarian, Vol. 25, No. 3, September, 1977, p. 245.

[Philippa Pearce's **The Shadow-Cage**] takes on a difficult task. The stories are genuinely frightening, investing nice safe familiar things like grandmothers and vegetables with the unspeakable. But because she writes them for children, she talks each one down into the daylight again, not leaving it on a sinister peak. There is one exception, **The Running Companion,** which makes no concessions to a younger audience. Mr. Adamson—the name is significant—murders his brother and is pursued by a nameless fury of his own. And (delicious shudder) he is caught! But in all the other stories, we wake from the nightmare in time and have the bad dream interpreted for us.

Some of the revenants are very moral, like the late vegetable-grower who frightens his successor away from wasted hours in front of the television set and out into the garden. Others, as in the title story, are motiveless malignants. It's a fine collection, with an assured M. R. Jamesian touch. . . .

> Mary Hoffman, "Pearls," in The Times Educational Supplement, No. 3258, November 18, 1977, p. 35.*

Foreshadowing and the building of tension are skillfully handled in these stories, though sometimes the climax is so subtle that readers may be left wondering what happened. Still, they are the best answer yet for those who want more by the author of **Tom's Midnight Garden.** . . .

> Margaret Chatham, in a review of "The Shadow Cage and Other Tales of the Supernatural," in School Library Journal, Vol. 24, No. 4, December, 1977, p. 50.

The strength of Philippa Pearce's collection lies in its very credible linking of the "real" world and the spirit world, and

in the variety of experience it describes: the stories are never merely "spooky."

The spirit world insinuates itself into a very everyday world because it needs to: quite suddenly, easily almost, it is there, because some task has to be completed, some wrong put right. Its arrival is often a familiar experience—the listening for a creaking stair in the night, the loss of a personal belonging. When the visited person has overcome his fear and responded to the need (without necessarily recognizing it), the spirit is released from its restlessness. And in the process there is often an access of some good in the real world—the care of the young for the old, for example.

The range of the collection is wide: each of the ten stories is totally different in setting, in its group of characters (though the family and the mutual feelings of its members are strongly present in most), and in its tone. A climbing frame in a playground, an open hearth, ordinary houses, a mill, a school: it is in these everyday places, often in broad daylight, and to very ordinary people, that the experience happens. Perhaps the weakest story—**Her Father's Attic,** with its unnecessary spelling out of the moral—is the one that takes place in the most traditional location.

The collection is not without comedy: **The Dog Got Them** is a marvellous comic treatment of the otherwise unbearable reality of D.T.'s, and **The Strange Illness of Mr. Arthur Cook** is a very pleasant light-hearted end to the book.

As you would expect, the stories are simply and elegantly written. In the tiny compass of some of them there is even space for a minor background character vividly presented; and there are two memorable animals.

It is a fine collection, brilliantly illustrating the theme: "it wasn't a mystery, it was a muddle." It is the untangling of the muddles that makes the book valuable. (pp. 125-26)

> Frederic Smith, in a review of "The Shadow Cage and Other Tales of the Supernatural," in Children's literature in education, Vol. 12, No. 3 (Autumn), 1981, pp. 125-26.

---

## THE BATTLE OF BUBBLE AND SQUEAK  (1978)

Philippa Pearce has long been acknowledged as one of the best writers we have for children. Her stories are always about themes which children will readily understand but they are also always very subtle. On the face of it this is the story about the difficulties of keeping pets at home and some of the dramas that can result. But as with all Philippa Pearce's books, from the very first sentence that hooks you into the plot immediately to the final climax, you are also caught up unconsciously in much bigger dramas that have to do with the difficulties sharing your life, your joys, your pains, your interests and your pleasures with other people.

> A review of "The Battle of Bubble & Squeak," in Books for Your Children, Vol. 13, No. 4, Autumn, 1978, p. 9.

The successive stages in [the attitude of Alice Sparrow's son, Sid Parker, to the gerbils, Bubble and Squeak,]—enthusiasm, indifference, a fury of protectiveness, desperate misery—accompany and give point to each chapter of this small, significant domestic drama. There is enough colour and movement in the narrative, enough precise detail of sound, venue and personality, to hold the reader's attention. There is, though, much more. Alice Sparrow's reaction to the gerbils, a necessary guiding line for the plot, is also part of a silent, secret, continuing battle between this house-proud, inhibited woman and her warm-hearted second husband, who once kept white mice and whose sympathy with the children involves him in divided loyalties. This is no deep marital probe but a suggestion of family tensions as quiet and inexorable as the definition of parental roles in that memorable short story, **"In the Middle of the Night"**. Philippa Pearce has always written expandable books, direct and open in style, simple in plot, but with so much in them of wisdom and humour that they offer new insights at every reading. Her new story could be understood and greatly enjoyed by children as young as seven or eight, as the tale of a pair of gerbils and their disruption of the family life of the Parkers and Sparrows. But when one has said that, one has only just begun. (p. 3415)

> Margery Fisher, in a review of "The Battle of Bubble and Squeak," in her Growing Point, Vol. 17, No. 4, November, 1978, pp. 3414-15.

Except for **The Children of the House,** which is a special case, Philippa Pearce has not written a major novel for children for fifteen years. But a writer of her unmatched integrity can do nothing trivial, and even her slightest book has the Pearce fingerprints all over it. In this nice little tale . . . , she demonstrates the famous use of language. Each word is weighed, measured and then fitted into place with a craftsman's precision; nothing could be farther from the clichés and the second-best of much present-day writing, for children as for their elders. There is no cliché either of character or situation. The story works itself out in terms of people and their reactions to crisis and to one another.

This however is only the machinery. What matters is what it produces. The story of how the Parkers came to terms with their pets has warmth and tenderness and a little heartbreak. Above all it is the story of Mrs. Parker (now Mrs. Sparrow, for the children have a stepfather), not at all the conventional mother, who finds it hardest of all to love the gerbils and plays a key part in their salvation. Here in a little book is a big study.

> M. Crouch, in a review of "The Battle of Bubble and Squeak," in The Junior Bookshelf, Vol. 42, No. 6, December, 1978, p. 302.

**The Battle of Bubble and Squeak** is a children's book of the most superb and approachable quality. . . . The boy, his little sisters, his stepfather, their friends and neighbours are all so totally convincing, and, on the outside so very ordinary. We've all met people just like them but here we're not on the outside looking in we're taken really inside, we can identify with their misgivings, their failings as well as their virtues in a triumph of writing for children. . . .

[Both **The Battle of Bubble and Squeak** and David Henry Wilson's *The Fastest Gun Alive and Other Night Adventures*] represent everything that is good about the best in children's books. It is not just that they are well written, they are of course. It is that they capture a quality of observation and a caring for the feelings of childhood which at the same time respects the sensibilities of adults. Children do have to grow up into the adult world we know but we can still be thankful for writers like Philippa Pearce and David Henry Wilson who can cheer them on their way and perhaps stay with them long after childhood has passed.

> Anne Wood, in a review of "The Battle of Bubble and Squeak" and "The Fastest Gun Alive and Other Night Adventures," in Books for Your Children, Vol. 14, No. 1, Winter, 1978, p. 1.*

Page one indicates the quality of the book. The soft repetitions, creakings of the gerbils' wheel, the problem of the noise in the night attract and extend a young reader because of the writer's understanding, not because she wants to teach reading. . . . There are splendid, coaxing chapter-endings, funny or dramatic, notices to read in shop windows, jokes and lively domestic situations. Most remarkably, the recognisable characterisation of parents and children extends to cat and gerbils too ('a gerbil rested one front paw as if to begin public-speaking'). Children lying on the carpet provide tunnels of clothing for gerbil race-tracks: a joyful piece of writing. . . . [This] book is needed in classrooms. (pp. 39-40)

> Dorothy Atkinson, in a review of "The Battle of Bubble and Squeak," in The School Librarian, Vol. 27, No. 1, March, 1979, pp. 39-40.

[**The Battle of Bubble and Squeak**] is about a family whose mother hates having pets in the house. Her oldest child Sid is given a couple of gerbils, and supported by the rest of the family, he insists on keeping them. Mrs. Sparrow tries her best and her worst to get rid of them—and fails; only after their dramatic escape from the jaws of an invading cat does she finally come to terms with the gerbils' presence. In the meantime everyone in the family has learned to put up with each other a bit more tolerantly. This, at least, is the top tune. Beneath it are played variations on the themes of family relationships, developing independence in children, the learning of social give-and-take, and the urgency of emotional desires and compulsions.

It's not hard to see resemblances between this story and the author's earlier novel *A Dog So Small*. . . . A boy's desire for a pet, his distress at not being allowed one, a family living on an ordinary housing estate, an act of emotional and psychological withdrawal, and a happy resolution with everyone's honor satisfied—these are common elements in both books. But there is nothing tired or repetitive in the treatment. On the contrary, **Bubble and Squeak** feels fresh, vigorous, and contemporary and places its emphasis differently—on social interactions rather than on one character's point of view and interior life. The book is primarily about living together.

What one enjoys at once, as with anything she writes, is Philippa Pearce's pellucid style. Someone, I forget who, called her the mistress of the short sentence. In a television interview with me recently, she told me how hard she works for that quality and how she loves getting the rhythms right—which means drafting and redrafting again and again and reading everything aloud at least three times as the work progresses. It is a skill she learned during her many years of working in radio for children. (pp. 229-30)

Another of the qualities that impresses me about this short book is the way the author opens up an adult's interior life for quite young readers. . . . Mrs. Sparrow is very nearly a central character, along with Sid—it's as much her story as his. She has remarried after the death of her first husband, who was the father of all the children.

Thus, another thread is added to the tale, giving it a richer texture. The delicate position that Bill Sparrow, the new husband, finds himself in as a kind of buffer between his wife and Sid; the way his sympathies are all on Sid's side, while his loyalties lie on his wife's; not to mention the danger of his intruding unasked and ham-fistedly into the battle between mother and son—are all beautifully suggested and handled. And because Bill is not the natural father and must behave circumspectly, Mrs. Sparrow feels all the more keenly her tussle with her family.

Philippa Pearce shows the strength of Mrs. Sparrow's aversion to animals, her hesitancy, her worry, and the inner struggle caused by a mother's instinct to please her children at odds with her natural temperament and fastidiousness. It would have been easier and more sensational—and the line most children's writers would have taken—to let Mrs. Sparrow be seen only in externals, an adult behaving selfishly against her children's entirely reasonable desire to keep pets.

The harder, more worthwhile, and truthful thing is to show why the adult behaves as she does and to gain sympathy and understanding for her without losing any of the young reader's preference for the child hero. The author does this with apparent ease and absorbs it all so completely into the story that at first one doesn't notice what she has achieved. (p. 230)

[We are] persuaded that in this story everyone matters, not just the hero or the other children. Adults have rights and three dimensions, too, and more in them than meets the eye. Most children's novels remind me of the father who told Paul Hazard, "the time will come when men will be oppressed by the children." But not this one. (pp. 231-32)

It is the contemplation of the narrative, the *why* of life, that this story is really about—not the *what*. Bravo to that. (p. 232)

[The author writes] carefully arranged variations on basic English orchestrated for tunefulness and elegance of line. No one does this better than Philippa Pearce, and she produces writing of precisely the kind she told me she is always striving for. What she wants, she said, is that the reader feel her writing is like an open window through which he can reach and touch what lies on the other side.

She carries that intention through into her plotting and structure. Each chapter is patterned so that we get another satisfying stage in the story and are led on in our understanding of the characters, and through story and characters, to a deepening appreciation of the thematic underlays. Elegant is indeed the modish critical word that comes at once to mind. If you wanted a handbook demonstration of how to arrange and handle narrative material in this dominant traditional manner, you couldn't find a better one than this.

The disadvantages are obvious. Life gets to seem all too neat and sequential. The characters are a mite too trim and explainable. The resolution is overly pat. There's plenty to think about, but the reader is given little room for maneuver within the text. And although the themes are subtly handled, they are finespun, their presence easily ignored. You can read this book without ever breaking through the surface—as no more than an amusing story about a kid who wins his fight to keep a couple of pets—something you cannot do with the story of *Tom's Midnight Garden.* . . . There the top tune leads you below the surface; otherwise you might soon find the book unsatisfying, which is why most of us would call it a more difficult and challenging novel. (pp. 232-33)

*The Battle of Bubble and Squeak* is exactly what it set out to be and is a fine example of that order of novel which begins by accepting children as they are—their likes and dislikes, their superficial preferences, and their predictable tastes—and then takes them on in literary terms by shifting the gears of their reading to match the participation demanded by a multifaceted story.

That's putting it far too pedagogically, and Philippa Pearce won't thank me, I think, for doing so. She doesn't set out to be a writer providing literary training courses for children. And, indeed, what I mainly want to do here is give straightforward expression to the pleasure I take in knowing that she and her books are there for all of us to enjoy. (p. 233)

*Aidan Chambers, "Letter from England: Reaching through a Window" in* The Horn Book Magazine, *Vol. LVII, No. 2, April, 1981, pp. 229-33.*

### THE WAY TO SATTIN SHORE   (1983)

In recent years Philippa Pearce's output has been slender by comparison with that of many writers, but she has never let her reputation down. *The Way to Sattin Shore* is her first full-length novel for more than 20 years. It is memorable; it has some splendid characters and finely evoked settings; it has atmosphere. It is not, I think, a total success.

Kate Tranter is the youngest of her family; it seems that her father died on the day of her birth. Picking up hints and puzzling over things observed, Kate tries to find out what happened to him; and as the story is unravelled the threads lead back to Sattin Shore, a desolate fringe of estuary where, 10 years ago, the tide welled up to cover the face of a man lying unconscious on the sand. The shadow of tragedy, of past hatreds and jealousies, falls on the present and is personified by Kate's grudging, watchful, almost sinister Granny.

The mystery from the past is complex, dark, and intricately plotted. The best things in the book are more cheerful, and are mostly independent of the story-line. Kate and her two brothers—direct, practical Lenny and almost grown-up Randall—are living, breathing people; so are dogged Mum and Lenny's inquisitive friend Brian. And there is Syrup the cat, weaving in and out of the story in cool pursuit of his own interests. . . . Philippa Pearce's sense of place is acute, and she has a vivid gift for catching the heightened moments of life: there is a chapter on tobogganing in which you can feel the bite of snow and the heady peril of downhill speed.

Kate is a child coping as best she can with situations that are too much for her. Though a good deal of the story is sombre and even melodramatic, there's a happy if farfetched ending for her and her family. Yet it seems to me that the strengths of *The Sattin Shore* lie in the way it conveys the flavour of life, the subtle and changing nature of human relationships. It does not gain from the intricacies of its plot. (pp. 41, 43)

*John Rowe Townsend, "Flavour of Life," in* The Times Educational Supplement, *No. 3509, September 30, 1983, pp. 41, 43.*

This new book hides in its lucid, direct narrative the same hints and implications of emotion and relationship which made that light-hearted family story, *The Battle of Bubble and Squeak*, outstanding in its kind. *The Way to Sattin Shore* has the virtues we have come to expect from Philippa Pearce—a finely wrought, smooth-running prose, characters realised to the full (even Syrup the family cat is an absolute, undeniable individual), a mystery illuminated bit by bit, an unobtrusive developing of emotion sparked off by action and of action resulting from emotion.

People matter in the book and so does place. The Tranter house and the village, the route to the wide estuary and its scattered dwellings, gradually reveal their secrets and become immediate and complex. Moments of relaxed fun and sudden explosions of pent-up anger, the bickering and unexpected kindness of brothers—these and many other threads are woven together in a classic tale for the young. (pp. 4150-51)

> *Margery Fisher, in a review of "The Way to Sattin Shore," in her* Growing Point, *Vol. 22, No. 4, November, 1983, pp. 4150-51.*

There can be no finer writer for children than Philippa Pearce. Latterly she seemed to have lost her true instinct for children's response though everything she touches is fine in a literary sense. Now with *The Way to Sattin Shore* . . . she has created a contemporary children's story that surpasses even *Tom's Midnight Garden*. . . . *The Way to Sattin Shore* cries out to be filmed—Philippa Pearce is a master both of the close-up and of the atmospheric location. Slowly and gently, deceptively quiet it starts with Kate Tranter coming home from school in the January dusk "Up three steps to the front door, and feel for the key on the string in her pocket. Unlock, and then in."—almost Dylan Thomas like in its detailed opening. . . . [Kate] doggedly tracks down the solution to a plot which no other writer could have handled with such brilliance. In other hands it would have been diminished to the point of cliché. Philippa Pearce's observation of character and ability to portray feelings—even those of the true murderer—invest it with truth.

> *Anne Wood, in a review of "The Way to Sattin Shore," in* Books for Your Children, *Vol. 18, No. 3, Autumn-Winter 1983, p. 28.*

Here is a literary event. Philippa Pearce has always been one of those rare writers who write only when they have something significant to say. She has not published a major novel since *A Dog So Small* in 1962, and the book now to hand must surely be regarded as her best since *Tom's Midnight Garden* in 1958. This then is a matter for much rejoicing. . . .

[The plot] is not . . . of the first importance. Miss Pearce is not the best plot-maker in the world. But she is, at her best, a writer without equal among the children's authors of this country. Her understanding of the human heart and of the human condition is profound, yet her drawing of characters like Kate and her brother Ran, however true, is not what lifts her into a class all her own. That is achieved by her mastery of language. With the simplest of means—without, for example, the verbal gymnastics of William Mayne or Leon Garfield—she gives life to her theme, her setting and her characters by using words as if she has just discovered them, with a freshness and a strength which springs from her deep respect for the medium she uses, as much as from her command of it. She is outstandingly the writer's writer, but she is the reader's writer too, and there is wealth in this tender and mysterious tale for the reader, child and adult, to discover. A very good

book indeed, a trifle slow, perhaps, in the early stages, but with growing momentum and a fine sense of timing in its build-up to a moving climax.

> *M. Crouch, in a review of "The Way to Sattin Shore," in* The Junior Bookshelf, *Vol. 48, No. 1, February, 1984, p. 36.*

[Philippa Pearce] is well-known in America (especially for *Tom's Midnight Garden*) and for good reason; she turns a neat sentence and her characters are memorable. [In *The Way to Sattin Shore*] it is only the plotting which brings on the problems. . . .

The unravelling of [the plot] requires much suspension of disbelief on the reader's part. The characters, early drawn so convincingly, must twist unnaturally to fulfill the plot's demands, and a number of improbabilities scar the conclusion. Still, Kate remains an appealing heroine; any young reader who has ever felt lonely, and shut out from the concerns of the adults in his life, will identify with her strongly. And Kate's lessons in friendship with classmate Anna, plus a charming chapter on sledding, let us believe whole-heartedly in the parts of her life that go forward outside the troublesome plot-line.

> *Natalie Babbitt, "Writings of Passage: The Young and the Restless," in* Book World—The Washington Post, *May 13, 1984, p. 18.\**

[Artistic], intuitive writers have always tried to present in terms comprehensible to children both the tragedy and the exaltation of life. Now, in a long-awaited major novel such a writer has fashioned an ingeniously plotted story of secrecy and suspense and has told it with limpid clarity.

Unobtrusively, with disarming simplicity, Philippa Pearce leads the reader into the book. (p. 316)

The clear, almost chastened prose allows room for many suggestive details—to be absorbed by the reader and recalled later on. Indigenous to the story are the settings; for as the action moves from the house in the town to the tiny village of Sattin and its deserted estuary shore—the scenes of both the dramatic background events and the stunning climax of the book—vivid graphic images incise themselves on the mind. All the characters are vital, their significance perhaps dimly perceived at first but fully recognized in the final clarification of the plot. Powerful rather than grim, the story has its moments of exhilaration and good-humored relief. But most important of all, Kate's fear, anger, resentment, longing, and love are echoed in the passionate feelings of her brothers and of the grownups: child, adolescents, and adults all caught up in a storm of circumstances and emotions in a rare example of contemporary fiction for children. (pp. 316-17)

> *Ethel L. Heins, in a review of "The Way to Sattin Shore," in* The Horn Book Magazine, *Vol. LX, No. 3, June, 1984, pp. 316-17.*

# Dr. Seuss

## 1904-

(Pseudonym of Theodor Seuss Geisel; has also written as Theo. LeSieg and Rosetta Stone) American author/illustrator and author of picture books.

Seuss is perhaps the most popular and well-known American creator of books for younger children. Considered a literary institution, he has been writing and illustrating picture books for nearly fifty years; many of his works feature characters now accepted as part of contemporary folklore, such as the Cat in the Hat, the Grinch who stole Christmas, Horton the faithful elephant, and Bartholomew Cubbins. Seuss is recognized for his originality, inventiveness, diversity, humor, and lack of inhibition; he is also credited with initiating a new type of children's literature—pleasure reading for beginning and reluctant readers. Seuss is regarded as a truly childlike author, one who distinguishes himself by his innate understanding of children and genuine respect for their individuality and imagination.

Beginning most of his books with simple ideas, Seuss builds them into fabulous concepts through repetition, suspense, and surprise. He combines words and pictures to fashion a series of complex situations which border on the lunatic but retain an integral logic. Writing in a variety of forms ranging from allegories and cautionary tales to folktales and pure fantasies, Seuss often narrates his works in rhythmic verse which includes many examples of wordplay and word invention.

Seuss usually uses line drawings and vivid primary colors to create illustrations which match the absurdity of his texts. Capitalizing on his lack of training, he often depicts preposterous creatures endowed with curious physical attributes in a natural style considered both suitable for and appealing to his young audience. Several of Seuss's books, such as *On Beyond Zebra* and *Hop on Pop*, extend the meaning of the texts through visual clues which help young readers to decipher word meanings.

Even at his most extravagant, Seuss invests his works with positive values. Many of his books contain veiled moral statements which balance the zaniness of his characters and situations. Concerned thematically with creativity, tenacity, loyalty, and self-confidence, Seuss also treats political and social issues such as racial and religious prejudice, conservation, and the nuclear arms race. Seuss usually leaves his readers with a lighthearted optimism. In *The Cat in the Hat* and *Green Eggs and Ham*, for example, he pushes the limits of good behavior and common sense, permits the chaotic consequences, then careens back to a safe and familiar world. His recent satire on the possibility of nuclear war, *The Butter Battle Book*, deviates from this approach. A thinly disguised portrayal of the United States and Russia, the work presents readers with an open ending: two characters from opposing countries stand poised on a dividing wall, each figure holding a bomb. Seuss has said that the ending of *The Butter Battle Book* is up to the adults of the world, a philosophy which has generated much controversy but has not affected the book's popularity.

Originally intending to become a teacher of English literature and a novelist, Seuss combined his scholarship with an affec-

tion for animals and drawing cartoons. As editor of the Dartmouth College humor magazine, *Jack-o'-Lantern*, he gave regular space to his drawings of eccentric animals. Seuss attended Oxford University and other European institutions, but abandoned his doctoral studies to become a full-time cartoonist. He returned to the United States to work as a freelance humorist for several major magazines. One of his cartoons won him a contract with Standard Oil to create the ads for Flit, an insect spray; Seuss's slogan, "Quick, Henry, the Flit!" became an advertising classic and prompted the consistent use of humor in ads. Seuss's contract prohibited all outside writing except children's books, a loophole which led to his first book, *And to Think That I Saw It on Mulberry Street*. Written in verse inspired by the rhythm of the ship's engines on a return voyage from Europe, *Mulberry Street* introduces Seuss's fascination with the potential of the child's imagination and is often regarded as his best work. The immediate success of *Mulberry Street* and such books as *The Five Hundred Hats of Bartholomew Cubbins* and *Horton Hatches the Egg* catapulted Seuss to fame under the pseudonym he formed from his middle name and the doctorate he stopped pursuing when he became a cartoonist.

During World War II, Seuss moved to Hollywood to write and design training films for the Information and Education Division of the U.S. Army. He received the Legion of Merit award for his work as well as an Academy Award for his documentary, "Hitler Lives." Two later films also won Academy Awards—"Design for Death," a documentary on Japan, and "Gerald McBoing-Boing," an animated cartoon. Seuss later admitted, "I learned more about children's books when I worked in Hollywood than anywhere else, for in films everything is based on coordination between pictures and words." Seuss also worked briefly in Japan as a correspondent for *Life* magazine during the Occupation, an experience he reflects in *Horton Hears a Who!*.

At the height of the "Why Johnny Can't Read" educational furor of the mid-1950s, author John Hersey published an article in *Life* magazine objecting to the exclusive use of unimaginative "Dick-and-Jane" primers in schools; he suggested that fanciful writers like Seuss be recruited to create more stimulating controlled vocabulary books. Responding to Hersey's challenge, Seuss published *The Cat in the Hat* in 1957. *The Cat in the Hat* is generally regarded as a revolutionary work for demonstrating that books for beginning readers can entertain children as well as teach them to read. Because of its success, Seuss founded Beginner Books, a publishing company that was later acquired by Random House with the author as its president. Seuss continued to publish books for the fledgling reader; by the late 1960s he was writing and illustrating "Bright and Early Books for Beginning Readers," a series for preschoolers which includes a more reduced vocabulary and Seuss's characteristically frantic, phonetic, and repetitive wordplay. Although Seuss eventually relaxed the rules for restricted vocabulary, his supplementary books consistently emphasize the importance of simple language and sentence structure as well as subject matter appropriate for very young readers.

Critics admire Seuss's works for their remarkable ingenuity as well as for their excellent integration of text and illustration. Praised as an outstanding nonsense poet and storyteller whose books are ideal for reading aloud, he is also considered a natural moralist who offers children a positive and enthusiastic view of life. Some observers see Seuss's involvement with beginning readers as limiting his creativity; others disapprove of his unconventional English and unschooled art. The preponderance of reviewers, however, esteem Seuss as an imaginative genius whose oeuvre has captivated readers for over two generations.

Three of Seuss's works have been chosen as Caldecott Honor Books—*McElligot's Pool* in 1948, *Bartholomew and the Oobleck* in 1950, and *If I Ran the Zoo* in 1951; he also received the Lewis Carroll Shelf Award for *Horton Hatches the Egg* in 1958 as well as for *And to Think That I Saw It on Mulberry Street* in 1961. Presented with the Laura Ingalls Wilder Award in 1980 and the Regina Medal in 1982, he also received a special Pulitzer Prize citation in 1984.

(See also *Children's Literature Review*, Vol. 1 [as Theodor Seuss Geisel]; *Something about the Author*, Vols. 1, 18; *Contemporary Authors New Revision Series*, Vol. 13; and *Contemporary Authors*, Vols. 13-16, rev. ed.)

---

### AUTHOR'S COMMENTARY

*[In the following excerpt, Peter Bunzel interviews Seuss, who comments on his drawing style, his imagination, and his writing habits.]*

"My animals look the way they do because I can't draw," explains Theodor Seuss Geisel, a man far better known as Dr. Seuss. But because his drawing and imagination are so outlandish, the weird menagerie of potbellied, strangely named creatures . . . has put Geisel in a class by himself as the creator of children's books and of a wacky world.

Geisel has been misdrawing animals since his childhood. . . . (p. 107)

"My animals all have a way of looking somewhat drunk." (p. 108)

"I've loved animals for as long as I can remember. The first thing I do when I'm traveling is to visit the nearest zoo. It's a wonder that after all the animals I've seen, I can't make them true to life. When I do an elephant the poor beast usually winds up not only with too many joints in his legs but with too many legs." (p. 110)

If you should ask Ted Geisel how he ever thought up an animal called a Bippo-no-Bungus from the wilds of Hippo-no-Hungus or a tizzle-topped Tufted Mazurka from the African island of Yerka, his answer would be disarmingly to the point: "Why, I've been to most of these places myself so the names are from memory. As for the animals, I have a special dictionary which gives most of them, and I just look up the spellings." Helen Geisel, Ted's chief editor, chief critic, business manager and wife, has another explanation. "His mind," she says of Ted, "has never grown up."

Mrs. Geisel goes on: "Ted doesn't sit down and write for children. He writes to amuse himself. Luckily what amuses him also amuses them." Her husband emphatically agrees. "Ninety percent of failures in children's books," says he, speaking with the authority of 16 successes, "come from writing to preconceptions of what kids like. When I'm writing a book I do it to please Helen and me. But when it finally comes out I take one look and think 'Oh, my God!'"

Most of Geisel's books point a moral, though he insists he never starts with one. "Kids," he says, "can see a moral coming a mile off and they gag at it. But there's an inherent moral in any story." *Horton Hatches the Egg* whose theme is *I meant what I said and I said what I meant, an elephant's faithful, one hundred percent!*, teaches dedication. Despotism gets the works in *Yertle the Turtle*, while *McElligot's Pool* extols unity in nature.

For every book completed, Geisel throws out enough material to fill 35 others. Each book takes about 18 months to write because Geisel, a meticulous craftsman, runs into log jams that last for days. The problem may be a single line or even a word. Stuck in this situation, Geisel will pace the studio floor or throw himself on a bed where he thrashes convulsively, "Every once in a while it comes easily," says he. "Sometimes a lovely flow of words will carry me four whole lines." His troubles and intensity arise chiefly from his high regard for children who, he says, "have as much right to quality as their elders," or, in the immortal words of Horton the Elephant, "a person's a person no matter how small."

All Dr. Seuss's books . . . proceed from the simple premise that children will believe a ludicrous situation if pursued with relentless logic. "If I start with a two-headed animal I must never waver from that concept. There must be two hats in the closet, two toothbrushes in the bathroom and two sets of spectacles on the night table. Then my readers will accept the poor fellow without hesitation and so will I." . . .

[The] postman brings him testimonials from a legion of vicarious offspring, his real-life fans. "Dr. Seuss has an imagination with a big long tail," said one child. ("That fellow will go places," says Geisel.) A 9-year-old wrote, "It's the funniest book I ever read in nine years." But the accolade Geisel cherishes above all is a single word set down in a childish hand, "Whew!" (p. 113)

Peter Bunzel, "Wacky World of Dr. Seuss," in Life Magazine, Vol. 46, No. 14, April 6, 1959, pp. 107-08, 110, 113.

## GENERAL COMMENTARY

### LORRENE LOVE ORT

[Though] this son of a zoo-keeping father *should* be able from his youthful associations to draw *reasonably real* animals, he doesn't draw *reasonably real* animals—not at all, and the reasonable answer to all this is . . . —he can't! Whenever artist Seuss commences to draw a *reasonably real* horse, or moose, or elephant, these uncooperative beasts somehow end up on his titillated drawing board all out of kilter and laughing hilariously at their amazed creator who tried his pencil-chewing best to make them look *reasonably real.* (pp. 135-36)

He capitalizes on what he considers to be his artistic and graphic deficiencies, and then he proceeds to create worlds of wonder, delight, and true merriment for all children from six to sixty. . . . (p. 136)

The "deficiencies" that Dr. Seuss considers to be his are certainly compensated (if, indeed, they exist at all!) by clean and virile color, simplicity and strength of line, a vibrant rhythm of composition, a wonderful and versatile ability to suggest action, daring, and emotion, and his own special wherewithal to capture graphically the imaginative flight of a true teller of tales. Although much of his art form suggests cartoon work, his is a variety that teases and stretches the imagination much further than most current cartooning attempts to do.

As one aspect of this author's graphic work, consider the matter of movement. Dr. Seuss secures much story momentum through illustration, and particularly is this so in books that have a reviewing-stand and dress-parade nature, such as: *The 500 Hats of Bartholomew Cubbins* (somewhat), *McElligot's Pool, And To Think That I Saw It On Mulberry Street, If I Ran The Zoo, Thidwick The Big Hearted Moose* (to some degree), and *Scrambled Eggs Super.* In these stories swiftness of motion depends largely on a rapid succession and addition of things—a sequence of incredible and incessant hats, a finny review of the sea's saltier characters, a colossal parade of animal-drawn vehicles, an introduction to the eye-popping members of swaggering Gerald McGrew's new zoo, a miscellaneous assortment of some persistent and parasitic guests, and a pilfering peek at a clutch of mighty good eggs that get cleverly "fowled" in the drawing! In most of the other tales, and in parts of some of the afore-mentioned, the plot seems to take the dominant lead in setting the pace and the environment in which the illustrative material operates, but in all Seuss publications there is a splendid unification in the total format of text, type, illustration, placement, and an over-all just-rightness which is certainly laudatory, if the spontaneous acclaim given by children to all Seuss tales is any gauge of merit.

Secure suspense is another necessary ingredient which Seuss champions with his brush. If, for example, Seuss baits his young audience with the lip-pursing drama of danger, he also adds a saucy feather of fun to his illustrations to serve as a sure and satisfying leaven of levity. (pp. 136-37)

[Horton and Thidwick] know a thing or two about dangerous living, and it is this noble and generous twosome who, on different occasions, face the terrors of a firing squad and manage to survive quite nicely! Horton's portly but heroic self is well suited to illustrations representing secure suspense, for it is quite apparent from the very beginning of the tale (*Horton Hatches the Egg*) that if Horton can be drawn withstanding as many different temperatures as a U. S. postal carrier in order to protect one mere Mayzie Bird egg he can *and will weather a threatening* storm of ballistic adversity and do it all with folded arms and a stoic countenance. Thidwick, on the other hand, is aided and abetted by both nature and Dr. Seuss in his once-in-a-lifetime escape from a fate worse than that of a Bingle Bug, but even when Thidwick is portrayed (and almost betrayed) while facing five exuberant hunters there is certainly enough of Thidwick & Co. to withstand falling rocks and sighting snipers. Here the text also comes to the rescue with these suggestive lines concerning the big-hearted and well-stocked moose:

> He gasped! He felt faint! And the whole
> world grew fuzzy!
> Thidwick was finished, completely. . . .
> . . . or WAS he. . .?

Suspense? Yes, but *secure* suspense.

Seuss also brings to his pages of illustration a subtle but gentle brush sense of satire. Consider well the hoydenish Wickershams, the perplexed and concerned Twiddler Owls, the nonchalant and totally fly-by-night Mayzie Bird, and the dour and doubting farmer of McElligot's Pool.

Sometimes the use of color in Seuss's illustrations takes on a new dimension, also. Green, for example, has come to have a new and very special meaning for at least one group of young children. "Oobleck! Oobleck!" they piped and chortled to a perplexed cook in the school cafeteria when she served them small mounds of steaming green peas! (p. 137)

Often there is a quiet and knowing touch of sensitivity, too, as well as the always abundant and rollicking sense of humor which spills exuberantly over most of the pages. This dimension for beauty is expressed very charmingly in the illustration of the Kwigger in *Scrambled Eggs Super,* and many little children think Dr. Seuss did a lovely bit of piscatorial painting in the picture of the fish that likes flowers in *McElligot's Pool.*

But the important thing about Seuss's paintings is that they so happily reflect the text—or the text so beautifully expresses the illustrations—that the total effect is a little like an old riddle, for surely Dr. Seuss has achieved a "which came first?" type of fine unity and blending.

For children there is, indeed, another vital view-point concerning the artistic talents of Dr. Seuss. As one second-grader happily pointed out, "Why, he draws just like ME!" Many a reluctant child who has been fearful of expressing himself either graphically or verbally has been so "taken in" by Seuss's casual charm and random and joyous sampling of form, words, and color that he finds himself daring to sample these media for himself. Part of this inspired confidence seems to be in the fact that there is never—in the magical land of Seuss—a talking down to the young reader either in words or through the art form, but, rather, both seem to have that generous hospitality that genuinely invites the reader and/or listener to "come on in and just make yourself at home and, above all, enjoy yourself!'', and this they most certainly do.

Sincere graciousness and hospitality which the Seuss stories represent are arts which, unfortunately, are not perfected over night, nor is a writer's grace and skill. . . . To achieve the smoothness of the finished product which the Mulberry Street story finally represented when sent to the publishers took almost one year of work—or ''sweat,'' as Seuss is wont to refer to it. One year for thirty pages! Nearly every line of Seuss print is worked and re-worked sixteen or seventeen times like a pliable lump of dough until at last it emerges all smooth and satiny, and then it's ready. But, though the process is painstakingly done, Seuss is as steadfast to his tale-telling as willing Horton was to his egg-hatching—and with results just as delightful and amazing. (p. 138)

Sound! It's a tantalizing trickster when Seuss manipulates it. It's as if the words so neatly pinned down to the pages by clean, clear type were just on tip-toe with excitement to be turned loose by being read aloud, for it's the reading, the showing, the sharing and all that makes the Seuss books ''shine.''

The shine that glimmers on all sorts of young faces when a Seuss tale is shared reflects a personality that knows and understands the intricacies and delights of childhood. Here is an author whose full-blown fling with fantasy has veered sharply away from the pudding-sweet, ''dear child'' tales and has produced instead some exceptionally fine ''honest injun'' and mirth-tickling stories that bring into a front-and-center focus the scuff-toed young male of our society in all his fishin' pole and day-dreaming glory. (pp. 140-41)

Into the woof and weft of several of the stories come nudging little thoughts that do a bit of mental nibbling and provide a germ or so of wisdom on which to contemplate. It is often the kindly and considerate Horton who voices these sentiments, and in *Horton Hears a Who!* the kindly pachyderm reiterates time and again this humane belief: ''A person's a person, no matter how small.''

In *Horton Hatches the Egg* the elephant dares to brave all manner of danger in order to fulfill his commitment with a bird and an egg, and this he does by reminding himself at constant intervals of his own staunch credo:

> I meant what I said
> And I said what I meant. . . .
> An elephant's faithful
> One hundred per cent!

In *Bartholomew and the Oobleck* the Kingdom of Didd is saved from becoming totally submerged in a sea of sticky green ''oobleck'' . . . when Bartholomew prevails upon proud King Derwin to admit that he is truly sorry for wishing that a new weather element might be added to the tried-and-true everyday varieties.

Even put-upon Thidwick, though he had five hundred pounds of reason to doubt it, staunchly maintains throughout his saga that ''. . . a host, above all, must be nice to his guests.''

True, the small nudges are there, but the tales supporting them are always wonderfully and deliciously funny. It's the light touch and the frivolous plights of the ridiculous characters that keep small nudges from becoming musty morals.

Anyone knows what the proof of a good pudding is, and in Dr. Seuss's case his ''puddings'' have certainly been ''plum'' good. Read aloud a Seuss book *once* to a young audience and there is a well-eared and big-eyed quiet, but read the book through *twice* and the audience will have disappeared! The second-time-'round everybody gets into the act and recites the yarn in snatches or by the yard! (p. 142)

> *Lorrene Love Ort, ''Theodore Seuss Geisel—The Children's Dr. Seuss,'' in* Elementary English, *Vol. XXXII, No. 3, March, 1955, pp. 135-42.*

### DAVID C. DAVIS

When reputable authors, who normally keep in balance the elements of integrity, originality, and plausibility, and who have a long record of healthy books to their credit, slip, it is disheartening. And unfortunately, the matter doesn't always end with one slipshod story being published. More often, that one story becomes a Typhoid Mary and unwittingly spreads the killer germ.

The backsliding that Theodor Geisel experienced when he began his romance with restricted vocabulary illustrates an interesting point. Dr. Seuss is a great humorist, and those who know him as such can forgive him for his minor errors (if he keeps them minor); but it is up to him to determine whether future historians of children's literature will credit him with being a children's humorist or an easy-to-read opportunist. (p. 269)

> *David C. Davis, ''Who'll Kill the Mockingbirds?'' in* The Horn Book Magazine, *Vol. XXXIX, No. 3, June, 1963, pp. 265-71.**

### J. H. DOHM

There is no doubt that Dr. Seuss, whose books have recently been introduced into England, is the favourite author of American children today. There is some doubt about why and whether books should be so enthusiastically received, though the why is not altogether mysterious—the books make an immediate impact, have an easy-to-recognise style and an author with an easy-to-remember name. (p. 323)

[The books] have a tall tale flavour as each idea tries to overtop the one before, a facile sort of knock-about word play and occasional moments of triumph which seem simple when analysed but make even his more reluctant admirers say, ''Who but Dr. Seuss would have thought of that?''

There is much in the books to make some of us reluctant, for most of the pictures are downright ugly and the texts are often tiresome and sometimes vulgar, yet in a country where children's books are fairly critically reviewed they are sure of a glowing critical reception and immense sales. An effect of wild activity is achieved partly by the pictures which are drawn with tremendous assurance and verve, endless variations on several species, most having wisps of hair sprouting on their heads, long lashed eyes, either wobbly cotton-filled legs and necks or none at all and horribly inebriated grins or scowls. The rest is achieved by the text, especially in the books with their tum-tati-tum ''Night before Christmas'' rhythm, colloquial speech and constant exclamatory remarks. (p. 324)

[*And to think that I saw it on Mulberry Street*] is now considered his best work by many librarians, who may feel ill at ease about some of his later work. It is an unpretentious affair with an appealing moral. . . . Next came *The 500 Hats of Bartholomew Cubbins*, one of three books in prose about kings and castles, not a very characteristic background though it was soon filled with Seuss ingredients, a steadfast persecuted hero and the inexplicable multiplication of increasingly magnificent hats with someone by to keep a tally. After a second prose tale came the most general favourite, **Horton Hatches the Egg,** and when **McElligott's Pool** appeared in 1949, all the Seuss specialities had been presented: everything since has been an elaboration or simplification of the same themes. The first Horton book is probably the best of his moralities, with the simple-minded, single-minded elephant staying on the bird's nest he has promised to tend, refusing to desert it despite ridicule, capture, seasickness and publicity, and being rewarded in a grand finale when the fledgling hatches "with ears and a tail and a trunk just like his." **McElligott's Pool** provided the first opportunity to give full play to a gift for inventing fabulous monsters with attributes to match.

Although these books and their successors were well received their sales first began to soar and the creator's name became a household word in 1957, when he wrote **The Cat in the Hat.** . . . Few attempts had then been made to present primary material in non-text book form but the demand had been growing for years and the Cat appeared at the very best moment. It was the first of many books in the Beginner Books series. . . . [None] of the newer titles rivals the first for popularity. It may not seem remarkable to some adults, but it is not surprising that children find it so when it is compared with the typical "school readers" used by primary classes in America. Set beside them, **The Cat in the Hat** seems a miracle of action and wit. . . . After the inanities of all the primers about Dicks and Susans and Babies, the Cat comes as a revelation: the first intimation to many children that books actually tell *stories* and that they themselves can read and enjoy reading. And after seeing children of so many types light up over that hideous cat, it is impossible to feel that Dr. Seuss is simply a mistake. False claims are made in the back of the book, where the publishers not only state that there is no need to read to children, once they have discovered the cat, but add that this is "as lively and amusing a book as the best that has ever been read to them," an ignorant and arrogant remark.

But although better books may be produced in this field, it was Dr. Seuss who made the first major breakthrough and whose name will probably continue to mean most to the children. He may not fancy the notion that this might prove his chief claim to immortality, but he continues to write for the series. . . . (pp. 324-26)

[It] would be interesting, if irritating, to see what a psychologist would make out of the Seuss books, especially those with morals. The morals are unexceptionable in themselves, although like so many they seem heavy-handed at times and likely to backfire. In **Horton Hears a Who** when the elephant guards a speck of dust because he is sure it is a world full of tiny beings and says "A person's a person no matter how small," the crowd-followers amongst the readers are sure to notice that it is the animals in the unsympathetic crowd who jeer at Horton and who have a good time and no troubles and plenty of company easily gained. Others may well object that when "the whole world was saved by the Smallest of All" it was only because the Smallest was found malingering and coerced into adding the last iota of sound which all the other Whos had already been making so that the animals could hear them and admit their existence on the dust-speck. There are even more doubts about the title piece in **The Sneetches,** which also contains the most unpropitious start of any juvenile now in print: "Now the Star-Belly Sneetches / Had bellies with stars / The Plain-Belly Sneetches / Had none upon thars"— *can* anything worse be brought forward? The tricky monkey, the image of the cat in the hat, may be seen by some as the

hero of the piece since he plays on the snobbishness of the two factions and gets all their money by adding and subtracting stars in turn until the impoverished Sneetches realise snobbishness is silly, something few children will believe, as snobbishness is one of the hallmarks of immaturity.

Perhaps the books without morals would provide even more grist for a psychologist's mill. They *could* represent a retreat from reality, though I don't believe it for a moment, and it is true that both the people and the "people, sort-of" in the Seuss books are often displayed as very foolish, fallible, unlovable and unattractive, but it seems that the artist's facility in doodling odd shapes and playing about with sounds and words combine to make and label new creatures all the time without reference to his feelings about life or his book of the moment. . . . [He] obviously delights in using actual words in a new context mixed with nonsense words, thinking up things like "The Chippendale Mupp in the Valley of Vail." Some of the names are clumsy and obvious (Gertrude McFuzz, Ziffer-Zoof seeds), but this word play proves useful in the little primary books: "In yellow socks / I box my Gox / I box in yellow / Gox box socks."

Trivial perhaps, but a welcome change from "See funny, funny Baby," and the picture books often seem just as welcome a discovery to adult readers-aloud, who all too frequently know of only two kinds of books for chilren—the run-of-the-mill series typified by the Bobbsey Twins and the standard classics which are usually presented too soon and without enthusiasm. It seems likely that the most ardent Seuss supporters in America are the fathers who have already tried the picture books which offer little beyond a mood or arty pictures, or mild little tales about shopping with mother or dragons who turn out to be friendly. Suddenly they find books they feel a man can read aloud with gusto. . . . They seem to relish the gratuitous ugliness of the pictures, the phrases like "It sure was a terrible place that he hid it . . . Cage the big dope . . . Here is a Hoodwink who winks in his winkhood / without a good winkhood / a Hoodwink can't wink good . . . Then that Voom / it went VOOM! / And, oh boy! / What a Voom!" and the idea that the twenty-three sons of Mrs. McCave might have had names like Snimm, Stinky and Putt-Putt instead of all being called Dave strikes them as richly comic.

To those who have their doubts about all this, it is reassuring to find that, unlike most authors known for their popularity with the uncritical, Dr. Seuss does not seem to render any of his readers less able and willing to tackle something more demanding. It is also reassuring to think how unlikely it is that anyone else will ever have to make Seuss-like books: there have been remarkably few imitations and it would seem that he has made the field his own. To some of us, one seems quite enough, but it is unfashionable to decry him, and I do not remember ever seeing any adverse criticism of his work. No wonder, for it is singularly difficult to assess. It is easy to see why comic books or the Disneys, with their hack work by anonymous hands flat on the pages, or the enervating Blytons or the ridiculous Hardy Boys fall below the average library standard. But Dr. Seuss refuses to be placed below the line, Sneetches and all: there is something alive and kicking here that the others lack, something that won't be defined or denied either. Misgivings may be justified or simply another indication of the over-ladylike influence pervading most libraries; in any case the books are generally purchased in quantity. How they will do in England is impossible to predict: to those unsure of his merits it is rather like seeing a jolly uncle through the eyes of a new friend whose judgment is valued. Suddenly he seems just an advertising man, a commercial artist with a knack of raising a quick laugh with his buffoonery. Compared with Lear and Carroll he seems madly common, slick, unmemorable, and yet Lear seems no better to some people—might the good doctor prove the all-American Lear? Perhaps his brashness, the very consistency of his singular world give a helpful jolt to those who would otherwise miss (or dismiss) even the Lears and Carrolls as sheer nonsense, something to be outgrown. (pp. 327-29)

> *J. H. Dohm, "The Curious Case of Dr. Seuss," in* The Junior Bookshelf, *Vol. 27, No. 6, December, 1963, pp. 323-29.*

## PHYLLIS COHEN

[*Peter Rabbit*] is easy enough for a little one to follow, but it certainly excites the imagination and expands his horizons to include even such phrases as "implored him to exert himself." There is humor and excitement and even justice. . . .

In a completely different vein we have **Horton Hatches the Egg.** Dr. Seuss' very funny book has enthralled children for a completely different reason. The incongruity of an immense elephant hatching an egg on a tiny sapling tickles the funny bone. And the steady cumulation of incident, each one more emotional than the previous one, builds to the ridiculous, but satisfying and rightful ending. The implied meaning, "It takes more than laying an egg to be a 'mother,'" pleases the parents as well as the children. Yet, this is not a "preachy" book. Though the difficulties of fulfilling a trust are not sloughed off, and Dr. Seuss appeals to and re-inforces the child's sense of fair play and justice, the humor saves the book from being a 19th century sermon.

Both of the previous books were written to entertain. But a whole new field of books, with limited vocabularies, was opened up, and a great many books are written with the primary purpose being to use as few words as possible, and so give the beginning reader a sense of accomplishment as he reads a complete book. . . .

A typical example of the majority of these controlled vocabulary books is Dr. Seuss' **One Fish, Two Fish, Red Fish, Blue Fish.** How the man who could write **And To Think That I Saw It on Mulberry Street** and **The 500 Hats of Bartholomew Cubbins** could do this, surpasseth understanding. As an introduction to poetry or art, it is more likely to kill a child's aesthetic development than aid it. There is no unity in the book, and the nonsense which was spontaneous, joyful and imaginative in his previous books is forced, stilted, and tiresome here. A child will remember Horton the Elephant all his life, but will a Nook with a hook cook book provide anything except an exercise in phonics? There is no emotional experience at all anywhere in the entire 64 pages. The one image which had possibilities is not developed at all. In fact it is murdered. Sheep, sleepwalking, "By the light of the moon, by the light of a star, they walked all night from near to far. I would never walk. I would take a car." Why do we waste children's precious time (childhood is very short!) with this kind of thing? Is the "sense of accomplishment" so much more important than every other sense and sensibility? Is the feeling of accomplishment lessened very much by the child having to ask for help with a few words?

> *Phyllis Cohen, "Complexity in Simplicity," in* Young Readers Review, *Vol. I, No. 6, February, 1965, p. 12.**

## DOROTHY M. BRODERICK

Best known of the more recent books in the field of easy reading is **Cat in the Hat** by Dr. Seuss. We can all be grateful that a man of Dr. Seuss's genius was willing to turn his hand to working with a controlled vocabulary and thus demonstrate in a dramatic way that it was possible to use few words to create real books. . . . Dr. Seuss proved with subsequent titles such as **Cat in the Hat Comes Back** and an easier volume, **Hop on Pop,** that he had mastered the technique of vocabulary control with the same degree of competency with which he had earlier mastered the absurd fantasies of the child's world. To be able to combine the two competencies as Dr. Seuss does is a talent not found in any other writer of our time. (p. 122)

> *Dorothy M. Broderick, "Easy Reading," in her* An Introduction to Children's Work in Public Libraries, *The H. W. Wilson Company, 1965, pp. 118-28.**

## BARBARA BADER

Piper, prophet, magician, priest—these are the words for Dr. Seuss; and for Geisel, entertainer-in-chief.

Self-portrayed as an upstart, an interloper, Geisel was, rather, a welcome recruit. On the one hand "the timid and oversentimentalized American approach"—Margaret Wise Brown's charge—was coming into question, on the other the popularity of the comics and especially, since their introduction in 1933, of comic books, drew attention to possible substitutes. (p. 302)

Obviously, [Marco's] father cannot be entrusted with Marco's latest tall tale [in **And to Think That I Saw It on Mulberry Street**], and so it remains a secret between Dr. Seuss and his audience "How"—to quote the jacket—"a plain horse and wagon on Mulberry Street / Grows into a story that no one can beat." Call it a conspiracy against adulthood, maybe, but not a lesson . . . or, conversely, an instance of being forced to lie. . . . Geisel and his spokesmen have steadfastly disclaimed any moral or psychological 'message' . . . and, just as consistently, he has been interpreted and reinterpreted, accused of purveying candy-coated medicine or, alternatively, wormy apples. My hunch is that, in common with children, he is a natural moralizer; that it comes to him as unselfconsciously (and unambiguously) as rhyming lines from an engine's beat.

*Seuss entertains first- and second-graders at La Jolla Country Day School in La Jolla, California. John Bryson, Life Magazine © 1959 Time Inc.*

*The 500 Hats of Bartholomew Cubbins* is hors de combat—folkloric fantasy of a spoofing sort with a happy open end. (pp. 303-04)

*The 500 Hats* had a plucky young hero who fancies his red hat for its upstanding feather and faces even the executioner with aplomb. . . ; it has straight-faced ceremonial nonsense and, as a foil, a convincingly obnoxious brat; and it has a clipped, loaded text set precisely to pictures. Indeed, the very notion is visual and ideally suited to a two-color treatment—by all appearances, conceived in terms of it. Against the black, white and gray of the cartoons (done in tone, not line), the red hats have, rightly, a life of their own.

So, in *Bartholomew and the Oobleck*. . . , has the sticky green stuff, the oobleck, that King Derwin, bored with ordinary rain, fog, sunshine and snow, prompts his magicians to bring down from the sky. First a vaporous cloud in the distance, it pelts against the palace like peanuts, then cupcakes, then footballs, glues birds to their nests and farmers to their plows, pours through windows, drips through ceilings, seeps through keyholes . . . and spreading over King Derwin, clings to his royal eyebrows, oozes into his royal ears. . . . [The] King has forgotten the magic words. "YOU ought to be saying some plain *simple* words!" blurts out Bartholomew, meaning it's all the King's fault and the least he can say is, "I'm sorry." And bellowing, then sobbing, the King complies. "And the moment the King spoke those words, something happened . . . Maybe there *was* something in those simple words 'I'm sorry.' Maybe there *was* something in those simple words, 'It's all my fault.' Maybe there was and maybe there wasn't." But as soon as the King speaks them, the sun begins to shine, the blobs grow smaller, and the oobleck starts to melt away.

No doubt about it, those simple words turned the trick. Geisel was deep into morality tales by this time, and *Bartholomew and the Oobleck* is similarly tinged—or, if you will, tainted. But if it is a lesser work than *The 500 Hats,* the cause is not so much the genial moralizing as the tidy disposition of untoward events. Besides, how can a gooey Midas touch compare with 500 irrepressible red feathered hats?

The book that kicked off the morality tales, *Horton Hatches the Egg,* is also—paradoxically? characteristically?—the first truly wild thing Geisel did. *Mulberry Street,* for all its gusto and carnival colors, is conventional in design, and notwithstanding a certain loose energy in the drawing, *The 500 Hats* is as orderly a book as any. But *Horton,* along with many of its successors, looks like something funny that happened on the way to the printer. . . . (pp. 304-06)

Horton stays at his post through rain and hail and constant derision, repeating: "I meant what I said / And I said what I meant . . . / An elephant's faithful / One hundred per cent!". . . . Horton at last has his reward: from the egg that Mayzie, chancing by, claims as her own, "*Horton the Elephant saw something whizz! / IT HAD EARS AND A TAIL AND A TRUNK JUST LIKE HIS!*" With the Elephant-Bird perched on his trunk—"And it should be, it *should* be, it SHOULD be like that!"—Horton heads home, "Happy, / One hundred per cent!"

'And it should be, it *should* be, it SHOULD be like that': iced on a cake or written in the sky, it could be the official Seuss credo.

*Thidwick the Big-Hearted Moose* . . . is another lovable chump, put upon by pests he won't, he can't get rid of because, hold on, "*They're guests!*" (p. 306)

There isn't the satisfaction, though, in the mass retribution that there is in Mayzie's comeuppance, nor is Thidwick's loss of the pests a triumph on a par with Horton's gaining the Elephant-Bird. But then Horton has a mission—as against Thidwick's dubious obligation—and in sticking by the egg until it hatches he's as much a hero as a sap.

In *Horton Hears a Who!* he is a hero. . . . [There] was more to it than meets the eye. The intention was to encourage tolerance—in the first place, tolerance for the Japanese, whom Geisel had gotten to know on a post-World War II assignment. But Horton's dogged protection of the microscopic Whos, his firm "A person's a person, no matter how small," were taken rather as a plea for minority rights, and the book was faulted for its moralizing (where ten years earlier, before the McCarthy era, it would have been hailed). That children, always ready to champion the small against the large, ever took it as anything but that, is doubtful—the more so because it concludes by extolling the contribution of "the Smallest of All!" (pp. 306-07)

[While] *Mulberry Street* is the story of a boy with big dreams, *If I Ran the Zoo* is about the dreams a boy has. . . .

The rhyme and the rhythm are hyper-contagious, the pace is somewhere between hightail and hurtle, and the content, at last, is pure Nonsense. (p. 308)

Like Lear, with whom he is most often compared, [Seuss's] Nonsense is native to him, the expression of an angle of vision, a cast of mind, different from other people's. But quite apart from the fact that Lear could draw in the usual sense, it is not, like Lear's in the limericks and stories, an assemblage of incongruities, of the inherently irreconcilable. The Obsk from the far-away Mountains of Tobsk 'who eats only rhubarb and corn-on-the-cobsk' is a different order of Nonsense—nutsky—from the Blue-Bottle Fly who subsists "Mainly on Oyster-patties . . . and, when these are scarce, on Raspberry Vinegar and Russian leather boiled down to a jelly" ("The Story of Four Little Children. . ."). (p. 310)

If, however, one leaves Lear to his singularities and turns to the American scene, one finds an abundance of word play and doggerel . . . of bravado and, too, cockalorum, as a precedent, from "Yankee Doodle" to Mike Fink to the comic spurt at the turn of the century. The last embraces the work of George Thomas Lanigan ("The Akhoond of Swat"), John Kendrick Bangs, Oliver Herford, Carolyn Wells, Peter Newell . . . and the like of "The Brick Bat" and "The Round Robin" (Carolyn Wells's *Phenomenal Fauna*)—out of an accident of language, something new, whole, even operative.

Still more functional, however fantastic, are the inventions of Paul Bunyan natural history: the Gillygaloo, a hillside plover that laid square eggs so they wouldn't roll down the steep incline; the Hoop Snake, to be avoided only by jumping through its hoop as it approached; the Goofang, a fish that swam backward to keep the water out of its eyes; the Hangdown, the Hidebehind, the Sidehill Dodger (short-legged on the uphill side).

Geisel too is a teller of tall tales and as such, thoroughly American. They're expansive, immoderate, uninhibited, preposterous—along the way they did diverge from what others were doing. But not until *The Cat in the Hat* does chaos take over, and a brash slapbang humor; there's almost nothing in the earlier books construable as violence, physical or emotional, except some of the miscreants' misdeeds. (pp. 310-11)

*The Cat in the Hat* made Geisel a celebrity and sent the sales of the earlier books soaring; by picturebook standards, however, they had always done well. That it also presaged—or caused—a decline in the subsequent picturebooks, as often alleged, is less demonstrable. On the whole they are more frantic, more forced, and it is fair to say that they add very little to what he had done before. But one need not deplore them to value more "the natural truthful simplicity of the untruthfulness" that Beatrix Potter praised in *Mulberry Street* [see excerpt below] and the natural exuberance of the **"Horton"** books. (p. 312)

> Barbara Bader, "Dr. Seuss," in her American Picture Books from Noah's Ark to the Beast Within, *Macmillan Publishing Company, 1976, pp. 302-12.*

## EVELYN SCHROTH

[An] integral part of reading (or experiencing) Dr. Seuss is sensitivity to the language medium.

Much could be stated about the story line tactics that Dr. Seuss uses—inclusion of the fantastic in a familiar framework, stacking-procedures, the accrumental devices used over and over, logical phenomena to make the illogical plausible (such as having two dinners for a two-headed animal), poetic justice, extolling virtues such as perseverance and fidelity and enterprise. Many of the qualities of fairy tales are carried over into the Seuss tales, and all embellished with sumptuous, supporting artwork.

Here, discussion will be confined to the language use of Dr. Seuss, where many of these same tactics are applied, in an attempt to isolate in part the "undefinable something" that makes the Seuss books so delightful, with the hope that such knowledge will be recognized as an essential which the teacher must bring to teaching any reading content, whether it is reading to delight or inform or persuade.

It is obvious that Dr. Seuss is writing to be read aloud, and nowhere is this better evidenced than in the pleasurable sonorous effects, achieved through controlled rhyme, repetition, and intonation. From his earliest books, Dr. Seuss has shown awareness of the major role of intonation in reading. He has consistently marked stress for the reader by italicizing a word or a phrase or by capitalizing it (comic strip approaches) to give the word a special twist or emphasis. He controls rhythm, too, with such devices as end punctuation which isolates and emphasizes falling and rising voice contours, as in "He was shortish. And oldish. And brownish. And mossy."

He uses open juncture to coin words whose length and mixture of forms and non-forms might otherwise prove too formidable. "Thing-a-ma-Bokob," "Moota-fa-Potta-fa-Pell," "Ham-ikka-Schnim-ikka-Schnam-ikka-Schnopp." Such nonsensical forms exhibit a definite pattern and create a rhythmic feel and sound.

This patterned use of sounds appears in his beginner reading books, where a series of words may have the same vowel with only a single consonant change: "Tobok, nobok, obok;" "nungos, dungos;" the "Drummers, Zummers, Strummers;" "laws, paws, thaws." To this he adds generous alliteration, and we have "tizzle-topped Mazurka," "the Valley of Ving," "sneezed and snuffed," "zizzerzoofing." It is such devices, coupled with rhyme, which delight the ear of his reader.

In addition to compounding words by mixing non-forms and bona fide forms, Seuss compounds known words to make new ones: a family of "What-do-you-know," "Snore-a-snoot-Band," a "Bad-Animal-Catching-Machine," the "Who's-Asleep-Score," and "Happy-Way-Home-Bus"—all seemingly logical and sensible and useful, if unorthodox, and all perfectly meaningful. He also takes a few highly productive bound morphemes, such as *un-, -ish, -ly, -ed, -ler, -est,* and constructs vocabulary which though non-standard is logical and meaningful, since these morphemes are part of children's linguistic competence: "unthink," "gladish," "sharpishly," "Onceler," "biggered."

He uses functional shift with abandon: "cooked by my cooks in my Cookermobile," "turned on her Unthinker and unthinks the thing away," "the smog you smogged up," "the wubble wubbled in a wubble-some way"—shades of Jabberwocky, but also a return to classical rhetoric, where polyptoton was a play upon words by taking a base form and exploiting its varying functions. Its use here is reminiscent of its use then—to turn and tease language in order to approximate the turnings and twistings of thought which the form provides. It is another example of repetition, and it too is well used for listeners.

Another ploy to involve the reader approximates a trying-out of word patterns in the manner of small children, using a pivot word to test combinations: "keen shooter, bean shooter;" "Horseback, Bird-back, Hiffer-back."

Not only do the nonsensical words clearly evidence their form category but the connotation of positive or negative value is also revealed by the choice of sound. We have "jubbulous pay," "unshlump," "some unkerish place," "a cruffulous croak," "the Perilous Poozer of Pomplemoose Pas," but "the Truffula Trees" and "the City of Solla Sollew" and "the banks of Wa-Hoo." Onomatopoetic effects, too, abound: "spuggle it," "gluppity-glupp," "schloppity-schloop," "slurp."

Some cleverisms—or we might call them Seussisms—appear: "I thunked up quite a meth," cats become more "demo-catic," to read "Jivvanese," berries "Rasp," tail is "entailed with unsolvable know," "the Marvelous-He," and "Mustard-Off Pools."

He tickles us with unexpected collocations—"fresh butterfly milk"—and with ingenious concoctions—"peppermint cucumber sausage-paste butter." He tantalizes us with an enchanting once-upon-a-time beginning: "Way back in the olden, golden days; (In the Year one Thirty-nine) / A fancy cat named Looie / Was the King of Katzen-stein."

With overexaggeration, he exuberantly embroiders pattern upon pattern: "the Russian Palooski / Whose headski is redski and belly is blueski / . . . for my Zooski McGrewski." He plays upon words, backwards and forwards: "bird called the Bustard / Who eats only custard with sauce made of mustard; / and also a beast called Flustard / Who only eats mustard with a sauce made of custard." He loves tongue twisters enroute: "Clip and clip with clopping clippers. / Nip and snip with clipping cloppers; / Snip and snop with snipping snoppers." Repetitions abound: "I tossed and I flipped and I flopped and I flepped; and Everyone seemed to be yapping and yipping / Everyone seemed to be beeping or bipping."

In a list of words, Dr. Seuss slips in one that is incongruous but, because it is familiar to the child, imparts a sense of meaning to the whole: "They sparkled like diamonds and *gumdrops* and gold! Like silk! Like *spaghetti!* Like satin! Like lace!"

All the upmanshipping that children love is reflected in Seuss with superlatives like "East of the East-est to West of the West-est," "the best-est," "the top tallest," "the allest of all-est,'' ''The Night-of-all-Nights-of-all-Nights,'' ''Scrambled Eggs Super-dee-Dooper-dee-Booper / Special de luxe à-la-Peter T. Hooper,'' and ''Ninety-nine zillion nine trillion and three.''

He often captures the disarmingly simple nature of children's expression with a ''sort-of-a-hen'' or ''a-what-do-you-know,'' but other times he uses the same indefiniteness as a sophisticated art form, in the manner of e. e. cummings, as in ''Whoville'' with its ''Who-ville Town Square'' and ''you might be a Wasn't'' or ''You might be an Isn't.''

Interspersed infrequently among the ''out'' forms are some colloquial expressions of everyday speech. We encounter ''the young twirp,'' ''good gracious alive,'' ''a fast-moving bloke,'' ''a klunker-klunk,'' and ''head screwed on.'' These provide immediacy and keep us earthbound in our heady encounter with Seuss-land adventure.

In all areas of the language, then—the phonetic, lexical, syntactic, stylistic, and semantic—we have the versatile Dr. Seuss making his own imprint. What emerges is certain to be a flavorful, delightful, enthralling experience for the young reader. If teachers know the components of the form and are able to pinpoint them for young readers, this will do nothing to diminish and everything to enrich the reading experience. (pp. 748-50)

*Evelyn Schroth, "Dr. Seuss and Language Use," in The Reading Teacher, Vol. 31, No. 7, April, 1978, pp. 748-50.*

## ALISON LURIE

It is the particular gift of some writers to remain in one sense children all their lives: to continue to see the world as boys and girls see it, and take their side instinctively. One author who carries on this tradition today in America is Dr. Seuss, who like Twain and Carroll has adopted a separate literary personality.... Seuss's picture books, though extremely popular with children, have yet to be recognized as classics; they are not even mentioned in many surveys of the ''best'' children's books. (p. 70)

[From *And to Think That I Saw It on Mulberry Street*] onward, Dr. Seuss has not only celebrated the power and richness of the child's imagination, but suggested that children may do well to conceal their flights of fancy, and possibly other things, from their elders. The boy and girl in his best-known book, *The Cat in the Hat,* shut indoors on a rainy day, completely wreck the house with the help of the devilish-looking cat, then tidy it up again just before their mother gets home to ask

> ''Did you have any fun?
> Tell me. What did you do?''
>
> And Sally and I did not know
>     What to say.
> Should we tell her
> The things that went on there
>     that day?
> Should we tell her about it?
> Now, what should we do?
>
> Well . . .
> What would YOU do
> If your mother asked you?

The implication is that mother will never find out what went on in her absence—and just as well, too. (p. 72)

*Alison Lurie, "Vulgar, Coarse, and Grotesque: Subversive Books for Kids," in Harper's, Vol. 259, No. 1555, December, 1979, pp. 66-8, 70, 72.* *

## MAY HILL ARBUTHNOT, MARGARET MARY CLARK, RUTH M. HADLOW AND HARRIET G. LONG

[Theodor Seuss Geisel] can turn humorous fantasy into beauty both in his stories and his pictures. His pop-eyed heroes, his impossible hats, fish, or birds, his stilt-loving royalty, or his wizards and nizzards have about them a beauty of line, a sudden splash of color, or a grace of movement that is utterly captivating. This is true of his landscapes as well.... [Nothing] except his own creative genius can account for the unique quality of his nonsense, which, at its most hilarious peak, has also beauty.

*May Hill Arbuthnot, Margaret Mary Clark, Ruth M. Hadlow, and Harriet G. Long, "The Artist and Children's Books: Theodor Seuss Geisel," in their Children's Books Too Good to Miss, revised edition, University Press Books, 1979, p. 64.*

## JONATHAN COTT

''Useless trumpery'' is the way John Locke condemned fairy tales, ballads, and chapbook romances in the eighteenth century; his disciple John Newbery might have applied the same epithet to Marco's Mulberry Street hallucinations, as well as to the book that preserves them. But just as *A Little Pretty Pocket-Book* opened up new possibilities for children's literature in its time, so did *Mulberry Street* in ours. One could say that while Newbery created the children's book industry in England, Dr. Seuss—two centuries after its inception—has, astonishingly, been able to create his own microcosmic publishing universe: Walk into most children's bookstores today and you will find sections devoted to ''Fairy Tales,'' ''Picture Books,'' and ''Dr. Seuss.'' He has become a genre, a category, an institution. . . .

''What exactly is it that makes this stuff immortal?'' asked Rudolf Flesch (author of *Why Johnny Can't Read*) about Dr. Seuss's work. ''There is something about it,'' Flesch tried to explain. ''A swing to the language, a deep understanding of the playful mind of a child, an undefinable something that makes Dr. Seuss a genius pure and simple.''

*And To Think That I Saw It on Mulberry Street* immediately provides several other answers to Flesch's question, striking as it does the characteristic Seussian chord and rhythm, and ringing their changes. There is, first of all, the unflagging momentum, feeling of breathlessness, and swiftness of pace, all together acting as the motor for Dr. Seuss's pullulating image machine that brings to life—through rhymes and pictures—what William James describes as our earliest experiences of the world (''The baby, assailed by eyes, ears, nose, skin, and entrails at once, feels that all is one great blooming, buzzing confusion''), as well as what, more specifically, Selma G. Lanes calls ''Marco's rapidly expanding universe.'' All of this expansiveness expresses itself through Seuss's unique, children's-drawing style of illustration and through a theme-and-variations technique (the theme is usually that of searching for, discovering, or inventing something *new*) that the author uses in many of his books, including *Scrambled Eggs Super!* (in which the hero cook searches for new and different birds whose eggs will create a unique mélange) and *On Beyond Zebra* (in which the hero creates a new alphabet beyond the letter Z with invented animals representing each new letter). It is a technique that features the use of visual exaggeration. (p. 8)

In *Mulberry Street,* Dr. Seuss's illustrations are less exaggerated than they would become several years later—as in the books mentioned above—but you can already observe incipient signs of this tendency in the way he portrays the bibulous faces of his animals—zebras, reindeer, giraffes, and elephants. . . . Indeed, more than any other children's-book artist—except perhaps for Edward Lear (think of the Dong with a Luminous Nose and the Quangle Wangle)—Dr. Seuss has created the most extraordinary variety of ingeniously named, fantastical-looking animals and composite beasts. (pp. 9-11)

Also extremely characteristic of Seuss's work—in this and almost all of his other books—is his habitual use of anapestic tetrameter verse. Geisel claims that in 1936, when he was returning from Europe on an ocean liner, he became entranced by the rhythm of the ship's engines: "Da, da, *da,* da de *dum* dum de *da* de de *da.*" The words that to him seemed to match the boat's beat were: "And to think that I saw it on Mulberry Street"—the line that set him off writing and illustrating the book, and was a promise of the musical energy and excitement to be found in all of Dr. Seuss's poetry. For the anapest line embodies movement and swiftness, as in: "Oh, he flies through the air with the greatest of ease" and "O who rides by night thro' the woodland so wild?" (p. 11)

[Simply] and unselfconsciously, Dr. Seuss has retained a fresh perceiving system, naturally communicating an understanding of children's energies, needs, and desires.

Nowhere is this more obvious than in *The Cat in the Hat.* . . . "It's the book I'm proudest of," Geisel told me, "because it had something to do with the death of the *Dick and Jane* primers." (p. 25)

Dr. Seuss, in *The Cat in the Hat,* created one of the great *bouleversements* in the history of children's reading. (p. 26)

Like Coyote of many American Indian tribes and like Rabbit of Afro-American folklore, the Cat in the Hat is nothing less than an archetypal trickster hero, whose manifestation is perfectly suited—as is Bugs Bunny—for mid-twentieth-century appreciation and delight. (p. 27)

[I interviewed Theodor Geisel in July 1980:] "You seem quite recusant yourself, and I think a lot of your books *are* subversive." . . . "Don't you?"

"I'm subversive as hell!" Geisel replied. "I've always had a mistrust of adults. And one reason I dropped out of Oxford and the Sorbonne was that I thought they were taking life too damn seriously, concentrating too much on nonessentials. Hilaire Belloc, whose writings I liked a lot, was a radical. *Gulliver's Travels* was subversive, and both Swift and Voltaire influenced me. *The Cat in the Hat* is a revolt against authority, but it's ameliorated by the fact that the Cat cleans everything up at the end. It's revolutionary in that it goes as far as Kerensky and then stops. It doesn't go quite as far as Lenin."

"Like many of your books," I suggested, "*The Cat in the Hat* is quite anarchistic."

"It's impractical the way anarchy is, but it works within the confines of a book," Geisel agreed.

"Without pushing you further down the revolutionary path," I said, laughing, "I've always wondered about the concluding lines of *Yertle the Turtle:* 'And today the great Yertle, that Marvelous he, / Is King of the Mud. That is all he can see. / And turtles, of course . . . all the turtles are free / As turtles

and, maybe, all creatures should be.' Why 'maybe' and not 'surely'?"

"I qualified that," Geisel explained, "in order to avoid sounding too didactic or like a preacher on a platform. And I wanted *other* persons, like yourself, to say 'surely' in their minds instead of my having to say it."

"Within the confines of your books," I added, "you've written some very moral and political tales. The two books about Horton the elephant praise the virtues of loyalty and faithfulness. And you once said that the idea for *The 500 Hats of Bartholomew Cubbins* came about when you were 'taking a railroad train through Connecticut, sitting in a smoky, stuffy car, and ahead of me sat a smoky, stuffy Wall Street broker, wearing a derby and reading the *Wall Street Journal.* I was fascinated with his hat, and wondered what his reaction would be if I took his hat off his head. And then, half an hour later, I wondered how he'd react if there was still another hat on his head.'"

"Yes," Geisel responded, "children's literature as I write it and as I see it is satire to a great extent—satirizing the mores and the habits of the world. There's *Yertle the Turtle* (about the turtle dictator who becomes the 'ruler of all that I can see' by sitting on the backs of hundreds of subject turtles, his throne brought down by the simple burp of the lowliest and lowest turtle), which was modeled on the rise of Hitler; and then there's *The Sneetches* (about Star-Belly Sneetches who ostracize Plain-Belly Sneetches who pay to become Star-Belly Sneetches who then have to become Plain-Belly Sneetches, etc.), which was inspired by my opposition to anti-Semitism. These books come from a different part of my background and from the part of my soul that started out to be a teacher. Every once in a while I get mad. *The Lorax* (about a rapacious Once-ler who despoils the land of its Truffula Trees, leading to the total pollution and destruction of the environment) came out of my being angry. The ecology books I'd read were dull. But I couldn't get started on that book—I had notes but was stuck on it for nine months. Then I happened to be in Kenya at a swimming pool, and I was watching a herd of elephants cross a hill; why that released me I don't know, but all of a sudden all my notes assembled mentally. I grabbed a laundry list that was lying around and wrote the whole book in an hour and a half. In *The Lorax* I was out to attack what I think are evil things and let the chips fall where they might; and the book's been used by ministers as the basis of sermons, as well as by conservation groups."

"Aside from works like *Yertle the Turtle* and *The Sneetches,* which have the power of the great fables," I said, "there's a certain folktale quality to a few of your stories—I'm thinking particularly of **"The Big Brag"** in *Yertle the Turtle*—about the pomposity and egomania of a bear and a rabbit and of how they are cut down to size by a little worm—and **"The Zax"** in *The Sneetches*—about two Zaxs who bump into each other in the prairie and who each stubbornly refuse to let the other one pass until, eventually, highways are built over and around them. This last tale is similar to an African tale I recently read about two goats who bump into each other on a bridge and refuse to budge, each of them finally throwing the other into the water below."

"It just proves that there's nothing new," Geisel replied. "People are always reacting to the same stimuli. You could probably find duplications of all my stuff. But I used to read a lot of

Uncle Remus and a lot of Belloc, . . . so maybe there's some influence there." (pp. 28-30)

[Aside] from *The Cat in the Hat* and its brilliant sequel *The Cat in the Hat Comes Back,* most of Dr. Seuss's Beginner and Bright and Early Books have often been overlooked, patronized, and undervalued.

One of the most difficult tasks is to create a book meant to be read by very young children that will prove instructive to the child and also exciting to adults who might be reading over their shoulders. John Newbery's books were pleasing in form and generally rigid and boring in content. Dr. Seuss's books perfectly mate form and content, using nonsense, rhyme, and illustration to strengthen in the child's mind—and to confirm in the adults—a sense not of the "required" but of the "possible." (In Dr. Seuss's moral universe, what "should" happen is always connected to the heart's desires—as when Horton the faithful elephant hatches the elephant-bird, "it should be, it *should* be, it SHOULD be like that!''; and what "could" or "might" happen is limited only by one's patience and the powers of one's imagination—as when the hero of *McElligot's Pool* says: "'*Cause you never can tell / What goes on down below! / This pool might be bigger / Than you or I know!*''')

*Dr. Seuss's ABC* (one of the freshest additions to this centuries-old genre), *Hop on Pop* (subtitled **"The Simplest Seuss for Youngest Use"**), and *Fox in Socks* (a volume of mind-boggling tongue twisters) are among the most innovative, amusing, and audacious teaching books I have ever seen. *One Fish Two Fish Red Fish Blue Fish* and *There's a Wocket in My Pocket!* feature some of Dr. Seuss's most remarkable animal creations. And books like *Green Eggs and Ham, Mr. Brown Can Moo! Can You?* and *Marvin K. Mooney, Will You Please Go Now!* remind us that Dr. Seuss is one of the great creators of nonsense verse in the English language—verse in which you can almost hear an unmistakable musical accompaniment.

These last three books—along with *The Cat in the Hat Songbook* (which includes titles like "My Uncle Terwilliger Waltzes with Bears," "Beeper Booper," and "Rainy Day in Utica, N.Y.")—are in fact part of the wonderful tradition of American nonsense songs represented by "Old Aunt Kate," "Chick-a-Li-Lee-Lo," and "Risselty-Rosselty." (pp. 31-4)

> *Jonathan Cott, "The Good Dr. Seuss," in his* Pipers at the Gates of Dawn: The Wisdom of Children's Literature, *Random House, 1983, pp. 3-37.*

### BRIAN SUTTON-SMITH

I think that Dr. Seuss is packaging flexibility and possibility, and it's a new kind of thing in children's literature, which used to be much more staid. His books reflect a recognition—at least implicitly by intelligent people—that flexibility of thinking and brightness and associations and combinations, etc., are what mental development is about these days—it's as much a part of achievement as anything else. The notion that you can capture people's souls just by pressing the basics on them is nonsense and terrifying and stupid. . . . Seuss breaks barriers. What happens is that some person like him comes along who's intuitively a bit more in touch with the younger generation, he's nearer to his childhood and he expands the danger zones a little; and because kids love it, gradually parents come to accept it. It's the *adults* who have to be comforted.

> *Brian Sutton-Smith, in a conversation with Jonathan Cott, in* Pipers at the Gates of Dawn: The Wisdom of Children's Literature *by Jonathan Cott, Random House, 1983, p. 14.*

### HOWARD GARDNER

Dr. Seuss really seems to be tuned into both the form and the content that constitute the child's world, and he can approach the world through the child's conscious and unconscious abilities or faculties.

To fill that out a bit: There are some people who write works that appeal formally to children because they have certain rhythms, certain words, certain structures, certain visual patterns. You can enjoy Dr. Seuss's books, for example, even if you don't understand some of the words, even if you don't know English, and even if you don't follow the plots—some of them are fairly complicated. But there's enough regularity and sequence built into them so that even if you don't get all the words or all the points, it doesn't matter. You don't have to get the moral of *The Sneetches* in order to enjoy it.

There are also people who can produce works which appeal to kids in terms of content—something little overpowers something big, for example, or somebody goes on an adventure and comes home and becomes secure. Or you can take a book like Robert McCloskey's *Make Way for Ducklings*—the content is something very close to kids (animals, mothers, etc.), but the form isn't the sort of thing kids produce themselves—there isn't that metrical wordplay. And what I think is special about Dr. Seuss is that he's exploited both of these things—form and content—at the same time.

*Seuss poses with one of his sculptures, a blue-green abelard. John Bryson,* Life Magazine © *1959 Time Inc.*

Now, as far as 'conscious' and 'unconscious' elements are concerned: I think that Dr. Seuss has read his Freud, at least implicitly; I think his works are polymorphously perverse—they play with kids' desire to muck things up, to get dirty, to overpower authority. No kid would talk about this explicitly, but Dr. Seuss is sensitive to the unconscious strivings of kids in the same way that Bettelheim describes fairy tales as being responsive to kids' concerns.

But Dr. Seuss also writes about things and objects kids are consciously concerned with. In *The Cat in the Hat,* for example, a mother goes away, and what do the kids do then? They play, but all the time are worrying about what their mother will think when she comes back and finds out what they've been doing. So he's right in the center of two very important intersections—the kinds of formal properties of work that children like and the kinds of content they're interested in, and kids' unconscious and conscious concerns.

*Sesame Street* could also be described in a similar way, though I don't think the program does very much with the child's unconscious because it's 'pro-social'—as is *Mister Rogers' Neighborhood* . . . they want to make kids behave well so they don't deal very much with kids' aggressive desires. And, in a way, Dr. Seuss can be said to capture not only this kind of *Sesame Street* approach but also things that you find in Saturday morning cartoons, which play a lot more with aspects of a child's unconscious.

In a way, of course, any good work of art has got to play with those two dimensions I spoke about before. And for society today—at least in the West—Dr. Seuss has been as effective as anybody in doing this. (pp. 32-3)

> *Howard Gardner, in a conversation with Jonathan Cott, in* Pipers at the Gates of Dawn: The Wisdom of Children's Literature *by Jonathan Cott, Random House, 1983, pp. 32-3.*

**MARY LYSTAD**

About two-thirds of [Dr. Seuss's] books portray human characters, usually in some form of interaction with animal friends. Major human characters are exclusively male and white and usually middle-class. Dr. Seuss seems to admire the ingenuity and spirit of young boys; if young girls appear at all they are uncommonly quiet, even silent. Non-white human characters appear in only two books (although animal characters come in all colors). The socioeconomic class is clear from the settings in which characters live: The youngsters enjoy modest but comfortable homes in orderly and quiet neighborhoods.

Many of the animal friends, however, are quite the opposite: immodest, disorderly and noisome. The reader has rarely, if ever, seen the likes of them before. . . .

What do these characters, human or animal, need and want? In well over half the books, the needs are primarily for play and adventure. A few books reveal concern for the needs of physical safety, some for love and friendship, and a few for strength and achievement. Dr. Seuss' overwhelming emphasis on play and adventure is quite uncharacteristic of 20th century American books for children, most of which emphasize love and friendship or strength and achievement. Furthermore, Dr. Seuss' characters encounter few real problems in satisfying their needs. Children, especially male children, are rarely frustrated by confrontation with insuperable barriers, either physical or psychological.

How do Seussian characters satisfy their needs? First of all, it is the character himself who satisfies his own needs, primarily through creative self-direction rather than through conformity to traditional social norms. Moreover, the characters usually satisfy their needs in unique ways. These features distinguish Dr. Seuss' books from most 20th century books for children, for in most, needs are met primarily through conformity to adult norms. Dr. Seuss encourages children to believe that they are in control, that they can change themselves and their environment and even the whole world if they choose!

Dr. Seuss, by and large, views the world as a friendly place. In about two-thirds of his books, characters are really quite congenial, although in the others they do exhibit hostility along with congeniality. In only one book, his latest one, is the tone of hostility overwhelming. *The Butter Battle Book* . . . takes nuclear war as its theme, and it ends without resolution of the issues. While the format of this book—size, print, illustrations—resembles that of his other children's books, the message does not. In this book Dr. Seuss turns didactic and calls up many moral arguments adults make against nuclear proliferation. In only two other books does the spectre of death appear: *The Lorax*. . . , where the threat is environmental, and *The 500 Hats of Bartholomew Cubbins* . . . , where the threat is political.

Of the 50 children's books with stories to tell, 35 focus on the individual character and his unique needs, eight on the individual character as he relates to other characters, and seven on the individual interacting with and dependent upon a larger society. . . .

Most of the books feature a young boy exploring his universe. He explores it, questions it, seeks to change it. And when he is finished, he is satisfied that he has improved upon this universe. (p. 20)

Although most of Dr. Seuss' characters are loving, kind and generous toward each other and toward others, some are hostile, aggressive and selfish. In this he is consistent with the views of child development specialists, who have learned that portrayal of one type of character without the other leaves the child with a distorted sense of reality. Child development specialists have suggested that a major fault in books for children is the failure to deal directly with people's aggressive drives. Depiction of greater complexity in personality helps the child-reader better to understand both the direction these diverse drives can take him and the direction in which he can take them. (p. 21)

Individual characters are linked to larger social contexts in a few of Dr. Seuss's books. Some deal with threats to individual freedom in the forms of tyrannical, profiteering rulers, environmental hazards and nuclear war. Others extol friendship between differing racial, ethnic and national groups.

*The Lorax* is a story of greed and power personified in a character called the Once-ler. . . .

*The Butter Battle Book* is about two groups of animals who live on either side of a stone wall and who fear the threat to their safety that each poses for the other. . . .

There is no closure: It is left for the Yooks and the Zooks and the reader to answer the question.

On a much different note is *Come Over To My House*. . . . This is the only book by Dr. Seuss in which children of both sexes and a number of ethnic and racial groups interact. They explore each other's homes in a spirit of love and friendship. Children appear with white and black and brown faces, straight and curly hair, round and oval eyes. Children live in houses of brick, straw, paper, wood, clay and ice-block. Some of the houses float in the water and some sit on stilts. Children play, eat, work and sleep in different modes, but always with dignity and with a sense of the commonalities between them.

Wit and wisdom populate the world of Dr. Seuss. He provides the child-reader with many scenarios for play and adventure, and his creative imagination enriches and enlarges their world. He entices the child to read on, because the next page is unpredictable and so is the one after that. He entices the child to think on, because there is always more than a horse and wagon to be found on Mulberry Street. Generations of children and parents and grandparents are fortunate that the good Dr. takes them so seriously. (p. 22).

> *Mary Lystad, "The World According to Dr. Seuss,"* in Children Today, *Vol. 13, No. 3, May-June, 1984, pp. 19-22.*

---

### AND TO THINK THAT I SAW IT ON MULBERRY STREET (1937)

Is there no book so completely spontaneous that the American child can take it to his heart on sight? Dr. Seuss, the artist-author of **And To Think That I Saw It on Mulberry Street** . . . has provided one—an American picture-storybook in rhyme, as original in conception, as spontaneous in the rendering, as it is true to the imagination of a small boy. The drawings, in bright color, have the dynamic quality of the comic strip, but are without vulgarity. The verses have a rhythm and swing born of familiarity with good nonsense verse and a sure knowledge of cumulative effect.

> *Anne Carroll Moore, in a review of "And to Think That I Saw It on Mulberry Street,"* in The Atlantic Bookshelf, *a section of* The Atlantic Monthly, *Vol. 160, No. 5, November, 1937.*

Highly original and entertaining, Dr. Seuss's picture book partakes of the better qualities of those peculiarly American institutions, the funny papers and the tall tale. It is a masterly interpretation of the mind of a child in the act of creating one of those stories with which children often amuse themselves and bolster up their self-respect.

Little Marco has been chided by his father for his lack of observance in the ordinary routines of life, and, on his way home from school one day, he determines to have something of importance to tell. There is nothing very outstanding about a rattle-trap cart and horse on Mulberry Street, yet Marco, once aroused, is not to be balked by mere realism. Tentatively he experiments, substituting in his rehearsed story a zebra for the horse. Fancy, unleashed, climbs to further heights. "Why not a chariot?" says Marco to himself. Logic, which has nothing to do with cold facts, intervenes, and with every step homeward the original report grows into a caravan of startling size and character, until a grand climax is reached, with its inevitable anticlimax in perfect keeping with Marco's character. The whole is told in rollicking verse, and in bright pictures, which though a bit crude in coloring are as spirited and comic as is the young hero's imagination. It is a book which will divert older readers as well as little children. (pp. 14, 37)

> *Ellen Lewis Buell, "The Startling Parade,"* in The New York Times Book Review, *November 14, 1937, pp. 14, 37.*

Those whose work it is to examine the new children's books as they are published are always looking for a surprise, for the truly fresh and original book. This year some of us have found one in this amusing picture book, so true to the thoughts of childhood, and with a far clearer suggestion to parents than can be had from many pages in child psychology books. (pp. 373-74)

> *A review of "And to Think That I Saw It on Mulberry Street,"* in The Horn Book Magazine, *Vol. XIII, No. 6, November-December, 1937, pp. 373-74.*

The cleverest book I have met with for many years. . . . The swing and movement of the pictures and the natural, truthful simplicity of the untruthfulness—spontaneous, natural, barefaced. Too many story books for children are condescending, self-conscious invention, and then some trivial oversight, some small, incorrect detail, gives the show away. Dr. Seuss does it thoroughly. (pp. 32-3)

> *Beatrix Potter, in an extract from a letter to Anne Carroll Moore in 1938,* in The Horn Book Magazine, *Vol. XIV, No. 1, January-February, 1938, pp. 32-3.*

Both in text and illustrations this is a most delightfully funny book. The verses have a spontaneity that is as welcome as the spring sunshine, and are a perfect picture of a small boy's extravagant imaginings as he lets his fancy roam. . . . [Imagination] embroiders a picture that contains everything—and more—that could possibly have been built up on so ordinary a thing. The pictures, all in colour, have an irresponsibly humorous gaiety. Dr. Seuss deserves our thanks. (pp. 27-8)

> *A review of "And to Think That I Saw It on Mulberry Street,"* in The Junior Bookshelf, *Vol. 4, No. 1, October, 1939, pp. 27-8.*

**And to Think That I Saw It on Mulberry Street** has its roots deep in the humor and originality of its author-artist's mind. The book's unique contribution is an accurate diagram of a complex situation in which the best elements of a fire, a circus, a parade, the Fourth of July, are combined in celebration of a dream. All the events of this story must have occurred, for here, incident by incident, with mechanical perfection, the interlocking fantasy is demonstrated in line, color, and exaltation of the mood. (p. 438)

> *Frances Clarke Sayers, "'Through These Sweet Fields',"* in The Horn Book Magazine, *Vol. XVIII, No. 6, November-December, 1942, pp. 436-43.\**

---

### THE 500 HATS OF BARTHOLOMEW CUBBINS (1938)

Once again Dr. Seuss has given us a completely hilarious story in the **500 Hats of Bartholomew Cubbins**. . . . It is nonsense, but so original, so full of surprise, that just to think of the book makes one laugh. There is no doubt that the children's reactions to it will be as spontaneous as the book itself.

> *Ruth A. Hill, in a review of "The 500 Hats of Bartholomew Cubbins,"* in Library Journal, *Vol. 63, No. 19, November 1, 1938, p. 818.*

The only thing I had against Dr. Seuss's exuberant debut in children's books last year with **"And to Think That I Saw It** on Mulberry Street" was that he made it, so to speak, on a shoestring. There was a gorgeous idea in that book, but not more than enough for one thoroughly good comic strip. In this one there is a gorgeous, brand-new idea, developed into a complete tale, not too long, not too short, just right. . . .

Somewhere between the Sunday supplements and the Brothers Grimm. Dr. Seuss has produced a picture-book combining features of both. The instant appeal of his cartoons for grown-ups is to the small-boy delight in other people's difficulties by no means lost in growing up. In drawing for small boys Dr. Seuss need not change style.

> *"Fifteen Hounds and Five Hundred Hats," in* New York Herald Tribune Books, *November 13, 1938, p. 22.\**

This new book by Dr. Seuss is a worthy successor to **"And to Think That I Saw It on Mulberry Street."** It is not, perhaps, quite so startling, but it is just as original in its conception, and the extraordinary dilemma of Bartholomew Cubbins with his superfluity of hats is built up with the same flair for narrative. . . .

It is a lovely bit of tomfoolery which keeps up the suspense and surprise until the last page, and of the same ingenious and humorous imagination are the author's black and white illustrations in which a red cap and then an infinite number of red caps titillate the eye. (p. 32)

> *Ellen Lewis Buell, "A Humorous Tale," in* The New York Times Book Review, *November 13, 1938, pp. 11, 32.*

I would trade everything else Dr. Seuss has written for this one nonsense story, whimsical and original, with its spiky, casual pictures and its cheeky young hero. Nearly thirty years old, and still bursting with life and humour.

> *Margery Fisher, in a review of "The 500 Hats of Bartholomew Cubbins," in her* Growing Point, *Vol. 5, No. 6, December, 1966, p. 825.*

Dr. Seuss has been for some years the most popular author of children's books in America, mostly on the basis of his pleasant, rhyming books written to replace the moribund Dick-and-Jane primers. My impression is that the more popular Dr. Seuss has become, the less seriously he has been taken by those who take children's literature seriously, and it is true that his recent books seem to be rapidly written and increasingly inconsequential. But before *The Cat in the Hat* and the others came a long series of pleasant, rhyming books such as *Horton Hatches the Egg* and *How the Grinch Stole Christmas,* and even before that, back in the thirties, he wrote two major books of my youth, *The 500 Hats of Bartholomew Cubbins* and *The King's Stilts,* both pleasant, but in prose, and not really inconsequential either. There has always been a strain of bubbling whimsicality in Dr. Seuss; in these early books there is plenty of bubble, but the whimsicality is channeled by the tracing of unsentimental narrative propositions: the really hard thing about getting from one to five hundred is to get from one to two; a king who works and plays equally well is bound to earn someone's enmity.

It now seems to me that the second of these two propositions, the one that underlies *The King's Stilts,* is the stronger, but the other, for *The 500 Hats,* is the one that entranced me when I was young. . . . The name of the hero, the fact of the monarchy as well as a world where objects were handed down through

the generations, all make it much unlike my world. Dr. Seuss, however, is clearly not trying to transport his reader to the Other, the foreign, or magical, because he quite openly states the fact that what he seeks is a story, and a story that can get us from one hat to five hundred. Our concern is with hats. (pp. 8-9)

You get from one hat to five hundred by counting. One is released into the simplicity of getting from two hats to five hundred by just playing past the difficulty of getting from one to two, so that focusing on red hats and counting will carry us along. . . . Bartholomew's hats . . . level the court; he himself is not in the least raised up by all this, and no claims are offered for his pluck, cleverness, or courage, because he has these virtues only in ordinary quantities. Dr. Seuss's whimsical artistic skills are lavished on all the other characters, and their frustration offers one focus. Meanwhile Bartholomew remains small, wide-eyed, and counting, and he of course offers a second focus. But he and the others keep meeting on the hats. Dr. Seuss does not, as Hans Christian Andersen so often does, fire satiric shafts at monarchies, and he does not, as Milne does in the Christopher Robin books, imply extra points to readers who can count. (p. 10)

It all seems too simple, the sort of story that must please much more the first time one reads it than any subsequent time. Yet I have never tired of reading this story, and, so far as I can tell, my pleasure now is not only as great as it once was, but is pretty much the same, as Dr. Seuss continues his leveling by making the near forty years between my first and my most recent reading indistinguishable. I still stare at the hats, flying off the turrets of the castle with arrows in them, piling up around the startled, friendly executioner, lining the stairs to the tallest tower as Bartholomew tears hats off furiously because he is about to be shoved from the tower, hat and all. We know, as Bartholomew does not, that after he gets well past four hundred he is approaching a crisis, but Bartholomew knows he can think of nothing else to do except tear hats off. The story works, and keeps on working, because it insists on two apparently contrary feelings: first, we are in control here, well ahead of both Bartholomew and the court, because we know the book's essential journey is one hat to five hundred and no one in the story knows this; second, there is a problem, a mystery here, that will never be solved: how did all these hats get on Bartholomew's head? The effect of the two feelings on each other is to rob our control of complacence and to transform our sense of mystery into fun.

Following from all this, it is the last line that has always meant more to me than any other. After Bartholomew climbs the tower he takes off his five hundredth hat, and of course his life is saved because there isn't going to be a five hundredth and first hat, and so he can return home, happy and relieved to feel the breeze blowing in his hair at last:

> But neither Bartholomew Cubbins, nor King Derwin himself, nor anyone else in the Kingdom of Didd could ever explain how the strange thing had happened. They could only say it just "happened to happen" and was not very likely to happen again.

I carry that last line with me and use it often to "explain" strange events in this sublunary sphere. I do so not just because it is a good line, but because it is how Dr. Seuss slays the dragon of explanation: by walking between its legs. It isn't "once upon a time" at the start, and so it isn't "they lived happily ever after'' at the end, but ''it just happened to happen and is not very likely to happen again,'' as in a world, like mine, where the best that could be done was to get back alive to the point where I began. Not fairy, not heroic, but not antifairy or antiheroic either. How wonderful, when things just happened to happen, to get not only from one hat to two and thence to five hundred, but to get back home again, the only price exacted being the loss of one hat. It is more wonderful than I have ever been able to ask for or to expect, but not so wonderful I could not hope for it, and in this feeling the child I was and the man I am agree.

The story of *The 500 Hats* offers a narrative cradle, not for rocking one to sleep, but to encourage one with the knowledge that when one confronts angry kings and cavernous castles one goes on being oneself, taking one's hat off, and counting, and that all that one needs one also has. It was this rather than vivid or brilliant details that made this book alive and important to me; even as a child I could see how rudimentary Dr. Seuss's drawing is, how much every face resembles every other because, like me, Dr. Seuss has only one face he can draw. For sheer vividness in the memory there were frightening moments in other books and pictures that stayed with me longer than anything in *The 500 Hats,* compared to which this book has to seem rather tame. But as a whole, as an enterprise undertaken and completed, it offered and offers a residual sense of wonder and possibility that lies deeper than any single scary memory taken from other, ''more powerful'' books. (pp. 10-12)

> *Roger Sale, "Introduction: Child Reading and Man Reading," in his* Fairy Tales and After: From Snow White to E. B. White, *Cambridge, Mass.: Harvard University Press, 1978, pp. 1-21.\**

---

### THE KING'S STILTS   (1939)

''Naturally,'' Dr. Seuss assures us gravely, ''the King *never* wore his stilts during business hours,'' and with that provocative statement we are plunked right into the middle of another one of those fantastic, one-syllabled kingdoms which he creates out of thin air and a fertile imagination.

The very existence of the Kingdom of Binn depended on the Dike Trees, which on three sides twined their sturdy roots together to keep out the hungry ocean. Fortunately the citizens rejoiced in one of the most simple-hearted, hardest-working kings on record. . . .

Naturally no one begrudged King Birtram his 5 o'clock hour on stilts, even though it did look a little odd. No one, that is, but Lord Droon, who disapproved of fun in any form, and he it was who stole the King's stilts. . . .

Following on the heels of **"The Five Hundred Hats of Bartholomew Cubbins,"** and **"And to Think That I Saw It on Mulberry Street,"** this is just a little anticlimactic. There is the same suspense, the same breath-taking pace, and, although no one can gainsay its originality, the fantasy does not seem quite so spontaneous nor absurd. Yet Dr. Seuss at his second-best is much better and funnier than no Dr. Seuss.

> *Ellen Lewis Buell, in a review of "The King's Stilts," in* The New York Times Book Review, *October 15, 1939, p. 12.*

A thoroughly amusing yarn. Dr. Seuss's first two books were so totally different that we had expected him to turn out a third

equally unique. In make-up and illustrations this is very similar to *The 500 Hats of Bartholomew Cubbins.*

> *Eunice G. Mullan, in a review of "King's Stilts," in* Library Journal, *Vol. 64, No. 19, November 1, 1939, p. 370.*

Dr. Seuss's latest extravaganza has a meaning so good it makes its madness all the merrier. . . . How [the Prime Minister hides the king's stilts] and the king droops, and the cats relax discipline, and the Nizzards all but wreck the place, makes the plot. How the page comes to the rescue makes a triumphant conclusion. . . . For, as the text concludes after all these hilarious pictures: ''When they played they really PLAYED. And when they worked they really WORKED.'' This is the best Dr. Seuss so far, and tha's no small praise.

> *A review of "The King's Stilts," in* New York Herald Tribune Books, *November 12, 1939, p. 22.*

A king who liked walking on stilts, birds who pecked the roots of trees that were planted to keep out the ocean, patrol cats (with special badges of office) who kept out the birds, a miserable old spoil-sport of a courtier who stole the stilts—these are the ingredients that make up Dr. Seuss' latest nonsensical story. His pictures are in keeping. There are few author-artists who can let themselves go with such gusto, few who can accomplish such boisterous and spirited humour in a book, as can Dr. Seuss.

> *A review of "The King's Stilts," in* The Junior Bookshelf, *Vol. 6, No. 3, November, 1942, p. 94.*

---

### HORTON HATCHES THE EGG   (1940)

Horton was an elephant, but such an elephant as only the creator of Mulberry Street and Bartholomew Cubbins could invent and draw. Gigantic and comfortably baggy, he may not have been very bright, but he was kind and easy-going and he meant what he said. Mayzie, a lazy bird, must have known that, for when she wanted a vacation it was Horton whom she asked to sit on her egg.

Horton propped up the tree and sat down, and continued to sit, for Mayzie, charmed by Palm Beach, didn't come back. Not rain, nor snow, nor hunters, not even the jeers of his jungle friends could discourage him, for an elephant is faithful—one hundred per cent. How Horton, still treed, came to America, joined a circus, met Mayzie and finally hatched a winged surprise, is told in swinging metrics which move along much faster than poor Horton could, but which still have time to point up a lesson in faithfulness.

A moral is a new thing to find in a Dr. Seuss book, but it doesn't interfere much with the hilarity with which he juggles an elephant up a tree. To an adult the tale seems a little forced in comparison to his first grand yarns, less inevitable in its nonsense, but neither young nor old are going to quibble with the fantastic comedy of his pictures.

> *"Elephant's Egg," in* The New York Times Book Review, *October 13, 1940, p. 10.*

We are well used to allowing for divergent tastes in humorous books. There is generally an audience to declare itself, definitely, not amused. But humor is too dignified a term to apply to this present subject. It is that greater rarity, a funny book, and it is impossible to imagine any reader of any age getting

*From* Horton Hatches the Egg, *written and illustrated by Dr. Seuss. Random House, 1940. Copyright 1940, renewed 1960 by Dr. Seuss. All rights reserved. Reprinted by permission of Random House, Inc.*

far into it without hilarious laughter. . . . In text and pictures this is pure comedy. Possibly it lacks the aesthetic quality of this author's earlier stories, and some children's librarians may therefore feel it calls for special tolerance, or even disapproval. For my part, I think we should be abjectly grateful for a funny book this year. It will do families good to laugh, as everyone of them will have to laugh at this ridiculous yarn.

> *Irene Smith, in a review of "Horton Hatches the Egg," in* Library Journal, *Vol. 65, No. 19, November 1, 1940, p. 929.*

Young or old, if there is a knot in your nerves, the chances are that this will loosen it enough to let you laugh.

[More than half the story] is made up of wild luxuriant pictures in several colors, so funny nobody forgets them. The story rumbles along in verse you find yourself repeating.

> *"Animals, Little Children, Mother Goose," in* New York Herald Tribune Books, *November 10, 1940, p. 11.**

Probably, **Horton Hatches the Egg** is the most beloved and enjoyed of all the Seuss animals. . . . The incongruity of a great big elephant sitting on a nest in a tree tickles the funny bone of the child in all of us. Horton believes so thoroughly in the

responsibility of his task that he convinces the reader of the seriousness of this utterly ridiculous situation. The ending of this hilarious story represents poetic justice as only Dr. Seuss could imagine it! (pp. 308-09)

> *Charlotte S. Huck and Doris A. Young, "Children Enjoy Folk, Fun, and Fancy," in their* Children's Literature in the Elementary School, *Holt, Rinehart and Winston, 1961, pp. 272-318.**

The American offering will be familiar to those who remember the picture-books which came in small numbers into this country early in the war. We have seen Dr. Seuss lately at less than his best in the "Beginner Books." *Horton Hatches the Egg* is a nice example of his zest for the ridiculous. Gloriously funny—and ever so slightly vulgar—drawings and doggerel text tell the moving story. . . .

> *A review of "Horton Hatches the Egg," in* The Junior Bookshelf, *Vol. 26, No. 5, November, 1962, p. 248.*

Two qualities are basic to cartoonism, and these qualities provoke laughter, or at least a smile, from the reader. Incongruous and incompatible characteristics or situations are depicted. . . . For example, the situations which Horton, the faithful and persistent elephant, faces in **Horton Hatches the Egg** send youngsters into gales of laughter. Seuss sketched numerous wonderfully humorous and expressive pictures of this long-suffering creature. Horton, sitting on a small nest in a tree, at times looks bewildered, frightened, cold, or embarrassed. His facial expressions are indeed a delight to behold. The incongruity of such a situation as an elephant stranded on top of a tree in itself would amuse children. Scenes in which the tree, with Horton still sitting on the nest, is moved from the jungle and carried by boat across rolling and tossing ocean waters to America only to be sold to a circus and the picture of the elephant-bird bursting out of the shell of the egg that Horton sat on so long and so faithfully are other incongruities and incompatibilities in Seuss' cartoons that help to make this narrative enjoyable. Even primary-age children recognize how ridiculous these situations are. (p. 50)

> *Patricia Cianciolo, "Styles of Art in Children's Books," in her* Illustrations in Children's Books, *second edition, Wm. C. Brown Company Publishers, 1976, pp. 28-57.**

---

### McELLIGOT'S POOL (1947)

[The author-artist] has produced another book of hilarious non-sense in his inimitable imaginative pictures and rhyme, similar in treatment to **Mulberry street.** It is a fish story to end all fish stories. A little boy is called a fool for thinking he can catch any fish in McElligot's pool. Says he: "If I wait long enough; if I'm patient and cool, who knows *what* I'll catch in Mc-Elligot's pool!" A natural for picture-book hours and for reading aloud.

> *A review of "McElligot's Pool," in* The Booklist, *Vol. 44, No. 3, October 1, 1947, p. 53.*

Like the boy in **"And to Think That I Saw It on Mulberry Street,"** this one has an active imagination, and he proceeds to exercise it. . . . There *might* be all sorts of strange and beautiful fish that would come up [the] river to the Pool. So, in a series of drawings in color and in black and white that are a fascinating mixture of beauty and humor, we follow these fish up the river; we even see the people who live above it. Children will have nothing but admiration for this boy who heard that there were no fish in McElligot's Pool and then saw them swimming in from the sea.

*A review of "McElligot's Pool," in The Saturday Review of Literature, Vol. XXX, No. 46, November 15, 1947, p. 38.*

In the seven years since his last book, **"Horton Hatches the Egg,"** and in the ten since his first book, **"And to Think That I Saw It on Mulberry Street,"** a whole new audience has been born and growing for Dr. Seuss' comic genius, and with **"McElligot's Pool"** he snares them, every one.

Politely unmindful of the farmer who declares it folly to drop a baited hook into McElligot's Pool, a young angler with imagination fishes of what *might be*. Instead of old shoes or empty bottles, he visualizes a possible catch of jelly fish, Eskimo fish (with fur parkas), sea horses, whales, and even a Thing-a-ma-jigger—all drawn in Dr. Seuss' benign style (which characteristically represents the worm as never pierced but obligingly knotting himself upon the hook) and described in fantastically funny rhymes.

*Sarah Chokla Gross, in a review of "McElligot's Pool," in The New York Times Book Review, November 16, 1947, p. 45.*

We needed laughter, and we have it in the return of Dr. Seuss in *McElligot's Pool* . . . with its rhymes, which are sheer delight to read aloud . . . and its pictures of fishes which gave me nostalgia for the old Aquarium at the Battery. May all halting rhymesters, of whom there are legion, study Dr. Seuss as he in his turn must have studied the best of nonsense poetry before he wrote *Mulberry Street*.

*Anne Carroll Moore, in a review of "McElligot's Pool," in The Horn Book Magazine, Vol. XXIII, No. 6, November-December, 1947, p. 436.*

Marco fishes in McElligot's Pool without success: like many a committed angler, he sits and thinks—is the pool connected to an underground river? Dr. Seuss' singular illustrations provide the answer as they trace the stream under the state highway, under Sneedon's Hotel and out to sea. Here is an abundance of fish of all sorts and sizes, humorously and characteristically imagined by Dr. Seuss: page after page of delightful creatures, finny and funny, with appropriate faces and features. He would be a very dull soul who was not hooked by this piscatorial fantasy!

*G. Bott, in a review of "McElligot's Pool," in The Junior Bookshelf, Vol. 41, No. 1, February, 1976, p. 18.*

Flowing, moving, and vibrant describe both text and illustration for *McElligot's Pool*.

The text, typically in rhyme, is as lively and imaginative as the watercolor and black and white illustrations. Geisel creates a unique species on nearly every page, and though his word invention is kept to a minimum in this text, he does not avoid it completely: A "THING-A-MA-JIGGER!!" is quite some fish.

During this period of picturebook production, the imagination and frivolity of this book undoubtedly insured it a warm welcome from an audience that was predominantly presented with more serious themes. The sheer nonsense of *McElligot's Pool* and the sense of fun in the plethora of Geisel books that follow

appeal to the lighter side of childhood and eventually become books that children themselves turn to read. The evolution into *I-Can-Read-It-All-By-Myself* books is an indication of the "readability," which is facilitated by the rhyming text and unforgettable illustrations of the artist's imagination. All this ensures a continual audience and popularity far beyond the picture-book age.

*Linda Kauffman Peterson "The Caldecott Medal and Honor Books, 1938-1981: 'McElligot's Pool'," in* Newbery and Caldecott Medal and Honor Books: An Annotated Bibliography *by Linda Kauffman Peterson and Marilyn Leathers Solt, G. K. Hall & Co., 1982, p. 273.*

---

## THIDWICK, THE BIG-HEARTED MOOSE (1948)

### AUTHOR'S COMMENTARY

Thidwick did not come into the world through inspiration. Thidwick was an accident, pure and simple—a scribble.

Over a year ago, the piece of paper on which this scribble was scribbled was a clean, fresh piece of white paper. I was sitting at my typewriter in my studio in Hollywood, where I live. I had put a clean piece of paper in my machine and had typed a few words in the upper left-hand corner. I was trying to write a story for the movies, but my ideas weren't coming very fast that day. I didn't like the words I had typed at all. So I took my pencil and scratched them out. Then, for a long time, I just sat there, staring at the paper and waiting for some idea that would be important enough to write down on the paper. But no ideas would come—not a single one!

Well—along about one-thirty the telephone rang. It was an old friend, Joe Warwick, whom I hadn't seen for almost ten years. He was going to be in Hollywood for a day or two, and he asked if we could have dinner together the next night—Thursday—at eight o'clock.

"Wonderful, Joe," I told him. "I'll see you at eight o'clock." Not having my engagement book handy, I pulled the paper out of the typewriter and made a note of the date. Then we talked on for about twenty minutes more. While we talked, I did what almost everyone else in the world does when he talks on the phone. I doodled—just absent-minded, meaningless scribbles, here and there on the paper.

It wasn't until after Joe had hung up that I realized that one of the scribbles looked somewhat like a moose, with some other peculiar animals sitting on his horns. Then I began to wonder how a moose would like it if some animals *did* move in to live on his horns.

That's what started off the story of Thidwick. Only, at the beginning, his name wasn't Thidwick. His name was Warwick, in honor of my friend Joe. How the name finally was changed to Thidwick is something I don't exactly recall. But I do remember that the whole thing began with a doodle which was started by Joe's phone call. So, if by any chance there are some of you who don't like the book, *Thidwick: The Big-Hearted Moose*, please remember that you can't blame me. You'll have to blame Joe Warwick. It's really all *his* fault. (pp. 71-2)

*Dr. Seuss, "'Where Do You Get Your Story Ideas?' They Ask," in* Writing Books for Boys and Girls, *edited by Helen Ferris, Doubleday & Company, Inc., 1952, pp. 71-3.*

The fable of the camel in the Arab's tent hasn't a patch on what happened to Thidwick the moose when he kindly gave a ride to a Bingle Bug. That was a fine gesture, but the guest invited a Tree-Spider who invited a Zinn-a-zu Bird, who brought his wife, who invited . . . Well, the community which was soon established in Thidwick's antlers has to be seen for itself and even then can only be believed because of the persuasive powers of Dr. Seuss, who is an old hand at cooking up impossible situations and always knows a new trick or two. How Thidwick asserted himself is told in verses which march in double-quick time. The pictures are scenes of happy confusion, a little difficult to see at first, but as madly absurd as anything Dr. Seuss has done. This is pure entertainment for almost anyone over 5.

> *Ellen Lewis Buell, in a review of "Thidwick the Big-Hearted Moose," in* The New York Times Book Review, *October 10, 1948, p. 25.*

The author's rollicking verse is perfectly suited to this comical tale. His pictures in red, blue, and black are expressive and funny, and though they appear slightly confusing at first glance, they are well adapted to the spirit of the story. For little children it is splendid read-aloud nonsense.

> *Virginia H. Mathews, in a review of "Thidwick, the Big-Hearted Moose," in* New York Herald Tribune Weekly Book Review, *November 14, 1948, p. 12.*

[In "**Thidwick: the Big-Hearted Moose,**"] Seuss builds sympathy for the animal who lets himself be used by others. ("For a host, above all, must be nice to his guests" is the refrain which is repeated, satirically, throughout the tale.) . . .

"**Thidwick**" is a masterpiece of economy, and a shrewd satire of the "easy mark" who lets the conventions of society get the better of him. The genius of the story, however, lies in its finale. A man of less consistency than Seuss would have let Thidwick be rescued by the creatures he is befriending (this is the customary Disney riposte in similar situations) but Seuss' logic is rooted in principle, rather than sentiment, and the sponging animals get what they deserve. Incidentally, this is also what the child expects.

> *David Dempsey, "The Significance of Dr. Seuss," in* The New York Times Book Review, *May 11, 1958, p. 30.*

Like Edward Lear's old man with a beard, Thidwick allows a colony of creatures to take up residence in his antlers. . . . Such cheerful nonsense must disarm all but the fossilized, and this one, circa 1948 and one of Seuss's best, shows no sign of growing old.

> *J. Jackson, in a review of "Thidwick the Big-Hearted Moose," in* Children's Book News, *Vol. 3, No. 6, November-December, 1968, p. 313.*

---

## BARTHOLOMEW AND THE OOBLECK (1949)

### AUTHOR'S COMMENTARY

My mail is full of letters that go like this:

"This oobleck—this green stuff that comes down from the sky—how did you think it up?" they all ask in their letters. "Did you *dream* it?"

Now some writers, I am told, really do dream their stories. . . But I never had any luck with my dreams.

It was in a rainstorm that the idea for *Bartholomew and the Oobleck* came to me—not just an ordinary American rainstorm, but one in France, way back during World War II. It always seems to rain when wars are going on, and this was the wettest rain I had ever seen. It had been pouring out of the sky for weeks, and everyone in the whole Army was mighty cold and soaked and, of course, unhappy.

One night while splashing through the drenching rain and deep mud of a little French town, I was wondering whether the rain would ever stop. Just then out of the dark ahead two American soldiers came splashing toward me.

"Rain! Always *rain* comes down!" one soldier was muttering as he passed me. "Why can't something new, something different, come down?"

That's all I heard, for the next moment the men disappeared in the dark behind. But there I stood in the wet with an exciting idea running around and around in my head. Maybe something new *could* come down! Maybe someday something *would* come down that was different from rain or snow, sunshine or fog, something strange that had never before fallen from the sky to the earth. For a long time I stood there alone in the storm, wondering what kind of stuff might come down. And I decided then and there that after the war I would write a story about it.

So it was in France, five years ago, that I first got the idea for *Bartholomew and the Oobleck*. I finished it this year at my home in California, six thousand miles from the spot in France where I got the idea.

If anyone tells you the story started in a dream, you can tell him that it just isn't so. Tell him I got it from a soldier in a rainstorm, a soldier whose face I never even saw. And if you like the story, don't thank me. Thank that soldier, whoever he is. *He's* the one who really started the story going, while I'm merely the one who put it down on paper. (pp. 72-3)

> *Dr. Seuss, "'Where Do You Get Your Story Ideas?' They Ask," in* Writing Books for Boys and Girls, *edited by Helen Ferris, Doubleday & Company, Inc., 1952, pp. 71-3.*

---

Bartholomew Cubbins, he of the *500 Hats* and a long time favorite, has more adventures in this sequel. The story [is about] how he became a courtier in the kingdom of Didd . . . and a good tale it is, though funnier to children than to adults. For it is a story of how the court magicians attempted to please the king, bored with the weather, by producing a new substance, called oobleck, which inundates the kingdom and results in nonsensical misadventures. Just how the king gets rid of it is a bit on the silly side, but that won't worry Bartholomew's friends.

> *A review of "Bartholomew and the Oobleck," in* Virginia Kirkus' Bookshop Service, *Vol. XVII, No. 17, September 1, 1949, p. 465.*

In one of the funniest books ever written for children young Bartholomew Cubbins nearly lost his head because he simply couldn't remove his hat—or rather his 500 hats—to bow before the king. Now, praise be! he's back. . . . How the redoubtable Bartholomew saves the day, . . . how the king becomes a re-formed character, and how the people have a brand-new holiday is all told and pictured in as happily cockeyed fashion as the best of Dr. Seuss. You'll love it.

> *Polly Goodwin, "Hurrah! Dr. Seuss Gives Us Oobleck," in* Chicago Tribune, *Part 4, November 13, 1949, p. 17.*

If Bartholomew Cubbins doesn't become King Bartholomew of Didd when he outgrows his role as page boy, the citizens of Didd will miss a fine bet. For Bartholomew . . . is the only astute person in the whole tale of what happened when the oobleck descended.

Dr. Seuss gives us the fun of watching the calamity develop, picture by picture, and pleases us with a simple, happy ending. Not quite up to **"The Five Hundred Hats,"** it does prove without intention that Bartholomew should be King! Especially for the 6-to-9-year-olds.

> *Gladys Crofoot Castor, "King and Page," in* The New York Times Book Review, *November 13, 1949, p. 12.*

Though more text is included in this tale than is customary of Seuss's style, the illustrations remain characteristic. More and more green is added to the black and white illustrations as the oobleck continues to fall throughout the story, and Seuss's expressive illustrations transform the imaginary tale into a setting convincingly appropriate. The movement in the illustrations, within pages and across pages, keeps up with the pace of the story, and the careful placement of green oobleck helps the eye travel in a path as hectic as Bartholomew's wild attempts to warn the people of the Kingdom of the oobleck's arrival.

Seuss's style of art and prose, unique and original as it is, undoubtedly accounts for the wide appeal his work holds. The silly, unimaginable events momentarily become real at his hand and even possess a touch of moralism to balance the frivolity of the story.

> *Linda Kauffman Peterson "The Caldecott Medal and Honor Books, 1938-1981: 'Bartholomew and the Oobleck'," in* Newbery and Caldecott Medal and Honor Books: An Annotated Bibliography *by Linda Kauffman Peterson and Marilyn Leathers Solt, G. K. Hall & Co., 1982, p. 283.*

---

## IF I RAN THE ZOO   (1950)

Many thousands of youngsters will shout with joy for a new "Dr. Seuss" book, whatever it may be. **"And To Think That I Saw It on Mulberry Street"** is a little American classic, in the form of a big picture book. It is very gentle nonsense, however, compared with this riotous new masterpiece. Here the good "doctor" out-draws, out-rhymes, out-imagines himself.

[We] meet in startling side-splitting portraits: flustards, joats, lunks, deer with connected horns, the scraggle-foot mulligatawny, the iota, the thwerll, tufted mazurka, wild tick tock-toe and many others. A few quite new machines, useful in their pursuit, also will demand delighted study.

As you turn the pages, the imaginings get wilder and funnier, the rhymes more hilarious. There will be no age limits for this book, because families will be forced to share re-reading and quotation, for a long, long time.

Hurrah for you, Dr. Seuss, and thank you for one of the funniest children's books in a blue moon.

> *"Wonderful Trucks, Trains, Squirrels, Alps, Cats, Boats and Thwerlls," in* New York Herald Tribune Book Review, *November 12, 1950, p. 8.\**

All the Dr. Seuss books are popular with children as well as with the adults who read them aloud, because the imagination darts along as rapidly as a child's would, and the humor is high spirited. And of course the pictures keep perfect pace with the story.

This newest one is among the best. Told in terse rhyme, it is the wild tale of a boy who, noting a zoo keeper's pride, imagines what sort of a zoo he himself will keep. . . . The amazement of the zoo audience is a wonder to see and the names of the new creatures roll out hilariously.

> *Frances Chrystie, "Ideal Zoo," in* The New York Times Book Review, *November 19, 1950, p. 42.*

Not only does [Gerald M. McGrew] capture the most outrageous animals of the imagination—a ten-footed lion, an elephant cat, a scraggle-footed Mulligatawny—but the places in and means by which he traps these unique species are just as inventive. . . .

As is customary, Seuss's text demands the attention of the reader, for the words are an invention in and of themselves. The hyphenated words help produce such a rapid verbal pattern that it is often easy to wind up tongue-tied before the end of a page.

The rhythm of the twisting word patterns demands as much attention as do the red, yellow, blue, and black and white illustrations. If the text is outrageous, then Seuss's visual interpretation is equally so. The primary colors produce rapid, successive eye movements across and around the pages, and the use of black and white is just as integral to the illustrations as the color.

It is no surprise that Seuss's work remains so popular; he creates worlds where the impossible becomes ordinary and the underdog, child or animal, is for a time in command—the hero. (p. 287)

> *Linda Kauffman Peterson "The Caldecott Medal and Honor Books, 1938-1981: 'If I Ran the Zoo'," in* Newbery and Caldecott Medal and Honor Books: An Annotated Bibliography *by Linda Kauffman Peterson and Marilyn Leathers Solt, G. K. Hall & Co., 1982, pp. 286-87.*

---

## SCRAMBLED EGGS SUPER!   (1953)

When the one and only Dr. Seuss unleashes his famous imagination to run riot across the pages of a large-size picture book, hurrahs sound from every quarter. And so they will again at this wildly nonsensical account of the most astounding egg hunt in history.

[Any] child from 8 to 80 will gleefully accompany Peter T. Hooper, a boy tired of ordinary hen's eggs, on his global search for new kinds of eggs. . . . A lovely book.

> *Polly Goodwin, in a review of "Scrambled Eggs Super!" in* Chicago Tribune, *Part 4, March 29, 1953, p. 14.*

The Rabbit who started in business as escort to the Goddess Ostara will be happier this Easter season for the fertility rampant in the brain of Dr. Seuss.

The good Doctor, a leading expert in the field of un-Natural Science, has been, of course, a graphic advocate of the Unfettered Mind since the days of Clara Bow, having started his great body of work in that late and lamented journal of research, College Humor Magazine. He has now come up with help for a presumably over-wrought animal who has been trying to make the eggs of this earth go far enough round at Easter time. No simple solution such as more productive mash or better home environment for chickens is proposed by Dr. Seuss. Such measures are pedestrian in the winged world of the Doctor. He, it can now be revealed, has discovered completely new eggs—with birds to match.

It is clear to this observer that the Doctor speaks in this book through a child, one Peter T. Hooper, in rolling verse (to be read aloud in ringing tones), so as to bemuse the less alert.

The whole story is proved with bona fide drawings and it is hard to deny their authenticity. Old scholars may note some resemblance to certain commercial associates of Dr. Seuss who were once wont to flee the ministrations of a famous insecticide. Despite that, all look fine.

The thoughtful parent may wish to buy the children a television set or a limousine to divert their attention while he pussyfoots into his den with this latest collection of Dr. Seuss' fabulous findings.

> *Walt Kelly, "A La Peter T. Hooper," in* The New York Times Book Review, *April 5, 1953, p. 21.*

How one man can make up such marvelous names and also draw pictures that surpass the names in fantastic imagery is a mystery. The "very best fowls" in this book are just as wild and funny as the animals in **"If I Ran the Zoo."** To an adult, the precise quality in the tall-tale style of young Peter T. Hooper adds to the fun of a hilarious creation.

> *A review of "Scrambled Eggs Super!" in* New York Herald Tribune Book Review, *May 17, 1953, p. 10.*

---

### HORTON HEARS A WHO! (1954)

This is the story of a humane elephant, a town of tiny creatures named Whos, and various intolerant animals. It is probably the most moral tale since the first "Elsie Dinsmore," but since it is written and illustrated by Dr. Seuss it is a lot more fun.

Horton, a big-eared, Seuss-type elephant was taking a bath in a jungle pool one day when he distinctly heard a call for help. It was coming from a speck of dust. When he told the other animals about it they ganged up on him. They thought Horton was crazy, and tried in every way to dispose of what they couldn't understand. . . . Horton's efforts to keep life intact on the Who's dust-speck would have daunted a lesser elephant, but Horton keeps going by telling himself:

> I simply must help them,
> because, after all,
> A person's a person no
> matter how small.

Children, parents, relatives and friends need not come whimpering to this reviewer to find out what the Whos and their

*From* How the Grinch Stole Christmas, *written and illustrated by Dr. Seuss. Random House, 1957. Copyright © 1957 by Dr. Seuss. All rights reserved. Reprinted by permission of Random House, Inc.*

town look like. She knows the limits of her powers of description. Buy the book and find out.

> *Jane Cobb, "A Handful of Dust," in* The New York Times Book Review, *September 12, 1954, p. 32.*

The verses are full of the usual lively, informal language and amazing rhymes that have delighted such a world-wide audience in the good "doctor's" other books. The story, with its moral, does not match the gayety of some of the older books. But the pictures are as wildly original and funny as ever. Horton will make many thousands of new friends, and bring that special kind of Seuss fun to the many homes where he is shared by young and old.

> *Louise S. Bechtel, in a review of "Horton Hears a Who!" in* New York Herald Tribune Book Review, *October 24, 1954, p. 20.*

This book seems recent to children, while Andersen's "Ugly Duckling" seems long ago and faraway. Not that a twelve-year-old would be caught carrying this Seuss picture book unless he had the excuse of reading it to the small fry in the family. But if you happen to have it in your library, persuade him to look at it again to see if the story suggests anything current in our world today. In his usual light vein, Dr. Seuss has turned out a fable about the little people trying to be heard in a world-society\where the huge ones make all the noise. Not only is this true of obscure peoples everywhere, but of the little nations today, trying to have a voice in world affairs. This light-hearted picture book, once the children catch its application, is an easy introduction to other more complex satires for our generation.

> *May Hill Arbuthnot, "Magic and Make-Believe for Adolescents, 12-13-14: 'Horton Hears a Who!',"' in her Children's Reading in the Home, Scott, Foresman and Company, 1969, p. 199.*

[*Horton Hears a Who!*] is a fantasy in form, but its ideology is very goal-oriented and socially concerned. While *Winnie the Pooh* centered on the on-going happiness of a group of mutually respectful but self-contained individuals, and *The Little House* on a nostalgic recreation of a lost rural past, *Horton* is, above all, concerned with the individual's crucial role as a member of society. And it is a society full of conflicts and antagonism, with constant crises and dangers, and social pressures of every sort.

The plot of *Horton* is very simple. A benevolent elephant hears a voice from a small speck of dust and immediately feels obligated to help and protect it "Because, after all, / A person's a person, no matter how small." This refrain is repeated again and again as the elephant faces one crisis after another. First some kangaroos mock him, then some monkeys steal the clover with the speck of dust on it. They give it to Vlad Vlad-i-koff the "black-bottomed eagle" who obligingly flies off with it and drops it in a 100-mile wide field of clover. Horton toils after it "with groans, over stones / That tattered his toenails and battered his bones" and then picks three million clovers before he discovers his speck of dust. The people on the speck are in real trouble . . . because they had "landed so hard that our clocks have all stopped. / Our tea-pots are broken. Our rocking-chairs smashed. / And our bicycle tires all blew up when we crashed." Horton promises once again to "stick by you small folks through thin and through thick!" But the kangaroos have decided to rope and cage the elephant for "chatting with persons who've never existed" and for "Such carryings-on in our peaceable jungle!" Furthermore, they are going to boil the dust speck in Beezle-Nut oil. (p. 170)

The action now shifts to the people of *Who*-ville on the speck, since Horton can no longer protect them. Their only hope, and his, lies in shouting enough to make even the kangaroos hear. As Horton puts it, "you very small persons will not have to die / If you make yourselves heard! *So come on, now, and TRY!*" They do try—desperately—but without success, until the Mayor "discovered one shirker," a very small one who "Was standing, just standing, and bouncing a Yo-Yo!" He lectured the lad that this was the "town's darkest hour! The time for all *Whos* who have blood that is red / To come to the aid of their country!" Finally, "that one small, extra Yopp put it over" and the Whos "proved they ARE persons, no matter how small. / And their whole world was saved by the Smallest of ALL!"

The ideological message of this story is so blatant that one is tempted to interpret it almost too specifically. For example, it seems to reflect the Cold War mentality of the Fifties—especially in the name of the arch-villain, the Eagle. It also teaches the general virtue of responsible paternalism—the big should take care of the little, the comfortable should protect the op-

pressed, no matter how great the cost. And then it further preaches that an individual's value is determined not by his own pleasure (playing with Yo-Yo's), but only by his contribution to the whole, his active participation in achieving the goals of his society.

*Horton* is not a "middle-of-the-road" story. The preservers of the status quo are the kangaroos, and they are clearly evil. They also represent the pressures for social conformity and against "hearing voices." The ideal which Horton represents is that of the sensitive, spiritual, artistic, dedicated lone defender of humanity with all the world against him. There is a similarity to the Little Engine of 1930, but Horton is far less humble and the stakes are much higher. This is a life-and-death struggle, not just a matter of toys and good food. Horton's non-conformism is shown as right because it is in a good cause benefiting others—just playing and minding one's own business like the *Who* with the Yo-Yo is clearly immoral. (pp. 170-71)

One may suggest that Horton represents the messianic idealism which has been for so long a part of American tradition—with periodic eruptions on both the right and the left in internal affairs, and, in the twentieth century especially, on the international scene as well. Nixon, Johnson, and Kennedy could claim to be identified with Dr. Seuss's dedicated elephant just as well as Ellsberg, Dr. Spock, and Daniel Berrigan. Radical fighters for social justice come right out of the mainstream of American ideology, and violent confrontations are an accepted part of our world view.

In another way, *Horton* reveals the two main themes of a mass democratic society—the paradoxical importance of individual resistance to mass pressure for evil but cooperation with mass pressure for good. In such a society neither the large "elephant" nor the small "Who" is safe without the help of the other—and both are always in danger. (p. 171)

> *Ruth B. Moynihan, "Ideologies in Children's Literature: Some Preliminary Notes," in Children's Literature: Annual of the Modern Language Association Seminar on Children's Literature and The Children's Literature Association, Vol. 2, edited by Francelia Butler, Temple University Press, 1973, pp. 166-72.\**

## ON BEYOND ZEBRA (1955)

It *would* be Dr. Seuss who had the fantastic idea of telling a small boy who knows all the letters of the alphabet that "*My* alphabet starts when *your* alphabet ends." He begins drawing his new letters in lovely Chinese designs, and explaining the wonderful new words in which they are used. A too-logical child can see that his new letters use old letters, but what difference! For the fun of it all is in the ridiculous word play, even more inventive this time than in his other recent rhymes. As for the beasts, it is incredible, but he has dreamed up still more, large and small, male and female, each somehow connected with a feeling you yourself wish you could have put into a new word.

Haven't you, too, worried like the Quandary? You won't worry so long, after you see the little cross-eyed red one in his lonely hole in the ocean. Wait till you hear the troubles of the Nutches, for whom there never are enough Nitches: there's Miss Fuddle-dee-Duddle who needs six helpers to get her wonderful tail out of muddle-dee-puddles; the letter Zatz is necessary to spell Zatz-it, see the "Three-Seater Zatz-it Nose-Patting Extension." In a wild round-up at the end, young Conrad is beginning to invent letters, too, and it's up to you to guess their use. It takes the wits of "good readers" to laugh with the current Seuss output, but there is proof that plenty of boys even up to twelve welcome his nonsense with joy.

> Louise S. Bechtel, in a review of "On Beyond Zebra!" in New York Herald Tribune Book Review, *November 13, 1955, p. 3.*

Like most writers Dr. Seuss probably has his troubles, but there is one worry from which he must be free. When he is putting a book together he need never get into a cold sweat wondering if some other author-illustrator might be working on the same idea. *Nobody* could possibly have ideas in any way resembling those that occur to this talented man. The one complaint to be made is that his themes are so bizarre that it is hard to make them clear to anyone who does not have the book right in his hands. **"On Beyond Zebra,"** for example, involves a whole new alphabet. . . .

Without the Seuss letters there would be no way to spell the names of creatures who look like brooms, or who live in tiny hutches, or like to sing in grottos. What these creatures look like *is* indescribable, but they are delightful and it is difficult to imagine how we ever managed without them.

> Jane Cobb, "Transalphebetica," in The New York Times Book Review, *Part II, November 13, 1955, p. 45.*

Conrad Cornelius o'Donald o'Dell has mastered the standard twenty-six letters of the alphabet, but finds them inadequate for his needs. He thereupon creates an addendum to the basic alphabet in order to write about the wonderous creatures he knows whose names are currently unspellable. The improbable Yuzz-a-Ma-Tuzz obviously requires a Yuzz; the mountain-climbing Wumbus clearly needs a Wum, and the rare High-Gargel-orum must be spelled with a Hi! As the additions to the menagerie get more outlandish, so does their orthography, until absurdity is raised to a high art form. The summary list of new letters in the back of the book is a further bit of tom-foolery. Seuss has devised new symbols that borrow rather freely from alphabetic forms already known by children; that is, he has overlapped and intertwined standard letters to create new forms. Thus, the "Spazz" contains a recognizable "s" and "p," and the "Nuh" reveals, after careful scrutiny, convoluted shapes of "n," "u," and "h." The list of new alphabetic forms concludes with a stupendous fabrication representing the ultimate letter and leaves it to the young reader to assign it a sufficiently spectacular name.

Seuss' flamboyant signature illustrations contribute to the sense of fun. He manipulates, in this case, not only the illustrations but the orthography. His consummate skill is in taking a seemingly reasonable idea and elaborating on it until it attains outrageous levels of hyperbole. The humor in this work is preposterous but contagious. Obvious end and internal rhymes, pronounced rhythms, and extensive alliteration characterize the narrative. To call this bad poetry is to miss the point—it is terrible poetry, but it is superlative doggerel. The obvious course of action is for readers to continue where Seuss left off, inventing new letters and expanding this unlikely but enviable zoo. (pp. 231-32)

> Barbara H. Baskin and Karen H. Harris, "A Selected Guide to Intellectually Demanding Books: 'On Beyond Zebra'," in their Books for the Gifted Child, *R. R. Bowker Company, 1980, pp. 231-32.*

## *IF I RAN THE CIRCUS* (1956)

Dr. Seuss fans can have a circus even if the greatest show on earth is no more. In a mad riot of pink, yellow and blue inventions the Circus McGurkus makes its debut. It's super-stoopendus. Young Morris McGurkus thinks it up, and his star performer is Sneelock who does odds and ends like taming a spotted atrocious. On it goes in a riot of Seussian nonsense which, as usual, will bring happy grins to the faces of young and old. . . . Our own favorites are the "to and fro marchers who march in five layers. The Fros march on Tos and the Tos march on Fros. Don't know how they do it but that's how it goes." That last, we might add, applies to Dr. Seuss himself in this fine wacky book with more unity and order than is usual in his nonsense.

> *"Jolly Stories: Gay Pictures,"* in New York Herald Tribune Book Review, *November 18, 1956, p. 4.**

This Dr. Seuss creation does not start with so bizarre a premise as some of his other extravaganzas. The idea of a small boy dreaming up an ideal circus is not in itself startling. However when the great man gets going, he turns on his own free-wheeling fantasy, which is both peculiar to himself and just plain peculiar. It is also just plain wonderful. . . .

All of Morris' animals are in the best weird Seuss tradition, and the composite illustrations are, if possible, even more elaborately outlandish than usual.

> Jane Cobb, "Snumms, Foons & Jotts," in The New York Times Book Review, *Part II, November 18, 1956, p. 47.*

In one of his best efforts since **Mulberry Street,** Dr. Seuss presents the fabulous Circus McGurkus. . . . There are the expected number of strange creatures with nonsensical names, but the real humor lies in the situations, and especially those involving Mr. Sneelock. There is fun for the entire family here.

> *"'If I Ran the Circus',"* in Good Books for Children: A Selection of Outstanding Children's Books Published 1948-57, *edited by Mary K. Eakin, The University of Chicago Press, 1959, p. 198.*

Dr. Seuss's peculiar attraction is the sheer nonsense of ridiculous names and creatures. Here there are Truffles, Flummoxes and Fibbels, but the framework of If I Ran The Circus . . . is the daydream of a small boy about his circus in the field behind Sneelock's Store, with Sneelock as the acrobatic star. The admixture of reality somehow makes the nonsense less acceptable, though the compulsive rhythms and audacious rhymes which make such a cheerful business of learning to read are as evident as ever.

> A review of "If I Ran the Circus," in The Junior Bookshelf, *Vol. 33, No. 6, December, 1969, p. 365.*

Here is a pleasantly mad book about a dream circus, 'The Circus McGurkus', which transmogrifies a waste plot. The drum-tummied snum, the remarkable foon, the hoodwink, and the spotted atrocious are among the weird performers who parade themselves in rollicking, predictable rhyme and crude, inventive illustrations. Though the madness never rises to the heights of nonsense, it will surely entertain.

> Timothy Rogers, in a review of "If I Ran the Circus," in The School Librarian, *Vol. 18, No. 1, March, 1970, p. 126.*

## *THE CAT IN THE HAT* (1957)

### AUTHOR'S COMMENTARY

Every year, just a moment before Christmas, millions of Americans named Uncle George race into a book store on their only trip of the year.

"I want a book," they tell the salesman, "that my nephew Orlo can read. He's in the first grade. Wants to be a rhinosaurus hunter."

"Sorry," said the salesman. "We have nothing about rhinosauri that Orlo could possibly read."

"O.K.," say the millions of Uncle Georges. "Gimme something he can read about some other kind of animal."

And on Christmas morning, under millions of Christmas trees, millions of Orlos unwrap millions of books . . . all of them titled, approximately, "Bunny, Bunny, Bunny."

This causes the rhinosaurus hunters to snort, "Books stink!" And this, in turn, causes philosophers to get all het up, and to write essays entitled "Why Orlo Can't Read," in which they urge that we all rush out and burn down the nearest school house.

Of course this would be just as silly as it would be to rush out and burn down the nearest Uncle George.

The reason Orlo says "Nuts to Books" is because practically every book that he is able to read is far beneath his intellectual capacity. Orlo, in the first grade, is a mighty hep guy. When he twists the knob of his television set he meets everyone from Wyatt Earp to Governor Faubus. He attends the launchings of Intercontinental Ballastic Missiles. He observes the building of the Pyramids, flies across the South Pole and he knows what tools you have to use if you want to defang a cobra. Orlo, at 6, has seen more of life than his great-grandfather had seen when he died at the age of 90.

Yet, if you go out to get Orlo a good book he can read, even if you search the great New York Public Library, you can bring all the available books back home in a paper bag and still have room in the paper bag for three oranges and a can of tuna.

So . . . one day I got so distressed about Orlo's plight, that I put on my Don Quixote suit and went out on a crusade. I announced loudly to all those within earshot, "Within two short weeks, with one hand tied behind me, I will knock out a story that will thrill the pants right off all Orlos!"

My ensuing experience can best be described as not dissimilar to that of being lost with a witch in a tunnel of love. The only job I ever tackled that I found more difficult was when I wrote the Baedeker that Eskimos use when they travel in Siam.

In writing for kids of the middle first grade, the writer gets his first ghastly shock when he learns about a diabolical little thing known as "The List." School book publishing houses all have little lists. Lists of words that kids can be expected to read, at various stages in their progress through the elementary grades. How they compile these lists is still a mystery to me. But somehow or other . . . with divining rods or something . . . they've figured out the number of words that a teacher can ram into the average child's noodle. (Also the approximate dates on which these rammings should take place.)

Poor Orlo! At the age of 6½, his noodle has scarcely been rammed at all!

He can, of course, recognize some 1500 *spoken* words when they enter his head through the holes in his ears. But *printed* words . . . *ugh!* He can recognize only about 300 when they try to get into his head through his eyes. All the other printed words in the world all look, to Orlo, like Appomatox.

And there I was, in my shining armor, with my feet nailed down to a pathetic little vocabulary that I swear my Irish setter could master.

After the first couple hours of staring at my Word List, I did discover a few words that might come in handy in writing a story. Words like *am* and *are* and *is*. But when you want to thrill the pants off a rhinosaurus hunter, that takes a bit of doing with words like *daddy* and *kitten* and *pot*.

After the first few weeks, I was still looking for a subject to write about. Then, suddenly one night, I dreamed the answer. Two simple little romantic words! Every last kid in the United States knew them! They were even printed on kindergarten building blocks!

I leapt from my beddie house. I rushed for my typewriter. Even before I got there, my happy fingers were already typing in the air. "The Queen Zebra" was the title of my story!

I had dashed off thirty-two red hot pages when, suddenly, I felt sort of all-over-queasy. Out of the corners of my eyes, I snuck a look at the Word List. *Queen* and *Zebra* weren't there after all!

Then, to make things even more befuddling, I noticed something new that had escaped my attention up to now. Maybe the letters *Q* and *Z* were perfectly kosher in kindergarten, but there were no *Q* and *Z* words on my first-grade list whatever. *Q* and *Z* had been purged and sent to Siberia!

Befuddled? At the end of the first four months, my Befuddlement Index had zoomed so high that my befuddlement thermometer blew up in my mouth. I was now trying to sweat out a story about a bird . . . at the same time refraining from using the word *bird*. (The list, you see, declares a permanent closed season.)

But *wing* was on the list. And *thing* was on the list. So I COULD write about a bird IF I called the bird a WING THING! And then I discovered I could use the word *fly!* Now, at last, I could really be moving! This enabled me to write one sentence.

That first sentence was also the last sentence of that story. After six weeks of trying to get my *wing thing* off the ground and into the sky, I had to give up due to numerous unbelievable reasons. *Ground* and *sky* were both taboo. Furthermore, my *wing thing* couldn't have *legs* or a *beak* or a *tail*. Not even a *foot!* Neither a *left* foot nor a *right* foot. And she couldn't lay *eggs*. Because *eggs*, according to the word list, are to be eaten, not read. . . .

I solved my problem by writing **"The Cat in the Hat."** How I did this is no trade secret. The method I used is the same method you use when you sit down to make apple stroodle without stroodles.

You forget all about time. You go to work with what you have! You take your limited, uninteresting ingredients (in my case 223 words) and day and night, month after month, you mix them up into thousands of different combinations. You bake a batch. You taste it. Then you hurl it out of the window. Until finally one night, when it is darkest just before dawn, a plausible stroodle-less stroodle begins to take shape before your eyes!

Since **"The Cat"** I've been trying to invent some easier method. But I am afraid the above procedure will always be par for the course. At least it will be just as long as the course is laid out on a word list. (pp. 2, 60)

> *Dr. Seuss, "How Orlo Got His Book," in* The New York Times Book Review, *November 17, 1957, pp. 2, 60.*

---

Beginning readers and parents who have been helping them through the dreary activities of Dick and Jane and other primer characters are due for a happy surprise. Dr. Seuss, that old master of nonsense, has turned his special talents to an easy-reading book. The result is a madly tumultuous tale about two children home alone on a dull, wet afternoon, a cat from no-where who knows a lot of zany tricks; two indescribable Things—also full of tricks—and a fish who is in constant protest against all the commotion.

It's fine, furious slapstick, told in rolling rhythms and lots of conversation. Dr. Seuss has used only 223 different words,

according to the publisher, and, according to my count, less than a dozen of these are two-syllable, all chosen with an eye to the knowledge and ability of the first and second grade reader. And there are Dr. Seuss' own illustrations to help make this one of the most original and funniest of books for early readers.

> *Ellen Lewis Buell, "High Jinks at Home," in* The New York Times Book Review, *March 17, 1957, p. 40.*

Hurray for Dr. Seuss! He's done it again, only differently this time. You'll not find here the extravagant vocabulary of his other creations. No, indeed. From a list of 300 words known to middle first-graders, he has taken just 223, juggled them about, and come up with a hilarious story.... All the old delightful rimes and rhythms, the zany illustrations are here. Together they make a book to rejoice 7 and 8 year olds and make them look with distinct disfavor on the drab adventures of standard primer characters.

> *Polly Goodwin, "Hurray for Dr. Seuss!" in* Chicago Tribune, *Part 4, May 12, 1957, p. 7.*

**"The Cat in the Hat"** is elegant nonsense. We were afraid that the limitations Dr. Seuss put upon himself might have shackled his marvelous inventiveness. Quite the contrary. Restricting his vocabulary to a mere 223 words (all in the reading range of a six or seven year old) and shortening his verse story has given a certain riotous and extravagant unity ... that is pleasing. "All the swing and merriment of the pictures and the natural truthful simplicity of the untruthfulness" that [Beatrix Potter noted in her letter to Anne Carroll Moore] are still there. [see excerpt above] It is a case of "all this and heaven too."

Mothers, fathers, teachers. Courage. Resist the temptation to read this to your five, six or seven year old. It will be hard, for you'll love the foolish cat and his tricks. You'll want to share this jolly book. But let your child have the fun of dis-covery. Let him read it to himself. Read **"Horton Hatches the Egg,"** or **"McElligot's Pool"** or **"On Beyond Zebra"** to him but not **"The Cat in the Hat."** This is his book.

> *"Fun, Beauty, Fancy for First Readers," in* New York Herald Tribune Book Review, *May 12, 1957, p. 24.\**

A rhyming story whose vocabulary is limited to 223 simple words. Thus it cannot have the absurd excellence of the early Seuss books, but it is remarkably successful.... The drawings are fun, and children admire the ingenious and useful car at the end. I wish "For Beginning Readers" were not so obvious on jacket and cover—this is a fine book for remedial purposes, but self-conscious children often refuse material if it seems meant for younger children.

> *Heloise P. Mailloux, in a review of "The Cat in the Hat," in* The Horn Book Magazine, *Vol. XXXIII, No. 3, June, 1957, p. 215.*

*The Cat in the Hat* is one of Dr. Seuss' best. It is a preposterous, nonsensical fantasy about Cat, who takes over a house in the absence of the mother and does all the appalling things the children might *dream* of doing but would never really do. Readers are, of course, horrified at the increasing mess and are also happily titillated that it is so terrific with mother liable to walk in any moment! The serene conclusion is a gem of wishful thinking that brings every young reader back to a re-reading of this completely satisfying nightmare.

> *May Hill Arbuthnot, "Reading Begins, 6-7-8: 'The Cat in the Hat'," in her* Children's Reading in the Home, *Scott, Foresman and Company, 1969, p. 86.*

[*The Cat in the Hat*] is pure Seuss. The text consists of short, snappy rhymes with a metronomic beat that doesn't fail. The pictures are his cartoons: absurd, poised between cute and ugly, always about to explode from one silly situation to another, sillier one. There is nothing lovely about the worlds Dr. Seuss presents to us. But that is not his aim. His books are crazy little planets, fast and often funny, that deal exclusively in visual and verbal gags. Sensitive aunts will not exclaim over Seuss, art directors won't whip out their awards, but a lot of children you and I are fond of will yell the words aloud and chortle happily at the foolish carryings-on in those nutty pictures. (p. 74)

> *Karla Kuskin, "Dick, Jane, and Dr. Seuss," in* Saturday Review, *Vol. LV, No. 50, December 9, 1972, pp. 74-6.\**

---

### HOW THE GRINCH STOLE CHRISTMAS (1957)

Not since Scrooge has there been such a downright, out-and-out Christmas-hater as the Grinch. . . . Repulsive but fascinating in his very horridness, the Grinch lived just north of Who-ville. . . .

He tries [to stop Christmas from coming], in most demoniacal fashion, masquerading as Santa Claus, but even when he has stolen all the presents and Christmas goodies, the Whos still celebrate and the Grinch begins to realize that "maybe Christmas doesn't come from a store. Maybe Christmas . . . perhaps . . . means a little bit more."

Even if you prefer Dr. Seuss in a purely antic mood, you must admit that if there's a moral to be pointed out, no one can do it more gaily. The reader is swept along by the ebullient rhymes and the weirdly zany pictures until he is limp with relief when the Grinch reforms and, like the latter, mellow with good feeling.

> *Ellen Lewis Buell, "Yuletide in Who-Ville," in* The New York Times Book Review, *October 6, 1957, p. 40.*

Mr. Scrooge has nothing on Dr. Seuss' Grinch "who had a heart two sizes too small" which made him try to stop Christmas coming. . . . But not even the hardened Grinch could remain unaffected by the spirit of Christmas, which Dr. Seuss captures in an unsentimental way such as only he knows.

A splendid warmhearted book just right for the Christmas season. Like last year's great success book *How Santa had a Difficult Journey to Deliver His Presents* by Krahn . . . it uses brilliant patches of single colour to highlight the illustrations. It is a pity that we have not had this book, available in America since 1957, sooner as there is a dearth of good non-religious books to read at this season. (pp. 387-88)

> *J. Russell, in a review of "How the Grinch Stole Christmas," in* The Junior Bookshelf, *Vol. 37, No. 6, December, 1973, pp. 387-88.*

---

### THE CAT IN THE HAT COMES BACK! (1958)

A year ago last March there appeared a thin, red-white-and-blue volume which immediately made publishing history. Dr. Seuss' monosyllabic fantasy was not the first book to beguile the tedium of beginning readers . . . , but this deft combination of easy words, swift rhymes and batty nonsense convinced thousands of hitherto skeptical children that reading could be fun—just as the grown-ups said.

Now Dr. Seuss has not only presented his converts with a sequel, **"The Cat in the Hat Comes Back,"** but has also edited four other stories on the same first-grade and second-grade reading level which, with the two Cat books, comprise a new series, "Beginner Books." . . .

First off, I should like to report that the new antics of the Cat in the Hat are just as funny and unexpected as in the original story. There are the same hypnotic rhythms, and the same kind of cumulative action, building at jet speed to suspense and surprise. The mysterious, magical Cat, raising Cain in a normally peaceful household, is just as debonair as ever and somehow, in the midst of some indescribable hocus-pocus involving pink snow, he manages to introduce the letters of the alphabet in a manner to disarm the most suspicious of nonscholars.

> *Ellen Lewis Buell, in a review of "The Cat in the Hat Comes Back," in* The New York Times Book Review, *October 5, 1958, p. 36.*

[The trick-playing cat of *The cat in the hat* makes a return visit], . . . again wreaking havoc and then restoring order in a most ingenious manner. While not quite so rib-tickling as the first story, this one is still well above the average book for beginning readers both in imaginativeness and humor and in narrative and pictorial interest. First graders should be able to read it by themselves.

> *A review of "The Cat in the Hat Comes Back!" in* The Booklist and Subscription Books Bulletin, *Vol. 55, No. 5, November 1, 1958, p. 136.*

The chief difficulty with the new series of "Beginner Books" under Dr. Seuss' editorship is . . . : the problem of keeping misguided parents, teachers and older children (who enjoy them immensely) from reading them aloud to children who have not yet begun to read and so spoiling all the fun and profit for them. . . . It will be no news to anybody that the Dr. Seuss book is the best of the [five books reviewed, which also include "A Fly Went By," by Mike McClintock; "The Big Jump, and Other Stories," by Benjamin Elkin; "Sam and the Firefly," by P. D. Eastman; and "A Big Ball of String," by Marion Holland]; the semi-smooth jingles, the irresistibly funny situations, the exaggerations in text and pictures that are [Seuss'] alone, all are there, no more hampered by a small vocabulary than a bird is hampered in making an attractive song by being able to sing only a few notes.

> *A review of "The Cat in the Hat Comes Back!" in* New York Herald Tribune Book Review, *Part II, November 2, 1958, p. 8.*

There are five books so far in the Beginner Book series recently published by Random House; all are edited by Dr. Seuss, whose rules for vocabulary control keep the stories well within the grasp of a beginning reader. Dr. Seuss's own contribution, *The Cat in the Hat Comes Back,* is by far the pick of the lot, with that zany cat and a hatful of kittens named for letters of the alphabet cavorting in a story that moves at a fast clip, with comic pictures that almost talk. (pp. 97-8)

> *Charlotte Jackson, in a review of "The Cat in the Hat Comes Back!" in* The Atlantic Monthly, *Vol. 202, No. 6, December, 1958, pp. 97-8.*

## HAPPY BIRTHDAY TO YOU!  (1959)

In Katroo (where they really know how to do such things) a birthday celebration is a whizz-bang of a to-do that starts at dawn when the Birthday Bird, especially trained for the job, calls for the birthday child. Then, for 18 hours it leads on thru frolic and feasting that only the wonderfully zany verse and pictures of Dr. Seuss can describe adequately. It's a story of lilting vitality from which birthday joy will burst forth every day in the year.

> *Robert L. Shebs, in a review of "Happy Birthday to You!" in* Chicago Tribune, *Part 4, November 1, 1959, p. 12.*

If you are at all acquainted with the children's literature currently being produced, you don't need to be told that Dr. Seuss is the most popular, most individualistic, most acceptable children's writer around today. We have the feeling however that in his latest he nears the point of self-parody. May he soon seek out new territory. Meanwhile the smaller boy at our fireside never seems to tire of his rhythms. Every day is a birthday with Dr. Seuss's gang.

> *"Joys for Many Days," in* The Christian Century, *Vol. LXXVI, No. 48, December 2, 1959, p. 1405.\**

This multicolored excursion is a gay and festive one, though perhaps a little too long and involved. The rhyming text and imaginative illustrations, however, will delight not only Dr. Seuss fans, but birthday boys and girls as well.

> *Nancy B. Childs, in a review of "Happy Birthday to You!" in* Junior Libraries, *an appendix to* Library Journal, *Vol. 6, No. 5, January 15, 1960, p. 33.*

## ONE FISH, TWO FISH, RED FISH, BLUE FISH  (1960)

Though humorous and imaginative, these episodes are too numerous, almost to the point of boredom despite all that is clever and unique about them. The book's greatest value will come in its simple vocabulary (designed for beginning readers) and in its repetition of similar sounds. Sentences, such as, "He (the Yink) likes to wink and drink pink ink," will help those learning to read to see the sameness of suffixes and prefixes. Recommended, but not with the enthusiasm which earlier Seuss books have generated.

> *Nancy Childs, in a review of "One Fish, Two Fish, Red Fish, Blue Fish," in* Junior Libraries, *an appendix to* Library Journal, *Vol. 6, No. 9, May 15, 1960, p. 50.*

Dr. Seuss has made a tremendous effort to pretend that reading is dead easy. This American book is of the *mad* kind, where freakish (and rather unpleasant) pictures illustrate crazy remarks about crazy creatures, linked only by the order of the alphabet. The book, and its companion volumes, are advertised as containing only a hundred words: the only possible comment is 'Which hundred?'

> *Margery Fisher, in a review of "One Fish, Two Fish," in her* Growing Point, *Vol. 1, No. 2, July, 1962, p. 25.*

## GREEN EGGS AND HAM  (1960)

Would you like them anywhere?—Well, try them before you finally refuse. Only Dr. Seuss could break down the resistance, and he does it with a contagious use of repeat words and phrases—and winds up with complete capitulation. Here's a tale with a moral—but done so engagingly and absurdly that the reluctant beginning reader may find himself hoist by his own petard. Try for yourself. Here's a book an adult will use— that will be taken over by the young fry until the oldsters cry for mercy.

> *A review of "Green Eggs and Ham," in* Virginia Kirkus' Service, *Vol. XXVIII, No. 16, August 15, 1960, p. 679.*

The old master has done it again—this time with fifty, count them fifty, words. The happy theme of refusal-to-eat changing to relish will be doubly enjoyable to the child who finds many common edibles as nauseating as the title repast. The pacing throughout is magnificent, and the opening five pages, on which the focal character introduces himself with a placard: "I Am Sam," are unsurpassed in the controlled-vocabulary literature.

> *A review of "Green Eggs and Ham," in* Saturday Review, *Vol. XLIII, No. 45, November 12, 1960, p. 103.*

This fall Dr. Seuss has tried a new and daring experiment, writing not for "beginning readers" but for "beginning beginner readers." Lest those uninitiated in the reading abilities of first graders be alarmed and expect this sort of thing to be run into the ground with indefinite beginnings until we have a game of dumb crambo, we hasten to say that this series uses not a hundred, but fifty words in the hope that by Christmas six-year-olds alias the "beginning beginner readers" can read them alone. Dr. Seuss has entitled his book **"Green Eggs and Ham"** . . . and, not to be outdone by "The House that Jack Built" in forty-one words, concocts a similar bit of cumulative, repetitive foolishness with fifty. His choice is necessarily less picturesque and colorful than "shaven and shorn" and "tattered and torn," as he limits himself to monosyllables, but his pictures and the wonderful dead-pan humor are superb.

> *"Few Words, but Lively Ones," in* New York Herald Tribune Book Review, *November 13, 1960, p. 16.\**

One cannot help object, I think, to the streams and streams of "easy-to-read" books, which took over as suddenly and completely as singing commercials and are often as over-ingratiating. (The publishers hold the limited number of words out like bait—only fifty words! only a hundred and fifty words!) There are two conspicuous exceptions this year ["**Green Eggs and Ham**" and Else Holmelund Minarik's "Little Bear's Friend"]. The first is . . . by Dr. Seuss, who was, I guess, the originator of the genre, and who has been able from the beginning to work a limited vocabulary into narrative poems of astounding virtuosity. . . . [The] very persistant Sam-I-Am, who doesn't know the meaning of "No," keeps offering a big, shaggy character in a ruined top hat some poached eggs and a ham butt, both arsenic green. Dr. S. can play so many tunes on his simplified keyboard that, reading him, one is hardly aware that there *are* more than fifty words. The big character

Sam!

If you will let me be,

I will try them.

You will see.

55

*From* Green Eggs and Ham, *written and illustrated by Dr. Seuss. Beginner Books, 1960. Copyright ©*
*1969 by Dr. Seuss. All rights reserved. Reprinted by permission of Beginner Books, Inc., a Division of*
*Random House, Inc.*

gets crosser and crosser, but Sam-I-Am, never more than momentarily dismayed, bounces back. . . . This is the best thing on being forced to eat since "What is the matter with Mary Jane?" (p. 226)

*Emily Maxwell, "Scottish Fairies, the Chair Wind,*
*and How to Talk to a Firefly," in* The New Yorker,
*Vol. XXXVI, No. 40, November 19, 1960, pp. 223-48.\**

One of the most successful authors of children's books is Theodor Geisel or Dr. Seuss, and perhaps his best seller is *Green Eggs and Ham*. . . . Why is this book popular? Probably one reason is that it is by Dr. Seuss, and that many parents and children reach for another book by an author they know and like. Once a writer becomes popular, the popularity will linger for a good number of years, particularly if the author keeps on producing new books. . . . But *Green Eggs and Ham* needs to have more than its author's reputation to become one of the most popular of his books. We suspect that among those qualities are the fact that Dr. Seuss tells a funny tale of a pest— and pests are around children all the time—the fact that it deals with food and liking food, the fact that it uses extravagant lists of words that are fun and close to nonsense, the fact that it uses repetition to establish a pattern and break it and the fact that it uses bright colors and cartoonlike illustrations. We also

suspect that, like the folk tale, *Green Eggs and Ham* shows the triumph of the "little person," the one who has common sense. All of these appear to be qualities especially appealing to a five-to-seven year old (and to a younger child if it is read aloud). There is another reason, too: it is different from other Dr. Seuss books. . . . *Green Eggs and Ham,* then, is one of those books that, through a combination of writing and visual artistry, was initially popular with all sorts of children and has remained so. (pp. 31, 33)

*Alan C. Purves and Dianne L. Monson, "Folk Tales,*
*Popular Literature, and Myth," in their* Experiencing Children's Literature, *Scott, Foresman and Company, 1984, pp. 23-56.\**

### THE SNEETCHES AND OTHER STORIES (1961)

Four stories by Dr. Seuss are not necessarily four times as good as one Dr. Seuss story—but they are probably four times as good as somebody else's stories. Anyhow they are sure of an ecstatic welcome and the fact that they are uneven in quality is something readers will find out for themselves. *The Sneetches* and *What Was I Scared Of* have plenty of laughs—and some underlying truths which may find their lodging places in small listeners' minds. *The Zax* and *Too Many Daves* are just plain goofy nonsense, but their brevity will recommend them for those small fry with concentration problems.

> *A review of "The Sneetches and Other Stories," in* Virginia Kirkus' Service, *Vol. XXIX, No. 28, September 15, 1961, p. 842.*

Dr. Seuss was a genius, until he got on to the easy-reader bandwagon. *The Sneetches* harks back to his earlier manner, and he has a good idea here. The Plain-Belly Sneetches, trying hard to keep up with the Star-Belly Joneses, are very funny, and there is sound, if slightly laboured, social comment in the course of the story. There is, however, something incurably vulgar here which gets in the way of enjoyment. (pp. 345-46)

> *A review of "The Sneetches and Other Stories," in* The Junior Bookshelf, *Vol. 29, No. 6, December, 1965, pp. 345-46.*

---

## TEN APPLES UP ON TOP!   (1961)

The Dust Cover describes this book as a 'delightfully funny story in rhyme for the young reader just mastering the art of reading'. This is exactly what the book is—63 pages of sheer fun pitched at the precise level required for children of this age and stage.... [What] wonders the author has done with a mere 75 different words! *Ten Apples Up On Top* should be required reading for all budding 'reading scheme' writers, for here is a real story, with a beginning, a middle and a satisfactory ending, yet full of interest throughout....

[It] is perhaps too much to expect that large quantities of this book (and its eleven companions) will be found in every infants' classroom, but there ought to be at least one copy. Genuinely funny books for young children are a rare treat, and this is one of them.

> *A. Bullough, in a review of "Ten Apples Up On Top," in* The School Librarian and School Library Review, *Vol. 11, No. 5, July, 1963, p. 559.*

---

## DR. SEUSS'S SLEEP BOOK   (1962)

[A] rarity among books—one deliberately calculated to make its readers yawn. And anyone who has followed Dr. Seuss' twenty-five-year career as author-artist knows how persuasive he is. No one could resist those zillions of astonishing sleepyheads, such as the Hoop-Soup-Snoop Group and the Biffer-Baum Birds, which only he could have invented, pictured and described in hypnotic rhythms which bring yawns right on top of the chuckles. He had me nodding at 8:30 P.M.

> *Ellen Lewis Buell, in a review of "Dr. Seuss's Sleep Book," in* The New York Times Book Review, *September 9, 1962, p. 30.*

The new Dr. Seuss, hardly a classic, at least has the considerable virtue of being continually silly and unflaggingly inventive. Like all of T. S. Geisel's Seuss books, it abounds in the kind of word play which seems to fascinate children in the early stages of learning to read.... Whether the thought of Biffer-Baum Birds and Collapsible Frinks nesting down will promote drowsiness in young humans I do not know. In a test on one seven-year-old, the result was giggling. The drawings are, if anything, more frazzled, more rubbery than ever.

> *Earl W. Foell, "Quiet Please," in* The Christian Science Monitor, *November 15, 1962, p. 2B.\**

---

## HOP ON POP   (1963)

As for Dr. Seuss, that wizard is bent on removing reading frustrations before they start and he deserves a special fanfare for *Hop on Pop.*... Here he introduces phonic elements by showing word groups in smashing large type and then combining the words in phrases set in smaller but still easily-read type, thus UP and PUP are coupled with the statement "Pup is up" and so on through cunningly contrived and carefully built word patterns to such relatively complicated sentences as "We like to hop on top of Pop." Sentiments like that should turn any reading lesson into a ball, especially when the children see the illustrations. These are as funny as ever; they also provide clues for figuring out the meanings of words. Dr. Seuss thinks of everything.

> *Ellen Lewis Buell, in a review of "Hop on Pop," in* The New York Times Book Review, *April 14, 1963, p. 56.*

"The simplest Seuss for youngest use," as the words on jacket and book cover suggest, is exactly what this new book is. Superb, simple Seuss. Funny, phonic, fantastic. It groups one syllable rhythmic and rhyming words together, uses them in brief sentences and illustrates the idea hilariously with the Doctor's ever fresh and amusing oddities.... A splendid teaching device which is a bit cheaper than a $400,000 Automated Responsive Environments typewriter. Try it on your 4-year-old now that it's pedagogically respectable to allow that age to attempt to read! Or forget about teaching them anything and have fun.

> *A review of "Hop on Pop," in* New York Herald Tribune, *May 12, 1963, p. 24.*

---

## DR. SEUSS'S ABC   (1963)

Only Dr. Seuss would have an alphabet book with:

> Big M
> little m
> Many mumbling mice / are making /
> midnight music / in the moonlight ...
> mighty nice.

It is "to add new pleasures," to help a child enjoy the sounds, he says—not to help a child merely memorize his ABCs.

But Dr. Seuss is crafty—and he knows that children will listen to or read the funny rhymes so many times that the alphabet may also stick.

> *A review of "Dr. Seuss's ABC," in* Saturday Review, *Vol. XLVI, No. 45, November 9, 1963, p. 58.*

*Dr. Seuss's A.B.C.* presents the usual supercilious, laughing or sly animals, but thank goodness there are few imaginary creatures; in fact Z is the only letter for which the author *depends* on one ('I'm a Zigger-Zagger-Zuz, as you can plainly see'), and his solution of the problem of X is much better than this. The captions vary from the laconic list to the mad statement, and there is one charmingly smooth one ('Many mumbling mice are making midnight music in the moonlight ... mighty nice') which those not wholly addicted to zany books will like best. (pp. 297-98)

*Margery Fisher, in a review of "Dr. Seuss's A.B.C.," in her* Growing Point, *Vol. 2, No. 9, April, 1964, pp. 297-98.*

[*Dr. Seuss's ABC*] earned my respect—at first grudgingly, for the goofiness is so familiar, and so commercially successful, that it's easy to overlook the achievement of a line like: "O is very useful. You use it when you say: 'Oscar's only ostrich oiled an orange owl today.'" Here Seuss has managed to use (and illustrate in his own play-dough colors) just about every sound O can make, without the slightest hint of struggle or ennui; and he does the same for every letter in a series of varied, tight-fitting rhythms, a current of nervous energy running from Aunt Annie's alligator to the Zizzer-Zazzer-Zuzz.

*Janice Prindle, in a review of "Dr. Seuss's ABC," in* VLS, *No. 7, May, 1982, p. 12.*

---

### THE CAT IN THE HAT BEGINNER BOOK DICTIONARY, BY THE CAT HIMSELF AND P. D. EASTMAN (1964)

The latest offering of the "**Cat in the Hat**" is not so much a dictionary as a rather clever device for presenting a basic vocabulary of 1350 words. . . . A story thread carrying several characters through a number of definitions adds appeal. It seems unfortunate that this is called a dictionary, for, in spite of its format, it does not truly define words. For example, the word "luck" is illustrated by a four-leaf clover; the word "still" pictured by five soldiers standing still, and "pockets" shows the pocket of a kangaroo—this is funny, yes, but not a common picture definition of a pocket. This is a book to be read by the beginning reader after it has been read to him, for there are too many unfamiliar words for him to tackle it himself. It is full of fun and nonsense, but it is not a beginning dictionary and should not be bought as such.

*Christine B. Gilbert, in a review of "The Cat in the Hat Beginner Book Dictionary," in* School Library Journal, *an appendix to* Library Journal, *Vol. 11, No. 3, November, 1964, p. 56.*

Admirers of *The Cat in the Hat* will welcome this amusing dictionary of the thousand or so words a child must know to read it. It is all in color, all in cartoons [by P. D. Eastman], and has a method all its own for presenting such "difficult" words as "after," "before," "beside," etc., as well as the tenses of verbs, which are presented quite painlessly. . . . The dictionary is also, and naturally, quite skilfully geared to Beginner Books.

*A review of "The Cat in the Hat Beginner Book Dictionary," in* Saturday Review, *Vol. XLVII, No. 45, November 7, 1964, p. 51.*

There is no doubt who has had a hand in this dictionary: "the Cat Himself" (alias Dr. Seuss). . . . If there were any question at all, it would be dispelled by a glance at the last page where the letter Z is illustrated by a nest of *zyxuzpf* birds. Who but Dr. Seuss would try that? . . .

Despite all the solemn accolades quoted from educators, we think this book should be considered as plain fun. Then any incidental educational improvement in the child enjoying it will be the result of pure serendipity.

*Margaret Sherwood Anderson, "From the Horse's Mouth," in* Book Week—The Sunday Herald Tribune, *January 24, 1965, p. 15.**

Dr. Seuss's copious **Dictionary** makes fascinating reading. . . . Mostly to its credit is the amiable ingenuity with which basic words are depicted: several running characters—Aaron the alligator, bespectacled Abigail and so on—maintain a flow of familiarity. I find I have noted down a pretty formidable list of items to cavil at. It's surely an unnecessarily cute and baleful offshoot of Lear and nonsense-namings to offer under Z 'a nest full of zyxuzpf birds' and Americanisms still abound.

*John Coleman, "Tender Minds," in* New Statesman, *Vol. LXX, No. 1809, November 12, 1965, p. 750.**

[I] am delighted to recommend [this] **Beginner Book Dictionary**. It is a dictionary of pictures and phrases, designed to introduce very young readers to a growing vocabulary; nobody could call the pictures pretty, but in their weird way they grow on one, like Yogi Bear, and children who do not care much for prettiness are delighted by the typical Seuss babies, hideously bald and furious, which scream wide-mouthed to illustrate loud, louder, and loudest. The text is always entertaining, and full of useful phrases such as "We own our own owl."

*Margaret Drabble, "Ten for Tots," in* Punch, *Vol. CCXLIX, No. 6536, December 15, 1965, p. 899.**

---

### FOX IN SOCKS (1965)

This is an amusing exercise for beginning readers, especially those who are inadequately equipped to skim or guess at words and who need a gentle brake applied. The sentence length, word shape and sounds employed require reader alertness and word-by-word recognition. One example will serve to show this as a strength of the book—"Clocks on fox tick. Clocks on Knox tock . . . Six sick bricks tick. Six sick chicks tock." This same example also shows the weakness of many of these when considered purely as twisters. They can seldom survive a glance away from the Dr.'s characteristic, boldly colored drawings. Seen with the illustrations, however, they make for a certain kind of verbal/visual nonsense. (pp. 172-73)

*A review of "Fox in Socks," in* Virginia Kirkus' Service, *Vol. XXXIII, No. 4, February 15, 1965, pp. 172-73.*

Although some children may feel like the Fox in Socks's straight man, poor Mr. Knox, who can't "blab such blibber blubber," most will find this great fun. These tongue twisters, despite a blurb prophecy by a language expert, seem unlikely to replace hoary favorites, since much of both their humor and meaning depend on Seuss's zany drawings of characters and situations. Garish use of color gives the book a Sunday supplement appearance.

*Elva Harmon, in a review of "Fox in Socks," in* School Library Journal, *an appendix to* Library Journal, *Vol. 11, No. 9, May, 1965, p. 96.*

Reporting his own response, [a second-grader] wrote: "I like the pictures. I think sometimes you get mixed up. I think it is funny. I like the words and rhymes and words that sound alike."

This confirmed a parental impression that a young reader will persist in something new and difficult—even tongue-twisters like these—if there are pleasures to pull him along. . . . [Dr. Seuss] continues to supply such pleasures.

*Roderick Nordell, "Grades from a Second-Grader," in* The Christian Science Monitor, *May 6, 1965, p. B2.**

[*Fox in Socks*] lacks all charm. It is mere calisthenics. The phonic guile shows: "Slow Joe Crow sews / Knox in box now." It raises an important question: When we have an effective intellectual implement to give a child, why set up elaborate situations so that the child "finds" the implement, "discovers" that it *is* an implement, and "explores" its effects? If you have a door-key a child needs, why hand it to him buried in a boxful of hairpins, clips and coins? Why not say, "Here is a key"? Our schools are full of this counterfeit induction, part of the current mystique of discovery. There is a trickiness about it that at best is smarmy and at worst may contaminate a child's best pride with doubt. (p. 19)

*Donald Barr, "Read, Dick, Read," in* Book Week— The Sunday Herald Tribune, *June 27, 1965, pp. 1, 19.*

---

## I HAD TROUBLE IN GETTING TO SOLLA SOLLEW (1965)

It's an epic lament of a little, ratty-looking, yellow creature, for whom "nothing, not anything ever went wrong" until he had an accident, and then another . . . And the harder he concentrated on escaping his troubles, the more they expanded. His dilemmas are of the broadly farcical, Tom and Jerry variety, which draw a fast big laugh but don't have the fantastic memorability of what was once seen on *Mulberry Street*. Dr. Seuss' brightly colored, universally familiar illustrations are as always.

*A review of "I Had Trouble in Getting to Solla Sollew," in* Virginia Kirkus' Service, *Vol. XXXIII, No. 17, September 1, 1965, p. 898.*

Whatever his limitations as a creator of children's literature, Dr. Seuss almost always puts on a good show—at least when he abandons the repetitive dreariness that mars a limited-vocabulary book like *Green Eggs and Ham.* With the limited-vocabulary handcuffs off, he comes on strong and shows us all his razzmatazz: the bold colors, the crazy names, the hapless narrators sorely beset by wacky tormentors, the funny if forced rhymes. You almost forget while you're in headlong transit through his latest madcap misadventure that you've seen all the tricks before, and that the new routines are only slight variations on the old. Still, a Seuss variation is more fun than most of the plodding picture books we get for boys and girls.

Seuss has two basic storytelling strategies. The more traditional one is simply, to tell a story—of heightening suspense or deepening woe—but embellished by his own special sense of the ridiculous. It is with this form, I think, that he has done his most memorable work: *The 500 Hats of Bartholomew Cubbins, The Cat in the Hat, Yertle the Turtle.* His other technique is to exhibit his menagerie of hairy or feathered (or hairy-feathered) creatures in two dozen or so set pieces, like blackouts in a vaudeville routine, and to hold the book together with sheer zaniness, as in *If I Ran the Zoo* or *The Sleep Book.* The latter technique may require more virtuosity, but too often with Seuss it seems to degenerate into repetitive exhibitions.

The new Seuss book tries to bridge the techniques: it is a breathless picaresque about one of his forlorn little critters—a sort of all-purpose animal, part mongrel pup, part alleycat—who has a great deal of trouble getting to Solla Sollew, an Oz-like town "where they never have troubles, at least very few." The fellow starts off just minding his business and before you know it, he's being assaulted on all sides. . . . When he finally evades his troubles enroute, it turns out Solla Sollew wasn't

worth all the bother: they can't open the door to the place—a dirty trick, on all of us. So the narrator heads back where he came from, game as ever but more determined not to be an easy mark: "But I've bought a big bat. / I'm all ready, you see. Now my troubles are going / To have troubles with *me*."

It's a limp ending to a pointless journey—though, one of Professor Crews' Pooh-Plexers might argue the very pointlessness is, well, you know—*existential*. But the hi-jinks along the way are vintage Seuss. Everything is hyperbole. . . . [When] disaster strikes in the narrative, it is catastrophic, drawings and rhymes bursting at you in unison.

Hyperbole aside, Seuss can be characterized as inventive—he is tirelessly, and sometimes tiresomely, inventive. He is both in *Solla Sollew.* You can't do better than hitching a ride on a One-Wheeler Wubble, a camel-drawn vehicle of precarious design, driven by a mountebank perched on a flimsy chair, that traverses hostile, indeed impassable, terrain. Less successful are those Perilous Poozers in Pompelmoose Pass, typical snub-nosed and toothsome varmints in the Seuss bestiary whose names are their only distinctive feature. (pp. 6, 12)

*Richard Kluger, "Hi-Jinks, and Low," in* Book Week—The Sunday Herald Tribune, *October 31, 1965, pp. 6, 12, 16.*

The common Dr. Seuss features are present in this book—impossible characters and situations coupled with the usual absurdly plausible illustrations of a wild tale. Some elements that we might expect from the talented author are rather scarce. . . . The brilliant, sparkling spontaneity that the author is capable of is noticeably lacking. As intriguing as many children will find the odd words, animals, and colorful illustrations, they deserve more than this book offers them. "Maisie, the lazy bird" of *Horton* fame will be remembered, but the chap who ". . . rumbled up in a One-Wheeler Wubble" and incited the fruitless travels will most likely be forgotten before the last page is turned.

The animals introduced in this book are nowhere nearly so cleverly conceived and executed as those in *If I Ran the Zoo,* and the story does not measure up to the standard we expect of the man who gave us *And to Think That I Saw It on Mulberry Street* or *The 500 Hats of Bartholomew Cubbins.*

*Phyllis Cohen, in a review of "I Had Trouble Getting to Solla Sollew," in* Young Readers Review, *Vol. II, No. 5, January, 1966, p. 4.*

---

## I WISH THAT I HAD DUCK FEET (1965)

My initial response to [*I Wish That I Had Duck Feet*] was one of delight at the way the author, and the artist, Barney Tobey, had made use of primitive aggressive and sexual fantasy material in their presentation of a series of thwarted daydreams for their child protagonist. First, the unnamed boy imagines that he has duck feet, which allow him to play in a pond with ducks and to laugh at the bully, Big Bill Brown, and say, "YOU don't have duck feet! These are all there are in town!" The duck feet, however, are rejected by his mother because they track water on her clean floor, and they are replaced in his imagination by antlers (which he calls "horns"), that provide another way of one-upping Big Bill Brown, a useful offensive weapon when playing football and a means of carrying all kinds of things to school, including an apple for his teacher. This daydream, however, is thwarted by the boy's recognition

All the rest of that day, on those wild screaming beaches,
The Fix-it-Up Chappie kept fixing up Sneetches.
Off again! On again!
In again! Out again!
Through the machines they raced round and about again,
Changing their stars every minute or two.
They kept paying money. They kept running through
Until neither the Plain nor the Star-Bellies knew
Whether this one was that one . . . or that one was this one
Or which one was what one . . . or what one was who.

*From* The Sneetches and Other Stories, *written and illustrated by Dr. Seuss. Random House, 1961.*
*Copyright © 1953, 1954, 1961 by Dr. Seuss. All rights reserved. Reprinted by permission of Random*
*House, Inc.*

that such "horns" would make it impossible for him to enter the school bus.

A yet more obviously phallic fantasy is embodied in the daydream of having a "whale spout" on his head, to keep him cool at school and when playing tennis with Bill Brown, to the latter's discomfiture; but as with the boy's mother, who in his daydream angrily asserts, "'I don't want that spout about!'" and, says the boy, "When Mother does not want a thing, it's O-U-T. It's out!" So as a less messy alternative, the child wishes for a "long, long tail," which will enable him to play jump-rope with the girls (making Big Bill jealous), and "to ride down State Street pulling girls behind my bike," as well as swatting flies in the schoolroom and pleasing his teacher. This time Big Bill Brown thwarts the wish in the daydream by tying the boy up in a tree with his own tail. "AND SO . . . if I can't have a tail, I'll have a long, long, nose! A nose just like an elephant's, the longest nose that grows," which enables him to reach up high for forbidden cookies, to knock down Big Bill with a sneeze, to help firemen to put out fires, and to impress the boys and girls in the playground. Authority intervenes again, this time in the form of the father, enforcing the reality principle by putting the boy to work washing the car and house-windows with his extraordinarily long nasal member.

Upon contemplating the dangers in all of these daydreams, the boy in his frustration imagines having *all* the extra bodily appendages at once, becoming a "Which-What-Who," and frenetically jumping, splashing, and spouting, to "give the town a scare." This time the consequences are more serious, as he imagines himself arrested and locked up in the zoo. So he decides that he does not wish to be any of those things, but to be only himself; and the final, wordless illustration shows duck feet, horns, spout, tail, and elephant's nose in the garbage can, with the boy walking contentedly away from his daydream fantasy-objects.

After some reflection, my initial response of pleasure at the amusing way in which the author and artist employed such obviously "Freudian" material gave way to my disturbance at the story's didacticism, the message that daydreams about oneself are dangerous. I now tend to suspect that the primitive aggressive and sexual fantasies are not themselves the objects of attack, but that they function to provide for the reader what Freud called the pleasure effected by a rediscovery of the once-familiar—that is, the repressed—while the real message is insidiously directed at a later period of individual development: the dangers of being "different," or even imagining yourself to be different—the dangers of nonconformity and the need to

190

accept the realities of a world dominated by adults who generally do not tolerate imagination.

Whatever their conscious intentions, Geisel and Tobey have produced a book that is in the tradition of the cautionary tale, and a consideration of that genre, its possible source in child-parent relationships, and its historical transformations may throw some light on the way in which, for the reader, imaginative literature may operate on several developmental levels simultaneously. (p. 138)

[One] might say that the cautionary tale, in whatever guise, is a transformation of parental commands and warnings, of which the simplest form is the negative imperative, "Don't!" Parental commands operate upon children through tacit aspects of the relationship, such as love and fear, rather than through the evident rationality of the edict, but such a simple command lacks any bonus of aesthetic pleasure such as the most primitive cautionary tale provides. Thus, if a parent says, "Don't go near the well; a little girl about your age leaned over the edge last year, fell in, and drowned," there is added to the basic "Don't!" a *frisson* of pleasure deriving from the idea of *someone else's* getting killed, as well as a fantasy of its happening to oneself that has a concreteness lacking in the response to a mere negative command.

It is a short step from this model of the parental caution to the actual cautionary tale. . . . (pp. 138-39)

"The Giddy Girl" and many more violent cautionary tales of the late eighteenth and early nineteenth centuries are pretty tame stuff . . . compared to Heinrich Hoffmann's *Struwwelpeter.* . . . It may be (though I doubt it) that few children have had nightmares as a result of the fate of Conrad's thumbs, or the cremation in "The Dreadful Story About Harriet and the Matches," but I find it hard to believe that the increase in the intensity and variety of both crimes and punishments (in contrast to traditional cautionary tales) can have functioned solely through their absurdity to distance children from the emotional reality of what is depicted. For in Hoffmann's poems and pictures the child's most fearsome fantasies are acted out almost literally. (p. 139)

My suspicion is that in a family setting, where the poems are read aloud and the adults and older children laugh, the younger child is under a kind of social pressure to act grown-up and laugh as well. The ultimate pleasures for all are, surely, due to the evoking of primitive modes of thinking in which love and punishment, sexual stimulation and pain, sex and death or violence are not clearly distinguished. For the adult, this may include a strong overlay of sadism and *Schadenfreude*, things the child learns to appreciate in the process of acculturation. Hoffmann also goes beyond earlier cautionary tales in suggesting the dangers of imagination: I refer to "The Story of Johnny Head-in-the-Air," whose transgression is failing to concentrate on the "real" world—for what else does it mean to have your head in the clouds?

Geisel and Tobey's post-Freudian version of the cautionary tale warns against daydreaming and imagining oneself to be different. Its method is much subtler than that of the *Struwwelpeter* because it speaks overtly and directly to childhood anxieties about getting along socially, dealing with social rivals, pleasing the teacher, and pleasing one's parents. At the same time, however, the particular content of the boy's daydreams, all of which have to do with parts of the body, appeals to more primitive, less consciously held fantasies, to earlier modes of thinking, when an elephant's trunk and a penis were not fully

distinguished, when one's own body could seem like a collection of interchangeable extremities, and when fantasies about sexual and aggressive feelings, and parental recognition, dominated dreams and unconscious mental life.

I think it is fair to say that the didactic content of *I Wish That I Had Duck Feet* is more oppressive than the vocalized parental edict or the traditional cautionary tale, even though the author and artist may have been unaware of any hostility toward children. Unlike the *Struwwelpeter*, which hints at such things only intermittently, *I Wish That I Had Duck Feet* is directed not at the child's overt behavior but at his inner thoughts and feelings and his imagination, and it is of some interest that in Dr. Seuss's first children's book, *To Think That I Saw It on Mulberry Street*, the stand-off is between the father's insistence on empirical observation and the child's over-active imagination. I have always felt the author's sympathy to be with the child in that early book, but it is more difficult to locate the sympathy in *I Wish That I Had Duck Feet*. The later book may achieve its appeal, not because children are all that anxious about their daydreams, but because the bright, funny pictures conveying sexual and aggressive images are, so to speak, the first line of attack. The emotional sequence of the story as a whole is a build-up to a state of extreme tension, a discharge in frenzy, and a subsequent depression; and these feelings are resolved into calm self-satisfaction when the child accepts his place in the family and community and consigns his dreams, literally, to the garbage can. It is a subtle form of (possibly unintended) propaganda for conformity and far outdoes the ordinary cautionary tale and even the *Struwwelpeter* in manipulating deep fantasies in the service of acculturation to a society where imagination is often an object of distrust. That the author and illustrator drew brilliantly upon their own imaginations to achieve this effect is one of the paradoxes of any didactic literature which is ultimately directed against the failure to conform to social codes. (pp. 139-40)

> *Michael Steig, "Dr. Seuss's Attack on Imagination: 'I Wish That I Had Duck Feet' and the Cautionary Tale," in* Proceedings of the Ninth Annual Conference of The Children's Literature Association: The Child and the Story, an Exploration of Narrative Forms, *edited by Priscilla A. Ord, The Children's Literature Association, 1983, pp. 137-41.*

---

*MY BOOK ABOUT ME: BY ME, MYSELF. I WROTE IT! I DREW IT! WITH A LITTLE HELP FROM MY FRIENDS DR. SEUSS AND ROY McKIE* (1969)

Pure ridiculous fun is always a winner, when it works: and it certainly does in the latest of the admirable Dr. Seuss Beginner Books, *My Book About Me*. . . . This is full of odd lively questions for a child to answer, on the dotted lines provided or by putting ticks in little boxes. Example: "I eat like a horse" (box), "I eat like a bird" (box), "I eat like a ———". I liked especially (you tick Yes or No) "My feet are ticklish."

> *Edward Blishen, in a review of "My Book about Me," in* The Spectator, *Vol. 231, No. 7582, October 20, 1973, p. xv.*

[Lear] would, I am sure, have been among those who approve of the Doctor—both for his zany humour and role as zealous, if unorthodox educationist.

This latest addition to the Beginner Books series involves reading, writing and calculating. It demands a one child/one book relationship as it is in the form of a questionnaire which is a cross between a census form . . . and a passport form . . . and a market research project. . . . Would that our adult questionnaires were illustrated by Seuss.

The reader is sometimes asked a question which involves him in counting: 'How many teeth?' 'How many windows?'; or decision making: 'My favourite food is . . .', 'Please don't give me any . . .' and at other times is asked to select an answer from a number of choices including having green, purple or no hair, for example. He must draw round his foot and hand to show their size, but merely copy his nose shape from the five provided.

Great fun and painless learning, but something of a liability on a public library shelf as the temptation might well prove too great for the first borrower.

> *Margot Petts, in a review of "My Book about Me,"*
> *in* Children's Book Review, *Vol. IV, No. 1, Spring,*
> *1974, p. 10.*

---

### THE LORAX (1971)

The greening of Dr. Seuss, in an ecology fable with an obvious message but a savingly silly style. In the desolate land of the Lifted Lorax, an aged creature called the Once-ler tells a young visitor how he arrived long ago in the then glorious country and began manufacturing anomalous objects called Thneeds from "the bright-colored tufts of the Truffula Trees." Despite protests from the Lorax, a native "who speaks for the trees," he continues to chop down Truffulas until he drives away the Brown Bar-ba-loots who had fed on the Truffula fruit, the Swomee-Swans who can't sing a note for the smogulous smoke, and the Humming-Fish who had hummed in the pond now glumped up with the Gluppity-Glupp. As for the Once-ler, "I went right on biggering, selling more Thneeds. / And I biggered my money, which everyone needs"—until the last Truffula falls. But one seed is left, and the Once-ler hands it to his listener, with a message from the Lorax: "UNLESS someone like you / cares a whole awful lot, / nothing is going to get better. / It's not." The spontaneous madness of the old Dr. Seuss is absent here, but so is the boredom he often induced (in parents, anyway) with one ridiculous invention after another. And if the Once-ler doesn't match the Grinch for sheer irresistible cussedness, he is stealing a lot more than Christmas and his story just might induce a generation of six-year-olds to care a whole lot.

> *A review of "The Lorax," in* Kirkus Reviews, *Vol.*
> *XXXIX, No. 15, August 1, 1971, p. 804.*

[It] takes an old master like Dr. Seuss to jump on the [conservation] bandwagon and really show us the way. In *The Lorax* he cunningly uses broad humour, fantastic characters, sub-Carrollian nonsense doggerel, crude comic-strip line and colours more appropriate to ice-cream and sugared almonds, to tell of a Garden of Eden denuded of trees and blighted by smog and 'glump'—and all for the manufacture of absurdly useless but highly salable garments called 'thneeds'. It is a cautionary tale that will certainly get young eyes sparkling, young lips trembling and young indignations smouldering—and in so doing will prove more valuable educationally than any number of elegant junior reference books. (p. 649)

> *Wallace Hildick, "Popularisations," in* The Lis-
> tener, *Vol. 88, No. 2275, November 9, 1972, pp.*
> *648-49.\**

Dr. Seuss' zany imagination and his inventive ingenuity with words are here harnessed to a more serious subject than usual, the prevention of pollution. . . . [The Lorax is] a conception worthy of Mervyn Peake. . . . This brilliant fantasy, which rolls off the tongue, is more likely to be effective than libraries of junior reference books on the subject.

> *M. Hobbs, in a review of "The Lorax," in* The Junior
> Bookshelf, *Vol. 36, No. 6, December, 1972, p. 371.*

"The Lorax" is a bold, brilliant and beautiful allegory. (p. 46)

The whole is marvellously drawn, particularly the machinery of the Thneed factory, with the productivity breakthrough invention of the Super Axe-Hacker. Dr Seuss is a very natty word coiner, so that one wonders how the English language could have survived without the verb "to bigger." Dr Seuss is in real life Mr Ted Geisel, who lives on a mountain in California, where the landscape is now being destroyed for a housing development. One can see why he is a convert to conservation. Still, Mr Geisel, one man's view is another man's chance of a home; we never learnt where the Once-ler's employees were living before. (p. 47)

> *"Do You Need a Thneed?" in* The Economist, *Vol.*
> *245, No. 6748, December 23, 1972, pp. 46-7.\**

The danger to our environment posed by technological growth . . . appears as the key theme in *The Lorax*. . . . Typical of the Seuss books, attractive illustrations and humorous rhyme are joined into an exciting book, one that also makes an important statement against thoughtless industrial growth. (p. 274)

> *Myra Pollack Sadker and David Miller Sadker,*
> *"Spaceship Earth: Ecology in Children's Litera-*
> *ture," in their* Now Upon a Time: A Contemporary
> View of Children's Literature, *Harper & Row, Pub-*
> *lishers, 1977, pp. 269-85.\**

---

### IN A PEOPLE HOUSE (1972)

With the forced animation and routinely disorderly conduct of a played out *Cat in the Hat*, a *Bright-and-Early* bird flits through a mouse-guided tour of the objects—bananas and bathtubs, teapots and trash—to be found *In A People House*. Seuss' successors are just going through the motions here—mechanical writing in a series that set out to prevent mechanical reading.

> *A review of "In a People House," in* Kirkus Re-
> views, *Vol. XL, No. 17, September 1, 1972, p. 1025.*

[*In a People House*] provides a vehicle for teaching many familiar household words as mouse shows Mr. Bird through a house: "banana/bathtub/bottles/brooms / That's what you find / in people's rooms." Though it's not another *Cat in the Hat* . . . , it is a perfect pre-school read aloud and teachers can use this with beginners who have difficulty reading with expression, as its tight rhyme and fast-paced rhythm make it easy to mimic. Though the text is silly, more power to Dr. Seuss for reminding us once more that reading doesn't have to be a sober experience. (pp. 70-1)

A review of "In a People House," in School Library Journal, *an appendix to* Library Journal, *Vol. 19, No. 4, December, 1972, pp. 70-1.*

## THE MANY MICE OF MR. BRICE   (1973)

Mr. Brice's mice have names beginning with each letter of the alphabet, from Ann to Zeke, and their crazy doings are illustrated in pictures that incorporate lift-out or press-out devices, so that you can see Harriet hiding behind the furniture, Eddie drinking soda pop, Waldo riding round the clock and so on. An amusing and unusual way to temper the effects of learning to read; words are simple, though not graduated, and sentences rhyme agreeably, while the pictures are riotous in the extreme.

*Margery Fisher, in a review of "The Many Mice of Mr. Brice," in her* Growing Point, *Vol. 14, No. 7, January, 1976, p. 2809.*

One of my grandchildren, then not yet two, was fascinated by Theo Le Sieg's **The Many Mice of Mr Brice** . . . , which I'd bought for her six-year-old brother. It is a delightful book that, through fun and action, leads to actual reading, but for a younger child it invites a touching and a grabbing, and a shouting of words. This toddler's finger movements were by now astonishingly delicate and precise, unlike a clutching baby, and she moved the tabs and turned the wheel with care as well as delight, and plucked new words as she went along.

*Leila Berg, "Knowing the Story: Leila Berg on Pre-reading," in* The Times Educational Supplement, *No. 3396, July 24, 1981, p. 26.**

## OH, THE THINKS YOU CAN THINK!   (1975)

"You can think about red, / You can think about pink.
You can think up a horse. / Oh, the THINKS you can
   think!"
Think of prattling in print, never mind that it's rot.
If you've got the right name you can sell quite a lot.
Think how far you can go without THINKING A
   THOUGHT!

*A review of "Oh! The Thinks You Can Think!" in* Kirkus Reviews, *Vol. XLIII, No. 19, October 1, 1975, p. 1128 [the excerpt of Dr. Seuss's work used here was taken from* Oh, the Thinks You Can Think!, *Beginner Books, 1975].*

Beginner Books are intended to be simple enough for abecedarians to read by themselves. Dr. Seuss is one of the most popular contributors to this genre and this one, which is simpleminded as well as simple, will probably be undeservedly read, reread, even memorized. One wonders how long the vogue for this substandard nonsense, featuring ". . . a day in Da-Dake. / The water is blue / and the birds are awake." and nonthings like the tail of a zong, a jibboo, snuvs and their gloves, all jiffy made for the sake of a rhyme, can last. Probably as long as substandard reading levels prevail.

*A review of "Oh, the Thinks You Can Think!" in* Publishers Weekly, *Vol. 208, No. 18, November 3, 1975, p. 72.*

[**"Oh, the Thinks You Can Think!"**] is not exactly the master's Seusstine Ceiling, but it contains, as usual, one of his solid-gold morals, the joy of letting one's imagination rip. In my opinion Dr. Seuss deserves the Nobel Prize. Think of the in-fluence he has had on the human race! And all of it good! Can Henry Kissinger say the same? (p. 40)

*Jane Langton, "Snatchibility and the GPQ," in* The New York Times Book Review, *November 16, 1975, pp. 40, 42.**

The doctor's nonsense may become its own worst enemy, as this addition to the seemingly endless catalog of creatures indicates. . . . Still, there's life in the old pop schlopp blop plop yet, and Seuss' fanciful color pictures are familiarly wacky. The combination of controlled vocabulary and phonetic nonsense words keeps the verses readable.

*Judith Goldberger, in a review of "Oh, the Thinks You Can Think!" in* The Booklist, *Vol. 72, No. 8, December 15, 1975, p. 583.*

## THE CAT'S QUIZZER   (1976)

Dr. Seuss is at it again. Pages of witty questions varying from the absurd (Where would you go to learn to play the stethoscope?) to the informative (What do they call a one-wheeled Bicycle?) are amusingly illustrated. For the benefit of learned but impractical uncles there are answers at the back. What a splendid example of painless learning!

*D. A. Young, in a review of "The Cat's Quizzer," in* The Junior Bookshelf, *Vol. 41, No. 5, October, 1977, p. 292.*

[**The Cat's Quizzer**] lacks the anarchic zest of many of its predecessors. Dr Seuss has made such a substantial contribution to beginners' books since 1954, when **The Cat in the Hat** first appeared, that one almost hesitates to apply ordinary critical standards to his work. But the format of the present volume is poor and its humour less than inspiring. Even the most risible youngster is unlikely to find himself welling over with laughter at dialogue of this quality: Question: "Are there a few ducks on the moon?" Answer: "No ducks on the moon. (No elephants, either.)"

*Suzanne Wiener, "Pachyderms," in* The Times Educational Supplement, *No. 3259, November 25, 1977, p. 25.**

## OH, SAY CAN YOU SAY?   (1979)

[**"Oh Say Can You Say?"**] seems a self-parody. I have always thought that later Seuss (not Bartholemew Cubbins, never Bartholemew Cubbins) is really dumb, even though it is currently popular among the intellectual elite to cite him for clever invention. This book, purporting to be full of tongue twisters, is wrapped in the familiar bumpity-bump Seuss verse and the familiar Seuss cartoons, and makes the other easy-reads look great. Still, it will out-sell them all, which says a lot for taste—and reading—today. (p. 60)

*Jane Yolen, "Easy and Early," in* The New York Times Book Review, *November 11, 1979, pp. 55, 60.**

The usual Dr. Seuss fun shines in **Oh Say Can You Say?** . . . but its "terrible tongue twisters" ("The greener green grapes are, the keener keen apes are to gobble green grape cakes.") lose their novelty long before the book ends. Brevity of text might pack a pithier punch.

*Kathy Coffey, in a review of "Oh Say Can You Say?" in* School Library Journal, *Vol. 26, No. 4, December, 1979, p. 94.*

## MAYBE YOU SHOULD FLY A JET! MAYBE YOU SHOULD BE A VET! (1980)

The range is from serious to silly (maybe you should be a "talker"? A "bride" is a *career* choice?) in a text that consists only of a string of job possibilities punctuated by the occasional frenzied comment about having to "BE someone sooner or later." It seems dated to have the book refer to "Fireman, Tireman, Telephone wireman," failing to recognize occupational title changes (surely LeSieg, of all people, could have found a rhyme for "fire-fighter"?). Granted, this is a semi-humorous look at jobs, and women *are* shown in some non-traditional roles, but their gross under-representation (the illustrations [by Michael J. Smollin] show over three times as many men workers) seems oddly ignorant. No nonwhites are shown, period.

*Nancy Palmer, in a review of "Maybe You Should Fly a Jet! Maybe You Should Be a Vet!" in* School Library Journal, *Vol. 27, No. 4, December, 1980, p. 71.*

Humorous drawings and catchy rhymes introduce youngsters to the variety of career choices in **Maybe You Should Fly a Jet!**. . . . Stressing that "You've got to do something," LeSieg suggests over 80 possible careers, some absurd to create interest (hammock tester), but most realistic and viable. Readability in this "Beginner Book" is generally appropriate for independent reading, although some terms will require explanation. Illustrations and content are sexually (but not racially) balanced, despite the "bride" choice and others ending with "man".

*"Guides to Life Planning," in* Curriculum Review, *Vol. 20, No. 1, January, 1981, p. 39.\**

## THE TOOTH BOOK (1981)

In the familiar bouncy, breezy Dr. Seuss style, this is both a rhapsodic paean to teeth and a reminder that they have to be taken care of—both in the sense of oral hygiene and in the sense of refraining from such abuse as opening bottles by biting off caps. . . . [The] rhyming text sacrifices sense to convenience occasionally, but for many children that's part of the Seuss appeal.

*Zena Sutherland, in a review of "The Tooth Book," in* Bulletin of the Center for Children's Books, *Vol. 35, No. 2, October, 1981, p. 33.*

We already have the foot, eye, and ear books in what was previously called the 'Beginning Beginner Books' series. These offerings from the Dr Seuss stable are perfect for making 'fonics phun' because they are energetic, comic-style books which appeal to large numbers of children who enjoy playing with words and rhymes. . . . **The tooth book** will probably prove to be the most popular in the quartet because all children are intrigued by these things which keep dropping out . . . just at the time when many of them are learning to read!

*Cliff Moon, in a review of "The Tooth Book," in* The School Librarian, *Vol. 30, No. 3, September, 1982, p. 227.*

## HUNCHES IN BUNCHES (1982)

What happens when a Dr. Seuss kid can't make up his mind turns out to be an exaggerated and slap-happily visualized version of what might happen to anyone. First the kid gets a Happy Hunch that he should be outside, but then a Real Tough Hunch reminds him of his homework. Both hunches are personified as the familiar, Seussian, goofy human-animal figures in union-suit costumes and large hand-shaped hats—as are the subsequent Better, Sour, Very Old, Spookish, Four-Way, Nowhere, Up, Down, and Super hunches that have the boy running around in circles, climbing slablike stairs in space, and going through all the other frenzied motions now routine for Seuss. The kid finally follows a Munch Hunch to the kitchen for a six-hot-dog lunch. The bearded purple Down Hunch is a silly extravagance dealt with a touch of *éclat,* but mostly this is just one more product of the Dr. Seuss machine set on automatic.

*A review of "Hunches in Bunches," in* Kirkus Reviews, *Vol. L, No. 20, October 15, 1982, p. 1152.*

It seems unlikely that any but the most devoted Seuss fans will find this bit of froth palatable: it has silliness without humor, it has an overextended plot about the difficulty of making up one's mind, it has a protagonist who responds to anthropomorphized (if fantastic) characters called Hunches, and it is faulty in scansion and padded to achieve rhymes.

*Zena Sutherland, in a review of "Hunches in Bunches," in* Bulletin of the Center for Children's Books, *Vol. 36, No. 5, January, 1983, p. 97.*

## THE BUTTER BATTLE BOOK (1984)

Ever since our children were young, my wife and I have enjoyed reading Dr. Seuss's stories. Yearly on Christmas Eve we have read the now-tattered copy of **How the Grinch Stole Christmas,** and agreed, at least until we opened packages the next day, that Christmas doesn't come from a store. It is something more. Through hearing this story and seeing the Grinch in our mind's eyes (because we did not have a television), our hearts, like the Grinch's, grew a size or two. Now our grandson likes to "read," and we have discovered again through **Horton Hears a Who** that "a person's a person no matter how small." These are morals to my liking.

When we heard of the recent celebration of Dr. Seuss's 80th birthday and the concurrent publication of his newest book, **The Butter Battle Book,** we went to the bookstore and bought a copy to read to our grandson, who is now two and a half. . . . Lucas, his three-month-old sister, his mother and dad came to visit on a Saturday. After eating fresh-baked whole wheat bread warm from the oven, Grandma announced that we had a new book to read. So we all sat by the wood stove while "Grandmom" read **The Butter Battle Book.**

I became uneasy when I began to realize that the grandfather in the book was engaged in a primitive form of military escalation. Then Lucas's parents said, "This doesn't sound like a children's book." When we reached the last page, we found that the story had no resolution. No Grinch carved the "roast beast." No Horton finally saved the world of the "Whos." No "Cat in the Hat" put the house in order. We could not tell Lucas that Grandpa decided to get rid of his "Bitsy Big-Boy Boomeroo." Instead, we faced a blank final page—leaving the Yooks and Zooks face to face, about to destroy each other either by intent or by the tremor of an aging hand.

"Grandpa!" I shouted. "Be careful! Oh, gee!
Who's going to drop it?
Will *you*...? Or will *he*...?"
"Be patient," said Grandpa. "We'll see.
We will see..."

*From* The Butter Battle Book, *written and illustrated by Dr. Seuss. Random House, 1984. Copyright © 1984 by Dr. Seuss and A. S. Geisel. All rights reserved. Reprinted by permission of Random House, Inc.*

We were all distressed that we had read such a book to our grandson. And Lucas, not comprehending fully what it meant, but feeling uneasy, wanted to read the book again.

We did not read it again. We found another book on birds so that we could look at pictures and put our world back in order. But my world would not go back into a secure pattern. Recalling my initial outrage at the "Yooks" grandfather standing there, not heeding the plea of his grandson, I wondered how many of those who support mutual assured destruction are grandfathers, or grandmothers or parents. I was also angry at Dr. Seuss, the storyteller, for tricking me into telling Lucas of the "MAD" reality of our arms race. I blamed myself for not checking the story before we read it aloud.

Then I recalled the story of Nathan's telling a parable to David, the killer of the giant Goliath. David, seeing Bathsheba in her bath, sent for her and made her pregnant. Seeking to hide his act of adultery, he recalled her husband from the battlefront and tried to manipulate him into sleeping with his wife. Loyal to his comrades in the field and loyal to the cleanliness code which protected the "holy" army of God, Uriah refused, even when made drunk on David's wine. Unable to hide his adulterous act, David added murder to adultery by instructing Joab, the army commander, to place Uriah in the thickest fighting and then to call a retreat. The plan worked, Uriah was killed, and David married Bathsheba.

The prophet Nathan did not rush to David, point his finger and accuse him directly of murder and adultery. Instead he told a story which captured the king's imagination and evoked his judgment. A rich man with many sheep stole a poor man's one beloved ewe lamb to serve as the main course of a banquet for a guest. Outraged at such moral callousness, David declared that the rich man deserved to die. When Nathan said, "You are the man," David realized that he had judged himself. . . .

I heard in my inner ear the words of Dr. Seuss to all giant-killers: "You are the one." I was captured in his parable. In judging his characters, I discovered that I had judged myself. I am the grandfather who through paying taxes and through insufficient opposition to the arms race has not done enough to make a different ending to the parable of *The Butter Battle Book*.

Repentance is more than sorrow and regret. It is a turning away and a turning toward. My repentance must now include a turn away from inaction born of frustration and toward vigorous and imaginative deeds—to make sure that the last page of the book of life for Lucas, his sister and all the children and grandchildren of this world is neither blank nor filled with destruction.

> *Daniel R. Bechtel, "Dr. Seuss, Prophet to Giant-Killers," in* The Christian Century, *Vol. 101, No. 12, April 11, 1984, p. 359.*

Dr. Seuss chronicles the long-standing feud between the Yooks (who eat their bread butter-side up) and the Zooks (who prefer it butter-side down). The war escalates from slingshots through more and more sophisticated weaponry until each side possesses a tiny bomb that resembles an Easter egg but has the capacity to destroy the world. The book ends with a Yook and a Zook standing on the wall that divides the two countries, each clutching a bomb daintily between two fingers. When the child narrator asks, "Who's going to drop it?" he is told, "We'll see. We will see. . . . " The language of the story rhymes and amuses in customary Seuss fashion, and the colorful cartoon drawings are zesty and humorous. Seuss is in a category of his own in both originality and popularity, and the demand for this book will undoubtedly be large. One wonders, however, if a book for young children is a suitable vehicle for such an accurate and uncloaked description of the current stalemate in nuclear disarmament. Even very young children are aware of the potential for doom inherent in the present buildup of nuclear arms, and a book may be useful as a means of dealing with the feelings evoked, or as a tool for discussion. But this story ends without the slightest glimmer of hope that a solution to the standoff will be found, and as such can only contribute to a child's sense of helplessness. On this issue, perhaps above all others, it is critical to communicate to children the possibility of finding solutions beyond those immediately visible.

> *Anne L. Okie, in a review of "The Butter Battle Book," in* School Library Journal, *Vol. 30, No. 9, May, 1984, p. 72.*

Provocative as it is, [*The Butter Battle Book*'s] open-ended conclusion is sure to frustrate younger viewers, who prefer concrete wrap-ups. More successful is the parade of increasingly elaborate (and ridiculous-looking) armaments and uniforms, which amuses and makes a telling point at the same time. An abrupt, unsignaled shift in narrators brings attentive readers up short, and there are bothersome inconsistencies between the story's beginning and end.

*Karen Stang Hanley, in a review of "The Butter Battle Book," in* Booklist, *Vol. 80, No. 17, May 1, 1984, p. 1254.*

**The Butter Battle Book** is a trivialization of an already oversimplified world view—that of the nuclear-freeze movement. The adherents of that movement—Dr. Seuss evidently among them—see the U.S.-Soviet rivalry as an unfortunate misunderstanding over not very important cultural differences, e.g., which side bread should be buttered on; a misunderstanding fueled by a senseless arms race driven by technological imperatives alone. Quite obviously, the Yooks should have let the Zooks butter their bread however they pleased; if the United States would only stop modernizing its own arsenals, the Soviet Union would surely do the same, and the whole senseless dispute would wind down and cease. Live and let live—Yooks and Zooks and Kooks alike.

**The Butter Battle Book,** however, contains a number of subtle messages that could do grave damage to the cause Seuss is professing. Seuss makes the mistake, for example, of explaining that a great wall divides the Yooks and the Zooks. This is all too likely to evoke memories of the Berlin Wall—that stark prison boundary reminding the world that the heart of the East-West struggle is human liberty versus totalitarian tyranny, not American failure to comprehend Russian food, music, and poetry. Seuss also makes the serious mistake of not ending the book with an arms-control agreement or a nuclear holocaust. By ending inconclusively, with neither side having fired a serious shot and with each side wary of the nuclear weapons of the other, Seuss reminds us that nuclear weapons have kept the peace for nearly forty years now. The last page of **The Butter Battle Book** is an eloquent, albeit unintended, affirmation of the value of nuclear deterrence—the Zooks do not dare nuke the Yooks for fear of being nuked themselves. Children, in particular, are not likely to conclude from the story that the whole dispute is senseless—Seuss's books are always ridiculous, after all. Children will conclude, instead, that the Yooks are lucky they invented the bomb, so that the Zooks dare not attack them first. They may well infer—to Seuss's chagrin—that remaining strong is the surest way of achieving peace. Give that man the Committee on the Present Danger Award. (pp. 15-16)

*A review of "The Butter Battle Book," in* National Review, *Vol. XXXVI, No. 14, July 27, 1984, pp. 15-16.*

[Dr. Seuss has just published a book] which introduces children to the arms race. I wonder how much our attempt to make our children politically aware, politically correct, is in reality a way of assuaging our own guilts. If we have produced moral children we ourselves must be pure, or at least on the right track . . . this, anyway, is a tempting thought for a lot of us. It backfires. . . .

Children are violent like the rest of us. Violence is something which is civilized out of us. It is often a losing battle, civilization involving both Chartres and the Crusades, the Sermon on the Mount and the Jihad. Anyone who has watched babies play with one another knows that if it weren't for civilization it would be all Crusades, all Jihad. (p. 423)

**The Butter Battle** is, I suppose, an effort to begin this civilization by doing a kind of consciousness-raising among children before the militarists get to them. Fair enough. The idea that children should be dragged early into the political arena is one I am willing to bracket. Something else bothers me about the

book. The book's description of the illogical nature of the arms race is uncomfortably true: there really is something crazy about what we have done and continue to do.

My discomfort isn't with that part of the story. It is rather with the cute conceit which precedes it. If life were only a matter of two fuzzy bunches of warm bodies whose difference consisted in which sides of the bread they liked to put their butter on, things would be so much simpler—almost as simple as they are in **The Butter Battle.** In a world in which all values are matters of taste, subjective preference, it really is crazy to think of killing or dying for anything at all. If it all comes down to which side of the bread you butter, of course it is mad (or, in child-terms, just plain silly) to build weapons and aim them at one another.

Let's rewrite the book. On one side of the wall people who don't believe in butter at all are put into prison, and some of them are killed. On the other side, people whose color is wrong are forced into poverty, and those who protest are tortured.

I don't mean any analogies here between existing superpowers, except to say that each has plenty with which to charge the other, and that the differences are quite serious. They matter deeply, much more than the difference involved in buttering bread on the top or on the bottom. Neither superpower, of the two that now threaten to grind the rest of the world underneath, is blameless. Far from it. The American presence in Vietnam, the Russian presence in Afghanistan, the American support of right-wing dictators and the Russian support of left-wing dictators, all of this is ugly—but it involves something substantial, something which in fact matters deeply. The world may burn in a conflict between Soviet paranoia and American innocence, but what it suffers for and maybe dies for will be something rather more important than what side of the bread gets buttered.

We are responsible for doing what we can do about evils on both sides of whatever borders exist; but this means, at the very least, admitting that there are evils. And inasmuch as there are evils, there are also goods. There are standards against which we must measure things. It is right to delight in the victory of an Alfonsin in Argentina, and to protest the imprisonment of Father Gleb Yakunin and the persecution of Sakharov in the Soviet Union. It is right to protest the funding of terrorists in Nicaragua, and to encourage the hope which Solidarity brings to the people of Poland.

It may seem unfair to poor Dr. Seuss to single him out as an object lesson in liberal sentimentality. But in fact his latest book suggests something that exists at certain levels of liberal thought, and has existed there for years. The major problem, according to this line of thinking, is that we don't understand one another. What if we do? What if we do, and hate what the other guy thinks? What if our understanding of the other's values is based on such real and ugly things as the Gulag, or Vietnam, or genocide? There are, after all, things worth caring a lot about. I agree that the arms race is a tragic absurdity. But it isn't there for any frivolous reason. No one is good here, no one innocent. The innocence of butter up or down, nice as it would be, isn't anywhere close to what is true about our world. The values that divide us from the Soviet system, as well as the actions which contradict our own professed devotion to freedom and democracy, are important—it isn't a matter of learning simply to accept our differences.

The question is rather whether we can learn and teach forms of resistance to evil which will not inevitably lead to violence. There are examples, in our century, of effective nonviolent resistance: the Danish resistance to the Nazis, Gandhi's role in the liberation of India, and the continuing existence of Solidarity. (If Solidarity had decided on violence as a tool, it would have been crushed at birth.) We must indeed teach our children that the arms race is something which cannot be allowed to continue; but at the same time we must teach them that there are values which cannot be compromised and evils which must be resisted. To believe that nonviolent resistance is necessary for our world may seem utopian, until you face the fact that the alternative is racial suicide. The truly utopian belief is that we can go on as we are, and nothing will go wrong. (p. 424)

> *John Garvey "Guns & Butter: Dr. Seuss's Liberal Sentimentality" in* Commonweal, *Vol. CXI, No. 14, August 10, 1984, pp. 423-24.*

["**The Butter Battle Book"**] is really a grownup's book in child's clothing. . . . [The book] is a satire designed to inform the young and remind their elders of the consequences of mindless hostility coupled with escalating invention. In "Gulliver's Travels," Swift satirized opposing religious factions (he called them Big-Endians and Little-Endians), which clashed over the best way to open a boiled egg. Seuss uses buttered bread to serve his polemical purpose. (p. 184)

What to think about a story that pulls out of a hat not a cat but the most frightening apparition of all time? I found it strangely flat. The verses race along with the felicitous lilt of other Seuss books, but this book cannot be funny. Even Seuss's drawings, lively and ridiculous as ever, couldn't overcome my sinking feeling. Whereas his other books deal with morality in the abstract, this one is aimed at an immediate and horrible reality more complex than butter side up or butter side down. To reduce it to that seems not quite honest. I thought as well about the propriety and wisdom of starting a propaganda war in the kindergarten. Might not the Radical Right take up the challenge and produce persuasive stories about nuclear deterrence and the right to life? Perhaps it already has, and I've been spared the knowledge, but the thought of escalating weaponry in children's books is a scary one. Wondering what a child would make of **"The Butter Battle Book,"** I tried it on a small sample—a five-year-old girl and a seven-year-old boy. The girl heard it out solemnly and seemed puzzled at the end. When queried, she said the story was about fighting. She preferred Yooks to Zooks, insisting, sensibly, that butter side up *is* best—butter side down gets your fingers messy. The seven-year-old found the story interesting. He, too, preferred Yooks to Zooks. His eyes lighted with creative thought as he pointed out ways the Yooks might have improved their tactics and won the war by preëmptive strike. With sadness, I put the book away. (pp. 184, 187)

> *Faith McNulty, in a review of "The Butter Battle Book," in* The New Yorker, *Vol. LX, No. 42, December 3, 1984, pp. 184, 187.*

# Seymour Simon

## 1931-

**American author of nonfiction and fiction.**

Simon is a prolific writer best known for creating informational books which cover a wide range of topics in the pure and applied sciences. His natural curiosity and experiences as a teacher influence Simon's writing style and provide him with ideas for books in such fields as astronomy, zoology, and the life sciences. Because he believes in the personal rewards of learning by doing, Simon structures his works to follow the scientific method of observation and experimentation. Gearing his succinctly organized texts mainly toward middle graders, he tries to provide the conversational tone of the classroom. A common thread in Simon's works is his effort to grab and keep the child's interest throughout each book. He attempts to do this by centering on subjects which are naturally attractive to children, by beginning every book with an absorbing story or fact, by providing varied projects, and by asking many thought-provoking and open-minded questions.

Simon has moved from writing nonfiction exclusively to producing fictional works that emphasize science and computers. Observers see many of his early books as useful adjuncts to such curricular topics as animal behavior and ecology. Among these titles are his *Discovering* series, which presents guides to the study and care of animals often used as classroom pets, and the *On Your Street* series, which prompts city children to become more aware of their surroundings. Simon conceived his later, more diverse books as enticements for leisure reading and browsing rather than as classroom resources. Readers are drawn to such subjects as poisonous snakes, earthquakes, and optical illusions, and are particularly attracted to Simon's novel series of books, such as *Animal Fact/Animal Fable* and *Body Sense/Body Nonsense*, which separate fact from myth. Simon has also produced several photoessays, usually centering on outer space, in which he provided the explanatory text for photographs from reputable scientific institutions. With the *Einstein Anderson* series and *Chip Rogers, Computer Whiz*, Simon ventures into realistic fiction. Einstein Anderson is a brilliant, pun-loving youngster whose command of scientific facts enables him to solve mysteries contained in the ten stories which comprise each book. Frequently compared to Donald Sobol's *Encyclopedia Brown* books, Simon's series invites readers to interpret the clues as well as become knowledgeable about science. *Chip Rogers* is a mystery story which introduces readers to computer concepts and basic programming. The solution to the mystery is contained not only in textual clues but in an actual program which can be run on most computers.

Attracted to science since childhood, Simon credits science fiction magazines for sparking his fascination with astronomy and technology. He pursued his interests by attending the Bronx High School of Science and becoming president of the Junior Astronomy Club at the American Museum of Natural History. Following graduate work at City College of New York, where he concentrated on animal studies, Simon became a teacher in 1955. For more than twenty years he taught science, creative writing, and other subjects to intermediate grade and junior high school students in the New York City school system. A lifelong fondness for writing led Simon to compose

© William P. Gottlieb. Courtesy of Seymour Simon

articles and a science supplement for *Scholastic* magazine. In 1968, he wrote his first book, *Animals in Field and Laboratory: Science Projects in Animal Behavior*, to satisfy a curriculum need. Since then, Simon has produced more than ninety books, often working on several of them at one time. He also reviews juvenile science books and writes occasional scientific articles for teachers. Though he is now a full-time author, Simon still regards himself as a teacher and often visits classrooms to discuss his books.

Critics commend Simon for his clear and stimulating writing style and for his ability to lead children gradually into complex ideas. While some reviewers object to minor points in Simon's books, his works are considered good introductions to many subjects. Simon is recognized as a scientist who successfully couples his enthusiasm with a knowledge of teaching skills to conceive authoritative and interesting books for children.

The National Science Teachers Association has named more than thirty of Simon's books as Outstanding Science Trade Books for Children.

(See also *Something about the Author*, Vol. 4; *Contemporary Authors New Revision Series*, Vol. 11; and *Contemporary Authors*, Vols. 25-28, rev. ed.)

## AUTHOR'S COMMENTARY

**[Geraldine De Luca]:** How did you get involved in writing science books for children?

**[Seymour Simon]:** I've always written—even while I was a high school student. When I started to teach, I wrote for the kids I was teaching. . . . I attended the Bronx High School of Science and was very interested in science when I was younger, so after I began to teach, I decided to try to write while I was teaching. I sent some articles to *Scholastic* magazines and although they didn't accept the articles, the editor of one of the magazines asked me to come in and he gave me an assignment, which happened to be for an article about the moon. The editors were very interested that I taught science because they were having a very difficult time finding anyone who could write who also knew something about science.

**[Roni Natov]:** When was this?

**[SS]:** In the early sixties. I then began writing regularly for them. . . . I did that for a number of years until I decided to do a book. Since my field in graduate school was mostly animal behavior, the first book that I wrote was called *Animals in Field and Laboratory: Science Projects in Animal Behavior.* I was teaching ninth grade then and a lot of kids in my classes were doing projects. I would tend to influence them to do work on animal behavior. So I did quite a long book for McGraw-Hill. Interestingly enough, my book, which was written for junior and senior high school students, wound up in college libraries. Evidently it's very useful for psychology courses. . . . The first book came out in 1968, and within a year or two, I was doing four to six books a year.

**[GD]:** You're writing full-time now?

**[SS]:** Right. I taught until about five years ago. When I stopped teaching, I had published about forty or fifty books. But I found that I wanted to spend more time in selecting the types of books that I would do. I had been doing books that were very curriculum-oriented. They were not textbooks by any means, but they were books which were tied in with class work. What I really wanted was to write the kinds of books that a kid might pick up in a library or in a bookstore, and I found that I needed more time to do that kind of book. My newer books are different from the earlier ones.

**[RN]:** Did publishers ask you to do the books you've done or did you simply write them?

**[SS]:** All the recent books have been my own doing. Generally, I approach my publishers with an idea. I always think of the idea—I think they rely upon me primarily to do that because most of my editors are not strong in science and ideas are always coming to me for one reason or another. I'll jot it down. It may go through some changes; I may simply get rid of it completely, or I may not do anything with it for a number of years or I may change it slightly. (pp. 10-11)

I'm always working on several books at the same time. I may be writing a book and researching another book and writing for information about a third book and thinking about plans for still a fourth book. . . . It's really much easier for me to work that way because then I don't have to do just one type of work—all research or all writing for a long period of time. I would find it impossible to sit at a typewriter for eight hours. To write for a few hours each day and then to go to a library, or to visit somebody to talk about something that I'm going to do, and then to think for a while is really far more pleasant.

**[RN]:** When you conceive of these books, do you think about illustrations?

**[SS]:** Well, when I do a photo essay book I obviously have to think in terms of illustrations as well. I got the illustrations for *The Long View into Space* before I wrote the text. I wrote the text to the illustrations, which I collected myself. I've also done a follow-up of this book, titled *The Long Journey from Space,* for which I've written the text and gathered the photos. It's about comets—because of Halley's comet coming in around 1985-6—and it is the same kind of photo essay book. For most other books, though, I don't think of illustrations in advance. (pp. 11-12)

**[GD]:** Is the technique of starting out with common misconceptions something that you use often?

**[SS]:** The techniques of writing nonfiction and fiction are very similar. When you write fiction, you try to get the reader hooked on your story so you start out with something that's interesting in some way. Exactly the same thing is true of writing an informational book. You want to start out with something that interests the reader so you begin with a story. For example, I wrote a book called *The Secret Clocks,* which is about the biological time senses. I started out with a story about grunions, which are small fish that spawn on the California beaches so precisely that local newspapers print the time the grunions are going to come onto the beach to spawn, so that people can gather them and eat them. It's a fascinating thing, a kind of happening. . . .

Almost every chapter in every book that I've written begins with some kind of narrational hook to get the reader involved in what's going to follow. In books that I write for younger kids, I use this technique throughout the entire book. (p. 16)

**[GD]:** Do many of the subjects that you think about exploring come from your own curiosity?

**[SS]:** Absolutely. That's the single biggest source of ideas for my books. If I'm curious about something—I have a very childlike imagination and interests—I'm sure that kids are going to be curious. (p. 18)

**[RN]:** How do you gauge what basic age group you are going to write for?

**[SS]:** Well, sometimes it's suggested by the topic. For example, with my book about mirrors, I was not interested in writing on the level on which I used to teach optics, because that's really quite technical—involving the angle of incidence and the angle of reflection and information like that. That's almost like a textbook. So if I wanted to write a simpler book about mirrors, it really had to be for younger kids; it seems to me that it was more appropriate. Sometimes, the age choice is arbitrary. The *Long View into Space,* I suppose, could have been written for any level from very young to adult. I made the choice because I thought that the age group that I wrote it for, children in younger elementary grades, would find it most accessible because they are the ones who I think are interested in space and know the least about it. I also think it's very important to get kids to read science books from a very young age. If they're not reading books about science by the time they're twelve, you've probably lost them. When they grow up, they will view science with a great deal of fear and misinformation. Thus, if we want a literate citizenry, we have to start children on science books when they're young. They have no fear at a young age, and they will stay familiar with science all of their lives. (pp. 18-19)

[GD]: Do you have a favorite subject that you like to write about?

[SS]: I write about a variety of subjects. When I first started to write, I wrote a lot of books about animals. I wrote a whole series of books called *Discovering What Earthworms Do, Discovering What Frogs Do, Discovering What Puppies Do,* and so on. . . . By this time, I think every animal has been covered in children's books so I no longer write about particular animals and neither does anybody else. I go through cycles. When I was a kid, I was an amateur astronomer. I was president of the Junior Astronomy Club at the Museum of Natural History, and I ground my own telescope mirror, but I didn't do any astronomy books until a few years ago. And then after I did one, I did another, and now I've done a third; all of a sudden I seem to be doing astronomy books.

[GD]: And what about the future? What are you interested in?

[SS]: Well, it's not so much a particular subject that I'm interested in. It's the way in which books are presented. I want to write books that are very accessible to children, so that a child seeing the book will want to pick it up and read it. And I try, whatever the subject is, to slant the book so that it will interest the kid. I try to give it a title that will be exciting. For example, I recently did a book on army ants. . . . [Instead] of calling it army ants, I called it *Deadly Ants,* to give it a little sense of menace. I figure if children pick up one of my books, and start to read it, they're going to read it. But I have to get them to pick it up. . . . I'm going to continue to write imaginative books about science, and continue to present them in ways that I think are interesting or novel. I'm willing to try any kind of a new technique. *Einstein Anderson,* for example, represents a new technique for me—teaching science through fiction. Then there are pop-up books. I've seen a lot of these books, and I thought, wouldn't it be great to do a science book like this. I really am open to lots of different kinds of things. (pp. 21-2)

*Geraldine De Luca and Roni Natov, "Who's Afraid of Science Books? An Interview with Seymour Simon," in* The Lion and the Unicorn, *Vol. 6, 1982, pp. 10-27.*

---

GENERAL COMMENTARY

**LEONE R. HEMENWAY**

Because of the growing concern for environmental quality, this well-written pair of books [*Science Projects in Ecology* and *Science Projects in Pollution*] which includes experiments to test, and sometimes counteract, pollutants and projects to study ecosystems will be useful for middle-school students.

Many of the projects in . . . *Ecology* rely on materials collected in woodlands, fields, deserts, bogs, or swamps which may be inaccessible to many. However, they provide for the effective study of plant and animal communities and their concomitant food chains and oxygen and nitrogen cycles.

. . . *Pollution* includes a mixed bag of experiments, some new. The use of vaseline-covered paper to trap air-polluting particles is probably familiar to most readers, but the adaptation of this technique to measure the exhausts of different automobiles is unique, and the determination of thermal pollution by varying aquarium temperatures and then counting the gill movements of goldfish is certainly different. However, the experiments with water pollution require some expertise, as well as access

to polluted sources and the ability to measure trash and garbage production.

Although these experiments are addressed to the young scientist at home, most of them require adult supervision and a science lab for the needed materials. Therefore, these books will provide good supplementary material for science lessons on ecology and pollution.

*Leone R. Hemenway, in a review of "Science Projects in Ecology" and "Science Projects in Pollution," in* School Library Journal, *an appendix to* Library Journal, *Vol. 19, No. 7, March, 1973, p. 112.*

### KIRKUS REVIEWS

Evidently aimed at city kids and intended, according to Simon's introductions, to encourage habits of "scientific" observation, [*A Building on Your Street* and *A Tree on Your Street,* include] a minimum of information. . . , a few suggestions. . . , and a number of questions. . . . Of the two, the tree book is closer to other city field guides; the one on buildings, though it does set its readers a few mindless chores ("measure the width and height of each foundation stone"), tries its best to encourage an investigative habit of mind. We suspect that kids who need this kind of prod are not inclined to take their behavioral cues from books, but elementary teachers at a loss for creative direction might find Simon's questions a starting point.

*A review of "A Building on Your Street" and "A Tree on Your Street," in* Kirkus Reviews, *Vol. XLI, No. 8, April 15, 1973, p. 461.*

### KIRKUS REVIEWS

[The purpose of *Birds On Your Street* and *Water On Your Street*] is to stimulate curiosity rather than answer questions, and the likely danger is that readers will get ahead of the author and grow impatient with his too-limited aims. Of the two books, the *Water* volume is the most diffuse, mixing desultory observations of condensation, perspiration and precipitation ("How does the sidewalk look different after a rainfall?") with a brief description of plumbing and water supply systems. . . . [Too] many of the questions are either undirected and dull ("Where do you find puddles?") or insultingly calculated (after making the distinction between sewage systems that dump raw waste and those that treat them, Simon asks, "Which do you think is the better kind?"). Birds are a more promising subject for open-ended observation, and by limiting himself to enumerating the kinds most likely to be watched by city kids (pigeons, sparrows, jays . . . ) and giving brief directions for feeding and nest watching, Simon is on firmer ground. Yet aside from warning that nests should never be collected or disturbed, he offers very little that nest-watchers can't easily think up on their own. And it's doubtful whether the more sluggish among them can be effectively motivated by the slight push Simon offers. (pp. 430-31)

*A review of "Birds on Your Street" and "Water on Your Street," in* Kirkus Reviews, *Vol. XLII, No. 8, April 15, 1974, pp. 430-31.*

**ZENA SUTHERLAND, DIANNE L. MONSON, and MAY HILL ARBUTHNOT**

Seymour Simon's many years as a public school science teacher are reflected in his books both by the knowledgeable ease with which he adapts his style to the comprehension level of the intended audience and by the fact that in many of his books he includes experiments that are clearly explained and that illustrate the principles he is discussing. He moves from the familiar to the less familiar, from the simple to the more complex, in the best tradition of teaching, but his writing has a natural, informal flow that has no didactic tone.

In *The Rock-Hound's Book* . . . Simon encourages the novice collector, pointing out that rocks are everywhere, that they are composed of minerals, and that rock-collecting is a safe, pleasant, endlessly interesting hobby. He describes qualities that identify mineral components, and supplies advice on where and how to collect with effective zeal. In *The Long View Into Space* . . . he creates a photographic essay that is handsome, accurate, lucid, and serious: an excellent introduction to astronomical bodies and the phenomena peculiar to each. It is typical of Simon's writing that he carefully explains, in this book, such subjects as novae or spiral galaxies without telling middle-grade readers so much that they are confused or so little that the subjects are not comprehensible. (p. 461)

> *Zena Sutherland, Dianne L. Monson, and May Hill Arbuthnot, "Informational Books," in their* Children and Books, *sixth edition, Scott, Foresman and Company, 1981, pp. 442-501.\**

## BERNICE E. CULLINAN WITH MARY K. KARRER AND ARLENE M. PILLAR

A rare combination of talent and knowledge of children, science, and teaching, Seymour Simon is a believer in the hands-on approach of leading children to discoveries about their world. For example, he used the appeal of making paper airplanes to teach the concepts of aerodynamics in *The Paper Airplane Book.* The diagrams explain thrust, lift, gravity, and how movable wing surfaces, like flaps, affect flight. . . .

[Simon] knows what readers are interested in and how to relate science to their interests. He involves the child as scientist as well as reader by providing projects, experiments, and things to observe in every book. . . .

The practical activities that he provides for children to try on their own lead to greater understanding because they make the children active participants in the learning process. Simon knows, and shows that he knows, that children learn by doing. (p. 388)

> *Bernice E. Cullinan with Mary K. Karrer and Arlene M. Pillar, "Informational Books," in their* Literature and the Child, *Harcourt Brace Jovanovich, Inc., 1981, pp. 383-426.\**

## JEFFREY A. FRENCH

[For brief] introductions to our planet and moon, it would be hard to beat [*Earth: Our Planet in Space* and *The Moon*]. . . . The texts, while very brief, provide good coverage of the basics. *Earth* discusses the earth's surface, the sun and other planets, the atmosphere and the cause of seasons; *The Moon* features the Apollo explorations while explaining the moon's phases, the lunar environment, surface and geologic activity and the 4.5 billion-year-old "Genesis Rock." Well organized, the texts have a smooth transition between topics, though some passages are slightly choppy to read. Both titles are useful as beginning nonfiction, but because of their visual appeal, neither would be out of place in picture book collections. A pair of winners!

> *Jeffrey A. French, in a review of "Earth: Our Planet in Space" and "The Moon," in* School Library Journal, *Vol. 30, No. 7, March, 1984, p. 151.*

## LAVINIA C. DEMOS

[*Earth: Our Planet in Space* and *The Moon* are] in every way suited to the beginning reader. . . . Their format and content would make these ideal volumes also for older, language disabled readers. (p. 35)

Sentences are short, even choppy, but the information is conveyed in real chunks of prose rather than as mere captions to the large black and white photographs. . . . Neither book has an index or table of contents. (pp. 35-6)

> *Lavinia C. Demos, in a review of "Earth: Our Planet in Space" and "The Moon," in* Appraisal: Science Books for Young People, *Vol. 18, No. 1, Winter, 1985, pp. 35-6.*

---

## ANIMALS IN FIELD AND LABORATORY: SCIENCE PROJECTS IN ANIMAL BEHAVIOR   (1968)

This is one of the more exciting little books in science to come along for some time: twenty-five projects involving the behavior of a wide variety of animals that encourage genuine inquiry and almost assure success. The instructions for the investigations are thorough: the instructions for maintaining the animals range from useful to almost negligible, but since most of these will be done under the supervision of a teacher (whether in school or at home) this is a minor aspect. So, for the same reason, is the brevity of the list of biological supply houses. Interesting information introduces a section of questions and suggestions for real study at the close. Eminently worthwhile, with projects that are likely to be started before the book is finished.

> *A review of "Animals in Field and Laboratory: Science Projects in Animal Behavior," in* Kirkus Reviews, *Vol. XXXVI, No. 8, April 15, 1968, p. 475.*

From its lively descriptions of classic animal behavior experiments to its practical suggestions for field and laboratory research that can be done by children, this is an excellent book for every child who asks why and is willing to find out for himself. The text and projects cover the senses, time and direction indicators, responses to environmental changes, means of communication, learning patterns, and courtship, parental, and group behavior in various animals, insects, birds, and fish. At the end of each chapter is an excellent bibliography, which includes magazine articles. This book offers the most extensive suggestions for scientific, field, and laboratory work at this age level.

> *Barbara S. Waters, in a review of "Animals in Field and Laboratory: Science Projects in Animal Behavior," in* School Library Journal, *an appendix to Library Journal, Vol. 14, No. 9, May, 1968, p. 82.*

With specific language and precision of style, the author leads his young readers through scores of projects. . . . All fall within the ability of young readers to perform rather easily (but not too much so), and are complemented by "open-ended" experiments at the end of each section. Students are afforded the opportunity to make conclusions on the basis of their own observations, a somewhat rare but essential quality in books of this type. There are no technical terms, large financial investments, or impractical suggestions to deter the young experimenter from "getting his hands dirty" doing actual, scientific work. . . . The list of references is far too brief. The list of biological supply houses lacks accurate addresses for correspondents.

*A review of "Animals in Field and Laboratory: Science Projects in Animal Behavior," in* Science Books, *Vol. 4, No. 2, September, 1968, p. 129.*

### *DISCOVERING WHAT EARTHWORMS DO* (1969)

*Discovering what earthworms do* involves many observations miscalled experiments and some quasi-experiments that prove very little (which kinds of leaves an earthworm prefers, and whether your findings jibe with an expert's list), others that are of dubious justification (cutting up earthworms at various points to see how they regenerate). The book assumes that the child will be able to watch earthworms at night, after a rain, etc. and be able to keep some at hand; the first is difficult in the city, the second is hampered here by slipshod instructions. In this area, as in most others, the Dorothy Hogner *Earthworms* is more precise and methodical (the Simon . . . fails to identify types). Only in regard to mating, which Hogner omits, does this have an edge.

*A review of "Discovering What Earthworms Do," in* Kirkus Reviews, *Vol. XXXVII, No. 10, May 15, 1969, p. 563.*

An interesting book for intermediate grade children. . . . [The author] provides an abundance of information about [the earthworm's] anatomy, performance of basic life functions, where and under what conditions people can find and keep worms, and what these little creatures do for the soil. In addition, he includes many easily performed experiments (notable for their clarity and directness of instruction, and the informative results obtainable from them) that children can do themselves. . . . Technical terms are explained lucidly and phonetically. . . .

*Harold F. Desmond, Jr., in a review of "Discovering What Earthworms Do," in* School Library Journal, *an appendix to* Library Journal, *Vol. 16, No. 5, January, 1970, p. 61.*

These [experiments] are well thought out, require little equipment and are well within the scope of the average kitchen or classrooom for younger children.

The narrative style may not be easy for the youngest children to follow and the lack of an index makes quick reference a problem. . . .

*A review of "Discovering What Earthworms Do," in* The Junior Bookshelf, *Vol. 34, No. 6, December, 1970, p. 359.*

### *DISCOVERING WHAT FROGS DO* (1969)

[Not as complete] as Hogner's *Frogs and Polliwogs* (Crowell, 1956), this adequately covers all phases of frog development, reproduction and reaction to stimulus, and in each area provides suitable experiments. A question approach is used throughout to motivate experimentation and involvement; the presentation is scientific but elementary and clear enough for young readers. The author fails to stress the importance of the frog to the balance of nature. Instead, Simon pleads for frog conservation on a live-and-let-live platform. . . . An acceptable supplement, but Hogner's book should be the first choice.

*Pat Barnes, in a review of "Discovering What Frogs Do," in* School Library Journal, *an appendix to* Library Journal, *Vol. 16, No. 9, May, 1970, p. 79.*

A good introduction to the topic. . . . The information given is useful. . . ; the writing is marred by an occasional excursion into exclamation points and by some patronizing questions ("How is this an advantage for the egg?" the author asks just after stating that a certain color pattern makes the egg difficult to see from below.) A final page, headed **"A Note on the Names of Frogs"** gives the common and scientific names for the leopard frog described in the text, and for three others. (p. 168)

*Zena Sutherland, in a review of "Discovering What Frogs Do," in* Bulletin of the Center for Children's Books, *Vol. 23, No. 10, June, 1970, pp. 167-68.*

### *DISCOVERING WHAT GOLDFISH DO* (1970)

Practical aspects of goldfish care are capably discussed here, such as tank size, preparing the aquarium, feeding and breeding, etc. Then, simple, harmless experiments that will lead children to discover the fish's ability to hear, distinguish color, and learn, as well as its reaction to groups, are suggested. Use of the scientific method is encouraged, and probable results for each experiment are examined. The text is written in a clear, interesting style. . . . Other pet books also devote space to care of goldfish but do not include experimentation. All in all, youngsters may find this valuable not only as a pet guide, but also as a potential source of simple science fair material or just experiments to do for the fun of it.

*Lea R. Pastorello, in a review of "Discovering What Goldfish Do," in* School Library Journal, *an appendix to* Library Journal, *Vol. 17, No. 6, February, 1971, p. 59.*

[This] little book cannot be recommended. . . . [The booklet] describes and suggests that the readers carry out many experiments with sentient vertebrate animals and this portion incorporates two major failings. The lesser failing is that the meaning of controls is never described and that many of the training and discrimination sequences are so simplistic that one learns nothing about the scientific method. Even more important is the question of harm to the animals. Slight misunderstandings of instructions, such as would be expected from readers of this age group, will expose these creatures to severe stress or physical harm. Cautions are mentioned but these are hardly enough. Experiments of the kind described here should only be carried out under supervision and if more than passing interest is involved.

*A review of "Discovering What Goldfish Do," in* Science Books, *Vol. 7, No. 1, May, 1971, p. 60.*

While the experiments suggested are clearly and simply explained, I object to a couple of them which, if not carefully done, endanger the life of the goldfish. I don't think any fish should be handled, and the author does not warn against this. In the above-mentioned experiments, I would prefer that an adult supervise the child since the oxygen supply of the fish is being tampered with. The rest of the experiments are fine and test the senses of the goldfish group behavior, and the development of the eggs. . . . [With] the above reservations, I recommend this book to school and public libraries. (pp. 39-40)

Esther L. Steffens, in a review of "Discovering What Goldfish Do," in Appraisal: Children's Science Books, Vol. 5, No. 1, Winter, 1972, pp. 39-40.

If you think of goldfish as the helpless denizens of a plastic water-filled bag clutched in the fingers of a fairground prize-winner and destined to a short life in a small bowl Seymour Simon's book will lift the fishy scales from your eyes. . . . It suggests in true scientific manner how you should observe, record and make deductions from what you have seen. It is an indispensable adjunct to the classroom aquarium.

D. A. Young, in a review of "Discovering What Goldfish Do," in The Junior Bookshelf, Vol. 37, No. 3, June, 1973, p. 191.

## SCIENCE IN A VACANT LOT (1970)

An excellent handbook on life in an open lot that teaches how to make observations, and utilize them. . . . Questions encourage the reader to observe, reach conclusions, and be encouraged to make further investigations. . . . Experiments and activities are simple and thoroughly described.

Jane Granstrom, in a review of "Science in a Vacant Lot," in Appraisal: Children's Science Books, Vol. 4, No. 3, Fall, 1971, p. 24.

**Science in a Vacant Lot** is a very professionally written book that explains scientific thinking and steps clearly yet simply with activities that are interesting and fun. The last two pages are devoted to a list of "books for reading and research". This reading list gives the young investigator a good start along the path or paths of interest that the book has opened for him.

Ryan B. Walden, in a review of "Science in a Vacant Lot," in Appraisal: Children's Science Books, Vol. 4, No. 3, Fall, 1971, p. 24.

## SCIENCE AT WORK: EASY MODELS YOU CAN MAKE (1971)

Simon has thrown together a group of rather simple little projects through which he attempts to teach some science. There is uniformity in style of presentation but no continuity in content. Each of the thirty exercises has the same three sections: YOU WILL NEED, in which equipment is specified; WHAT TO DO, in which adequately explicit directions are given. . . ; and WHAT TO LOOK FOR, in which attention is focused on particular facets of the model and the reader is told what he should see as well. Topics jump from Altimeter to Static Electricity Detector to Weather Front Model, and each piece stands independently of all the others. The exercises are similar to those in Milgrom's *Explorations in Science: A Book of Basic Experiments*. . . . [In Simon's book] there is a sense of more freedom in the investigations (although there is still not much), and more information accompanies each exercise than in Milgrom's book. Most of the materials for the models are easily available; when they are not, as for example when a lens is needed, the reader often is not directed to a source. If you are interested in a potpourri of science exercises, then this one is as good or better than the others, but it is not nearly so satisfying as similar single topic books.

A review of "Science at Work: Easy Models You Can Make," in Kirkus Reviews, Vol. XXXIX, No. 5, March 1, 1971, p. 241.

All of the models are teaching devices, for the student learns scientific principles by making them and from the experiments in which he uses them. Directions are minimum yet sufficiently explicit. Open-ended questions abound to stimulate thinking and experimentation. Wherever necessary, the author has inserted warnings so that the student will not injure himself by thoughtless acts. The materials that are needed for making the models will be available in the average household or can be secured easily. A few well-chosen books are recommended for further reading and there is an index. The . . . [author's] head is brimful of good ideas, as evidenced by eight previous books on science activities and observations. . . . (pp. 19-20)

A review of "Science at Work: Easy Models You Can Make," in Science Books, Vol. 7, No. 1, May, 1971, pp. 19-20.

Here is a fine collection of thirty simple and interesting science projects. . . . Projects center around the areas of astronomy, optics, electricity, magnetisim, meteorology, geology, and Newtonian and nuclear physics. It is essential that the reader have either an elementary knowledge of general science or a reasonably high level of reading comprehension in order to carry out these activities. . . . Overall organization and materials-oriented approach make it a very good resource for the school library or even for the classroom. (pp. 35-6)

Thomas A. Butler, in a review of "Science at Work: Easy Models You Can Make," in Appraisal: Children's Science Books, Vol. 5, No. 2, Spring, 1972, pp. 35-6.

## CHEMISTRY IN THE KITCHEN (1971)

It is unfortunate that the inclusion of one dangerous experiment spoils an otherwise fine book. As an introduction to chemical change, author Simon has prepared a thought-provoking manual using equipment and materials generally found in most kitchens. In a few instances, simplification for the young child has led to distortion of scientific principles, but the slight misconceptions which could result are largely outweighed by the good features of the book. Questions guiding children to think critically about what they observe are found throughout the book, although there are fewer in the later chapters than in the earlier ones. The concluding experiment in the chapter **"Soaps and Detergents"** involves dissolving lye in water and heating the resulting solution. The solution is used to prepare soap from butter. The author suggests giving pieces of soap to friends! Although the reader is cautioned not to handle the solid sodium hydroxide with the hands, no mention is made of the heat generated during dissolution or of the danger to the eyes of spattering sodium hydroxide solution as a result of possible overheating. Further, the product will undoubtedly be contaminated by entrained sodium hydroxide and could cause eye damage if used by children. A list of references for further reading is appended, but over half of the works cited are 10 or more years old. A complete index is included. (pp. 128-29)

A review of "Chemistry in the Kitchen," in Science Books, Vol. 7, No. 2, September, 1971, pp. 128-29.

Although the book is intended to interest the seven-to-ten-year-old reader, the text lacks appeal for several reasons. 1. Chapters are not broken down into subheadings; 2. New words are not included in a glossary; 3. The inside margin is too narrow. It is doubtful that the book would hold the interest of the young reader because it is not one which invites you to read on. (p. 34)

*Judith E. Trenholm, in a review of "Chemistry in the Kitchen," in Appraisal: Children's Science Books, Vol. 5, No. 3, Fall, 1972, pp. 33-4.*

This book is better than most I have seen with respect to its emphasis on safety, yet it does not go far enough to allow me to consider it more than conditionally acceptable. Experiments by budding young chemists surely ought to be conducted with the full knowledge and approval of a parent, and it is wise for chemists of any age never to be alone, yet this is not stressed. The experiment on soap making ought to be rewritten or deleted. How about a few safety instructions about what to do in case something goes wrong—water washing, fire fighting, inducing vomiting, and reading labels beforehand?

*Frank Fish, in a review of "Chemistry in the Kitchen," in Appraisal: Children's Science Books, Vol. 5, No. 3, Fall, 1972, p. 34.*

### DISCOVERING WHAT GERBILS DO   (1971)

Although this gives information about the care and feeding of gerbils, neither the text nor the illustrations [by Jean Zallinger] provides the details of Dobrin's *Gerbils.* . . . Both books suggest ways of experimenting to learn more about the animal's behavior, but this is less smoothly incorporated here, with more brief questions but with more suggestions. Less useful than the Dobrin, which has the index lacking here, this is nevertheless a good additional book on the topic.

*Zena Sutherland, in a review of "Discovering What Gerbils Do," in Bulletin of the Center for Children's Books, Vol. 25, No. 2, October, 1971, p. 33.*

While much fundamental information about the care and habits of gerbils is presented, basically, the text is meant to motivate children to conduct simple experiments and make observations on the behavior of their pet gerbils. The ideas, suggestions and questions are most thought-provoking, and seemingly would arouse any reader's curiosity enough so that he would attempt some of their activities.

*M. Letita Kelley, in a review of "Discovering What Gerbils Do," in Appraisal: Children's Science Books, Vol. 5, No. 2, Spring, 1972, p. 35.*

[The] text is good. It seems to be easily readable by fourth, possibly even third graders. While informative and practical, it also raises many open-ended questions relating to gerbil behavior. Presumably an interested gerbil owner could spend many enjoyable hours attempting to describe and explain specific aspects of gerbil behavior patterns. This is a strong point of the text, although it does seem to read like a college lab manual in places. But why doesn't Simon discuss sexual activity? . . . The author cops out, I'm afraid. He mentions fertilization and then goes on to birth. This omission seriously weakens the text. One final comment: this book is a mixed blessing. With its high and low points it ends up being just Fair.

*Thomas A. Butler, in a review of "Discovering What Gerbils Do," in Appraisal: Children's Science Books, Vol. 5, No. 2, Spring, 1972, p. 35.*

### THE PAPER AIRPLANE BOOK   (1971)

For the young reader with any interest at all in flying paper airplanes, this . . . little book should provide hours of entertainment along with some basic facts on the theory of flight. . . . The reader is shown how to make rudders, elevators, and flaps with simple cuts in the paper and is encouraged to investigate their effects on the model's flight characteristics. This reviewer, who many years ago considered himself an expert on paper airplanes, thoroughly flight-tested all the models presented and will attest that they fly.

*A review of "The Paper Airplane Book," in Science Books, Vol. 7, No. 4, March, 1972, p. 327.*

[This is] an exemplary home demonstration book. The author uses the process approach, suggesting variations on the airplane and asking the reader to consider *why* a certain effect is obtained, or which change is most effective for a desired result. The book does, of course, show the reader how to make paper airplanes, but it is really used (and very deftly) to discuss what makes a real airplane fly, and how the various parts of a plane contribute to or affect its flight.

*Zena Sutherland, in a review of "The Paper Airplane Book," in Bulletin of the Center for Children's Books, Vol. 25, No. 9, May, 1972, p. 146.*

### SCIENCE AT WORK: PROJECTS IN SPACE SCIENCE   (1971)

The principles and scientific facts upon which space exploration is based are introduced here by 39 simple experiments. They can be set up with common household materials and those available from hobby shops or mail-order suppliers. The experiments are divided into three groups: (i) how we get into space, (ii) how we exist in space, and (iii) how we explore space. Each experiment is divided into three parts: (i) materials, (ii) methods, and (iii) what to look for with leading questions to encourage thinking. . . . The experimenter will gain knowledge and confidence as well as develop skill in reading, observing, recording, and explaining verbally or in writing. Most data are given in round figures. Some approximate mathematical formulae, graphs, and a chemical equation are given. The index is adequate and the bibliography is appropriate. Most beginning students of astronautics should benefit from this book. (pp. 79-80)

*A review of "Science at Work: Projects in Space Science," in Science Books, Vol. 8, No. 1, May, 1972, pp. 79-80.*

*Science at Work* is written in a non-technical style that encourages the reader to think and to perform the experiments. The book provides a good source of leisure activities and classroom experiments. There is a fine reading list and a very good list of supply sources at the back of the book. The author also does an excellent job of stressing safety in each experiment.

*Ryan B. Walden, in a review of "Science at Work: Projects in Space Science," in Appraisal: Children's Science Books, Vol. 6, No. 1, Winter, 1973, p. 31.*

### SCIENCE PROJECTS IN ECOLOGY   (1972)

Though there are instructions here for setting up an aquarium and different kinds of terrariums, and some suggestions that might serve as a starting point for a teacher short of ideas who has other sources of basic information, this wide-ranging col-

*Simon visits a classroom for one of his frequent book talks. Here he involves children in his presentation on* The Paper Airplane Book, *one of his most popular works. Xenia* Daily Gazette. *Courtesy of Seymour Simon.*

lection of nature "experiments" is spread so thin that no one topic is illuminated or procedure elaborated. Whether readers are exploring woodland, desert, grassland, pond, or bog communities, the directions are on the order of "look for the living things" or "try to identify the different plants you see." The questions for experimenters are so vague as to offer no direction at all ("what happens when conditions change?") and after the initial activity for each ecosystem is an offhand list of "more things to try" ("Try growing cactuses from seed . . . follow the instructions of the package for their care"). Typically, Simon suggests keeping a garter snake and gives brief instructions for its care but offers no hints as to the nature of the animal or how or what children might learn from the experience. The very thoroughness, precision, and directed inquiry that distinguished Simon's *Animals in Field and Laboratory* . . . are just the qualities that are fatally lacking here. (pp. 483-84)

> *A review of "Science Projects in Ecology," in* Kirkus Reviews, *Vol. XL, No. 8, April 15, 1972, pp. 483-84.*

All the projects can be done at home or in the classroom using few and inexpensive materials. For each exercise, needed materials are listed and simple instructions ("project pointers") are given. . . . A list of 23 "books for research" is presented at the end. In general the exercises are not particularly imaginative and some directions are not specific enough for ele-

mentary grades. . . . Words like "conifer" and "humus" are used freely but not defined; a glossary is needed. Simon can hardly expect a child to know what a liverwort or a partridge-berry is. Also, the reader should not be subjected to the pun: "[keeping] a daily log of a rotting log" (p. 27), and he should be told about larvae, not "larvas." On the other hand, many helpful hints are provided, and the many questions that are posed throughout the text should develop observational and analytical capabilities among young readers. (pp. 140-41)

> *A review of "Science Projects in Ecology," in* Science Books, *Vol. 8, No. 2, September, 1972, pp. 140-41.*

Each "project" consists of two or three pages of suggested materials and ideas for study, most of which are found in other books already published. This is predominately a starter book for helping young people begin projects, but the child investigator would need to know much about field identification, collecting, and care of organisms. . . . The physical environment is slighted in favor of plant and animal study of field, forest, pond, and soil habitats. A project book which encourages self-study would be expected to contain . . . detailed explanations on techniques for conducting field activities. This book does not.

> *John R. Pancella, in a review of "Science Projects in Ecology," in* Appraisal: Children's Science Books, *Vol. 6, No. 2, Spring, 1973, p. 35.*

*SCIENCE PROJECTS IN POLLUTION* (1972)

[Similar to *Science Projects in Ecology*] in its vague and superficial treatment of the topics, this has the further disadvan-
tage of including much exposition on pollution (merely repeating the oft-told tales of Donora, Pa., detergents and algae,
etc.), didactic lectures on littering, and extraneous, too familiar
lists of "what you can do" about air, water, and land pollution.
Opening suggestions for collecting "particles" from the air or
vacuum cleaner on index cards or for viewing "pollutants from
cars" ignore such questions as what the particles are made of
or how they pollute or what a dusty index card might signify
or measure. Simon then asks "Should people who work in
heavy traffic wear nose and mouth masks?" without providing
or even asking readers to obtain the information they'd need
for an intelligent answer, and sometimes he actually encourages
glib oversimplification about complex and controversial subjects—a glance at crowded guppies leads to the questions, "Is
there a difference in aggressiveness (in a crowded jar)? In your
opinion, is overcrowding harmful to guppies? How about people?" [Charles Jakubowski's pictures] are no more than mildly
pleasant decorations—understandable since there is so little to
elucidate.

> *A review of "Science Projects in Pollution," in* Kir-
> kus Reviews, *Vol. XL, No. 8, April 15, 1972, p.*
> *484.*

[The projects] can be performed for the most part with simple,
easily obtainable equipment and supplies: and generally require
little more than straightforward observation for drawing conclusions. For example, gelatin in baby food jars substitutes for
agar in petri dishes: manure furnishes the inoculum; and the
resulting growth of bacterial colonies demonstrates contami-
nation. Each experiment is divided into three sections: "Materials You Will Need," "Project Pointers," and "More Things
to Try," thereby offering a simple guide to teachers in their
choice of experiments. Unfortunately the accompanying text
provides only a superficial treatment of many topics. In addition, Simon often fails to adequately explain the implications
of the experiment results—the child using this book on his own
might easily miss the real point or be led to an over-simplified
analysis of a particular issue.

> *A review of "Science Projects in Pollution," in* Sci-
> ence Books, *Vol. 8, No. 2, September, 1972, p. 141.*

Arranged in three parts—air, water, and earth pollution—this
book has a bibliography and index. The material is well-organized. . . . Experiments are simple, with cautions italicized,
or with recommendations to enlist the help of an adult. In
addition to the effective projects in the text, there are many
questions for the thoughtful reader. Without being sensational
or emotional, Mr. Simon presents clear evidence of pollution
in a manner which encourages a positive scientific approach.
Adults working with children should find this a valuable book.

> *Frances Doughty, in a review of "Science Projects*
> *in Pollution," in* Appraisal: Children's Science Books,
> *Vol. 5, No. 3, Fall, 1972, p. 34.*

Seymour Simon has drawn together a great collection of experiments that permit children to investigate pollution problems
in their immediate environment. . . . Each experimental procedure is carefully explained, required materials are listed, and
caution is advised where appropriate. The experiments do not
lead to closure but rather expose the student to a wider arena
of investigation. Following each experiment there is a good

list of "More Things to Try." *Science Projects in Pollution*
will definitely provide students with some very meaningful
environmental experiences, while developing some basic laboratory skills. (pp. 34-5)

> *Harry O. Haakonsen, in a review of "Science Proj-*
> *ects in Pollution," in* Appraisal: Children's Science
> Books, *Vol. 5, No. 3, Fall, 1972, pp. 34-5.*

*LET'S TRY IT OUT: HOT AND COLD* (1972)

In a good book for the child who is curious about scientific
phenomena, [Simon] includes in his discussion of heat and
cold many simple projects that require no special equipment.
Written in a succinct, direct style, the text describes how we
feel and dress in response to temperature, how animate and
inanimate objects react, and the way in which heat is conducted
or retained by objects of different consistencies and colors.

> *Zena Sutherland, in a review of "Let's Try It Out*
> *. . . Hot and Cold," in* Bulletin of the Center for
> Children's Books, *Vol. 26, No. 5, January, 1973,*
> *p. 82.*

Guiding a child's examination of the qualities of heat and cold
is the excuse for this book which is designed to be read to
small children. Its virtue lies in its use of commonplace objects
for study. . . . The book does not seem well organized, and
it's usefulness is diminished by its attempt to be at once poetic,
conversational and instructional—the result is a confusion of
tone and voice and a diffusion of focus.

> *A review of "Let's-Try-It-Out: Hot & Cold," in* Sci-
> ence Books, *Vol. 8, No. 4, March, 1973, p. 318.*

*SCIENCE AT WORK: PROJECTS IN OCEANOGRAPHY* (1972)

This science project book encompasses experiments dealing
with salinity, differences between fresh and salt-water properties, wave motion, tides, ocean currents, seashore life, salt-
water aquariums, the ocean floor, cores, icebergs and even
messages in bottles. A useful list of aquarium suppliers and a
brief reading list are included. Approximately one-fourth of
the suggested projects require a seashore which limits the book's
use in landlocked areas. Nevertheless, this is comprehensive
in scope and combines many oceanographic concepts for the
age group.

> *Leone R. Hemenway, in a review of "Science at*
> *Work: Projects in Oceanography," in* School Library
> Journal, *an appendix to* Library Journal, *Vol. 19,*
> *No. 6, February, 1973, p. 72.*

Without a doubt many elementary teachers will be grateful to
Mr. Simon for this book. Several laboratory manuals are available for the high school student, but this is one of the first
prepared specifically for use in the elementary school classroom. The projects selected for inclusion have been wisely
chosen; when taken collectively they effectively represent a
notable cross-section of oceanic phenomena and characteristics. Mr. Simon avoids the use of "laboratory-type" scientific
equipment for experiments; rather he has chosen to utilize everyday "household" items which are familiar to the elementary
school student. This allows the student to participate in obtaining the materials and equipment as well as in doing the
experiment itself. Twenty-nine projects are described. Each

specifies what you will need, what to do, and what to look for in language suitable for the average fourth grade student. For the elementary teacher who has been seeking a project book to help illustrate marine science and to make it "come alive" in the classroom, this is it! Well done! Every elementary school attempting to include environmental science as a classroom topic should insure that this book is available in their library.

A review of "Science at Work: Projects in Oceanography," in Science Books, Vol. IX, No. 1, May, 1973, p. 71.

**Science at Work** ... provides some very interesting questions and activities for the curious child. The text has a blend of information and unanswered challenges that gives the child a structure of operation, yet will encourage him to explore on his own. Even children away from the ocean will be stimulated to explore the nature of salt water, depth of water bodies, action of winds, etc. This book is useful for school libraries.

Ann E. Matthews, in a review of "Science at Work: Projects in Oceanography," in Appraisal: Children's Science Books, Vol. 6, No. 3, Fall, 1973, p. 35.

---

## A BUILDING ON YOUR STREET (1973)

This marginal title purports to teach observation, measurement, and other basic scientific skills. The vehicle for presenting these concepts is a walk along the street with numerous suggestions of things to look for which apply almost exclusively to urban dwellers. Several of the activities require special equipment, but children are not instructed to take any along. The answers to some of the series of questions which comprise the text require additional information not provided in the book, and youngsters out for a walk cannot look-it-up.... Phyllis S. Busch's *Exploring As You Walk in the City* (Lippincott, 1972) is more effective but deals almost entirely with the observation of city plant and animal life.

Carole P. Haro, in a review of "A Building on Your Street," in School Library Journal, an appendix to Library Journal, Vol. 20, No. 1, September, 1973, p. 62.

The questions are often narrow and somewhat uninspiring: "Are some of the buildings taller than others?" "Are some wider than others?" "Of what use are fire escapes?" Answers to these questions should require direct observation, but they will probably be generated during class discussions—not quite what the author had in mind. A great deal of information is given concerning shapes, sizes and materials used in buildings. Building materials are dealt with more extensively than other topics, and this information is not normally offered in the science curriculum. The organization of the book is not very coherent—topics such as preserving natural resources are injected without contextual justification.... The book does not teach "scientific method" in the strict sense of the term, but it is reasonably accurate and could serve as a resource book for elementary science.

A review of "A Building on Your Street," in Science Books, Vol. IX, No. 4, March, 1974, p. 324.

---

## PROJECTS WITH PLANTS (1973)

The usual round of experiments on seed germination, osmosis, and the effects of light on plant growth is embellished here with a few tests that seem hardly worth bothering with (try watering a plant only on the leaves and stems—in a day or two "it will begin to wilt and die") and a more promising series on tropisms that, however, require access to an inexpensive record player turntable. With 27 concepts to cover—including bread mold and bacteria which is a subject in itself—Simon has little use for style or continuity, and few kids will be satisfied with the breezy explanations of difficult topics (like those "chemicals called auxins" that tell roots which direction to grow in—"Gravity usually pulls the auxins downward"). Readers are continually referred to the list of "further reading" for help in straightening things out; indeed, one might just as well begin there.... (pp. 1102-03)

A review of "Projects with Plants," in Kirkus Reviews, Vol. XLI, No. 19, October 1, 1973, pp. 1102-03.

The clearly explained projects use readily available materials and most are simple and safe enough to be conducted independently by students. Only a few require teacher/parental supervision, and some of the more complex concepts may require additional information to be fully understood. Simon's book is less difficult than *Experimenting with Seeds and Plants* by Ware T. Budlong (Putnam, 1970) which contains more elaborate projects.

Judith Eisinger, in a review of "Projects with Plants," in School Library Journal, an appendix to Library Journal, Vol. 20, No. 7, March, 1974, p. 111.

---

## FROM SHORE TO OCEAN FLOOR: HOW LIFE SURVIVES IN THE SEA (1973)

Seymour Simon has produced another excellent and interesting book for children, this one on the struggle for survival in the sea. He effectively presents in this true perspective the story of the "eat and be eaten" life of marine animals. Mr. Simon has wisely chosen to begin with certain species which are in some degree familiar to children (the whale, the seal, and the seahorse); he then systematically introduces other selected organisms which exhibit the particular life cycle and activity characteristics that relate to the chapter topic under discussion. For emphasis (and the teacher's convenience), words which are unique or new to the average 10- to 12-year old reader are italicized; a definition or explanation accompanies each.... The final chapter introduces man's effect on (threat to) marine life; it covers in succinct fashion the three major areas of concern: the pollution problem (oil and pesticides); overfishing; and waste disposal (dumping). A good index is provided, as is a list of references (including several advanced books apparently intended for teachers). About half of the sources cited pre-date 1965. Better coverage may be available in more recent material, yet Simon's new book is an excellent introduction to marine biology for the elementary school student.

A review of "From Shore to Ocean Floor: How Life Survives in the Sea," in Science Books, Vol. IX, No. 3, December, 1973, p. 257.

**From Shore to Ocean Floor** is a very good overview or general introduction to every level of marine life. It is amazing to consider just how much information has been arranged in these few pages.... The only detracting feature of this otherwise fine volume is its "cutesy" chapter headings which offer no clue as to their contents.

*Sonja Wieta Coleman, in a review of "From Shore
to Ocean Floor: How Life Survives in the Sea," in
Appraisal: Children's Science Books, Vol. 7, No. 2,
Spring, 1974, p. 42.*

This interesting text is full of fascinating information about
ways in which life survives in the sea. The chapter headings
are particularly appealing, each communicating an important
concept; for example, **"A Parade of Winners," "Survival Under Pressure,"** etc. However, as a science trade book it disappoints in that an explanation of scientific methods is not
integrated with the text. One may well ask when reading, how
do we know?

*Ann E. Matthews, in a review of "From Shore to
Ocean Floor: How Life Survives in the Sea," in
Appraisal: Children's Science Books, Vol. 7, No. 2,
Spring, 1974, p. 42.*

---

### A TREE ON YOUR STREET   (1973)

This book is a pedestrian attempt at stimulating a child's interest
in observation through examination of trees. It contains little
specific information and is instead a series of unoriginal projects and questions intended to guide the child. Some of the
suggested activities are: measuring a tree by comparing it with
buildings; noticing the kinds of leaves and when they appear
(seven varieties are given as examples); watching animals and
insects that inhabit trees; looking for damaged trees; finding
out how to plant a new tree; and watering a tree. This last
project filled me with dismay at the thought of rotting roots
resulting from solicitous overwatering with larger "pails" than
the ones Mr. Simon evidently envisions in his generous instructions. . . . The book could have some use on schoolroom
shelves as an aid to students needing concrete directions for
an independent ecology project, but its informational use is
very limited. It is unpaged and unindexed. Through its generality and glib movement from one project to another, it hardly
fulfills the promise of the introduction, in which the author
claims that the book will familiarize the child with the scientific
method.

*Carole Cochran Wilson, in a review of "A Tree on
Your Street," in Appraisal: Children's Science Books,
Vol. 7, No. 1, Winter, 1974, p. 37.*

[Simon's] suggestions for observation are both practical and
imaginative, and the activities are well suited to children of
this age. Descriptions of leaves for identification could be more
precise. . . . It is a good book, on the whole, for city children.

*Pearl B. Care, in a review of "A Tree on Your
Street," in Appraisal: Children's Science Books, Vol.
7, No. 1, Winter, 1974, p. 37.*

There is a minimum amount of facts and theory in this book
and a maximum of enthusiasm and encouragement for personal
participation. Although the projects described are not original
or unusual (leaf rubbings, plaster casting of bark), they sound
like fun and could be carried out with little or no adult help. . . .
Second- to fourth-graders will enjoy the book.

*A review of "A Tree of Your Street," in Science
Books, Vol. X, No. 1, May, 1974, p. 71.*

---

### BIRDS ON YOUR STREET   (1974)

Simon offers suggestions for bird watching in the city (pigeons
and starlings) and in suburbs (catbirds and robins). Little specific information about birds is given. Instead, Simon suggests
what young observers should look for—the bird's size, style
of flying, behavior, etc.—by asking questions like "Does it
walk or hop along the ground?"; "Do you see the bird all year
round or only during one season?" Also included are suggestions for investigating old nests, setting up a bird-feeding shelf,
etc. The text is clearly written. . . ; however, Glen Blough's
*Bird Watchers and Bird Feeders* (McGraw, 1963) contains
more detailed information on birds and more suggestions for
observation activities.

*Juliet Kellogg Markowsky, in a review of "Birds on
Your Street," in School Library Journal, an appendix
to Library Journal, Vol. 21, No. 1, September, 1974,
p. 70.*

Any child in the primary grades will delight in reading **Birds
on Your Street**. It's a book that poses many questions for elementary and kindergarten students concerning the birds of their
environment. It shows the birds in their new natural element—
the city streets and lots, and it will help students be more
observant and think in terms of the birds' sizes, colors and
descriptions. The author stresses that birds are wild animals
which should be left alone—particularly at nesting time—but
which should be fed during the winter and protected as necessary. Having raised many young birds and banded thousands,
this reviewer found this a delightfully enlightened book for his
youngest neighbors, and it is recommended to any parent or
school library.

*A review of "Birds on Your Street," in Science Books,
Vol. X, No. 3, December, 1974, p. 259.*

Pigeons, house sparrows, and blue jays are revealed as the
fascinating creatures they are through Simon's suggestions of
what characteristics and behavioral traits one should look for.
All suggestions can be carried out by any city child without
any expenditure of money, thus making the joy of observation
available to the poorest. A sound and practical book which
develops the powers of observation that make the commonplace
the marvel it truly is. (pp. 34-5)

*Wayne Hanley, in a review of "Birds on Your Street,"
in Appraisal: Children's Science Books, Vol. 8, No.
1, Winter, 1975, pp. 34-5.*

---

### LIFE IN THE DARK: HOW ANIMALS SURVIVE AT NIGHT
(1974)

Children who are really interested in pursuing the subjects of
bat sonar, bioluminescence or the physiology of vision, for
example, will find fuller and more fascinating introductions
elsewhere; for those everyday school reports, however, Simon
offers a quick survey of some common nocturnal animals'
habits and equipment, along with a few relevant anecdotes for
diversion. . . .

*A review of "Life in the Dark: How Animals Sur-
vive," in Kirkus Reviews, Vol. XLII, No. 17, September 1, 1974, p. 948.*

Two chapters, **"Seeing in the Dark"**, and **"Sounds in the
Dark"**, are excellent in their descriptions of how the eyes and
ears work in dim light. Subsequent chapters on bats, biolu-

minescence, and cave dwellers are particularly interesting. . . . [This book has a] clear and precise text. An index is included.

*Sallie Hope Erhard, in a review of "Life in the Dark: How Animals Survive at Night," in* Appraisal: Children's Science Books, *Vol. 8, No. 2, Spring, 1975, p. 42.*

Seymour Simon has produced a beautiful little volume that makes night a most inviting period, and the animals of night emerge as engaging creatures, equal to our diurnal cousins in interest. He wisely included the niches of darkness as well as the astronomical darkness, and his chapter on cave creatures becomes an elegant introduction to ecology.

*Wayne Hanley, in a review of "Life in the Dark: How Animals Survive at Night," in* Appraisal: Children's Science Books, *Vol. 8, No. 2, Spring, 1975, p. 42.*

An extremely well-written account of nocturnal animals, both vertebrate and invertebrate. . . . The account of echo location by bats and the induced evasive action by moths is not only better than that in many adult texts, but is a model of how a complex subject can be presented to a juvenile audience. Chapters devoted to the nocturnal animals of cities and suburbs greatly increase the utility of this excellent book. It should be in every school library and would be a welcome gift for any young naturalist.

*Peter Gray, in a review of "Life in the Dark: How Animals Survive at Night," in* Science Books & Films, *Vol. XI, No. 1, May, 1975, p. 36.*

---

## WATER ON YOUR STREET (1974)

Mr. Simon is trying to do two things at the same time in his little book about how water gets in and out of our houses. He talks about rain and reservoirs, water mains and drain pipes, condensation and evaporation, and urges the reader to look, think, and ask questions in a scientific way. The format of the book . . . and the information it contains seems to be for one age child, but the unanswered "observation" questions, which are supposed to make the reader think scientifically, are definitely for someone older. The book, therefore, is uneven. The information and ideas are good, but it doesn't quite come off.

*Heddie Kent, in a review of "Water on Your Street," in* Appraisal: Children's Science Books, *Vol. 7, No. 3, Fall, 1974, p. 41.*

There is one misconception. The bend in the drain pipe under the sink is not for trapping things like rings which can then be retrieved. (Many bends have no means of being opened.) The primary function of the bend is to keep the trap full of water so that the sewer gas does not back up into the sink and cause foul odors. Simple questions are asked in the text and will spur the reader to think about water and its importance. Suggestions are made for various simple demonstrations which the pupil can do alone yet still get accurate results. . . . The book makes excellent supplementary reading and should be available for study with any unit on water.

*A review of "Water on Your Street," in* Science Books, *Vol. X, No. 3, December, 1974, p. 248.*

---

## PROJECTS WITH AIR (1975)

Twenty-seven experiments; from the very simple demonstrations that air has weight and occupies space (which are explained less simply . . . than in other easy project books) to the ubiquitous tests for air pollution (e.g., counting the number of particles trapped on index cards), with investigations of convection currents, air pressure and Bernoulli's principle in between. But neither his overly familiar experiments, his unbending vocabulary (*withdraw, inverted* and *place* for take out, upside down and put are typical) nor his method of starting right in on directions with no orienting background or motivating questions (you don't even know what you're looking for until you've gone through what could seem like a lot of meaningless motions) indicate that Simon has taken any trouble to improve on existing collections.

*A review of "Projects with Air," in* Kirkus Reviews, *Vol. XLIII, No. 9, May 1, 1975, p. 520.*

Simon has done a marvellous job of bringing together 27 inspiring and meaningful kitchen science projects on a single subject—air. Only a few of the projects are classics that have been appearing in similar books for generations, and some of them are so unique that I had to interrupt my reading to try them out for myself. Each project occupies less than two pages, so it is unlikely a child will lose interest before finishing an experiment. . . . The concluding part of each project not only describes the results, but asks some relevant questions and, in many instances, relates the observations to things the child can see in the world at large. The book includes an excellent index and a page of suggested readings on the subject of air and the atmosphere.

*David L. Heiserman, in a review of "Projects with Air," in* Science Books & Films, *Vol. XI, No. 4, March, 1976, p. 209.*

---

## PETS IN A JAR: COLLECTING AND CARING FOR SMALL WILD ANIMALS (1975)

*A Zoo in Your Room* [by Roger Caras] and *Pets in a Jar* are complementary. . . . Of the two books, Caras' is the broader and more enjoyable to read. (p. 400)

Although Seymour Simon includes facts commonly available, he also offers valuable information not readily found elsewhere on collecting and maintaining hydras, planaria, several water insects, crickets, ants, saltwater brine shrimp, hermit crabs, and starfish. Moreover, he suggests experiments such as causing a planarian to generate two heads. Had he entitled one chapter "Water Insects" instead of **"Water Bugs,"** he would have avoided the confusion between bug as insect and bug as the common name for one specific group of insects. The author's personal experiences as teacher come out when he warns about wearing old clothing and using extreme caution with a razor. (p. 401)

*Sarah Gagné, "Insects, Animals, and Man," in* The Horn Book Magazine, *Vol. LI, No. 4, August, 1975, pp. 400-01.**

Not only a simple how-to book for would-be pet owners but also an on-the-spot observer's guide to small wildlife. Succinctly and logically, the author answers questions of anatomy, ecology, propagation, and other habits peculiar to certain wild animals. . . . [This] is a must for young naturalists. (pp. 111-12)

*Barbara Gerson, in a review of "Pets in a Jar: Collecting and Caring for Small Wild Animals," in* School Library Journal, *Vol. 22, No. 1, September, 1975, pp. 111-12.*

[This is a] well-executed book. . . . The responsibility for the creatures' needs and comfort is stressed, as well as safety precautions for the child. . . . Each chapter is laden with interesting and pertinent facts. The final chapter offers ecological guidance on how to release the pet if the child decides he no longer wants it. . . . Bibliography and index round out a book which makes good reading even if one never braves the elements and translates the words into action.

*Ethanne Smith, in a review of "Pets in a Jar: Collecting and Caring for Small Wild Animals," in* Appraisal: Children's Science Books, *Vol. 9, No. 1, Winter, 1976, p. 39.*

---

## LIFE ON ICE: HOW ANIMALS SURVIVE IN THE ARCTIC (1976)

This is a carefully written introduction to life in the Arctic Circle. In addition to describing the animals' physical characteristics and habits, Simon explains their place in the food chain. There is also some material on plant life and the peoples of the Far North and a chapter on the cycle of the seasons which is almost lyrical in tone. . . . A good replacement for Goetz's *The Arctic Tundra* (Morrow, 1958) and complement to Liversidge's *The First Book of the Arctic* (Watts, 1967) which is more general in scope.

*John D. Boniol, in a review of "Life on Ice: How Animals Survive in the Arctic," in* School Library Journal, *Vol. 23, No. 1, September, 1976, p. 125.*

In general, the text is clearly written; however, the chapter on cyclic population changes in lemmings and other species is written for an older audience than the rest of the book. Although the reasons for these cyclic changes are not yet well understood, Simon's explanations lack clarity. . . . As an elementary text to illustrate the relationships between some of the Arctic fauna and their interactions with their environment, this book would be suited to classroom use.

*Janet Dando, in a review of "Life on Ice: How Animals Survive in the Arctic," in* Science Books & Films, *Vol. XII, No. 4, March, 1977, p. 213.*

---

## THE OPTICAL ILLUSION BOOK (1976)

[Few] authors have explained as diligently and as lucidly as Simon does, *why* we think, seeing lines of equal length, that one is longer or why one circle seems larger than another of the same size. . . . Simon is careful to distinguish between conjecture and proven theory; he discusses how what we think we see may be affected by past experience, familiarity with perspective, how light or color can effect illusion, and how much of our visual impression may be determined by the brain rather than the eye. There is also an interesting chapter on optical illusions in art, and several suggestions for readers' experiments. An index is appended.

*Zena Sutherland, in a review of "The Optical Illusion Book," in* Bulletin of the Center for Children's Books, *Vol. 30, No. 3, November, 1976, p. 48.*

Here is another book which is fascinating because it has so much for the reader to do and to try. It is also open-ended; the existing explanations given for many types of optical illusion are far from satisfactory, and it is quite possible that even a young investigator, with a strong and disciplined imagination, may come up with better ones. The book does not contain any examples of theories which I have not seen elsewhere, but it conveniently brings them together. Also, the author does not expend words on uncertain theory; he says just enough and leaves the reader to decide whether or not to feel satisfied.

*Harry C. Stubbs, in a review of "The Optical Illusion Book," in* The Horn Book Magazine, *Vol. LII, No. 6, December, 1976, p. 650.*

More than 80 examples of classic optical illusions and fascinating visual phenomena are . . . discussed in convenient sequence. The commentary is written in a common-sense style rather than in the more esoteric terms usually employed by scientists. Although intended as juvenile literature, the book is quite suitable as informative reading for anyone wishing an easy but reliable introduction to the topic. . . . The short chapter on the illusory nature of color perception is inadequate because the reader has to supply his own colored materials such as papers, filters, lights, and crayons. Except for the lack of bibliographic identification of the occasionally mentioned scientific work supporting one or another assertion, this book is useful as easy collateral reading in a variety of courses. (pp. 38-9)

*H. W. Hofstetter, in a review of "The Optical Illusion Book," in* Science Books & Films, *Vol. XIII, No. 1, May, 1977, pp. 38-9.*

Here is one of those extraordinary, one-a-year, "must buy" books. . . . In eminently readable style, Mr. Simon explains why we see optical illusions and some basics about how sight works. . . . Even if you have Kettlekamp's *Tricks of Eye and Mind*, this is a good addition, since it is shorter and easier to read. This is a high-interest, low-vocabulary book which can be confidently offered to the child, teenager, and adult alike.

*Carole Cochran, in a review of "The Optical Illusion Book," in* Appraisal: Children's Science Books, *Vol. 10, No. 3, Fall, 1977, p. 39.*

---

## EVERYTHING MOVES (1976)

The basic concept that everything, from the smallest atom to the largest star, is always in motion is presented here in a clear and engaging fashion. Starting with common occurrences in a child's environment—e.g., cars whizzing down a highway and leaves tumbling in the breeze—Simon progresses to more complex movements—e.g., the revolution of the earth, moon, and sun and the perpetual motion of molecules, atoms, and electrons. The few simple experiments included are appropriate for the age group and illustrate the concept well.

*Diane Holzheimer, in a review of "Everything Moves," in* School Library Journal, *Vol. 23, No. 3, November, 1976, p. 51.*

[The] author starts out with a very simple concept, allowing the young child to realize that, indeed, everything (or *almost* everything) moves. . . . Unfortunately, about halfway through the book, the concept of movement suddenly becomes more complex and requires a greater background of knowledge. For example, while the first half of the book shows movement with examples of a car moving on a highway and a mouth moving when one eats or talks, later pages deal with light moving at 186,000 miles per second and electrons moving to produce electricity. By isolating each of the more advanced experiments, a teacher can spend time developing specific concepts. The presentation of many experiments with unrelated concepts and the inconsistency in the levels of difficulty may result in confusion and minimize the value of this book. However, the book can be used satisfactorily for incidental learning and for expanding science vocabulary.

> *John L. Hubisz, in a review of "Everything Moves,"* in Science Books & Films, *Vol. XIII, No. 1, May, 1977, p. 41.*

Simple sentences and clear illustrations explain the concept of motion to young readers in a direct, logical manner. . . . Experiments to test the reality of heat and sound waves and molecular motion are easy and require no special equipment. So lucid is *Everything Moves* that sections of it, with a teacher or parent helping, could be used with preschoolers.

> *Mary Johnson-Lally, in a review of "Everything Moves,"* in Appraisal: Children's Science Books, *Vol. 10, No. 3, Fall, 1977, p. 38.*

### LIFE AND DEATH IN NATURE (1976)

In this slight account of the life and death cycle, a single idea—that "without death and decay in nature there can be no new life"—is incessantly hammered home. Simon indicates that nutrients released from decaying matter are used by living things but the process is not explained, and the brief description of overcrowding and the balance of life is vague.

> *Cynthia K. Richey, in a review of "Life and Death in Nature,"* in School Library Journal, *Vol. 23, No. 6, February, 1977, p. 58.*

The major portion of this book deals with the processes of thinning and nutrient cycles. The discussion of these two topics is adequate for the intended audience level. Also included are a few simple exercises which could help a child appreciate the process of decay and the complexity of the soil detritus pathway. Unfortunately, the author fails to discuss some major topics which should be introduced at this time. The most obvious omission is the lack of any discussion of aging. There is no attempt to relate the processes of reproduction, birth, senescence, and death. (p. 164)

> *William P. Hanratty, in a review of "Life and Death in Nature,"* in Science Books & Films, *Vol. XIII, No. 3, December, 1977, pp. 164-65.*

### ANIMALS IN YOUR NEIGHBORHOOD (1976)

This book is a pleasant invitation to younger children to explore their neighborhoods and observe the different types of animals that live there. The neighborhood depicted is urban, but the suggested activities will apply equally well to suburban neighborhoods. The easy-to-read text is accessible to young readers. . . . Arranged according to the different animals noticed, the text offers many questions to guide the child's own observations. This light, enjoyable ramble will encourage children to be more aware of their environment. (p. 38)

> *Christine McDonnell, in a review of "Animals in Your Neighborhood,"* in Appraisal: Children's Science Books, *Vol. 10, No. 3, Fall, 1977, pp. 37-8.*

A well-balanced mixture of information and simple yet thought-provoking questions make this book readable and pedagogically sound. The sections dealing with insects and birds are the most thorough, but adequate coverage is also given to common rodents (rats, mice, squirrels). . . . *Animals in Your Neighborhood* should open the eyes of any child who reads it, and I recommend it for the home or classroom library.

> *Sandra Haggard, in a review of "Animals in Your Neighborhood,"* in Science Books & Films, *Vol. XIII, No. 3, December, 1977, p. 167.*

### BENEATH YOUR FEET (1977)

After a muddled introduction, the text settles down to talk about three kinds of soil—sandy, clay, and silty—and covers their consistencies, their origins, the effects of rain, and the need for conservation. Words such as topsoil, humus, erosion, and lichen are introduced; and interest is generated with simple and worthwhile experiments: these are the book's strength, as most are ones children can do alone or within the confines of the classroom. Simon asks questions to provoke curiosity but often doesn't provide the concrete answers this age group requires; hence, the book's greatest usefulness is with teacher or other adult guidance.

> *Barbara Elleman, in a review of "Beneath Your Feet,"* in Booklist, *Vol. 74, No. 2, September 15, 1977, p. 199.*

At appropriate intervals throughout the easy-to-read text suggestions are given for some simple but highly effective experiments . . . using readily available materials. Children who "read and do" will gain a firm understanding of soil and an appreciation of the need for soil conservation. This is a perky little book that will revitalize your science discovery corner and enrich your classroom library. (pp. 114-15)

> *A review of "Beneath Your Feet," in* Teacher, *Vol. 95, No. 7, March, 1978, pp. 114-15.*

This is a well-crafted book providing information in nontechnical terms on a range of topics related to soil. . . . Simon relies on short, simple syntactic patterns that he tends to repeat to make for easy reading; he builds in questions and imperatives to encourage readers to think and do. New vocabulary is italicized for clarity and emphasis. There are a few minor problems in using the book in classroom situations. For example, soil is generally not defined to include that material which covers the ocean bottoms. . . . Another suggestion is to include metric units of measuring. The overall thoroughness and simplicity of the presentation, however, make *Beneath Your Feet* a useful addition to library collections for children. (pp. 41-2)

> *George Hennings, in a review of "Beneath Your Feet," in* Science Books & Films, *Vol. XIV, No. 1, May, 1978, pp. 41-2.*

### WHAT DO YOU WANT TO KNOW ABOUT GUPPIES? (1977)

Simon Tells All about these colorful, varied, small, inexpensive, and relatively easy to care for fish. History (the name derives from Dr. Robert Guppy), physical description, feeding, housing (jam jars will do in a pinch), life cycle, ailments, breeding habits (frequent) are discussed in a thorough manner. Simon also deals with scientific experiments and observation methods but cautions against causing guppies discomfort. A list of books and magazines for serious guppy-fanciers and an index are included in this informative guide. . . .

> *Patricia Manning, in a review of "What Do You Want to Know About Guppies?" in* School Library Journal, *Vol. 24, No. 3, November, 1977, p. 63.*

This book may not find many readers among the young audience the author seeks unless they own guppies or plan to get some. . . . The accuracy of information is good, and the scope is very thorough. Unfortunately, so much information is presented, and much of it in a dry manner, that potential readers may lose interest.

> *Albert C. Jensen, in a review of "What Do You Want to Know About Guppies?" in* Science Books & Films, *Vol. XIV, No. 3, December, 1978, p. 185.*

### LOOK TO THE NIGHT SKY: AN INTRODUCTION TO STAR WATCHING (1977)

A clear, attractive introduction. . . . [Indicative] of the book's preprimer intent is the shortage of sky charts . . . to accompany the orienting discussion of pole-circling constellations, seasonal changes, planet tracking, moon features, and "special sights" such as eclipses. Thus acclimated, sky watchers will certainly want to go on to Rey, Joseph, or another of the fuller, systematic guides. (And why, in a book so geared, devote a chapter to telescopes? Or bother at any level with the astrological addenda?) But this brisk and eminently readable orientation will surely succeed in making almost any youngster feel right at home with the night skies.

> *A review of "Look to the Night Sky: An Introduction to Star Watching," in* Kirkus Reviews, *Vol. XLV, No. 23, December 1, 1977, p. 1269.*

Simon's excellent introduction to astronomy is an example of books that parents are grateful to share with children. The adults should also enjoy star-and-planet gazing with their youngsters after absorbing the author's lucid, extraordinarily interesting information about the night sky. . . . In differentiating between astronomy and astrology, Simon is one of the few writers who explains *why* the latter does not meet the test of a true science. . . .

> *A review of "Look to the Night Sky: An Introduction to Star Watching," in* Publishers Weekly, *Vol. 215, No. 25, June 18, 1979, p. 93.*

[This book] is an observational primer rather than an elementary astronomy textbook. The author clearly drew on his experiences as a young stargazer to write a book that he would have enjoyed and used. The first chapter is an excellent overview of the night sky as a naked-eye observatory and covers the hourly drift of the stars, the seasonal progression of the constellations, and the perils of light pollution. . . . The text is clear and concise throughout. . . . Only two minor shortcomings are evident. The oft-cited lists of references and periodicals should have been updated, and the chapter on buying a telescope should have covered binoculars and richest-field reflectors. In sum, my 12-year-old daughter and I find much to recommend in this slim volume.

> *David J. Lipiro, in a review of "Look to the Night Sky: An Introduction to Star Watching," in* Science Books & Films, *Vol. 19, No. 4, March-April, 1984, p. 216.*

### EXPLORING FIELDS AND LOTS: EASY SCIENCE PROJECTS (1978)

This short book is designed to encourage young children to explore fields and lots near their homes or schools. The investigative activities are simple and do not require expensive equipment. If used as group projects with adequate leadership, these numerous activities would result in much learning. The text is readable and understandable, though some words are used without adequate definition. . . . Some experiments, such as comparison of plants grown on window sills with those grown on a dark shelf, suggest that effects of a single variable (light) has been isolated when that is not the case. Sentences such as, "What do these surroundings tell you about a plant's needs?" were not written or edited by a thinking scientist, and a science educator should not ask a six-year-old child, "Which kind is better able to survive over a long time: plants that need particular surroundings or plants that can grow in many different surroundings?" Overall, however, the book is useful and can be recommended.

> *Bernadette Menhusen, in a review of "Exploring Fields and Lots: Easy Science Projects," in* Science Books & Films, *Vol. XIV, No. 4, March, 1979, p. 230.*

### KILLER WHALES (1978)

Mr. Simon tells of the natural habits of these mammals and their domestic life. He accurately describes the enigma of their cruelty and ferociousness with natural prey compared with their playful, friendly behavior in captivity. . . . The writing contains information about the studies of the animals from as early as 1862 to the first capture in 1964. This is easy and interesting reading. . . . The author writes with authority and accuracy. Included are a table of contents, index and bibliography. (pp. 58-9)

> *John R. Pancella, in a review of "Killer Whales," in* Appraisal: Children's Science Books, *Vol. 12, No. 2, Spring, 1979, pp. 58-9.*

The author immediately captures the reader's attention with a report of a January, 1911 sighting of killer whales by Antarctic explorer Robert Falcon Scott. Fortunately, this alarmist type of introduction is followed by a more realistic portrayal of this intelligent animal. The remainder of the book contains a thorough description of whale biology, physiology, capture and training. Cetaceans of all types are discussed, with main emphasis on the largest cetacean of all: the killer whale. In a clear, concise text, the author discusses size, behavior, senses and communication of the killer whale. Chapter 6 (**"Are Killer Whales Dangerous to Humans?"**) is a rebuttal of several myths; some responses here may be oversimplified. . . . The final chapter (**"The Future of the Killer Whale"**) is a weak plea for conservation.

> *Henry A. Mitchell, in a review of "Killer Whales," in* Science Books & Films, *Vol. XV, No. 1, May, 1979, p. 42.*

## ANIMAL FACT/ANIMAL FABLE (1979)

Simon's intelligently delivered information should find eager readers. The humorous aspects of facts and fables are judiciously stressed . . . in an outstanding book. . . . Every entry is a surprise in the best kind of book—one that entertains while it educates.

> *A review of "Animal Fact/Animal Fable," in Publishers Weekly, Vol. 215, No. 7, February 12, 1979, p. 127.*

Old beliefs about animals—ostriches hide their heads in sand, camels store water in their humps, bats are blind, and elephants fear mice—are disproved in a simple, clear narrative that replaces fable with fact. Scientific information about porcupines' quills, crickets' chirps, cats' nine lives, goats' eating habits, and raccoons' washing their food is given on the verso of the page stating the folklore, so that guessing games can be played. . . . Children able to read the text may want more substantial data, and younger children will need help in interpretation. But teachers and librarians working with children will find a worthwhile sharing experience.

> *Barbara Elleman, in a review of "Animal Fact/Animal Fiction," in Booklist, Vol. 75, No. 14, March 15, 1979, p. 1160.*

Children at the intermediate elementary level who are curious about animals will enjoy this book. Unfortunately there is no table of contents and there are no page numbers so it cannot be used conveniently to look up particular animals. This book is more for entertainment than for any serious classroom use.

> *Katharine C. Payne, in a review of "Animal Fact/Animal Fable," in Science Books & Films, Vol. XV, No. 5, May, 1980, p. 278.*

---

## DANGER FROM BELOW: EARTHQUAKES, PAST, PRESENT, AND FUTURE (1979)

The most valuable feature of this title is a list of safety rules to follow during and after earthquakes. Information on the history of earthquakes presents graphic descriptions of deaths; however, the explanation of the causes and measurement of earthquakes is over-simplified and unclear. The writing is weakened by poor transitions and short, choppy sentences. Both Asimov's *How Did We Find Out About Earthquakes* (Walker, 1978) and Matthews' *The Story of Volcanoes and Earthquakes* (Harvey, 1969) are better introductions to this topic.

> *Jo Ann Carr, in a review of "Danger from Below: Earthquakes, Past, Present, and Future," in School Library Journal, Vol. 25, No. 8, April, 1979, p. 63.*

I must admit to a personal prejudice against the use of disasters or other atypical and sensational phenomena as devices to attract attention to topics of serious and objective scientific study. Here, however, the author has used this device skillfully and effectively; capitalizing upon the "gee whiz" impact of earthquake accounts, yet consistently using these narratives to highlight pertinent empirical evidence, and never dwelling needlessly upon the human tragedy that accompanies these geological phenomena. . . . The reader is left with a very positive feeling of aroused, concerned, and not-quite-satisfied curiosity, which is likely to be manifested in further reading, discussion, and consideration. Unfortunately the book does not grasp the opportunity, or meet the responsibility, of providing a list of suggested readings to encourage and guide such further exploration.

> *Robert J. Stein, in a review of "Danger from Below: Earthquakes, Past, Present, and Future," in Appraisal: Children's Science Books, Vol. 12, No. 3, Fall, 1979, p. 54.*

Although generally accurate and up-to-date, the book could have been more complete. The explanation of the relationship between plate tectonics and earthquakes is a bit too sketchy—similar books have done better. Simon also leaves unexplained the extremely large number of earthquakes he has listed for Hawaii on a chart of U.S. earthquakes. The index lacks a listing for the important term "epicenter" and includes only one reference to the several pages on China. All in all, still one of several acceptable books on this ever popular topic for children.

> *Joseph Hannibal, in a review of "Danger from Below: Earthquakes, Past, Present, and Future," in Science Books & Films, Vol. XV, No. 4, March, 1980, p. 226.*

---

## THE SECRET CLOCKS: TIME SENSES OF LIVING THINGS (1979)

A well-organized, non-technical presentation of the time senses of living things—the daily and seasonal rhythms of plants and animals—and the total harmony of the rhythms of the earth. . . . Human rhythms, studies of people in isolation, and even the currently popular biorhythms are touched upon. The experiments conducted by scientists are explained clearly, and a final chapter encourages readers to perform simple experiments and make observations. A fascinating subject, well handled through Simons' open-ended questions and try-it-and-see approach.

> *Connie Tyrrell, in a review of "Secret Clocks: The Time Senses of Living Things," in School Library Journal, Vol. 25, No. 9, May, 1979, p. 67.*

Simon's treatment here won't enlarge the understanding of anyone who's [read Selsam's *How Animals Tell Time* or the Silversteins's *Sleep and Dreams*], though [Simon] does put things simply and report on the classic experiments . . . in logical sequence, with frequent leading questions to keep readers alert. . . . He does, however, seem unduly attentive to the intricacies of biorhythm charts, especially as he acknowledges that "almost all scientists think they are about as much use as fortune telling with cards." Undemanding.

> *A review of "The Secret Clocks: Time Senses of Living Things," in Kirkus Reviews, Vol. XLVII, No. 14, July 15, 1979, p. 795.*

Mr. Simon has written an engrossing book. . . . [Evidence] of the "secret clocks" within living things is presented in a fascinating manner. These discoveries, along with the many questions still to be answered, make exciting reading. He uses clear, but not condescending, language. Complete, easily understood directions are given for experiments the child can conduct. . . . Books and articles for further reading as well as an index are included.

> *Etha D. Miller, in a review of "The Secret Clocks," in Appraisal: Children's Science Books, Vol. 13, No. 1, Winter, 1980, p. 50.*

A strong point is the citing of the research on which internal rhythms are based. A weak point is the time spent on human biorhythms after the author admits that there is little scientific value in them. The book has a high vocabulary level and sometimes offers almost incomprehensible explanations (for example the one given to allow students to calculate their own biorhythms). Suggested experiments may be interesting to some students; the references will be difficult for most. The work in general is too difficult for young readers but too simple for a more sophisticated audience. Neither reading level nor content is suited to the abilities of the intended audience.

> *William V. Mayer, in a review of "The Secret Clocks: Time Senses of Living Things," in* Science Books & Films, *Vol. XV, No. 5, May, 1980, p. 262.*

### THE LONG VIEW INTO SPACE   (1979)

[This] lucid and serious text serves as a good introduction to the universe for middle grades readers. Simon begins with the members of our own solar system, moves out to stars, meteors, and comets, and into the nebulae and galaxies of our universe. When he mentions such subjects as novae or spiral galaxies, they are clearly explained but not over-explained. . . .

> *Zena Sutherland, in a review of "The Long View into Space," in* Bulletin of the Center for Children's Books, *Vol. 33, No. 4, December, 1979, p. 81.*

*Long View Into Space* is a collection of photographs; the text is merely a series of extended captions. . . . The pictures are very good; the text is less so, however, and in some places it appears to have been quite carelessly done. The "model of Mars" seems to be, judging by the shadows, a mosaic of photographs of the actual planet from orbit. The "dark shape at the bottom" of a photo of the crater Copernicus is actually the crater Fauth well outside Copernicus, not a "small crater that is inside Copernicus." Whether Pluto has any rock in its make-up is decidedly questionable; the recent discovery of its moon and consequent determination of its mass would seem to favor ice or frozen-gas composition. And someone living on Mars would not see Phobos "rise and set three times a day" unless Mars's own rotation were stopped first. (p. 688)

> *Harry C. Stubbs, "Astronomy and Space," in* The Horn Book Magazine, *Vol. LV, No. 6, December, 1979, pp. 687-88.\**

This is, in some ways, quite a good introduction to the universe, simple enough for the eight- to ten-year-old to understand. But it will not satisfy for long. . . . The editing is terrible. . . . 'A satellite is an object that moves around another object'; but 'binary stars circle around each other'. 'Nebulae do not shine by themselves'; but 'some nebulae glow brightly'. It is only remotely implied that the Milky Way galaxy is ours; and some of the Americanisms jar. One turns towards other, better introductory books. This one is just not up to it. (pp. 147, 149)

> *Peter Sanderson, in a review of "The Long View into Space," in* The School Librarian, *Vol. 29, No. 2, June, 1981, pp. 147, 149.*

### DEADLY ANTS   (1979)

Emphasizing army ants and fire ants, Simon describes those species that can have poisonous and sometimes fatal effects on animals and humans. Discussion covers where they live; what their breeding, attacking, and feeding habits are; and what control measures are being used against them. The author's tendency to remark on the grisly aspects of ant bites, his occasional use of scare tactics ("it is certainly possible that a young child may not be able to flee fast enough [and] could be overrun and killed by hundreds of thousands of biting army ants"), and his digression to summarize the plot of an adult short story concerning deadly ants disrupts his otherwise factual and readable text.

> *Barbara Elleman, in a review of "Deadly Ants," in* Booklist, *Vol. 76, No. 8, December 15, 1979, p. 617.*

The book left me with a vivid impression of the two types of ants it deals with—fire ants and army ants. I therefore recommend it, in spite of some improvements I could suggest. . . . [A] reader impressed with the severe threat fire ants pose to humans wants to know more about their range in this country and perhaps more, too, about army ants. But caveats aside, the book is fascinating for its description of ant attacks and habits. . . .

> *Sarah Gagné, in a review of "Deadly Ants," in* The Horn Book Magazine, *Vol. LVI, No. 1, February, 1980, p. 86.*

Simon's smoothly written narrative focuses on the behavior of fire and army ants. . . . Physiological information lacks detail in some instances; children may wonder, for instance, about the sex of worker ants which is implied to be neither male nor female but is not actually explained.

> *Margaret Bush, in a review of "Deadly Ants," in* School Library Journal, *Vol. 26, No. 8, April, 1980, p. 116.*

### MEET THE GIANT SNAKES   (1979)

Simon's subject—boas and pythons—is inherently interesting to children. Unfortunately his book does not maximize the appeal. The text begins with an overview of the two families and moves on to a page or so of information on each of six species. There is a heavy emphasis on size (including averages, speculations, actual records) and eating habits. Very little specific information on physiology and behavior is provided— digestion and disposal of waste, molting, and locomotion are among the omissions. . . . The reiteration of information . . . leaves readers with a general impression of the giant snakes, but many other sources are more interesting and informative. (pp. 61-2)

> *Margaret Bush, in a review of "Meet the Giant Snakes," in* School Library Journal, *Vol. 26, No. 6, February, 1980, pp. 61-2.*

This is an interesting introduction. . . . Accurate descriptions are given of six members of the [boa and python] families. The text is written in a simple, entertaining way to appeal to young readers. Range, life habits, food, enemies and economic value are all discussed. The author seeks to allay common fears of these snakes and to debunk certain superstitions relating to them. In describing some of the physical features, such as eye coverings and senses, more care might have been taken to explain to the young readers that most of these features apply to most, if not all, snakes and not just to giant snakes.

*Douglas B. Sands, in a review of "Meet the Giant Snakes," in* Appraisal: Children's Science Books, *Vol. 13, No. 2, Spring, 1980, p. 77.*

The author does an excellent job of dispelling the mythology built up around these giants by highlighting the role of scientists in determining the authenticity of facts. . . . Unfortunately, no point is made as to their current or future status in relation to hunting, exploitation (skins and pet trade) or habitat destruction.

*Wade C. Sherbrooke, in a review of "Meet the Giant Snakes," in* Science Books & Films, *Vol. XV, No. 5, May, 1980, p. 279.*

## ABOUT THE FOODS YOU EAT   (1979)

This informative and thorough account of the inner workings of the digestive system is unfortunately marred. . . . Although the publisher recommends it for grades 1-3, the 6.5 reading level (Fry scale) will make the text incomprehensible to all but the best readers below fourth grade; yet its short sentences and casual tone may make it seem too childish to readers above sixth grade. Simon's descriptions of the digestive organs and processes are clear and accurate, as are his explanation of food groups, nutrients, and sensible diet habits. . . . The book's saving grace is a series of very simple but interesting **"Try This"** experiments which are scattered throughout the first part of the text but inexplicably disappear about half way through.

*Anne M. Rath, in a review of "About the Foods You Eat," in* Curriculum Review, *Vol. 19, No. 2, April, 1980, p. 125.*

The section on nutrition endorses a low-fat diet with special mention of roughage and the usual warnings on the evils of "junk food." However, scare tactics are not used and the book avoids a didactic tone. There are many unfamiliar words used and, although each is in italics when first encountered and defined adequately in the text, a glossary containing a pronunciation guide is lacking. . . . The humor, which makes the book so appealing to younger students, will limit its usefulness to the older crowd. (pp. 115-16)

*Cathleen Lemmer, in a review of "About the Foods You Eat," in* School Library Journal, *Vol. 26, No. 8, April, 1980, pp. 115-16.*

Written in clear and simple language. . . . There is a real depth of content to the material, but the language is very simple, considering the underlying mechanisms and chemical changes. The digestive system is explained, and the author offers simple and interesting approaches to eating for balanced nutrition, while bearing in mind what children are offered at home and through the media and the market. . . . [The book is] suitable as collateral reading for advanced young students as well as general classroom reading for older ones.

*Molly Schuchat, in a review of "About the Foods You Eat," in* Science Books & Films, *Vol. 16, No. 2, November-December, 1980, p. 97.*

In the friendly informative style he has brought to scores of science books for children, Seymour Simon here introduces six-to-ten-year-olds to food. . . . A particularly nice feature are the several experiments or demonstrations included in the text to involve the reader and illustrate points being made. . . . The text is unbroken by headings and there is no index, but given the brevity of the book these are not serious drawbacks, since other books about food are for older readers or take a different tack, this is recommended for all libraries.

*Diane Holzheimer, in a review of "About the Foods You Eat," in* Appraisal: Science Books for Young People, *Vol. 14, No. 1, Winter, 1981, p. 58.*

## MIRROR MAGIC   (1980)

Simon's new book is a good example of why his 60-plus works on scientific subjects attract boys and girls of all ages. His personalized approach and the uncomplicated sentences in this text for beginners tell exactly how mirrors are made and how they make images. . . . [Simon provides] experiments readers will have fun with and learn from.

*A review of "Mirror Magic," in* Publishers Weekly, *Vol. 218, No. 3, July 18, 1980, p. 61.*

[This] author has taken full advantage of the many uncomplicated but interesting experiments possible. They are described cleverly. . . . The explanation in the beginning on how mirrors work does not really show how the displaced and reversed image is formed for an observer. It is curious that the author also left out the perplexing observation that mirrors reverse left and right but not up and down for the viewer. However, the quality of the book is excellent and appropriate for the level of reader to which it is directed. The "magic" of mirrors will have to be explained scientifically later . . . or challenge the imagination of the child now.

*David G. Hoag, in a review of "Mirror Magic," in* Appraisal: Science Books for Young People, *Vol. 14, No. 1, Winter, 1981, p. 59.*

## STRANGE MYSTERIES FROM AROUND THE WORLD   (1980)

A potpourri of oddments: the raining down of frogs or of fish, the mysterious image on the shroud of Turin, the crystal skull found in a Mayan city, the (reputedly) lost treasure of Oak Island, and of course the strange lights in the sky that are sometimes reported as UFOs. The subjects are intriguing; most of them have been described in other, similar books for children. This isn't quite up to Simon's usual standard of cohesion and authoritativeness; however, he does distinguish between documented fact and unverified reporting, and the writing style is adept, casual but never cute or condescending.

*Zena Sutherland, in a review of "Strange Mysteries from Around the World," in* Bulletin of the Center for Children's Books, *Vol. 33, No. 11, July-August, 1980, p. 224.*

[Ten long-standing puzzles] are presented briefly and without bias in this cleanly designed book. Although some information is repetitious in the chapter on the Mayan crystal skull, the text is generally clear. . . . Too bad no bibliography is included to allow extended investigation, especially of modern (UFO's, Kirlian photography) subjects.

*Ann G. Brouse, in a review of "Strange Mysteries from Around the World," in* School Library Journal, *Vol. 27, No. 4, December, 1980, p. 62.*

Young readers are sure to enjoy this book of ten strange mysteries in the tradition of Ripley's *Believe It or Not*. . . . Simon clearly reports each mystery and gives several theories which scientists have advanced to explain it. Since none of the mysteries has been solved and perhaps never will be, the reader is challenged to think through his/her own explanations. This book will motivate students to become involved in the scientific process of hypothesizing.

> *Martha T. Kane, in a review of "Strange Mysteries from Around the World," in* Appraisal: Science Books for Young People, *Vol. 14, No. 1, Winter, 1981, p. 60.*

### EINSTEIN ANDERSON, SCIENCE SLEUTH; EINSTEIN ANDERSON SHOCKS HIS FRIENDS (1980)

[In *Einstein Anderson: Science Sleuth* and *Einstein Anderson Shocks His Friends,*] Simon turns to story form to present a series of science puzzles. Einstein Anderson is a 12-year-old science whiz who is continually being challenged by friends, relatives, and enemies. In each chapter of these basically plotless narratives, Einstein solves a mystery as readers try to do the same. Elementary knowledge of biological, chemical, physical, and other scientific phenomena will be brought into play. The writing is fairly smooth, situations are amusing, and characterization solid if a little flat. Good light reading for those with a taste for science. .

> *Judith Goldberger, in a review of "Einstein Anderson: Science Sleuth" and "Einstein Anderson Shocks His Friends," in* Booklist, *Vol. 77, No. 3, October 1, 1980, p. 257.*

With ten cases per volume, modeled closely after the popular Encyclopedia Brown puzzle-solving episodes, [*Einstein Anderson, Science Sleuth* and *Einstein Anderson Shocks His Friends*] are less ingenious and more didactic, though possibly less flabbergasting to readers. Here, if you know the elementary science, the answers are obvious. If you don't know, you get a small lesson with the explanation. . . . Einstein parallels Encyclopedia right down to the tough-guy enemy (here Pat the Brat) whom the hero consistently outsmarts. Twelve-year-old Einstein also upstages several episodes showing up his older (high school) friend Stanley, who is also described as a science buff but behaves like a science dud. Purely mechanical, though perhaps reinforcing for other would-be Einsteins.

> *A review of "Einstein Anderson, Science Sleuth" and "Einstein Anderson Shocks His Friends," in* Kirkus Reviews, *Vol. XLVIII, No. 23, December 1, 1980, p. 1517.*

Einstein and his friends provide a framework for the rather pedestrian stories [*Einstein Anderson, Science Sleuth* and *Einstein Anderson Shocks His Friends*]. . . . While the writing is adequate, the characters are secondary to the translation of scientific principles into terms that elementary students can understand.

> *Lee Beasley, in a review of "Einstein Anderson, Science Sleuth" and "Einstein Anderson Shocks His Friends," in* Children's Book Review Service, *Vol. 9, No. 5, January, 1981, p. 39.*

### POISONOUS SNAKES (1981)

Simon starts with a dramatic report, which he then reveals "couldn't possibly be true," of a black mambo overtaking two galloping horses and killing both the horses and the children riding them. He goes into poisonous snakes' appearance and

distribution by way of debunking other fallacious beliefs, which injects some life into the descriptive material, and then on to the business of venom glands, fangs, and the effects of snakebites, topics that are lure enough in themselves. Most of the book is a sharp but unsensationalized review of the world's poisonous snakes. . . . Finally, he makes clear that though snakes are responsible for more deaths than all other dangerous animals in the world combined, they are needed to control the rodent population. . . . [The] text and subject should hook readers. (pp. 681-82)

> *A review of "Poisonous Snakes," in* Kirkus Reviews, *Vol. XLIX, No. 11, June 1, 1981, pp. 681-82.*

[Simon describes the four main venomous groups] in a catalog approach to their poison potential that sometimes gets repetitive but does serve to separate fact from fearful fiction. The style is cut-and-dried, though the information may intrigue researching students.

> *Betsy Hearne, in a review of "Poisonous Snakes," in* Booklist, *Vol. 77, No. 21, July 1, 1981, p. 1396.*

Although the writing is choppy (lots of short sentences), a great deal of information is included. The Index even includes the scientific name of each snake discussed. The bibliography is all too brief. . . .

While there are numerous other books on snakes, most include only brief chapters specifically on poisonous snakes, so Simon's book is one of very few devoted exclusively to this subject, especially for this age group.

> *Arlene Bernstein, in a review of "Poisonous Snakes," in* Appraisal: Science Books for Young People, *Vol. 15, No. 2, Spring-Summer, 1982, p. 66.*

[*Poisonous Snakes*] is an interesting and factual account. . . . I enjoyed *Poisonous Snakes* very much and feel it is an honest and accurate representation of the species covered. It is also written in a style that is understandable and interesting to the young reader.

> *Peter Stowe, in a review of "Poisonous Snakes," in* Appraisal: Science Books for Young People, *Vol. 15, No. 2, Spring-Summer, 1982, p. 66.*

### EINSTEIN ANDERSON MAKES UP FOR LOST TIME (1981)

Science sleuths who enjoyed Einstein Anderson's agile-minded acrobatics in the first two books will find these 10 puzzlers similar in format and style. Presented in story form, various incidents centering around physical, biological, and chemical properties allow young Einstein to show off his expertise and give readers the opportunity to unravel the "mysteries" as well. Related with spirit and peppered with puns, these will intrigue science buffs and offer entertaining possibilities for group presentation in the classroom.

> *Barbara Elleman, in a review of "Einstein Anderson Makes Up for Lost Time," in* Booklist, *Vol. 77, Nos. 22 & 23, July 15 & August, 1981, p. 1450.*

There's humor in the writing (Einstein loves bad puns) and the lure of the poser in each anecdote, but these kinds of books are, while appealing to readers, appealing more because of this game element than for any literary quality. (pp. 16-17)

*Zena Sutherland, in a review of "Einstein Anderson Makes Up for Lost Time," in* Bulletin of the Center for Children's Books, *Vol. 35, No. 1, September, 1981, pp. 16-17.*

Einstein Anderson, whose hometown must be right next to Encyclopedia Brown's Idaville, continues to confront science mysteries. . . . Fans of Encyclopedia Brown will find the transition to Einstein Anderson easy, and a few may even be inspired to pursue the oddments of science fact given here.

*Margaret L. Chatham, in a review of "Einstein Anderson Makes Up for Lost Time," in* School Library Journal, *Vol. 28, No. 1, September, 1981, p. 130.*

---

### EINSTEIN ANDERSON TELLS A COMET'S TALE (1981)

Ten further story-puzzles are easily solved by Simon's sixth-grade science whiz—who relies not on ingenuity but on common scientific knowledge. . . . In some of the cases, readers might expose the fraud from evidence that Einstein overlooks. Matching wits with Einstein is the whole game here, as the cocky kid is not personable nor the stories more than exercises in one-upmanship.

*A review of "Einstein Anderson Tells a Comet's Tale," in* Kirkus Reviews, *Vol. XLIX, No. 19, October 1, 1981, p. 1236.*

Adam "Einstein" Anderson is the science lover's Encyclopedia Brown. . . . The mysteries, liberally sprinkled with bad puns, are clever, readable, and sometimes guessable. As a further aid, Simon lists at the beginning of the book the scientific areas of knowledge used to arrive at the answers.

*Ilene Cooper, in a review of "Einstein Anderson Tells a Comet's Tale," in* Booklist, *Vol. 78, No. 4, October 15, 1981, p. 311.*

There is no plot as such—just a series of puzzles strung together in the manner of the *Encyclopedia Brown* series. Characterization is equally scanty, but it really doesn't matter. Children who have run out of new titles in Sobol's series will find this an acceptable substitute. The science principles used to solve the puzzles are simple enough for any reasonably alert youngster to figure out easily. Not great literature by any means, but fun reading for the science-minded.

*Elaine Fort Weischedel, in a review of "Einstein Anderson Tells a Comet's Tale," in* School Library Journal, *Vol. 28, No. 3, November, 1981, p. 98.*

---

### STRANGE CREATURES (1981)

Twenty-two fish, birds, reptiles, amphibia and mammals are featured, most of them not well known. . . . Seymour Simon has chosen just the language and tone six to eleven year olds will appreciate, describing each selection's odd appearance, ability or behavior in an informative and direct manner, and clearly putting each animal in a context a child can relate to.

My only objections are that the short sentences just occasionally sound choppy, and that a table of contents and index would have enabled a quick check to see if a particular creature was included, but these drawbacks are minor in such a . . . distinguished book which will be a pleasure to read from start to finish.

*Diane Holzheimer, in a review of "Strange Creatures," in* Appraisal: Science Books for Young People, *Vol. 15, No. 1, Winter, 1982, p. 61.*

All of the creatures described here have been discussed in other books, but this is the sort of browsing compendium that serves well as an introduction and can also, because of the combination of brief treatment, simple style, and dignified tone, be useful for slow older readers.

*Zena Sutherland, in a review of "Strange Creatures," in* Bulletin of the Center for Children's Books, *Vol. 35, No. 9, May, 1982, p. 178.*

The information is interesting, accurate, and well written. . . . The book will intrigue inquisitive young naturalists. It does have several minor shortcomings: there is neither a table of contents nor an index, so each entry must stand on its own. There is no list of references or suggested reading so the reader's curiosity is stimulated and then abandoned. The entries are not complete enough to be definitive.

*Norman A. Engstrom, in a review of "Strange Creatures," in* Science Books & Films, *Vol. 17, No. 5, May-June, 1982, p. 272.*

---

### BODY SENSE/BODY NONSENSE (1981)

*Body Sense, Body Nonsense* is a tastefully written book about the truth or "nonsense" inherent in 22 familiar sayings about health. . . . Although the book is intended for elementary school students, others might enjoy it also. . . . In general, the book is fun to read and should capture a juvenile audience readily. It might be a useful aid in a health class.

*Ruth G. Mullins, in a review of "Body Sense, Body Nonsense," in* Science Books & Films, *Vol. 17, No. 5, May-June, 1982, p. 273.*

I was delighted to discover an amount of intriguing information sprinkled through this little volume. The format of a question with [Dennis Kendrick's] cartoon illustration on the right hand page and the answer "nonsense" or "sense" explained on the following left hand page but with no index makes this book useless for scientific research. BUT for browsing and casual reading, it was great fun. . . . [What] this book intends to do, it does very well.

*Sallie Hope Erhard, in a review of "Body Sense, Body Nonsense," in* Appraisal: Science Books for Young People, *Vol. 15, No. 2, Spring-Summer, 1982, p. 65.*

For the most part, the treatment is clever, attention-getting, and reasonably accurate. I would think that most kids would find this a fascinating way to learn some basic, if often trivial, information about the way their bodies function. I am slightly concerned that every statement selected by the author has to be classified as *right* ("sense") or *wrong* ("nonsense"). Many folk sayings contain a grain of truth, but cannot be taken too literally. These statements are difficult to classify as purely correct or incorrect. For example, it *is* true to say that "Carrots are good for your eyesight," but only in a rather limited way (in the prevention of night-blindness, as the author explains). . . .

All in all, a pleasant, well-written . . . addition to a child's health library.

*David E. Newton, in a review of "Body Sense, Body Nonsense," in* Appraisal: Science Books for Young People, *Vol. 15, No. 2, Spring-Summer, 1982, p. 65.*

### HOW TO BE A SPACE SCIENTIST IN YOUR OWN HOME   (1982)

Simon writes in a lucid, appealing style here as he details 24 experiments for would-be astronauts to try.... [The text] is grounded firmly in immutable laws that the author explains carefully. He tells what the home space scientist needs to make a launcher and a water-powered rocket, and to fuel the craft during stages of the flight. The text emphasizes caution in handling several steps in the procedures and makes it a pleasure to learn about reasons for attention to these matters and to understand Newton's law and other foundations on which the space age is built.

*A review of "How to Be a Space Scientist in Your Own Home," in* Publishers Weekly, *Vol. 221, No. 10, March 5, 1982, p. 71.*

Each experiment follows the same pattern of a funny drawing [by Bill Morrison] and a catchy title followed by two headings in bold type: *Here's What You Will Need* and *Here's What You Do,* but there's never an equally clear sign post to what you're trying to find out.... The text is very clear and precise, however, and in every chapter the discussion ends with a good series of thought-provoking questions.

This is not new material. Simon published it all over ten years ago in a book called **Science at Work: Projects in Space Science**.... [The older book] has a nearly identical text, but with more diagrams, clearer chapter titles and a third heading— *What To Look For*—which guides the reader to the objective of each experiment.... Keep the older book if you have it. (p. 46)

*Lavinia C. Demos, in a review of "How to Be a Space Scientist in Your Own Home," in* Appraisal: Science Books for Young People, *Vol. 15, No. 3, Fall, 1982, pp. 45-6.*

You have to admire this author for creating so many simple experiments for a youngster to do that are related to astronautics. The relationship is a little strained at times and some of the experiments are almost trivial in content. Others are quite interesting, albeit some a little dangerous for an unsupervised youth, with possibilities of glass jars exploding, melting wax catching fire, or fingers getting burned on a hot plate. The author supplies suitable cautions with emphasis, however.... The science taught by the text discussions is ofttimes shallow and sometimes misleading. However, the author to his credit attempts over and over to make the young scientist think by asking significant questions related to the experiment. On the whole a worthwhile book, but it could have been better.

*David G. Hoag, in a review of "How to Be a Space Scientist in Your Own Home," in* Appraisal: Science Books for Young People, *Vol. 15, No. 3, Fall, 1982, p. 46.*

[Simon is a] prolific, dependable science writer.... As usual, Simon avoids using laboratory equipment in favor of simple household materials or items found in inexpensive chemistry sets.... With adequate detail and a nontechnical style, Simon allows children to discover scientific principles for themselves. His **Science at Work: Projects in Space Science** ... touches on different aspects of space travel (devising a space language, psychological implications of space travel, etc.)

*Connie Tyrrell, in a review of "How to Be a Space Scientist in Your Own Home," in* School Library Journal, *Vol. 29, No. 5, January, 1983, p. 79.*

### EINSTEIN ANDERSON GOES TO BAT   (1982)

Punning painfully all the way, sixth-grade superbrain Einstein Anderson sees through [several supposedly true stories].... He coaches little brother Dennis for a sword-balancing challenge, helps out mean classmate Pat the Brat on two occasions, and tricks him on another. For these mental feats, Einstein calls on his knowledge of Newton, Archimedes, photosynthesis, the center of gravity, and a number of odd facts. The episodes still tend to center on competition and one-upmanship of one sort or another, though Einstein seems to be toning down his tendency to rub it in.

*A review of "Einstein Anderson Goes to Bat," in* Kirkus Reviews, *Vol. L, No. 6, March 15, 1982, p. 347.*

Careful reading and a fair knowledge of science is necessary to be able to figure out the puzzles. Even if they can't be figured out, it's fun to read the solution and then go back to locate the clues that were overlooked. Each chapter is complete in itself and contains several jokes and puns that will delight young readers. An excellent volume for reading aloud or silent enjoyment.

*Paulette Sparks, in a review of "Einstein Anderson Goes to Bat," in* Catholic Library World, *Vol. 55, No. 2, September, 1983, p. 89.*

### THE SMALLEST DINOSAURS   (1982)

Even though most books briefly mention that not all dinosaurs were large, this is the only one that concentrates exclusively on small specimens of the species.... Unlike the stilted language and inaccurate drawings in Peggy Parish's *Dinosaur Time* (Harper, 1974), both text and [Anthony Rao's] illustrations are flowing and substantial in detail. This book also provides something unique to the subject at this grade level: frequent indications of what scientists do not yet know about dinosaurs and might discover in the future.... [A *Book to Begin on Dinosaurs* (Holt, 1959) by Eunice Holsaert and Robert Gartland] and this one will provide beginning dinosaur enthusiasts with a sound basic knowledge of the subject.

*Ann G. Brouse, in a review of "The Smallest Dinosaurs," in* School Library Journal, *Vol. 28, No. 8, April, 1982, p. 63.*

Beginning readers clamoring for dinosaur material will find Simon's simple approach, straightforward manner, and easy wording helpful in ferreting out needed information. Pronunciation keys to long scientific names make difficult words easy to comprehend and say.

*Barbara Elleman, in a review of "The Smallest Dinosaurs," in* Booklist, *Vol. 78, No. 20, June 15, 1982, p. 1372.*

The single most annoying feature of the book is its use and its translation of scientific names without any real explanation of this taxonomy. The reader is told, for example, that Saurornithoides means "lizard like a bird." The rather natural responses "to whom?" or "in what language?" have not been anticipated or dealt with.

> *Ronald J. Kley, in a review of "The Smallest Dinosaurs," in* Appraisal: Science Books for Young People, *Vol. 15, No. 2, Spring-Summer, 1982, p. 67.*

## THE LONG JOURNEY FROM SPACE (1982)

Spectacular space photographs, elegant design, and a clean, straightforward text make Simon's introduction to comets and meteors a sure pick for the astronomy shelf. A companion to *The Long View into Space* . . . , this describes in nontechnical language what comets and meteors are, how we came to know about them, [and] what their special characteristics are. . . . The level of discussion and information is strictly introductory. . . . But the introduction is striking and sure to lure many readers on to more substantial fare.

> *Denise M. Wilms, in a review of "The Long Journey from Space," in* Booklist, *Vol. 79, No. 3, October 1, 1982, p. 250.*

Simon has misinterpreted one of the historical prints he chose, mistaking the constellation Corvus for a live bird. This is an attractive introduction, but readers who want a diagram of comet orbits or a short list of annual meteor showers will have to go elsewhere, such as to the more difficult but far more inclusive *Comets, Meteoroids, and Asteroids* (Crowell, 1974) by Franklyn Branley.

> *Margaret L. Chatham, in a review of "The Long Journey from Space," in* School Library Journal, *Vol. 29, No. 3, November, 1982, p. 91.*

Seymour Simon has written a solid and interesting narrative describing the relationship between human thought about and scientific data regarding the heavenly phenomena, comets and meteors. He clearly defines those two entities. . . . [The book has] straightforward yet elegant prose. . . . This short work is immensely satisfying from scientific and aesthetic viewpoints. It is accessible to a broad age group, and is highly recommended.

> *Deborah Robinson, in a review of "The Long Journey from Space," in* Appraisal: Science Books for Young People, *Vol. 16, No. 1, Winter, 1983, p. 55.*

## EINSTEIN ANDERSON LIGHTS UP THE SKY (1982)

Einstein spends his time in the sixth grade solving puzzles and foiling the school bullies via his knowledge of science. There are ten new mysteries here based on seven areas of science, including meteorology and electrostatics. The answers are obtainable through observation or general reference material. Einstein's jokes and puns continue to make the puzzles fun to read and the nonstereotyped characterizations are also a plus. Fans of the "Encyclopedia Brown" series will enjoy Einstein Anderson even though the format is slightly different.

> *Carolyn Caywood, in a review of "Einstein Anderson Lights Up the Sky," in* School Library Journal, *Vol. 29, No. 5, January, 1983, p. 79.*

In his latest adventures, Einstein Anderson once again solves the scientific mysteries of stars like grains of sand, science

stamps, lunar olympics, bulbs that won't freeze and mysterious lights. Einstein's puns are corny yet humorous and are certain to please the joke telling group of the elementary grades. Einstein's fans will not be disappointed in this new one.

> *Susan Melcher, in a review of "Einstein Anderson Lights Up the Sky," in* Catholic Library World, *Vol. 54, No. 10, May-June, 1983, p. 425.*

## LITTLE GIANTS (1983)

The book provides less than a page of text for each "little giant," and the creatures range from insects that are larger than most of their kind to such animals as the ostrich or beluga sturgeon. The material is accurate and interesting, but the fact that the arrangement seems haphazard and that the book has neither an index nor a table of contents limits access and indicates that the primary use will be for browsing.

> *Zena Sutherland, in a review of "Little Giants," in* Bulletin of the Center for Children's Books, *Vol. 36, No. 9, May, 1983, p. 179.*

With his usual clarity and fluidity, Seymour Simon writes about the biggest little animals in the world. . . . (pp. 47-8)

Other books about strange animals abound, such as I. Akimushkin's *Rare Animals,* and the Reader's Digest *Marvels and Mysteries of Our Animal World.* But there's nothing quite like *Little Giants.* The subject matter is whimsically original, it's fun to read and beautiful to look at. What more can you ask for? (p. 48)

> *Lee Jeffers, in a review of "Little Giants," in* Appraisal: Science Books for Young People, *Vol. 17, No. 1, Winter, 1984, pp. 47-8.*

## EINSTEIN ANDERSON SEES THROUGH THE INVISIBLE MAN (1983)

The jokes will appeal to both boys and girls, and the friendly competition between Einstein and his fellow sixth-grade classmate, Margaret Michaels . . . adds to the fun. While readers are enjoying themselves with the easy story lines, they will also be learning a little bit about science. This is a good book for readers beyond the easy reader stage, especially for those reluctant to spend much time with a book in hand. The jokes and puns are entertaining, as are the characters' reactions to all of Einstein's scientific solutions. (pp. 82-3)

> *Sondra Vandermark, in a review of "Einstein Anderson Sees Through the Invisible Man," in* School Library Journal, *Vol. 30, No. 3, November, 1983, pp. 82-3.*

Ten puzzles, each several pages long (including the solutions), are easily read yet thought-provoking. In this volume, Einstein unmasks an invisible man, outsmarts a bully, and figures out the ups and downs of ball playing along with other scientific feats. The series continues operating at its usual high level.

> *Ilene Cooper, in a review of "Einstein Anderson Sees Through the Invisible Man," in* Booklist, *Vol. 80, No. 11, February 1, 1984, p. 817.*

*HIDDEN WORLDS: PICTURES OF THE INVISIBLE*  (1983)

Assorted objects and events "that your eyes just cannot see"—assembled as if such "hidden worlds," very large, very small, or very fast, had something intrinsically in common. The section-topics—**"Around You," "Inside the body," "Time," "Earth," "Space"**—constitute another kind of meaningless classification. **"Around You,"** in turn, we find: diatoms, snowflakes, whirls of soap; insect parts, bread mold, "a dye called acetotoluidine." (And much more.) The magnifications are all different, and presented without scale or comparison.... The accompanying information is over-technical for the young pictorial format, over-specific for the few words of explanation provided, and generally a catchall of unrelated facts.... Add old-fashioned gee-whiz twaddle about "these weird-looking objects" (magnified pollen grains) and "some distant worlds in space" (that acetotoluidine dye, crystallized), and the whole thing's a muddle.

> *A review of "Hidden Worlds: Pictures of the Invisible," in* Kirkus Reviews, *Vol. LI, No. 21, November 1, 1983, p. J-199.*

Accompanying the photographs are careful explanations of the methodologies that were used to produce the pictures.... Simon's explanations of these techniques are concise and easy to understand.... Readers desiring more examples and explanations of a particular methodology will prefer the approach of *Small Worlds Close Up.* **Hidden Worlds** is, however, an entertaining and fact-filled introduction to a wide variety of scientific techniques that will be new to most readers.

> *Julia Rholes, in a review of "Hidden Worlds: Pictures of the Invisible," in* School Library Journal, *Vol. 30, No. 6, February, 1984, p. 77.*

[Several] terms that are used are not explained clearly enough for elementary age children to understand (e.g., the definition for polarized light includes the terms, "filter," "plane," "fractures" within a crystal) and a few terms which are used repeatedly are never defined.

The National Geographic Society's book of the same title (*Hidden Worlds,* 1981) is a much more detailed and expanded treatment of this same subject.... In comparison with that book, Simon's seems slight and insufficient.

> *Arlene Bernstein, in a review of "Hidden Worlds: Pictures of the Invisible," in* Appraisal: Science Books for Young People, *Vol. 17, No. 2, Spring-Summer, 1984, p. 43.*

[The] book does not have an index or suggestions for further reading or viewing. At the end, Simon presents four paragraphs of summary and suggested hidden mysteries that are on the verge of being solved, but the book's simple organization would have been more complete if these statements and questions had been placed under the formal heading of "Summary" rather than being tacked onto the last chapter. Overall, this compilation of excellent photographs is an excellent source of ancillary information for third through sixth grade science classes.

> *Benjamin Barnhart, in a review of "Hidden Worlds: Pictures of the Invisible," in* Science Books & Films, *Vol. 20, No. 1, September-October, 1984, p. 31.*

*EARTH: OUR PLANET IN SPACE*  (1984)

Black and white photographs of good quality are carefully combined with textual references to achieve a maximum level of conveyance of information. There are many books about our planet and its solar system; this additional title should be welcome because of ... the careful and accurate marshalling of facts, the directness of style, and the combination of good coverage and controlled scope, as Simon discusses such topics as the earth's place in the solar system, its topography, erosion, atmosphere, and other aspects, in a lucid continuous text.

> *Zena Sutherland, in a review of "Earth: Our Planet in Space," in* Bulletin of the Center for Children's Books, *Vol. 37, No. 8, April, 1984, p. 155.*

[The author] has done an interesting job of maintaining an external viewpoint, that is, of concentrating on the appearance of our world from the outside—making extensive use of photographs taken from space, well selected to go with the text, thus stressing its status as a planet....

[The] author has undertaken a job that is difficult because of the combination of the intended readership and the available space in the book, and he has accomplished it well.

> *Harry C. Stubbs, "Earth," in* The Horn Book Magazine, *Vol. LX, No. 4, August, 1984, p. 500.*

---

*THE DINOSAUR IS THE BIGGEST ANIMAL THAT EVER LIVED AND OTHER WRONG IDEAS YOU THOUGHT WERE TRUE* (1984)

Two pages are devoted to each popular fallacy, in a book that is admirably suited—by subjects, by level of reading difficulty ...—to the middle grades audience. Simon, an authoritative science writer, gives careful explanations of why it's not true that quicksand drags you down, or that lightning never strikes twice. Informative, intriguing.

> *Zena Sutherland, in a review of "The Dinosaur Is the Biggest Animal That Ever Lived: And Other Wrong Ideas You Thought Were True," in* Bulletin of the Center for Children's Books, *Vol. 37, No. 11, July-August, 1984, p. 212.*

This is a collection of twenty-nine corrections to commonly mistaken factual beliefs about natural phenomena....

Several of the corrections serve an educative function. The fact that the Earth is nearer to the sun in winter, ... and that one can be sunburned on a cloudy day, are counter intuitive.... They are puzzling and may provoke questions about other assumptions. (p. 39)

It is difficult to understand, at least for this reader, what criteria were used to assemble the other facts. It is even more difficult to understand why all the facts are given equal space. Is the composition of a pencil really as important as human diversity?

The treatment of the information is inconsistent. The author makes a plea for the blue whale, but not for withholding judgment on the basis of people's physical characteristics. The facts about lightning and the cracking of glass are explained, but no explanation is offered for the fact that the largest animal lives in water, not on land. The explanation of the blue sky includes an experiment the reader can do, but no experiment is suggested to test the notion that food spoils when stored in open cans.

The validity of two items is, at best, doubtful. "A chocolate bar is also a good source of energy." The sugar content of chocolate bars ranges from about twenty to more than fifty percent. Is it wise to encourage children to consume sugar? The second item concerns the classification of protozoans. It has been entirely respectable for the past twenty years to classify life forms, not into two kingdoms, plants and animals, but into five: Monera, Proctista, Fungi, Animalia, and Plantae. In this classification, plants do not move about.

The absence of an intellectual framework, the implied equal importance of various bits of information, the inconsistency of treatment, and the questionable validity of two of these bits, results in a book that will contribute little to the reader's understanding of the natural world. The author has written many fine science books for young readers, and he will, I am confident, write many more such books. This one is not to be counted among them. (pp. 39-40)

> *Lazer Goldberg, in a review of "The Dinosaur Is the Biggest Animal That Ever Lived and Other Wrong Ideas You Thought Were True," in* Appraisal: Science Books for Young People, *Vol. 17, No. 3, Fall, 1984, pp. 39-40.*

Some of the "wrong ideas" are not actually wrong, just oversimplified ("the sky is blue") and others fall into the "so what" category ("you can see a million stars on a clear night"). Some explanations are themselves misleading. In the section on sunburn, Simon states that "Tanning the skin is not the same as burning the skin," but recent research has shown that the only difference in skin damage between tanning and burning is one of degree and that even a slight tan damages the skin. Still, . . . [this has a] very readable text.

> *Ann G. Brouse, in a review of "The Dinosaur Is the Biggest Animal That Ever Lived: And Other Wrong Ideas You Thought Were True," in* School Library Journal, *Vol. 31, No. 2, October, 1984, p. 162.*

I cannot recommend this book, but with changes in its title and chapter headings, it would be more than "acceptable" for young readers. The topics are well chosen and pertinent to children in the third through sixth grades. . . . However, considering that children are apt to unquestioningly consider anything that is printed as "truth" and that many children read only the first part of sentences, I highly question the title and chapter headings—they could easily leave the wrong impression in young readers' minds. The book also contains a few scientifically questionable statements. For example, in the discussion of the octopus, the black liquid used for protection is referred to as "ink": "If poked by a diver, an octopus will give off a cloud of ink and try to escape instead of attacking." Also, "there would be no seasons as we know them if the earth were straight up in space." What does "up" in space mean? With some changes, this would be a good book.

> *Dora Wood Dean, in a review of "The Dinosaur Is the Biggest Animal That Ever Lived: And Other Wrong Ideas You Thought Were True," in* Science Books & Films, *Vol. 20, No. 3, January-February, 1985, p. 157.*

---

## COMPUTER SENSE, COMPUTER NONSENSE (1984)

Veteran science writer Simon tackles computers, taking an approach akin to that of his earlier *Body Sense, Body Nonsense.* . . . The result is rather a hodgepodge of computer lore,

but the popularity of the subject and the friendly, browsable treatment should make this a happy addition to larger computer book collections. In a series of mostly two-page spreads, 24 statements about computers are labeled "SENSE" or "NONSENSE," with accompanying explanatory discussions. Occasionally Simon stretches a little, as in his contention that "the heart of a computer is made from sand"—i.e., silicon—but other facts and fallacies are cleverly framed and sometimes surprising. This is not the best resource for a rank beginner, but kids with a smattering of computer background are almost sure to pick up something new. A detailed contents listing compensates to some degree for the lack of an index. (p. 1629)

> *Karen Stang Hanley, in a review of "Computer Sense, Computer Nonsense," in* Booklist, *Vol. 80, No. 22, August, 1984, pp. 1629-30.*

Simon's contribution to computer literacy is up-to-date but breaks no new ground. . . . Information is scattered: for example, word processors are treated in **"Computers Can Help You Do Your Homework"** and **"Computers Are Good Only at Working Numbers."** Since there is no index, readers will not be able to locate the information easily, and this book will be better as a browsing item. Simon's *Body Sense, Body Nonsense* . . . answered a need to clear up misconceptions, but *Computer Sense, Computer Nonsense* rehashes ideas readily available elsewhere: computers can take over the world, are smarter than people, can run without a program, etc. . . . Teachers could use this title to add a little spice to their computer literacy presentation.

> *Sharen Lee Wagner, in a review of "Computer Sense, Computer Nonsense," in* School Library Journal, *Vol. 31, No. 3, November, 1984, p. 128.*

[This is done in Simon's] usual brisk and authoritative fashion. . . . This not only debunks fallacies but gives a considerable amount of information about computers lucidly. It gives facts about function and use and limitations, and even provides some information about programming.

> *Zena Sutherland, in a review of "Computer Sense, Computer Nonsense," in* Bulletin of the Center for Children's Books, *Vol. 38, No. 6, February, 1985, p. 116.*

---

## CHIP ROGERS, COMPUTER WHIZ (1984)

Computer-crazy eighth-grader Chip Rogers and his best friend, Katie Williams, discover a museum jewel theft and, after a sleuthing expedition, rely on a computer to tell them who the culprit is. Simon's thin but entertaining mystery is designed to introduce computer capabilities and some elementary BASIC programming to young readers as painlessly as possible. Computer concepts and terminology are woven deliberately but naturally into the story, which has Chip setting up several programs and thereby actively demonstrating some beginning programming. As a mystery, this is slight, but there's no denying its success at making the subject of computers approachable—even if the story's critical mystery-solving program seems a little dense to the uninitiated.

> *Denise M. Wilms, in a review of "Chip Rogers, Computer Whiz," in* Booklist, *Vol. 81, No. 8, December 15, 1984, p. 592.*

Fine literature it isn't, but it certainly serves to acquaint young people with the rudiments and uses of computer programming and presents them with a challenging program to solve. Computer terms listed in the book's preface are explained within the story. Even beginning computer operators with computer access can copy and run the book's programmed solution to find the answer to the mystery. (Programs can be run as is on Apple, Atari, Commodore, IBM PC and TRS 80 models.) Clues provided in the text enable those readers who have no access to a computer to solve the mystery using logic. First of a projected series, this bit of enrichment material will have the same appeal as an educational computer game.

> *Susan Scheps, in a review of "Chip Rogers: Computer Whiz," in* School Library Journal, *Vol. 31, No. 5, January, 1985, p. 80.*

# Mildred D(elois) Taylor

## 19??-

**Black American author of fiction.**

The author of three realistic stories that juxtapose the security of family love against the evils of racism—*Song of the Trees, Roll of Thunder, Hear My Cry,* and *Let the Circle Be Unbroken*—Taylor is recognized for her original interpretation of the black experience. Inspired by her father's oral account of the struggle of their ancestors to establish themselves as landowners after the abolition of slavery, Taylor depicts heroic men and women who face oppression with fortitude and imagination. Her themes—self-respect, integrity, independence, strong family bonds, and love of nature and the land—underscore works that powerfully express the indomitability of the human spirit in lyrical prose and vivid dialogue. Writing in the first person, Taylor describes life in rural Mississippi during the Depression through the observations and reactions of Cassie Logan, a vibrant young girl who learns what it means to be black in America and how to cope with bigotry.

Taylor structures her books around the efforts of Cassie's family to keep their land from prejudiced white neighbors. Placing her stories in the climate of events that preceded the Civil Rights movement of the 1950s and 1960s, she endeavors to show the impact of Cassie's generation on issues of racial equality. Throughout the series, Taylor relates the personal impressions of her protagonists and provides historical perspective by touching on the larger socioeconomic issues of the day. She presents graphic accounts of experiences in the lives of the Logans and their friends that range from racial friction among classmates to the execution of a black boy for a crime he did not commit.

Born in Jackson, Mississippi, Taylor moved with her family to Toledo, Ohio after her father was involved in a racial incident. She grew up in a supportive environment that stressed pride and self-confidence, much like the one she created for the Logans. Throughout her school days, Taylor sensed the discrepancy between what she learned at home and what she was taught in class. Her father, a gifted storyteller, told her tales about himself and their relatives which emphasized how they retained their dignity despite sorrow and defeat. Taylor discovered that her history books portrayed blacks as weak and vulnerable, when they were mentioned at all. By the time she reached high school, Taylor was convinced that she would write the truth about her people.

After her graduation from the University of Toledo, Taylor joined the Peace Corps and went to Ethiopia for two years to teach English and history. Living in Africa, she observed black pride and independence and was reminded of the stories she had heard from her father. Taylor returned to the United States to teach and recruit for the Peace Corps before attending the University of Colorado to study journalism. There, as a member of the Black Student Alliance, she helped create a black studies program, becoming study skills coordinator after receiving her master's degree. Resigning her position to move to Los Angeles, Taylor worked at a nominal day job and wrote *Song of the Trees* at night. She entered the novella in the

Council on Interracial Books for Children competition, where it won first prize in the African-American category in 1973.

After *Song of the Trees* was published in 1975, Taylor decided to continue the story of the Logans with *Roll of Thunder, Hear My Cry* and *Let the Circle Be Unbroken*, which further incorporate her father's teachings and stories and combine them with actual historical incidents. Taylor plans to complete the series with a fourth volume that takes the Logan children into adulthood. "It is my hope," she has said, "that to the children who read my books, the Logans will provide those heroes missing from the schoolbooks of my childhood. Black men, women, and children of whom they can be proud."

Critics hail Taylor as a talented writer, and many regard *Roll of Thunder* as a classic. They commend the powerful yet sensitive manner with which she writes, the realism of her characters, the authenticity of her descriptions, and the evocative, emotional experience her works provide for readers. Reviewers applaud Taylor's proud depiction of the Logans and look forward to the continuation of their saga.

*Roll of Thunder, Hear My Cry* won the Newbery Medal, was a National Book Award finalist, and was named a *Boston Globe-Horn Book* Honor Book in 1977. In 1982, *Let the Circle Be Unbroken* was nominated for the American Book Award in the hardcover fiction category and also won the Coretta Scott King Award.

(See also *Contemporary Literary Criticism*, Vol. 21; *Something about the Author,* Vol. 15; and *Contemporary Authors*, Vols. 85-88.)

---

AUTHOR'S COMMENTARY

I was blessed with a special father, a man who had unyielding faith in himself and his abilities, and who, knowing himself to be inferior to no one, tempered my learning with his wisdom. In the foreword to **Roll of Thunder, Hear My Cry** I described my father as a master storyteller; he was much more than that. A highly principled, complex man who did not have an excellent education or a white-collar job, he had instead strong moral fiber and a great wealth of what he always said was simply plain common sense. Throughout my childhood he impressed upon my sister and me that we were somebody, that we were important and could do or be anything we set our minds to do or be. (p. 402)

Through him my growing awareness of a discriminatory society was accompanied by a wisdom that taught me that anger in itself was futile, that to fight discrimination I needed a stronger weapon. When my family was refused seating in a Wyoming restaurant, he taught me that I must gain the skill to destroy such bigotry; when "For Sale" signs forested the previously all-white neighborhood into which we had moved, he taught me pride in our new home as well as in myself by reminding me that how I saw myself was more important than how others saw me; and when I came home from school one day versed in propaganda against the Soviet Union, he softly reminded me that Black people in the United States of the fifties had no more rights than I had been told the citizens of the Soviet Union had. From that I learned to question, to reason. (pp. 402-03)

The effects of those teachings upon me are evident to anyone reading **Roll of Thunder, Hear My Cry**. Also evident are the strong family ties. Through David Logan have come the words of my father, and through the Logan family the love of my own family. If people are touched by the warmth of the Logans, it is because I had the warmth of my own youthful years from which to draw. If the Logans seem real, it is because I had my own family upon which to base characterizations. And if people believe the book to be biographical, it is because I have tried to distill the essence of Black life, so familiar to most Black families, to make the Logans an embodiment of that spiritual heritage; for, contrary to what the media relate to us, all Black families are not fatherless or disintegrating. Certainly my family was not. (p. 403)

[At the many gatherings we had when I was a child], there was always time for talk, and when we children had finished all the games we could think to play, we would join the adults, soon becoming enraptured by their talk, for it would often turn to a history which we heard only at home, a history of Black people told through stories.

Those stories about the small and often dangerous triumphs of Black people, those stories about human pride and survival in a cruelly racist society were like nothing I read in the history books or the books I devoured at the local library. There were no Black heroes or heroines in those books; no beautiful Black ladies, no handsome Black men; no people filled with pride, strength, or endurance. There was, of course, always mention of Booker T. Washington and George Washington Carver; Marian Anderson and occasionally even Dr. Ralph Bunche. But that hardly compensated for the lackluster history of Black people painted by those books, a history of a docile, subservient people happy with their fate who did little or nothing to shatter the chains that bound them, both before and after slavery. There was obviously a terrible contradiction between what the books said and what I had learned from my family, and at no time did I feel the contradiction more than when I had to sit in a class which, without me, would have been all white, and relive that prideless history year after year.

As I grew, and the writers of books and their publishers grew, I noticed a brave attempt to portray Black people with a white sense of dignity and pride. But even those books disturbed me, for the Black people shown were still subservient. Most often the Black characters were housekeepers and, though a source of love and strength to the white child whose story it was, they remained one-dimensional because the view of them was a white one. Books about Black families by white writers also left me feeling empty, not because a white person had attempted to write about a Black family, but because the writer had not, in my opinion, captured the warmth or love of the Black world and had failed to understand the principles upon which Black parents brought up their children and taught them survival. It was not that these writers intentionally omitted such essential elements; it was simply that not having lived the Black experience, they did not know it.

But I did know it. And by the time I entered high school, I had a driving compulsion to paint a truer picture of Black people. I wanted to show the endurance of the Black world, with strong fathers and concerned mothers; I wanted to show happy, loved children about whom other children, both Black and white, could say: "Hey, I really like them! I feel what they feel." I wanted to show a Black family united in love and pride, of which the reader would like to be a part.

I never doubted that one day I would grasp that bright spark of life in words for others to see, for hadn't my father always said I could do anything I set my mind to do? But as the years passed and what I wrote continued to lack the vitality of the world I knew, there began to grow within a very youthful me an overwhelming impatience, and the question: *when?*

Well, the *when* was not to come until almost four years ago, after I had seen much of the world, returned to school for graduate study, and become a Black student activist. It was then that on a well-remembered day in late September a little girl named Cassie Logan suddenly appeared in my life. Cassie was a spunky eight-year-old, innocent, untouched by discrimination, full of pride, and greatly loved, and through her I discovered I now could tell one of the stories I had heard so often as a child. From that meeting came **Song of the Trees**.

If you have met Cassie and her brothers—Stacey, the staunch, thoughtful leader; Christopher-John, the happy, sensitive mediator; and Little Man, the shiny clean, prideful, manly six-year-old—then perhaps you can understand why, when I sent that final manuscript off to Dial, I did not want to give them up. Those four children make me laugh; they also make me cry, and I had to find a way of keeping them from fading into oblivion. In August, 1974, came the answer: I would write another book about the Logans, one in which I could detail the teachings of my own childhood as well as incorporate many of the stories I had heard about my family and others. Through artistic prerogative I could weave into those stories factual incidents about which I had read or heard, as well as my own childhood feelings to produce a significant tapestry which would portray rural Black southern life in the 1930s. I would write *Roll of Thunder, Hear My Cry*.

Writing is a very lonely business. It is also a very terrifying one emotionally if a writer knows and cares about the people of her novel as well as I know and care about the Logans. Cassie's fears were my fears and what she feared from the night men, so did I. More than once my dreams were fraught with burnings and destruction, with faceless men coming in the night, with a boy being beaten, with a boy about to die. (pp. 404-06)

[In the first draft of my book] I had attempted to make Cassie play too big a part in the climax. I had wanted her to be with David when his leg was broken, to be with him when the fire started, to fight the fire. After all, it was she who had to tell the story and how could she if she wasn't there? But the character of David Logan wouldn't let me put her into the center of the action. I thought of my own father and what he would have done. He, like David, would never have taken his young daughter on such dangerous missions. It was clear to me now. All I had to do was allow my characters to remain true to themselves; that was the key.

I believe that that key served me well in the writing of *Roll of Thunder, Hear My Cry,* and I hope that it will continue to guide me through the next two books about the Logans, which will chronicle the growth of the Logan children into adolescence and adulthood. . . . I will continue the Logans' story with the same life guides that have always been mine, for it is my hope that these four books, one of the first chronicles to mirror a Black child's hopes and fears from childhood innocence to awareness to bitterness and disillusionment, will one day be instrumental in teaching children of all colors the tremendous influence that Cassie's generation—my father's generation—had in bringing about the great Civil Rights movement of the fifties and sixties. Without understanding that generation and what it and the generations before it endured, children of today and of the future cannot understand or cherish the precious rights of equality which they now possess, both in the North and in the South. If they can identify with the Logans, who are representative not only of my family but of the many Black families who faced adversity and survived, and understand the principles by which they lived, then perhaps they can better understand and respect themselves and others. (pp. 407-08)

> *Mildred D. Taylor, in the Newbery Award Acceptance Speech given at the meeting of the American Library Association in Detroit, Michigan, on June 18, 1977, in* The Horn Book Magazine, *Vol. LIII, No. 4, August, 1977, pp. 401-09.*

---

### GENERAL COMMENTARY

#### PHYLLIS J. FOGELMAN

"A natural writer" is an overused expression I don't particularly like, but in speaking of Mildred Taylor it seems absolutely appropriate. Mildred's words flow smoothly, effortlessly, it seems, and they abound in richness, harmony, and rhythm. Her stories unfold in a full, leisurely way, well suited to and evocative of her Southern settings. Her ability to bring her characters to life and to involve her readers is remarkable. In short, Mildred is one of the few people of whom I have felt: This woman was born to write. (pp. 410-11)

> *Phyllis J. Fogelman, "Mildred D. Taylor," in* The Horn Book Magazine, *Vol. LIII, No. 4, August, 1977, pp. 410-14.*

#### SHARON L. DUSSEL

After reading the words of Mildred Taylor, one can't help but be impressed by the talent and style of this young author; yet she is the first to admit that her strengths, convictions, and successes are all directly related to the love and support she received from her wonderful family—and chiefly her father. Her words should make parents pause to consider just what kind of impact (both positive and negative) they are unconsciously having on their own children. For in a world that is quickly changing, a loving family seems to be more important than ever. The influence a strong, supporting family can have on a child's development is most definitely seen in the life and work of Mildred D. Taylor. (p. 604)

> *Sharon L. Dussel, "Profile: Mildred D. Taylor," in* Language Arts, *Vol. 58, No. 5, May, 1981, pp. 599-604.*

---

### *SONG OF THE TREES*  (1975)

First are the trees behind the house. Hickory, pine, beech, sturdy walnut, sweet alligator gum, they are the joy of young Cassie's life—trunks to hug, leaves that sing, branches that protect. With such a forest, a girl can feel rich even though this is the Depression and money is scarce, particularly in Mississippi for black people. Cassie's father has to go clear to Louisiana to find work, and sometimes when he sends money home it is taken from the envelope before the family gets it. Still, no matter what happens, the trees sing their song, and that is a comfort.

But then come the white crosses on the trees, and the white men come. . . . Sweet talk and scare talk until they get their way. So the axes ring and the old friends fall. For a while.

This is a slender book and so moving, the temptation is to tell the whole story. But the important thing is that Cassie's father, David, comes home and that we, the readers, meet him. We are not likely to forget him. He is a man who knows the full measure of his manhood. . . .

So at the end the white men go away (at least for a time), and part of the forest is saved. Still, the sounds of those axes ring on long after the last page of this triumphant book. And well they may, for this is a true story and truly told. A story to linger over.

> *Jean Fritz, in a review of "Song of the Trees," in* The New York Times Book Review, *May 4, 1975, p. 39.*

Based on an experience of the author's family, this is a moving story that manifests two simple, strongly felt emotions: a love of nature and a sense of self-respect. . . . The writing style, although at times self-conscious, smoothly backs up the element of dignity in the story's message and in its well-drawn black characters.

> *A review of "Song of the Trees," in* The Booklist, *Vol. 71, No. 22, July 15, 1975, p. 1193.*

The dedication of this book—thirteen lines which end "To my grandparents . . . who bridged the generations between slavery and freedom; and To the Family, who fought and survived"—immediately sets the tone of black pride that permeates every page.... [The] book is almost written to formula: Blacks encounter evil whites who attempt to rob them of their possessions and dignity, but a strong, black man counteracts with force. But what could have been a banal, trite book has been saved by its description of a child's feeling for nature which elevates the story from the socio-political realm.... The simple story has been written with great conviction and strength, and Cassie's descriptions of the trees add a poetic touch.

> *Anita Silvey, in a review of "Song of the Trees," in* The Horn Book Magazine, *Vol. LI, No. 4, August, 1975, p. 384.*

The confrontation [between the Logan family and the white work crew] symbolizes much of the history of Black struggle. Its components—economic defenselessness, Black bravery in the face of white power, the forced assumption of adult responsibility by children, and the children's fears—speak volumes. Furthermore, the author's handling of these factors encourages readers to struggle against their own and/or others' oppression—a most rare and welcome quality in children's books. (p. 109)

> *"Middle Grades: 'Song of the Trees'," in* Human—And Anti-Human—Values in Children's Books: A Content Rating Instrument for Educators and Concerned Parents, *edited by the Council on Interracial Books for Children, Inc., Racism and Sexism Resource Center for Educators, 1976, pp. 109-10.*

*Song of the Trees* is so beautifully told, the prose rings poetry....

The children are charming, disarming, personal, and not too private in their love and appreciation for the "sharp-needled pines," the "shaggy-bark hickories," and the "sweet alligator gum trees" which tower helplessly on "Big Ma's" land. They forebodingly await their devastation with their song quieted in an implied anticipation of their destruction.

The story builds smoothly and culminates in a clash of willfulness between Mr. Anderson, a White man who sees the trees as lumber, and David Logan, the Black father of the homestead, and of the aesthetic forest which captures the reader with its tender personality.

The book has much to recommend it. Mildred Taylor handles her characters with a fine sensitivity. It is a story not only of trees but of children, and an interplay of their personalities is carefully woven into the text. (p. 434)

> *Ruby Martin, in a review of "Song of the Trees," in* Journal of Reading, *Vol. 20, No. 5, February, 1977, pp. 433-35.*

---

### ROLL OF THUNDER, HEAR MY CRY (1976)

[*Roll of Thunder, Hear My Cry*] describes a year during which Cassie Logan learns to handle the indignities inflicted upon herself, her family and neighbors. She also learns the importance of her family's struggle to keep their land and their economic independence....

Throughout the book, the reader is moved to tears by Ms. Taylor's vibrant, exquisite and simple style. The dialogue is lightly seasoned with Southern colloquialisms.

After reading Cassie's last lines—"And I cried for those things which had happened in the night and would not pass. I cried

for T. J. For T. J. and the land"—you want to turn back and start all over again.

*Roll of Thunder, Hear My Cry* deserves to become a classic in children's literature.

> *Emily R. Moore, in a review of "Roll of Thunder, Hear My Cry," in* Interracial Books for Children Bulletin, *Vol. 7, No. 7, 1976, p. 18.*

The book presents injustice and several ways of dealing with it; the children cleverly avenge their tormentors, but the adults are not able to dismiss their problems as easily. There is little relief from the tension of frightening events, and the reader is able to identify with Cassie's frustration and anger as she experiences great unfairness and witnesses crimes against Black people. The events and settings of the powerful novel are presented with such verisimilitude and the characters are so carefully drawn that one might assume the book to be autobiographical, if the author were not so young.

> *Sally Holmes Holtze, in a review of "Roll of Thunder, Hear My Cry," in* The Horn Book Magazine, *Vol. LII, No. 6, December, 1976, p. 627.*

Phyllis Fogelman, writing in the Horn Book about Mildred Taylor on the occasion of her acceptance of the Newbery Award for *Roll of Thunder, hear my cry,* spoke of her as a "natural writer" [see excerpt above in General Commentary]. This is a dangerous phrase to use of anyone and it would be a pity if this author, new to the sphere of children's books, should take it at all seriously, for in fact her book is too natural altogether. Burningly honest as the book undoubtedly is, it has the air of autobiography in its crowded details and assumptive descriptions, while the raw emotionalism needs to be disciplined and channelled if it is to make a proper impact as fiction. There is much talent in this extended chronicle of a negro family in Mississippi in the early 'thirties, and a very evident truth in episodes derived from the author's father which show up the bigotries and brutal social alignments of the time. But the strength of feeling in the book has been too much for the characters. They remain dim, stiff figures manipulated for the sake of certain key situations, and they are so far based on the author's own family history that they never achieve the independent identity essential to a novel. (pp. 3286-87)

> *Margery Fisher, in a review of "Roll of Thunder, Hear My Cry," in her* Growing Point, *Vol. 16, No. 9, April, 1978, pp. 3286-87.*

Although in literature symbols are communicated through words, they are more than words, which is why their meanings cannot be looked up in dictionaries. Also they are more complex than metaphors. For example, the semantic feature or meaning common to the word *thunder* and the metaphorical phrase *thunderous applause* is that of a big noise. But in Mildred Taylor's title *Roll of Thunder, Hear My Cry* there is no such simple explanation. The idea of noise is still there, but added to it is the idea of size and relativity. It is the power of all nature contrasted to the smallness of one human voice. Additionally, there's the negativeness, the ominous feeling that is communicated through the mention of a storm and the word *cry* which has a negative or at least a serious connotation as compared, for example, with *shout* or *yell*. Yet, in spite of this, the title has an optimistic ring to it, probably because the reader intuitively recognizes the strength of the voice behind the *my*. Weak characters hide under the bedcovers during a thunderstorm. Only the strong stand in the storm and yell back. (pp. 48-9)

*Kenneth L. Donelson and Alleen Pace Nilsen, "Literary Aspects of Young Adult Books," in their* Literature for Today's Young Adults, *Scott, Foresman and Company, 1980, pp. 24-54.\**

Mildred Taylor, in *Roll of Thunder, Hear My Cry,* comes closer than anyone else to giving us a really good novel about racial prejudice. She is perhaps not so strong on its origins as James Vance Marshall [is in *Walkabout*]; and, like him, she does not put her story in modern urban terms, opting to set it in the rural American south in the nineteen-thirties. But she is excellent on the *effects* of racial prejudice. She may not analyze in depth the motives behind the actions of her white characters, but their nastiness, their selfishness and greed, their inability to see blacks as human beings, come over vividly to the reader. It's impossible not to feel anger and a sense of burning injustice in reading this book, and the fact that one does so is a measure of the author's success in bringing to life in words both the petty nuisances the blacks have to put up with in her story—shop-keepers serving white people first; black children obtaining copies of school books that are considered no longer fit for white children to use; blacks walking to school while the whites have their own bus—but also the really vile horrors: blacks being hanged for crimes whites would not even be prosecuted for; attacks at night on homes, houses burned down; people maimed and crippled for life.

As literature *Roll of Thunder, Hear My Cry* is undoubtedly superior to *Walkabout;* characterization, narrative skill, command of English, are all of a higher order than in James Vance Marshall's novel. Its only weakness is that Mildred Taylor seems uncertain about how much she can involve the children—Cassie and Stacey Logan, the central characters—in areas that are the preserve of the adults: the result is that she is obliged, too often, to make them eavesdrop at keyholes or through floorboards on their parents' discussions of what atrocities have recently occurred, and what actions should be taken in reprisal. In the incidents where the children are directly involved and the adults are absent, the writing has a freshness and a directness that is not always so evident in those parts of the story where they are listeners. Their father's talks with the lawyer, Mr. Jamison, for instance, or Mama's plans for boycotting the Wallaces' shop, are not so exciting as Little Man's confrontation with his teacher over the tattered book, or Stacey's highly successful plan to get his own back on the odious bus driver by digging a pot-hole in the road. And the scene where Cassie, as a result of devious plotting and controlling her anger for weeks, gives Lillian Jean her come-uppance, has a marvelous feeling of relief and release, of the sweetness of revenge. . . . (pp. 108-09)

Cassie and Stacey may not be direct participants in the worst evils that occur but they are eye-witnesses to some of them. The spine-tingling fear, the awful insecurity that life in the South—or any place where racial prejudice is so strong—can produce in the victims is conveyed to the reader in no uncertain terms. (pp. 109-10)

Cassie's family, more than most blacks in the area, are marked out for victimization. They aren't poverty-stricken illiterate cotton-pickers; they're intelligent, educated people, owners of four hundred acres of land. . . . They are much more of a threat to white supremacy than the blacks who accept the status quo, who mind their own business and bow like reeds before the

storm. A great deal of the tension in the story is produced by the feeling that the Logans may have overreached themselves and become the obvious targets for the next burning or killing. True, Papa is fired at and his leg broken as the result of the horse bolting in fright when it hears the gun-shot, but the family escapes the worst atrocities one fears may be in store for them. This does not mean that Mildred Taylor has shirked the issue, feeling, perhaps, that it isn't a suitable subject for a children's book; rather it is a tribute to the skill and cunning one particular family exercises in self-defense and deflecting the attacks on itself. The full weight of racist violence falls on the hapless lad, T. J. Avery, and here the author does perhaps make a concession to the fact that she is writing a children's book rather than a novel for adults. T. J.'s fate—a trial on a murder charge and hanging as the almost inevitable result—would have been exceptionally harrowing for the child reader if it had been made the fate of a member of the Logan family, and Mildred Taylor may well have felt that she did not want to put her audience through such an experience. Perhaps that is an underestimation of what the young can take, but as the book is to a large extent based on real events that happened to the author's father and his family, it would be quite absurd to fault her for telling the truth!

Though T. J. is only fourteen, and the white boys, who are more responsible than he is for Mr. Barnett's death, escape unpunished, the full horror of the tragic waste of a young life is mitigated to some extent by the fact that T. J. is on the whole a thoroughly detestable person; a cheat, a liar, and a thief; the cause of Mrs. Logan losing her job; someone who will side with the whites to the detriment of the blacks when it furthers his own selfish aims. The uneasy friendship between him and Stacey turns to open hostility when T. J. obtains Stacey's winter overcoat under false pretences, and for most of the book the Logan family dislike and disapprove of him, realizing that he is as much of a threat to them as the whites are. The Logans are, of course, as appalled as anyone else by what happens to him, and the ambivalence Cassie feels about this is very well rendered. The last paragraphs of the book show an interesting stage in Cassie's growing up—a discovery that all is not, metaphorically speaking, black and white, that there are grey areas which are very hard to pinpoint, to sum up, which do demand contradictions of feeling. . . . (pp. 110-12)

*David Rees, "The Color of Skin: Mildred Taylor," in his* The Marble in the Water: Essays on Contemporary Writers of Fiction for Children and Young Adults, *The Horn Book, Inc., 1980, pp. 104-13.*

The claim that I think must underlie some of the most imaginative kinds of fiction for young people today must be that to treat [contemporary themes] at all, and at all well, is fully possible, and that fiction at its best can provide a unique and valuably private experience of some of the central issues of modern life. Mildred Taylor's *Roll of Thunder, Hear My Cry* achieves this, set in the race-riot torn Southern States during the 1930s, seen from the viewpoint of nine-year-old Cassie, and full of episodes of emotional power which eventually crash over in a crescendo of horror. The deep insults implied in simple events, like walking along a road and being splashed by the white man's car, like being ignored in the local store for being black, are seen and confronted with a fresh innocence which grows into a fresh and hating disillusionment, and then into pure terror as the lynch mob come after Cassie's folks. There is, too, just a hint of the adult view at the end as Cassie 'cries for T. J. For T. J. and the land'. . . . Moving on beyond the obvious can sometimes benefit from this implied adult perspective, since it suggests larger issues, the element of the unknown in the future, the disturbing thought that perhaps the future will not be able to find easy answers either, and that the narrator himself / herself is still around (in fiction or reality), still brooding thoughtfully on the event. (p. 175)

*Stuart Hannabuss, "Beyond the Formula: Part II," in* The Junior Bookshelf, *Vol. 46, No. 5, October, 1982, pp. 173-76.**

---

### LET THE CIRCLE BE UNBROKEN  (1981)

**"Let the Circle Be Unbroken"** is a powerful novel, marketed for young adults but capable of touching readers of any age. It focuses attention on large-scale issues and events as well as smaller happenings and personal emotions, interweaving the intimate details of family life and growing up with dramatic and chilling lessons on racism.

It is a book that balances by contrast. The strength, love, dignity, and integrity of the close-knit black community stand out in sharp distinction against the greed, corruption, cruelty, and hatred they face. (p. B1)

Overpowering the bitter and dramatic examples of oppression and racism, the rich, strong love of the Logan family carries the story. Like **"Roll of Thunder, Hear My Cry,"** this is a celebration of black family strength and continuity.

It is also a story of emerging adolescence. Stacey strains to be grown, eager to help support the farm. His impatience causes him to act foolishly, and he is rescued only through his family's perseverence. Cassie struggles with maturity, wishing things could remain unchanged. She begins to learn what it means to be a black woman in the South. Though many of Cassie and Stacey's experiences happen because they are black, their growing pains and self-discovery are universal.

This story is shaped by Mildred Taylor's clear, smooth, and graceful language, which evokes the wide rolling fields and stands of trees, the wooden cabins warmed by fires; children and adults alike come to life, each unique and charged with individuality. The dialogue is sharp and quick, filled with emotion and often with humor. Cassie relates the story with understanding, compassion, and vitality.

**"Let the Circle Be Unbroken"** draws us into the circle of an inspiring black family, nourishes us with their strength and love, and shows us their sustaining traditions, heritage, and community. This is a novel that has so much of what we need today: hard truth courageously told, deep love that binds and strengthens, dignity in the face of oppression, and warmth and humor rooted in compassion. The Logans' story will strengthen and satisfy all who read it. (p. B11)

*Christine McDonnell, "Powerful Lesson of Family Love," in* The Christian Science Monitor, *October 14, 1981, pp. B1, B11.*

Most children are not juvenile, most of the time. It is not their nature. Writers as diverse as Jean Piaget and Herbert Kohl have made this truth widely available. Nonetheless, because Mildred Taylor recognizes that children, to use an expression of a friend of mine, are as serious as snakebite, her books represent an exceptional achievement. The children in them do not trifle or dally or "kid around," whether they're gambling for marbles or teaching somebody how to comprehend the Constitution of the State of Mississippi. . . .

Cassie occupies the foreground as the storyteller; we hear, see, move and retrace events in step with her unpredictable, but always fast, pace. Such a complicated, agile and irrepressible live wire!

I would suppose that readers of all ages will constitute the audience for this hilarious and harrowing work. The language remains accessible to the relatively young, the plot never convolutes into the unfathomable, and the issues examined (Federal entry into local arrangements for land use and distribution, class versus race unity) should readily compel the willing attention of the thoughtful reader. (p. 55)

Miss Taylor provides her readers with a literal sense of witnessing important American history. Through a narrative laden with dramatic tension and virtuoso characterization we come, humbly, to understand what it was like when a white boy of 14 could call a black child's mother by her first name and rightly expect her to answer him as *Sir,* or when an elderly black woman, hoping "to qualify" to vote, might spend hours memorizing the State Constitution under the tutelage of an 11-year-old girl only to be met with public humiliation.

Moreover, Miss Taylor never neglects the details of her volatile 11-year-old heroine's interior life. The daydreams, the jealousy, the incredible ardor of that age come alive. . . . (pp. 55, 58)

The character of Cassie Logan bids fair to become a folk favorite on the level of Huckleberry Finn, even as this new series by Mildred Taylor creates its own place next to such classics as Wilder's "Little House on the Prairie." (p. 58)

*June Jordan, "Mississippi in the Thirties," in* The New York Times Book Review, *November 15, 1981, pp. 55, 58.*

When did life experience become history? A musical biography of Jackie Robinson was greeted with bafflement by the generation in which minorities dominate sports. Martin Luther King, Jr.'s strategy, as well as his "dream," need no explaining to one who witnessed George Wallace on the schoolhouse steps, and Bull Connor's dogs, by way of the television news. But what about white youngsters who know only busing and affirmative action? And black youngsters with a 1981 militant sensibility who do not see the courage and dignity in passive resistance? Mildred Taylor's saga of the Logan family can help fill the void between the generations. . . .

The narrative unfolds from the viewpoint of eleven-year-old Cassie. When this girl, who has never seen indoor plumbing before, innocently sends her younger brothers to a restroom, and drinks from the "wrong" fountain, only to be hastily warned away, her incredulity and fear are our own. Cassie's viewpoint is consistently and skillfully maintained, enhancing the illusion of life as it is happening, with its shock of the unexpected, and its suspense about the unknown future. . . .

My one reservation about this book may be inherent in its nature as a sequel. There is a sense of crowding in the first few pages, of re-introducing numerous characters and recapitulating facts from the previous book. Apart from recommending reading the other book first, I would urge young readers to hold on through those initial awkward pages, and then to go on to enjoy a reading adventure.

*Melanie Eiger, in a review of "Let the Circle Be Unbroken," in* Best Sellers, *Vol. 41, No. 11, February, 1982, p. 444.*

Years of oppression and cruelty are recalled strongly in *Let the Circle be Unbroken,* not from first-hand but with the force, the authenticity and, above all, the bitterness of family history. . . . A book of tighter construction than its predecessors, this one has the same occasional hysterical note which, however much one may attribute it to the youthful narrator, does make for a certain artistic monotony; as a whole, the book could benefit from an occasional relaxing of tension and a greater isolation of the most dramatically telling moments. Sincerity and documentation of this calibre deserves the best possible literary presentation.

> *Margery Fisher, in a review of "Let the Circle Be Unbroken," in her* Growing Point, *Vol. 20, No. 6, March, 1982, p. 4033.*

[In *Let the Circle Be Unbroken,* as in *Roll of Thunder, Hear My Cry,*] the fear, the cruelty and the bewildering injustice of a hopelessly racist society are transcended by a family's strength, self-respect, and determination. The characters, both young and old, in all their variety and individuality come alive with penetrating humanness, while the effect of the storytelling is intensified by a lean, understated style and made more poignant by touches of lyrical sensitivity. (p. 174)

> *Ethel L. Heins, in a review of "Let the Circle Be Unbroken," in* The Horn Book Magazine, *Vol. LVIII, No. 2, April, 1982, pp. 173-74.*

This second chronicle of the Logans, a black Mississippi family, is remarkably powerful and moving. It is a horrifyingly authentic indictment of the white landowners in the worst depression of the mid-thirties. . . . Because Mildred Taylor understands her people from within, she draws her characters with passionate sympathy, and because she is a first-rate writer, she avoids all suggestion of preaching and lets the facts speak for themselves. She has found a way of reproducing the Southern manner of speech without making the reader aware of effort or unnaturalness. And she is fair—there are good whites as well, though they too are powerless against the landowners. . . . Memorable among many striking characters are the mysterious strong silent Wardell, with dog-like devotion to Cassie, and his mother Mrs Lee Annie, who teaches herself the law, to attempt to exercise her legal right to vote—with tragic consequences. The changing seasons and the countryside are depicted beautifully, and make bearable the strong tensions and harrowing incidents.

> *M. Hobbs, in a review of "Let the Circle Be Unbroken," in* The Junior Bookshelf, *Vol. 46, No. 3, June, 1982, p. 112.*

# Vera B. Williams

## 1927-

American author/illustrator and illustrator of picture books.

Williams's picture books convey the warmth of family love and the importance of shared experience. She is best known for her "Rosa" series—*A Chair for My Mother, Something Special for Me,* and *Music, Music for Everyone*—which features an urban Hispanic family whose concern for each other helps them to meet financial difficulties with equanimity. A strong supporter of the feminist, peace, and nuclear freeze movements, Williams champions feminism in her books by portraying strong, caring women who overcome odds to accomplish their goals.

*A Chair for My Mother* recounts the efforts of Rosa, her hardworking mother, and resourceful grandmother to save enough money to purchase a comfortable overstuffed chair. *Something Special for Me* describes Rosa's dilemma in deciding what she wants for her birthday, while *Music, Music for Everyone* finds Rosa forming a band to earn money for her grandmother who is ill. Told in Rosa's simple yet expressive words, the series communicates the harshness of living with economic limitations while emphasizing life's inherent richness. These books also highlight the special relationship between generations in Rosa's community, and portray her as a particularly thoughtful child. Williams translates the heartfelt emotions of the stories into her illustrations. Using a primitive folk art technique and bright colors, she creates childlike watercolors which are surrounded with cheerful borders that incorporate related motifs.

Two of Williams's earlier works, *Three Days on a River in a Red Canoe* and *The Great Watermelon Birthday,* also reflect her interest in family and community solidarity. Inspired by Williams's 500-mile trip on the Yukon River, *Three Days* details the experiences of two young cousins and their mothers who are depicted as independent people with a sense of adventure and a desire to keep nature unpolluted. The story combines fiction with nonfiction by the inclusion of recipes, wildlife identifications, and instructions for putting up a tent and building a fire. Illustrated with soft crayon drawings, the book reads like an enthusiastic child's journal. In *The Great Watermelon Birthday,* an elderly couple who own a fruit market celebrate the birth of their first great-grandchild by offering free watermelons to any child born on the same day. The owners' generosity prompts a party attended by one thousand neighborhood residents. Williams has also created a cookbook, *It's a Gingerbread House: Bake It! Build It! Eat It!,* that is noted for being simple yet complete.

Raised in New York City during the Depression, Williams was often supported by her mother, who also found time to assist the needy of their neighborhood; *A Chair for My Mother* is dedicated to her and is based on an incident from Williams's childhood. After attending New York's High School of Music and Art, where she produced her first children's book, Williams received a degree in graphic arts from Black Mountain College, an experimental school where learning was considered a group activity. She believes that all her avocations are a result of the holistic philosophy she learned at Black Mountain.

Photograph by Susan Hirschman. By permission of Greenwillow Books (A Division of William Morrow

After graduation, Williams helped to found an alternative school for children as well as The Gate Hill Cooperative, which she calls an "intentional community." Williams has also run a bakery and has been a cook in schools and restaurants; food is central to *It's a Gingerbread House* and plays a subsidiary role in *Three Days on a River in a Red Canoe.*

Critics commend the engaging simplicity, spontaneity, depth of feeling, and positive messages which pervade Williams's works. Applauding her verbal and artistic ability to capture a range of emotions without melodrama, reviewers especially note the gaiety and exuberance of her paintings in the "Rosa" series. Williams's natural and objective presentation of family life and her attention to universal values has brought her acclaim as a sensitive and vibrant contributor to contemporary children's literature.

In 1983, *A Chair for My Mother* was a Caldecott Honor Book and received the *Boston Globe-Horn Book* Award for illustration; in 1984, it won the Other Award.

(See also *Something about the Author,* Vol. 33.)

------

*IT'S A GINGERBREAD HOUSE: BAKE IT! BUILD IT! EAT IT!*
(1978)

Complete directions for making a gingerbread house, with all the trimmings, form the bulk of this attractive book. It begins as a story, in which three children receive an irresistible house and, after nibbling it down to plainness, find instructions for duplicating it inside. The directions are thorough and careful, from pattern making, dough mixing, and baking to building and decorating. Bright-colored pictures are a useful guide.

> *A review of "It's a Gingerbread House: Bake It, Build It, Eat It!" in* Booklist, *Vol. 75, No. 6, November 15, 1978, p. 553.*

[*It's a Gingerbread House: Bake It! Build It! Eat It!*] is my favorite cookbook of the season. . . . I can assure you that your young reading friends will run to the store for all the ingredients needed to build these fabulous houses which, heretofore, have remained mainly bakery shop items. . . . P.S. If I can follow the directions given in this "Read-Alone Guide," you can be sure that you can, too! Yum! Yum!

> *Barbara Ann Kyle, "It's a Gingerbread House: Bake It! Build It! Eat It!" in* The Babbling Bookworm, *Vol. 6, No. 11, December, 1978, p. 2.*

[*It's a Gingerbread House*] is reminiscent of those elaborate holiday projects in women's magazines: admiringly one reads all the complicated directions, then surreptitiously, turns the page. The directions for this project are clearly presented in story format, but it's obviously a time-consuming undertaking requiring patient adult help. This reviewer unashamedly, unprofessionally admits to not trying it out: deep down, she knew her roof would crack.

> *A review of "It's a Gingerbread House," in* School Library Journal, *Vol. 25, No. 4, December, 1978, p. 65.*

---

## THE GREAT WATERMELON BIRTHDAY (1980)

This enumeration of children and relatives, what they bring to a community birthday party, and how they celebrate one summer evening might hold some interest for youngsters. The small, scratchy drawings are suited to the text, and could be enjoyed by one child, but not by a group. Overall this is a gentle episode in the style of *Jenny's Birthday*, but it is not a "grabber," in spite of some nice touches.

> *Jody Berge, in a review of "The Great Watermelon Birthday," in* Children's Book Review Service, *Vol. 8, No. 6, February, 1980, p. 52.*

The watermelon pink end papers scattered with large black seeds, may be the best part of the book. . . . [The] text seems to pull more punches than it lands, and its laid-back, deadpan, low-keyed style seems contrary to its purpose. . . . The author uses fine line drawings to depict the celebrants and color for the melons. There's a quality of humor here which tries too hard, and that may be what's wrong.

> *Joan W. Blos, in a review of "The Great Watermelon Birthday," in* School Library Journal, *Vol. 26, No. 7, March, 1980, p. 126.*

99 watermelons, two large honeydew melons, 100 birthday children, 1000 guests, and no story whatever. . . . [It] takes more than balloons and a general good time to make a picture book. Though Williams' casual line drawings show crowds of people enjoying themselves, they're not the sort of crowd scenes that have little individual jokes or dramas packed in for the amusement of observant viewers. Though tricky and pleasant,

they seem better suited to birthday-party paper table ware than to hard-cover production.

> *A review of "The Great Watermelon Birthday," in* Kirkus Reviews, *Vol. XLVIII, No. 6, March 15, 1980, p. 361.*

There really isn't much to this, yet it generates such warm feelings of family participation and community enterprise, and such cheerfulness and simplicity in conception that it's engaging. . . . Children should enjoy the listing of participants ("82 little brothers . . . 70 fathers, 22 stepfathers . . . 51 grandmothers . . . 133 friends and neighbors . . . 41 aunts . . . and 1 great-great-grandmother"). The small line drawings, black and white, have green and pink (whole and cut) watermelons and balloons in festive contrast. (pp. 163-64)

> *Zena Sutherland, in a review of "The Great Watermelon Birthday," in* Bulletin of the Center for Children's Books, *Vol. 33, No. 8, April, 1980, pp. 163-64.*

---

## THREE DAYS ON A RIVER IN A RED CANOE (1981)

The fun, excitement, and sometimes scary experiences of a canoe trip are enthusiastically related as the young narrator, his cousin, and their mothers set off on a three-day holiday. Through crisp journal-style entries (jarred by frequent tense changes) and affectionately rendered, soft, Crayola-colored illustrations, the practicalities of putting up a tent, making dumplings, and preparing fruit stew (recipes included) are shown. The relaxed camaraderie of catching fish, telling stories, and feeding ducks balances the suspense of an unexpected dunking and a fierce storm. Knowledgeable as well as would-be campers will enjoy following the red canoe as it skims its way through the pages to a happy-to-be-home conclusion.

> *Barbara Elleman, in a review of "Three Days on a River in a Red Canoe," in* Booklist, *Vol. 77, No. 19, June 1, 1981, p. 1302.*

The jacket simulates an exercise-book cover, the crayon drawings are suggestive of a child's, the opening words put you in her place—"I was the one who first noticed the red canoe for sale in a yard on the way home from school." And then we are off on a three-day canoe trip, picture-mapped at the outset, with "My mom and my aunt Rosie and my cousin Sam." As presented, it's an adventure for the reader or looker-on too. The words "We drove and drove / and drove and drove . . ." rise and dip, with the little car, across the top and bottom of the wide page; **"Our First Morning on the River"** brings a double-page spread of multiple activities. . . . Fish jump around—pictured and labeled; an accident occurs—after which Sam, the culprit, "gets up as though the canoe were a baby's cradle." The resonant wordings, the eventfulness, the information—plus the spontaneity and contagious delight—combine into an experience that can be relived, with new discoveries, again and again.

> *A review of "Three Days on a River in a Red Canoe," in* Kirkus Reviews, *Vol. XLIX, No. 12, June 15, 1981, p. 737.*

In an unusually attractive book a canoe trip for two children and two adults is recorded with all its interesting detail in a spontaneous first-person account and engaging full-color drawings on carefully designed pages. . . . The profusion of disarmingly naïve pictures shows the progress of the journey—along with such essential procedures as assembling supplies, packing,

building a fire, cooking . . . , knot-tying, and putting up a tent—and accurately delineates the fish, waterfowl, and other wildlife encountered on the way. (pp. 418-19)

> *Ethel L. Heins, in a review of "Three Days on a River in a Red Canoe," in* The Horn Book Magazine, *Vol. LVII, No. 4, August, 1981, pp. 418-19.*

What could have been a jumble of facts and fiction succeeds because of its careful incorporation of information into the text via cheerful crayon pictures (excuse the cut-off caption in the pictorial map of **"Our First Morning on the River"**) and a childlike text certain to have young readers begging for their own three days.

> *Marilyn Payne Phillips, in a review of "Three Days on a River in a Red Canoe," in* School Library Journal, *Vol. 28, No. 4, December, 1981, p. 58.*

---

### *A CHAIR FOR MY MOTHER* (1982)

#### AUTHOR'S COMMENTARY

[There are] deeply moving aspects of this occasion [winning The *Boston Globe-Horn Book* Award for illustration] I want to tell you of, and I expect I'll have a somewhat harder time explaining just where these feelings are rooted than I have with the obvious joy and celebration of the experience.

It has something to do with being welcomed and honored by a community I respect, owe much to, and love. . . . [About fifty years ago], I was entered into the community of the library. At once I went and took out a book called *The Poppy Seed Cakes* (Doubleday). . . . I loved the pictures. It occurs to me to note that the borders of *A Chair for My Mother,* though so different from the borders in *The Poppy Seed Cakes,* probably owe their dim beginnings to this book. Of course, there's no way to be certain of such origins, but it is exciting to look back over the years and see the strands braiding up their many ways.

One strand I do feel certain about is my mother. I dedicated *A Chair for My Mother* to her, but that was just the final naming. I had, in a way, made the whole book for her. . . . It's not that my book is about her in a biographical way. She was not tall and dark-haired but short and carrot-topped. There was never a fire in our house as there is in my book. Although I have worked in restaurants, my mother worked most of her life in shops, offices, and hospitals. And I doubt that she or any other real parent (certainly not I) was ever as patient as were the mother and the grandmother in the book. Truthfully, we never had a chair covered in velvet with roses all over it. In fact, the book is a re-formed story about a chair we actually did have in our lives. The story went like this.

Like many families during the Depression, we often moved. And we had very little furniture; my parents did not much value possessions. They looked critically at those suites of heavy dark furniture crammed into the small flats of our neighbors. They knew how painfully these suites were acquired by struggling young families, often to be repossesed for default of a month's payment or set out on the street in an eviction for overdue rent. Such chairs and sofas made me sad. They came to symbolize the unjust and depressing facts of economic life. I saw the lack of such furniture in our own apartments (some twelve in all by the time I grew up) as a refreshing offer of freedom.

But one day my sister and I came home from school, and there was a new chair. It was green and upholstered. A real chair, not just a kitchen chair. My mother had recently found a job . . . and so made a down payment on the chair. After that, it seemed, when my sister or I would ask for a nickel or some pennies to get something or to go somewhere, my mother would say we had to save our money to make the monthly chair payments. I hated to hear how worried she sounded, so one day I yelled at her in my uncompromising way, "But why did you buy the chair now? Why didn't you wait till we really had money to pay for it?" And she told me with great dignity, "I don't intend to work all my life and have nowhere to sit down."

Of course I felt that terrible mixture of guilt and righteousness that a person—child or adult—feels in such a situation. I knew as sure as I knew anything that my mother should have a chair. . . . My father often had no job, and she supported us; but she was also busy—as so many people were—helping to carry back the chairs (or the boxes used as chairs) for evicted families or trying to find a free dentist for some child, free piano lessons for another, or summer camps for the whole neighborhood.

By the time I got around to making my book, she richly deserved a super real chair—one with roses all over it. . . . As you can probably tell, I have a particular affection for this little book I've made. It's embarrassing, but it's true. I've liked my other books, too, but in this one I take particular pride. And it is because I became very involved in trying to express these childhood emotions, along with a certain wholeness I value greatly—a kind of amalgam that is so well named for me by the phrase "Bread and Roses."

I take this good-smelling and good-tasting phrase from a song. . . . It was written for and sung by the women of the textile mills of Lawrence, Massachusetts, around 1928 in a strike both famous and infamous. The song is about how the women and the girls, who banded together with great constancy and devotion at that time, were doing it not only for the bread they so desperately needed for their families but also for the roses. They were telling that they needed, just as desperately, a chance to have some beauty and joy in their overworked lives. And, of course, this is what my parents' lives were very much about, and it has been part of my life, too. . . . (pp. 35-7)

Now, I don't mean to say I had anything like a developed intention to express all this when I set upon making this book. But I *did* have the feeling that some long-gestating baby was trying to be born. I sensed it as I worked at my drawing board day afer day, as cups and saucers, salt shakers and roses, checkered borders and onions, jars of money, neighbors bearing gifts, fire engines, and sad faces confronting the ashes of their home all took form upon the pages—scenes I did not know I knew. I saw myself using more colors than I had ever used before, searching out the brightest I could buy and working out ways to make them appear even brighter. Then, . . . when I stayed up all night painting roses to go on the back of the jacket and then yet another night when it turned out that those roses wouldn't reproduce properly because, in my passion to make pink pinker and red redder, I had used some ink that was fluorescent—well, then I knew I had indeed been trying to make something really full, a testament to my feeling for the values and people of my childhood. (p. 38)

*Vera B. Williams, in the Boston Globe-Horn Book Award Acceptance Speech given at the meeting of the New England Library Association in Hyannis, Massachusetts, on October 31, 1983, in The Horn Book Magazine, Vol. LX, No. 1, February, 1984, pp. 34-8.*

---

Color-splashed watercolors recalling the patterns of Matisse and the primitive quality of Gauguin evoke the love and warmth among a child, her mother, and her grandmother. Sitting in their kitchen, with its mottled linoleum and old-fashioned white appliances, they count the tips the mother earned as a waitress at the Blue Tile Diner. The money—like all their spare change—is put into a large glass jar; when they "can't get a single other coin into the jar," they will take the money and buy "a won-

derful, beautiful, fat, soft armchair" to replace the chairs and sofa the family lost in a fire. At last, the jar is full, and the three set out to shop for the chair, stopping only when they find one that lives up to their dreams—a gloriously overstuffed armchair covered in red upholstery splashed with large pink roses. The cheerful paintings take up the full left-hand page and face, in most cases, a small chunk of text set against a modulated wash of a complementing color; a border containing a pertinent motif surrounds the two pages, further unifying the design. The result is a superbly conceived picture book expressing the joyful spirit of a loving family.

*Kate M. Flanagan, in a review of "A Chair for My Mother," in The Horn Book Magazine, Vol. LVIII, No. 5, October, 1982, p. 514.*

A tender knockout—from the author/illustrator of, most recently and auspiciously, *Three Days on a River in a Red Canoe.* "My mother works as a waitress in the Blue Tile Diner," the little-girl narrator begins—and to the accompaniment of vividly colored, direct, proto-primitive pictures, the real-life-like story comes out. . . . [The sequence in which the mother, grandmother, and child shop for the chair] is a glory: Grandma feeling like Goldilocks, trying out all the chairs; the very rose-covered chair "we were all dreaming of," plump in the middle of the floor; the little girl and her mother, snuggled in it together . . . and she can reach right up "and turn out the light if I fall asleep in her lap." It's rare to find so much vitality, spontaneity, *and* depth of feeling in such a simple, young book.

*A review of "A Chair for My Mother," in Kirkus Reviews, Vol. L, No. 19, October 1, 1982, p. 1104.*

If the plot is scant, . . . the atmosphere of anticipation and family warmth is strong. Williams' illustrations are energetic watercolor paintings brimming with color and a cozy, indulgent expressionism. Intense roses, blues, yellows, and greens vie for attention in the picures' blocky compositions, where natty patterning adds extra spice. A striking, offbeat backdrop for a loving story.

*Denise M. Wilms, in a review of "A Chair for My Mother," in Booklist, Vol. 79, No. 5, November 1, 1982, p. 375.*

[Almost every page] vibrates with primary colors so intense and warm you can almost feel them physically. They're so strong that they come near to overpowering the slight story. . . . Cleverly designed borders around each pair of facing pages are keyed to the text, and there are many charming spot drawings, as well. The only pictures with diminished color are those showing the apartment fire that burned up the comfortable furniture; before that, Williams utilized a hazy gray shading to foreshadow the tragedy. Getting over such an experience with the loving help of family and friends is one of the author-artist's themes, as is also the simple pleasure of working toward an obtainable goal.

*Michele Slung, "Picture Palettes," in Book World—The Washington Post, November 7, 1982, p. 16.\**

*A Chair for My Mother* is a sensitively written, beautifully illustrated story about a working-class family. . . . The characters are sympathetically and believably portrayed, with a mother who is sometimes so tired she falls asleep at the kitchen table after a long work day. . . .

There is a gentle, loving quality to the relationships between the characters in this small family, especially as we see them

Right outside our house stood two big fire engines. I could see lots of smoke. Tall orange flames came out of the roof. All the neighbors stood in a bunch across the street. Mama grabbed my hand and we ran. My uncle Sandy saw us and ran to us. Mama yelled, "Where's Mother?" I yelled, "Where's my grandma?" My aunt Ida waved and shouted, "She's here, she's here. She's O.K. Don't worry."

Grandma was all right. Our cat was safe too, though it took a while to find her. But everything else in our whole house was spoiled.

*From* A Chair for My Mother, *written and illustrated by Vera B. Williams. Greenwillow Books, 1982.*

counting coins together at the end of the day. The highlight of the story is, of course, when enough is saved to shop for the long-awaited chair, and the warm, cheerful illustrations contribute to the pleasure of watching the family try out all the chairs in the store.

Working-class children will recognize the joy of saving to buy something special; and those who are more affluent may be made aware that comfort is not always a matter of immediate gratification, but sometimes has to be worked and waited for. All children will see a family and community of people who care about and support one another in hard times.

> *Leonore Gordon, in a review of "A Chair for My Mother," in* Interracial Books for Children Bulletin, *Vol. 14, No. 6, 1983, p. 19.*

The whole of each page in this picture story book from America glows with colour and warmth. The text is printed over a colour wash which tones with the full-colour illustration on the opposite page, and the border around each double-page spread attracts a second and third look. There is a glow in the story too. . . . The writing is as important as the pictures: it could only be this particular girl telling this particular story in a voice all her own.

> *Mary Steele, "Picture Books & Illustrated Stories 6 to 9: 'A Chair for My Mother'," in* The Signal Review of Children's Books 2: A Selective Guide to Picture Books, Fiction, Plays, Poetry, Information Books Published during 1983, *edited by Nancy Chambers, The Thimble Press, 1984, p. 12.*

---

### SOMETHING SPECIAL FOR ME   (1983)

The coins accumulating in the jar first bought *A Chair for My Mother* . . . ; now the coins are to be used for Rosa's birthday present. She and her mother go downtown so Rosa can pick out what she wants most. She has difficulty choosing but when the right present appears, Rosa is quick to know it. A street-

corner musician playing the accordion brings memories of Rosa's grandmother making ". . . even the chairs and tables dance" when she played the accordion. Rosa's gift of an accordion and lessons is exactly right. This is a sensitive depiction of a warm and loving family; much depth of feeling is shown by the characters. The illustrations are bright, splashy watercolors which aptly convey the liveliness of the story. The format echoes that of the first book about Rosa: full-page paintings oppose paragraphs of text set on a watercolor background; both pages are surrounded by a border that creates a unified spread. A visual and emotional treat.

> *Ellen Fader, in a review of "Something Special for Me," in* School Library Journal, *Vol. 29, No. 8, April, 1983, p. 108.*

As in *A Chair for My Mother,* the sense of family love is strong; so are implicit values, as Rosa struggles to spend her money wisely. The accompanying full-color paintings are dense and colorful, with eclectic borders and a parade of appealingly homely faces that reflect the story's abundance of love. (p. 1099)

> *Denise M. Wilms, in a review of "Something Special for Me," in* Booklist, *Vol. 79, No. 16, April 15, 1983, pp. 1098-99.*

Repeating oneself is always risky, above all when it involves a sequel to something prized for its inventiveness. Vera B. Williams takes this gamble in her follow-up to **"A Chair for My Mother,"** last autumn's enjoyable tale of Rosa, a young Hispanic girl. . . .

Unnecessary efforts to connect that story with this new one make for a slow beginning, but our attention is deftly shifted to the dilemma Rosa faces on her birthday: What can she buy as a gift for herself with the hard-earned money the family has given her from the replenished jar? . . .

The prose is skillfully plain. It is through the book's pictures—framed watercolor compositions in Rosa's folk tradition, each denying poverty with its richness of color and detail—that we sense Rosa's real problem: whether she can enjoy a solitary treat at communal expense. With the help of a patient, playful mother, a street corner musician, some luck and her own good nature, Rosa discovers a glorious way to give a present to her family and herself.

*Janice Prindle, in a review of "Something Special for Me," in* The New York Times Book Review, *May 29, 1983, p. 18.*

Rosa, the engaging small heroine of *A Chair for My Mother* . . . , appears again in a delightful sequel. . . . Overall, the book suggests a quilt pieced together from family reminiscences; the warmth of the story is reflected in exuberant full-page illustrations executed with childlike naïveté. As in the first book, each one is integrated with the text by means of a border design derived from an implicit motif—a device which underscores the book's folk art quality. Simple yet effective, the story creates an impression of a household rich in love if not in possessions.

*Mary M. Burns, in a review of "Something Special for Me," in* The Horn Book Magazine, *Vol. LIX, No. 3, June, 1983, p. 296.*

Once again, Williams portrays a close extended family, successfully countering the stereotypical image of either the "complete" nuclear family or the "broken," "fatherless" family.

The story is primarily about the choices Rosa faces as she shops for her birthday present. What comes through, above all, is the adventure of Rosa's special outing with her mother, and Rosa's ability to accept and enjoy the challenge of having only enough to buy one thing she wants, difficult as that choice is. Rosa finally decides on a gift she can share with the entire family, and it is clear that she relishes the prospect of doing so.

Again, the author succeeds in making the reader sensitive to the struggles and decisions inherent in being poor, while not romanticizing it (as some writers are prone to do). We look forward to more of her books.

*Leonore Gordon, in a review of "Something Special for Me," in* Interracial Books for Children Bulletin, *Vol. 14, No. 6, 1983, p. 19.*

The many illustrations are in bold, strong colour and child-like style, with rather ugly caricature-like people, but the detail is lively and amusing. The spelling is American, but it is easily read and understood. Many little girls will sympathize with Rosa's predicament, but, apart from that the book is not very appealing and consequently rather expensive.

*A. Thatcher, in a review of "Something Special for Me," in* The Junior Bookshelf, *Vol. 48, No. 3, June, 1984, p. 123.*

---

*MUSIC, MUSIC FOR EVERYONE* (1984)

You might just well-up from the emotional charge of Williams' successor to *A Chair for My Mother* and *Something Special for Me*. It's the luminous tremor of the pictures, combined with what happens, that gives this a special vibrance. Grandma is sick, so the big, rose-print chair in the living room is often empty. Upstairs in bed, she likes it when Rosa and her friends play music for her: "Leora plays the drums, Mae plays the flute, Jenny plays the fiddle and I play my accordion." Worried because the big money jar is empty . . . , Rosa recalls her mother telling her about her other grandma, who played the accordion at parties and weddings, and was paid. Grandma's all for it. The Oak Street Band is formed; gets help, practices. And their first job is to play at a party for Leora's great-grandparents, to celebrate the 50th anniversary of their corner market. . . . The children are first shy, then they play and play "like a real band"—while a whirl of dancers young and old fills two wordless pages. The book closes in quiet exultation, with Rosa putting her share of the evening's money into the big jar. Brimming to look at—see Grandma calling out the

*From* Music, Music for Everyone, *written and illustrated by Vera B. Williams. Greenwillow Books, 1984. Copyright © 1984 by Vera B. Williams. All rights reserved. By permission of Greenwillow Books (A Division of William Morrow & Company, Inc.).*

window, with big snowflakes in her hair—and heart-catching, sometimes, to listen to.

> *A review of "Music, Music for Everyone," in* Kirkus Reviews, *Juvenile Issue, Vol. LII, Nos. 10-17, September 1, 1984, p. J-67.*

Exuding human caring, warmth, and love, the book is closely linked to its predecessors in characters, format, color, and style. Yet, its attractiveness and emotional truth notwithstanding, one does hope that the author-artist will now turn her impressive talents to something fresh and new.

> *Ethel L. Heins, in a review of "Music, Music for Everyone," in* The Horn Book Magazine, *Vol. LX, No. 5, September & October, 1984, p. 587.*

"The whole house seemed so empty and so quiet." And Rosa, in **"Music, Music for Everyone,"** is uneasy in empty, quiet rooms. . . .

But emptiness doesn't last long in Vera B. Williams's books. This is her sixth, the third featuring Rosa, and, like the earlier ones, it is a story of replenishment. When things get too quiet, Rosa takes out her accordion and fills the room with music. . . .

In Miss Williams's lovely watercolor illustrations, everyday things look special. Objects are lifted from the background of one picture and seen anew in another: the swan sprouting flowers from his back was Grandma's ceramic planter on an earlier page. A radio and a can of tomatoes seem out of the ordinary. Each illustration is framed, the frame itself fashioned from elements in the various pictures—tangerines, crackers, roses, stars. Miss Williams knows the kind of detail that children will spot as a sign of delight in the world. She spreads a picnic table; piles it high with pies, fruit, casseroles; sets in the middle a giant pink cake; and tops the cake with a miniature of the Oak Street Market, its tiny awning unfurled, pennants flying.

If Rosa's victory seems magically easy, that is the charm of the book. What seems magical isn't—a child really could do what Rosa does. There *is* a magic in real things, in food, music, friendship, love among the generations. Despite some ambiguity at the beginning (an ominous first page that could make you think Grandma has died), **"Music, Music for Everyone"** is a gently exuberant book.

> *Josephine Humphreys, in a review of "Music, Music for Everyone," in* The New York Times Book Review, *October 21, 1984, p. 35.*

This author-illustrator is a national treasure. This third book in a series . . . is as delicious as the first book . . . and that's saying it's superb. The art is beautiful, with many details and emotions young readers will enjoy. And the messages are all positive—family love, community cooperation, interracial friendship, and sharing among friends. Buy it for libraries and schools. Give it as a gift.

> *Lyla Hoffman, in a review of "Music, Music for Everyone," in* Interracial Books for Children Bulletin, *Vol. 15, Nos. 7 & 8, 1984, p. 33.*

[*A Chair for My Mother, Something Special for Me,* and *Music, Music for Everyone* all] have similar illustrations, watercolors smaller than page size surrounded by a watercolor border, which give the effect of a homemade book, a vividly personal child's album of pictures glued on colorful wrapping paper. This third story . . . is complete in itself, but it will have additional meaning when read with the previous books. . . . The last pages of Rosa's narrative are extraordinary pleasures: two pages surrounded by night and stars show families and neighbors caught up in joyous celebration. Then, as the text continues, in each corner of the next pages, families hug their girls proudly. Finally, as Rosa brings the story to an end, the tired musicians divide up the money they have earned. Community, family and personal triumphs converge, making unforgettable music for everyone. Rarely do books for young readers show multiracial, working class life with such ease and love.

> *Anna Biagioni Hart, in a review of "Music, Music for Everyone," in* School Library Journal, *Vol. 31, No. 4, December, 1984, p. 78.*

Williams's splashy, childlike, flower-strewn watercolors illustrate the latest enterprise by little Rosa. . . . Williams is unbeatable as an author-illustrator of simple, heartening stories with the implicit meaning: we are human and must be concerned with each other.

> *A review of "Music, Music for Everyone," in* Publishers Weekly, *Vol. 227, No. 1, January 4, 1985, p. 70.*

# APPENDIX

The following is a listing of all sources used in Volume 9 of *Children's Literature Review*. Included in this list are all copyright and reprint rights and acknowledgments for those essays for which permission was obtained. Every effort has been made to trace copyright, but if omissions have been made, please let us know.

**THE EXCERPTS IN CLR, VOLUME 9, WERE REPRINTED FROM THE FOLLOWING PERIODICALS:**

v. 59, March, 1982 for "Profile: Gerald McDermott" by David E. White; v. 59, May, 1982 for a review of "The Keeper of the Isis Light" by Ruth M. Stein; v. 60, March, 1983 for a review of "Howliday Inn" by Ruth M. Stein; v. 60, September, 1983 for a review of the "Jafta" books by Ronald A. Jobe; v. 61, January, 1984 for a review of "The Isis Pedlar" by Ronald A. Jobe; v. 61, January, 1984 for "On the Writing of 'The Isis Pedlar'" by Monica Hughes; v. 61, February, 1984 for a review of "A Medieval Feast" by Geneva T. VanHorne; v. 61, February, 1984 for a review of "A Medieval Feast" by Ronald A. Jobe; v. 61, September, 1984 for a review of "The Celery Stalks at Midnight" by Frances Graham. Copyright © 1976, 1980, 1981, 1982, 1983, 1984 by the National Council of Teachers of English. All reprinted by permission of the publisher and the respective authors.

*Library Journal,* v. 63, November 1, 1938; v. 64, November 1, 1939; v. 65, November 1, 1940; v. 77, September 15, 1952./ v. 91, November 15, 1966. Copyright © 1966 by Xerox Corporation. Reprinted from *Library Journal,* published by R.R. Bowker Co. (a Xerox company), by permission.

*The Library Quarterly,* v. 37, January, 1967. © 1967 by The University of Chicago. All rights reserved. Reprinted by permission.

*Life* Magazine, v. 46, April 6, 1959 © 1959 Time Inc. Reprinted with permission.

*The Lion and the Unicorn,* v. 4, Summer, 1980; v. 4, Winter, 1980-81; v. 6, 1982. Copyright © 1980, 1981, 1982 *The Lion and the Unicorn.* All reprinted by permission.

*The Listener,* v. 88, November 9, 1972 for "Popularisations" by Wallace Hildick. © British Broadcasting Corp. 1972. Reprinted by permission of the author.

*Maclean's Magazine,* v. 95, June 28, 1982. © 1982 by *Maclean's Magazine.* Reprinted by permission.

*National Review,* v. XXXVI, July 27, 1984. © by National Review, Inc., 150 East 35th Street, New York, NY 10016; 1984. Reprinted with permission.

*New Statesman,* v. LXIII, May 18, 1962; v. LXX, November 12, 1965; v. 85, May 25, 1973; v. 94, November 4, 1977; v. 106, December 2, 1983; v. 108, December 7, 1984. © 1962, 1965, 1973, 1977, 1983, 1984 The Statesman & Nation Publishing Co. Ltd. All reprinted by permission.

*New York Herald Tribune,* May 12, 1963. © 1963 I.H.T. Corporation. Reprinted by permission.

*New York Herald Tribune Book Review,* November 12, 1950; September 7, 1952; May 17, 1953; October 24, 1954; November 13, 1955; November 18, 1956; May 12, 1957; November 17, 1957; March 9, 1958; p. II, November 2, 1958; November 1, 1959; November 13, 1960. © 1950, 1952, 1953, 1954, 1955, 1956, 1957, 1958, 1959, 1960 I.H.T. Corporation. All reprinted by permission.

*New York Herald Tribune Books,* November 13, 1938; November 12, 1939; November 10, 1940. © 1938, 1939, 1940 I.H.T. Corporation. All reprinted by permission.

*New York Herald Tribune Weekly Book Review,* November 14, 1948. © 1948 I.H.T. Corporation. Reprinted by permission.

*New York Times Book Review,* November 14, 1937; November 13, 1938; October 15, 1939; October 13, 1940; November 16, 1947; October 10, 1948; November 13, 1949; November 19, 1950; September 7, 1952; April 5, 1953; September 12, 1954; p. II, November 13, 1955; p. II, November 18, 1956; March 17, 1957; October 6, 1957; November 17, 1957, May 4, 1958; May 11, 1958; October 5, 1958; August 30, 1959; August 28, 1960; September 9, 1962; p. II, November 11, 1962; April 14, 1963; January 26, 1964; November 8, 1964; December 20, 1964; January 30, 1966; p. II, November 6, 1966; January 29, 1967; April 30, 1967; February 11, 1968; p. II, November 3, 1968; p. II, May 4, 1969; August 24, 1969; December 14, 1969; November 7, 1971; March 12, 1972; January 20, 1974; May 4, 1975; November 16, 1975; July 11, 1976; February 26, 1978; April 8, 1979; September 30, 1979; November 11, 1979; November 18, 1979; April 27, 1980; November 9, 1980; March 8, 1981; November 15, 1981; May 29, 1983; October 16, 1983; October 21, 1984. Copyright © 1937, 1938, 1939, 1940, 1947, 1948, 1949, 1950, 1952, 1953, 1954, 1955, 1956, 1957, 1958, 1959, 1960, 1962, 1963, 1964, 1966, 1967, 1968, 1969, 1971, 1972, 1974, 1975, 1976, 1978, 1979, 1980, 1981, 1983, 1984 by the New York Times Company. All reprinted by permission.

*The New Yorker,* v. LX, December 3, 1984 for a review of "The Butter Battle Book" by Faith McNulty. © 1984 by the author. Reprinted by permission./ v. XXXIII, November 23, 1957; v. XXXV, November 21, 1959; v. XXXVI, November 19, 1960; v. XLIII, December 16, 1967; v. XLVI, December 14, 1968; v. LV, December 3, 1979. © 1957, 1959, 1960, 1967, 1968, 1979 by The New Yorker Magazine, Inc. All reprinted by permission.

*The Observer,* December 10, 1978; November 25, 1984. Both reprinted by permission of The Observer Limited.

*Publishers Weekly,* v. 224, July 22, 1983 for an interview with Aliki Brandenberg by Dulcy Brainard. Copyright © 1983 by Xerox Corporation. Reprinted by permission of the publisher and Dulcy Brainard./ v. 181, March 19, 1962; v. 191, May 15, 1967; v. 192, August 7, 1967. Copyright © 1962, 1967 by R.R. Bowker Company. All reprinted from *Publishers Weekly,* published by R.R. Bowker Company, by permission./ v. 196, November 24, 1969; v. 198, September 14, 1970; v. 198, December 7, 1970; v. 199, February 15, 1971; v. 207, February 3, 1975; v. 208, November 3, 1975; v. 208, December 15, 1975; v. 211, March 14, 1977; v. 215, February 12, 1979; v. 215, March 19, 1979; v. 215, June 18, 1979; v. 216, September 10, 1979; v. 216, October 15, 1979; v. 217, February 1, 1980; v. 217, May 30, 1980; v. 218, July 18, 1980; v. 221, March 5, 1982; v. 221, March 19, 1982; v. 221, May 21, 1982; v. 221, June 4, 1982; v. 223,

**THE EXCERPTS IN CLR, VOLUME 9, WERE REPRINTED FROM THE FOLLOWING BOOKS:**

Arbuthnot, May Hill, Sutherland, Zena, and Monson, Dianne L. From *Children and Books*. Sixth edition. Scott, Foresman, 1981. Copyright © 1981, 1977, 1972, 1964, 1957, 1947 by Scott, Foresman and Company. All rights reserved. Reprinted by permission.

Arbuthnot, May Hill, Margaret Mary Clark, Ruth M. Hadlow, and Harriet G. Long. From *Children's Books Too Good to Miss*. Revised edition. University Press Books, 1979. Copyright © 1979 by Educational Shipping Company. Reprinted by permission.

Arbuthnot, May Hill. From *Children's Reading in the Home*. Scott, Foresman, 1969. Copyright © 1969 by Scott, Foresman and Company. All rights reserved. Reprinted by permission.

Bader, Barbara. From *American Picture Books from Noah's Ark to the Beast Within*. Macmillan, 1976. Copyright © 1976 by Barbara Bader. All rights reserved. Reprinted with permission of Macmillan Publishing Company.

Baskin, Barbara H. and Karen H. Harris. From *Books for the Gifted Child*. Bowker, 1980. Copyright 1980 by Xerox Corporation. All rights reserved. Reprinted with permission of R. R. Bowker Company.

Bennett, Jill. From "Picture Books for Learning to Read: 'Avocado Baby'," in *The Signal Review 1: A Selective Guide to Children's Books, 1982*. Edited by Nancy Chambers. Thimble Press, 1983. Copyright © 1983 The Thimble Press. Reprinted by permission.

Broderick, Dorothy M. From *An Introduction to Children's Work in Public Libraries*. The H. W. Wilson Company, 1965. Copyright © 1965 by Dorothy M. Broderick. Reprinted by permission.

Cameron, Eleanor. From *The Green and Burning Tree: On the Writing and Enjoyment of Children's Books*. Little, Brown, 1969. Copyright © 1962, 1964, 1966, 1969 by Eleanor Cameron. All rights reserved. Reprinted by permission of Little, Brown and Company.

Chambers, Nancy, ed. *The Signal Review of Children's Books 2: A Selective Guide to Picture Books, Fiction, Plays, Poetry, Information Books Published during 1983*. Thimble Press, 1984. Copyright © 1984 The Thimble Press. Reprinted by permission.

Cianciolo, Patricia Jean. From *Books for Children*. Revised edition. American Library Association, 1981. Copyright © 1981 by the American Library Association. All rights reserved. Reprinted by permission.

Cianciolo, Patricia. From *Illustrations in Children's Books*. Second edition. Brown, 1976. Copyright © 1970, 1976 by Wm. C. Brown Company Publishers. All rights reserved. Reprinted by permission of the author.

Cott, Jonathan. From *Pipers at the Gates of Dawn: The Wisdom of Children's Literature*. Random House, 1983. Copyright © 1981, 1983 by Jonathan Cott. All rights reserved. Reprinted by permission of Random House, Inc.

Crouch, Marcus. From *The Nesbit Tradition: The Children's Novel in England 1945-1970*. Ernest Benn Limited, 1972. © Marcus Crouch 1972. Reprinted by permission of the author.

Crouch, Marcus. From *Treasure Seekers and Borrowers: Children's Books in Britain 1900-1960*. The Library Association, 1962. © Marcus Crouch, 1962. Reprinted by permission.

Cullinan, Bernice E., with Mary K. Karrer and Arlene M. Pillar. From *Literature and the Child*. Harcourt Brace Jovanovich, 1981. Copyright © 1981 by Harcourt Brace Jovanovich, Inc. Reprinted by permission of the publisher.

Donelson, Kenneth L., and Alleen Pace Nilsen. From *Literature for Today's Young Adults*. Scott, Foresman, 1980. Copyright © 1980 Scott, Foresman and Company. All rights reserved. Reprinted by permission.

Dreyer, Sharon Spredemann. From *The Bookfinder, a Guide to Children's Literature about the Needs and Problems of Youth Aged 2-15: Annotations of Books Published 1975 through 1978, Vol. 2*. American Guidance Service, Inc., 1981. © 1981 American Guidance Service, Inc. All rights reserved. Reprinted by permission.

Eaton, Mary K., ed. *Good Books for Children: A Selection of Outstanding Children's Books Published 1948-57*. University of Chicago Press, 1959. © 1959 by The University of Chicago. Reprinted by permission of The University of Chicago Press.

Eaton, Mary K., ed. *Good Books for Children: A Selection of Outstanding Children's Books Published 1950-65*. Third edition. Edited by

Mary K. Eakin. University of Chicago Press, 1966. © 1959, 1962, and 1966 by The University of Chicago. All rights reserved. Reprinted by permission of The University of Chicago Press.

Egoff, Sheila A. From *Thursday's Child: Trends and Patterns in Contemporary Children's Literature*. American Library Association, 1981. Copyright © 1981 by the American Library Association. All rights reserved. Reprinted by permission.

Eyre, Frank. From *British Children's Books in the Twentieth Century*. Revised edition. Longman Books, 1971, Dutton, 1973. Copyright © 1971 by Frank Eyre. All rights reserved. Reprinted by permission of the publisher, E.P. Dutton, a division of New American Library. In Canada by Penguin Books Ltd.

Fisher, Margery. From *Intent Upon Reading: A Critical Appraisal of Modern Fiction for Children*. Hodder & Stoughton Children's Books (formerly Brockhampton Press), 1961. Copyright © 1961 by Margery Fisher. Reprinted by permission.

Fisher, Margery. From *Who's Who in Children's Books: A Treasury of the Familiar Characters of Childhood*. Weidenfeld & Nicolson, 1975. Copyright © 1975 by Margery Fisher. All rights reserved. Reprinted by permission.

Gardner, Howard. From a conversation with Jonathan Cott in *Pipers at the Gates of Dawn: The Wisdom of Children's Literature*. By Jonathan Cott. Random House, 1983. Copyright © 1981, 1983 by Jonathan Cott. All rights reserved. Reprinted by permission of Random House, Inc.

Georgiou, Constantine. From *Children and Their Literature*. Prentice-Hall, Inc., 1969. © 1969 by Prentice-Hall, Inc. All rights reserved. Reprinted by permission of the author.

Helbig, Alethea K. From ''Trends in Poetry for Children,'' in *Children's Literature: Annual of the Modern Language Association Seminar on Children's Literature and The Children's Literature Association, Vol. 6*. Edited by Francelia Butler. Temple University Press, 1977. © 1977 by Francelia Butler. All rights reserved. Reprinted by permission of Francelia Butler.

Hoban, Russell. From "Beyond the Last Visible Dog," in *Painted Desert, Green Shade: Essays on Contemporary Writers of Fiction for Children and Young Adults*. Edited by David Rees. The Horn Book, Inc., 1984. Copyright © 1984 by David Rees. All rights reserved. Reprinted by permission.

Huck, Charlotte S., and Doris A. Young. From *Children's Literature in the Elementary School*. Holt, Rinehart and Winston, 1961. Copyright © 1961 by Holt, Rinehart and Winston. All rights reserved. Reprinted by permission of CBS College Publishing.

Huck, Charlotte S., and Doris Young Kuhn. From *Children's Literature in the Elementary School*. Second edition. Holt, Rinehart and Winston, 1968. Copyright © 1961, 1968 by Holt, Rinehart and Winston, Inc. All rights reserved. Reprinted by permission of Holt, Rinehart and Winston, Publishers, CBS College Publishing.

*Human—And Anti-Human—Values in Children's Books: A Content Rating Instrument for Educators and Concerned Parents*. Edited by the Council on Interracial Books for Children, Inc. Racism and Sexism Resource Center for Educators, 1976. Copyright © 1976 by the Council on Interracial Books for Children, Inc. All rights reserved. Reprinted by permission.

Hürlimann, Bettina. From *Three Centuries of Children's Books in Europe*. Edited and translated by Brian W. Alderson. Oxford University Press, Oxford, 1967. © Oxford University Press 1967. Reprinted by permission.

Jan, Isabelle. From *On Children's Literature*. Edited by Catherine Storr. Allen Lane, 1973. Translation copyright © Allen Lane, 1973. Reprinted by permission of Penguin Books Ltd.

Lanes, Selma G. From *Down the Rabbit Hole: Adventures and Misadventures in the Realm of Children's Literature*. Atheneum Publishers, 1972. Copyright © 1971 by Selma G. Lanes. All rights reserved. Reprinted by permission of the author.

Lonsdale, Bernard J., and Helen K. Mackintosh. From *Children Experience Literature*. Random House, 1973. Copyright © 1973 by Random House, Inc. All rights reserved. Reprinted by permission of the publisher.

Meek, Margaret. From ''Speaking of Shifters,'' in *Changing English: Essays for Harold Rosen*. Edited by Margaret Meek and Jane Miller. University of London, 1984. Copyright © 1984 The Institute of Education. Reprinted by permission of The Institute of Education and Margaret Meek.

Moss, Elaine. From ''Picture Books: 'The Baby','' in *Children's Books of the Year: 1974*. Edited by Elaine Moss. Hamish Hamilton, 1975. © Elaine Moss 1975. All rights reserved. Reprinted by permission.

Moss, Elaine. From *Picture Books for Young People: 9-13*. The Thimble Press, 1981. Copyright © 1981 Elaine Moss. Reprinted by permission.

Moynihan, Ruth. B. From "Ideologies in Children's Literature: Some Preliminary Notes," in *Children's Literature: Annual of the Modern Language Association Seminar on Children's Literature and The Children's Literature Association, Vol. 2*. Edited by Francelia Butler. Temple University Press, 1973. © 1973 by Francelia Butler. All rights reserved. Reprinted by permission of Francelia Butler.

Pearce, A. Philippa. From "'Tom's Midnight Garden'," in *Chosen for Children: An Account of the Books Which Have Been Awarded the Library Association Carnegie Medal, 1936-1975*. Edited by Marcus Crouch and Alec Ellis. Third edition. The Library Association, 1977. © Marcus Crouch and Alec Ellis, 1977. Reprinted by permission.

Pearce, Philippa. From "Writing a Book: 'A Dog So Small'," in *The Thorny Paradise: Writers on Writing for Children*. Edited by Edward Blishen. Kestrel Books, 1975. Collection copyright © 1975 by Edward Blishen. Reprinted by permission of Penguin Books Ltd.

Peterson, Linda Kauffman. From "The Caldecott Medal and Honor Books, 1938-1981: 'Anansi the Spider: A Tale From the Ashanti', 'Arrow to the Sun', 'Bartholomew and the Oobleck', 'If I Ran the Zoo', 'McElligot's Pool'," in *Newbery and Caldecott Medal and Honor Books: An Annotated Bibliography*. By Linda Kauffman Peterson and Marilyn Leathers Solt. G.K. Hall & Co., 1982. Copyright © 1982 by Marilyn Solt and Linda Peterson. Reprinted by permission.

Purves, Alan C., and Dianne L. Monson. From *Experiencing Children's Literature*. Scott, Foresman, 1984. Copyright © 1984 Scott, Foresman and Company. All rights reserved. Reprinted by permission.

Rees, David. From *The Marble in the Water: Essays on Contemporary Writers of Fiction for Children and Young Adults*. The Horn Book, Inc., 1980. Copyright © 1979, 1980 by David Rees. All rights reserved. Reprinted by permission.

Sadker, Myra Pollack, and David Miller Sadker. From *Now Upon a Time: A Contemporary View of Children's Literature*. Harper & Row, 1977. Copyright © 1977 by Myra Pollack Sadker and David Miller Sadker. All rights reserved. Reprinted by permission of Harper & Row, Publishers, Inc.

Sale, Roger. From *Fairy Tales and After: From Snow White to E. B. White*. Cambridge, Mass.: Harvard University Press, 1978. Copyright © 1978 by the President and Fellows of Harvard College. All rights reserved. Excerpted by permission.

Salway, Lance. From "A Selection of Novels: 'Ring-Rise Ring-Set'," in *The Signal Review 1: A Selective Guide to Children's Books, 1982*. Edited by Nancy Chambers. Thimble Press, 1983. Copyright © 1983 The Thimble Press. Reprinted by permission.

Schneiderman, Leo. From "A Miscellany. 'Arrow to the Sun' and Others," in *Children's Literature: Annual of the Modern Language Association Seminar on Children's Literature and The Children's Literature Association, Vol. 4*. Edited by Francelia Butler. Temple University Press, 1975. © 1975 by Francelia Butler. All rights reserved. Reprinted by permission of Francelia Butler.

Schwarcz, Joseph H. From *Ways of the Illustrator: Visual Communication in Children's Literature*. American Library Association, 1982. Copyright © 1982 by the American Library Association. All rights reserved. Reprinted by permission.

Seuss, Dr. From *Oh, the Thinks You Can Think!* Beginner Books, 1975. Copyright © 1975 by Dr. Seuss and A. S. Geisel. All rights reserved. Reprinted by permission of Beginner Books, a division of Random House, Inc.

Seuss, Dr. From "'Where Do You Get Your Story Ideas?' They Ask," in *Writing Books for Boys and Girls*. Edited by Helen Ferris. Doubleday, 1952. Copyright © 1952 by Doubleday & Company, Inc. Renewed 1980 by Dr. Seuss. All rights reserved. Reprinted by permission of the publisher.

Steele, Mary. From "Picture Books & Illustrated Stories 6 to 9: 'A Chair for My Mother'," in *The Signal Review of Children's Books 2: A Selective Guide to Picture Books, Fiction, Plays, Poetry, Information Books Published during 1983*. Edited by Nancy Chambers. Thimble Press, 1984. Copyright © 1984 by The Thimble Press. Reprinted by permission.

Steig, Michael. From "Dr. Seuss's Attack on Imagination: 'I Wish that I Had Duck Feet' and the Cautionary Tale," in *Proceedings of the Ninth Annual Conference of the Children's Literature Association: The Child and the Story, an Exploration of Narrative Forms*. Edited by Priscilla A. Ord. Children's Literature Association, 1983. Copyright © 1983 by The Children's Literature Association. All rights reserved. Reprinted by permission.

Sutton-Smith, Brian. From a conversation with Jonathan Cott in *Pipers at the Gates of Dawn: The Wisdom of Children's Literature*. By Jonathan Cott. Random House, 1983. Copyright © 1981, 1983 by Jonathan Cott. All rights reserved. Reprinted by permission of Random House, Inc.

Townsend, John Rowe. From *A Sense of Story: Essays on Contemporary Writers for Children*. J.B. Lippincott Company, 1971. Copyright © 1971 by John Rowe Townsend. All rights reserved. Reprinted by permission of Harper & Row, Publishers, Inc.

Townsend, John Rowe. From *Written for Children: An Outline of English Children's Literature*. J. Garnet Miller Ltd., 1965. Copyright © 1965 by John Rowe Townsend. Reprinted by permission.

# CUMULATIVE INDEX TO AUTHORS

This index lists all author entries in *Children's Literature Review* and includes cross-references to them in other Gale sources. References in the index are identified as follows:

| | |
|---|---|
| **AITN:** | *Authors in the News,* Volumes 1-2 |
| **CA:** | *Contemporary Authors* (original series), Volumes 1-114 |
| **CANR:** | *Contemporary Authors New Revision Series,* Volumes 1-15 |
| **CAP:** | *Contemporary Authors Permanent Series,* Volumes 1-2 |
| **CA-R:** | *Contemporary Authors* (revised editions), Volumes 1-44 |
| **CLC:** | *Contemporary Literary Criticism,* Volumes 1-33 |
| **CLR:** | *Children's Literature Review,* Volumes 1-9 |
| **DLB:** | *Dictionary of Literary Biography,* Volumes 1-40 |
| **DLB-DS:** | *Dictionary of Literary Biography Documentary Series,* Volumes 1-4 |
| **DLB-Y:** | *Dictionary of Literary Biography Yearbook,* Volumes 1980-1984 |
| **NCLC:** | *Nineteenth-Century Literature Criticism,* Volumes 1-9 |
| **SATA:** | *Something about the Author,* Volumes 1-39 |
| **TCLC:** | *Twentieth-Century Literary Criticism,* Volumes 1-16 |
| **YABC:** | *Yesterday's Authors of Books for Children,* Volumes 1-2 |

**Adkins, Jan** 1944-.....7
See also SATA 8
See also CA 33-36R

**Adoff, Arnold** 1935-.....7
See also SATA 5
See also CA 41-44R
See also AITN 1

**Aiken, Joan** 1924-.....1
See also SATA 2, 30
See also CANR 4
See also CA 9-12R

**Alcott, Louisa May** 1832-1888.....1
See also NCLC 6
See also YABC 1
See also DLB 1

**Alexander, Lloyd (Chudley)** 1924-.....1, 5
See also SATA 3
See also CANR 1
See also CA 1-4R

**Aliki (Liacouras Brandenberg)** 1929-.....9
See also Brandenberg, Aliki (Liacouras)

**Andersen, Hans Christian** 1805-1875.....6
See also NCLC 7
See also YABC 1

**Anglund, Joan Walsh** 1926-.....1
See also SATA 2
See also CANR 15
See also CA 5-8R

**Anno, Mitsumasa** 1926-.....2
See also SATA 5, 38
See also CANR 4
See also CA 49-52

**Ardizzone, Edward (Jeffrey Irving)**
1900-1979.....3
See also SATA 1, 28
See also obituary SATA 21
See also CANR 8
See also CA 5-8R
See also obituary CA 89-92

**Armstrong, William H(oward)** 1914-.....1
See also SATA 4
See also CANR 9
See also CA 17-20R
See also AITN 1

**Aruego, Jose** 1932-.....5
See also SATA 6
See also CA 37-40R

**Ashley, Bernard** 1935-.....4
See also SATA 39
See also CA 93-96

**Aylesworth, Thomas G(ibbons)** 1927-.....6
See also SATA 4
See also CANR 10
See also CA 25-28R

**Babbitt, Natalie** 1932-.....2
See also SATA 6
See also CANR 2
See also CA 49-52

**Bacon, Martha (Sherman)** 1917-1981.....3
See also SATA 18
See also obituary SATA 27
See also CA 85-88
See also obituary CA 104

**Bang, Garrett** 1943-
See Bang, Molly (Garrett)

**Bang, Molly (Garrett)** 1943-.....8
See also SATA 24
See also CA 102

**Bawden, Nina** 1925-.....2
See also Kark, Nina Mary (Mabey)
See also DLB 14

**Baylor, Byrd** 1924-.....3
See also SATA 16
See also CA 81-84

**Bemelmans, Ludwig** 1898-1962.....6
See also SATA 15
See also CA 73-76
See also DLB 22

**Bendick, Jeanne** 1919-.....5
See also SATA 2
See also CANR 2
See also CA 5-8R

**Bethancourt, T(homas) Ernesto** 1932-.....3
See also Paisley, Tom
See also SATA 11

**Bland, Edith Nesbit** 1858-1924
See Nesbit, E(dith)

**Blume, Judy (Sussman Kitchens)**
1938-.....2
See also CLC 12, 30
See also SATA 2, 31
See also CANR 13
See also CA 29-32R

**Bond, (Thomas) Michael** 1926-.....1
See also SATA 6
See also CANR 4
See also CA 5-8R

**Bontemps, Arna (Wendell)** 1902-1973.....6
See also CLC 1, 18
See also SATA 2
See also obituary SATA 24
See also CANR 4
See also CA 1-4R
See also obituary CA 41-44R

**Boston, L(ucy) M(aria Wood)** 1892-.......3
  See also SATA 19
  See also CA 73-76

**Bova, Ben(jamin William)** 1932-.........3
  See also SATA 6
  See also CANR 11
  See also CA 5-8R
  See also DLB-Y 81

**Brandenberg, Aliki (Liacouras)** 1929-
  See Aliki (Liacouras Brandenberg)
  See also SATA 2, 35
  See also CANR 4, 12
  See also CA 1-4R

**Bruna, Dick** 1927-.....................7
  See also SATA 30
  See also CA 112

**Brunhoff, Jean de** 1899-1937............4
  See also SATA 24

**Brunhoff, Jean de** 1899-1937 and
    **Laurent de Brunhoff** 1925-.........4

**Brunhoff, Laurent de** 1925-.............4
  See also SATA 24
  See also CA 73-76

**Brunhoff, Laurent de** 1925- and
    **Jean de Brunhoff** 1899-1937........4

**Burnford, Sheila (Philip Cockrane Every)**
  1918-1984........................2
  See also SATA 3
  See also obituary SATA 38
  See also CANR 1
  See also CA 1-4R
  See also obituary CA 112

**Burningham, John (Mackintosh)**
  1936-...........................9
  See also SATA 16
  See also CA 73-76

**Burton, Hester (Wood-Hill)** 1913-.......1
  See also SATA 7
  See also CANR 10
  See also CA 9-12R

**Byars, Betsy** 1928-.....................1
  See also SATA 4
  See also CA 33-36R

**Cameron, Eleanor (Butler)** 1912-........1
  See also SATA 1, 25
  See also CANR 2
  See also CA 1-4R

**Carroll, Lewis** 1832-1898...............2
  See also Dodgson, Charles Lutwidge
  See also NCLC 2
  See also DLB 18

**Charlip, Remy** 1929-....................8
  See also SATA 4
  See also CA 33-36R

**Chauncy, Nan(cen Beryl Masterman)**
  1900-1970........................6
  See also SATA 6
  See also CANR 4
  See also CA 1-4R

**Christie, (Ann) Philippa (Pearce)** 1920-
  See Pearce (Christie), (Ann) Philippa
  See also CANR 4

**Christopher, John** 1922-................2
  See also Youd, (Christopher) Samuel

**Cleary, Beverly (Atlee Bunn)** 1916-.... 2, 8
  See also SATA 2
  See also CANR 2
  See also CA 1-4R

**Cleaver, Bill** 1920-1981 .................6
  See also SATA 22
  See also obituary SATA 27
  See also CA 73-76

**Cleaver, Bill** 1920-1981 and
    **Vera Cleaver** 1919-.................6

**Cleaver, Vera** 1919- ....................6
  See also SATA 22
  See also CA 73-76

**Cleaver, Vera** 1919- and
    **Bill Cleaver** 1920-1981.............6

**Clifton, Lucille** 1936- ..................5
  See also CLC 19
  See also SATA 20
  See also CANR 2
  See also CA 49-52
  See also DLB 5

**Coatsworth, Elizabeth** 1893-............2
  See also SATA 2
  See also CANR 4
  See also CA 5-8R
  See also DLB 22

**Cobb, Vicki** 1938-.....................2
  See also SATA 8
  See also CANR 14
  See also CA 33-36R

**Cohen, Daniel** 1936- ...................3
  See also SATA 8
  See also CANR 1
  See also CA 45-48

**Cole, Joanna** 1944- ....................5
  See also SATA 37

**Collier, James Lincoln** 1928-............3
  See also CLC 30
  See also SATA 8
  See also CANR 4
  See also CA 9-12R

**Collodi, Carlo** 1826-1890...............5
  See also Lorenzini, Carlo

**Conly, Robert L(eslie)** 1918-1973
  See O'Brien, Robert C.
  See also SATA 23
  See also CA 73-76
  See also obituary CA 41-44R

**Cooper, Susan** 1935-...................4
  See also SATA 4
  See also CANR 15
  See also CA 29-32R

**Corbett, Scott** 1913- ...................1
  See also SATA 2
  See also CANR 1
  See also CA 1-4R

**Crews, Donald** 1938-...................7
  See also SATA 30, 32
  See also CA 108

**Dahl, Roald** 1916- ................... 1, 7
  See also CLC 1, 6, 18
  See also SATA 1, 26
  See also CANR 6
  See also CA 1-4R

**de Angeli, Marguerite** 1889- ............1
  See also SATA 1, 27
  See also CANR 3
  See also CA 5-8R
  See also DLB 22
  See also AITN 2

**DeJong, Meindert** 1906-.................1
  See also SATA 2
  See also CA 13-16R

**de Paola, Thomas Anthony** 1934-
  See de Paola, Tomie
  See also SATA 11
  See also CANR 2
  See also CA 49-52

**de Paola, Tomie** 1934- .................4
  See also de Paola, Thomas Anthony

**Dodgson, Charles Lutwidge** 1832-1898
  See Carroll, Lewis
  See also YABC 2

**Donovan, John** 1928- ...................3
  See also SATA 29
  See also CA 97-100

**du Bois, William (Sherman) Pène**
  1916-...........................1
  See also SATA 4
  See also CA 5-8R

**Emberley, Barbara (Anne)** 1932- .........5
  See also SATA 8
  See also CANR 5
  See also CA 5-8R

**Emberley, Barbara (Anne)** 1932- and
    **Ed(ward Randolph) Emberley**
    1931-...........................5

**Emberley, Ed(ward Randolph)** 1931-......5
  See also SATA 8
  See also CANR 5
  See also CA 5-8R

**Emberley, Ed(ward Randolph)** 1931- and
    **Barbara (Anne) Emberley** 1932- .....5

**Engdahl, Sylvia Louise** 1933-............2
  See also SATA 4
  See also CANR 14
  See also CA 29-32R

**Enright, Elizabeth** 1909-1968 ...........4
  See also SATA 9
  See also CA 61-64
  See also obituary CA 25-28R
  See also DLB 22

**Estes, Eleanor** 1906- ...................2
  See also SATA 7
  See also CANR 5
  See also CA 1-4R
  See also DLB 22

**Farmer, Penelope (Jane)** 1939-..........8
  See also SATA 39
  See also CANR 9
  See also CA 13-16R

**Feelings, Muriel (Grey)** 1938-
  See Feelings, Muriel L.
  See also SATA 16
  See also CA 93-96

**Feelings, Muriel L.** 1938-...............5
  See also Feelings, Muriel (Grey)

**Feelings, Muriel L.** 1938- and
    **Tom Feelings** 1933- ................5

**Feelings, Thomas** 1933-
  See Feelings, Tom
  See also SATA 8
  See also CA 49-52

**Feelings, Tom** 1933- ...................5
  See also Feelings, Thomas

**Feelings, Tom** 1933- and
    **Muriel L. Feelings** 1938-............5

Fitzgerald, John D(ennis)  1907- ..........1
    See also SATA 20
    See also CA 93-96

Fitzhardinge, Joan Margaret  1912-
    See Joan Phipson
    See also SATA 2
    See also CANR 6
    See also CA 13-16R

Fitzhugh, Louise  1928-1974.............1
    See also SATA 1
    See also obituary SATA 24
    See also CAP 2
    See also CA 29-32
    See also obituary CA 53-56

Fleischman, (Albert) Sid(ney)  1920-.......1
    See also SATA 8
    See also CANR 5
    See also CA 1-4R

Foster, Genevieve (Stump)  1893-1979 .....7
    See also SATA 2
    See also obituary SATA 23
    See also CANR 4
    See also CA 5-8R
    See also obituary CA 89-92

Fox, Paula  1923- ......................1
    See also CLC 2, 8
    See also SATA 17
    See also CA 73-76

Fritz, Jean (Guttery)  1915- ..............2
    See also SATA 1, 29
    See also CANR 5
    See also CA 1-4R

Gág, Wanda (Hazel)  1893-1946 .........4
    See also YABC 1
    See also CA 113
    See also DLB 22

Geisel, Theodor Seuss  1904-  ...........1
    See Seuss, Dr.
    See also SATA 1, 28
    See also CANR 13
    See also CA 13-16R

George, Jean Craighead  1919-  ..........1
    See also SATA 2
    See also CA 5-8R

Gibbons, Gail (Gretchen)  1944-  .........8
    See also SATA 23
    See also CANR 12
    See also CA 69-72

Giovanni, Nikki  1943-..................6
    See also CLC 2, 4, 19
    See also SATA 24
    See also CA 29-32R
    See also DLB 5
    See also AITN 1

Glubok, Shirley (Astor)  1933-............1
    See also SATA 6
    See also CANR 4
    See also CA 5-8R

Goffstein, M(arilyn) B(rooke)  1940-.......3
    See also SATA 8
    See also CANR 9
    See also CA 21-24R

Grahame, Kenneth  1859-1932...........5
    See also YABC 1
    See also CA 108
    See also DLB 34

Greenaway, Catherine  1846-1901
    See Greenaway, Kate
    See also CA 113

Greenaway, Kate  1846-1901 .............6
    See also Greenaway, Catherine
    See also YABC 2

Greene, Bette  1934-....................2
    See also CLC 30
    See also SATA 8
    See also CANR 4
    See also CA 53-56

Greenfield, Eloise  1929-.................4
    See also SATA 19
    See also CANR 1
    See also CA 49-52

Gripe, Maria (Kristina)  1923-...........5
    See also SATA 2
    See also CA 29-32R

Hamilton, Virginia (Edith)  1936-  .......1
    See also CLC 26
    See also SATA 4
    See also CA 25-28R
    See also DLB 33

Haskins, James  1941-...................3
    See also SATA 9
    See also CA 33-36R

Henry, Marguerite  1902-................4
    See also SATA 11
    See also CANR 9
    See also CA 17-20R
    See also DLB 22

Hentoff, Nat(han Irving)  1925-  ..........1
    See also CLC 26
    See also SATA 27
    See also CANR 5
    See also CA 1-4R

Hergé  1907-1983 .....................6
    See also Rémi, Georges

Hinton, S(usan) E(loise)  1950-.........3
    See also CLC 30
    See also SATA 19
    See also CA 81-84

Hoban, Russell (Conwell)  1925-  .........3
    See also CLC 7, 25
    See also SATA 1
    See also CA 5-8R

Hogrogian, Nonny  1932-................2
    See also SATA 7
    See also CANR 2
    See also CA 45-48

Houston, James A(rchibald)  1921-........3
    See also SATA 13
    See also CA 65-68

Howe, James  1946-....................9
    See also SATA 29
    See also CA 105

Hughes, Monica (Ince)  1925-............9
    See also SATA 15
    See also CA 77-80

Hughes, Ted  1930-....................3
    See also CLC 2, 4, 9, 14
    See also SATA 27
    See also CANR 1
    See also CA 1-4R
    See also DLB 40

Hunt, Irene  1907-.....................1
    See also SATA 2
    See also CANR 8
    See also CA 17-20R

Hunter, Kristin (Eggleston)  1931-........3
    See also SATA 12
    See also CANR 13
    See also CA 13-16R
    See also DLB 33
    See also AITN 1

Isadora, Rachel  1953(?)- ...............7
    See also SATA 32
    See also CA 111

Iwamatsu, Jun Atsushi  1908-
    See Yashima, Taro
    See also SATA 14
    See also CA 73-76

Jansson, Tove (Marika)  1914-...........2
    See also SATA 3
    See also CA 17-20R

Jarrell, Randall  1914-1965..............6
    See also CLC 1, 2, 6, 9, 13
    See also SATA 7
    See also CANR 6
    See also CA 5-8R
    See also obituary CA 25-28R

Kark, Nina Mary (Mabey)  1925-
    See Bawden, Nina
    See also SATA 4
    See also CANR 8
    See also CA 17-20R

Kästner, Erich  1899-1974 ..............4
    See also SATA 14
    See also CA 73-76
    See also obituary CA 49-52

Keats, Ezra Jack  1916-1983 ............1
    See also SATA 14
    See also obituary SATA 34
    See also CA 77-80
    See also obituary CA 109
    See also AITN 1

Kellogg, Steven  1941-..................6
    See also SATA 8
    See also CANR 1
    See also CA 49-52

Klein, Norma  1938-....................2
    See also CLC 30
    See also SATA 7
    See also CANR 15
    See also CA 41-44R

Konigsburg, E(laine) L(obl)  1930-  .......1
    See also SATA 4
    See also CA 21-24R

Korinetz, Yuri (Iosifovich)  1923- ........4
    See also SATA 9
    See also CANR 11
    See also CA 61-64

Kotzwinkle, William  1938-..............6
    See also CLC 5, 14
    See also SATA 24
    See also CANR 3
    See also CA 45-48

Krahn, Fernando  1935- ................3
    See also SATA 31
    See also CANR 11
    See also CA 65-68

Krementz, Jill  1940-...................5
    See also SATA 17
    See also CA 41-44R
    See also AITN 1, 2

**Krüss, James (Jacob Hinrich)** 1926-.......9
See also SATA 8
See also CANR 5
See also CA 53-56

**Kurelek, William** 1927-1977 ............2
See also SATA 8
See also obituary SATA 27
See also CANR 3
See also CA 49-52

**Kuskin, Karla (Seidman)** 1932-..........4
See also SATA 2
See also CANR 4
See also CA 1-4R

**Lagerlöf, Selma (Ottiliana Lovisa)**
1858-1940.........................7
See also TCLC 4
See also SATA 15
See also CA 108

**Langstaff, John (Meredith)** 1920-........3
See also SATA 6
See also CANR 4
See also CA 1-4R

**Lawson, Robert** 1892-1957 .............2
See also YABC 2
See also DLB 22

**Lear, Edward** 1812-1888 ...............1
See also NCLC 3
See also SATA 18
See also DLB 32

**Lee, Dennis (Beynon)** 1939-.............3
See also SATA 14
See also CANR 11
See also CA 25-28R

**Le Guin, Ursula K(roeber)** 1929-........3
See also CLC 8, 13, 22
See also SATA 4
See also CANR 9
See also CA 21-24R
See also DLB 8
See also AITN 1

**L'Engle, Madeleine** 1918-..............1
See also CLC 12
See also SATA 1, 27
See also CANR 3
See also CA 1-4R
See also AITN 2

**LeShan, Eda J(oan)** 1922- ..............6
See also SATA 21
See also CA 13-16R

**LeSieg, Theo** 1904-
See Seuss, Dr.

**Lester, Julius B.** 1939- .................2
See also SATA 12
See also CANR 8
See also CA 17-20R

**Lewin, Hugh (Francis)** 1939-............9
See also CA 113

**Lewis, C(live) S(taples)** 1898-1963 .......3
See also CLC 1, 3, 6, 14, 27
See also SATA 13
See also CA 81-84
See also DLB 15

**Lindgren, Astrid** 1907-.................1
See also SATA 2, 38
See also CA 13-16R

**Lindsay, Norman (Alfred William)**
1879-1969........................8
See also CA 102

**Lionni, Leo(nard)** 1910-................7
See also SATA 8
See also CA 53-56

**Little, (Flora) Jean** 1932-...............4
See also SATA 2
See also CA 21-24R

**Lively, Penelope (Margaret)** 1933-........7
See also CLC 32
See also SATA 7
See also CA 41-44R
See also DLB 14

**Livingston, Myra Cohn** 1926-............7
See also SATA 5
See also CANR 1
See also CA 1-4R

**Lobel, Arnold (Stark)** 1933-.............5
See also SATA 6
See also CANR 2
See also CA 1-4R
See also AITN 1

**Lorenzini, Carlo** 1826-1890
See Collodi, Carlo
See also SATA 29

**Lowry, Lois** 1937-.....................6
See also SATA 23
See also CANR 13
See also CA 69-72

**Macaulay, David (Alexander)** 1946-.......3
See also SATA 27
See also CANR 5
See also CA 53-56

**Mahy, Margaret (May)** 1936-............7
See also SATA 14
See also CANR 13
See also CA 69-72

**Manley, Seon** 19??-....................3
See also SATA 15
See also CA 85-88

**Mathis, Sharon Bell** 1937-...............3
See also SATA 7
See also CA 41-44R
See also DLB 33

**McCloskey, (John) Robert** 1914-..........7
See also SATA 2, 39
See also CA 9-12R
See also DLB 22

**McCord, David (Thompson Watson)**
1897-...........................9
See also SATA 18
See also CA 73-76

**McDermott, Gerald (Edward)** 1941- ......9
See also SATA 16
See also CA 85-88
See also AITN 2

**McHargue, Georgess** 1941- ..............2
See also SATA 4
See also CA 25-28R

**Milne, A(lan) A(lexander)** 1882-1956......1
See also TCLC 6
See also YABC 1
See also CA 104
See also DLB 10

**Mitsumasa Anno** 1926-
See Anno, Mitsumasa

**Monjo, F(erdinand) N(icolas, III)**
1924-1978........................2
See also SATA 16
See also CA 81-84

**Montgomery, L(ucy) M(aud)**
1874-1942........................8
See also YABC 1
See also CA 108

**Myers, Walter Dean** 1937-...............4
See also SATA 27
See also CA 33-36R
See also DLB 33

**Nesbit, E(dith)** 1858-1924...............3
See also YABC 1

**Ness, Evaline (Michelow)** 1911-..........6
See also SATA 1, 26
See also CANR 5
See also CA 5-8R

**Norton, Mary** 1903- ...................6
See also SATA 18
See also CA 97-100

**Oakley, Graham** 1929-.................7
See also SATA 30
See also CA 106

**O'Brien, Robert C.** 1918-1973 ..........2
See also Conly, Robert L(eslie)

**O'Connor, Patrick** 1915-
See Wibberley, Leonard

**O'Dell, Scott** 1903- ...................1
See also CLC 30
See also SATA 12
See also CANR 12
See also CA 61-64

**Paisley, Tom** 1932-
See Bethancourt, T(homas) Ernesto
See also CANR 15
See also CA 61-64

**Paterson, Katherine (Womeldorf)**
1932-...........................7
See also CLC 12, 30
See also SATA 13
See also CA 21-24R

**Pearce (Christie), (Ann) Philippa**
1920-...........................9
See also Christie, (Ann) Philippa (Pearce)
See also CLC 21
See also SATA 1
See also CA 5-8R

**Peyton, K. M.** 1929-...................3
See also Peyton, Kathleen (Wendy)

**Peyton, Kathleen (Wendy)** 1929-
See Peyton, K. M.
See also SATA 15
See also CA 69-72

**Phipson, Joan** 1912- ...................5
See also Fitzhardinge, Joan Margaret

**Pieńkowski, Jan** 1936- .................6
See also SATA 6
See also CANR 11
See also CA 65-68

**Pinkwater, D(aniel) Manus** 1941-.........4
See also CANR 12
See also CA 29-32R

**Pinkwater, Manus** 1941-
See Pinkwater, D(aniel) Manus
See also SATA 8

**Polder, Markus** 1926-
See Krüss, James (Jacob Hinrich)

**Potter, (Helen) Beatrix** 1866-1943 ........1
See also YABC 1
See also CA 108

**Pringle, Laurence P.** 1935- .............4
See also SATA 4
See also CANR 14
See also CA 29-32R

**Ransome, Arthur (Michell)**
1884-1967.........................8
See also SATA 22
See also CA 73-76

**Raskin, Ellen** 1928-1984................1
See also SATA 2, 38
See also CA 21-24R
See also obituary CA 113

**Rau, Margaret (Wright)** 1913- ...........8
See also SATA 9
See also CANR 8
See also CA 61-64

**Rémi, Georges** 1907-1983
See Hergé
See also SATA 13
See also obituary SATA 32
See also CA 69-72
See also obituary CA 109

**Rey, H(ans) A(ugusto)** 1898-1977.........5
See also SATA 1, 26
See also CANR 6
See also CA 5-8R
See also obituary CA 73-76
See also DLB 22

**Rey, H(ans) A(ugusto)** 1898-1977 and
Margret (Elisabeth) Rey 1906- .......5

**Rey, Margret (Elisabeth)** 1906- ..........5
See also SATA 26
See also CA 105

**Rey, Margret (Elisabeth)** 1906- and
H(ans) A(ugusto) Rey 1898-1977 .....5

**Rockwell, Thomas** 1933- .................6
See also SATA 7
See also CA 29-32R

**Rodman, Maia** 1927-
See Wojciechowska, Maia

**Sachs, Marilyn (Stickle)** 1927- ............2
See also SATA 3
See also CANR 13
See also CA 17-20R

**Sasek, M(iroslav)** 1916-1980 .............4
See also SATA 16
See also obituary SATA 23
See also CA 73-76
See also obituary CA 101

**Scarry, Richard (McClure)** 1919- .........3
See also SATA 2, 35
See also CA 17-20R

**Schwartz, Alvin** 1927-....................3
See also SATA 4
See also CANR 7
See also CA 13-16R

**Schweitzer, Byrd Baylor** 1924-
See Baylor, Byrd

**Selden (Thompson), George** 1929- ........8
See also Thompson, George Selden

**Selsam, Millicent E(llis)** 1912-............1
See also SATA 1, 29
See also CANR 5
See also CA 9-12R

**Sendak, Maurice (Bernard)** 1928-.........1
See also SATA 1, 27
See also CANR 11
See also CA 5-8R

**Serraillier, Ian (Lucien)** 1912-............2
See also SATA 1
See also CANR 1
See also CA 1-4R

**Seuss, Dr.** 1904-.........................9
See also Geisel, Theodor Seuss

**Showers, Paul C.** 1910- .................6
See also SATA 21
See also CANR 4
See also CA 1-4R

**Shulevitz, Uri** 1935-.....................5
See also SATA 3
See also CANR 3
See also CA 9-12R

**Silverstein, Shel(by)** 1932- ..............5
See also SATA 27, 33
See also CA 107

**Simon, Seymour** 1931- ..................9
See also SATA 4
See also CANR 11
See also CA 25-28R

**Singer, Isaac Bashevis** 1904- .............1
See also CLC 1, 3, 6, 9, 11, 15, 23
See also SATA 3, 27
See also CANR 1
See also CA 1-4R
See also DLB 6, 28
See also AITN 1, 2

**Slote, Alfred** 1926-......................4
See also SATA 8

**Sneve, Virginia Driving Hawk** 1933- ......2
See also SATA 8
See also CANR 3
See also CA 49-52

**Sobol, Donald J.** 1924- .................4
See also SATA 1, 31
See also CANR 1
See also CA 1-4R

**Southall, Ivan (Francis)** 1921-...........2
See also SATA 3
See also CANR 7
See also CA 9-12R

**Speare, Elizabeth George** 1908- ........8
See also SATA 5
See also CA 1-4R

**Spier, Peter (Edward)** 1927- .............5
See also SATA 4
See also CA 5-8R

**Steig, William** 1907- ....................2
See also SATA 18
See also CA 77-80
See also AITN 1

**Steptoe, John (Lewis)** 1950-..............2
See also SATA 8
See also CANR 3
See also CA 49-52

**Sterling, Dorothy** 1913- .................1
See also SATA 1
See also CANR 5
See also CA 9-12R

**Stren, Patti** 1949-.......................5

**Suhl, Yuri** 1908- .......................2
See also SATA 8
See also CANR 2
See also CA 45-48

**Sutcliff, Rosemary** 1920- ................1
See also CLC 26
See also SATA 6
See also CA 5-8R

**Taylor, Mildred D(elois)** 19??-............9
See also CLC 21
See also SATA 15
See also CA 85-88

**Thomas, Ianthe** 1951-...................8

**Thompson, George Selden** 1929-
See Selden (Thompson), George
See also SATA 4
See also CA 5-8R

**Tobias, Tobi** 1938-......................4
See also SATA 5
See also CA 29-32R

**Townsend, John Rowe** 1922-.............2
See also SATA 4
See also CA 37-40R

**Travers, P(amela) L(yndon)** 1906- ........2
See also SATA 4
See also CA 33-36R

**Treece, Henry** 1911-1966................2
See also SATA 2
See also CANR 6
See also CA 1-4R
See also obituary CA 25-28R

**Tunis, Edwin (Burdett)** 1897-1973 ........2
See also SATA 1, 28
See also obituary SATA 24
See also CANR 7
See also CA 5-8R
See also obituary CA 45-48

**Uchida, Yoshiko** 1921- .................6
See also SATA 1
See also CANR 6
See also CA 13-16R

**Uncle Gus** 1898-1977
See Rey, H(ans) A(ugusto)

**Uncle Shelby** 1932-
See Silverstein, Shel(by)

**Ungerer, Jean Thomas** 1931-
See Ungerer, Tomi
See also SATA 5, 33
See also CA 41-44R

**Ungerer, Tomi** 1931-....................3
See also Ungerer, Jean Thomas

**Van Allsburg, Chris** 1949-...............5
See also SATA 37
See also CA 113

**Viorst, Judith** 1931- ...................3
See also SATA 7
See also CANR 2
See also CA 49-52

**Walsh, Gillian Paton** 1939-
See Walsh, Jill Paton
See also SATA 4
See also CA 37-40R

**Walsh, Jill Paton** 1939-..................2
See also Walsh, Gillian Paton

**Watanabe, Shigeo** 1928-.................8
See also SATA 32, 39
See also CA 112

**Watson, Clyde** 1947-....................3
See also SATA 5
See also CANR 4
See also CA 49-52

**Weiss, Harvey**  1922-....................4
  See also SATA 1, 27
  See also CANR 6
  See also CA 5-8R

**Wersba, Barbara**  1932- .................3
  See also CLC 30
  See also SATA 1
  See also CA 29-32R

**White, E(lwyn) B(rooks)**  1899- ..........1
  See also CLC 10
  See also SATA 2, 29
  See also CA 13-16R
  See also DLB 11, 22
  See also AITN 2

**White, Robb**  1909- ....................3
  See also SATA 1
  See also CANR 1
  See also CA 1-4R

**Wibberley, Leonard**  1915-1983..........3
  See also SATA 2
  See also obituary SATA 36
  See also CANR 3
  See also CA 5-8R
  See also obituary CA 111

**Wilder, Laura Ingalls**  1867-1957 ........2
  See also SATA 15, 29
  See also CA 111
  See also DLB 22

**Wildsmith, Brian**  1930- .................2
  See also SATA 16
  See also CA 85-88

**Willard, Barbara (Mary)**  1909-...........2
  See also SATA 17
  See also CANR 15
  See also CA 81-84

**Willard, Nancy**  1936- ...................5
  See also CLC 7
  See also SATA 30, 37
  See also CANR 10
  See also CA 89-92
  See also DLB 5

**Williams, Jay**  1914-1978 ...............8
  See also SATA 3
  See also obituary SATA 24
  See also CANR 2
  See also CA 1-4R
  See also obituary CA 81-84

**Williams, Kit**  1948-...................4
  See also CA 107

**Williams, Vera B.**  1927-................9
  See also SATA 33

**Wojciechowska, Maia (Teresa)**  1927-......1
  See also CLC 26
  See also SATA 1, 28
  See also CANR 4
  See also CA 9-12R

**Wrightson, Patricia**  1921- ..............4
  See also SATA 8
  See also CANR 3
  See also CA 45-48

**Yashima, Taro**  1908-...................4
  See also Iwamatsu, Jun Atsushi

**Yep, Laurence (Michael)**  1948-...........3
  See also SATA 7
  See also CANR 1
  See also CA 49-52

**Yolen, Jane H(yatt)**  1939- ..............4
  See also SATA 4
  See also CANR 11
  See also CA 13-16R

**Youd, (Christopher) Samuel**  1922-
  See Christopher, John
  See also SATA 30
  See also CA 77-80

**Zei, Alki**  1928-........................6
  See also SATA 24
  See also CA 77-80

**Zim, Herbert S(pencer)**  1909-............2
  See also SATA 1, 30
  See also CA 13-16R

**Zimnik, Reiner**  1930- ...................3
  See also SATA 36
  See also CA 77-80

**Zindel, Paul**  1936-......................3
  See also CLC 6, 26
  See also SATA 16
  See also CA 73-76
  See also DLB 7

**Zolotow, Charlotte (Shapiro)**  1915- .......2
  See also SATA 1, 35
  See also CANR 3
  See also CA 5-8R

# CUMULATIVE INDEX TO NATIONALITIES

**AMERICAN**

Adkins, Jan  7
Adoff, Arnold  7
Alcott, Louisa May  1
Alexander, Lloyd  1, 5
Aliki  9
Anglund, Joan Walsh  1
Armstrong, William H.  1
Aruego, Jose  5
Aylesworth, Thomas G.  6
Babbitt, Natalie  2
Bacon, Martha  3
Bang, Molly  8
Baylor, Byrd  3
Bemelmans, Ludwig  6
Bendick, Jeanne  5
Bethancourt, T. Ernesto  3
Blume, Judy  2
Bontemps, Arna  6
Bova, Ben  3
Byars, Betsy  1
Cameron, Eleanor  1
Charlip, Remy  8
Cleary, Beverly  2, 8
Cleaver, Bill  6
Cleaver, Vera  6
Clifton, Lucille  5
Coatsworth, Elizabeth  2
Cobb, Vicki  2
Cohen, Daniel  3
Cole, Joanna  5
Collier, James Lincoln  3
Corbett, Scott  1
Crews, Donald  7
de Angeli, Marguerite  1
DeJong, Meindert  1
de Paola, Tomie  4
Donovan, John  3

du Bois, William Pène  1
Emberley, Barbara  5
Emberley, Ed  5
Engdahl, Sylvia Louise  2
Enright, Elizabeth  4
Estes, Eleanor  2
Feelings, Muriel L.  5
Feelings, Tom  5
Fitzgerald, John D.  1
Fitzhugh, Louise  1
Fleischman, Sid  1
Foster, Genevieve  7
Fox, Paula  1
Fritz, Jean  2
Gág, Wanda  4
Geisel, Theodor Seuss  1
George, Jean Craighead  1
Gibbons, Gail  8
Giovanni, Nikki  6
Glubok, Shirley  1
Goffstein, M. B.  3
Greene, Bette  2
Greenfield, Eloise  4
Hamilton, Virginia  1
Haskins, James  3
Henry, Marguerite  4
Hentoff, Nat  1
Hinton, S. E.  3
Hoban, Russell  3
Hogrogian, Nonny  2
Howe, James  9
Hunt, Irene  1
Hunter, Kristin  3
Isadora, Rachel  7
Jarrell, Randall  6
Keats, Ezra Jack  1
Kellogg, Steven  6
Klein, Norma  2

Konigsburg, E. L.  1
Kotzwinkle, William  6
Krementz, Jill  5
Kuskin, Karla  4
Langstaff, John  3
Lawson, Robert  2
Le Guin, Ursula K.  3
L'Engle, Madeleine  1
LeShan, Eda J.  6
Lester, Julius  2
Lionni, Leo  7
Livingston, Myra Cohn  7
Lobel, Arnold  5
Lowry, Lois  6
Manley, Seon  3
Mathis, Sharon Bell  3
McCloskey, Robert  7
McCord, David  9
McDermott, Gerald  9
McHargue, Georgess  2
Monjo, F. N.  2
Myers, Walter Dean  4
Ness, Evaline  6
O'Brien, Robert C.  2
O'Dell, Scott  1
Paterson, Katherine  7
Pinkwater, D. Manus  4
Pringle, Laurence  4
Raskin, Ellen  1
Rau, Margaret  8
Rey, H. A.  5
Rey, Margret  5
Rockwell, Thomas  6
Sachs, Marilyn  2
Scarry, Richard  3
Schwartz, Alvin  3
Selden, George  8
Selsam, Millicent E.  1

Sendak, Maurice  1
Seuss, Dr.  9
Showers, Paul  6
Shulevitz, Uri  5
Silverstein, Shel  5
Simon, Seymour  9
Singer, Isaac Bashevis  1
Slote, Alfred  4
Sneve, Virginia Driving Hawk  2
Sobol, Donald J.  4
Speare, Elizabeth George  8
Spier, Peter  5
Steig, William  2
Steptoe, John  2
Sterling, Dorothy  1
Suhl, Yuri  2
Taylor, Mildred D.  9
Thomas, Ianthe  8
Tobias, Tobi  4
Tunis, Edwin  2
Uchida, Yoshiko  6
Van Allsburg, Chris  5
Viorst, Judith  3
Watson, Clyde  3
Weiss, Harvey  4
Wersba, Barbara  3
White, E. B.  1
White, Robb  3
Wibberley, Leonard  3
Wilder, Laura Ingalls  2
Willard, Nancy  5
Williams, Jay  8
Williams, Vera B.  9
Wojciechowska, Maia  1
Yashima, Taro  4
Yep, Laurence  3
Yolen, Jane  4

Zim, Herbert S.   2
Zindel, Paul   3
Zolotow, Charlotte   2

**AUSTRALIAN**
Chauncy, Nan   6
Lindsay, Norman   8
Phipson, Joan   5
Southall, Ivan   2
Travers, P. L.   2
Wrightson, Patricia   4

**AUSTRIAN**
Bemelmans, Ludwig   6

**BELGIAN**
Hergé   6

**CANADIAN**
Burnford, Sheila   2
Houston, James   3
Hughes, Monica   9
Kurelek, William   2
Lee, Dennis   3
Little, Jean   4
Montgomery, L. M.   8
Stren, Patti   5

**CHILEAN**
Krahn, Fernando   3

**CZECHOSLOVAKIAN**
Sasek, M.   4

**DANISH**
Andersen, Hans Christian   6

**DUTCH**
Bruna, Dick   7
DeJong, Meindert   1
Lionni, Leo   7
Spier, Peter   5

**ENGLISH**
Aiken, Joan   1
Ardizzone, Edward   3
Ashley, Bernard   4
Bawden, Nina   2
Bond, Michael   1
Boston, L. M.   3
Burningham, John   9
Burton, Hester   1
Carroll, Lewis   2
Chauncy, Nan   6
Christopher, John   2
Cooper, Susan   4
Dahl, Roald   1, 7
Farmer, Penelope   8
Greenaway, Kate   6
Grahame, Kenneth   5
Hughes, Monica   9
Hughes, Ted   3
Lear, Edward   1
Lewis, C. S.   3
Lively, Penelope   7
Macaulay, David   3
Milne, A. A.   1
Nesbit, E.   3
Norton, Mary   6
Oakley, Graham   7
Pearce, Philippa   9
Peyton, K. M.   3
Pieńkowski, Jan   6

Potter, Beatrix   1
Ransome, Arthur   8
Serraillier, Ian   2
Sutcliff, Rosemary   1
Townsend, John Rowe   2
Travers, P. L.   2
Treece, Henry   2
Walsh, Jill Paton   2
Wildsmith, Brian   2
Willard, Barbara   2
Williams, Kit   4

**FILIPINO**
Aruego, Jose   5

**FINNISH**
Jansson, Tove   2

**FRENCH**
Brunhoff, Jean de   4
Brunhoff, Laurent de   4
Ungerer, Tomi   3

**GERMAN**
Kästner, Erich   4
Krüss, James   9
Rey, H. A.   5
Rey, Margret   5
Zimnik, Reiner   3

**GREEK**
Zei, Alki   6

**ISRAELI**
Shulevitz, Uri   5

**ITALIAN**
Collodi, Carlo   5
Munari, Bruno   9

**JAPANESE**
Anno, Mitsumasa   2
Watanabe, Shigeo   8
Yashima, Taro   4

**NEW ZEALAND**
Mahy, Margaret   7

**POLISH**
Pieńkowski, Jan   6
Shulevitz, Uri   5
Singer, Isaac Bashevis   1
Suhl, Yuri   2
Wojciechowska, Maia   1

**RUSSIAN**
Korinetz, Yuri   4

**SCOTTISH**
Burnford, Sheila   2

**SOUTH AFRICAN**
Lewin, Hugh   9

**SWEDISH**
Gripe, Maria   5
Lagerlöf, Selma   7
Lindgren, Astrid   1

**WELSH**
Dahl, Roald   1, 7

# CUMULATIVE INDEX TO TITLES

*A and THE; or, William T. C. Baumgarten Comes to Town* (Raskin)  **1**:155
*A Apple Pie* (Greenaway)  **6**:134
*ABC* (Burningham)  **9**:39
*ABC* (Lear)  **1**:126
*ABC* (Munari)  **9**:125
*ABC* (Pieńkowski)  **6**:233
*The ABC Bunny* (Gág)  **4**:90
*ABCDEFGHIJKLMNOP-QRSTUVWXYZ* (Kuskin)  **4**:138
*A Building on Your Street* (Simon)  **9**:207
*A Chair for My Mother* (Williams)  **9**:232
*A Dog So Small* (Pearce)  **9**:149
*A Flower with Love* (Munari)  **9**:130
*A Is for Always* (Anglund)  **1**:19
*A Tree on Your Street* (Simon)  **9**:208
*About the B'nai Bagels* (Konigsburg)  **1**:119
*About the Foods You Eat* (Simon)  **9**:215
*About the Sleeping Beauty* (Travers)  **2**:176
*Abraham Lincoln* (Foster)  **7**:94
*Abraham Lincoln's World* (Foster)  **7**:92
*The Acorn Quest* (Yolen)  **4**:268
*Across Five Aprils* (Hunt)  **1**:109
*Across the Sea* (Goffstein)  **3**:57
*Adam Clayton Powell: Portrait of a Marching Black* (Haskins)  **3**:63
*Adler und Taube* (Krüss)  **9**:86
*Adventures in Making: The Romance of Crafts around the World* (Manley)  **3**:145

*The Adventures of Pinocchio* (Collodi)  **5**:69
*Africa Dream* (Greenfield)  **4**:100
*The Age of Giant Mammals* (Cohen)  **3**:37
*Air in Fact and Fancy* (Slote)  **4**:199
*Akavak: An Eskimo Journey* (Houston)  **3**:84
*Alan Mendelsohn, the Boy from Mars* (Pinkwater)  **4**:169
*Album of Dogs* (Henry)  **4**:112
*Album of Horses* (Henry)  **4**:112
*The Alchemists: Magic into Science* (Aylesworth)  **6**:50
*Alexander and the Terrible, Horrible, No Good, Very Bad Day* (Viorst)  **3**:207
*Alexander and the Wind-Up Mouse* (Lionni)  **7**:133
*Alexander Soames: His Poems* (Kuskin)  **4**:137
*Alice's Adventures in Wonderland* (Carroll)  **2**:31
*All about Horses* (Henry)  **4**:114
*All Around You* (Bendick)  **5**:36
*All Day Long: Fifty Rhymes of the Never Was and Always Is* (McCord)  **9**:100
*All in the Woodland Early* (Yolen)  **4**:265
*All My Men* (Ashley)  **4**:15
*All Sizes of Noises* (Kuskin)  **4**:137
*All the Colors of the Race: Poems* (Adoff)  **7**:37
*All Upon a Stone* (George)  **1**:89
*All Us Come Cross the Water* (Clifton)  **5**:54

*The Alley* (Estes)  **2**:73
*The Alligator Case* (du Bois)  **1**:62
*Alligator Pie* (Lee)  **3**:115
*Alligators All Around* (Sendak)  **1**:167
*Alligators and Crocodiles* (Zim)  **2**:225
*All-of-a-Sudden Susan* (Coatsworth)  **2**:53
*Allumette: A Fable, with Due Respect to Hans Christian Andersen, the Grimm Brothers, and the Honorable Ambrose Bierce* (Ungerer)  **3**:199
*The Almost All-White Rabbity Cat* (DeJong)  **1**:55
*Alone in the Wild Forest* (Singer)  **1**:173
*Along Came a Dog* (DeJong)  **1**:56
*The Alphabet Tree* (Lionni)  **7**:133
*Altogether, One at a Time* (Konigsburg)  **1**:119
*Always Reddy* (Henry)  **4**:110
*Amanda, Dreaming* (Wersba)  **3**:215
*The Amazing Laser* (Bova)  **3**:31
*American Colonial Paper House: To Cut Out and Color* (Ness)  **6**:208
*Amifika* (Clifton)  **5**:58
*Amos and Boris* (Steig)  **2**:158
*Amy and Laura* (Sachs)  **2**:131
*Amy Moves In* (Sachs)  **2**:131
*Anansi the Spider: A Tale from the Ashanti* (McDermott)  **9**:110

*Anastasia Again!* (Lowry)  **6**:195
*Anastasia at Your Service* (Lowry)  **6**:196
*Anastasia Krupnik* (Lowry)  **6**:194
*Ancient Monuments and How They Were Built* (Cohen)  **3**:37
*The Ancient Visitors* (Cohen)  **3**:38
*And It Rained* (Raskin)  **1**:155
*And So My Garden Grows* (Spier)  **5**:219
*And Then What Happened, Paul Revere?* (Fritz)  **2**:79
*And to Think That I Saw It on Mulberry Street* (Seuss)  **1**:84; **9**:172
*Andrew Jackson* (Foster)  **7**:95
*Andy (That's My Name)* (de Paola)  **4**:55
*Angels and Other Strangers: Family Christmas Stories* (Paterson)  **7**:237
*Angie's First Case* (Sobol)  **4**:212
*Animal Fact/Animal Fable* (Simon)  **9**:213
*The Animal Family* (Jarrell)  **6**:162
*Animal Superstitions* (Aylesworth)  **6**:56
*Animal Territories* (Cohen)  **3**:38
*The Animals and the Ark* (Kuskin)  **4**:135
*Animals and Their Niches: How Species Share Resources* (Pringle)  **4**:183
*Animals as Parents* (Selsam)  **1**:159

*The Animals' Conference*
(Kästner)  **4**:125

*Animals for Sale* (Munari)  **9**:124

*Animals in Field and Laboratory: Science Projects in Animal Behavior* (Simon)  **9**:201

*Animals in Your Neighborhood*
(Simon)  **9**:211

*Annaluise and Anton*
(Kästner)  **4**:123

*Anne of Avonlea*
(Montgomery)  **8**:134

*Anne of Green Gables*
(Montgomery)  **8**:131

*Anne of Ingleside*
(Montgomery)  **8**:139

*Anne of the Island*
(Montgomery)  **8**:137

*Anno's Alphabet: An Adventure in Imagination* (Anno)  **2**:1

*The Ants Who Took Away Time*
(Kotzwinkle)  **6**:183

*Any Me I Want to Be: Poems*
(Kuskin)  **4**:140

*The Apple and Other Fruits*
(Selsam)  **1**:160

*Apples* (Hogrogian)  **2**:87

*April Fools* (Krahn)  **3**:103

*Apt. 3* (Keats)  **1**:113

*Arabel's Raven* (Aiken)  **1**:2

*Archimedes and the Door of Science* (Bendick)  **5**:40

*Are All the Giants Dead?*
(Norton)  **6**:225

*Are You There God? It's Me, Margaret.* (Blume)  **2**:15

*Arm in Arm: A Collection of Connections, Endless Tales, Reiterations, and Other Echolalia* (Charlip)  **8**:28

*The Arm of the Starfish*
(L'Engle)  **1**:129

*Armitage, Armitage, Fly Away Home* (Aiken)  **1**:2

*Armored Animals* (Zim)  **2**:225

*The Armourer's House*
(Sutcliff)  **1**:183

*Around Fred's Bed*
(Pinkwater)  **4**:165

*Around the World in Eighty Days*
(Burningham)  **9**:44

*Arrow to the Sun: A Pueblo Indian Tale*
(McDermott)  **9**:111

*Art and Archaeology*
(Glubok)  **1**:95

*The Art and Industry of Sandcastles: Being an Illustrated Guide to Basic Constructions along with Divers Information Devised by One Jan Adkins, a Wily Fellow* (Adkins)  **7**:18

*The Art of America from Jackson to Lincoln* (Glubok)  **1**:95

*The Art of America in the Gilded Age* (Glubok)  **1**:95

*The Art of Ancient Mexico*
(Glubok)  **1**:96

*The Art of Ancient Peru*
(Glubok)  **1**:96

*The Art of China* (Glubok)  **1**:97

*The Art of India* (Glubok)  **1**:97

*The Art of Japan* (Glubok)  **1**:97

*The Art of Lands in the Bible*
(Glubok)  **1**:98

*The Art of the Etruscans*
(Glubok)  **1**:98

*The Art of the New American Nation* (Glubok)  **1**:99

*The Art of the North American Indian* (Glubok)  **1**:99

*The Art of the Northwest Coast Indians* (Glubok)  **1**:99

*The Art of the Spanish in the United States and Puerto Rico* (Glubok)  **1**:100

*Arthur Mitchell* (Tobias)  **4**:215

*Arts and Crafts You Can Eat*
(Cobb)  **2**:64

*Ash Road* (Southall)  **2**:147

*Astercote* (Lively)  **7**:151

*Astrology and Foretelling the Future* (Aylesworth)  **6**:50

*At Mary Bloom's* (Aliki)  **9**:25

*At the Beach* (Tobias)  **4**:217

*Attar of the Ice Valley*
(Wibberley)  **3**:224

*August the Fourth* (Farmer)  **8**:86

*Augustus Caesar's World, a Story of Ideas and Events from B.C. 44 to 14 A.D.* (Foster)  **7**:93

*Auno and Tauno: A Story of Finland* (Henry)  **4**:109

*Autumn Street* (Lowry)  **6**:195

*Avocado Baby*
(Burningham)  **9**:50

*Away and Ago: Rhymes of the Never Was and Always Is*
(McCord)  **9**:102

*The BFG* (Dahl)  **7**:82

*B is een beer* (Bruna)  **7**:50

*B Is for Bear: An ABC*
(Bruna)  **7**:50

*Babar and Father Christmas*
(Brunhoff)  **4**:32

*Babar and His Children*
(Brunhoff)  **4**:32

*Babar and the Old Lady*
(Brunhoff)  **4**:37

*Babar and the Professor*
(Brunhoff)  **4**:34

*Babar and the Wully-Wully*
(Brunhoff)  **4**:39

*Babar at Home* (Brunhoff)  **4**:32

*Babar at the Seashore*
(Brunhoff)  **4**:38

*Babar at the Seaside*
(Brunhoff)  **4**:38

*Babar Comes to America*
(Brunhoff)  **4**:36

*Babar Goes on a Picnic*
(Brunhoff)  **4**:38

*Babar Goes Skiing*
(Brunhoff)  **4**:38

*Babar in the Snow*
(Brunhoff)  **4**:38

*Babar Loses His Crown*
(Brunhoff)  **4**:37

*Babar the Gardener*
(Brunhoff)  **4**:38

*Babar the King* (Brunhoff)  **4**:31

*Babar Visits Another Planet*
(Brunhoff)  **4**:38

*Babar's Birthday Surprise*
(Brunhoff)  **4**:38

*Babar's Castle* (Brunhoff)  **4**:35

*Babar's Childhood*
(Brunhoff)  **4**:37

*Babar's Coronation*
(Brunhoff)  **4**:37

*Babar's Cousin: That Rascal Arthur* (Brunhoff)  **4**:33

*Babar's Day Out*
(Brunhoff)  **4**:38

*Babar's Fair* (Brunhoff)  **4**:34

*Babar's French Lessons*
(Brunhoff)  **4**:35

*Babar's Mystery*
(Brunhoff)  **4**:39

*Babar's Picnic* (Brunhoff)  **4**:34

*Babar's Trunk* (Brunhoff)  **4**:38

*Babar's Visit to Bird Island*
(Brunhoff)  **4**:34

*The Baby* (Burningham)  **9**:46

*A Baby Sister for Frances*
(Hoban)  **3**:75

*A Baby Starts to Grow*
(Showers)  **6**:244

*Backstage* (Isadora and Maiorano)  **7**:104

*The Bad Island* (Steig)  **2**:158

*The Bad Speller* (Steig)  **2**:159

*The Baker and the Basilisk*
(McHargue)  **2**:117

*The Bakers: A Simple Book about the Pleasures of Baking Bread* (Adkins)  **7**:22

*The Ballad of St. Simeon*
(Serraillier)  **2**:135

*The Ballad of the Pilgrim Cat*
(Wibberley)  **3**:224

*Bang Bang You're Dead*
(Fitzhugh and Scoppettone)  **1**:71

*Barefoot in the Grass*
(Armstrong)  **1**:22

*A Bargain for Frances*
(Hoban)  **3**:75

*Bartholomew and the Oobleck*
(Seuss)  **9**:177

*The Baseball Trick*
(Corbett)  **1**:42

*Bass and Billy Martin*
(Phipson)  **5**:182

*The Bastable Children*
(Nesbit)  **3**:161

*The Bat-Poet* (Jarrell)  **6**:158

*The Battle for the Atlantic*
(Williams)  **8**:223

*The Battle of Bubble and Squeak*
(Pearce)  **9**:156

*Battleground: The United States Army in World War II*
(Collier)  **3**:44

*The Bear and the People*
(Zimnik)  **3**:242

*A Bear Called Paddington*
(Bond)  **1**:27

*Bear Circus* (du Bois)  **1**:62

*The Bear Who Saw the Spring*
(Kuskin)  **4**:136

*The Bear's House* (Sachs)  **2**:131

*The Bears of the Air*
(Lobel)  **5**:164

*Bear's Picture*
(Pinkwater)  **4**:162

*The Beast of Monsieur Racine*
(Ungerer)  **3**:200

*The Beast with the Magical Horn*
(Cameron)  **1**:39

*The Beasts of Never*
(McHargue)  **2**:117

*Beauty and the Beast*
(Pearce)  **9**:154

*The Beckoning Lights*
(Hughes)  **9**:77

*Bed-knob and Broomstick*
(Norton)  **6**:222

*Bedtime for Frances*
(Hoban)  **3**:75

*The Beethoven Medal*
(Peyton)  **3**:171

*Beezus and Ramona*
(Cleary)  **2**:45; **8**:47

*Before You Came This Way*
(Baylor)  **3**:13

*Before You Were a Baby*
(Showers and Showers)  **6**:244

*Beneath Your Feet*
(Simon)  **9**:211

*Benjamin West and His Cat Grimalkin* (Henry)  **4**:110

*Ben's Dream* (Van Allsburg)  **5**:240

*Ben's Trumpet* (Isadora)  **7**:104

*Benson Boy* (Southall)  **2**:148

*Beowulf* (Sutcliff)  **1**:183

*Beowulf the Warrior*
(Serraillier)  **2**:135

*Bertie's Escapade*
(Grahame)  **5**:135

*Bess and the Sphinx*
(Coatsworth)  **2**:53

*Best Word Book Ever*
(Scarry)  **3**:182

*Betje Big gaat naar de markt*
(Bruna)  **7**:52

*Betrayed* (Sneve)  **2**:143

*Beyond the Burning Lands*
(Christopher)  **2**:37

*Beyond the Dark River*
(Hughes)  **9**:71

*Beyond the Tomorrow Mountains*
(Engdahl)  **2**:69

*Beyond the Weir Bridge*
(Burton)  **1**:30

*Big Anthony and the Magic Ring*
(de Paola)  **4**:62

*The Big Cleanup* (Weiss)  **4**:224

*The Big Joke Game*
(Corbett)  **1**:43

*The Big Orange Splot*
(Pinkwater)  **4**:166

*Big Sister Tells Me That I'm Black* (Adoff)  **7**:33

*The Big Six* (Ransome)  **8**:180

*The Biggest House in the World*
(Lionni)  **7**:132

*Bill and Pete* (de Paola)  **4**:61

*Bill Bergson and the White Rose Rescue* (Lindgren)  **1**:135

*Bill Bergson Lives Dangerously*
(Lindgren)  **1**:135

*Bill Bergson, Master Detective*
(Lindgren)  **1**:135

*Bill's Garage* (Spier)  **5**:228

*Bill's Service Station*
(Spier)  **5**:228

*Billy Goat and His Well-Fed Friends* (Hogrogian)  **2**:87

*Billy's Balloon Ride*
(Zimnik)   **3**:242
*Billy's Picture* (Rey)   **5**:196
*Binary Numbers* (Watson)   **3**:211
*The Bird and the Stars*
(Showers)   **6**:246
*The Bird Smugglers*
(Phipson)   **5**:184
*Birds at Home* (Henry)   **4**:109
*Birds on Your Street*
(Simon)   **9**:208
*Birds: Poems* (Adoff)   **7**:37
*Birkin* (Phipson)   **5**:180
*Birth of a Forest* (Selsam)   **1**:160
*Birth of an Island*
(Selsam)   **1**:160
*Birthday* (Steptoe)   **2**:162
*The Birthday Present*
(Munari)   **9**:125
*The Birthday Visitor*
(Uchida)   **6**:257
*A Birthday Wish*
(Emberley)   **5**:100
*Birthdays of Freedom: America's
Heritage from the Ancient
World* (Foster)   **7**:95
*Birthdays of Freedom: From the
Fall of Rome to July 4, 1776,
Book Two* (Foster)   **7**:97
*The Bishop and the Devil*
(Serraillier)   **2**:136
*The Black BC's* (Clifton)   **5**:53
*The Black Cauldron*
(Alexander)   **1**:11; **5**:18
*The Black Death, 1347-1351*
(Cohen)   **3**:39
*Black Folktales* (Lester)   **2**:112
*Black Gold* (Henry)   **4**:113
*Black Hearts in Battersea*
(Aiken)   **1**:2
*Black Is Brown Is Tan*
(Adoff)   **7**:32
*The Black Island* (Hergé)   **6**:148
*The Black Pearl* (O'Dell)   **1**:145
*Black Pilgrimage*
(Feelings)   **5**:106
*The Blanket* (Burningham)   **9**:47
*The Blonk from Beneath the Sea*
(Bendick)   **5**:38
*Blood* (Zim)   **2**:225
*The Bloody Country* (Collier and
Collier)   **3**:44
*Blowfish Live in the Sea*
(Fox)   **1**:76
*Blubber* (Blume)   **2**:16
*Blue Moose* (Pinkwater)   **4**:163
*The Blue Thing*
(Pinkwater)   **4**:166
*Blue Trees, Red Sky*
(Klein)   **2**:97
*Blueberries for Sal*
(McCloskey)   **7**:205
*Bo the Constrictor That Couldn't*
(Stren)   **5**:231
*Boat Book* (Gibbons)   **8**:95
*Body Sense/Body Nonsense*
(Simon)   **9**:217
*The Body Snatchers*
(Cohen)   **3**:39
*Boek zonder woorden*
(Bruna)   **7**:51
*Bones* (Zim)   **2**:226

*Bonhomme and the Huge Beast*
(Brunhoff)   **4**:39
*The Book of Dragons*
(Nesbit)   **3**:162
*The Book of Nursery and Mother
Goose Rhymes* (de
Angeli)   **1**:52
*A Book of Scary Things*
(Showers)   **6**:247
*The Book of Three*
(Alexander)   **1**:12; **5**:18
*Border Hawk: August Bondi*
(Alexander)   **5**:17
*Bored—Nothing to Do!*
(Spier)   **5**:226
*Borka: The Adventures of a
Goose with No Feathers*
(Burningham)   **9**:38
*Born to Trot* (Henry)   **4**:111
*The Borrowers* (Norton)   **6**:220
*The Borrowers Afield*
(Norton)   **6**:221
*The Borrowers Afloat*
(Norton)   **6**:222
*The Borrowers Aloft*
(Norton)   **6**:223
*The Borrowers Avenged*
(Norton)   **6**:226
*Boss Cat* (Hunter)   **3**:97
*The Boundary Riders*
(Phipson)   **5**:178
*A Box Full of Infinity*
(Williams)   **8**:231
*A Boy Had a Mother Who Bought
Him a Hat* (Kuskin)   **4**:141
*The Boy Who Didn't Believe in
Spring* (Clifton)   **5**:54
*The Boy Who Spoke Chimp*
(Yolen)   **4**:268
*The Boy Who Was Followed
Home* (Mahy)   **7**:183
*Boy without a Name*
(Lively)   **7**:159
*Brady* (Fritz)   **2**:79
*Brainstorm* (Myers)   **4**:157
*Brave Buffalo Fighter (Waditaka
Tatanka Kisisohitika)*
(Fitzgerald)   **1**:69
*The Brave Cowboy*
(Anglund)   **1**:19
*Bread and Honey*
(Southall)   **2**:149
*Bread and Jam for Frances*
(Hoban)   **3**:76
*Break in the Sun* (Ashley)   **4**:17
*Brian Wildsmith's ABC*
(Wildsmith)   **2**:208
*Brian Wildsmith's Birds*
(Wildsmith)   **2**:208
*Brian Wildsmith's Circus*
(Wildsmith)   **2**:209
*Brian Wildsmith's Fishes*
(Wildsmith)   **2**:210
*Brian Wildsmith's Mother Goose:
A Collection of Nursery
Rhymes* (Wildsmith)   **2**:210
*Brian Wildsmith's 1, 2, 3's*
(Wildsmith)   **2**:211
*Brian Wildsmith's Puzzles*
(Wildsmith)   **2**:211
*Brian Wildsmith's The Twelve
Days of Christmas*
(Wildsmith)   **2**:212

*Brian Wildsmith's Wild Animals*
(Wildsmith)   **2**:212
*Bridge to Terabithia*
(Paterson)   **7**:232
*Briefe an Pauline* (Krüss)   **9**:87
*Brighty of the Grand Canyon*
(Henry)   **4**:112
*The Bronze Bow* (Speare)   **8**:208
*Brother Dusty-Feet*
(Sutcliff)   **1**:184
*Brothers of the Wind*
(Yolen)   **4**:268
*Bruno Munari's ABC*
(Munari)   **9**:125
*Bruno Munari's Zoo*
(Munari)   **9**:127
*Bubbles* (Greenfield)   **4**:96
*The Bug That Laid the Golden
Eggs* (Selsam)   **1**:160
*Bulbs, Corms, and Such*
(Selsam)   **1**:161
*Bunnicula: A Rabbit-Tale of
Mystery* (Howe and
Howe)   **9**:56
*The Burglar Next Door*
(Williams)   **8**:235
*The Buried Moon and Other
Stories* (Bang)   **8**:19
*The Burning of Njal*
(Treece)   **2**:182
*Burt Dow, Deep-Water Man: A
Tale of the Sea in the Classic
Tradition* (McCloskey)   **7**:210
*The Bus under the Leaves*
(Mahy)   **7**:182
*Busiest People Ever*
(Scarry)   **3**:183
*The Butter Battle Book*
(Seuss)   **9**:194
*By the Great Horn Spoon!*
(Fleischman)   **1**:73
*By the Shores of Silver Lake*
(Wilder)   **2**:205
*C.O.L.A.R.: A Tale of Outer
Space* (Slote)   **4**:203
*A Calf Is Born* (Cole)   **5**:64
*Calico Captive* (Speare)   **8**:205
*Call Me Bandicoot* (du
Bois)   **1**:63
*Camilla* (L'Engle)   **1**:129
*Can I Keep Him?*
(Kellogg)   **6**:170
*Candy* (White)   **3**:220
*Cannonball Simp*
(Burningham)   **9**:41
*The Capricorn Bracelet*
(Sutcliff)   **1**:184
*Captain Kidd's Cat*
(Lawson)   **2**:109
*Captain of the Planter: The Story
of Robert Smalls*
(Sterling)   **1**:177
*Cargo Ships* (Zim and
Skelly)   **2**:226
*Carousel* (Crews)   **7**:61
*Carrie's War* (Bawden)   **2**:10
*Cars, Boats, Trains, and Planes
of Today and Tomorrow*
(Aylesworth)   **6**:52
*The Case of the Gone Goose*
(Corbett)   **1**:43
*The Case of the Silver Skull*
(Corbett)   **1**:43

*The Castle Number Nine*
(Bemelmans)   **6**:65
*A Castle of Bone* (Farmer)   **8**:80
*The Castle of Llyr*
(Alexander)   **1**:12; **5**:19
*The Castle of Yew* (Boston)   **3**:26
*Castors Away* (Burton)   **1**:30
*The Cat and the Captain*
(Coatsworth)   **2**:54
*The Cat in the Hat* (Seuss)   **1**:84;
**9**:182
*The Cat in the Hat Beginner
Book Dictionary, by the Cat
Himself and P. D. Eastman*
(Seuss and Eastman)   **9**:188
*The Cat in the Hat Comes Back!*
(Seuss)   **9**:184
*The Cat Who Went to Heaven*
(Coatsworth)   **2**:54
*The Cat Who Wished to Be a
Man* (Alexander)   **1**:12; **5**:22
*Caterpillars* (Sterling)   **1**:178
*Cathedral: The Story of Its
Construction*
(Macaulay)   **3**:140
*The Cats* (Phipson)   **5**:184
*A Cat's Body* (Cole)   **5**:68
*The Cat's Quizzer* (Seuss)   **9**:193
*The Cave above Delphi*
(Corbett)   **1**:43
*CDB!* (Steig)   **2**:159
*Cecily G. and the Nine Monkeys*
(Rey)   **5**:192
*The Celery Stalks at Midnight*
(Howe)   **9**:59
*Cells: The Basic Structure of Life*
(Cobb)   **2**:64
*Centerburg Tales*
(McCloskey)   **7**:207
*Central City/Spread City: The
Metropolitan Regions Where
More and More of Us Spend
Our Lives* (Schwartz)   **3**:188
*The Centurion* (Treece)   **2**:183
*Ceramics: From Clay to Kiln*
(Weiss)   **4**:223
*Chains, Webs, and Pyramids:
The Flow of Energy in Nature*
(Pringle)   **4**:179
*The Challenge of the Green
Knight* (Serraillier)   **2**:136
*Chancy and the Grand Rascal*
(Fleischman)   **1**:73
*The Changing Earth*
(Viorst)   **3**:207
*Chariot in the Sky: A Story of the
Jubilee Singers*
(Bontemps)   **6**:82
*Charity at Home*
(Willard)   **2**:216
*Charlie and the Chocolate
Factory* (Dahl)   **1**:49; **7**:69
*Charlie and the Great Glass
Elevator: The Further
Adventures of Charlie Bucket
and Willy Wonka, Chocolate-
Maker Extraordinary*
(Dahl)   **1**:50; **7**:73
*"Charlie Needs a Cloak"* (de
Paola)   **4**:55
*Charlotte Sometimes*
(Farmer)   **8**:78
*Charlotte's Web* (White)   **1**:193

*Chasing the Goblins Away* (Tobias) 4:216

*Chaucer and His World* (Serraillier) 2:137

*Chemistry in the Kitchen* (Simon) 9:203

*Chester Cricket's New Home* (Selden) 8:202

*Chester Cricket's Pigeon Ride* (Selden) 8:201

*The Chewing-Gum Rescue and Other Stories* (Mahy) 7:186

*The Chichi Hoohoo Bogeyman* (Sneve) 2:144

*A Chick Hatches* (Cole) 5:64

*Chicken Soup with Rice* (Sendak) 1:167

*Child of the Owl* (Yep) 3:235

*The Children Come Running* (Coatsworth) 2:54

*The Children of Green Knowe* (Boston) 3:26

*The Children of Noisy Village* (Lindgren) 1:135

*The Children of the House* (Pearce and Fairfax-Lucy) 9:152

*Childtimes: A Three-Generation Memoir* (Greenfield and Little) 4:101

*The China People* (Farmer) 8:76

*Chinaman's Reef Is Ours* (Southall) 2:149

*Chip Rogers, Computer Whiz* (Simon) 9:221

*Chipmunks on the Doorstep* (Tunis) 2:191

*The Christmas Book* (Bruna) 7:49

*Christmas in Noisy Village* (Lindgren) 1:136

*Christmas in the Stable* (Lindgren) 1:136

*Christmas Is a Time of Giving* (Anglund) 1:19

*Christmas Manger* (Rey) 5:194

*Christmas Time* (Gibbons) 8:94

*Chronicles of Avonlea, in Which Anne Shirley of Green Gables and Avonlea Plays Some Part* (Montgomery) 8:136

The Chronicles of Narnia (Lewis) 3:126

*The Church Cat Abroad* (Oakley) 7:215

*The Church Mice Adrift* (Oakley) 7:217

*The Church Mice and the Moon* (Oakley) 7:216

*The Church Mice at Bay* (Oakley) 7:218

*The Church Mice at Christmas* (Oakley) 7:220

*The Church Mice in Action* (Oakley) 7:223

*The Church Mice Spread Their Wings* (Oakley) 7:217

*The Church Mouse* (Oakley) 7:213

*Les Cigares du Pharaon* (Hergé) 6:148

*The Cigars of the Pharaoh* (Hergé) 6:148

*Cinnabar, the One O'Clock Fox* (Henry) 4:113

*A Circle of Seasons* (Livingston) 7:174

*The Circus in the Mist* (Munari) 9:128

*City: A Story of Roman Planning and Construction* (Macaulay) 3:142

*City and Suburb: Exploring an Ecosystem* (Pringle) 4:180

*City of Darkness* (Bova) 3:32

*The City of Gold and Lead* (Christopher) 2:38

*City Seen from A to Z* (Isadora) 7:108

*Clancy's Cabin* (Mahy) 7:183

*The Clashing Rocks: The Story of Jason* (Serraillier) 2:137

*Clay, Wood, and Wire: A How-To-Do-It Book of Sculpture* (Weiss) 4:220

*Clocks and How They Go* (Gibbons) 8:90

*The Cloud Book: Words and Pictures* (de Paola) 4:57

*The Clown of God: An Old Story* (de Paola) 4:61

*Cluck Baa* (Burningham) 9:51

*The Coat-Hanger Christmas Tree* (Estes) 2:73

*Cockroaches* (Cole) 5:61

*Cockroaches: Here, There, and Everywhere* (Pringle) 4:176

*A Cold Wind Blowing* (Willard) 2:216

*Coll and His White Pig* (Alexander) 1:13; 5:19

*Collage and Construction* (Weiss) 4:225

*Colonial Craftsmen and the Beginnings of American Industry* (Tunis) 2:192

*Colonial Living* (Tunis) 2:192

*A Color of His Own* (Lionni) 7:137

*Colors* (Pieńkowski) 6:230

*A Colour of His Own* (Lionni) 7:137

*Colours* (Pieńkowski) 6:230

*Come Away* (Livingston) 7:170

*Come Away from the Water, Shirley* (Burningham) 9:47

*Comet in Moominland* (Jansson) 2:93

*Coming Home from the War: An Idyll* (Krüss) 9:87

*Commercial Fishing* (Zim and Krantz) 2:226

*The Complete Adventures of Charlie and Mr. Willy Wonka* (Dahl) 7:77

*The Complete Book of Dragons* (Nesbit) 3:162

*Computer Sense, Computer Nonsense* (Simon) 9:221

*Confessions of an Only Child* (Klein) 2:97

*The Controversial Coyote: Predation, Politics, and Ecology* (Pringle) 4:182

*The Cookie Tree* (Williams) 8:229

*Coot Club* (Ransome) 8:176

*Corals* (Zim) 2:226

*Corn Is Maize: The Gift of the Indians* (Aliki) 9:24

*Cornelius* (Lionni) 7:140

*Count Up: Learning Sets* (Burningham) 9:50

*The Counterfeit African* (Williams) 8:221

*The Country of the Heart* (Wersba) 3:215

*The Court of the Stone Children* (Cameron) 1:39

*The Courtship of Animals* (Selsam) 1:161

*Cowboy and His Friend* (Anglund) 1:19

*The Cowboy's Christmas* (Anglund) 1:20

*Cowboy's Secret Life* (Anglund) 1:20

*Coyote Cry* (Baylor) 3:14

*Coyote in Manhattan* (George) 1:89

*Crabs* (Zim and Krantz) 2:227

*The Craft of Sail* (Adkins) 7:20

*The Crane* (Zimnik) 3:242

*Crash! Bang! Boom!* (Spier) 5:221

*A Crazy Flight and Other Poems* (Livingston) 7:169

*The Creoles of Color of New Orleans* (Haskins) 3:63

*The Cricket in Times Square* (Selden) 8:196

*Crisis on Conshelf Ten* (Hughes) 9:69

*A Crocodile's Tale: A Philippine Folk Tale* (Aruego and Aruego) 5:30

*The Crooked Snake* (Wrightson) 4:240

*Cross Your Fingers, Spit in Your Hat: Superstitions and Other Beliefs* (Schwartz) 3:188

*Crow Boy* (Yashima) 4:251

*The Cruise of the Arctic Star* (O'Dell) 1:145

*The Cuckoo Tree* (Aiken) 1:3

*The Cupboard* (Burningham) 9:47

*Curious George* (Rey) 5:193

*Curious George Flies a Kite* (Rey) 5:198

*Curious George Gets a Medal* (Rey) 5:198

*Curious George Goes to the Hospital* (Rey) 5:199

*Curious George Learns the Alphabet* (Rey) 5:199

*Curious George Rides a Bike* (Rey) 5:196

*Curious George Takes a Job* (Rey) 5:196

*The Curse of Cain* (Southall) 2:150

*Cutlass Island* (Corbett) 1:44

*Da lontano era un'isola* (Munari) 9:129

*Daedalus and Icarus* (Farmer) 8:79

*Daisy* (Coatsworth) 2:54

*Daisy Summerfield's Style* (Goffstein) 3:58

*Dance in the Desert* (L'Engle) 1:130

*The Dancing Camel* (Byars) 1:35

*The Dancing Kettle and Other Japanese Folk Tales* (Uchida) 6:250

*Danger from Below: Earthquakes, Past, Present, and Future* (Simon) 9:213

*Danger Point: The Wreck of the Birkenhead* (Corbett) 1:44

*Danny Dunn and the Anti-Gravity Paint* (Williams and Abrashkin) 8:222

*Danny Dunn and the Automatic House* (Williams and Abrashkin) 8:227

*Danny Dunn and the Fossil Cave* (Williams and Abrashkin) 8:225

*Danny Dunn and the Heat Ray* (Williams and Abrashkin) 8:225

*Danny Dunn and the Homework Machine* (Williams and Abrashkin) 8:223

*Danny Dunn and the Smallifying Machine* (Williams and Abrashkin) 8:230

*Danny Dunn and the Swamp Monster* (Williams and Abrashkin) 8:232

*Danny Dunn and the Universal Glue* (Williams and Abrashkin) 8:236

*Danny Dunn and the Voice from Space* (Williams and Abrashkin) 8:229

*Danny Dunn and the Weather Machine* (Williams and Abrashkin) 8:223

*Danny Dunn, Invisible Boy* (Williams and Abrashkin) 8:233

*Danny Dunn on a Desert Island* (Williams and Abrashkin) 8:223

*Danny Dunn on the Ocean Floor* (Williams and Abrashkin) 8:224

*Danny Dunn, Scientific Detective* (Williams and Abrashkin) 8:234

*Danny Dunn, Time Traveler* (Williams and Abrashkin) 8:226

*Danny Goes to the Hospital* (Collier) 3:44

*Danny: The Champion of the World* (Dahl) 7:74

*The Dark Bright Water* (Wrightson) 4:246

*The Dark Canoe* (O'Dell) 1:146

*The Dark Is Rising* (Cooper) 4:44

*Darlene* (Greenfield) 4:103

*Daughter of Earth: A Roman Myth* (McDermott) 9:119

*David's Witch Doctor* (Mahy) 7:184

*Dawn* (Bang)   **8**:23
*Dawn* (Shulevitz)   **5**:206
*Dawn from the West: The Story of Genevieve Caulfield* (Rau)   **8**:185
*A Dawn in the Trees: Thomas Jefferson, the Years 1776 to 1789* (Wibberley)   **3**:224
*Dawn of Fear* (Cooper)   **4**:43
*Dawn Wind* (Sutcliff)   **1**:184
*A Day of Pleasure: Stories of a Boy Growing Up in Warsaw* (Singer)   **1**:173
*The Day the Gang Got Rich* (Kotzwinkle)   **6**:181
*The Day the Numbers Disappeared* (Bendick and Simon)   **5**:40
*The Day the Teacher Went Bananas* (Howe)   **9**:59
*Daydreamers* (Greenfield)   **4**:103
*Daylight Robbery* (Williams)   **8**:235
*Days with Frog and Toad* (Lobel)   **5**:173
*Dead Man's Light* (Corbett)   **1**:44
*Deadly Ants* (Simon)   **9**:214
*Deadmen's Cave* (Wibberley)   **3**:225
*Dear Mr. Henshaw* (Cleary)   **8**:59
*Dear Readers and Riders* (Henry)   **4**:115
*Death Is Natural* (Pringle)   **4**:181
*Deathwatch* (White)   **3**:221
*Deenie* (Blume)   **2**:16
*Delpha Green and Company* (Cleaver and Cleaver)   **6**:108
*Department Store* (Gibbons)   **8**:98
*Desert Dan* (Coatsworth)   **2**:55
*The Desert Is Theirs* (Baylor)   **3**:14
*Devil on My Back* (Hughes)   **9**:78
*The Devil Rides with Me and Other Fantastic Stories* (Slote)   **4**:203
*Devil's Hill* (Chauncy)   **6**:90
*The Devil's Storybook* (Babbit)   **2**:5
*Dick Bruna's Animal Book* (Bruna)   **7**:51
*Dick Bruna's Word Book* (Bruna)   **7**:53
*Dick Foote and the Shark* (Babbitt)   **2**:5
*Did I Ever Tell You How Lucky You Are?* (Geisel)   **1**:85
*Died on a Rainy Sunday* (Aiken)   **1**:3
*Dierenboek* (Bruna)   **7**:51
*Digging Up Dinosaurs* (Aliki)   **9**:28
*Dinner Ladies Don't Count* (Ashley)   **4**:18
*Dinner Time* (Pieńkowski)   **6**:231
*The Dinosaur Is the Biggest Animal That Ever Lived and Other Wrong Ideas You Thought Were True* (Simon)   **9**:220

*Dinosaur Story* (Cole)   **5**:63
*Dinosaurs* (Zim)   **2**:227
*Dinosaurs and People: Fossils, Facts, and Fantasies* (Pringle)   **4**:184
*Dinosaurs and Their World* (Pringle)   **4**:174
*Diogenes: The Story of the Greek Philosopher* (Aliki)   **9**:21
*The Disappearing Dog Trick* (Corbett)   **1**:44
*Disaster* (Sobol)   **4**:211
*Discovering the Royal Tombs at Ur* (Glubok)   **1**:100
*Discovering What Earthworms Do* (Simon)   **9**:202
*Discovering What Frogs Do* (Simon)   **9**:202
*Discovering What Gerbils Do* (Simon)   **9**:204
*Discovering What Goldfish Do* (Simon)   **9**:202
*Do Tigers Ever Bite Kings?* (Wersba)   **3**:216
*Do You Have the Time, Lydia?* (Ness)   **6**:207
*Dr. Anno's Magical Midnight Circus* (Anno)   **2**:2
*Dr. Merlin's Magic Shop* (Corbett)   **1**:45
*Dr. Seuss's ABC* (Seuss)   **1**:85; **9**:187
*Dr. Seuss's Sleep Book* (Seuss)   **1**:85; **9**:187
*The Dog* (Burningham)   **9**:47
*A Dog and a Half* (Willard)   **2**:217
*The Dog Days of Arthur Cane* (Bethancourt)   **3**:18
*The Dog That Could Swim under Water: Memoirs of a Springer Spaniel* (Selden)   **8**:196
*Dogs and Dragons, Trees and Dreams: A Collection of Poems* (Kuskin)   **4**:144
*The Dolphin Crossing* (Walsh)   **2**:197
*Dom and Va* (Christopher)   **2**:39
*Dominic* (Steig)   **2**:159
*The Dong with the Luminous Nose* (Lear)   **1**:127
*''Don't Play Dead Before You Have To''* (Wojciechowska)   **1**:196
*Don't You Remember?* (Clifton)   **5**:55
*The Door in the Wall* (de Angeli)   **1**:53
*Door to the North* (Coatsworth)   **2**:55
*Dorrie's Book* (Sachs)   **2**:132
*A Double Discovery* (Ness)   **6**:203
*The Double Quest* (Sobol)   **4**:206
*Down Half the World* (Coatsworth)   **2**:55
*Down to Earth* (Wrightson)   **4**:242
*Dragon Night and Other Lullabies* (Yolen)   **4**:266
*The Dragon of an Ordinary Family* (Mahy)   **7**:179

*The Dragon Takes a Wife* (Myers)   **4**:156
*Dragonfly Summer* (Farmer)   **8**:79
*Dragonwings* (Yep)   **3**:236
*Dream Days* (Grahame)   **5**:128
*Dream of Dark Harbor* (Kotzwinkle)   **6**:183
*The Dream Time* (Treece)   **2**:183
*The Dream Watcher* (Wersba)   **3**:216
*Dream Weaver* (Yolen)   **4**:265
*Dreams* (Keats)   **1**:114
*Dreams, Visions and Drugs: A Search for Other Realities* (Cohen)   **3**:39
*Drei Mal Drei: An Einem Tag* (Krüss)   **9**:85
*The Driftway* (Lively)   **7**:154
*The Drinking Gourd* (Monjo)   **2**:120
*A Drop of Blood* (Showers)   **6**:243
*Drummer Hoff* (Emberley)   **5**:94
*Duck on a Pond* (Willard)   **2**:217
*The Dueling Machine* (Bova)   **3**:32
*The Dunkard* (Selden)   **8**:199
*Dust of the Earth* (Cleaver and Cleaver)   **6**:110
*ESP* (Aylesworth)   **6**:50
*E.T.: The Extra-Terrestrial* (Kotzwinkle)   **6**:184
*E.T.: The Extra-Terrestrial Storybook* (Kotzwinkle)   **6**:185
*Eagle and Dove* (Krüss)   **9**:86
*Eagle Mask: A West Coast Indian Tale* (Houston)   **3**:85
*The Eagle of the Ninth* (Sutcliff)   **1**:185
*Early Thunder* (Fritz)   **2**:80
*Earth: Our Planet in Space* (Simon)   **9**:220
*Earthdark* (Hughes)   **9**:69
*The Earthsea Trilogy* (Le Guin)   **3**:118
*The Easter Cat* (DeJong)   **1**:56
*Eats: Poems* (Adoff)   **7**:35
*Ecology* (Bendick)   **5**:48
*Ecology: Science of Survival* (Pringle)   **4**:175
*Ed Emberley's A B C* (Emberley)   **5**:100
*Ed Emberley's Amazing Look Through Book* (Emberley)   **5**:101
*Ed Emberley's Big Green Drawing Book* (Emberley)   **5**:102
*Ed Emberley's Big Orange Drawing Book* (Emberley)   **5**:102
*Ed Emberley's Big Purple Drawing Book* (Emberley)   **5**:103
*Ed Emberley's Crazy Mixed-Up Face Game* (Emberley)   **5**:103
*Ed Emberley's Drawing Book: Make a World* (Emberley)   **5**:98
*Ed Emberley's Drawing Book of Animals* (Emberley)   **5**:97

*Ed Emberley's Drawing Book of Faces* (Emberley)   **5**:99
*Ed Emberley's Great Thumbprint Drawing Book* (Emberley)   **5**:100
*The Edge of the Cloud* (Peyton)   **3**:172
*Egg Thoughts and Other Frances Songs* (Hoban)   **3**:76
*Egg to Chick* (Selsam)   **1**:161
*The Eggs: A Greek Folk Tale* (Aliki)   **9**:20
*Ego-Tripping and Other Poems for Young People* (Giovanni)   **6**:116
*Eight for a Secret* (Willard)   **2**:217
*The Eighteenth Emergency* (Byars)   **1**:35
*Einstein Anderson Goes to Bat* (Simon)   **9**:218
*Einstein Anderson Lights Up the Sky* (Simon)   **9**:219
*Einstein Anderson Makes Up for Lost Time* (Simon)   **9**:216
*Einstein Anderson, Science Sleuth* (Simon)   **9**:216
*Einstein Anderson Sees Through the Invisible Man* (Simon)   **9**:219
*Einstein Anderson Shocks His Friends* (Simon)   **9**:216
*Einstein Anderson Tells a Comet's Tale* (Simon)   **9**:217
*Electronics for Boys and Girls* (Bendick)   **5**:34
*Elephant Boy: A Story of the Stone Age* (Kotzwinkle)   **6**:180
*The Elephant's Wish* (Munari)   **9**:125
*Elidor and the Golden Ball* (McHargue)   **2**:117
*Elijah the Slave* (Singer)   **1**:174
*Elisabeth the Cow Ghost* (du Bois)   **1**:63
*Elizabite: The Adventures of a Carnivorous Plant* (Rey)   **5**:194
*Eliza's Daddy* (Thomas)   **8**:213
*Ellen Dellen* (Gripe)   **5**:148
*Ellen Grae* (Cleaver and Cleaver)   **6**:101
*Ellen Tebbits* (Cleary)   **2**:45; **8**:45
*The Elm Street Lot* (Pearce)   **9**:153
*Eloquent Crusader: Ernestine Rose* (Suhl)   **2**:165
*Elvis and His Friends* (Gripe)   **5**:148
*Elvis and His Secret* (Gripe)   **5**:148
*Elvis! Elvis!* (Gripe)   **5**:148
*Elvis Karlsson* (Gripe)   **5**:148
*The Emergency Book* (Bendick)   **5**:41
*Emil and Piggy Beast* (Lindgren)   **1**:136
*Emil and the Detectives* (Kästner)   **1**:121
*Emil's Pranks* (Lindgren)   **1**:136
*Emily of New Moon* (Montgomery)   **8**:138

Emily's Runaway Imagination (Cleary) 2:45; 8:50
Emma in Winter (Farmer) 8:78
Emmet Otter's Jug-Band Christmas (Hoban) 3:76
The Emperor and the Kite (Yolen) 4:257
The Emperor's Winding Sheet (Walsh) 2:197
The Enchanted: An Incredible Tale (Coatsworth) 2:56
The Enchanted Castle (Nesbit) 3:162
The Enchanted Island: Stories from Shakespeare (Serraillier) 2:137
Enchantress from the Stars (Engdahl) 2:69
Encounter Near Venus (Wibberley) 3:225
Encyclopedia Brown and the Case of the Dead Eagles (Sobol) 4:210
Encyclopedia Brown and the Case of the Midnight Visitor (Sobol) 4:211
Encyclopedia Brown and the Case of the Secret Pitch (Sobol) 4:207
Encyclopedia Brown, Boy Detective (Sobol) 4:207
Encyclopedia Brown Carries On (Sobol) 4:212
Encyclopedia Brown Finds the Clues (Sobol) 4:208
Encyclopedia Brown Gets His Man (Sobol) 4:208
Encyclopedia Brown Lends a Hand (Sobol) 4:210
Encyclopedia Brown Saves the Day (Sobol) 4:209
Encyclopedia Brown Shows the Way (Sobol) 4:209
Encyclopedia Brown Solves Them All (Sobol) 4:208
Encyclopedia Brown Takes the Case (Sobol) 4:209
Encyclopedia Brown's Record Book of Weird and Wonderful Facts (Sobol) 4:211
End of Exile (Bova) 3:32
An Enemy at Green Knowe (Boston) 3:27
Energy: Power for People (Pringle) 4:179
The Enormous Crocodile (Dahl) 7:77
The Epics of Everest (Wibberley) 3:226
The Erie Canal (Spier) 5:220
Estuaries: Where Rivers Meet the Sea (Pringle) 4:178
Ever Ride a Dinosaur? (Corbett) 1:45
Everett Anderson's Christmas Coming (Clifton) 5:54
Everett Anderson's Friend (Clifton) 5:57
Everett Anderson's Nine Month Long (Clifton) 5:59
Everett Anderson's 1-2-3 (Clifton) 5:58

Everett Anderson's Year (Clifton) 5:55
Every Time I Climb a Tree (McCord) 9:100
Everybody Needs a Rock (Baylor) 3:15
Everyone Knows What a Dragon Looks Like (Williams) 8:235
Everything Moves (Simon) 9:210
Exactly Alike (Ness) 6:201
Exiled from Earth (Bova) 3:33
The Expeditions of Willis Partridge (Weiss) 4:222
The Exploits of Moominpappa (Jansson) 2:93
Explorers on the Moon (Hergé) 6:148
Exploring Fields and Lots: Easy Science Projects (Simon) 9:212
Fables (Lobel) 5:174
Facts, Frauds, and Phantasms: A Survey of the Spiritualist Movement (McHargue) 2:118
A Fall from the Sky: The Story of Daedalus (Serraillier) 2:138
Fall Is Here! (Sterling) 1:178
Family (Donovan) 3:51
The Family Christmas Tree Book (de Paola) 4:65
The Family Conspiracy (Phipson) 5:179
The Family Tower (Willard) 2:217
Famous Negro Athletes (Bontemps) 6:84
Fanny and the Battle of Potter's Piece (Lively) 7:163
Fanny's Sister (Lively) 7:161
Fantastic Mr. Fox (Dahl) 1:51; 7:73
Far and Few: Rhymes of the Never Was and Always Is (McCord) 9:98
Far Out the Long Canal (DeJong) 1:57
The Far Side of Evil (Engdahl) 2:70
Farmer Palmer's Wagon Ride (Steig) 2:160
The Farthest Shore (Le Guin) 3:123
Fast Sam, Cool Clyde, and Stuff (Myers) 4:156
The Fast Sooner Hound (Bontemps and Conroy) 6:79
Fast-Slow, High-Low: A Book of Opposites (Spier) 5:222
Fat Elliot and the Gorilla (Pinkwater) 4:162
Fat Men from Space (Pinkwater) 4:168
Father Fox's Pennyrhymes (Watson) 3:211
A Father Like That (Zolotow) 2:233
The Fearsome Inn (Singer) 1:174
The Feather Star (Wrightson) 4:241
Feelings (Aliki) 9:32
Fiddlestrings (de Angeli) 1:53

Fierce: The Lion (Ness) 6:209
Fifteen (Cleary) 2:46; 8:48
Fighting Men: How Men Have Fought through the Ages (Treece and Oakeshott) 2:184
Fighting Shirley Chisholm (Haskins) 3:64
Fin M'Coul: The Giant of Knockmany Hill (de Paola) 4:66
Find a Stranger, Say Goodbye (Lowry) 6:193
Find Out by Touching (Showers) 6:241
Find the Constellations (Rey) 5:196
Find the Hidden Insect (Cole) 5:66
Finding Out about Jobs: TV Reporting (Bendick and Bendick) 5:48
Finn Family Moomintroll (Jansson) 2:93
Finn's Folly (Southall) 2:150
Fire! Fire! (Gibbons) 8:98
The Fire Station (Spier) 5:228
The Firehouse (Spier) 5:228
The Firemen (Kotzwinkle) 6:180
Fireweed (Walsh) 2:198
The First ABC (Lear) 1:127
First Adventure (Coatsworth) 2:56
The First Book of Airplanes (Bendick) 5:37
The First Book of Fishes (Bendick) 5:41
The First Book of How to Fix It (Bendick and Berk) 5:39
The First Book of Medieval Man (Sobol) 4:206
The First Book of Ships (Bendick) 5:38
The First Book of Space Travel (Bendick) 5:37
The First Book of Supermarkets (Bendick) 5:37
The First Book of Time (Bendick) 5:40
The First Four Years (Wilder) 2:205
A First Look at Birds (Selsam and Hunt) 1:162
A First Look at Leaves (Selsam) 1:162
A First Look at Mammals (Selsam and Hunt) 1:162
The First Margaret Mahy Story Book: Stories and Poems (Mahy) 7:181
The First Peko-Neko Bird (Krahn and Krahn) 3:103
First Pink Light (Greenfield) 4:99
The First Two Lives of Lukas-Kasha (Alexander) 5:24
First Words (Burningham) 9:51
The Fish (Bruna) 7:49
Fish for Supper (Goffstein) 3:58
A Fish Hatches (Cole) 5:65
Fish Head (Fritz) 2:80
Fish Is Fish (Lionni) 7:133
Five Children and It (Nesbit) 3:163

Five Down: Numbers As Signs (Burningham) 9:50
The 500 Hats of Bartholomew Cubbins (Seuss) 9:172
Flambards (Peyton) 3:172
Flambards in Summer (Peyton) 3:173
The Flambards Trilogy (Peyton) 3:173
Fleas (Cole) 5:62
Flicks (de Paola) 4:63
Flight of Exiles (Bova) 3:33
Flight 714 (Hergé) 6:149
Flight to the Forest (Willard) 2:218
Flint's Island (Wibberley) 3:226
Flocks of Birds (Zolotow) 2:234
The Flood at Reedsmere (Burton) 1:31
Fly by Night (Jarrell) 6:165
Fly into Danger (Phipson) 5:184
Fly-by-Night (Peyton) 3:176
A Flying Saucer Full of Spaghetti (Krahn) 3:104
Follow a Fisher (Pringle) 4:178
The Food Market (Spier) 5:228
The Fool of the World and the Flying Ship: A Russian Tale (Ransome) 8:184
The Fools of Chelm and Their History (Singer) 1:174
For Me to Say: Rhymes of the Never Was and Always Is (McCord) 9:101
Forest of the Night (Townsend) 2:169
Forever (Blume) 2:17
The Forever Christmas Tree (Uchida) 6:253
Forever Free: The Story of the Emancipation Proclamation (Sterling) 1:178
Forgetful Fred (Williams) 8:233
Fortunately (Charlip) 8:27
A Fortune for the Brave (Chauncy) 6:89
Fossils Tell of Long Ago (Aliki) 9:21
The Foundling and Other Tales of Prydain (Alexander) 1:13; 5:22
The Four Donkeys (Alexander) 1:14
Four Rooms from the Metropolitan Museum of Art (Ness) 6:208
Four Stories for Four Seasons (de Paola) 4:59
The Four-Story Mistake (Enright) 4:74
4-Way Stop and Other Poems (Livingston) 7:172
The Fox Friend (Coatsworth) 2:57
The Fox Hole (Southall) 2:151
Fox in Socks (Seuss) 1:85; 9:188
The Fox Went Out on a Chilly Night: An Old Song (Spier) 5:217
Franklin Stein (Raskin) 1:155
Frederick (Lionni) 7:131

Frederick Douglass: Slave-Fighter-Freeman (Bontemps) 6:83

Freedom Train: The Story of Harriet Tubman (Sterling) 1:179

Freight Train (Crews) 7:56

The Friend (Burningham) 9:47

Friend Dog (Adoff) 7:36

A Friend Is Someone Who Likes You (Anglund) 1:20

Friend Monkey (Travers) 2:177

Friend: The Story of George Fox and the Quakers (Yolen) 4:259

Frog and Toad All Year (Lobel) 5:170

Frog and Toad Are Friends (Lobel) 5:165

Frog and Toad Together (Lobel) 5:167

Frog Went A-Courtin' (Langstaff) 3:109

The Frogmen (White) 3:221

A Frog's Body (Cole) 5:66

From Afar It Is an Island (Munari) 9:129

From Anna (Little) 4:151

From Lew Alcindor to Kareem Abdul Jabbar (Haskins) 3:64

From Pond to Prairie: The Changing World of a Pond and Its Life (Pringle) 4:176

From Shore to Ocean Floor: How Life Survives in the Sea (Simon) 9:207

From the Mixed-Up Files of Mrs. Basil E. Frankweiler (Konigsburg) 1:120

Frontier Living (Tunis) 2:192

Funniest Storybook Ever (Scarry) 3:183

Funny Bananas (McHargue) 2:118

The Funny Thing (Gág) 4:89

The Further Adventures of Nils (Lagerlöf) 7:110

The Further Adventures of Robinson Crusoe (Treece) 2:184

The Gadget Book (Weiss) 4:226

The Gales of Spring: Thomas Jefferson, the Years 1789-1801 (Wibberley) 3:226

Games and Puzzles You Can Make Yourself (Weiss) 4:228

The Garden of Abdul Gasazi (Van Allsburg) 5:238

The Garden under the Sea (Selden) 8:196

Gases (Cobb) 2:65

The Gats! (Goffstein) 3:59

Gaudenzia, Pride of the Palio (Henry) 4:113

The Genie of Sutton Place (Selden) 8:200

The Gentle Desert: Exploring an Ecosystem (Pringle) 4:183

Geological Disasters: Earthquakes and Volcanoes (Aylesworth) 6:55

(George) (Konigsburg) 1:120

George and Red (Coatsworth) 2:57

George and the Cherry Tree (Aliki) 9:18

George Washington (Foster) 7:93

George Washington's Breakfast (Fritz) 2:81

George Washington's World (Foster) 7:91

George's Marvelous Medicine (Dahl) 7:80

Georgie Has Lost His Cap (Munari) 9:125

Geraldine, the Music Mouse (Lionni) 7:138

Get Set! Go! Overcoming Obstacles (Watanabe) 8:216

The Ghost Dance Caper (Hughes) 9:70

Ghost in a Four-Room Apartment (Raskin) 1:156

The Ghost in the Noonday Sun (Fleischman) 1:74

The Ghost of Thomas Kempe (Lively) 7:154

Ghost Paddle: A Northwest Coast Indian Tale (Houston) 3:85

The Giant (du Bois) 1:63

The Giant Golden Book of Cat Stories (Coatsworth) 2:57

Giant John (Lobel) 5:163

The Giant Panda at Home (Rau) 8:188

The Giants' Farm (Yolen) 4:263

The Giants Go Camping (Yolen) 4:265

A Gift for Sula Sula (Ness) 6:201

The Gift of Sarah Barker (Yolen) 4:267

Gigi cerca il suo berretto (Munari) 9:125

Ginger Pye (Estes) 2:73

The Gingerbread Rabbit (Jarrell) 6:158

A Giraffe and a Half (Silverstein) 5:209

The Girl and the Goatherd; or, This and That and Thus and So (Ness) 6:205

The Girl Who Cried Flowers and Other Tales (Yolen) 4:260

The Girl Who Loved the Wind (Yolen) 4:260

Girls Can Be Anything (Klein) 2:98

Give Dad My Best (Collier) 3:45

The Giving Tree (Silverstein) 5:209

Glasblasarns Barn (Gripe) 5:144

The Glassblower's Children (Gripe) 5:144

Glimpses of Louisa (Alcott) 1:9

Die Glücklichen Inseln Hinter dem Winde (Krüss) 9:83

Die Glücklichen Inseln Hinter dem Winde Bd. 2 (Krüss) 9:84

Go and Hush the Baby (Byars) 1:35

Gobble, Growl, Grunt (Spier) 5:220

The Goblins Giggle and Other Stories (Bang) 8:17

Goggles! (Keats) 1:114

Going Back (Lively) 7:159

Gold: The Fascinating Story of the Noble Metal through the Ages (Cohen) 3:40

The Golden Age (Grahame) 5:126

The Golden Basket (Bemelmans) 6:64

The Golden One (Treece) 2:185

The Golden Road (Montgomery) 8:136

The Golden Serpent (Myers) 4:160

Goldengrove (Walsh) 2:199

Gold-Fever Trail: A Klondike Adventure (Hughes) 9:68

Goldie, the Dollmaker (Goffstein) 3:59

Golly Gump Swallowed a Fly (Cole) 5:68

A Gondola for Fun (Weiss) 4:220

Gone Is Gone; or, The Story of a Man Who Wanted to Do Housework (Gág) 4:90

Gone-Away Lake (Enright) 4:75

Good Ethan (Fox) 1:77

The Good Knight Ghost (Bendick) 5:38

Good Luck Duck (DeJong) 1:57

Good Luck to the Rider (Phipson) 5:177

Good Morning (Bruna) 7:53

Good News (Greenfield) 4:96

Good Night, Prof, Dear (Townsend) 2:170

Good Old James (Donovan) 3:51

Good, Says Jerome (Clifton) 5:55

Good-bye to the Jungle (Townsend) 2:171

The Good-for-Nothing Prince (Williams) 8:230

Goodnight (Hoban) 3:77

Goody Hall (Babbitt) 2:6

The Gorgon's Head: The Story of Perseus (Serraillier) 2:138

Graham Oakley's Magical Changes (Oakley) 7:219

Grand Papa and Ellen Aroon (Monjo) 2:121

Grandfather Learns to Drive (Krüss) 9:88

Grandmother Cat and the Hermit (Coatsworth) 2:58

Granpa (Burningham) 9:52

Graphology: A Guide to Handwriting Analysis (Aylesworth) 6:53

Grasshopper on the Road (Lobel) 5:172

The Gray Kangaroo at Home (Rau) 8:189

The Great Blueness and Other Predicaments (Lobel) 5:165

The Great Brain (Fitzgerald) 1:69

The Great Brain at the Academy (Fitzgerald) 1:69

The Great Brain Reforms (Fitzgerald) 1:69

The Great Flood (Spier) 5:224

The Great Gilly Hopkins (Paterson) 7:235

The Great Millionaire Kidnap (Mahy) 7:184

Great Northern? (Ransome) 8:182

The Great Piratical Rumbustification & The Librarian and the Robbers (Mahy) 7:185

The Great Watermelon Birthday (Williams) 9:231

The Great Wheel (Lawson) 2:109

The Green Coat (Gripe) 5:148

Green Eggs and Ham (Seuss) 1:86; 9:185

The Green Flash and Other Tales of Horror, Suspense, and Fantasy (Aiken) 1:4

Green Grass and White Milk (Aliki) 9:23

Green Says Go (Emberley) 5:96

The Greentail Mouse (Lionni) 7:135

Greenwitch (Cooper) 4:45

Gregory Griggs and Other Nursery Rhyme People (Lobel) 5:172

The Gremlins (Dahl) 7:68

Greta the Strong (Sobol) 4:209

The Grey King (Cooper) 4:47

The Grey Lady and the Strawberry Snatcher (Bang) 8:20

Greyling: A Picture Story from the Islands of Shetland (Yolen) 4:257

The Groober (Byars) 1:36

Grossvater Lerner auf Fahren (Krüss) 9:88

The Grove of Green Holly (Willard) 2:218

Grover (Cleaver and Cleaver) 6:104

Growing Pains: Diaries and Drawings for the Years 1908-1917 (Gág) 4:91

The Guardian of Isis (Hughes) 9:73

The Guardians (Christopher) 2:39

Guarneri: Story of a Genius (Wibberley) 3:227

Guests in the Promised Land (Hunter) 3:98

Gull Number 737 (George) 1:89

Hadassah: Esther the Orphan Queen (Armstrong) 1:22

Half a World Away (Chauncy) 6:91

Halloween (Gibbons) 8:99

The Hand of Apollo (Coatsworth) 2:58

A Handful of Thieves (Bawden) 2:11

Handtalk: An ABC of Finger Spelling and Sign Language (Charlip, Mary Beth, and Ancona) 8:31

Title Index

Hang Tough, Paul Mather (Slote)  4:200
Hansi (Bemelmans)  6:63
Happy Birthday to You! (Seuss)  9:185
The Happy Islands behind the Winds (Krüss)  9:83
The Happy Place (Bemelmans)  6:69
Happy Times in Noisy Village (Lindgren)  1:137
Harbor (Crews)  7:60
Harbour (Crews)  7:60
The Hard Life of the Teenager (Collier)  3:45
The Hare and the Tortoise (Wildsmith)  2:212
The Hare and the Tortoise & The Tortoise and the Hare/La Liebre y la Tortuga y La Tortuga y la Liebre (du Bois and Lee Po)  1:63
Harlequin and the Gift of Many Colors (Charlip and Supree)  8:29
Harquin: The Fox Who Went Down to the Valley (Burningham)  9:41
Harriet the Spy (Fitzhugh)  1:71
Harry Cat's Pet Puppy (Selden)  8:200
The Hat (Ungerer)  3:200
The Hating Book (Zolotow)  2:234
Haunted House (Pieńkowski)  6:230
The Haunting (Mahy)  7:187
Have a Happy Measle, a Merry Mumps, and a Cheery Chickenpox (Bendick, Bendick, and Bendick)  5:38
Havelok the Dane (Serraillier)  2:139
Hawk, I'm Your Brother (Baylor)  3:15
The Hawkstone (Williams)  8:231
Hazel Rye (Cleaver and Cleaver)  6:114
Head in the Clouds (Southall)  2:152
Hear Your Heart (Showers)  6:243
Heat (Cobb)  2:65
Heat and Temperature (Bendick)  5:47
Heather, Oak, and Olive: Three Stories (Sutcliff)  1:185
Heavy Equipment (Adkins)  7:26
Heb jij een hobbie? (Bruna)  7:52
Hector Protector and As I Went over the Water (Sendak)  1:167
Heimkehr aus dem Kriege (Krüss)  9:87
Heinrich Schliemann, Discoverer of Buried Treasure (Selden)  8:198
Helga's Dowry: A Troll Love Story (de Paola)  4:59
Hell's Edge (Townsend)  2:172
Helping Horse (Phipson)  5:183

The Henchmans at Home (Burton)  1:31
Hengest's Tale (Walsh)  2:200
Henry and Beezus (Cleary)  8:46
Henry and Ribsy (Cleary)  2:46; 8:47
Henry and the Clubhouse (Cleary)  8:50
Henry and the Paper Route (Cleary)  2:47; 8:48
Henry Huggins (Cleary)  2:47; 8:44
Heracles the Strong (Serraillier)  2:139
Herbert Hated Being Small (Kuskin)  4:143
Here Comes Thursday! (Bond)  1:27
Here I Stay (Coatsworth)  2:58
Heritage of the Star (Engdahl)  2:70
Herman the Loser (Hoban)  3:77
The Hermit and Harry and Me (Hogrogian)  2:88
The Hero from Otherwhere (Williams)  8:232
Heroes and History (Sutcliff)  1:186
Hetty (Willard)  2:218
Hetty and Harriet (Oakley)  7:221
Hey, Lover Boy (Rockwell)  6:240
"Hey, What's Wrong with This One?" (Wojciechowska)  1:196
Hi, Cat! (Keats)  1:114
Hi! Ho! The Rattlin' Bog and Other Folk Songs for Group Singing (Langstaff)  3:109
Hi, Mrs. Mallory! (Thomas)  8:214
Hickory Stick Rag (Watson)  3:212
The Hidden World: Life under a Rock (Pringle)  4:181
Hidden Worlds: Pictures of the Invisible (Simon)  9:220
Hide and Seek (Coatsworth)  2:59
Hiding Out (Rockwell)  6:238
Higglety Pigglety Pop! or, There Must Be More to Life (Sendak)  1:168
High and Haunted Island (Chauncy)  6:92
The High Deeds of Finn MacCool (Sutcliff)  1:186
High Elk's Treasure (Sneve)  2:144
The High King (Alexander)  1:14; 5:21
The High World (Bemelmans)  6:72
The Highest Hit (Willard)  5:248
Hildegarde and Maximilian (Krahn)  3:104
Hills End (Southall)  2:152
Hisako's Mysteries (Uchida)  6:255
Hobo Toad and the Motorcycle Gang (Yolen)  4:259

The Hoboken Chicken Emergency (Pinkwater)  4:167
Hoists, Cranes, and Derricks (Zim)  2:227
Hold Zero! (George)  1:90
Holding Up the Sky: Young People in China (Rau)  8:194
The Hollywood Kid (Wojciechowska)  1:197
Home from Far (Little)  4:147
The Home Run Trick (Corbett)  1:45
Homer Price (McCloskey)  7:203
The Homework Machine (Williams and Abrashkin)  8:223
Hooray for Me! (Charlip and Moore)  8:31
Hop on Pop (Seuss)  1:86; 9:187
The Horn of Roland (Williams)  8:229
Horned Helmet (Treece)  2:185
The Horse and His Boy (Lewis)  3:134
A Horse Came Running (DeJong)  1:57
The Horse in the Camel Suit (du Bois)  1:64
Horse with Eight Hands (Phipson)  5:183
A Horse's Body (Cole)  5:66
Horton Hatches the Egg (Seuss)  9:174
Horton Hears a Who! (Seuss)  1:86; 9:179
The Hospital Book (Howe)  9:57
The Hotshot (Slote)  4:202
The Hound of Ulster (Sutcliff)  1:186
The House in Norham Gardens (Lively)  7:158
The House of Dies Drear (Hamilton)  1:103
The House of Secrets (Bawden)  2:12
The House of Sixty Fathers (DeJong)  1:58
The House of Wings (Byars)  1:36
The House with Roots (Willard)  2:218
How a House Happens (Adkins)  7:19
How Animals Behave (Bendick)  5:48
How Animals Live Together (Selsam)  1:162
How Animals Tell Time (Selsam)  1:163
How Beastly! (Yolen)  4:266
How Do I Eat It? (Watanabe)  8:216
How Do I Put It On? Getting Dressed (Watanabe)  8:216
How Heredity Works: Why Living Things Are As They Are (Bendick)  5:47
How It Feels When a Parent Dies (Krementz)  5:155
How Many Miles to Babylon? (Fox)  1:77

How Many Teeth? (Showers)  6:242
How Much and How Many: The Story of Weights and Measures (Bendick)  5:35
How Puppies Grow (Selsam)  1:163
How Santa Claus Had a Long and Difficult Journey Delivering His Presents (Krahn)  3:104
How the Doctor Knows You're Fine (Cobb)  2:65
How the Grinch Stole Christmas (Seuss)  1:86; 9:184
How the Whale Became (Hughes)  3:92
How to Be a Hero (Weiss)  4:225
How to Be a Space Scientist in Your Own Home (Simon)  9:218
How to Be an Inventor (Weiss)  4:230
How to Eat Fried Worms (Rockwell)  6:236
How to Eat Fried Worms and Other Plays (Rockwell)  6:239
How to Make a Cloud (Bendick)  5:44
How to Make Your Own Books (Weiss)  4:227
How to Make Your Own Movies: An Introduction to Filmmaking (Weiss)  4:227
How to Run a Railroad: Everything You Need to Know about Model Trains (Weiss)  4:228
How Tom Beat Captain Najork and His Hired Sportsmen (Hoban)  3:78
How We Got Our First Cat (Tobias)  4:218
How You Talk (Showers)  6:242
How Your Mother and Father Met, and What Happened After (Tobias)  4:217
Howliday Inn (Howe)  9:58
Hug Me (Stren)  5:230
Hugo (Gripe)  5:142
Hugo and Josephine (Gripe)  5:143
Hugo och Josefin (Gripe)  5:143
The Hullabaloo ABC (Cleary)  2:47
Human Nature-Animal Nature: The Biology of Human Behavior (Cohen)  3:40
Humbert, Mister Firkin, and the Lord Mayor of London (Burningham)  9:40
Hunches in Bunches (Seuss)  9:194
The Hundred Penny Box (Mathis)  3:149
The Hundredth Dove and Other Tales (Yolen)  4:264
Hunted in Their Own Land (Chauncy)  6:92
Hunter in the Dark (Hughes)  9:74

The Hunting of the Snark: An
  Agony in Eight Fits
  (Carroll)   2:34
Hurrah, We're Outward Bound!
  (Spier)   5:219
Hurry Home, Candy
  (DeJong)   1:58
I, Adam (Fritz)   2:81
I Am a Clown (Bruna)   7:52
I Am Papa Snap and These Are
  My Favorite No Such Stories
  (Ungerer)   3:201
I Am the Running Girl
  (Adoff)   7:35
I Can Build a House!
  (Watanabe)   8:217
I Can Count More (Bruna)   7:51
I Can Do It! (Watanabe)   8:217
I Can Read (Bruna)   7:50
I Can Ride It! Setting Goals
  (Watanabe)   8:217
I Can Take a Walk!
  (Watanabe)   8:217
I Go by Sea, I Go by Land
  (Travers)   2:178
I Had Trouble in Getting to Solla
  Sollew (Seuss)   9:189
I Klockornas Tid (Gripe)   5:145
I Love My Mother
  (Zindel)   3:248
I Never Loved Your Mind
  (Zindel)   3:248
I Own the Racecourse!
  (Wrightson)   4:242
I See What I See!
  (Selden)   8:197
I Want to Stay Here! I Want to
  Go There! A Flea Story
  (Lionni)   7:137
I Wish That I Had Duck Feet
  (Seuss)   1:87; 9:189
I Would Rather Be a Turnip
  (Cleaver and Cleaver)   6:106
The Ice Is Coming
  (Wrightson)   4:245
If All the Swords in England
  (Willard)   2:219
If I Had My Way (Klein)   2:98
If I Ran the Circus (Seuss)   1:87;
  9:181
If I Ran the Zoo (Seuss)   1:87;
  9:178
If It Weren't for You
  (Zolotow)   2:234
Iggie's House (Blume)   2:17
Ik ben een clown (Bruna)   7:52
Ik kan lezen (Bruna)   7:50
I'll Get There. It Better Be Worth
  the Trip. (Donovan)   3:52
The Illustrated Marguerite Henry
  (Henry)   4:116
I'm Hiding (Livingston)   7:168
I'm Only Afraid of the Dark (At
  Night!) (Stren)   5:235
I'm Really Dragged but Nothing
  Gets Me Down
  (Hentoff)   1:107
I'm the King of the Castle!
  Playing Alone
  (Watanabe)   8:217
I'm Trying to Tell You
  (Ashley)   4:18
I'm Waiting (Livingston)   7:169

The Impossible People: A History
  Natural and Unnatural of
  Beings Terrible and Wonderful
  (McHargue)   2:118
In a Beaver Valley: How Beavers
  Change the Land
  (Pringle)   4:175
In a People House
  (Seuss)   9:192
In My Garden (Zolotow)   2:235
In Search of Ghosts
  (Cohen)   3:40
In Spite of All Terror
  (Burton)   1:32
In the Company of Clowns: A
  Commedia (Bacon)   3:11
In the Country of Ourselves
  (Hentoff)   1:108
In the Flaky Frosty Morning
  (Kuskin)   4:140
In the Middle of the Trees
  (Kuskin)   4:135
In the Middle of the World
  (Korinetz)   4:130
In the Night Kitchen
  (Sendak)   1:168
In the Rabbitgarden
  (Lionni)   7:136
In the Time of the Bells
  (Gripe)   5:145
In-Between Miya (Uchida)   6:255
Inch by Inch (Lionni)   7:128
The Incredible Journey
  (Burnford)   2:19
The Incredible Television
  Machine (LeShan and
  Polk)   6:189
Indian Encounters: An Anthology
  of Stories and Poems
  (Coatsworth)   2:59
Indian Festivals
  (Showers)   6:245
Indian Mound Farm
  (Coatsworth)   2:59
Indian Summer (Monjo)   2:121
Indians (Tunis)   2:193
Inside Jazz (Collier)   3:45
Inside: Seeing Beneath the
  Surface (Adkins)   7:21
Intelligence: What Is It?
  (Cohen)   3:41
Into the Woods: Exploring the
  Forest Ecosystem
  (Pringle)   4:178
The Intruder (Townsend)   2:172
The Invaders: Three Stories
  (Treece)   2:185
The Inway Investigators; or, The
  Mystery at McCracken's Place
  (Yolen)   4:258
Irma and Jerry (Selden)   8:201
The Iron Giant: A Story in Five
  Nights (Hughes)   3:92
The Iron Lily (Willard)   2:220
Is This a Baby Dinosaur?
  (Selsam)   1:163
Isabel's Noel (Yolen)   4:257
Isamu Noguchi: The Life of a
  Sculptor (Tobias)   4:214
The Isis Pedlar (Hughes)   9:75
Island of the Blue Dolphins
  (O'Dell)   1:146

The Island of the Grass King:
  The Further Adventures of
  Anatole (Willard)   5:248
The Island of the Skog
  (Kellogg)   6:172
L'Isle noire (Hergé)   6:148
It Ain't All for Nothin'
  (Myers)   4:158
It Happened One Summer
  (Phipson)   5:178
It Looks Like Snow: A Picture
  Book (Charlip)   8:26
It's a Gingerbread House: Bake
  It! Build It! Eat It!
  (Williams)   9:230
It's Not the End of the World
  (Blume)   2:17
It's Not What You Expect
  (Klein)   2:98
Jacob Have I Loved
  (Paterson)   7:238
Jafta (Lewin)   9:90
Jafta—My Father (Lewin)   9:90
Jafta—My Mother (Lewin)   9:90
Jafta—The Journey
  (Lewin)   9:92
Jafta—The Town (Lewin)   9:92
Jafta—The Wedding
  (Lewin)   9:90
Jake (Slote)   4:199
Jambo Means Hello: Swahili
  Alphabet Book
  (Feelings)   5:107
James and the Giant Peach
  (Dahl)   1:51; 7:68
James and the Rain
  (Kuskin)   4:134
Jane, Wishing (Tobias)   4:216
Janey (Zolotow)   2:235
Jangle Twang
  (Burningham)   9:51
A Jar of Dreams (Uchida)   6:259
Jazz Country (Hentoff)   1:108
Jean and Johnny (Cleary)   2:48;
  8:49
Jennie's Hat (Keats)   1:115
Jennifer, Hecate, Macbeth,
  William McKinley, and Me,
  Elizabeth (Konigsburg)   1:121
Jesse and Abe (Isadora)   7:108
Jethro and the Jumbie
  (Cooper)   4:49
The Jezebel Wolf (Monjo)   2:122
Jim Along, Josie: A Collection of
  Folk Songs and Singing Games
  for Young Children (Langstaff
  and Langstaff)   3:110
Jimmy Has Lost His Cap: Where
  Can It Be? (Munari)   9:125
Jimmy of Cherry Valley
  (Rau)   8:186
Jimmy Yellow Hawk
  (Sneve)   2:145
Jingo Django (Fleischman)   1:74
Joan of Arc (Williams)   8:225
Jock's Island (Coatsworth)   2:59
Joe and the Snow (de
  Paola)   4:54
John Henry: An American Legend
  (Keats)   1:115
Johnny the Clockmaker
  (Ardizzone)   3:4

Jokes from Black Folks
  (Haskins)   3:65
Jonah, the Fisherman
  (Zimnik)   3:243
Josefin (Gripe)   5:142
Josefina February (Ness)   6:200
Josephine (Gripe)   5:142
Josh (Southall)   2:153
Journey behind the Wind
  (Wrightson)   4:247
Journey between Worlds
  (Engdahl)   2:70
Journey from Peppermint Street
  (DeJong)   1:58
Journey Home (Uchida)   6:258
Journey to Jericho
  (O'Dell)   1:147
Journey to Topaz: A Story of the
  Japanese-American Evacuation
  (Uchida)   6:256
Journey to Untor
  (Wibberley)   3:228
The Journey with Jonah
  (L'Engle)   1:130
Journeys of Sebastian
  (Krahn)   3:105
Juan and the Asuangs
  (Aruego)   5:28
Julia's House (Gripe)   5:147
Julias Hus och Nattpappan
  (Gripe)   5:147
Julie of the Wolves
  (George)   1:90
Jumanji (Van Allsburg)   5:239
June Anne June Spoon and Her
  Very Adventurous Search for
  the Moon (Kuskin)   4:139
June 7! (Aliki)   9:23
The Juniper Tree, and Other
  Tales from Grimm
  (Sendak)   1:169
Just Cats: Learning Groups
  (Burningham)   9:50
Just Like Everyone Else
  (Kuskin)   4:135
Justin Morgan Had a Horse
  (Henry)   4:109
To kaplani tis Vitrinas
  (Zei)   6:260
Kate (Little)   4:150
The Kate Greenaway Treasury:
  An Anthology of the
  Illustrations and Writings of
  Kate Greenaway
  (Greenaway)   6:135
Kate Greenaway's Book of
  Games (Greenaway)   6:135
Kate Greenaway's Language of
  Flowers (Greenaway)   6:133
Kate Rider (Burton)   1:32
Keep Calm (Phipson)   5:185
Keep Your Mouth Closed, Dear
  (Aliki)   9:19
The Keeper of the Isis Light
  (Hughes)   9:72
Kenny's Window (Sendak)   1:170
Kerstmis (Bruna)   7:49
The Kestrel (Alexander)   5:25
The Kids' Cat Book (de
  Paola)   4:63
Killer Whales (Simon)   9:212
Kilmeny of the Orchard
  (Montgomery)   8:135

Title Index

A Kind of Wild Justice
(Ashley)  4:16
The King and His Friends
(Aruego)  5:27
King George's Head Was Made
of Lead (Monjo)  2:122
King Grisly-Beard
(Sendak)  1:171
King of the Wind (Henry)  4:111
The Kingdom and the Cave
(Aiken)  1:4
A Kingdom in a Horse
(Wojciechowska)  1:197
The King's Beard
(Wibberley)  3:228
The King's Falcon (Fox)  1:78
The King's Fifth (O'Dell)  1:148
The King's Fountain
(Alexander)  1:15; 5:22
The King's Stilts (Seuss)  9:174
Kintu: A Congo Adventure
(Enright)  4:71
The Kissimmee Kid (Cleaver and
Cleaver)  6:113
Kiviok's Magic Journey: An
Eskimo Legend
(Houston)  3:86
Klippity Klop (Emberley)  5:98
The Knee-High Man and Other
Tales (Lester)  2:112
Kneeknock Rise (Babbitt)  2:6
The Knight and the Dragon (de
Paola)  4:64
The Knight of the Lion
(McDermott)  9:117
Knight's Fee (Sutcliff)  1:187
Knights in Armor
(Glubok)  1:100
Knights of the Crusades
(Williams)  8:225
Konta stis ragies (Zei)  6:262
Ladies of the Gothics: Tales of
Romance and Terror by the
Gentle Sex (Manley and
Lewis)  3:145
Lady Ellen Grae (Cleaver and
Cleaver)  6:102
The Lady of Guadalupe (de
Paola)  4:63
Lafcadio, the Lion Who Shot
Back (Silverstein)  5:208
The Land Beyond (Gripe)  5:145
The Land of Black Gold
(Hergé)  6:148
The Land of Forgotten Beasts
(Wersba)  3:217
Landet Utanfor (Gripe)  5:145
The Lantern Bearers
(Sutcliff)  1:187
The Lark and the Laurel
(Willard)  2:220
The Last Battle (Lewis)  3:135
The Last Battle
(Wibberley)  3:228
The Last Guru
(Pinkwater)  4:168
The Last Little Cat
(DeJong)  1:59
The Last Viking (Treece)  2:186
Laura's Luck (Sachs)  2:132
The Lazy Bear
(Wildsmith)  2:213

Lazy Tommy Pumpkinhead (du
Bois)  1:64
Learning to Say Good-By: When
a Parent Dies (LeShan)  6:188
The Legend of New Amsterdam
(Spier)  5:226
The Legend of Old Befana: An
Italian Christmas Story (de
Paola)  4:65
The Lemonade Trick
(Corbett)  1:46
Lens and Shutter: An Introduction
to Photography (Weiss)  4:226
Lentil (McCloskey)  7:200
Leonardo da Vinci
(Williams)  8:226
Leopard's Prey
(Wibberley)  3:229
The Leopard's Tooth
(Kotzwinkle)  6:182
Let Me Fall Before I Fly
(Wersba)  3:218
Let the Balloon Go
(Southall)  2:153
Let the Circle Be Unbroken
(Taylor)  9:228
Let's Make Rabbits: A Fable
(Lionni)  7:139
Let's Try It Out: Hot and Cold
(Simon)  9:206
A Letter to Amy (Keats)  1:115
Letterbox: The Art and History of
Letters (Adkins)  7:27
Letters to Horseface: Being the
Story of Wolfgang Amadeus
Mozart's Journey to Italy,
1769-1770, When He Was a
Boy of Fourteen
(Monjo)  2:123
Letters to Pauline (Krüss)  9:87
Der Leuchtturm auf den Hummer-
Klippen (Krüss)  9:82
Life and Death (Zim and
Bleeker)  2:228
Life and Death in Nature
(Simon)  9:211
The Life and Death of a Brave
Bull (Wojciechowska)  1:198
The Life and Death of Martin
Luther King, Jr.
(Haskins)  3:65
Life in Colonial America
(Speare)  8:210
Life in the Dark: How Animals
Survive at Night
(Simon)  9:208
Life in the Middle Ages
(Williams)  8:227
The Life of Winston Churchill
(Wibberley)  3:229
Life on Ice: How Animals Survive
in the Arctic (Simon)  9:210
Lift Every Voice (Sterling and
Quarles)  1:179
Light (Crews)  7:58
A Light in the Attic
(Silverstein)  5:212
Lighthouse Island
(Coatsworth)  2:60
The Lighthouse Keeper's Son
(Chauncy)  6:94
The Lighthouse on the Lobster
Cliffs (Krüss)  9:82

Lightning (Bendick)  5:39
Lightning and Thunder
(Zim)  2:228
A Likely Place (Fox)  1:78
Limericks by Lear (Lear)  1:127
Lines Scribbled on an Envelope
and Other Poems
(L'Engle)  1:131
A Lion in the Meadow
(Mahy)  7:178
The Lion, the Witch, and the
Wardrobe (Lewis)  3:135
Lisa and Lottie (Kästner)  4:124
Listen for the Fig Tree
(Mathis)  3:149
Listen for the Singing
(Little)  4:152
Listen to the Crows
(Pringle)  4:180
The Listening Walk
(Showers)  6:242
Little Babar Books
(Brunhoff)  4:37, 38
Little Blue and Little Yellow: A
Story for Pippo and Ann and
Other Children (Lionni)  7:127
Little Books (Burningham)  9:46,
47
The Little Brute Family
(Hoban)  3:78
The Little Cow and the Turtle
(DeJong)  1:59
A Little Destiny (Cleaver and
Cleaver)  6:112
The Little Drummer Boy
(Keats)  1:116
Little Giants (Simon)  9:219
Little House in the Big Woods
(Wilder)  2:205
Little House on the Prairie
(Wilder)  2:206
The Little Man (Kästner)  4:127
The Little Man and the Big Thief
(Kästner)  4:127
The Little Man and the Little
Miss (Kästner)  4:127
A Little Oven (Estes)  2:74
The Little Roaring Tiger
(Zimnik)  3:243
A Little Schubert
(Goffstein)  3:59
The Little Spotted Fish
(Yolen)  4:261
Little Tim and the Brave Sea
Captain (Ardizzone)  3:5
Little Town on the Prairie
(Wilder)  2:206
The Little Witch (Mahy)  7:180
Little Women (Alcott)  1:10
The Little Wood Duck
(Wildsmith)  2:213
Lives at Stake: The Science and
Politics of Environmental
Health (Pringle)  4:185
Living Things (Bendick)  5:42
Lizard Music (Pinkwater)  4:164
Lizzie Lights (Chauncy)  6:93
Lock, Stock, and Barrel
(Sobol)  4:207
Locks and Keys (Gibbons)  8:91
The Lollipop Princess: A Play for
Paper Dolls in One Act
(Estes)  2:74

A Lollygag of Limericks
(Livingston)  7:173
London Bridge Is Falling Down
(Emberley)  5:96
London Bridge Is Falling Down!
(Spier)  5:217
Lonesome Boy (Bontemps)  6:83
Long Ago When I Was Young
(Nesbit)  3:164
The Long and Short of
Measurement (Cobb)  2:66
Long, Broad, and Quickeye
(Ness)  6:205
The Long Journey from Space
(Simon)  9:219
Long Journey Home: Stories from
Black History (Lester)  2:113
The Long Lost Coelacanth and
Other Living Fossils
(Aliki)  9:23
The Long Secret (Fitzhugh)  1:72
The Long View into Space
(Simon)  9:214
The Long Winter (Wilder)  2:206
Look at Your Eyes
(Showers)  6:242
Look Through My Window
(Little)  4:149
Look to the Night Sky: An
Introduction to Star Watching
(Simon)  9:212
Look What I Can Do
(Aruego)  5:29
The Lorax (Seuss)  1:87; 9:192
Lordy, Aunt Hattie
(Thomas)  8:212
Lorry Driver (Munari)  9:125
The Lost Dispatch: A Story of
Antietam (Sobol)  4:206
Lotta on Troublemaker Street
(Lindgren)  1:137
Lottie and Lisa (Kästner)  4:124
The Lotus Caves
(Christopher)  2:40
Love and Tennis (Slote)  4:202
Love Is a Special Way of Feeling
(Anglund)  1:20
The Luckiest Girl (Cleary)  2:48
Lucky Chuck (Cleary)  8:61
The Lucky Stone (Clifton)  5:59
Lucretia Mott, Gentle Warrior
(Sterling)  1:179
Lucy Brown and Mr. Grimes
(Ardizzone)  3:5
Lumberjack (Kurelek)  2:101
Luther Tarbox (Adkins)  7:22
M. C. Higgins, The Great
(Hamilton)  1:104
MA nDA LA (Adoff)  7:31
Machine Tools (Zim and
Skelly)  2:229
The MacLeod Place
(Armstrong)  1:22
Madeline (Bemelmans)  6:66
Madeline and the Bad Hat
(Bemelmans)  6:73
Madeline and the Gypsies
(Bemelmans)  6:74
Madeline in London
(Bemelmans)  6:76
Madeline's Rescue
(Bemelmans)  6:69

*The Magic Bed-knob; or, How to Become a Witch in Ten Easy Lessons* (Norton)  **6**:219

*Magic Camera* (Pinkwater)  **4**:162

*The Magic City* (Nesbit)  **3**:164

*The Magic Finger* (Dahl)  **1**:52; **7**:72

*Magic for Marigold* (Montgomery)  **8**:139

*The Magic Gate* (Williams)  **8**:222

*The Magic Grandfather* (Williams)  **8**:237

*The Magic Listening Cap: More Folk Tales from Japan* (Uchida)  **6**:251

*The Magic Moscow* (Pinkwater)  **4**:171

*The Magic Pudding: Being the Adventures of Bunyip Bluegum and His Friends Bill Barnacle and Sam Sawnoff* (Lindsay)  **8**:101

*The Magic Stone* (Farmer)  **8**:77

*The Magic Tree: A Tale from the Congo* (McDermott)  **9**:110

*The Magician* (Shulevitz)  **5**:205

*The Magician's Nephew* (Lewis)  **3**:135

*The Magnificent Morris Mouse Clubhouse* (Gibbons)  **8**:92

*Mai contenti* (Munari)  **9**:125

*Make a Circle, Keep Us In: Poems for a Good Day* (Adoff)  **7**:32

*Make Way for Ducklings* (McCloskey)  **7**:200

*Making Music for Money* (Collier)  **3**:46

*The Making of an Afro-American: Martin Robison Delaney, 1812-1885* (Sterling)  **1**:180

*The Making of Man: The Story of Our Ancient Ancestors* (Collier)  **3**:46

*Making Sense of Money* (Cobb)  **3**:66

*Making the Movies* (Bendick)  **5**:34

*Makoto, the Smallest Boy: A Story of Japan* (Uchida)  **6**:256

*Malcolm X* (Adoff)  **7**:31

*The Malibu and Other Poems* (Livingston)  **7**:170

*Man Changes the Weather* (Bova)  **3**:34

*The Man Who Played Accordion Music* (Tobias)  **4**:218

*The Man Who Talked to a Tree* (Baylor)  **3**:15

*The Man Who Took the Indoors Out* (Lobel)  **5**:168

*The Man Whose Mother Was a Pirate* (Mahy)  **7**:180

*Man with a Sword* (Treece)  **2**:186

*The Man with the Purple Eyes* (Zolotow)  **2**:235

*The Many Lives of Benjamin Franklin* (Aliki)  **9**:25

*The Many Mice of Mr. Brice* (Seuss)  **9**:193

*The Maplin Bird* (Peyton)  **3**:177

*Marcella's Guardian Angel* (Ness)  **6**:208

*Maria Tallchief* (Tobias)  **4**:213

*Marian Anderson* (Tobias)  **4**:213

*The Mark of the Horse Lord* (Sutcliff)  **1**:188

*Marra's World* (Coatsworth)  **2**:60

*Martha, the Movie Mouse* (Lobel)  **5**:164

*The Marvelous Misadventures of Sebastian* (Alexander)  **1**:16; **5**:21

*Marvin K. Mooney Will You Please Go Now* (Geisel)  **1**:88

*Mary Jane* (Sterling)  **1**:180

*Mary McLeod Bethune* (Greenfield)  **4**:99

*Mary Poppins* (Travers)  **2**:178

*Mary Poppins from A to Z* (Travers)  **2**:179

*Mary Poppins in the Park* (Travers)  **2**:179

*The Marzipan Moon* (Willard)  **5**:249

*Masquerade* (Williams)  **4**:231

*The Master Puppeteer* (Paterson)  **7**:231

*Mathinna's People* (Chauncy)  **6**:92

*De matroos* (Bruna)  **7**:50

*Matt and Jo* (Southall)  **2**:155

*Matt Gargan's Boy* (Slote)  **4**:201

*Maurice's Room* (Fox)  **1**:79

*Max* (Isadora)  **7**:102

*Maybe You Should Fly a Jet! Maybe You Should Be a Vet!* (Seuss)  **9**:194

*Mazel and Shlimazel; or, The Milk of the Lioness* (Singer)  **1**:175

*McBroom Tells the Truth* (Fleischman)  **1**:75

*McBroom's Ghost* (Fleischman)  **1**:75

*McBroom's Zoo* (Fleischman)  **1**:75

*McElligot's Pool* (Seuss)  **9**:175

*Me and My Captain* (Goffstein)  **3**:60

*Me and My Family Tree* (Showers)  **6**:247

*Me and My Little Brain* (Fleischman)  **1**:70

*Me and Neesie* (Greenfield)  **4**:99

*Me and Willie and Pa: The Story of Abraham Lincoln and His Son Tad* (Monjo)  **2**:124

*Me Too* (Cleaver and Cleaver)  **6**:109

*Measuring* (Bendick)  **5**:45

*Medicine* (Zim)  **2**:229

*A Medieval Feast* (Aliki)  **9**:30

*Meet My Folks!* (Hughes)  **3**:93

*Meet the Austins* (L'Engle)  **1**:131

*Meet the Giant Snakes* (Simon)  **9**:214

*Ho megalos peripatos tou Petrou* (Zei)  **6**:261

*Mein Urgrossvater, die Helden und Ich* (Krüss)  **9**:87

*Mein Urgrossvater und Ich* (Krüss)  **9**:83

*The Mellops' Go Spelunking* (Ungerer)  **3**:202

*Men from the Village Deep in the Mountains and Other Japanese Folk Tales* (Bang)  **8**:18

*Men of the Hills* (Treece)  **2**:187

*The Mermaid and the Whale* (McHargue)  **2**:119

*The Merrymaker* (Suhl)  **2**:165

*Michael Bird-Boy* (de Paola)  **4**:57

*Microbes at Work* (Selsam)  **1**:163

*The Middle Moffat* (Estes)  **2**:74

*The Midnight Fox* (Byars)  **1**:36

*Midnight Is a Place* (Aiken)  **1**:4

*Miffy in the Hospital* (Bruna)  **7**:52

*Miffy's Dream* (Bruna)  **7**:52

*The Mighty Ones* (DeJong)  **1**:59

*Mik and the Prowler* (Uchida)  **6**:253

*Milkweed* (Selsam)  **1**:164

*The Milky Way Galaxy: Man's Exploration of the Stars* (Bova)  **3**:34

*Millions of Cats* (Gág)  **4**:87

*The Mills of God* (Armstrong)  **1**:23

*The Mimosa Tree* (Cleaver and Cleaver)  **6**:105

*Mine for Keeps* (Little)  **4**:147

*Ming Lo Moves the Mountain* (Lobel)  **5**:176

*The Minnow Family—Chubs, Dace, Minnows, and Shiners* (Pringle)  **4**:180

*The Minnow Leads to Treasure* (Pearce)  **9**:143

*Minnow on the Say* (Pearce)  **9**:143

*The Minority Peoples of China* (Rau)  **8**:193

*The Minstrel and the Mountain* (Yolen)  **4**:257

*Miranda the Great* (Estes)  **2**:74

*Mirror Magic* (Simon)  **9**:215

*Missee Lee* (Ransome)  **8**:180

*The Missing Maple Syrup Sap Mystery; or, How Maple Syrup Is Made* (Gibbons)  **8**:90

*The Missing Piece* (Silverstein)  **5**:211

*The Missing Piece Meets the Big O* (Silverstein)  **5**:212

*Mr. Bass' Planetoid* (Cameron)  **1**:40

*Mr Bidery's Spidery Garden* (McCord)  **9**:101

*Mr Gumpy's Motor Car* (Burningham)  **9**:45

*Mr Gumpy's Outing* (Burningham)  **9**:43

*Mr. Kelso's Lion* (Bontemps)  **6**:84

*Mr. Mysterious and Company* (Fleischman)  **1**:75

*Mr. Noah and the Second Flood* (Burnford)  **2**:20

*Mr. Revere and I* (Lawson)  **2**:110

*Mrs. Cockle's Cat* (Pearce)  **9**:149

*Mrs Discombobulous* (Mahy)  **7**:179

*Mrs. Frisby and the Rats of NIMH* (O'Brien)  **2**:127

*Mistresses of Mystery: Two Centuries of Suspense Stories by the Gentle Sex* (Manley and Lewis)  **3**:145

*Misty of Chincoteague* (Henry)  **4**:110

*Mitch and Amy* (Cleary)  **2**:48; **8**:52

*The Mock Revolt* (Cleaver and Cleaver)  **6**:107

*Model Buildings and How to Make Them* (Weiss)  **4**:229

*Model Cars and Trucks and How to Build Them* (Weiss)  **4**:227

*Moe Q. McGlutch, He Smoked Too Much* (Raskin)  **1**:156

*The Moffats* (Estes)  **2**:75

*Mog at the Zoo* (Pieńkowski and Nicoll)  **6**:233

*Mog's Mumps* (Pieńkowski and Nicoll)  **6**:230

*Moja Means One: Swahili Counting Book* (Feelings)  **5**:105

*Mojo and the Russians* (Myers)  **4**:157

*Mom, the Wolf Man, and Me* (Klein)  **2**:99

*Momo's Kitten* (Yashima and Yashima)  **4**:253

*Monkeys* (Zim)  **2**:229

*The Monsters' Ball* (de Paola)  **4**:54

*Monsters from the Movies* (Aylesworth)  **6**:49

*Moominpappa at Sea* (Jansson)  **2**:94

*Moominsummer Madness* (Jansson)  **2**:94

*Moominvalley in November* (Jansson)  **2**:94

*The Moon and a Star and Other Poems* (Livingston)  **7**:168

*The Moon by Night* (L'Engle)  **1**:132

*The Moon in Fact and Fancy* (Slote)  **4**:198

*Moon Man* (Ungerer)  **3**:202

*The Moon Ribbon and Other Tales* (Yolen)  **4**:262

*The Moon Walker* (Showers)  **6**:247

*The Mooncusser's Daughter* (Aiken)  **1**:5

*Moon-Whales and Other Moon Poems* (Hughes)  **3**:93

*More Adventures of the Great Brain* (Fitzgerald)  **1**:70

*More Tales from Grimm* (Gág)  **4**:94

*Morgan's Zoo* (Howe)  **9**:60

*Morning Is a Little Child* (Anglund)  **1**:21

*The Mortal Instruments* (Bethancourt)  **3**:18

*Mother Goose; or, The Old Nursery Rhymes* (Greenaway)  6:132
*Mother, Mother, I Feel Sick, Send for the Doctor Quick, Quick, Quick: A Picture Book and Shadow Play* (Charlip and Supree)  8:27
*Motion and Gravity* (Bendick)  5:45
*Motors and Engines and How They Work* (Weiss)  4:225
*Mountain Rose* (Stren)  5:234
*The Mouse and His Child* (Hoban)  3:78
*The Mouse and the Motorcycle* (Cleary)  2:48; 8:51
*Mouse Days: A Book of Seasons* (Lionni)  7:139
*Mouse Soup* (Lobel)  5:171
*Mouse Tales* (Lobel)  5:168
*Movie Monsters* (Aylesworth)  6:51
*Moving Day* (Tobias)  4:215
*Moving Heavy Things* (Adkins)  7:25
*Much Bigger than Martin* (Kellogg)  6:174
*Muley-Ears, Nobody's Dog* (Henry)  4:113
*Mummies* (McHargue)  2:119
*Mummies Made in Egypt* (Aliki)  9:27
*The Muppet Guide to Magnificent Manners: Featuring Jim Henson's Muppets* (Howe)  9:60
*Museum: The Story of America's Treasure Houses* (Schwartz)  3:189
*Music, Music for Everyone* (Williams)  9:235
*Musk Oxen: Bearded Ones of the Arctic* (Rau)  8:188
*Mustang, Wild Spirit of the West* (Henry)  4:115
*My Ballet Class* (Isadora)  7:105
*My Book about Me: By Me, Myself. I Wrote It! I Drew It! With a Little Help from My Friends Dr. Seuss and Roy McKie* (Seuss and McKie)  9:191
*My Brother Fine with Me* (Clifton)  5:56
*My Brother Sam Is Dead* (Collier and Collier)  3:47
*My Crazy Sister* (Goffstein)  3:60
*My Darling, My Hamburger* (Zindel)  3:249
*My Father, the Coach* (Slote)  4:200
*My Friend Jacob* (Clifton)  5:60
*My Friend John* (Zolotow)  3:236
*My Great-Grandfather and I: Useful and Amusing Occurrences and Inspirations from the Lobster Shack on Helgoland Told to the "Leathery Lisbeth" and Embellished with Verses from*

*My Great-Grandfather and Me, Carefully Put on Paper for Children of All Ages* (Krüss)  9:83
*My Great-Grandfather, the Heroes, and I: A Brief Study of Heroes in Verse and Prose, Made Up and Told in Several Attic Rooms by My Great-Grandfather and Myself* (Krüss)  9:87
*My Heart's in Greenwich Village* (Manley)  3:146
*My Heart's in the Heather* (Manley)  3:146
*My Mama Says There Aren't Any Zombies, Ghosts, Vampires, Creatures, Demons, Monsters, Fiends, Goblins, or Things* (Viorst)  3:208
*My Name Is Paula Popowich!* (Hughes)  9:77
*My Puppy Is Born* (Cole)  5:63
*My Robot Buddy* (Slote)  4:201
*My School* (Spier)  5:228
*My Side of the Mountain* (George)  1:91
*My Special Best Words* (Steptoe)  2:163
*My Street's a Morning Cool Street* (Thomas)  8:213
*My Trip to Alpha I* (Slote)  4:202
*My Visit to the Dinosaurs* (Aliki)  9:21
*The Mysterious Disappearance of Leon (I Mean Noel)* (Raskin)  1:156
*The Mysterious Tadpole* (Kellogg)  6:175
*The Mystery Beast of Ostergeest* (Kellogg)  6:170
*The Mystery of the Flying Orange Pumpkin* (Kellogg)  6:177
*The Mystery of the Giant Footsteps* (Krahn)  3:105
*The Mystery of the Loch Ness Monster* (Bendick)  5:49
*The Mystery of the Magic Green Ball* (Kellogg)  6:175
*The Mystery of the Missing Red Mitten* (Kellogg)  6:172
*The Mystery of the Stolen Blue Paint* (Kellogg)  6:178
*Names, Sets, and Numbers* (Bendick)  5:43
*Nana Upstairs and Nana Downstairs* (de Paola)  4:54
*Naomi in the Middle* (Klein)  2:100
*The Nap Master* (Kotzwinkle)  6:183
*The Nargun and the Stars* (Wrightson)  4:244
*Nathaniel Hawthorne: Captain of the Imagination* (Manley)  3:147
*Nattpappan* (Gripe)  5:146
*Natural Fire: Its Ecology in Forests* (Pringle)  4:184
*Near the Window Tree: Poems and Notes* (Kuskin)  4:142
*A Near Thing for Captain Najork* (Hoban)  3:81

*A Necklace of Raindrops* (Aiken)  1:6
*Nella nebbia di Milano* (Munari)  9:128
*The Neon Motorcycle* (Rockwell)  6:237
*Nessie the Monster* (Hughes)  3:94
*New Friends for Susan* (Uchida)  6:251
*New Road!* (Gibbons)  8:96
*New Year's Day* (Aliki)  9:20
*New York City Too Far from Tampa Blues* (Bethancourt)  3:19
*New Zealand: Yesterday and Today* (Mahy)  7:184
*Nicholas and the Fast Moving Diesel* (Ardizzone)  3:6
*Nicholas Knock and Other People* (Lee)  3:116
*Nicky Goes to the Doctor* (Scarry)  3:184
*Night Again* (Kuskin)  4:144
*Night Birds on Nantucket* (Aiken)  1:6
*The Night Daddy* (Gripe)  5:146
*Night Fall* (Aiken)  1:6
*A Night without Stars* (Howe)  9:58
*Night's Nice* (Emberley)  5:92
*Nijntje in het ziekenhuis* (Bruna)  7:52
*Nijntje's droom* (Bruna)  7:52
*Nils Holgerssons underbara resa genom Sverige* (Lagerlöf)  7:110
*Nine Lives* (Alexander)  5:18
*No, Agatha!* (Isadora)  7:106
*No Bath Tonight* (Yolen)  4:265
*No Beat of Drum* (Burton)  1:32
*No Kiss for Mother* (Ungerer)  3:202
*No Measles, No Mumps for Me* (Showers)  6:248
*No Promises in the Wind* (Hunt)  1:109
*No Way of Knowing: Dallas Poems* (Livingston)  7:174
*Noah's Ark* (Spier)  5:224
*The Noble Doll* (Coatsworth)  2:60
*Nobody Plays with a Cabbage* (DeJong)  1:60
*Nobody's Family Is Going to Change* (Fitzhugh)  1:73
*Noisy Words* (Burningham)  9:51
*Nonsense Book* (Lear)  1:127
*Nonstop Nonsense* (Mahy)  7:184
*Not What You Expected* (Aiken)  1:7
*Notes to a Science Fiction Writer* (Bova)  3:35
*Nothing at All* (Gág)  4:92
*Nothing Ever Happens on My Block* (Raskin)  1:157
*Nothing Like a Fresh Coat of Paint* (Spier)  5:225
*Now One Foot, Now the Other* (de Paola)  4:65
*Nuclear Power: From Physics to Politics* (Pringle)  4:185
*Number Play* (Burningham)  9:50

*The Nursery "Alice"* (Carroll)  2:35
*Nutshell Library* (Sendak)  1:171
*O Sliver of Liver: Together with Other Triolets, Cinquains, Haiku, Verses, and a Dash of Poems* (Livingston)  7:173
*Observation* (Bendick)  5:45
*Odyssey of Courage: The Story of Alvar Nunez Cabeza de Vaca* (Wojciechowska)  1:198
*Of Course Polly Can Ride a Bike* (Lindgren)  1:137
*Of Dikes and Windmills* (Spier)  5:219
*Of Nightingales That Weep* (Paterson)  7:230
*Oh, A-Hunting We Will Go* (Langstaff)  3:110
*Oh, Say Can You Say?* (Seuss)  9:193
*Oh, Were They Ever Happy!* (Spier)  5:225
*Oh What a Noise!* (Shulevitz)  5:204
*Ol' Dan Tucker* (Langstaff)  3:110
*Old Mrs. Twindlytart and Other Rhymes* (Livingston)  7:169
*Old Peter's Russian Tales* (Ransome)  8:170
*The Old Testament* (de Angeli)  1:53
*An Older Kind of Magic* (Wrightson)  4:244
*The Oldest Man and Other Timeless Stories* (Kotzwinkle)  6:181
*An Old-Fashioned Thanksgiving* (Alcott)  1:11
*Oliver Button Is a Sissy* (de Paola)  4:62
*On a marche sur la lune* (Hergé)  6:148
*On Beyond Zebra* (Seuss)  1:88; 9:180
*On Christmas Day in the Morning!* (Langstaff)  3:110
*On the Day Peter Stuyvesant Sailed into Town* (Lobel)  5:166
*On the Other Side of the Gate* (Suhl)  2:165
*On the Way Home* (Wilder)  2:206
*Once on a Time* (Milne)  1:142
*One at a Time: His Collected Poems for the Young* (McCord)  9:103
*The One Bad Thing about Father* (Monjo)  2:124
*One Big Wish* (Williams)  8:237
*One by Sea* (Corbett)  1:46
*One Earth, Many People: The Challenge of Human Population Growth* (Pringle)  4:175
*One Fine Day* (Hogrogian)  2:88
*One Fish, Two Fish, Red Fish, Blue Fish* (Seuss)  1:88; 9:185
*One I Love, Two I Love, and Other Loving Mother Goose Rhymes* (Hogrogian)  2:88

*One Monday Morning*
　(Shulevitz)　**5**:202
*One Morning in Maine*
　(McCloskey)　**7**:207
*The One Pig with Horns*
　(Brunhoff)　**4**:40
*One Small Blue Bead*
　(Baylor)　**3**:16
*One to Grow On* (Little)　**4**:149
*One Was Johnny: A Counting
　Book* (Sendak)　**1**:172
*One Wide River to Cross*
　(Emberley)　**5**:93
*The Only Earth We Have*
　(Pringle)　**4**:174
*The Optical Illusion Book*
　(Simon)　**9**:210
*The Orchard Cat*
　(Kellogg)　**6**:171
*Orlando, the Brave Vulture*
　(Ungerer)　**3**:203
*Oscar Lobster's Fair Exchange*
　(Selden)　**8**:196
*Otherwise Known as Sheila the
　Great* (Blume)　**2**:17
*Otis Spofford* (Cleary)　**8**:46
*Otto and the Magic Potatoes* (du
　Bois)　**1**:64
*Otto at Sea* (du Bois)　**1**:65
*Otto in Texas* (du Bois)　**1**:65
*Our Hungry Earth: The World
　Food Crisis* (Pringle)　**4**:181
*Our World: The People's
　Republic of China*
　(Rau)　**8**:187
*Outcast* (Sutcliff)　**1**:189
*OUTside INside Poems*
　(Adoff)　**7**:36
*The Outsiders* (Hinton)　**3**:70
*Over Sea, Under Stone*
　(Cooper)　**4**:42
*The Owl and the Pussycat*
　(Lear)　**1**:127
*The Owl and the Woodpecker*
　(Wildsmith)　**2**:213
*Owl at Home* (Lobel)　**5**:169
*Paddington Abroad* (Bond)　**1**:28
*Paddington at Large*
　(Bond)　**1**:28
*Paddington at Work*
　(Bond)　**1**:28
*Paddington Bear* (Bond)　**1**:28
*Paddington Helps Out*
　(Bond)　**1**:29
*Paddington Marches On*
　(Bond)　**1**:29
*Paddington Takes the Air*
　(Bond)　**1**:29
*Paint, Brush, and Palette*
　(Weiss)　**4**:223
*Palmistry* (Aylesworth)　**6**:53
*Pancakes for Breakfast* (de
　Paola)　**4**:60
*Papagayo, the Mischief Maker*
　(McDermott)　**9**:119
*The Paper Airplane Book*
　(Simon)　**9**:204
*Paper, Ink, and Roller: Print-
　Making for Beginners*
　(Weiss)　**4**:220
*Paper, Paper Everywhere*
　(Gibbons)　**8**:95

*Pappa Pellerin's Daughter*
　(Gripe)　**5**:143
*Pappa Pellerins Dotter*
　(Gripe)　**5**:143
*Parade* (Crews)　**7**:62
*The Parade Book*
　(Emberley)　**5**:91
*Pardon Me, You're Stepping on
　My Eyeball!* (Zindel)　**3**:250
*Parker Pig, Esquire* (de
　Paola)　**4**:54
*Parrakeets* (Zim)　**2**:229
*Parsley* (Bemelmans)　**6**:72
*A Pattern of Roses*
　(Peyton)　**3**:177
*Paul Robeson* (Greenfield)　**4**:98
*Paul Robeson: The Life and
　Times of a Free Black Man*
　(Hamilton)　**1**:104
*Pauline and the Prince of the
　Wind* (Krüss)　**9**:86
*Pauline und der Prinz im Wind*
　(Krüss)　**9**:86
*Paul's Horse, Herman*
　(Weiss)　**4**:221
*Pavo and the Princess*
　(Ness)　**6**:202
*The Peaceable Kingdom*
　(Coatsworth)　**2**:60
*The Pedaling Man and Other
　Poems* (Hoban)　**3**:81
*Pencil, Pen, and Brush Drawing
　for Beginners* (Weiss)　**4**:222
*The Penguin Book* (Rau)　**8**:186
*Pennington's Heir*
　(Peyton)　**3**:178
*Pennington's Last Term*
　(Peyton)　**3**:178
*People* (Spier)　**5**:227
*The People of New China*
　(Rau)　**8**:189
*The People of the Ax*
　(Williams)　**8**:234
*The People's Choice: The Story
　of Candidates, Campaigns, and
　Elections* (Schwartz)　**3**:190
*The People's Republic of China*
　(Rau)　**8**:187
*The Peppermint Pig*
　(Bawden)　**2**:12
*Perilous Pilgrimage*
　(Treece)　**2**:187
*Pet Show!* (Keats)　**1**:116
*The Pet Store* (Spier)　**5**:228
*Peter and Butch* (Phipson)　**5**:181
*Peter and Veronica*
　(Sachs)　**2**:132
*Peter Duck* (Ransome)　**8**:174
*Peter Graves* (du Bois)　**1**:65
*Peter Treegate's War*
　(Wibberley)　**3**:229
*Peter's Chair* (Keats)　**1**:116
*Petey* (Tobias)　**4**:217
*Petronella* (Williams)　**8**:233
*Petros' War* (Zei)　**6**:261
*Pets in a Jar: Collecting and
　Caring for Small Wild Animals*
　(Simon)　**9**:209
*Pezzettino* (Lionni)　**7**:137
*Philbert the Fearful*
　(Williams)　**8**:227
*Philip Hall Likes Me. I Reckon
　Maybe* (Greene)　**2**:85

*Phoebe's Revolt* (Babbitt)　**2**:6
*Pickle Creature*
　(Pinkwater)　**4**:169
*Picnic at Babar's*
　(Brunhoff)　**4**:34
*The Picts and the Martyrs; or,
　Not Welcome at All*
　(Ransome)　**8**:181
*A Piece of the Power: Four Black
　Mayors* (Haskins)　**3**:65
*Pierre: A Cautionary Tale*
　(Sendak)　**1**:172
*Pigeon Post* (Ransome)　**8**:177
*The Pigman* (Zindel)　**3**:251
*Pigs Plus: Learning Addition*
　(Burningham)　**9**:50
*The Pig-Tale* (Carroll)　**2**:35
*Pilyo the Piranha* (Aruego)　**5**:29
*Pinkerton, Behave!*
　(Kellogg)　**6**:176
*Pinky Pye* (Estes)　**2**:75
*Pipes and Plumbing Systems* (Zim
　and Skelly)　**2**:230
*Pippa Passes* (Corbett)　**1**:46
*Pippi Goes on Board*
　(Lindgren)　**1**:138
*Pippi in the South Sea*
　(Lindgren)　**1**:138
*Pippi Longstocking*
　(Lindgren)　**1**:138
*The Pirate Uncle* (Mahy)　**7**:185
*Pirate's Island*
　(Townsend)　**2**:173
*The Place* (Coatsworth)　**2**:61
*A Place to Live* (Bendick)　**5**:43
*The Plan for Birdsmarsh*
　(Peyton)　**3**:180
*The Planet of Junior Brown*
　(Hamilton)　**1**:104
*The Planet-Girded Suns: Man's
　View of Other Solar Systems*
　(Engdahl)　**2**:71
*Plants in Winter* (Cole)　**5**:63
*Plenty of Fish* (Selsam)　**1**:164
*Plink, Plink, Plink* (Baylor)　**3**:16
*A Pocket Full of Seeds*
　(Sachs)　**2**:133
*The Pocket Mouse*
　(Willard)　**2**:221
*Poems of Lewis Carroll*
　(Carroll)　**2**:35
*Poetry Is* (Hughes)　**3**:94
*Poisonous Snakes* (Simon)　**9**:216
*Polly's Tiger* (Phipson)　**5**:183
*The Pooh Story Book*
　(Milne)　**1**:142
*The Pool of Fire*
　(Christopher)　**2**:41
*Poor Richard in France*
　(Monjo)　**2**:129
*Poor Stainless: A New Story
　about the Borrowers*
　(Norton)　**6**:224
*The Popcorn Book* (de
　Paola)　**4**:60
*Popo and Fifina, Children of
　Haiti* (Bontemps and
　Hughes)　**6**:78
*Popol et Virginie au pays des
　lapinos* (Hergé)　**6**:149
*Popol Out West* (Hergé)　**6**:149
*Poppy Pig Goes to Market*
　(Bruna)　**7**:52

*Porko Von Popbutton* (du
　Bois)　**1**:65
*Portfolio of Horse Paintings*
　(Henry)　**4**:112
*Portfolio of Horses*
　(Henry)　**4**:112
*The Portmanteau Book*
　(Rockwell)　**6**:237
*Portrait of Ivan* (Fox)　**1**:79
*The Post Office Book: Mail and
　How It Moves* (Gibbons)　**8**:93
*The Potters' Kitchen*
　(Isadora)　**7**:103
*Practical Music Theory: How
　Music Is Put Together from
　Bach to Rock* (Collier)　**3**:48
*The Practical Princess*
　(Williams)　**8**:230
*The Practical Princess and Other
　Liberating Fairy Tales*
　(Williams)　**8**:236
*A Prairie Boy's Summer*
　(Kurelek)　**2**:103
*A Prairie Boy's Winter*
　(Kurelek)　**2**:103
*Pretty Pretty Peggy Moffitt* (du
　Bois)　**1**:66
*Pretzel* (Rey)　**5**:195
*Pretzel and the Puppies*
　(Rey)　**5**:195
*Prince Bertram the Bad*
　(Lobel)　**5**:163
*Prince Caspian: The Return to
　Narnia* (Lewis)　**3**:136
*The Prince in Waiting*
　(Christopher)　**2**:41
*The Prince of the Dolomites: An
　Old Italian Tale* (de
　Paola)　**4**:64
*Prince Rabbit and the Princess
　Who Could Not Laugh*
　(Milne)　**1**:143
*The Princess and the Clown*
　(Mahy)　**7**:180
*The Procession* (Mahy)　**7**:179
*Profiles in Black Power*
　(Haskins)　**3**:66
*Projects with Air* (Simon)　**9**:209
*Projects with Plants*
　(Simon)　**9**:207
*The Promised Year*
　(Uchida)　**6**:252
*The Proud Circus Horse*
　(Zimnik)　**3**:244
*A Proud Taste for Scarlet and
　Miniver* (Konigsburg)　**1**:122
*The Proud Wooden Drummer*
　(Krüss)　**9**:88
*The Prydain Chronicles*
　(Alexander)　**1**:16
*Psst! Doggie—* (Keats)　**1**:117
*Puddin' Poems: Being the Best of
　the Verse from "The Magic
　Pudding"* (Lindsay)　**8**:106
*Punch and Judy*
　(Emberley)　**5**:92
*Puppy Summer* (DeJong)　**1**:60
*Putting the Sun to Work*
　(Bendick)　**5**:49
*Pyramid* (Macaulay)　**3**:143
*Python's Party*
　(Wildsmith)　**2**:214

**Title Index**

*The Quangle Wangle's Hat*
(Lear)  **1**:127
*The Quarreling Book*
(Zolotow)  **2**:236
*The Queen Elizabeth Story*
(Sutcliff)  **1**:189
*Queen of Hearts* (Cleaver and
Cleaver)  **6**:111
*The Quest of Captain Cook*
(Selsam)  **1**:164
*The Question Box*
(Williams)  **8**:226
*Questions and Answers about
Ants* (Selsam)  **1**:165
*Questions and Answers about
Horses* (Selsam)  **1**:165
*The Quicksand Book* (de
Paola)  **4**:59
*Quips and Quirks*
(Watson)  **3**:213
*Quito Express*
(Bemelmans)  **6**:66
*The Quitting Deal*
(Tobias)  **4**:215
*The Rabbit* (Burningham)  **9**:46
*Rabbit Hill* (Lawson)  **2**:110
*A Racecourse for Andy*
(Wrightson)  **4**:242
*Rackety-Bang and Other Verses*
(Rockwell)  **6**:235
*Raffy and the Nine Monkeys*
(Rey)  **5**:192
*Raging Robots and Unruly Uncles*
(Mahy)  **7**:186
*The Railway Children*
(Nesbit)  **3**:164
*The Railway Engine and the
Hairy Brigands* (Mahy)  **7**:181
*Rain* (Spier)  **5**:228
*Rain Rain Rivers*
(Shulevitz)  **5**:203
*Rainbow Valley*
(Montgomery)  **8**:137
*Ralph Bunche: A Most Reluctant
Hero* (Haskins)  **3**:66
*Ralph S. Mouse* (Cleary)  **8**:58
*Ramona and Her Father*
(Cleary)  **8**:55
*Ramona and Her Mother*
(Cleary)  **8**:56
*Ramona Forever* (Cleary)  **8**:62
*Ramona Quimby, Age 8*
(Cleary)  **8**:57
*Ramona the Brave*
(Cleary)  **2**:49; **8**:55
*Ramona the Pest* (Cleary)  **2**:49;
**8**:52
*Rasmus and the Vagabond*
(Lindgren)  **1**:139
*Ray Charles* (Mathis)  **3**:151
*Read One: Numbers As Words*
(Burningham)  **9**:50
*Ready, Steady, Go!*
(Watanabe)  **8**:216
*The Real Hole* (Cleary)  **2**:50;
**8**:49
*The Real Thief* (Steig)  **2**:160
*The Rebel* (Burton)  **1**:33
*Rebels of the Heavenly Kingdom*
(Paterson)  **7**:242
*Recycling Resources*
(Pringle)  **4**:179

*Red Earth, Blue Sky: The
Australian Outback*
(Rau)  **8**:191
*Red Pawns* (Wibberley)  **3**:229
*The Red Room Riddle*
(Corbett)  **1**:46
*Religions* (Haskins)  **3**:66
*The Reluctant Dragon*
(Grahame)  **5**:135
*Remove Protective Coating a
Little at a Time*
(Donovan)  **3**:53
*The Renowned History of Little
Red Riding-Hood*
(Hogrogian)  **2**:89
*The Return of the Great Brain*
(Fitzgerald)  **1**:70
*Return of the Moose*
(Pinkwater)  **4**:169
*Return to Gone-Away*
(Enright)  **4**:76
*Return to the Happy Islands*
(Krüss)  **9**:84
*The Revenge of Samuel Stokes*
(Lively)  **7**:163
*Revolutionaries: Agents of
Change* (Haskins)  **3**:67
*The Reward Worth Having*
(Williams)  **8**:235
*Ribsy* (Cleary)  **2**:50; **8**:51
*Rich and Famous: The Future
Adventures of George Stable*
(Collier)  **3**:48
*Richard Scarry's Animal Nursery
Tales* (Scarry)  **3**:185
*Richard Scarry's Color Book*
(Scarry)  **3**:185
*Richard Scarry's Great Big Air
Book* (Scarry)  **3**:185
*The Richleighs of Tantamount*
(Cleary)  **3**:221
*Ride into Danger* (Treece)  **2**:188
*Ride Off: Learning Subtraction*
(Burningham)  **9**:50
*Riders of the Storm*
(Burton)  **1**:34
*Rilla of Ingleside*
(Montgomery)  **8**:138
*Ring Out! A Book of Bells*
(Yolen)  **4**:261
*Ring-Rise, Ring-Set*
(Hughes)  **9**:75
*The River and the Forest*
(Korinetz)  **4**:131
*River Winding* (Zolotow)  **2**:236
*The Road to Miklagard*
(Treece)  **2**:188
*Roald Dahl's Revolting Rhymes*
(Dahl)  **7**:81
*Roar and More* (Kuskin)  **4**:134
*The "Roaring 40"*
(Chauncy)  **6**:92
*Robert Fulton, Boy Craftsman*
(Henry)  **4**:109
*Robin and His Merry Men*
(Serraillier)  **2**:139
*Robin in the Greenwood: Ballads
of Robin Hood*
(Serraillier)  **2**:140
*Robot* (Pieńkowski)  **6**:232
*The Robot and Rebecca and the
Missing Owser* (Yolen)  **4**:268

*The Robot and Rebecca: The
Mystery of the Code-Carrying
Kids* (Yolen)  **4**:266
*Rock Star* (Collier)  **3**:48
*The Rocks of Honey*
(Wrightson)  **4**:241
*Roland the Minstrel Pig*
(Steig)  **2**:161
*Roll of Thunder, Hear My Cry*
(Taylor)  **9**:226
*The Roman Moon Mystery*
(Williams)  **8**:221
*A Room Made of Windows*
(Cameron)  **1**:40
*Rooster Brother*
(Hogrogian)  **2**:89
*The Rooster Who Understood
Japanese* (Uchida)  **6**:258
*Rosa Parks* (Greenfield)  **4**:97
*A Rose for Pinkerton*
(Kellogg)  **6**:177
*The Rose on My Cake*
(Kuskin)  **4**:138
*Rosebud* (Bemelmans)  **6**:67
*Rosebud* (Emberley)  **5**:93
*Rosie and Michael*
(Viorst)  **3**:208
*The Rotten Years*
(Wojciechowska)  **1**:198
*Rudi and the Distelfink*
(Monjo)  **2**:125
*Rudyard Kipling: Creative
Adventurer* (Manley)  **3**:147
*Rufus M.* (Estes)  **2**:75
*Rumble Fish* (Hinton)  **3**:71
*Run for the Money*
(Corbett)  **1**:47
*Run Softly, Go Fast*
(Wersba)  **3**:218
*Runaway Ralph* (Cleary)  **8**:54
*The Runaway Train*
(Farmer)  **8**:87
*Saber-Toothed Tiger and Other
Ice Age Mammals* (Cole)  **5**:65
*Sad-Faced Boy* (Bontemps)  **6**:79
*The Sailing Hatrack*
(Coatsworth)  **2**:61
*Sailing Small Boats*
(Weiss)  **4**:224
*Sailing to Cythera and Other
Anatole Stories*
(Willard)  **5**:245
*The Sailor* (Bruna)  **7**:50
*Sailor Jack and the 20 Orphans*
(Mahy)  **7**:179
*Saint George and the Dragon: A
Mummer's Play*
(Langstaff)  **3**:111
*Salvador and Mister Sam: A
Guide to Parakeet Care*
(Gibbons)  **8**:88
*Sam, Bangs, and Moonshine*
(Ness)  **6**:203
*Sam Patch: The High, Wide, and
Handsome Jumper* (Bontemps
and Conroy)  **6**:81
*Samurai of Gold Hill*
(Uchida)  **6**:257
*San Domingo: The Medicine Hat
Stallion* (Henry)  **4**:116
*San Francisco* (Fritz)  **2**:81
*Sand and Snow* (Kuskin)  **4**:139
*The Saturdays* (Enright)  **4**:73

*The School* (Burningham)  **9**:46
*School for Sillies*
(Williams)  **8**:230
*Science at the Ball Game*
(Aylesworth)  **6**:53
*Science at Work: Projects in
Oceanography* (Simon)  **9**:206
*Science at Work: Projects in
Space Science* (Simon)  **9**:204
*Science Experiments You Can Eat*
(Cobb)  **2**:66
*Science in a Vacant Lot*
(Simon)  **9**:203
*Science Looks at Mysterious
Monsters* (Aylesworth)  **6**:56
*Science Projects in Ecology*
(Simon)  **9**:204
*Science Projects in Pollution*
(Simon)  **9**:206
*Scrambled Eggs Super!*
(Seuss)  **9**:178
*The Sea Egg* (Boston)  **3**:28
*Sea Gull* (Farmer)  **8**:77
*The Sea Is All Around*
(Enright)  **4**:72
*The Sea of Gold and Other Tales
from Japan* (Uchida)  **6**:254
*Sea So Big, Ship So Small*
(Bendick)  **5**:40
*Sea Star, Orphan of
Chincoteague* (Henry)  **4**:111
*The Sea-Beggar's Son*
(Monjo)  **2**:125
*Seacrow Island*
(Lindgren)  **1**:139
*The Seagull* (Farmer)  **8**:77
*Search for a Stone*
(Munari)  **9**:129
*The Search for Delicious*
(Babbitt)  **2**:7
*The Search for Life*
(Aylesworth)  **6**:52
*Seashore Story* (Yashima)  **4**:254
*Season Songs* (Hughes)  **3**:95
*Seasons* (Burningham)  **9**:43
*The Seasons for Singing:
American Christmas Songs and
Carols* (Langstaff)  **3**:111
*The Sea-Thing Child*
(Hoban)  **3**:82
*The Second Margaret Mahy Story
Book: Stories and Poems*
(Mahy)  **7**:181
*The Secret* (Coatsworth)  **2**:61
*Secret Agents Four*
(Sobol)  **4**:208
*The Secret Box* (Cole)  **5**:61
*The Secret Clocks: Time Senses
of Living Things*
(Simon)  **9**:213
*The Secret Friends*
(Chauncy)  **6**:91
*Secret of the Hawk*
(Wibberley)  **3**:230
*The Secret of the Sachem's Tree*
(Monjo)  **2**:125
*Secret Sea* (White)  **3**:222
*Secret Water* (Ransome)  **8**:179
*See the Circus* (Rey)  **5**:198
*See through the Sea* (Selsam and
Morrow)  **1**:165
*See What I Found*
(Livingston)  **7**:168

*The Seeing Stick* (Yolen)   4:264
*The Self-Made Snowman*
   (Krahn)   3:105
*Sense of Direction: Up and Down*
   *and All Around* (Cobb)   2:67
*Serafina the Giraffe*
   (Brunhoff)   4:35
*The Serpent's Teeth: The Story of*
   *Cadmus* (Farmer)   8:80
*Servants of the Devil*
   (Aylesworth)   6:49
*Seventeen Kings and Forty-Two*
   *Elephants* (Mahy)   7:181
*Seventeen Seconds*
   (Southall)   2:155
*The Seventh Mandarin*
   (Yolen)   4:259
*Shadow of a Bull*
   (Wojciechowska)   1:199
*The Shadow-Cage and Other*
   *Tales of the Supernatural*
   (Pearce)   9:155
*Shadrach* (DeJong)   1:60
*Shaka, King of the Zulus: A*
   *Biography* (Cohen)   3:42
*Shaker Paper House: To Cut Out*
   *and Color* (Ness)   6:209
*Shapes* (Bendick)   5:42
*Sharks* (Zim)   2:230
*Shaw's Fortune: The Picture*
   *Story of a Colonial Plantation*
   (Tunis)   2:194
*She Come Bringing Me That*
   *Little Baby Girl*
   (Greenfield)   4:97
*The Shield Ring* (Sutcliff)   1:189
*Shimmy Shimmy Coke-Ca-Pop! A*
   *Collection of City Children's*
   *Street Games and Rhymes*
   (Langstaff and
   Langstaff)   3:112
*Ship Models and How to Build*
   *Them* (Weiss)   4:227
*The Ship That Came Down the*
   *Gutter* (Kotzwinkle)   6:181
*Shirlick Holmes and the Case of*
   *the Wandering Wardrobe*
   (Yolen)   4:267
*The Shopping Basket*
   (Burningham)   9:49
*Sia Lives on Kilimanjaro*
   (Lindgren)   1:140
*Sidewalk Story* (Mathis)   3:151
*The Sign of the Beaver*
   (Speare)   8:210
*The Sign of the Chrysanthemum*
   (Paterson)   7:230
*Silent Ship, Silent Sea*
   (White)   3:222
*Silky: An Incredible Tale*
   (Coatsworth)   2:61
*The Silver Branch*
   (Sutcliff)   1:190
*The Silver Chair* (Lewis)   3:136
*The Silver Crown*
   (O'Brien)   2:128
*Silver on the Tree* (Cooper)   4:47
*The Silver Sword*
   (Serraillier)   2:141
*The Silver Whistle*
   (Williams)   8:231
*Simon* (Sutcliff)   1:190

*Simon Boom Gives a Wedding*
   (Suhl)   2:166
*Simon's Song* (Emberley)   5:97
*Simple Gifts: The Story of the*
   *Shakers* (Yolen)   4:263
*Simple Pictures Are Best*
   (Willard)   5:247
*The Simple Prince*
   (Yolen)   4:264
*Sing Down the Moon*
   (O'Dell)   1:148
*The Singing Hill* (DeJong)   1:61
*A Single Light*
   (Wojciechowska)   1:199
*Sir Arthur Evans, Discoverer of*
   *Knossos* (Selden)   8:198
*Sister* (Greenfield)   4:97
*Sister of the Bride* (Cleary)   8:50
*Six and Silver* (Phipson)   5:178
*Skates!* (Keats)   1:117
*Skip Trip* (Burningham)   9:51
*The Sky Was Blue*
   (Zolotow)   2:236
*Slam Bang* (Burningham)   9:51
*Slappy Hooper, the Wonderful*
   *Sign Painter* (Bontemps and
   Conroy)   6:80
*Slater's Mill* (Monjo)   2:126
*The Slave Dancer* (Fox)   1:79
*Sleep Is for Everyone*
   (Showers)   6:246
*Sleepy People* (Goffstein)   3:61
*Sloan and Philamina; or, How to*
   *Make Friends with Your Lunch*
   (Stren)   5:231
*The Sly Old Cat* (Potter)   1:153
*Small Pig* (Lobel)   5:164
*The Smallest Dinosaurs*
   (Simon)   9:218
*Smeller Martin* (Lawson)   2:111
*Smoke from Cromwell's Time*
   (Aiken)   1:7
*Snail, Where Are You?*
   (Ungerer)   3:203
*Snails* (Zim and Krantz)   2:230
*A Snake's Body* (Cole)   5:67
*The Sneetches and Other Stories*
   (Seuss)   9:186
*Sniff Shout* (Burningham)   9:51
*Snippy and Snappy* (Gág)   4:89
*The Snow* (Burningham)   9:46
*The Snow Monkey at Home*
   (Rau)   8:190
*Snow Tracks* (George)   1:92
*The Snowy Day* (Keats)   1:117
*Snuffie* (Bruna)   7:51
*Snuffy* (Bruna)   7:51
*Social Welfare* (Myers)   4:157
*Socks* (Cleary)   2:51; 8:54
*The Soldier and Death: A Russian*
   *Folk Tale Told in English*
   (Ransome)   8:171
*Soldier and Tsar in the Forest: A*
   *Russian Tale*
   (Shulevitz)   5:205
*Soldier, Soldier, Won't You*
   *Marry Me?* (Langstaff)   3:112
*Solids, Liquids, and Gases*
   (Bendick)   5:47
*Some of the Days of Everett*
   *Anderson* (Clifton)   5:53
*The Something* (Babbitt)   2:8

*Something Special for Me*
   (Williams)   9:234
*Sometimes I Dance Mountains*
   (Baylor)   3:16
*The Song in My Drum*
   (Hoban)   3:82
*Song of the Trees* (Taylor)   9:225
*Songs of the Dream People:*
   *Chants and Images from the*
   *Indians and Eskimos of North*
   *America* (Houston)   3:86
*Songs of the Fog Maiden* (de
   Paola)   4:62
*Sonora Beautiful* (Clifton)   5:60
*Sophia Scrooby Preserved*
   (Bacon)   3:11
*The Sorely Trying Day*
   (Hoban)   3:82
*The Soul Brothers and Sister Lou*
   (Hunter)   3:99
*The Sound of the Dragon's Feet*
   (Zei)   6:262
*Sounder* (Armstrong)   1:23
*Sour Land* (Armstrong)   1:24
*South Swell* (Wibberley)   3:230
*Space and Time* (Bendick)   5:42
*A Space Story* (Kuskin)   4:143
*Space Trap* (Hughes)   9:77
*The Spanish Armada*
   (Williams)   8:228
*The Sparrow Bush*
   (Coatsworth)   2:62
*Sparrow Socks* (Selden)   8:198
*Speak Out in Thunder Tones:*
   *Letters and Other Writings by*
   *Black Northerners, 1787-1865*
   (Sterling)   1:181
*Speak Up: More Rhymes of the*
   *Never Was and Always Is*
   (McCord)   9:104
*A Spell Is Cast* (Cameron)   1:41
*Spiderweb for Two: A Melendy*
   *Maze* (Enright)   4:75
*Spin a Soft Black Song: Poems*
   *for Children* (Giovanni)   6:115
*The Spirit of the Lord: Revivalism*
   *in America* (Cohen)   3:42
*The Splintered Sword*
   (Serraillier)   2:188
*Spotty* (Rey)   5:195
*Die Sprechmachine* (Krüss)   9:86
*The Sprig of Broom*
   (Willard)   2:222
*Spring Begins in March*
   (Little)   4:148
*Spring Comes to the Ocean*
   (George)   1:92
*Spring Is a New Beginning*
   (Anglund)   1:21
*Spring Is Here!* (Sterling)   1:181
*Square as a House*
   (Kuskin)   4:136
*Squawwk!* (Rockwell)   6:236
*Squib* (Bawden)   2:13
*The Squirrel Wife*
   (Pearce)   9:153
*Squirrels* (Wildsmith)   2:214
*The Stained Glass Window*
   (Lively)   7:161
*Stand in the Wind* (Little)   4:151
*The Star in the Pail*
   (McCord)   9:102

*Star of Night: Stories for*
   *Christmas* (Paterson)   7:237
*The Star-Spangled Banner*
   (Spier)   5:222
*Stepmother* (Mahy)   7:182
*Steven Kellogg's Yankee Doodle*
   (Kellogg)   6:174
*Stevie* (Steptoe)   2:163
*Sticks, Spools, and Feathers*
   (Weiss)   4:223
*A Stitch in Time* (Lively)   7:160
*The Stolen Oracle*
   (Williams)   8:221
*The Stone Doll of Sister Brute*
   (Hoban)   3:83
*The Stonecutter: A Japanese Folk*
   *Tale* (McDermott)   9:115
*The Stone-Faced Boy* (Fox)   1:81
*Stoneflight* (McHargue)   2:120
*The Stones of Green Knowe*
   (Boston)   3:28
*Storie di tre uccellini*
   (Munari)   9:124
*Storm Alert: Understanding*
   *Weather Disasters*
   (Aylesworth)   6:55
*Storm from the West*
   (Willard)   2:222
*A Storm without Rain*
   (Adkins)   7:28
*Stormy, Misty's Foal*
   (Henry)   4:114
*The Story Girl*
   (Montgomery)   8:135
*The Story of a Puppet*
   (Collodi)   5:69
*The Story of Babar, the Little*
   *Elephant* (Brunhoff)   4:30
*The Story of George Washington*
   *Carver* (Bontemps)   6:82
*The Story of Johnny Appleseed*
   (Aliki)   9:17
*The Story of Paul Bunyan*
   (Emberley)   5:92
*The Story of Persephone*
   (Farmer)   8:85
*The Story of Stevie Wonder*
   (Haskins)   3:67
*The Story of the Amulet*
   (Nesbit)   3:165
*Story of the Negro*
   (Bontemps)   6:80
*The Story of Vampires*
   (Aylesworth)   6:53
*The Story of Werewolves*
   (Aylesworth)   6:54
*The Story of William Penn*
   (Aliki)   9:18
*The Story of William Tell*
   (Aliki)   9:17
*The Story of Witches*
   (Aylesworth)   6:54
*A Story to Tell* (Bruna)   7:51
*Storybook Dictionary*
   (Scarry)   3:186
*A Storybook from Tomi Ungerer*
   (Ungerer)   3:203
*The Stowaway to the Mushroom*
   *Planet* (Cameron)   1:41
*Strange Creatures*
   (Simon)   9:217
*Strange Mysteries from Around*
   *the World* (Simon)   9:215

**Title Index**

A Stranger at Green Knowe (Boston)  3:29
Stranger on the Ball Club (Slote)  4:199
Strangers' Bread (Willard)  5:247
Street Gangs: Yesterday and Today (Haskins)  3:68
Strega Nona: An Old Tale (de Paola)  4:57
Stuart Little (White)  1:195
The Sultan's Perfect Tree (Yolen)  4:263
Sumi and the Goat and the Tokyo Express (Uchida)  6:256
Sumi's Prize (Uchida)  6:253
Sumi's Special Happening (Uchida)  6:254
The Summer Birds (Farmer)  8:76
The Summer Book (Jansson)  2:95
The Summer Night (Zolotow)  2:237
Summer of My German Soldier (Greene)  2:86
The Summer of the Falcon (George)  1:93
The Summer of the Swans (Byars)  1:37
The Summer People (Townsend)  2:174
A Summer to Die (Lowry)  6:192
The Summer with Spike (Willard)  2:223
The Sun (Zim)  2:231
Sun Flight (McDermott)  9:118
Sun Up, Sun Down (Gibbons)  8:97
Sunday Morning (Viorst)  3:209
Sunshine (Bemelmans)  6:68
Super People: Who Will They Be? (Bendick)  5:50
Superpuppy: How to Choose, Raise, and Train the Best Possible Dog for You (Pinkwater and Pinkwater)  4:167
Supersuits (Cobb)  2:67
Suppose You Met a Witch (Serraillier)  5:142
The Supreme, Superb, Exalted and Delightful, One and Only Magic Building (Kotzwinkle)  6:182
Surrender (White)  3:222
The Survivor (White)  3:223
The Survivors (Hunter)  3:101
Swallowdale (Ransome)  8:174
Swallows and Amazons (Ransome)  8:171
Sweet Pea: A Black Girl Growing Up in the Rural South (Krementz)  5:150
Sweetwater (Yep)  3:238
Swimmy (Lionni)  7:129
The Sword and the Scythe (Williams)  8:221
The Sword of Esau (Southall)  2:156
The Sword of King Arthur (Williams)  8:229

The Sword of the Spirits (Christopher)  2:42
Sword of the Wilderness (Coatsworth)  2:62
Swords from the North (Treece)  2:189
Sylvester and the Magic Pebble (Steig)  2:161
Sylvie and Bruno (Carroll)  2:36
Symbiosis: A Book of Unusual Friendships (Aruego)  5:28
Symbols: A Silent Language (Adkins)  7:24
The Tailor and the Giant (Krüss)  9:88
The Tailor of Gloucester (Potter)  1:153
Takao and Grandfather's Sword (Uchida)  6:252
Take a Number (Bendick and Levin)  5:39
Take Sky: More Rhymes of the Never Was and Always Is (McCord)  9:99
Take Wing (Little)  4:148
Taking Care of Terrific (Lowry)  6:197
Taking Sides (Klein)  2:100
The Tale of the Faithful Dove (Potter)  1:153
The Tale of Three Landlubbers (Serraillier)  2:143
The Tale of Tuppenny (Potter)  1:154
Tales from Grimm (Gág)  4:91
Tales of a Fourth Grade Nothing (Blume)  2:18
The Tales of Olga da Polga (Bond)  1:29
Talk about a Family (Greenfield)  4:101
The Talking Machine: An Extraordinary Story (Krüss)  9:86
Talking with the Animals (Cohen)  3:42
Tallyho, Pinkerton! (Kellogg)  6:178
Tamar's Wager (Coatsworth)  2:62
Tangara: "Let Us Set Off Again" (Chauncy)  6:91
Taran Wanderer (Alexander)  1:17; 5:20
Tatsinda (Enright)  4:76
The Tavern at the Ferry (Tunis)  2:194
Teacup Full of Roses (Mathis)  3:151
Tear Down the Walls! (Sterling)  1:181
The Teddy Bear Habit; or, How I Became a Winner (Collier)  3:49
Teddy Bear's Scrapbook (Howe and Howe)  9:57
Teen-Age Treasury of Good Humor (Manley)  3:148
Teen-Age Treasury of Our Science World (Manley and Lewis)  3:148
Teen-Age Treasury of the Arts (Manley and Lewis)  3:148

Telboek no. 2 (Bruna)  7:51
Telephone Systems (Zim and Skelly)  2:231
Television Works Like This (Bendick and Bendick)  5:36
Ten Apples Up on Top! (Seuss)  9:187
Ten Black Dots (Crews)  7:56
Ten, Nine, Eight (Bang)  8:22
The Tenth Good Thing about Barney (Viorst)  3:209
The Terrible Churnadryne (Cameron)  1:41
The Terrible Roar (Pinkwater)  4:161
Terry and the Caterpillars (Selsam)  1:166
Terry on the Fence (Ashley)  4:15
Thanksgiving Day (Gibbons)  8:97
That Was Then, This Is Now (Hinton)  3:72
Then Again, Maybe I Won't (Blume)  2:18
Then There Were Five (Enright)  4:75
Theodore and the Talking Mushroom (Lionni)  7:135
Theodore Roosevelt, an Initial Biography (Foster)  7:97
There, Far Beyond the River (Korinetz)  4:129
There Was an Old Woman (Kellogg)  6:173
There's a Rainbow in My Closet (Stren)  5:232
These Happy Golden Years (Wilder)  2:207
They Found a Cave (Chauncy)  6:89
They Put on Masks (Baylor)  3:17
They Walk in the Night (Coatsworth)  2:63
Thidwick, the Big-Hearted Moose (Seuss)  9:176
The Thief (Rockwell)  6:239
Thimble Summer (Enright)  4:71
Things to Make and Do for Columbus Day (Gibbons)  8:89
Things to Make and Do for Halloween (Gibbons)  8:89
Things to Make and Do for Valentine's Day (de Paola)  4:58
Things to Make and Do for Your Birthday (Gibbons)  8:89
The Third Margaret Mahy Story Book: Stories and Poems (Mahy)  7:183
The Third Road (Bacon)  3:12
Thirteen (Charlip and Joyner)  8:32
The Thirteen Days of Yule (Hogrogian)  2:89
The Thirteen Moons (George)  1:93
The 35th of May; or, Conrad's Ride to the South Seas (Kästner)  4:123
This Is a River: Exploring an Ecosystem (Pringle)  4:176

This Is Australia (Sasek)  4:196
This Is Cape Kennedy (Sasek)  4:193
This Is Edinburgh (Sasek)  4:190
This Is Greece (Sasek)  4:194
This Is Historic Britain (Sasek)  4:196
This Is Hong Kong (Sasek)  4:194
This Is Ireland (Sasek)  4:193
This Is Israel (Sasek)  4:192
This Is London (Sasek)  4:188
This Is Munich (Sasek)  4:191
This Is New York (Sasek)  4:189
This Is Paris (Sasek)  4:187
This Is Rome (Sasek)  4:189
This Is San Francisco (Sasek)  4:192
This Is Texas (Sasek)  4:194
This Is the United Nations (Sasek)  4:195
This Is Venice (Sasek)  4:192
This Is Washington, D.C. (Sasek)  4:195
This Star Shall Abide (Engdahl)  2:71
Threat to the Barkers (Phipson)  5:179
Three and One to Carry (Willard)  2:223
Three Big Hogs (Pinkwater)  4:164
3 X 3: A Picture Book for All Children Who Can Count to Three (Krüss)  9:85
Three Days on a River in a Red Canoe (Williams)  9:231
Three Gay Tales from Grimm (Gág)  4:93
Three Gold Pieces: A Greek Folk Tale (Aliki)  9:20
Three on the Run (Bawden)  2:14
The Three Robbers (Ungerer)  3:204
Three Wishes (Clifton)  5:58
Through the Broken Mirror with Alice (Wojciechowska)  1:200
Through the Eyes of Wonder: Science Fiction and Science (Bova)  3:35
Through the Looking Glass and What Alice Found There (Carroll)  2:36
Thunder in the Sky (Peyton)  3:180
Tic, Tac, and Toc (Munari)  9:124
Tico and the Golden Wings (Lionni)  7:130
A Tide Flowing (Phipson)  5:186
A Tiger Called Thomas (Zolotow)  2:237
Tiger in the Bush (Chauncy)  6:89
The Tiger's Bones and Other Plays for Children (Hughes)  3:96
Tikta'liktak: An Eskimo Legend (Houston)  3:86
Till the Break of Day (Wojciechowska)  1:200
Tim All Alone (Ardizzone)  3:6

*Tim and Charlotte*
(Ardizzone)  3:6
*Tim and Ginger* (Ardizzone)  3:7
*Tim in Danger* (Ardizzone)  3:7
*Tim to the Lighthouse*
(Ardizzone)  3:7
*Tim to the Rescue*
(Ardizzone)  3:8
*Time and Mr. Bass: A Mushroom
Planet Book* (Cameron)  1:42
*Time Cat: The Remarkable
Journey of Jason and Gareth*
(Alexander)  5:18
*Time of the Harvest: Thomas
Jefferson, the Years 1801-1826*
(Wibberley)  3:230
*The Time of the Kraken*
(Williams)  8:235
*Time of Trial* (Burton)  1:34
*Time of Wonder*
(McCloskey)  7:209
*Time to Get Out of the Bath,
Shirley* (Burningham)  9:48
*Time-Ago Lost: More Tales of
Jahdu* (Hamilton)  1:105
*Time-Ago Tales of Jahdu*
(Hamilton)  1:106
*The Times They Used to Be*
(Clifton)  5:56
*Timm Thaler* (Krüss)  9:85
*Tim's Last Voyage*
(Ardizzone)  3:8
*Tin Cans* (Rockwell)  6:238
*Tin Lizzie* (Spier)  5:223
*Tintin au pays de l'or noir*
(Hergé)  6:148
*Tintin au Tibet* (Hergé)  6:148
*Tintin en Amérique*
(Hergé)  6:147
*Tintin in America* (Hergé)  6:147
*Tintin in Tibet* (Hergé)  6:148
*To Be a Slave* (Lester)  2:114
*To Market! To Market!*
(Spier)  5:218
*To the Wild Sky* (Southall)  2:156
*Toad of Toad Hall*
(Milne)  1:143
*Toc, toc, chi è? Apri la porta*
(Munari)  9:124
*Today We Are Brother and Sister*
(Adoff)  7:36
*Tom and the Two Handles*
(Hoban)  3:83
*Tom Fox and the Apple Pie*
(Watson)  3:213
*The Tombs of Atuan* (Le
Guin)  3:123
*Tomfoolery: Trickery and Foolery
with Words* (Schwartz)  3:190
*Tommy Helps, Too* (Rey)  5:194
*The Tomorrow City*
(Hughes)  9:70
*Tom's Midnight Garden*
(Pearce)  9:144
*Tony and Me* (Slote)  4:200
*The Too-Great Bread Bake Book*
(Gibbons)  8:91
*Tool Book* (Gibbons)  8:92
*Toolchest: A Primer of Woodcraft*
(Adkins)  7:21
*Toolmaker* (Walsh)  2:201
*The Tooth Book* (Seuss)  9:194

*Tooth-Gnasher Superflash*
(Pinkwater)  4:171
*The Toppling Towers*
(Willard)  2:223
*Topsy-Turvies: Pictures to Stretch
the Imagination* (Anno)  2:2
*The Topsy-Turvy Emperor of
China* (Singer)  1:175
*Tornado! Poems* (Adoff)  7:33
*The Tough Winter*
(Lawson)  2:111
*The Tournament of the Lions*
(Williams)  8:224
*The Town Cats and Other Tales*
(Alexander)  5:23
*The Toy Shop* (Spier)  5:228
*Tractors* (Zim and Skelly)  2:231
*Trail of Apple Blossoms*
(Hunt)  1:110
*Train Ride* (Steptoe)  2:164
*The Transfigured Hart*
(Yolen)  4:261
*The Travels of Babar*
(Brunhoff)  4:31
*The Treasure* (Shulevitz)  5:206
*The Treasure of the Long Sault*
(Hughes)  9:77
*The Treasure of Topo-El-Bampo*
(O'Dell)  1:148
*The Tree Angel: A Story and Play*
(Charlip and Martin)  8:26
*Tree House Island*
(Corbett)  1:47
*A Treeful of Pigs* (Lobel)  5:173
*The Treegate Series*
(Wibberley)  3:231
*Treegate's Raiders*
(Wibberley)  3:231
*Trial Valley* (Cleaver and
Cleaver)  6:111
*Tristan and Iseult*
(Sutcliff)  1:190
*Der Trommler und die Puppe*
(Krüss)  9:88
*Trouble in the Jungle*
(Townsend)  2:175
*The Trouble with Donovan Croft*
(Ashley)  4:14
*Trubloff: The Mouse Who Wanted
to Play the Balalaika*
(Burningham)  9:39
*Truck* (Crews)  7:57
*Trucks* (Gibbons)  8:92
*Trucks* (Zim and Skelly)  2:232
*True Sea Adventures*
(Sobol)  4:210
*The Trumpet of the Swan*
(White)  1:195
*Trust a City Kid* (Yolen and
Huston)  4:256
*The Truth about Mary Rose*
(Sachs)  2:133
*The Truthful Harp*
(Alexander)  1:18; 5:20
*Try It Again, Sam: Safety When
You Walk* (Viorst)  3:210
*Tuck Everlasting* (Babbitt)  2:8
*Tucker's Countryside*
(Selden)  8:199
*Tuned Out*
(Wojciechowska)  1:200
*Tunes for a Small Harmonica*
(Wersba)  3:220

*The Tunnel of Hugsy Goode*
(Estes)  2:75
*Tunnels* (Gibbons)  8:98
*Turkey for Christmas* (de
Angeli)  1:54
*The Turnabout Trick*
(Corbett)  1:47
*The Twelve Months: A Greek
Folktale* (Aliki)  9:26
*Twenty-Four and Stanley*
(Weiss)  4:219
*The Twenty-Four Days Before
Christmas* (L'Engle)  1:132
*The Twenty-One Balloons* (du
Bois)  1:66
*Twins: The Story of Multiple
Births* (Cole and
Edmondson)  5:62
*Twist, Wiggle, and Squirm: A
Book about Earthworms*
(Pringle)  4:177
*A Twister of Twists, a Tangler of
Tongues* (Schwartz)  3:190
*The Twits* (Dahl)  7:78
*Two Dog Biscuits* (Cleary)  8:49
*Two Laughable Lyrics*
(Lear)  1:128
*Two Love Stories* (Lester)  2:115
*The Two of Them* (Aliki)  9:26
*The Two Old Bachelors*
(Lear)  1:128
*Two Piano Tuners*
(Goffstein)  3:61
*Tye May and the Magic Brush*
(Bang)  8:21
*The Ultra-Violet Catastrophe! or,
The Unexpected Walk with
Great-Uncle Magnus Pringle*
(Mahy)  7:183
*Umbrella* (Yashima)  4:253
*Uncle Elephant* (Lobel)  5:175
*Uncle Lemon's Spring*
(Yolen)  4:267
*Uncle Misha's Partisans*
(Suhl)  2:166
*Under the Early Morning Trees:
Poems* (Adoff)  7:35
*Under the Green Willow*
(Coatsworth)  2:63
*Under the Window: Pictures and
Rhymes for Children*
(Greenaway)  6:131
*Underground* (Macaulay)  3:144
*The Underside of the Leaf*
(Goffstein)  3:61
*Understanding Body Talk*
(Aylesworth)  6:54
*The Unfriendly Book*
(Zolotow)  2:237
*The Universe* (Zim)  2:232
*University: The Students, Faculty,
and Campus Life at One
University* (Schwartz)  3:191
*L'uomo del camion*
(Munari)  9:125
*Up a Road Slowly* (Hunt)  1:110
*Up Periscope* (White)  3:223
*Up the Alley with Jack and Joe*
(Kotzwinkle)  6:182
*Upside-Downers: More Pictures
to Stretch the Imagination*
(Anno)  2:2
*Uptown* (Steptoe)  2:164

*Use Your Brain* (Showers)  6:245
*Use Your Head, Dear*
(Aliki)  9:31
*The Uses of Space* (Bova)  3:36
*Vacation Time: Poems for
Children* (Giovanni)  6:117
*Vaccination and You*
(Cohen)  3:43
*Vampires and Other Ghosts*
(Aylesworth)  6:49
*Vegetables from Stems and
Leaves* (Selsam)  1:166
*Il venditore di animali*
(Munari)  9:124
*Veronica Ganz* (Sachs)  2:134
*Very Far Away from Anywhere
Else* (Le Guin)  3:123
*A Very Young Circus Flyer*
(Krementz)  5:154
*A Very Young Dancer*
(Krementz)  5:151
*A Very Young Gymnast*
(Krementz)  5:153
*A Very Young Rider*
(Krementz)  5:152
*A Very Young Skater*
(Krementz)  5:154
*The Vicksburg Veteran*
(Monjo)  2:126
*Viking's Dawn* (Treece)  2:189
*Viking's Sunset* (Treece)  2:189
*Village Books* (Spier)  5:228
*The Village Tree*
(Yashima)  4:250
*De vis* (Bruna)  7:49
*A Visit to William Blake's Inn:
Poems for Innocent and
Experienced Travelers*
(Willard)  5:250
*Vol 714 pour Sydney*
(Hergé)  6:149
*The Voyage of Osiris: A Myth of
Ancient Egypt*
(McDermott)  9:116
*The Voyage of QV 66*
(Lively)  7:162
*The Voyage of the Dawn Treader*
(Lewis)  3:137
*W.E.B. DuBois: A Biography*
(Hamilton)  1:106
*Wagging Tails: An Album of
Dogs* (Henry)  4:112
*Wake Up and Goodnight*
(Zolotow)  2:237
*Walk a Mile and Get Nowhere*
(Southall)  2:157
*Walk Home Tired, Billy Jenkins*
(Thomas)  8:213
*Wall Street: The Story of the
Stock Exchange*
(Sterling)  1:182
*The Wanderers*
(Coatsworth)  2:63
*The War and the Protest: Viet
Nam* (Haskins)  3:68
*War Dog* (Treece)  2:190
*Warrior Scarlet* (Sutcliff)  1:191
*Watch Out for the Chicken Feet
in Your Soup* (de Paola)  4:56
*The Watcher in the Garden*
(Phipson)  5:186
*Watchers in the Wild: The New
Science of Ethology*
(Cohen)  3:43

**Title Index**

*The Water of Life*
(Williams)  **8**:238

*Water on Your Street*
(Simon)  **9**:209

*Water Plants* (Pringle)  **4**:179

*Watson, the Smartest Dog in the U.S.A.* (Kuskin)  **4**:139

*Waves* (Zim)  **2**:232

*The Way Home* (Phipson)  **5**:182

*The Way of Danger: The Story of Theseus* (Serraillier)  **2**:143

*The Way Things Are and Other Poems* (Livingston)  **7**:171

*The Way to Sattin Shore* (Pearce)  **9**:158

*We Are Best Friends* (Aliki)  **9**:29

*We Didn't Mean to Go to Sea* (Ransome)  **8**:178

*We Have Tomorrow* (Bontemps)  **6**:80

*We Hide, You Seek* (Aruego and Dewey)  **5**:30

*We Read: A to Z* (Crews)  **7**:55

*Weather* (Pieńkowski)  **6**:230

*The Weather Changes Man* (Bova)  **3**:36

*A Weed Is a Flower: The Life of George Washington Carver* (Aliki)  **9**:18

*Welcome Home!* (Bemelmans)  **6**:75

*The Well-Mannered Balloon* (Willard)  **5**:246

*Westmark* (Alexander)  **5**:24

*Westward to Vinland* (Treece)  **2**:190

*What a Good Lunch! Eating* (Watanabe)  **8**:216

*What Can You Do with a Word?* (Williams)  **8**:227

*What Color Is Love?* (Anglund)  **1**:21

*What Did You Bring Me?* (Kuskin)  **4**:141

*What Do People Do All Day?* (Scarry)  **3**:186

*What Do You Think? An Introduction to Public Opinion: How It Forms, Functions, and Affects Our Lives* (Schwartz)  **3**:191

*What Do You Want to Know about Guppies?* (Simon)  **9**:211

*What Does It Do and How Does It Work?* (Hoban)  **3**:83

*What Happens to a Hamburger* (Showers)  **6**:245

*What Holds It Together* (Weiss)  **4**:228

*What I'd Like to Be* (Munari)  **9**:125

*What Is a Man?* (Krahn)  **3**:106

*What It's All About* (Klein)  **2**:101

*What Made You You?* (Bendick)  **5**:44

*What Makes a Boat Float?* (Corbett)  **1**:47

*What Makes a Light Go On?* (Corbett)  **1**:48

*What Makes a Plane Fly?* (Corbett)  **1**:48

*What Makes Me Feel This Way? Growing Up with Human Emotions* (LeShan)  **6**:188

*What Shall We Do with the Land?* (Pringle)  **4**:186

*What the Neighbours Did and Other Stories* (Pearce)  **9**:154

*What to Do: Everyday Guides for Everyone* (Bendick and Warren)  **5**:41

*What's Going to Happen to Me? When Parents Separate or Divorce* (LeShan)  **6**:190

*The Wheel on the School* (DeJong)  **1**:61

*Wheels: A Pictorial History* (Tunis)  **2**:194

*When Clay Sings* (Baylor)  **3**:17

*When Everyone Was Fast Asleep* (de Paola)  **4**:57

*When I Have a Little Girl* (Zolotow)  **2**:238

*When I Have a Son* (Zolotow)  **2**:238

*When I Was a Boy* (Kästner)  **4**:126

*When I Was a Little Boy* (Kästner)  **4**:126

*When I'm Big* (Bruna)  **7**:52

*When Shlemiel Went to Warsaw and Other Stories* (Singer)  **1**:176

*When the City Stopped* (Phipson)  **5**:185

*When the Pie Was Opened* (Little)  **4**:148

*When the Wind Stops* (Zolotow)  **2**:238

*When Thunders Spoke* (Sneve)  **2**:145

*Where Does the Day Go?* (Myers)  **4**:155

*Where Does the Garbage Go?* (Showers)  **6**:245

*Where Is Everybody?* (Charlip)  **8**:26

*Where the Lilies Bloom* (Cleaver and Cleaver)  **6**:103

*Where the Sidewalk Ends* (Silverstein)  **5**:210

*Where the Wild Things Are* (Sendak)  **1**:172

*Where Was Patrick Henry on the 29th of May?* (Fritz)  **2**:81

*Where Wild Willie* (Adoff)  **7**:34

*Where's My Baby?* (Rey)  **5**:195

*Where's My Daddy?* (Watanabe)  **8**:217

*Which Horse Is William?* (Kuskin)  **4**:136

*The Whispering Knights* (Lively)  **7**:152

*The Whispering Mountain* (Aiken)  **1**:8

*Whispers and Other Poems* (Livingston)  **7**:167

*Whistle for Willie* (Keats)  **1**:118

*The White Archer: An Eskimo Legend* (Houston)  **3**:87

*The White Horse Gang* (Bawden)  **2**:14

*The White Marble* (Zolotow)  **2**:239

*The White Mountains* (Christopher)  **2**:43

*The White Mountains Trilogy* (Christopher)  **2**:43

*The White Room* (Coatsworth)  **2**:64

*White Stallion of Lipizza* (Henry)  **4**:114

*Whizz!* (Lear)  **1**:128

*Who I Am* (Lester)  **2**:115

*Who Really Killed Cock Robin?* (George)  **1**:94

*Who, Said Sue, Said Whoo?* (Raskin)  **1**:157

*Who Will Comfort Toffle?* (Jansson)  **2**:95

*Whoppers: Tall Tales and Other Lies* (Schwartz)  **3**:192

*Who's Out There? The Search for Extraterrestrial Life* (Aylesworth)  **6**:51

*Who's Seen the Scissors?* (Krahn)  **3**:106

*Who's That Stepping on Plymouth Rock* (Fritz)  **2**:82

*Who's There? Open the Door!* (Munari)  **9**:124

*Why Can't I?* (Bendick)  **5**:43

*Why Don't You Get a Horse, Sam Adams?* (Fritz)  **2**:82

*Why Noah Chose the Dove* (Singer)  **1**:176

*Why Things Change: The Story of Evolution* (Bendick)  **5**:46

*The Whys and Wherefores of Littabelle Lee* (Cleaver and Cleaver)  **6**:108

*The Wicked City* (Singer)  **1**:176

*The Wicked Tricks of Tyl Uilenspiegel* (Williams)  **8**:236

*Wide Awake and Other Poems* (Livingston)  **7**:167

*Wiggle to the Laundromat* (Lee)  **3**:116

*Wild and Woolly Mammoths* (Aliki)  **9**:25

*Wild Foods: A Beginner's Guide to Identifying, Harvesting, and Cooking Safe and Tasty Plants from the Outdoors* (Pringle)  **4**:183

*The Wild Hunt of Hagworthy* (Lively)  **7**:153

*The Wild Hunt of the Ghost Hounds* (Lively)  **7**:153

*Wild in the World* (Donovan)  **3**:54

*Wild Jack* (Christopher)  **2**:43

*Wildcat under Glass* (Zei)  **6**:260

*The Wildest Horse Race in the World* (Henry)  **4**:113

*Wiley and the Hairy Man: Adapted from an American Folktale* (Bang)  **8**:19

*Willaby* (Isadora)  **7**:103

*William and Mary: A Story* (Farmer)  **8**:85

*William's Doll* (Zolotow)  **2**:239

*Willie Blows a Mean Horn* (Thomas)  **8**:214

*Willy and His Wheel Wagon* (Gibbons)  **8**:88

*The Wind between the Stars* (Mahy)  **7**:184

*A Wind in the Door* (L'Engle)  **1**:132

*The Wind in the Willows* (Grahame)  **5**:128

*The Windswept City: A Novel of the Trojan War* (Treece)  **2**:191

*The Wing on a Flea: A Book about Shapes* (Emberley)  **5**:90

*The Winged Colt of Casa Mia* (Byars)  **1**:37

*Wingman* (Pinkwater)  **4**:163

*Winter Holiday* (Ransome)  **8**:175

*Winter Tales from Poland* (Wojciechowska)  **1**:200

*Winterthing* (Aiken)  **1**:8

*The Wish Workers* (Aliki)  **9**:17

*The Witch Family* (Estes)  **2**:76

*The Witch in the Cherry Tree* (Mahy)  **7**:182

*The Witch of Blackbird Pond* (Speare)  **8**:205

*The Witch Who Wasn't* (Yolen)  **4**:256

*Witchcraft, Mysticism, and Magic in the Black World* (Haskins)  **3**:69

*The Witches* (Dahl)  **7**:83

*The Witch's Brat* (Sutcliff)  **1**:191

*The Witch's Daughter* (Bawden)  **2**:15

*Witcracks: Jokes and Jests from American Folklore* (Schwartz)  **3**:192

*Wizard Crystal* (Pinkwater)  **4**:162

*The Wizard in the Tree* (Alexander)  **1**:18; **5**:23

*The Wizard Islands* (Yolen)  **4**:260

*A Wizard of Earthsea* (Le Guin)  **3**:124

*The Wizard of Op* (Emberley)  **5**:99

*The Wizard of Washington Square* (Yolen)  **4**:258

*Wobble Pop* (Burningham)  **9**:51

*Wolf Run: A Caribou Eskimo Tale* (Houston)  **3**:88

*The Wolves of Willoughby Chase* (Aiken)  **1**:8

*The Wonderful Adventures of Nils* (Lagerlöf)  **7**:110

*The Wonderful Dragon of Timlin* (de Paola)  **4**:53

*The Wonderful Flight to the Mushroom Planet* (Cameron)  **1**:42

*The Wonderful Story of Henry Sugar and Six More* (Dahl)  **7**:75

*Won't Somebody Play with Me?* (Kellogg)  **6**:171

*Wooden Ship* (Adkins)  **7**:23

*Wordhoard: Anglo-Saxon Stories* (Walsh and Crossley-Holland) **2**:201

*Working with Cardboard and Paper* (Weiss) **4**:229

*The World of Captain John Smith, 1580-1631* (Foster) **7**:98

*The World of Christopher Robin* (Milne) **1**:143

*The World of Columbus and Sons* (Foster) **7**:98

*The World of Pooh* (Milne) **1**:143

*The World of William Penn* (Foster) **7**:100

*World on a String: The Story of Kites* (Yolen) **4**:258

*World's End Was Home* (Chauncy) **6**:89

*The World's Greatest Freak Show* (Raskin) **1**:157

*The Worms of Kukumlina* (Pinkwater) **4**:171

*Would You Rather. . .* (Burningham) **9**:49

*A Wrinkle in Time* (L'Engle) **1**:133

*The Wuggie Norple Story* (Pinkwater) **4**:170

*The Yangtze River* (Rau) **8**:186

*Year of Columbus, 1492* (Foster) **7**:99

*Year of Independence, 1776* (Foster) **7**:99

*Year of Lincoln, 1861* (Foster) **7**:100

*The Year of the Horseless Carriage, 1801* (Foster) **7**:101

*Year of the Pilgrims, 1620* (Foster) **7**:99

*Yeck Eck* (Ness) **6**:208

*Yertle the Turtle and Other Stories* (Geisel) **1**:88

*Yobgorgle: Mystery Monster of Lake Ontario* (Pinkwater) **4**:170

*You Can't Make a Move without*

*Your Muscles* (Showers) **6**:248

*You Can't Pet a Possum* (Bontemps) **6**:79

*The Young Ardizzone: An Autobiographical Fragment* (Ardizzone) **3**:8

*Young Booker: Booker T. Washington's Early Days* (Bontemps) **6**:84

*The Young Landlords* (Myers) **4**:159

*Young Man from the Piedmont: The Youth of Thomas Jefferson* (Wibberley) **3**:232

*The Young Unicorns* (L'Engle) **1**:134

*The Young United States: 1783 to 1830* (Tunis) **2**:195

*Your Brain and How It Works* (Zim) **2**:232

*Your Heart and How It Works* (Zim) **2**:233

*Your Skin and Mine*

(Showers) **6**:242

*Your Stomach and Digestive Tract* (Zim) **2**:233

*Z for Zachariah* (O'Brien) **2**:129

*Zamani Goes to Market* (Feelings) **5**:105

*Zebulon Pike, Soldier and Explorer* (Wibberley) **3**:233

*Zeee* (Enright) **4**:77

*Zeely* (Hamilton) **1**:106

*Zeralda's Ogre* (Ungerer) **3**:204

*Zlateh the Goat and Other Stories* (Singer) **1**:177

*A Zoo for Mister Muster* (Lobel) **5**:163

*Zozo* (Rey) **5**:193

*Zozo Flies a Kite* (Rey) **5**:198

*Zozo Gets a Medal* (Rey) **5**:198

*Zozo Goes to the Hospital* (Rey) **5**:199

*Zozo Learns the Alphabet* (Rey) **5**:199

*Zozo Rides a Bike* (Rey) **5**:196

*Zozo Takes a Job* (Rey) **5**:196

**Title Index**